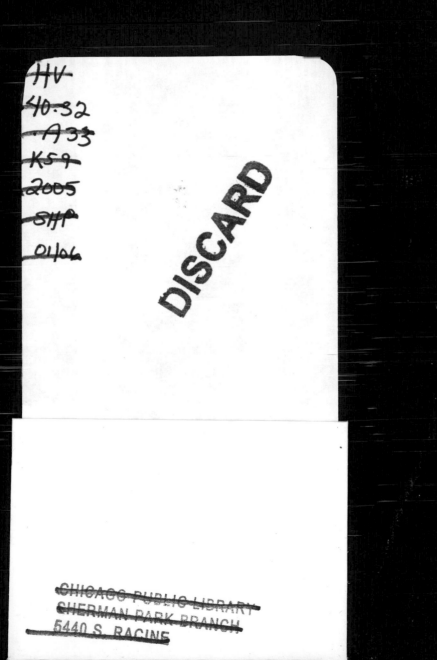

CITIZEN

Citizen

Jane Addams and the Struggle for Democracy

LOUISE W. KNIGHT

The University of Chicago Press Chicago and London

LOUISE W. KNIGHT
is an independent scholar whose articles on Jane Addams
have appeared in the *Journal of Women's History* and *Gender and History*
and in several collections of essays.

The University of Chicago Press, Chicago 60637
The University of Chicago Press, Ltd., London
© 2005 by The University of Chicago
All rights reserved. Published 2005
Printed in the United States of America

14 13 12 11 10 09 08 07 06 05   1 2 3 4 5

ISBN: 0-226-44699-9 (cloth)

Library of Congress Cataloging-in-Publication Data

Knight, Louise W.
    Citizen : Jane Addams and the struggle for democracy / Louise W. Knight.
        p.   cm.
    Includes bibliographical references and index.
    ISBN 0-226-44699-9 (cloth : alk. paper)
    1. Addams, Jane, 1860–1935. 2. Women social workers—United States—
Biography. 3. Social workers—United States—Biography. 4. Women social
reformers—United States—Biography. 5. Social reformers—United States—
Biography. I. Title.
HV40.32.A33K59 2005
361.92—dc22

2005008096

To my mother, Frances Berna Knight,
and the memory of my father, Augustus Knight Jr.,
whose support, in so many ways,
has made all the difference

*People are beginning to inquire how far public sentiment
should sanction or tolerate these unsexed women, who would step
out from the true sphere of the mother, the wife, and the daughter, and,
taking upon themselves the duties and the business of men, stalk
into the public gaze, and, by engaging in the politics, the rough
controversies and trafficking of the world, upheave existing
institutions, and overrun all the social relations of life.*
Albany Register, *March 7, 1854*

*Our hope of [social] achievement . . . lies in a complete
mobilization of the human spirit, using all our unrealized
and unevoked capacity.*
JANE ADDAMS, Second Twenty Years at Hull-House

CONTENTS

ILLUSTRATIONS

ACKNOWLEDGMENTS

My writing of this biography has been, in ways Addams would have appreciated, a cooperative venture. Although I have written it alone at my computer, the insights of many minds have profoundly shaped what I have been able to understand and capture on the page. Previous scholarship about Addams and the movements she was involved with has been essential. Readers interested in a history of that scholarship will find it summarized in this book's afterword. Colleagues and friends have helped in many different ways. I thank in particular Mary Lynn McCree Bryan, whose superb editing of the Jane Addams Papers and whose early encouragement made this project possible; Neil Coughlan for introducing me as a college student to Jane Addams; Sheila Tobias, whose example of an accomplished author was an early inspiration; Lucy Townsend, Charlene Haddock Seigfried, and Lois Rudnick, who taught me the meaning of scholarly collegiality and whose own scholarship laid foundations on which I could build; Robert Johnston, whose insightful comments improved every chapter; Kathleen Carpenter, Deborah Epstein, Leslie Johnson Harris, Jeanette LaCosse Mustacich, and Zephorene L. Stickney, whose excellent editorial eyes alerted me to snarled sentences, typos, and perplexing references; Susan Herbst, for every possible form of hearty encouragement; Leslie Johnson Harris (again), for her invaluable research assistance; and Michael Leff, for introducing me to the discipline of rhetoric and for believing in me and the book. My colleagues in Jane Addams scholarship, in addition to Bryan, Townsend, and Seigfried, have included Marilyn Fischer, Shannon Jackson, Bridget O'Rourke, and Rosemarie Redlich Scherman. Carolyn Gifford has been my colleague in studying the lives of great nineteenth-century women.

Many other people helped at crucial points along the way with advice, expert knowledge, resource support, or friendship. These include Peter Ascoli, Henry Binford, Ann Caldwell, Mina Carson, Paul Cimbala, Jill Ker Conway, Chris Cory, Joanne V. Creighton, Mary Dietz, Joseph Ellis, Ann Feldman, Joan Flanagan, Ann Fischbeck, Elzbieta Foeller-Pituch, Paul Fry, Penny Gill, Joan Gittens, Peggy Glowacki, Ann Gordon, Randy Holgate, Jennifer Hochschild, Helen Lefkowitz Horowitz, Shannon Jackson, Julia

W. Kramer, Jane Addams Morse Linn, John J. McCusker, Randall Miller, Julie Nebel, Ellie and Alan Pasch, Angela Ray, Leila J. Rupp, Anne Firor Scott, Richard Schneirov, Barbara Sicherman, Kathryn Kish Sklar, Carl Smith, Gloria Steinem, Glennis Stephenson, Carl Tomizuka, Jake Wachman, Carolyn Winterer, and Elisabeth Young-Bruehl.

In addition to my alma maters, Wheaton College (Massachusetts) and Wesleyan University, which nurtured my love of historical scholarship and writing, I am especially in debt to five educational institutions whose wonderful research resources were invaluable to me at different stages of this project: Duke University, Wheaton College (Massachusetts), Brown University, Mount Holyoke College, and Northwestern University. At these institutions, librarians of all sorts, from those in reference to those in acquisitions to the magicians in interlibrary loan, have been crucial partners. I am also grateful to Spertus Institute for interlibrary loan and research administration support while I was teaching there. At the archives where I did research, I thank Special Collections Librarian Mary Ann Bamberger and Professional Library Associate, Patricia Bakunas, Special Collections, The University Library, University of Illinois at Chicago; Head Sherrill Redmon, Sophia Smith Collection, Smith College; Curator Wendy Chmielewski, Swarthmore College Peace Collection; and Archivist Mary Pryor, Rockford College Archives. I am grateful to the Communication Studies Department at Northwestern University for its support. In Stephenson County, I especially thank volunteer Ruth Springer of the Local History Room, Freeport Public Library, Jean Joyce of Lena, Mary Mau of McConnell, and Ron Beam, Clyde Kaiser, and Moira and Thomas Fenwick of the Cedarville Historical Society for their hospitality and help with local history. In Berks County, Pennsylvania, I thank Paul Miller of the Sinking Spring Area Historical Society and Barbara Gill of the Historical Society of Berks County; in Northampton County, Pennsylvania, I think Jane S. Moyer of the Northampton Historical and Genealogical Society.

I am also grateful to the president of Rockford College, Paul Pribbenow, for granting permission for me to publish the oil painting of Addams that appears on the book's cover. The early part of the painting's provenance is undocumented, but it appears from the available evidence that Mary Rozet Smith commissioned the British portrait painter Harrington Mann to paint it in 1899. She apparently wanted to have a portrait of her friend to hang in her bedroom, just as Jane had one of Mary (by Alice Kellogg Tyler) hanging in hers. Mann, though based in London, also did portraits of wealthy clients in the United States and would open a New York City studio shortly thereafter. Among his Chicago subjects was Addams's and Smith's friend Lydia Coonley-Ward. For some reason, Addams was dreading the sittings, but when Smith was in London in 1899, she seems to have met Mann and found him charming (which by all accounts he was) and so wrote Jane to reassure her. Smith's letter does not survive, but Addams replied on July 28 that it brought her comfort and that "I don't drill at the portrait as much as I did." In 1922, the members of the class of 1881 of Rockford College decided to raise money among themselves to pay for a portrait of Addams to give to the college. Addams, who was about to leave for a trip around the world with Mary, suggested that she give the class this portrait instead and that her classmates donate the same amount of money to the college's endowment fund. Both were done, and the portrait has been at Rockford College ever since.

Funders have also been much-appreciated partners. The Ludwig Vogelstein Foundation, the Indiana University Center on Philanthropy, Indianapolis, on behalf of the Lilly Endowment, Inc., and other donors, and the Spencer Foundation all supported my research. An essential Independent Scholar Fellowship from the National Endowment for the Humanities in 2000 made it possible for me to make substantial progress in completing the manuscript. The Center for the Humanities at Northwestern University and the Five College Women's Studies Research Center at Mount Holyoke College provided research resources and colleagues.

My family has supported this project in many ways. My mother, Frances Berna Knight, astute reader of biographies, has understood what I was trying to do from the beginning, seen its value, and encouraged me. My sister Penny Knight not only read the manuscript but contributed her valuable psychological insights as well as her support. My other sister, Elizabeth Knight, has cheered me on. Initially, my father, Augustus Knight Jr., who died in January 2003 and is much missed, was perplexed by my decision to undertake a massively time-consuming, non-income-generating project of this sort—a skepticism that was certainly merited. But in time he came around. Believing in me, he believed in the book, too, which meant a great deal.

The last stage of any book (and a highly cooperative one) is its prepublication review by expert readers and its actual publication. I am grateful to the University of Chicago Press for being such a satisfyingly rigorous partner in this stage of the effort. The readers' comments were extremely helpful and Robert Devens has been the excellent editor I had hoped to find, someone who believed in the book and knew how to support me in my efforts to strengthen it.

Finally, it should be said that Jane Addams's cooperation has been essential. She contributed her voluminous papers and vast writings to the enterprise, but most of all she contributed her wisdom. A biographer herself, she was always at my elbow, helping me think clearly about how people grow and what obstacles they encounter, even when she did not understand (or at least disclose) her own story in those terms. It has been a privilege to get to know her.

Louise (Lucy) W. Knight
Evanston, Illinois
February 2005

INTRODUCTION

Early in my research for this book, I came across a passage in Jane Addams's writings that has remained one of my favorites. "[W]e are under a moral obligation in choosing our experiences," she wrote, "since the result of those experiences must ultimately determine our understanding of life."[1] Addams was thinking like a biographer, I mused; she was interested in how life changes people. But I knew she was also speaking personally. What choices did she make, I wondered, and what did she learn that was of such profound moral consequence?

This book attempts to answer those questions. It tells of the formative years of a person who began life, as most people do, unknown and who became one of America's most accomplished social reformers. Addams's subsequent fame, her reputation as the country's "most admired woman," and her numerous accomplishments—as a leader in immigrant and labor relations, as an advocate for children, low-income people, civil liberties, and peace, and as a 1931 recipient of the Nobel Peace Prize—compel our interest in her youth and young adulthood. We want to know more about her.

Sharp contrasts abound. She began life as a child from a small town, yet, driven by her sense of moral responsibility and hunger for adventure, she became a pioneer in urban reform, co-founding Hull House, the first settlement house in Chicago and one of the first in the United States. She was a dreamy book reader who dwelt happily in her imagination when young, yet she became an activist citizen, someone who applied ideas to life and who worked cooperatively with others, not alone. Two other facts of her childhood could have been limiting yet were overcome. Although she was a girl with big dreams who doubted that she, being female, could fulfill them, she achieved more than she could have dreamed. And although she was the daughter of a superior-minded, morally absolutist, Victorian upper-middle-class family, she developed into one of America's foremost social democrats and into one of its most pragmatic ethicists. Addressing all these stories, this book covers Jane Addams's early life from her birth in 1860 to 1898, the years of her becoming.

This book, however, is not simply about a person. It is also about the idea of democracy, the engine of our nation's political, economic, and social life. Democracy's eighteenth-century meanings were destabilized by many nineteenth-century developments. These included rapid industrialization, the concentration of wealth, the rise of labor unions, the arrival of millions of immigrants from non–northern European countries, and the expansion of the suffrage to working-class and some African American men but not to women. As a result, union workers, small farmers, and women joined with members of the populist, or radical, wing of the middle class in a struggle to increase democracy in the second half of the nineteenth century. In the 1890s their influence was felt in the city councils and state legislatures. After 1900 they emerged on the national scene as spokespersons, leaders, and foot soldiers for various voluntary organizations that constituted the democratic wing of the progressive movement. Despite their many defeats, their efforts reshaped the nation's political agenda and the distribution of political power.

Jane Addams was in a good position to become involved with white workers' and white women's issues in the 1890s (African Americans would not arrive in Chicago in substantial numbers until after 1900) because she was a woman and someone living in a working-class neighborhood. But that did not mean that her involvement was inevitable. It was because of her willingness to work cooperatively with others and because of the care with which she listened to and learned from others that her story and the story of the struggle for democracy became deeply intertwined.

Addams's given life, which began in the small town of Cedarville, Illinois, was one of wealth, books, a solemn morality of conscience and unselfishness, dreams of heroism, and expectations of public service. Her father, an agricultural businessman, a state senator, and a person of intense moral rectitude, was the center of her emotional life, her mother having died when she was two. The youngest of five surviving children, she was raised first by her oldest sister and later by her stepmother, whom her father married when she was eight. Jane was ambitious and idealistic when young; she dreamed of becoming a medical doctor and serving the poor, and at first she seemed likely to accomplish her dream. She earned a college degree when women rarely did so and then entered medical school. But she did not complete her studies. Instead, she floundered in her twenties, depressed by her father's sudden death, the burden of ill health, and her deep confusion about how best to meet family and societal expectations.

For eight years, until she was twenty-eight, she led the conventional female life to which she had been born—visiting family, traveling in Europe, and pursuing the study of culture.

To the outer world she seemed content, but on the inside, she was wrestling with the demons of her unfulfilled aspirations. Although she had decided to abandon medicine as a career, her great longing, shaped by her upbringing as a Christian and by her wide reading, remained to do something for "the poor." But what? In 1887 she read a magazine article about Toynbee Hall. Founded in a working-class neighborhood of London three years earlier, it was a new kind of social-educational institution called a settlement house that offered a way for educated people and the poor to live in the same community. From day to day, its residents and other volunteers provided classes in the humanities, opportunities for "civilized" social mingling, and friendship across class lines—those being what the settlement founders thought of as the best fruits of European high culture. Addams, already a passionate enthusiast for culture's benefits and still hoping to find a way to help the poor, decided to use the money she had inherited from her father to found a settlement house in Chicago. But she did not do it. Instead, at age twenty-seven, she left the United States for a second trip to Europe. Finally, in 1888, five months into her trip, she abruptly faced the fact that she had failed to act on her beliefs and, ashamed of her selfishness, changed course.

In 1889, shortly after her twenty-ninth birthday, Jane Addams entered her chosen life by moving into a heavily industrialized, working-class, mostly immigrant Chicago neighborhood and co-founding the settlement house Hull House with her friend Ellen Gates Starr. Focused on nurturing the human spirit, she and Starr offered clubs, parties, cultural events, and college extension classes to working-class people. They also helped them by taking care of their children, visiting them when they were sick, and assuaging their loneliness with social calls. Believing that only men could be active in politics because only men could vote and, in any case, more interested in social than political democracy, they were uninvolved in the political issues of the day.

Gradually, however, Addams's priorities shifted. Among the crucial influences were the momentous events taking place in her adopted city. Chicago in the 1890s saw the continuing rise of working-class union activism, the election in 1892 of Illinois's first progressive governor, its hosting of the 1893 World's Fair, the devastating depression of 1893–97, the tragedy of the Pullman Strike of 1894, the rise in political influence of Chicago's new Civic Federation from 1895 to 1898, the intensely contested aldermanic elections in the mid-to-late 1890s, and the eruption of the Spanish-American War in 1898. Also, Addams's friends among the working class, the lower- and upper-middle class, and the upper class set an example. A number of Chicago women, including Mary Kenney, Elizabeth Morgan, Florence Kelley, Lucy Flower, and Mary Wilmarth, responded to these developments by embracing political action. They inspired an initially reluctant Addams to follow in their footsteps. Rejecting her former assumption that public policy battles and politics were for men only, she began to fight for better labor laws for women and children, a state law establishing voluntary arbitration for labor disputes, better city sanitation services, a less corrupt city council, votes for women, and peace. These campaigns of the 1890s were her first political undertakings and transformed her understanding of her civic role.

Her experiences, along with key books she read, also transformed her ethics. By 1898 she had rejected the individualistic, absolutist, benevolent ethics of her father and her own class in favor of what she perceived to be the working-class ethic of cooperative justice, which she found less selfish and self-righteous. And her ethics became pragmatic. She came to believe that a nation's (and a person's) ethics ought to evolve. These conclusions were substantially shaped by the painful trauma of the Pullman Strike, which, she believed, revealed the arrogance, selfishness, and tyranny of George Pullman's out-of-date ethic of benevolence. She also learned that high ideals—ideals that were the product of reading and philosophizing—were not sufficient in themselves. She had brought with her to Hull House a commitment to Tolstoy's theory of nonresistance, Jesus Christ's theory of love, and the social Christian theory of cooperation, confident that if she kept those commitments, she would accomplish good. They were not enough. As she would write, "[F]ailure may come quite as easily from ignoring the adequacy of one's method as from selfish or ignoble aims."[2] She became a student of failure and studied experience as she had once studied the great classics of Western civilization. Addams earns our greatest respect as a profound student of life and as a moral and political philosopher of what it means to be fully human. As her nephew, Weber Linn, once observed, her "real eagerness" was for understanding.[3] Addams used the word "interpretation" to describe her soul-searching analysis of experience. It was hard work. "Many experiences in those early years," she later wrote, "although vivid, seemed to contain no illumination."[4]

She summed up the moral insights behind her hard-won lessons in an 1899 lecture series that eventually became her first book, *Democracy and Social Ethics* (1902). At bottom, it is about how living in a fully democratic way changes a person's ethics. Democracy, she wrote, is "a rule of living and a test of faith in the essential dignity and equality of all men."[5] It is attained and sustained, she argued, by developing a profound sense of connection with one's fellow human beings. "The identification with the common lot," she observed, "is the essential idea of Democracy."[6] For her that meant "includ[ing] all men in our hopes" and realizing that "all men are hoping and are part of the same movement of which we are a part."[7] By 1899 Addams had transformed herself and been transformed into a pragmatic, progressive social reformer and a skilled, compassionate, and engaged citizen. Her story illustrates what bears remembering and what she often stressed in her later writings: we are not born citizens; we must become them by means of experience.

To piece together her story I have relied on much previous scholarship, including several biographies of Addams written between her death in 1935 and 1973—for knowledge, inspiration, and a spur to unravel knotty puzzles. One puzzle is not about the biographies themselves but about the lack of biographies in the 1980s and 1990s. Was it merely a fluke or was there a reason for it? In the afterword to this book I explore that question and note the approach taken by a new biography of Addams published in 2004. I also consider the contributions that recent research in the burgeoning fields of women's history, social history, ethnic and racial history, and labor history, among others, have made to my interpretation of Jane Addams. We have a much greater understanding today both of the forces shaping Jane Addams and her world and the forces that she and her reform colleagues were challenging. I have tried, as every biographer must, to bridge the gap between the present and the past.

Jane Addams wrote often and profoundly throughout her life about what people learn from life and how they learn it. I came to realize, however, that she wrote very little about herself in this regard, not even in her famous memoir, *Twenty Years at Hull-House* (1910). Rather, she used the opportunity it provided her to embody and enact what she had learned. Its author was a wise woman, one of the wisest in our history. This book is about Jane Addams's journey to become that person.

PART ONE

THE GIVEN LIFE

1860–88

Our conceptions of morality, as all our ideas, pass through a course of development; the difficulty comes in adjusting our conduct, which has become hardened into customs and habits, to these changing moral conceptions. When this adjustment is not made, we suffer from the strain and indecision of believing one hypothesis and acting upon another.

JANE ADDAMS, Democracy and Social Ethics

CHAPTER I

SELF-RELIANCE

1822–60

In Cedarville, Illinois, within view of a creek winding through a sunken glade, Jane Addams was born on September 6, 1860. It was late summer in northern Illinois, a time when the windows were open to catch the breeze, the grain was ripe in the fields, and the apple trees in the family orchard were laden with fruit destined for cider and pies.

Yet distant events had brought foreboding to this peaceful place. The experiment of practicing slavery in a nation committed to individual freedom was proving untenable by slow degrees and had at last produced a fiercely polarized nation. Many southern states had threatened to leave the Union if Abraham Lincoln, the Republican presidential candidate who opposed extending slavery into the territories, was elected.

Jane Addams's father, John Huy Addams, was a friend and great admirer of Lincoln. He hung three pictures of him in his house and saved the letters he received from his hand. Their paths had crossed by way of politics. Both were Whigs, and then Republicans, and both had served in the Illinois state senate, although at different times. Addams came to elected office as Lincoln came to the presidency, because of slavery, and during the Civil War they both continued to oppose it. Lincoln issued the Emancipation Proclamation, freeing the slaves of the Confederate states. John Addams fought in the state senate to keep Illinois in the Union and, as a conductor in the Underground Railroad, sheltered African Americans escaping slavery.

As Jane Addams grew up and for the rest of her life, these two men were closely associated in her mind with the duty to relate to all people sympathetically. Her father, she observed in 1924, brought up his children in the belief that Lincoln's "kindliness and . . . understanding of all men, including his . . . enemies, [was] the highest point of civilization."[1] Jane Addams believed that her life was inspired by her father's and Lincoln's examples. In her 1910 memoir she gave them nearly equal places of honor. John

Addams's presence dominates the first chapter, "Earliest Impressions"; the second chapter is titled "Influence of Lincoln."

As future events would show, Jane Addams was indeed influenced by these men, but there were also other factors shaping the kind of person she would become. Perhaps the most central was that she was born female. If that influence had dominated, her life might have been like her mother's, organized around the home. Sarah Weber Addams had already given birth to seven children when Jane was born and, like most women of her time and place, had built a life centered on marriage, family, and neighborliness. Although she would die when Jane was two, she would be lovingly remembered in the family.

Another influence was Jane Addams's American heritage. She was born a citizen in a nation that placed a premium philosophically, if not always in practice, on the liberal values of individual freedom, human equality, freedom of conscience, self-development, and self-advancement. These values found powerful expression in the two interlocking and dominant theories, or ideologies, of the day: the economic theory of capitalism and the moral theory of individualism. Children of her generation were taught that they were responsible for improving their own circumstances, that their future depended on their ambition, their integrity, and their willingness to work hard.

This American lesson, however, contradicted the lessons of femininity. Women and girls were expected to limit their desire for personal accomplishment. Girls were instructed to be self-effacing, to serve others. Furthermore, law and custom dictated their dependence on males—on fathers, husbands, and grown sons. Considered ill-equipped to carry out the full responsibilities of citizenship, women could not serve on juries, vote, run for political office, or fight in wars. In the 1840s, the resulting tensions between the ideology of female limitations and the ideology of individualism gave rise to a women's rights movement. By 1860 its leaders had convened nine national women's rights conventions, persuaded male legislators in several states to amend divorce and married women's property laws, and petitioned numerous state legislatures for the right to vote, though none had yet granted it.

In the decades before the Civil War, the group that had reaped the benefits of the American ideology of individualism was working-class men. The United States was the first Western nation since the Athenian State to remove property ownership as a barrier to suffrage. The impact was, to be sure, uneven. Many states limited workingmen's votes by means of legal restrictions based on race, ethnicity, and religion and administrative procedures such as registration and fees. Male working-class African Americans had equal voting rights in only five states in 1860, all of them in New England, where only 4 percent of the nation's free blacks lived; Indians and paupers were unable to vote in most states. Recently arrived immigrants lost the vote in six states in the 1840s and 1850s.[2]

Those in the educated upper-middle class into which Jane Addams was born did not welcome the rise of white working-class men as a political force. John Addams was a Whig and a highly prosperous agricultural businessman; Americans of his party and background generally disliked propertyless and immigrant men voting.[3] The one exception John Addams made reflected his own ethnic background. Descended on both sides from German immigrants, he drew a firm distinction between immigrants from Germany, whom he befriended and hired, and those from countries such as Norway, whom he considered ignorant.

A small child in a small town in rural Illinois in the 1860s did not need to concern herself with women's rights, African American rights, or immigrant rights. Still, in the future she would need to answer the questions that underlay the argument for such rights. What was a good (female) citizen? Was it someone who was a politician like her father or a good neighbor like her mother? Was it a self-sufficient person or a person committed to a life of dependence and self-sacrifice? Was it someone who knew better than "the masses" or was it someone who thought class standing irrelevant to a person's right to have a public voice? Was it someone of Anglo-Germanic origins or were race and ethnicity irrelevant? The facts of Jane Addams's birth did not portend her fate so much as establish the questions that she would need to answer in her life.

At the beginning, Jane Addams's world was small and defined by her parents' love—particularly, after her mother's death before her third birthday, by that of her father. "My earliest recollection," Addams wrote in 1922, "was being held up in a pair of dusty hands to see the heavy stone mill wheels go round." The mill wheels belonged to her father's flour mill. Perhaps the dusty hands were also his. He was, she recalled, "the dominant influence" of her childhood, the subject of "my supreme affection."[4]

Jane Addams honored her father and his influence on her throughout her life. She dedicated her memoir, *Twenty Years at Hull-House with Autobi-ographical Notes*, published in 1910, when she was forty-nine, to his memory. To a question posed by a psychologist in the 1920s she replied that she believed she inherited "the dominant elements" of her character from him. In the 1930s she refused the invitation of the National Cathedral of Washington, D.C., to be interred beneath its august roof, preferring, as she told a friend, to be buried beside her father in the small Cedarville graveyard that was his resting place, and this is where her remains are today.[5]

Most of what we know about Jane Addams's devotion to her father is drawn from *Twenty Years at Hull-House*. On its opening page she writes that he is "directly connected" with all of the "impressions" of her childhood that she has recorded in the book. It was he, she explains, who "first drew me into the moral concerns of life." In the pages that follow she mostly recalls their conversations. Usually she tells stories in which he seems wise and all-knowing, larger than life, a man determined to be upright and good, a moral giant, at times too perfect to be human. Yet at other moments she abandons the child's viewpoint and with careful artistry reveals that she has a different perspective now. "It is hard," she observes at one point, "to account for the manifestations of a child's adoring affection, so emotional, so irrational, so tangled with the affairs of the imagination." In another place she calls her childish attempts to express her "doglike affection" for her father "grotesque."[6]

But if she dismisses her adoration at times, she does not attempt to correct for it by providing a realistic or factual view of her father. She calls him a "self-made man" and remembers being impressed as a child with the stories she heard of the "hardships" of his early life but mentions only one: that as a miller's apprentice he rose at 3 A.M. and used the early morning hours in the mill to read his way through the local library. She neglects to say where he was born or almost anything about his family. She reveals that he was a miller, a banker, and a Sunday school teacher but tells nothing more about his successful careers as a businessman and a leading citizen of their small town and the larger city of Freeport, six miles south, where his bank was located.[7] And although she mentions his service as a state senator, she only tells a few stories of his political experiences, all of them ones she learned as a child.

Knowledge of the flesh-and-blood John Huy Addams, the whole man that a small child could not know and that the adult daughter chose not to describe, must come not from her but from others. Glimpses of the man emerge from his 1844 diary, his letters, family stories, the list of books in his personal library, and descriptions in local histories.[8] It is important to round out the image of him that his daughter paints. Adoring him, she absorbed his civic conscience, his moral earnestness, and his passionate individualism into her very bones.

When Addams calls her father a "self-made man," she is invoking, as she notes, an ideal held in great admiration by young people of her generation. The phrase had at least three meanings. Addams seems to have in mind the economic meaning because she refers to her father's early "hardships." In the phrase's second meaning a man could "make himself" morally by starting with one set of moral principles and working out a new set on his own.[9] The third meaning was the broadest and was implicit in the other two: philosophically, a "self-made man" was a man convinced that he was responsible for the success or failure of his own life, a man who believed he should rely on his own reason and conscience, not tradition or inherited status, as the basis for his decisions and who had high expectations for his own achievements. By the second half of the nineteenth century, these views would be popularly summed up by two words: "self-reliance" and a new word, borrowed from the French, "individualism."[10]

As it happened, John Addams came from too prosperous a family and received too much help from it in his business to meet the economic definition. His daughter saw his early life as harder than it was. But he was indeed a self-made man in the other two senses of the phrase. In his religion, his moral principles, and his work, he was determinedly self-reliant and focused on the achievement of personal excellence. The ethic of individualism, along with the wealth her father would leave her, was part of Jane Addams's inheritance.

When John Addams was born in southeastern Pennsylvania in 1822, American society was thriving under postrevolution conditions of freedom from colonial rule.[11] As Alexis de Tocqueville was among the first to note, the country's new democratic political institutions and its egalitarian social conditions intensively nurtured the spread of trade and industry. Tocqueville was struck by the nation's obsession with economic growth. Americans' "principal interest," he wrote in 1831, is the "exploitation" of "a huge new country." He also astutely identified the passion that fueled this enormous undertaking: "Love of money serves the industrial expansion and prosperity of the nation." No one was embarrassed by this. In America, he reported, "love of money . . . is held in honor."[12] John Addams came to young manhood in these times, and all the choices of his adulthood resonate with these same goals—to earn public honor and advance his family's and his nation's fortunes by means of the personal acquisition of wealth. The strength of his passion can be gauged by his success.

Initially this effort was very much a family affair. When John Addams set out in 1844, at age twenty-two, to settle in northern Illinois, his father, Samuel Addams, did not accompany him but his money did. Their hometown of Sinking Spring had been in economic decline for years, partly because of the depression of 1837, and did not merit further investment. Enterprising Pennsylvania men of all ages, John Addams's extended family among them, were seeking profit in the west. Samuel Addams's first cousin George Ruth left for Chicago in 1836, when he was forty-seven. Soon afterward three other cousins, Jonathan and Philip Reitzel and Jonathan Flickinger, and their wives settled a bit further north, near the town of Freeport, in the region of Illinois that would become Stephenson County.[13]

Samuel Addams's economic situation was not dire. Although he owned one of the only two inns in Sinking Spring and therefore depended on the town's economy for that part of his business, he also owned extensive farmlands, inherited from his mother's side of the family. Aged sixty-two in 1844, he had wealth enough to retire comfortably. But his passion for making money was strong. His plan, events would reveal, was to send his seventh child and third son, John, to the area of northern Illinois where the Reitzels and Flickingers had settled.[14] He would give John enough cash for the down payment on a flour mill and come west himself to visit some months later and bring the rest of the money; perhaps he even considered moving himself and his wife there.

Grain milling was an obvious choice for John's trade. Two of John's uncles, Peter and William Addams, were millers, and it was an invaluable industry for a frontier settlement. In 1839 Samuel therefore apprenticed John, after he graduated from the Washington Hall Collegiate Institute, to a young Quaker miller, Enos Reiff, of Ambler, a town just north of Philadelphia and fifty miles southeast of Sinking Spring.[15]

Whether for economic or personal reasons or both, romance leading to marriage was next on John's agenda. Happily, under Enos Reiff's roof he met a young woman he wanted to marry. Sarah Weber (pronounced WEE-ber) was twenty-two and the sister of Reiff's new wife, Elizabeth. John was only seventeen, which is probably one reason it took five years for the couple to wed. Still, he must have been a poised young man to attract her interest. Photographs show that he was tall and slender, with wide-set gray eyes, thick, wavy brown hair, and a firm set to his jaw. Judging from various accounts, he did not laugh much, but his manners were excellent and his air of quiet purposefulness must have impressed Sarah.[16]

Sarah and John were a good match. Like John, she was well-educated for her day, having attended a female boarding school in Philadelphia. Like him, she came from a prosperous upper-middle-class family. Her father, George Weber, a miller in Kreidersville, Northampton County, in eastern Pennsylvania, was wealthy enough to own the most splendid house in town. She already knew mill life, therefore, and she would reveal herself to be masterful at household management and a hard worker. A sister of John's recalled her as a warm and appealing person. Their ethnic backgrounds were also similar. Hers, like John's, was mostly Germanic. And they had both been raised in the German Reformed Church. John continued to court Sarah after he completed his apprenticeship. Returning to Sinking Spring, he taught school for a time and, still seeking to improve himself, organized a literary society so that he and other young men could practice debating.[17]

Finally, on July 18, 1844, six days after John's twenty-second birthday and on Sarah's twenty-seventh birthday, they were married in Kreidersville and, eleven days later, left for Illinois. The circumstances were not entirely romantic. Traveling with them was Sarah's wealthy fifty-eight-year old father, who, predictably for the times, wanted to investigate money-making opportunities in the west. By carriage and train the three made their way to New York City, by boat north to Albany, and by train west to Buffalo, where, after a side trip to Niagara Falls, they boarded the steamer *St. Louis* for the trip across Lakes Erie, Huron, and Michigan. On August 8, after some serious seasickness, they arrived in Chicago.[18]

In 1844 Chicago was a booming, ramshackle frontier town of eight thousand people, most of them traders. Already it was the capital of speculation in the new American west. Located between Lake Michigan and the Mississippi River, it was obviously the place from which the commodities of the frontier would be sold and shipped, via the Great Lakes, to the markets back east and to Europe. John Addams understood as well as any the economic potential of Chicago, but he was pleased to move on. "Nearly every person [in Chicago] is engaged in . . . business," he noted, "in my opinion too many for the place." He paused long enough to buy a horse and buggy and attend a Whig political meeting, after which Sarah, George, and he headed

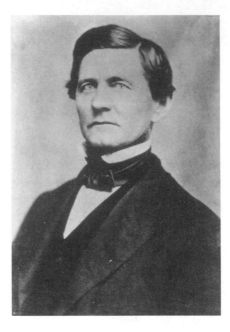

John Huy Addams, Jane Addams's father. The Jane Addams Papers Project, Fayetteville, NC.

north to Freeport, 120 miles northwest of Chicago, to find his cousins.[19] John Addams would build his wealth on Chicago's economic strength, but he would do it from the countryside, as a big fish in a small pond.

They moved in with Philip Reitzel, who lived ten miles north of Freeport, to wait until John could purchase his mill, or rather, as it turned out, mills. Soon after arriving, he found a flour mill with one grinding stone and a saw mill with one blade plus four hundred acres of land for sale on Cedar Creek, six miles north of Freeport in the tiny new hamlet of Harrison, soon to be renamed Cedarville. Now the problem became whether his father back in Pennsylvania would agree to pay the price.[20]

The mills' co-owners, Conrad Epley and John W. Shuey, were asking $4,000 for the property, $200 more than the $3,800 that Samuel Addams had authorized his son to offer. First John tried to persuade his father-in-law to join him in the investment.[21] George Weber refused. He wanted to buy his own mill in Como, a town more than a day's journey south of Freeport that he planned to visit shortly. Next John considered borrowing the money by taking out a loan, but that was expensive. Farmers and other

Sarah Weber Addams, Jane Addams's mother, around the time of her marriage.
The Jane Addams Papers Project, Fayetteville, NC.

rural businessmen in the region were currently borrowing money from land agents at annual interest rates of 25 to 30 percent. He decided against it, noting in his travel diary, in which he was keeping a careful record of his early days in Illinois, that he was unwilling to load himself with debt.[22]

He now did the only thing he felt he could do. He wrote a letter seeking his father's approval to pay the higher price for Cedar Creek Mills and waited impatiently for a reply. His ambition to succeed, having no outlet, worked on his mood. "The future looks gloomy," he wrote in his diary. This "makes my heart feel sad as I have a great desire to do well." He prayed about it, seeking reassurance, and received it. "I lifted up my soul to God," he wrote, "until my eyes filled with tears with the firm resolution that all would be alright." The fact that the money was not his own made the dilemma especially difficult. As the days dragged by without a letter, he wrote, "It is no trifling business to effect a purchase in which one is to make use of a kind father's money." Finally, in mid-October, the letter approving the price came. John recorded in his diary that he was "elated" and "thanked God." He would make the purchase, he vowed, "so that I will not disappoint my dear parents."[23]

But now there was a new snag. One of the co-owners refused to sell at the old price and proposed a new one of $4,200. John wrote his father again to ask for his approval and began another agonizing period of waiting. He was becoming depressed. "My future looks dark," he wrote at one point. "I hope and pray God some permanent light very soon [will] appear [and that Sarah and I can] settle down in life to do honor to God and selves." Finally, he could stand to wait no longer. Deciding to take out a loan if his father did not approve, in mid-December he offered to meet the new price and the mills' owners accepted the bid. He wrote Samuel, no doubt with some trepidation, telling him what he had done.[24] John's great distance from his father, a standard challenge of the frontier, had forced him to commit his first act of real self-reliance.

Samuel Addams not only approved the new price; by the time the sale was finalized in early January 1845, he had added more money to the pot. As a result more land was added to the package and the price went up, apparently with Samuel's approval, to $4,600. Whether the mills were wholly owned by Samuel Addams initially is not clear; in any case within months he appears to have given John some of the property as a gift. As of mid-1845, when the warranty deed for the property was filed, title records indicated that John owned half and his father owned half. Samuel, visiting John the following spring, bought more land that he later sold back to John at some profit to himself. That same year John added a second grinding stone, doubling the flour mill's output, perhaps aided by more of his father's money. John's older brother James, eager to join in the profit-making, would soon move to Cedarville to seek his own fortune. Samuel and his wife never moved west but George Weber did in 1845. Several of his adult children joined him although his wife did not. She died one year later, and he died in Como in 1854.[25]

John's worrying about his future was for naught. It did not take long for his mills to prosper. By 1850, he reported to the federal census taker that he possessed assets of $17,000. This made him the wealthiest man in fast-growing Cedarville, population four hundred, and its surrounding Buckeye Township. The next richest family in the township, his cousins the Reitzels, had assets of only $10,000. As these statistics illustrate, the wealth in the township was highly concentrated in the hands of a few. Of the 212 households in Buckeye Township in 1850, seven, or 3 percent, controlled nearly 20 percent of the township's wealth.[26] The myth of frontier equality notwithstanding, money brought from the class-stratified east quickly stratified the west.

Sarah struggled with loneliness at first. In a letter to Enos and Elizabeth Reiff in January 1845, written while her father was still back east selling his mill, she sounds wistful about the great distance that separated her from her family. She begins, "Here we are in the far west away from our relations." Making light of their hardships, she humorously describes their one-room log cabin. "I wish dear sister and brother you . . . could see us sit in our parlour and at the same time in our bed chamber and kitchen."[27] Her pen is silent about the burdens of primitive housekeeping and the fact that she is three months' pregnant with their first child.

John and Sarah's family grew as rapidly as his wealth. In the next eighteen years she gave birth to nine children; only five lived beyond their second year. These were Mary, born in 1845, Martha, in 1850, John Weber, called Weber, the first and only surviving son, in 1852, Sarah Alice, called Alice, in 1853, and Laura Jane, called Jennie, in 1860. Between the births of Mary and Martha a baby daughter, Georgiana, was born and died, and between the births of Alice and Jennie the family lost two small sons. The ninth child, a girl, was stillborn in 1863 and the cause of Sarah's death.[28]

John and Sarah were comforted in the loss of their four children by their strong religious faiths. Sarah did not keep a diary, but a few stray pieces of evidence, discussed below, suggest that she was an evangelical Christian. John's diary reveals his faith as prayerful, emotional, and devout; in other words, he, too, was an evangelical Christian. John's practice of private prayer, evident in the diary, would remain a lifelong habit. His faith was Christ-centered. After he died, his minister son-in-law was quick to remind Jane Addams that her father "desired you to live for . . . Christ." A story survives that John wept as he talked about Christ's sufferings in the Sunday school class he taught in Cedarville. Generally an unemotional man as he presented himself to others in later years, John Addams was not embarrassed to shed tears for Christ, knowing it was an acceptable sign of the depth of his faith.[29]

That he and Sarah were evangelical Christians was hardly surprising. They lived in an intensely religious period, that of the Second Great Awakening, when many thousands of people were experiencing religious conversion each year at revival meetings. Probably John and Sarah underwent a renewal of faith, called a conversion, sometime in their teens or early twenties. They felt themselves to have had an active experience of God and to have been saved in Jesus Christ.[30] John and Sarah's religion was profoundly important to them, as it was to many converts. For the rest of their lives, their faith would define their ethics, John's politics, and the influence they had on their children.

It also shaped their expectations of themselves. Evangelical Christians were intensely morally ambitious, believing that they would only enter heaven and avoid hell if they had actively sought salvation on earth through their own moral efforts. Charles Finney, the great preacher of the nondenominational wing of the evangelical movement in their day, wrote, "The first condition of moral obligation is the possession of the requisite powers of moral agency . . . and . . . the power of choice between possible courses to be chosen."[31] John agreed with Finney, and a surviving letter suggests that Sarah did, too. She wrote Enos and Elizabeth Reiff in 1841, "O if we only are prepared to meet our god in Judgment all is well. Earth's loss is Heaven's gain."[32]

John's path to his evangelical faith is difficult to reconstruct. His views concerning a single Christian ritual, baptism, provide the best clue. His parents baptized their children soon after birth in the German Reformed Church.[33] Infant baptism reflected the Calvinist belief in predestination. Samuel and Catherine Addams were confirming their hope that their offspring were among the Elect, that is, predestined to go to heaven when they died. Intended to emphasize God's sovereignty, predestination had the effect of denying the individual's responsibility for his salvation, or, more broadly, for the shape his life might take. Calvinism was at odds with the nation's rising individualism.

John Addams could not accept the doctrine of predestination. He would later tell Jane that he did not understand it and urged her not to pretend that she did.[34] In keeping with evangelical views and the Finney doctrine of moral choice, John and Sarah did not baptize their children. They believed that each child, as he or she grew older, would decide for himself or herself whether to "become a Christian," after which baptism would follow. The children felt this pressure. In 1864, Mary, nineteen, wrote to fourteen-year-old Alice, away at school, that she hoped "very soon you'll be one of Christ's lambs," adding that if "you make up your mind to follow Christ," perhaps Weber, their fifteen-year-old brother, would, too.[35] For Jane, the question of whether she would be baptized would hang like the sword of Damocles over her head in college and for years afterwards, placed there by her parents' evangelical faith.

John and Sarah relied on books to further their religious education. Sarah's books were about women's special responsibilities to perform works of charity and provide the moral example of self-sacrifice to the family. She and John owned the complete works of Hannah More, the influential British evangelist, founder of the British Sunday school movement, leading philanthropist and poet, and proponent of women's education, as well as Mrs. Ellis's *Guide to Social Happiness* and the evangelical Christian Margaret Coxe's *Claims of the Country on American Females*. The books John Addams brought west with him included a large number of evangelical Christian books, mostly about preaching and theology, including an 1832 edition of *Journal of the Life and Religious Labours of Elias Hicks*. In later years he would tell Jane that if he were forced to identify his preferred Protestant denomination, he would choose Hicksite Quakerism. The Hicksites were the evangelical branch of the Quakers and believed that men could prepare themselves for God's grace and that universal, personally achieved salvation was possible.[36]

When John Addams told Jane he was a Hicksite Quaker, he did not mean that he had joined that church. There was no Quaker meeting in the Freeport area for him to join. He meant that his religious ideas were closest to those of the Hicksites, who could be described as antidenominational. It was their central conviction that one's faith was guided by one's inner light. Elias Hicks, the founder of the sect, expected a man to frankly recognize and admit what he did not understand. John Addams agreed with this. When he told Jane that he did not understand predestination, he also told her to "always be honest with yourself inside." When Jane later praised her father's "mental integrity" regarding his religious beliefs, this was what she meant.[37]

Evangelical Christian faith was a faith of good works. Sarah was well known in the community for her compassionate efforts for others. After her death in 1863, others praised her "many deeds of charity to the poor[,] . . . the sick and unfortunate," her "constant willingness to . . . help . . . the suffering," and the way she "was always present when sympathy was needed or required." The local German newspaper spoke appreciatively of her work among German immigrant families.[38] Reading Hannah More's books certainly encouraged her in such efforts. In the famous poem "Sensibility" More wrote stirringly of "gen'rous sympathy's ecstatic hour" and "the bliss / Extracted from another's happiness" and about how it was the daughter's and wife's duty to give "the gift of minist'ring to others' ease." More's writings constituted an important influence on the women of the evangelical Anglo-American middle class to which Sarah belonged, and she seems to have lived up to More's expectations.[39]

John Addams's good works had a more reforming bent. Evangelical Christians in the mid-nineteenth century embraced a heroic task: to save the world by assisting Christ in his work of redeeming souls. Thus their primary focus was on reforming the individual by eradicating the personal vices of prostitution, drunkenness, and the absence of Christian faith. John Addams was a temperance man and served no alcohol in his home (Jane Addams would maintain that tradition at Hull House), but his greatest reform commitment in his early years in Illinois was to the Sunday school movement, a distinctly evangelical effort. Union, that is, interdenominational, Sunday schools were reform institutions intent on teaching literacy, improving personal morality, and inspiring Christian conversion in young people and adults of all ages. John Addams co-founded a Union Sunday school in Cedarville, taught the adult class every Sunday, and organized the annual Stephenson County Sunday School Convention in Freeport.[40]

Despite his interdenominational and Quaker enthusiasms, John Addams looked like a Presbyterian at first glance. He and his family were regular worshippers at the Presbyterian Church in Cedarville, and their neighbors generally thought of the Addams family as Presbyterian.[41] But he was not a member of the Presbyterian Church. That is, he was unwilling to sign the membership roster by professing to a belief in that denomination's creed. One obvious difficulty was the tenet of predestination, but that was not the only obstacle. His problem was with creeds in general. He did not join a church in Cedarville for the same reason that his friend and fellow Presbyterian weekly worshipper Abraham Lincoln did not. "I have never united myself with any church," Lincoln once said, "because I have found difficulty in giving my assent, without mental reservation, to the long, complicated statements of Christian doctrine which characterize their articles of belief and confessions of faith."[42]

John Addams's independent-minded approach to religion, or at least his willingness to mingle a private Quakerism with public worship at a non-Quaker denominational church, may have come from his mother, Catherine Huy Addams. Jane believed, apparently based on what her father told her, that his mother was a Quaker and taught the Quaker values of "plain living and high thinking" at home.[43] At the same time, Catherine's children were baptized in the German Reformed Church. She apparently was comfortable combining several versions of Protestantism in her own religious life.

The interesting question is why Jane Addams, who knew her father to be a deeply religious man, failed to capture this dimension in *Twenty Years*. In her stories about his views of predestination and Hicksite Quakerism, he sounds as if he approached religion with cool rationality. Perhaps the mystery of her silence about his faith was part of the mystery surrounding her own faith, which, by 1910, was, like her father's, highly personal and guided solely by her inner light. It is also mostly absent from the pages of her memoir.

———————

From his first day in northern Illinois, John Addams was a businessman with capital. As an early settler he was therefore positioned to help build the economy of the region, make a good deal of money, and win the respect of the community. One of his earliest entrepreneurial efforts was particularly effective in achieving all of these goals. In the late 1840s and early 1850s he was a leader in the campaign to attract the proposed Chicago-Galena Railroad to Freeport. After chairing a meeting in Freeport called to launch the local subscription drive, he traveled the countryside selling stock to citizens with little cash by persuading them that buying one of the $100 shares was a "public-spirited" act. He also headed off alternative routes twice. When a proposal pushed by the Mt. Carroll millers William and Nathaniel Haldeman and others to reroute the railroad south of Freeport seemed to be gaining ground, John Addams and several friends worked to defeat the plan. Months later, when the investors for the new north-south Illinois Central line offered a proposal that would have passed Freeport to the west, according to one newspaper, he "rallied all northern Illinois against it." The Board of Directors defeated the proposal by one vote, and Freeport was chosen for the Illinois Central route. Freeport had rail service on the Galena line by 1853 and on the Illinois Central line by 1854. In later years, the grateful citizens of Freeport would consider John Addams the "father of railroad enterprise in Stephenson County."[44]

The coming of the railroad made the nation's markets accessible at cheap transportation rates to the agriculturalists of the region, and John's businesses prospered. In 1858 he built a new flour mill with six grinding stones at a cost of $10,000. A year earlier, William Haldeman, abandoning his isolated Mt. Carroll mill, had opened a new steam mill in Freeport. After that, John Addams was careful to keep his flour prices competitive with those of Haldeman Mill.[45]

Although John Addams had been trained as a miller, he quickly became a multifaceted agricultural-industrial capitalist of the rural mid-nineteenth-century variety. To his core holdings of two mills and 675 acres of farmland, grazing land (for cattle), and timberland, he later added hundreds of acres of land and another manufacturing plant, the Cedar Creek Woolen Factory. Eventually he owned eighteen hundred acres in the county. As his assets accumulated, he moved into money-lending. In 1864 he co-founded the Second National Bank of Freeport, became its first president, and hired his friend Luther Guiteau to run it on a daily basis. He became involved in several fire insurance companies serving farmers, and by 1871 he was president of the Farmers' Insurance Company, the oldest such company in Freeport, with assets of $200,000. Real estate also beckoned. In 1869 he invested in a new building in Freeport, the Wilcox Opera House, and relocated his bank to its first floor. The eight-hundred-seat auditorium on the third floor became the best place in the county for holding concerts and lectures. By 1870 John Addams valued his personal estate at $80,000 and his real estate at $60,000 in the federal census.[46]

The Addams Homestead and Cedar Creek Mills. Combination Atlas Map of Stephenson County *(Geneva, IL: Thompson and Everts, 1871).*

Did his wealth mean that the Addams family was upper-class? In tiny Buckeye Township, yes. An 1871 publication featured John Addams as one of the township's eleven richest men. But if he was perceived as "very rich" in the township and perhaps also Stephenson County, his wealth positioned him as a member of the upper middle class in the state of Illinois and in the American economy. In an era in which an up-and-coming John D. Rockefeller Sr., still building his oil empire, was worth $5 million and the elderly Commodore Vanderbilt, whose transportation empire was complete, was worth $100 million, John Addams's wealth was relatively modest.[47]

John Addams was both a man of wealth and a civic leader, as was so often the case. In addition to founding the Sunday school, he helped organize the first public school in Cedarville, sat on the school board for the rest of his life, and contributed funds to support the teachers' salaries. He co-founded Cedarville's first library by lending out his own book collection and helped organize the town's first public cemetery, for which he donated the land. As churches began to be built in Cedarville, he served on their various building committees and made major donations towards their construction costs.[48] When the Civil War broke out, he did not fight because as a miller he was exempt from service, but he helped recruit men to serve from the county and supplied the unit with uniforms and equipment. When the war was over, he coordinated the fundraising effort to build a stone obelisk memorial in Freeport, the county seat, to the soldiers of Stephenson County who had given their lives for the cause.[49]

By the 1870s John Addams was greatly admired in Stephenson County. One story, still being repeated in the 1930s, serves to gauge the depth of the esteem in which he was held. According to the story, he passed a farmer one day and greeted him with the comment that it was fine weather and not cold at all. The farmer then turned up the earflaps on his cap. When another farmer came by and told him he'd freeze his ears off, the first replied, "No, I won't. I just saw John Addams and he says 'tain't cold."[50] Apocryphal or not, the story captures the way the average farmer felt about what John Addams said—that he must be right, even if common sense suggested otherwise.

No stories survive, on the other hand, to illustrate how wage-earners in the community felt toward John Addams. Nor is it known how he treated his own employees, who by the 1860s must have numbered between fifty and one hundred. Did he pay them well? How long were the work hours he required? Many wage-earners in these years were resentful of the way employers were exercising a new power over these matters in order to maximize profits. Wage labor was "slave labor," the workers said. Employers generally responded with the assurance that the young wage-earner would be a capitalist later. Further, they stressed that the employer's prosperity strengthened the regional economy on which wage-earners depended. In these ways, they argued, there was "a harmony of class interests," as the popular phrase held. The Pennsylvania Whig economist Henry Carey explained, "The interests of the capitalist and the laborer are . . . in perfect harmony with each other, as each derives advantage from every measure that tends to facilitate the growth of capital." The ideology denied the idea of distinct class interests. Calvin Colton, a Whig Party leader, was even more emphatic on the subject. "Every American laborer can stand up proudly and say," he wrote, "I AM A CAPITALIST, which is not a metaphor but literal truth."[51]

The ideology had some resonance with reality in the antebellum Whig-Republican (that is, rural) northern United States. Westward expansion created economic opportunities while economic competition offered a relatively even playing field, because most factories and businesses were fairly small. Abraham Lincoln had risen from poverty by working hard in an expanding economy. John Addams had used his family's wealth to create new jobs in northern Illinois. He likely believed what most employers believed: that he was doing his part to support wage-earners in their efforts to achieve success by providing them with jobs, even if the hours were long and the pay was low. Certainly, he thought his own prosperity was a just measure of his moral worth. In his day, the view was widely held that a wealthy man was a virtuous man. The popular evangelical Hartford minister Horace Bushnell stated the point concisely in 1847 when he declared, "A state of prosperity is itself one of the true evidences of character and public virtue."[52]

John Addams was too morally earnest, however, to rest on the laurels of material success. All the evidence suggests that he was intensely determined to be a good man. Perhaps the best evidence was the fact that his faith was not only evangelical but also "perfectionist." Perfectionism, a wing of the evangelical movement that was greatly increasing in popularity in the 1840s, held that once a person had been saved, or reborn, the new soul was without sin and that, henceforth, all of that person's deeds were for the benefit of others or, in the favorite word of the day, benevolent. In simplest terms, a perfectionist could do no wrong. Self-doubt, at least in theory, was eliminated. John Addams's library was full of the writings of evangelical perfectionists, including Elias Hicks, who was an evangelical Quaker perfectionist. John's friend Luther Guiteau, his bank manager, was a follower of John Noyes, founder of the perfectionist utopian Oneida Community in western New York State.[53] Apparently, John Addams was not put off by but was attracted to moral radicalism. Certainly, in his mature years he embodied moral perfection to others. Once full of self-doubt, he established a reputation in his community for being absolutely confident and correct in his moral judgments. He "was sure," as one friend recalled, "to be right on all moral questions, he was given to the right with his whole soul." Jane Addams recalled that her father "was the uncompromising enemy of wrong and of wrong doing." In his obituaries, the words "honorable," "high-minded," and "incorruptible" were repeated often.[54] John Addams bequeathed to Jane this passionate desire to be morally excellent.

Yet John was also known as a humble man. This was not a contradiction. In his day, a man of moral certitude like himself was not thought arrogant if he avoided putting on airs in his dealings with others. He was remembered as "a quiet, conscientious and dignified gentleman," a man of "genuine kindness" and "unassuming modesty," and as lacking "pretension." As he rode by in his carriage, pulled by a matched pair of gray horses, he would tip his black silk hat and greet and speak with everyone cordially. And he taught his children this American egalitarian etiquette. John's courtesy may have had its grounding in the political system. When Tocqueville asked a wealthy New York gentleman to explain to him America's "extreme equality of social relationships," the gentleman replied, "You must be polite to everybody since they all have political rights."[55]

In sum, John Addams's class relations were complicated. He was both a social democrat and a powerful man of wealth. He was both the equal of the less prosperous citizens of Stephenson County and their superior. The small farmers and wage-earners of the region understood, however, where the emphasis lay. They knew that in their relations with him the equality was limited and the superiority overriding. They spoke of him as "the king gentleman" of Stephenson County.[56] The sobriquet perfectly captures the mix of economic power, moral authority, and benevolence that John Addams exercised in his community.

By the 1860s, John Addams was a quintessentially successful man. His society had laid out the model by which he might "bring honor to God" and to Sarah and himself, and he had assiduously followed it. One might suppose, therefore, that he was content, but the historical record provides two hints otherwise. After his death, a local minister told a revealing story. Teaching Sunday school one day, John Addams had remarked as tears rolled down his cheeks that people who experience "the ingratitude of the human heart" must "take up Christ's cross" of suffering. The other hint was something his son-in-law once reminded Jane Addams about—that she "knew all [her father] suffered and tried to comfort him." John Addams's suffering could have had many causes but the story about his tears in Sunday school suggests that, among other things, he expected to receive more gratitude from others than he received. Perhaps he felt that his neighbors were not sufficiently grateful to him. If he did feel this, his expectations may well have been shaped by another common view—that the benevolent were owed gratitude by those they had helped. The Scottish moral philosopher Adam Smith, whose influence extended well into the nineteenth century, formulated the expectation precisely. Gratitude, he wrote in *A Theory of Moral Sentiments* (1759), is what the benevolent giver expects to receive from those who have benefited from his kindnesses.[57] Gratitude was not the same as respect; gratitude contained within it an acknowledgment of the power and superiority of the benevolent. Gratitude was what subjects owed kings, even a king of a minor realm, such as a county in northern Illinois.

The ultimate public service owed by a conscientious republican, wealthy man, and evangelical Christian was service in the state or national legislature. Conveniently, John Addams was already interested in politics. As a young man, he was a bit hot-headed on the subject. "At the P.O.," he wrote during his second month in Freeport, "got into the first violent political discussion since I am in the West, of which I was afterwards sorry." Presidential Election Day 1844 found him at the Freeport polls. He could not vote because state law required voters to have lived in the state for six months and he had not, so he went to watch. The voting was done by voice; the method was called "viva voce." The Democratic Party favored the method because it allowed the party to coerce the voter at the polls. John did not like it. He wrote in his diary that the "ballot is [the] proper way." In later years, he observed that the ballot was the best way for the people to rule "properly and fairly."[58]

The election results disgusted him. The Democratic Party's presidential candidate, James Polk, won both in Illinois and across the nation. John Addams was a Whig and, like many Illinois Whigs, he thought his newly adopted state entirely too "Democratic" or, as the slang expression went, too "Loco-Foco." It was, he wrote to Enos and Elizabeth Reiff, " 'Loco' to the core—every person who has been in the state six months has a right to vote." The voters included, to his disgust, unpropertied immigrant men. "An ignorant Norwegian . . . who knows nothing but says he has been here six months 1 day" can vote, he informed them, while "the Pennsylvanian who paid [property] tax in his native state and has been here five months and 29 days stands back at the polls. This is shameful."[59] He had, of course, been in Illinois for not quite four months. The Democratic Party's "Loco-Foco" version of democracy left a bitter taste in his mouth.

John Addams came by his interest in politics naturally. Although Samuel Addams does not appear to have run for office, other Addams men were legislators. John's grandfather Isaac served in the state assembly; his uncle Peter ran unsuccessfully for the U.S. Congress, and his uncle William served as a state assemblyman and a two-term Congressman. Once Jacksonian Democrats, by the 1840s the Addams men were Whigs. Sarah, too, came from a family active in politics. Her grandfather, John Weber, had

been a state legislator.[60] John Addams ran for no political office in his first
ten years in Illinois but through his many businesses and other undertakings he worked hard to build his political base.

His opportunity came in 1854, when the Whig Party split nationally over
the question of whether and how slavery could be regulated in the territories. John Addams's views concerning slavery, of which there is no written record, can be deduced from his other loyalties and from his actions.
Given that he was an enthusiast for republican government, an evangelical
Christian, and attracted to Hicksite Quakerism, he likely thought slavery
a morally corrupting practice for the slaveholder and the person enslaved.
This did not necessarily make him an abolitionist. Such views were compatible with an opposition solely to slavery's expansion. In any case, he was
willing to help African Americans escape slavery, though it meant breaking the federal Fugitive Slave Act of 1850 and risking a fine of $1,000 and
six months in jail. It is not known when he began to hide those fleeing to
freedom, but he hid at least one during the Civil War. Jane Addams recalled
discovering her father and an escaped slave in "quiet conversation" when
she was four. She "never forgot" the sight. This memory would become a
touchstone for her in later years, confirming her belief that her father was
committed to the principle of social justice.[61]

In 1854 the issue of slavery's expansion caused a political realignment
in Illinois and across the nation. In February 1854 John Addams joined
a group of northwestern Whigs at Ripon, Wisconsin, who vowed to create a new antislavery "Republican" party if Congress passed the Kansas-
Nebraska bill with the support of southern Whigs. The bill became law in
May, and by July angry Whigs had formed statewide Republican parties
across the northwest. In August, John Addams signed a call to Stephenson
County voters "of all parties" to attend a convention in Freeport to elect
delegates for the county's first Republican convention. Elected a delegate,
Addams then served on the committee at the convention that drafted a resolution, later adopted, that "slavery is destructive of the dearest rights of a
free people." Chosen by the party's local leadership to run as the Republican candidate for the state senate representing a newly designed district of
Stephenson and Jo Daviess Counties, he was carried into office in November on a wave of popular support for the new party. Repeatedly reelected,
he would serve for sixteen years.[62]

Addams's approach to representing his constituents was classically
Whig. Believing that he had been elected in recognition of his virtue, he

expected to use his own judgment and to stand free of political pressures, which he perceived to be corrupting. His grandson wrote, "John Addams did not so much care to know what the people wanted, as what would be good for them. He took advice only from his own conscience." Ralph Waldo Emerson, writing in the 1840s, expressed roughly the same view somewhat more poetically when he observed that the best politicians "do not need to inquire of their constituents what they should say, but are themselves the country which they represent."[63]

Addams would have an early opportunity to test his ideal against political reality. One of his first votes as a new state senator was to elect a U.S. senator to represent Illinois in Congress, as the U.S. Constitution then required. The term of one of the state's two senators, a pro-Nebraska Democrat named James Shield, had expired and he was seeking reelection. He had two opponents: Lyman Trumbull, a newly elected Congressman and anti-Nebraska Democrat, and Abraham Lincoln, a Springfield lawyer, former Illinois state senator and Congressman, and an anti-Nebraska Whig. In running for the Senate, Lincoln had the strong support of Elihu B. Washburne, his former colleague in Congress who had just been reelected as Congressman for Stephenson and Jo Daviess Counties under the new Republican Party banner. Washburne was the most powerful Republican in Addams's district.[64]

With the Senate prepared to vote on the question, Lincoln, counting his votes, wrote Washburne to ask about John Addams. Washburne, adept at sending messages between the lines, replied: "John Huy Addams certainly ought to be your friend. . . . You are . . . the choice of nearly every man who voted for him in Joe [*sic*] Daviess County. . . . He is a conscientious, excellent man and will do what he believes to be right. . . . Show to Addams what I have said about him." Whether Lincoln showed Addams the letter is not known, but when he wrote Addams to ask him how he would vote, he was careful to add, coached by Washburne, that he knew that Addams would "vote according to his conscience." Addams's reply also does not survive, but apparently his conscience and Elihu Washburne's preference coincided because he voted for Lincoln.[65]

Unwilling as he was to be lobbied, John Addams was even more horrified by bribes, which were common enough in the senate when he served. He soon became as famous in the Illinois General Assembly as he already was in Stephenson County for his incorruptibility. An "old political friend of his" once told Jane Addams that her father was so well-known for his unwillingness to take bribes that no one even dared offer him any.[66] From her father she acquired a view of politics that defined the crucial moment of political influence as taking place at the ballot box and that located political authority in the legislator's conscience.

Like other Whiggish Republicans, John Addams worked during his sixteen years as a state legislator to broaden the government's role in three areas: education, economic development, and care of dependents such as the "insane," the deaf, and the blind. At various times he served on the committees on education, public roads, township organization and counties, saline and swamplands, geology, agriculture, internal navigation, finance, banks and corporations, and state charity institutions. As a Republican, he favored women's suffrage—a policy the party platform finally endorsed in 1872. Eventually he became an influential leader in the twenty-four-person state senate and chair of the Senate Finance Committee.[67]

John Addams's ideas about the role of government in society were of a distinctly nineteenth-century sort. He was a liberal to the extent that he believed in individual autonomy, had a hatred of tyranny, and trusted the free market to benefit society. He was not, however, what some have called a "procedural liberal," that is, someone who wishes moral values to be excluded from shaping the political process. Instead he was a perfectionist, or evangelical, liberal—that is, he believed in society's perfectibility and in government's moral responsibility to aid those who were weaker.[68] He brought his morality to his politics because that is what his conscience required.

———————

Perhaps the most difficult part of John's political career, for himself and for Sarah, was that it kept him away from home for several months every other year. This left Sarah not only without his company but with a good deal of extra work to do, sometimes while she was pregnant. She was in the eighth month of her sixth pregnancy when John left Cedarville in January 1855 to serve his first term, and she gave birth on the last day of the session to a son who only lived two months. She was in the seventh and eighth months of her seventh pregnancy during the 1857 term, and the son who was born that spring lived only two years.[69] In January 1863, when John left for Springfield to serve his sixth term, she was seven months' pregnant with her ninth child.

Neither she nor the child would survive. A few weeks after John left, she received word in the middle of a cold January night that the wife of the

*John Huy Addams and colleagues (fellow Republican state legislators?),
ca. the late 1850s. JHA is in the back row on the far right. Illinois
State Historical Library, Old State Capitol Building, Springfield.*

miller who ran their flour mill was in labor and needed Sarah's help. As she climbed the hill toward town, clumsy in her state of advanced pregnancy, she slipped and fell. Though she continued on and delivered the neighbor's baby, she was bleeding heavily internally and collapsed soon afterward.[70] John, receiving an urgent telegram in Springfield, took the next train home and by morning he was at her bedside. She had slipped into a coma but later she regained consciousness and seemed to be improving. Two days later, however, her condition worsened. She was able to say the Lord's Prayer but not to find the words to speak to John. She died the following day.[71] She left five children, including Jane, who was two and a half.

John Addams's despair must have mingled with feelings of guilt. No man in his circumstances could have escaped the thought that if he had only been at home, he might have prevented the accident. Perhaps he might have stopped her from going out that night in her condition or he might have gone with her to give her his arm as she climbed the hill. Sarah's brother George, who was by then living in Freeport, wrote their sister Elizabeth that John took Sarah's passing "severely to heart."[72]

CHAPTER 2

THREE MOTHERS

1860–73

What we know about Jane Addams's childhood comes mostly from her own pen. In the sometimes lyrical, sometimes gently probing, sometimes skillfully obscure passages of her classic memoir, *Twenty Years at Hull-House*, Addams shared with the world her memories of her small-town American life. The situation for the biographer is at once delightful and dangerous—delightful because Addams is an evocative writer with a talent for telling stories, dangerous for the same reason and because the dearth of other sources leaves us too dependent on Addams's account.

But all texts reveal more than their authors intended, and none more so than autobiographies. While few can doubt that Addams crafted an artful tale of her Cedarville years, one that omits far more than it includes, the book escapes the boundaries of the universalizing story she sets out to tell.[1] She views herself as a typical child, sharing, for example, the expected tales of how her father helped her in her moments of embarrassment and moral perplexity. But her stories also provide glimpses of the unexpected—most significantly, of the unusual depth of her feelings of inadequacy and of her intense fear of, and fascination with, death. Like every child, Jane Addams had a particular childhood whose influence on her would ramify down the years.

The way she treats her parents is also hardly typical. Although she writes a good deal in the book's early chapters about her conversations with her father, she writes nothing at all about her relations with her mother. Her dilemma, in part, was that she had three. In addition to her deceased mother, she had a temporary mother in her oldest sister Mary and, beginning when she was eight, a new permanent mother in her stepmother, Anna Hostetter Haldeman Addams. Her failure to write about her mothers leaves us to puzzle about what she might have said and to consider the possibility that her silence embodied the profoundest truth of all—that she felt motherless most of her life.

Although Jane Addams was too young, at two and a half, to remember losing her mother, she remembered the tragic effects of Sarah's passing on the family. She writes in *Twenty Years*, although not in reference to her own circumstance, "[C]hildren whose mother is dead . . . perform unaccustomed offices for each other and awkwardly exchange consolations, as children in happier households never dream of doing."[2] The family's disbelief that Sarah was really gone mingled with a great longing that she not be forgotten.[3] Years later Addams described these feelings in a speech at a memorial service for the mother of a close friend: "The craving to . . . make tangible and enduring . . . the personality which has passed . . . beyond the reach of household affection is, perhaps, one of the oldest cravings of the hungry human heart." Three years after Sarah died, the Addams family was still struggling to absorb the reality of it. "It is all like a dream," twenty-one-year-old Mary wrote Alice, away at school. "I expect to see her."[4]

Sarah's death changed Jane's relations with her family. Mary, as the oldest sister, did her best to be a substitute mother. Not quite eighteen years old when Sarah died, Mary was considered by the family to be the daughter most like Sarah. A son remembered her as "thoughtful" and "affectionate," someone forgetful of her own needs. Family stories portrayed her as a person of "unfailing serenity and indulgent love." Many years later, Jane Addams would tell Mary's granddaughter of the devotion she felt to Mary as a child.[5] Mary's love, although not a mother's love, left a deep imprint.

After Sarah's death, the bond between Jane and her father also became stronger. The youngest child, she became his favorite, the one he feared the most to lose. He adored her, at times indulged her, even, some of her family thought, spoiled her.[6] His devotion was returned. Jane remembered, "I centered upon [my father] all that careful imitation which a little girl ordinarily gives to her mother's ways and habits." Most of all, Jane aspired to meet his high moral standards. "[C]hildren long 'to be good' with an intensity which they give to no other ambition," Addams wrote in 1898. "We can all remember that the earliest strivings of our childhood were in this direction and [that] we venerated grown people because they had attained perfection." Her father, she writes in *Twenty Years*, drew her "into the moral concerns of life," providing her with a "clew" that she afterwards "clung" to as she tried to find her way through life's "intricate mazes." The "clew," the reader gradually discovers, was to trust her conscience.[7]

As a child, Jane rarely felt that she achieved the moral perfection to which she aspired. She thought of herself as bad, not good. Her older sister Alice remembered that she "was always asking people to forgive her for the naughty things she fancied she had done." No doubt Jane was thinking of herself when she observed that all children suffer from "childish struggles in which a sense of hidden guilt, of repeated failure in 'being good,' . . . humbles a child to the very dust."[8]

Often she sought reassurance from her father. She recalled "constantly confiding my sins and perplexities." Astutely, he did not dismiss her worries. When she woke him in the middle of the night to confess that she had told a lie, he reassured her that he did not mind her unexpected visit. Speaking to her in the third person, as was his Quakerish habit, he told her that if he "had a little girl who told lies, [he was] glad that she felt too bad to go to sleep afterwards." When, after she had a temper tantrum, she asked her father, using his third-person syntax, whether he still loved "such a bad girl," he said he did but that she should try to control her temper. He also did not condescend. When she asked him to explain the thorny theological question of predestination, he flattered her intelligence by telling her, she writes, that he feared "he and I did not have the kind of mind" that could understand the concept. This sent her spirits soaring. "[A]ny intimation," she notes, "that our minds were on equality lifted me very high indeed."[9]

In all the stories about her conversations with him that Addams tells in *Twenty Years*, she seeks him out to question him. Apparently he was not one to initiate a conversation with a child. Yet children knew they could speak to him, though it took some courage, and that he would respond thoughtfully. A grandson, John Linn, remembered, "[He] was so very big to me and grave and I was always wondering what his thoughts must be— and yet I was so absolutely certain always of his love and that if I did dare to speak to him a certain look would come into his eyes and I felt he was never putting me off or only having to listen." Another grandson recalled his "serene reflectiveness."[10] Tall, silent, and solemn, John Addams was a daunting parent but also one a child could trust.

Sometimes he provided reassurance inadvertently. When small, Jane Addams thought of herself as "ugly," with a "crooked" body. Her general feelings of inadequacy no doubt contributed to this, but she was also mindful that she possessed a physical flaw. Although she was attractive, with large, wide-set gray eyes like her father's, a high square forehead, and slightly wavy, fine reddish-brown hair, she had a crooked back, having suffered from Pott's disease, or spinal tuberculosis, when she was small. The disease partially rigidified her spine, so that her head tilted sideways slightly and certain movements gave her pain. (A more minor flaw was that she was pigeon-toed.)[11] Convinced she was too unattractive to be seen with her elegant father among strangers, she suffered agonies of shame when she was forced to accompany him under such circumstances—for example, when visitors attended his Sunday school class. She was sure her presence profoundly embarrassed him. Eventually he managed, by accident, to undo the spell. Seeing her waiting for him as he was coming out of his bank in Freeport one day, he lifted his "high and shining silk hat" and, to her amazement, right there in front of "a mass of strange people," made an "imposing bow." Suddenly she realized that her worry was absurd; it "collapse[d] . . . into the limbo of forgotten specters."[12] The reasons for her obsession can only be guessed. Perhaps she intuited her father's substantial need for public admiration. The sensitive psyche of a child does not misread a parent's preoccupations.

Against the winds of self-doubt, Jane's most powerful anchor other than her family was the stable, interesting world in which she lived. Her father's grain mill, she remembered, was especially enticing, "full of dusky, floury places." Another pleasure was watching the enormous water wheel turn and pondering how the hard kernels of yellow wheat became white flour that then found its way into "myriad bowls of bread and milk." The sawmill, on the other hand, offered the enticement of a dangerous game. She and other children would take turns sitting on a log as it slowly approached the buzzing saw, a flashing, whining wheel of flying teeth, and jumping off at the last minute.[13]

The two mills stood in a beautiful wooded glen. Millennia ago an ancient river had carved a deep gouge through an up-thrusting limestone ridge, leaving behind eighty-foot cliffs that were, Jane recalled, "too perpendicular to climb without skill."[14] The relict creek could be seen from the Addams's front porch—a dancing ribbon of silver that ran, curving, from right to left at the feet of the encircling cliffs. Behind the largest cliff, Pine Hill, out of sight, was the town cemetery, where Sarah Weber Addams was buried.

The Addams's two-story brick homestead faced the glen, its back set into the gentle hill that formed the glen's fourth side. Running in front of the house was the road north out of town. Once it crossed the creek, it forked, one branch heading west between the cliffs to Galena and the other continuing north toward Wisconsin. Behind the house were the large barn, carriage house, poultry yard, and stable; to the south was the apple orchard, where white blossoms filled the air with fragrance in spring and apples loaded the tree boughs in late summer and fall.[15] Beyond the orchard,

up a hill, was the town of Cedarville, a prospering community of about
five hundred people when Jane Addams was born, and the second largest
town, after Freeport, in Stephenson County. The businesses, attracted to
the town because it had one of the busier flour mills in the county, included a carriage factory, a wagon factory, and a blacksmith shop. There
were three churches: Methodist, German Reformed–Lutheran, and Evangelical.[16] For a small child the bowl-shaped creek valley and the town of
Cedarville formed a satisfying, self-contained world.

But it was not a world from which human death could be banished. Having
first invaded Jane's life when she was two, it returned repeatedly in childhood and each time stirred fears that spilled out into terrifying nightmares.
She is silent about these events in *Twenty Years*, but not necessarily because
she was keeping them private; when she wrote the book in 1909–10, she
had forgotten them, or more precisely, had not yet remembered them. They
were restored to her when she visited Egypt in 1913 and found herself immersed in the ancient culture of the pharaohs, a culture deeply preoccupied
with death. As she studied the artwork in the tombs, with their many pictures of dead men's journeys to the afterlife, Addams's mind was suddenly
flooded with memories. Unnerved and fascinated, she made these fresh
recollections the focus of a powerfully evocative essay she published the
following year in the *Atlantic Monthly* titled "Unexpected Reactions of a
Traveler in Egypt."[17] The memories she describes, all dealing with death,
suggest the impact her mother's abrupt disappearance had had on her two-
year-old psyche—that it had been traumatized enough by the shock to re-
press them and that a feeling of helplessness had been seared into her soul.
In each memory, death was terrifying and a spur to action.

The earliest memory was of an event that happened when she was
roughly four years old. In Egypt, it came rushing back in rich detail. The
mother of one of the children in Jane's "ABC" class had died, and their
teacher took the class to attend the burial in a church cemetery next to
the school. Jane stood by the grave with the other children, looking upon
"the still face" of the mother in the open coffin and watching as the lid
was closed and the mother was put "into the ground."[18] Seeing the mother
abandoned in the cold earth frightened her. She did not want to be alone.
Afterwards, she walked along with the other mourners until their ways
parted. Then she ran terrified the rest of the way home.

At the homestead, finding no family to comfort her, she ended up in the kitchen, where, desperate to talk with someone, she asked the hired girl, who was baking a cake, what shape pan she would bake the cake in. She did not ask what she most wanted to ask. "Although the idle words were on my lips, I wanted to cry out, 'Their mother is dead; whatever, whatever will the children do?' " She had heard the sentence spoken as she had walked among the other mourners. As an adult, in Egypt, she understood the question, but she also knew that she had misunderstood it as a child. Back then, she thought the question was meant as "a demand" that the children take "definite action . . . against this horrible thing [that] had befallen their mother."

What followed next was also part of the memory she regained. For weeks afterward, her days were, she remembered, "heavy with a nameless oppression and the nights filled with horror." [19] The sight of the dead mother had apparently triggered her unconscious memories of her own mother's death and caused her fragile sense of safety to collapse. Fear of death—deep, terrifying, overwhelming, relentless fear—nearly drowned her four-year-old soul.

This terror of death was awakened again the following year, or perhaps the year after, by the mere threat of death. This memory, too, she regained in Egypt. Standing in a tomb, she suddenly remembered neighbors telling her about the exciting religious revival meetings taking place in town that she, being too young, was forbidden to attend. Night after night, they told her, people "shouted for joy or lay on the floor 'stiff with power' " while others, in a spiritual agony, "could not find salvation." Hearing about the unsaved ones, who were unprotected, she knew, from "the terrors of death," she felt terribly sad. "My heart was wrung for [them]," she writes. She decided that she could save them if she could find the right words in the Bible to say but she abandoned the project once she realized she did not read well enough to read the entire Bible out loud quickly. She also feared that she would die in the meantime. Her anguish lingered. In her memory that "cold winter" was one of "prolonged emotional stress." [20]

Jane's world fell apart again when she was six, and again death was the reason. The Egyptian trip brought back this memory, too. In the early spring of 1867, her sixteen-year-old sister Martha died of typhoid fever while attending Rockford Female Seminary in Rockford, Illinois, a city thirty miles east of Freeport. When her family went to Freeport for the funeral and left Jane behind with only Polly, the housekeeper, for company,

Jane kept a terrified vigil on the stairs. "Only the blank wall which flanked one side of the stairway," she wrote, "seemed to afford protection in this bleak moment against the formless peril." Again there were nightmares. In one she dreamed again and again that Mary would also die and there would be no one to love her.[21]

When that dream subsided, she had a new dream that, though not a nightmare, kept repeating itself. This dream she had always remembered. Without associating it with Martha's death, she describes it in detail in *Twenty Years*. "[E]veryone in the world was dead excepting myself, and . . . upon me rested the responsibility of making a wagon wheel . . . , [without which] the affairs of the world could not be resumed." The village streets of Cedarville were empty, but at the blacksmith shop a fire glowed upon the forge. Every night she dreamt that she stood in the same spot in the shop, "darkly pondering" how to make a wheel. She knew that everyone was "gone around the edge of the hill" to the village cemetery and that she alone remained alive "in the deserted world."

Daylight did not dispel her anxiety. "The next morning would often find me," she writes, "a delicate girl of six, with the further disability of a curved spine, standing in the doorway of the village blacksmith shop, anxiously watching the burly, red-shirted figure at work." She tried to memorize how he made the wheel and to learn more by asking questions. The hardest part, the step that she thought would be "horrid," was sizzling the iron in water. This step, the blacksmith assured her, he had to do in order to make the iron hard. The task struck her as particularly daunting. "I would sigh heavily and walk away, bearing my responsibility as best I could." She told no one. "There is something too mysterious [about dreams] to be communicated," she writes, "although it is at the same time too heavy a burden to be borne alone."[22]

The meaning of the dream unpacks in layers. Jane's days were filled with wagon wheels, carriage wheels, grinding stones, mill wheels, and saw mills, and their absence would indeed have marked the end of her world's affairs. As for making a wheel, one suspects that her subconscious concocted the task out of her familiarity with the nearby blacksmith shop and the cliché, no doubt overheard in conversation, that there was no need to reinvent the wheel. Finally, her motive in the wheel dream follows her motive in her earlier recovered memories, those about the mother's funeral and the suffering of the unsaved. In the wheel dream, too, she needed to do something to protect those whom death had hurt or threatened to hurt. And in the wheel dream, as in the earlier memories, her psyche was convinced that she could not perform the action proposed.[23] Addams's early loss of her mother seems to have taught her both that she would fail at any heroic action she attempted and that she urgently needed to try. Beneath those lessons lay the first lesson, the scar that had not fully healed—that she had failed to prevent her mother's death.

What happened next was revealing. Addams tells this story, too, in *Twenty Years*, noting that it took place before she turned seven but without mentioning that her sister's death preceded it. During a trip to Freeport with her father, she writes, she saw the city's poorer district for the first time. It was a kind of poverty she had not seen in the countryside. The rundown houses were strangely close together, cheek-by-jowl. When she asked her father why people lived in such houses, he told her they lacked enough money to live in better ones. "With much firmness" she replied that when she grew up she would have "a large house but it would . . . be built . . . in the midst of horrid houses like these."[24]

In telling this story, Addams, a skillful narrator, knew that readers would catch the implication—she never makes the point explicitly—that she, now living at Hull House, a large, elegant house in a rundown, working-class, crowded neighborhood of Chicago, was fulfilling her childhood vow. It all seems rather tidy, and several scholars have wondered whether she made up the story of the vow to strengthen the narrative force of her autobiography.[25] The evidence suggests that she did not. A Cedarville teacher remembered her father telling it in the 1870s. She told the story herself to two reporters in 1892.[26] Furthermore, the vow plausibly resonates with the troubles on her six-year-old mind in the weeks after Martha's death. Much evidence suggests that as a child and as an adult Addams subconsciously associated death with the poor, that is, those struggling to survive. If that is true, then her vow expressed the urgent need she always felt in death's presence to act on behalf of those at risk of dying.

Soon after Jane turned eight, her father made a decision that abruptly changed her life. "My father's second marriage . . . occur[red in] my eighth year," she writes in *Twenty Years* (precisely speaking, it was her ninth year). A few pages later she tells the story of a trip that she, her older sister, her stepbrother, and "my mother and father" took to Madison, Wisconsin. These are her only published references to her stepmother, Anna Hostetter Haldeman Addams. Some have thought her relative silence malevolent, a reasonable assumption given the tensions that developed between them.

Jane Addams at eight. Jane Addams Memorial Collection (JAMC neg. 2766), Special Collections, The University Library, University of Illinois at Chicago.

But in the text of *Twenty Years* Addams mentions no family member by name, not even her father, and he is the only one she writes about in any detail.[27] She does not name or describe her sister Mary, to whom she was devoted, or her sister Alice, to whom she was later close; she tells about her games with her stepbrother George, a loved childhood companion, but never mentions his name.

At the same time, there is no question that her failure to describe Anna leaves many questions. From the time Jane Addams was eight until she was twenty-eight years old, unless she was away at college or one of them was traveling, they lived together. Their relations were intimate and, because of Anna's forceful personality, necessarily intense. Anna's granddaughter Marcet Haldeman-Julius described her grandmother, whom she adored, as someone "alive in every fiber" and a person "whom people either loved rather extravagantly or disliked thoroughly." Without question, Jane Addams had strong feelings about Anna but she chose not to publish them. Those she expressed in correspondence with her family were probably lost to posterity when she destroyed certain letters because she thought them "too intimate" to be used for a biography.[28]

Anna Hostetter Haldeman, the wife of John Addams's competitor, the Freeport miller William Haldeman, had been a widow two years when John

Addams began to court her in the spring of 1868. Tall and stylish in her silks and satins, Anna was a striking, if not beautiful, woman with a high forehead, long nose, piercing dark hazel eyes, and thin, firm lips. Like John, she was a Pennsylvanian by birth and, like her two brothers, an early settler of Illinois. She was also a Swedenborgian. This Protestant sect believed strongly in free will, divided the living into two categories—those who are good and those who are evil—and believed in the reality of the spiritual world.[29]

Unlike many of the women of Freeport and perhaps unlike Sarah as well, Anna had intellectual interests. She loved literature; Byron, Scott, Shakespeare, and Goethe were among her favorite authors. She also played the piano and the guitar and sang. Anna's love of culture was no affectation but deeply felt. One of her favorite sayings was, "Whatever is beautiful— that belongs to me."

Anna had great personal charm, particularly with men. She was, Marcet wrote, "the type [of woman] . . . who instinctively wants men to love and protect them. . . . She understood men and loved to attract and please them."[30] Flattery was one of her methods. In a letter she wrote to John Addams a few months after their marriage, when he was in Springfield attending to legislative business, she closed with just the right words of modest subservience: "God's care be over you," she wrote. "This is the prayer of her who is now the *smaller* part of *your dear self*."[31] She had even adopted his habit of speaking of herself in the third person.

John Addams, at least as Anna remembered it, succumbed quickly to her charms and fell in love. The serious, dignified Addams, five years a widower, could not resist the flattering, vivacious, sophisticated Anna Haldeman. Her very oppositeness in temperament must have been what at first attracted him, though in time their differences would become a source of tension. Marcet writes of Anna, whom she called Ann, "This radiant and at times flaming woman—who first and last belonged to herself—was often a whirl of bewilderment to John Addams. . . . [She] brought an alien element of excitement, not to say confusion, into the previously placid household at Cedarville. . . . Accustomed to dominate quietly those around him, he found that Ann was one person who had unassailable individuality."[32]

In fact, Anna was as accustomed as John Addams was to dominating those around her, though she was intense and vocal in her methods where John was grave and quiet. Anna's brother, knowing his sister's temperament, took the opportunity when writing to congratulate her on her remarriage to advise "forbearance always; as in every family, there will sometimes

Anna Haldeman Addams and John Huy Addams. Jane Addams Collection,
Swarthmore College Peace Collection.

occur differences of opinion which require calm deliberate concessions on both sides. If you will, you can do much toward making others, as well as yourself, happy." It was good advice, but Anna was unable to follow it. As Marcet observed, she could not control her temper.[33]

If John Addams married for love, Anna did not. She told Marcet she had "qualms" about marrying John but decided to because "I thought he would make a good father for my sons and I *knew* I would make a good mother for his children." Anna had two sons. Harry, twenty, who was away studying music, and later medicine, in Germany, and George, seven. The Addams family consisted of Mary, twenty-three and still unmarried, Weber, sixteen, Alice, fifteen, and Jane, eight. Anna may have felt a special sympathy for Weber, Alice, and Jane because she had lost her own parents as a child— her mother when she was six, her father when she was fifteen. Anna also shared John's Pennsylvania roots and a love of reading (although not the same sort of books; John preferred history).[34] Furthermore, he was wealthy.

At the time Anna accepted John Addams's proposal she was in difficult financial straits. When William Haldeman died in 1866, he had left his estate burdened with debts.[35] William's wealthy brother Nathaniel, who had been named a co-executor of the estate with Anna, withdrew from that commitment, probably because he knew Anna's spendthrift ways. To his disgust, the court then required that he bond the estate with his own securities. Meanwhile, he and Anna tried to make money with the mill, but this effort only created more debt. In the fall of 1868, he petitioned the county court to require Anna to appear on the first day of the court's fall term, November 16, so that he could terminate the bond. This would leave Anna liable for the estate's debts.[36] Anna did not appear. Instead, on November 17 she married John Huy Addams at Freeport. She knew the implications for Nathaniel of her marriage. The Haldeman will required that if she remarried, she could no longer be executor of the estate and that Nathaniel must take that responsibility, which he subsequently did. It also stipulated that if she remarried her inheritance from the Haldeman estate would be reduced from 100 percent to one-third, the other two-thirds to go to her sons when they came of age, but this was no loss given the condition of the estate.[37]

The circumstances surrounding her second marriage illustrate the skill with which Anna used people as means to her own ends. In this case, the end she sought was financial security and the means was John Addams. Future events would confirm that she also hoped the marriage would provide her sons with the financial resources to do well in life, but in this she would fail to gain John Addams's cooperation. Anna understood the narrow options available to her as a woman and had concluded, as many women did in the same circumstances, that if she wanted financial security and personal status she would have to find ways to control the men in her life.

Jane Addams must have watched with amazement on moving day, when Anna and George arrived with their furniture and other belongings. These included several fine walnut beds and marble-topped dressers, large clothing wardrobes, gold-rimmed china, innumerable books and bound volumes of magazines, a guitar, and a piano.[38] The moment Anna arrived in Cedarville, she was quite possibly its most cultured citizen. Curiosity about her abounded. When she attended church for the first time, alone because John had left to attend the legislative session in Springfield, she discovered, she wrote John, "many piercing glances directed at me." She did not appreciate the scrutiny. She complained, "I trust I will some day cease to be an object of so much attraction." The neighbors' fascination was understandable. Aside from the fact that she was John Addams's new wife, there was a sharp contrast between Anna's culture and many of her Cedarville neighbors' rusticism.[39]

Happy to be the most elegant person in town, Anna set out to bring Jane's appearance up to the mark but ran into opposition. She bought Jane a new Sunday coat that Jane thought, she writes in *Twenty Years*, "gorgeous beyond anything I had ever worn before," but when Jane showed it to her father on Sunday morning, he told her to wear her old cloak. If she wore the new one, he explained, she would make the other girls at Sunday school, who did not have beautiful cloaks, feel bad. Unhappy but obedient, Jane changed cloaks and walked beside her father to church, her mind "busy with the old question . . . [of] the inequalities of the human lot." At the church door she announced her conclusion—that something should be done to make things more equal. John Addams replied that nothing could be done about "such things as clothes" but people could be equal in "the affairs of education and religion," which was why it was "very stupid" to wear "the sort of clothes that made it harder to have equality even there."[40]

Addams offers no interpretation of the story, preferring to let it speak for itself. Her silence allows it to be read as a tribute to her father's commitment to equality in education and religion and his desire to protect the poor from feelings of envy or shame. Yet there was a contradiction between her father's advice and his own and Anna's behavior. Neither he nor Anna "dressed down" when they went to church in Cedarville. Anna went in her best silk and John Addams wore his tall silk hat. Parents sometimes see their children's deeds in more symbolic terms than they see their own.

There were now nine in the Haldeman-Addams family, but with Anna's son Harry in Germany and Alice and Weber Addams often away at school, there were often only five in the house: Anna, John, Mary, Jane, and George, plus two live-in servants—the elderly housekeeper, Polly Beer, and a hired girl. For Jane Addams, who had to share her father with Anna now, the creation of a new family out of two separate ones could only have been deeply unsettling. To make matters worse, Anna was sterner in matters of discipline than Mary was, and Jane did not hide where her loyalties lay. A friend of Mary's who often visited the Addams homestead watched Jane in her relations with Mary and Anna. Years later she wrote to Addams, "I remember how much more acceptable to you was the service of love from your eldest sister than the word of authority from your stepmother."[41] Anna's arrival in Jane Addams's life must have felt to Jane like an unexpected plunge into cold water.

If Jane's new stepmother was an unpleasant disciplinarian, she was also, at times, delightful company, warmly affectionate and enthusiastic. Then again, she could explode with anger. She was a woman of fierce moods. No one could have been more opposite to Jane in temperament. Her granddaughter Marcet wrote in the 1920s about this difference, drawing on her mother Alice's and Anna's recollections. Although Marcet was devoted to her grandmother, she was also, by this time, devoted to her Aunt Jane and wished to understand both sides of the relationship. "Aunt Jane had the steady, reserved disposition of her mother and father; even in her young willfulness she was never dramatic. . . . [Ann's] outbursts of enthusiasm, while more agreeable or charming, were almost as disconcerting as the explosions of temper." Sudden emotional intensity of any kind caught Jane by surprise and made her uncomfortable. Still, she suffered more from Anna's anger. Marcet believed that Jane "resented . . . the conflicts" with Anna. Jane's more mellow temperament, however, did not mean that she could be easily dominated. In Marcet's judgment, "Jane, though quieter . . . and more equitable, had a strength and assertiveness that matched Ann's."[42]

To this already volatile mix, another unstable element was added. Anna doted on her younger son, seven-year-old George, who, as Marcet put it, was the "apple of her eye." Though Marcet claimed that Anna treated George and Jane equally, she adds the telling observation that Anna was "too honest to pretend that she loved them equally."[43] Jane's hurt at moments when Anna showered George with her overflowing affection must have added to her feelings of resentment toward her stepmother.

But if Jane was often angry with Anna, she also greatly benefited from having her in her life. Anna poured her considerable energies into entertaining and educating both children. Marcet wrote, "It was upon them that Ann concentrated the best of herself." In the evenings and on very cold or rainy days, when they could not be outside playing, Anna filled their time with card games, and later, chess, reading aloud, music, and social visiting.[44] Life became richer for Jane, and Anna was one reason.

George was the other. He was a bright, quiet boy who, like her, was lonely for a sibling close in age to play with. They became constant companions. She introduced him to her country world of fields, creek, and limestone cliffs, and he, a child fascinated by nature, showed her how to observe that world more closely. For the first time Jane had someone with whom to have adventures, concoct complicated imaginary games, and share confessions. Although in later life they would not be as close as they were as children, she would always retain a special affection for George and for the memories of their shared country childhood.[45]

Their most foolish adventure, which took place the summer when Jane was thirteen, involved an owl's nest. George, by then an amateur botanist, wanted to investigate the nest, which was lodged in the branches of a tree growing out of the side of one of the cliffs. Deciding to climb down to it, he enlisted Jane's help. For safety, he tied a rope around his waist and Jane tailed the other end around a tree on top of the cliff as George began to climb down to the nest. Suddenly, George lost his footing and fell, causing the rope to burn through and escape Jane's hands. Luckily his fall was broken by the tree. Jane retrieved the rope, wound the end around her tree again, and held on, though her hands were badly blistered, while George pulled himself back up. Anna was not pleased. Harry, hearing the story from her, wrote from Iowa, "I am quite astonished at the adventure of George and Jen—the owl's nest. Quite daring but quite too reckless for the comfort of others concerned." But Anna may have also felt some admiration for the grit Jane showed in rescuing George. In one of her few recorded words of praise for Jane, she remembered her as being "persistently brave."[46]

Addams did not include this adventure in *Twenty Years*, but she did write

lyrically in its pages about the quiet times she and George, whom she referred to only as her stepbrother, shared. At dusk they would sit in the
meadow and listen to the singing of the whippoorwill; the sound stirred
in them feelings of sadness and "vague longing." They had a strange sense
that this was not the first time they had lived. "The tales of children are
[long] when they sit down on the green grass and confide to each other
how many times they have remembered that they lived once before."[47]

Their interest in the mystical included a love of ritual sacrifice. "We
erected an altar beside the stream, to which for several years we brought
all the snakes we killed during our excursions." Sometimes they caught
a snake a good distance away but they always carried it back, however
long "the toilsome journey," the "limp snake dangling between two sticks."
Snake skins and snake bones soon littered the site. And they brought other
objects of value to the sacred spot. In the fall, they collected hundreds
of black walnuts and, placing them on the altar, poured a pitcher full of
cider over them as a way to honor the gods. Once, "solemnly," they burned
several favorite books. For this occasion, George, the high priest, wore a
necklace made of snake bones; Jane, the high priestess, wore a snake bone
bracelet.[48]

This was children's play but also something more. Children who have
suffered an early emotional shock, such as the loss of a parent, often play repeatedly a particular game whose origins lie in the initial trauma.[49] George
had been five when his father died. For him, as for Jane, the unconscious
purposes of the altar games were patently serious: to restore meaning to
death and to experience power over it by being death's agent rather than its
victim.

Their fascination with death was also apparent in the intensity of their
sympathy for village families who had lost loved ones in the Civil War. Jane
and George felt a special sadness for an elderly couple who lost four sons
in the war and a fifth in a hunting accident. "However much we were given
to talk of war heroes, we always fell silent as we approached [their] isolated
farmhouse," she writes. As they drove by in the family carriage, they felt
"overwhelmingly oppressed" by grief at "things as they are."[50]

Although Jane enjoyed the outdoors, as she grew older she was also
happy to stay inside. Reading was an early passion. Serious-minded and
imaginative, she found in books an enchanted world laden with meaning,
mystery, and intimate otherness. For school she read the textbooks of the
day—the McGuffey *Readers*. These offered selections of the "best" English

and American poetry and prose of the first half of the nineteenth century. Some selections promoted her father's ethics, the traditional Greco-Roman virtues of courage, cheerfulness, obedience, honesty, and self-control and the Christian ones of duty and forgiveness. Others, particularly the ones by the Romantic poets Wordsworth, Byron, Coleridge, and Shelley, whose works were promiscuously scattered among those of the sterner Christian moralists, taught what Anna believed—that private passions, nurtured by the flights of one's imagination, brought one closest to spiritual understanding and to happiness.[51] Jane absorbed it all, finding in her reading reinforcement for the two sides of her nature that her very different parents nurtured: her solemn moral earnestness and her fascination with the imaginary and mystical.

Encouraged by her father, she also browsed freely in his library, which contained much history and historical biography in addition to his religious books. Great men such as Washington, Jefferson, Franklin, Cromwell, and Napoleon were heavily featured. Among other books, he insisted that she read Plutarch's *Lives*, the many-volumed classic text that parents had been assigning boys for centuries to inspire in them dreams of greatness. Each essay was an extended historical commentary on the life and character of a political or military hero or antihero of ancient Greece or Rome. Believing that hard work should be financially recompensed, John Addams paid Jane five cents for each life about which she could report and twenty-five cents for reading each of the five volumes of Washington Irving's *Life of Washington*. Such reading not only instructed her in the virtues of courage, self-control, and good citizenship but transmitted a subtler message—that her gender was irrelevant to heroic dreams. Buoyed by her father's respect for her mind, she pushed herself, setting her own goals for reading. In imitation of him, she decided to read her way through his library, although she soon realized that it was more than she could accomplish.[52]

When Anna arrived at the homestead she brought with her more books and began consciously to develop Jane's taste for fiction. "I selected [Jane's] books," Anna recalled years later to a reporter interested in her famous stepdaughter, "and she was always satisfied with my choices. . . . We read as a family, discussing the book as we went along and encouraging the children to express their opinions freely." John Addams did not usually join in these evenings of reading (he disapproved of reading too many novels, which is what they mostly read), but it may have been just as well, given the austerity of his presence.[53] Lively, opinionated Anna was just the sort to draw out George and Jane's ideas.

They gathered around the dining room table, their faces lit by a golden pool of lamplight, as they took turns reading aloud. Anna read with flair, making the stories come alive. They read the sentimental romances of Mary Jane Holmes, whose novels were serialized in the *Atlantic Monthly*, and other popular writers of the day, including Dickens, a particular favorite. And Anna told her own stories. On at least one summer evening, if not many, she commanded Jane's and George's attention so completely that, long after the sun had set, they still sat in the moonlight with the lamp unlit, listening with rapt absorption.[54]

Anna's other great passion was music. She once wrote, "Music has been my abiding star—it sings to me." She taught Jane and George how to play the piano she brought from Freeport. Then, when Jane was fourteen, a man with bells on his wagon delivered a beautiful new ebony piano. Jane reported to her diary that one night, Alice, twenty-two, home from school, "hammered that everlasting Russian March and Bird Waltz" again and again and scratched the piano. Anna was not pleased. "All up with her fast," Jane laconically noted.[55] In the slang of the day, "all up" meant that Alice was in big trouble.

And Anna taught Jane etiquette. The family began having daily tea at 4 p.m., and Anna made a point of guiding conversations at dinner toward interesting topics. Anna's manners, as Marcet remembered them, were distinctly patrician, with just "a trace of imperiousness." A stranger once told Anna that she had the manners of "a lady of high birth." It was from Anna as well as her father that Jane gained her ability to move confidently in prosperous society and to meet strangers with poise.[56] And it was from Anna, as well as her father, that she acquired snobbery, that distinct sense of superiority derived from class and culture.

The lives of Jane's sisters were also reshaped by Anna's presence in the house. According to a friend, Mary had believed it "her duty to remain at home and preside over the home and care for Jane." She had attended Rockford Female Seminary for only a few months, feeling that she could not be spared for longer. Anna, eager to take charge of the household, pushed Mary to get out more and enjoy herself. Mary was obviously free to marry and in November 1871, at twenty-six, she did. Her father did not approve of her choice of husband, John Manning Linn, Cedarville's Presbyterian minister, for reasons that remain unclear but may have included what someone once described as Linn's "aggressive" personality. He would also prove an unreliable breadwinner. They moved to nearby Durand, Illinois, where he served a new church, and the following year Mary gave birth to their first child, John. With Mary's marriage, Jane lost the daily presence of her second "mother." Four years later, in October 1875, Alice married Anna's older son Harry and moved with him to Iowa, where he had established a medical practice, and Jane lost that sister's company as well. John Addams opposed the marriage because he disliked Harry. One reason was that Harry had a drinking problem.[57]

Anna's relations with Jane's only brother, Weber, who was eight years older than Jane, were stormy. It was becoming clear that he was a troubled young man. He enrolled at the University of Michigan in 1869 but soon dropped out. Eventually, he went to work for his father at the flour mill, then took over John's cattle stock farm of 512 acres, but his sisters remained worried about him. In August 1871, shortly before her marriage, Mary wrote Alice, "I think sometimes that Ma's death was more of a loss to [Weber] than any of the rest of us, much as it was to all."[58] In mid-May 1872, under strains that can only be guessed, Weber's mind gave way. For four awful weeks, the Addams family struggled to cope as they began to realize that Weber had temporarily gone insane. John Addams decided to commit him to one of the state mental hospitals for treatment. On June 17 the county court held a jury trial, as required by law; after hearing medical testimony, the jury confirmed Weber's condition as "temporarily insane" and the judge committed him to the Illinois State Hospital for the Insane in Jacksonville.[59]

In the court papers the cause of insanity was stated as "overexposure, physical exhaustion." This fit with the general theory of the time—that unnatural stresses of any kind, such as prolonged study or intense application to business, could bring on mental illness. The theory that insanity could be hereditary was just then coming into circulation. The Stephenson County jury specifically rejected it in Weber's case at the urging of the Addams's family doctor, Samuel Bucher.[60] Inheritable insanity was a controversial concept in the 1870s because it implied that the individual was not morally responsible for his actions. Such an idea contradicted everything that parents, ministers, teachers, and magazine editors were striving to teach; certainly it contradicted everything that John Addams believed and stood for in his community. Of course, if John could not accept the idea that Weber's illness was hereditary, then he had to believe that it was somehow due to a failure on Weber's part and therefore on his own. The shame that Weber's attack brought John Addams must have been profound.

The nature of Weber's mental instability cannot be known, but it is likely that he was suffering from paranoid schizophrenia, a disease which often first strikes when the patient is in his or her late teens or early twenties. Such patients are typically agitated, voluble, and irritable, characteristics Weber was described as possessing in later court records. Scientists still disagree about the cause, although some believe that the premature death of a parent can be a contributing factor.[61] Jane Addams left no record of what she thought of Weber's breakdown but, at eleven, she was old enough to have many questions about it and many complicated feelings—of sympathy for and disapproval of Weber, of embarrassment for herself, and of compassion for her father. Her brother's imperfection may have made it even more urgent that she be the "good" child.

Weber was released in November from the mental hospital after a stay of almost five months. If the Addams family responded like most families of the time, it no doubt welcomed him back, believing that if he took great care, avoided undue strain, and practiced better self-discipline, he could again lead a normal life. Bolstering the family in that hope was Weber's subsequent marriage in March 1876 to Laura Shoemaker, who was from a neighboring town. Weber seemed to be recovered. He soon was managing the stock farm again, was active in local politics, and in 1877, his marriage was blessed with a daughter.[62]

Anna's arrival also affected the deceased Sarah's place in the household, or at least Anna hoped it did. Mary Fry, a Cedarville woman who lived with Anna as her housekeeper from 1889 until Anna's death in 1919, told her nieces and nephews a remarkable story about the reason for a renovation Anna made to the house in the early years of her marriage. In 1873 she had a bolt installed on the door between the kitchen and the dining room, on the dining room side of the door. When thrown, the bolt made the rest of the house inaccessible from the kitchen, the sole room on the first floor that had been part of the original house. According to Mary, Anna's purpose in installing the bolt was to keep the ghost of Sarah Weber Addams from wandering the house at night, and for the rest of her life, Anna made sure before she went to bed that the door was bolted.[63]

As Jane entered adolescence, her relations with Anna remained difficult. Housekeeping was one point of friction. Although Anna herself did none, considering it beneath her, she was determined that Jane would learn the skills required. By the time Jane was fourteen, she was cleaning the house and making pies every Saturday. One Saturday Jane thought that the pies she made were fine but, as she noted tersely to a diary she kept briefly, "Ma

*Addams Homestead, with Anna H. Addams on the balcony. Jane Addams Memorial
Collection (JAMC neg. 1682), Special Collections, The University Library, University
of Illinois at Chicago.*

thought otherwise." Another time, to Jane's irritation, Anna required her
to cancel a visit to Mary's in order to fill in for the hired girl, who was away,
by cooking her father's breakfast.[64] It went without saying that Anna would
not cook it.

Jane's adolescent impatience also found other outlets. Her school-
teacher, C. W. Moore, was particularly irritating. In Latin class she got into
an argument with him about vocabulary. "I got my dander up," she confessed in her diary, "and everything went wrong." One evening at literary
club, Mr. Moore again did something infuriating. "I had my angry passions
stirred up considerably against Mr. Moore," she reported. On another day
she despaired of his weak attempts at humor in class. These diary entries
give glimpses of a bright girl's scornful impatience with her not-so-bright
teacher, whose salary, after all, was partially paid by her father.[65] They also
confirm what should not be surprising—that although Jane Addams was
rarely seen to be angry when older, she was angry often enough when she
was young.

Her goal was to control her temper, and her father was her model. Although he appeared calm and cool to Jane and others, there is some evidence that he had not always been so. He confessed in his 1844 diary that

he had gotten angry about politics and he may have been hot-headed about some other things, too. But he was mindful of the importance of controlling one's passions. A comment he makes in the diary about Sarah's brother George reveals his motive—to be more effective in his dealings with men. When they learned that George was planning to come west as a Christian missionary, John mused, "Would to God that he . . . not become excited but keep within bounds, that he may not get prejudice against him in his enthusiasm, and prevent him from doing good among his fellow beings."[66] It seems likely that the steady temperament that Jane found in her father was an accomplishment, not an inherent quality, of the man.

His ability to discipline his children benefited from his emotional control. For older children, his habit was to correct their misbehavior later, when he could obtain their complete attention and give his reasons. When twenty-year-old Alice, home for a visit from seminary, was late to breakfast every morning, he said little at the time. After she returned to school, however, Alice received a letter from her father. "I wish to allude to a subject that is not so pleasant to me," he wrote, "and . . . desire . . . you to pay attention to it. . . . I allude to your indifference to arise punctually in the morning. I believe [there was] not a single morning during your visit home [that] you were down to breakfast in time. It annoyed me although I did not say much. Hope you will break [this habit]." The reasons he gave her for his concern revealed his same practical desire to get along well with others. He wanted her to be effective in the world. "I am a businessman and know how annoying tardiness is—it is no small thing."[67]

For Jane, the contrast between John Addams, cool, firm, and predictable, and Anna Haldeman Addams, lively, demanding, affectionate, and capricious, could not have been greater. In her own way, however, Anna was an equal force to be reckoned with. What she gave Jane emotionally was complex. Her unpredictable temperament and her need to dominate unsettled and angered Jane, but her unflagging commitment to her responsibilities as stepmother and her sporadically affectionate ways provided Jane with an important stimulus. Anna was incapable of neglect or disinterest when it came to another human being. She attended to and engaged Jane at every turn, pushing, pulling, encouraging, criticizing, reacting with intensity to everything Jane did. For the solemn daughter of an austere father, such a stepmother was both a burden and a gift.

CHAPTER 3

DREAMS

1873-77

The early chapters of *Twenty Years at Hull-House* are filled with Jane Addams's childhood delight with heroes of a certain kind. Caught up in the enthusiasms of her day, she was fascinated by political heroes. In the realm of civic life, the confident, persuasive orator of the legislature and lecture circuit, like the self-made man in the realms of morality and economics, was much admired. He took responsibility; he pushed for what needed fixing and trusted in his ability to judge matters for himself. Political heroes were heavily featured in the books John Addams paid Jane to read. Indeed, his own political career brought the ideal to life. These were reasons enough for Jane's fascination. Deeper reasons are hinted at in the wheel dream.

There was, of course, the problem that most of the political heroes she knew about, whether real or fictitious, were male and she was female. Beneath this gender difference, but linked to it, was the question of whether heroism could only be pursued in the (male) public realm or whether women's private lot of suffering and self-sacrifice was also heroic. Negotiating these complexities was the task of Jane Addams's adolescence. In her day-to-day existence she was trained in the obedient, self-effacing feminine ideal; in her large imaginary life, she dwelt mostly among defiant, proud male heroes. In these years she formed grand dreams—and did her best to ignore her doubts about her right to dream them.

Jane Addams understood her interest in heroes to be generational. That is, she felt it had been sparked by the experience of growing up in the shadow of the Civil War. She was speaking of herself when she wrote, "Thousands of children in the sixties and seventies . . . caught a notion of imperishable heroism when they were told that brave men had lost their lives that the slaves might be free." She was surrounded at home by reminders of the war. Cedarville had sent its own unit to the front, financed by her father. A roster of the members of "Addams's Guard" and a portrait of its commanding officer hung on a wall in the house, attracting the attention of visitors. She and George knew which men of the guard had died and where each grieving family lived.[1]

Heroes were also important to her father. One of his political heroes was the martyred president Abraham Lincoln, three of whose portraits hung about the house. Jane was only four when, finding her father weeping as he read the newspaper and asking why, she learned that the "greatest man in the world" had died. After that, she writes in *Twenty Years*, "I never heard the great name without a thrill." John Addams had some letters from Lincoln tucked into one of the mysterious holes in his desk. He was usually, as she perceived it, too busy to read them to her but, on one red-letter day "of comparative leisure," he took the time to do so when she asked. She wanted to press him further, to ask him to reminisce, perhaps about the Lincoln-Douglas debate in Freeport. But she did not dare. As he folded the letters up, she simply waited "breathlessly." When she was young, her father was like an oracle to her, or a sphinx, full of wisdom and knowledge but also awesome in his silences. Her shyness and his distance often led to stillborn conversations. This frustrated her. "We long," she once wrote, "to interrogate the 'transfigured few' among our elders whom we believe to be carrying forward affairs of gravest import." When we fail to ask questions, she added, "we are dogged by a sense of lost opportunity, of needless waste and perplexity."[2]

Her intense curiosity about her father's political career seeps through many of the early pages of her memoir. Because her father was too busy to tell her his stories and she was too awed to ply him with questions, she learned what she could from eavesdropping. Once she overheard him telling how in 1861 he and some other legislators had helped prevent Illinois from seceding from the Union. In order to delay a planned vote on secession until the pro-Union side could rally support, they had taken a trip to St. Louis to create the absence of a quorum. She listened to the story, she recalls, "with breathless interest."[3] But this is the only story she tells in *Twenty Years* about his legislative work. Her silence suggests how little she actually knew.

John Addams's other political hero was Giuseppe Mazzini, the leader of Italy's failed struggle to overthrow the rule of France. Jane only learned about him because, when a bit older, she had more courage to question her father. When she was eleven, she found him one day "looking very solemn" as he read the *New York Tribune*, to which he subscribed. Asked by her why he appeared so serious, he told her that Giuseppe Mazzini, the "great Italian liberator," had died and that she should feel sad. The idea did not please her. Mazzini, after all, was Italian, not American. Growing "argumentative," she asked her father why. Perhaps John was mildly provoked or perhaps his sadness at Mazzini's death loosened his tongue. Whatever the reason, he laid down his paper and answered her at length, telling her about the political situation in Europe and explaining that men of different nationalities could share hopes and desires. As he talked, she recalled becoming "heartily ashamed of my meager notion of patriotism"; afterwards, she left the room "exhilarated" with the idea that international relations were "actual facts and not mere phrases" and impressed that her father felt a bond with a foreigner.[4]

Sometimes, to her delight, heroes walked the grounds of her very own home. Once "a certain general," probably the North's most famous general, Civil War hero, Republican, U.S. president, and native of nearby Galena, Illinois, Ulysses S. Grant, visited her father. Another time the governor of Illinois, Richard Oglesby, chatted with John under the pine trees in the front yard. These visits, like the stories her father told, were glorious and extraordinary occasions. "We felt on those days," she remembered, "a connection with the great world, . . . [one] much more heroic than the village world which surrounded us."[5]

Other moments of excitement came when John Addams himself stepped onto the public stage. These moments were fewer after he retired from the state Senate in 1870 but still took place because he remained active in the Illinois Republican Party.[6] In the fall of 1872, when Jane was twelve, Grant was running for reelection as president in a three-way race that was so hotly contested it brought the retired state senator back to the campaign stump.

Grant's fate was highly uncertain. He had easily won the Republican Party's endorsement the previous June, but then a splinter group of those long dissatisfied with the president's political cronyism and corruption had declared themselves a new party of Liberal (Radical) Republicans. Led by one of Illinois's longtime senators, Lyman Trumbull, and by Senator Carl Schurz of Missouri, the new third party held its own convention in May and nominated Horace Greeley, editor of the *New York Tribune*, as their candidate. Republicans had to choose sides. John Addams had been a Grant man but he was also a friend of Lyman Trumbull's.[7] Indeed, Grant's and Oglesby's visits to the Addams house probably took place in 1872, with

Grant coming to ask personally for John's support and Oglesby asking John to support Trumbull. It was Oglesby who failed in his mission. John Addams may have hated corruption but not enough to abandon Grant. At age fifty, he remained in what had become the conservative wing of his party. He was unwilling to join the rebellion.

After Trumbull gave a stump speech for Greeley in Freeport, Addams gave one for Grant. Jane undoubtedly read the speech, which was reprinted in the *Freeport Journal* the following week; it is possible that she was there to hear it. The event, held at the Opera House on Saturday night, October 19, was described as a Republican gathering of "ladies and gentlemen." In preparing his speech, John Addams's task was delicate. He knew that Greeley's success as a presidential candidate in Stephenson County depended on Trumbull's endorsement. This meant that before he attacked Greeley, he needed to undermine Trumbull's credibility. He would have to do that, however, without insulting the local Republican voters—including, most likely, nearly every man in the house—who had elected Trumbull three times as their senator. His first strategy was to invoke the voters' higher loyalties. Trumbull, he said, had "opposed and denounced" the party's greatest leader, Abraham Lincoln; despite endorsing the Grant administration's policies as "eminently wise" only a year earlier, four months later he was "plotting against the Republican Party." Then he attacked Trumbull's motives, implying they were self-serving. He asked sarcastically, "What came over the Senator? Was it not Presidency on the brain?" Having shredded Trumbull's reputation as an honest man, he did the same for Horace Greeley, using facts to mock the editor's commitment to his campaign positions. Intermittently, he spoke of Grant's accomplishments and rebutted the president's critics. The speech was a masterful performance and good evidence of John Addams's sure instinct for the political jugular. Thanks in part to his efforts, perhaps, the Republicans of Stephenson County, who represented 57 percent of the county's 4,986 voters, did their part on Election Day to give Grant a second term, while Greeley went down to defeat both in the county and nationally. For Jane Addams, the speech was a clear demonstration of her father's skill as an orator and a strong encouragement for her to master the skills of oratory herself.[8]

Jane Addams's fascination with the political hero occupied her imagination, but her days were shaped by the need to prepare for her life as a woman. In the midst of the presidential campaign of 1872, on September 6, her twelfth birthday, she spent part of the day in the kitchen on a most

Jane Addams at twelve. Jane Addams Collection, Swarthmore College Peace Collection.

apolitical task—kneading and baking bread. John Addams observed a tradition common in miller's families, requiring that each daughter when she turned twelve present him with a baked loaf for his approval. Jane found it difficult to satisfy his predictably high standards. She remembered, "He was most exigent as to the quality of this test loaf." Her first loaf was not even passable: it failed to rise. The second was full of holes; finally, the third was good enough. When it had cooled, she brought it to her father, who sliced it through with a knife and declared it satisfactory. She had demonstrated, at least symbolically, that she possessed the skills she would need as a married woman to keep her own house. The ritual at once confirmed her as a good daughter and marked her readiness to be a good wife.[9]

There were other, less formal rituals that the Addams daughters also performed for their father. These centered on his comfort and happiness. Mary, who had been trained by Sarah, trained her younger sisters. Mary wrote Alice at one point when their father was still a widower and she was traveling with Weber to distract him from his troubles, "Do not let Pa get lonesome; try to make it as pleasant as you can for him." Family correspondence also establishes that it was Mary's duty to bring her father his slippers.[10] Later, after Mary and Alice married and left home, Jane may have taken up the task.

John Addams's position at the center of the family universe, as the person whose every mood and comfort was lovingly attended to by the girls and women of the household, was conventional. In the mid-nineteenth century in middle-class families, the father was the head of the household and the person around whom the women of the house organized their lives. The Freeport press was happy to endorse the status quo. "It is a woman's business to please," the *Freeport Journal* asserted in 1878, reprinting a statement clipped from the *Atlantic Monthly*. "The woman who does not please is a false note in the harmony of nature."[11]

Women pleasing men may have been part of nature's system, but society took no risks: girls were carefully trained. As Jane Addams would later point out, women of her generation were taught from "babyhood" to be "self-forgetting and self-sacrificing." Jane's first teacher was her sister Mary, Mary's teacher was Sarah, and Sarah was instructed, in part, by the books she read, many brought west from Pennsylvania. Those books advised a woman to think "every hour" about the happiness of others and how to "make sacrifices" in order to increase her husband's enjoyment. The authors acknowledged that women's "circumstances" entailed suffering but viewed this painful reality as an opportunity for growth. As one female advice giver wrote, "Suffering to a woman occupies the place of labor to a man, giving a breadth, depth, and fullness not otherwise attained." Harriet Beecher Stowe advised a woman to view her "domestic trials as her haircloth, her ashes, her scourges—accept them, rejoice in them—smile and be quiet, silent, patient and loving under them."[12] According to this view, a woman's gender destined her for martyrdom.

Jane also encountered these lessons in novels. In this arena her favorite teacher was Charles Dickens. Dickens was enchanted with the ideal of the gentle, patient, loving, and self-sacrificing young woman and filled his novels with them. Characters such as Agnes Wickfield, Little Dorrit, Esther Summerson, and Florence Dombey were all angelic in their willingness to make any sacrifice for their families' sakes. The Dickens character of this sort that Jane liked best was Little Nell in *Old Curiosity Shop*. In the book, Nell loses her mother when she is very young and devotes her short life to taking tender care of her mentally confused, elderly father as they struggle to survive poverty. Spunky yet self-effacing, Nell struck Jane, who recorded the opinion in her diary, as "nearly perfect."[13]

As to what kind of example Anna Haldeman Addams set, an argument could be made in both directions. She was a traditionalist of the strongest sort when it came to ideas about male-female relations, but her intense personality and artistic passions, not to mention her temper tantrums, often prevented her from achieving the demure, self-sacrificing ideal. She modeled a self-centered independence even if her rhetoric argued otherwise. Similarly, she was fascinated by women of accomplishment even as she discouraged her stepdaughters from such aspirations. In a letter she wrote to Alice after reading the book *Eminent Women of the Age*, she sounded a note of caution against having big dreams. "We cannot all become eminent in a world-wide fame," she warned.[14] In more modern times a woman of Anna's intelligence, drive, and talents would have been proudly ambitious. Anna was admonishing herself first and foremost to keep her own dreams boxed up and stored beneath the bed.

Anna's conservative views about women were commonly held. But in the 1870s the women's rights movement was committed to spreading new ideas about women. Pro–women's rights lecturers were touring the country and having their speeches published in the *New York Tribune*, where Jane Addams could easily have read them. In 1872 in a popular lecture titled "Our Girls," Elizabeth Cady Stanton, a long-time advocate for women's rights, challenged the belief that a woman's life should "simply revolve around some man, [that she should] live only for him, in him, with him; to be fed, clothed, housed, guarded and controlled by him, today by Father or Brother, tomorrow by Husband or Son." Girls eventually realize that under such a regime they "are to have no individual character, no life purpose, . . . aim or ambition." They "may never utter it [but feel this] far more keenly than kind fathers imagine." Stanton hoped for the day when American women understood "their true dignity as citizens of a Republic."[15]

On the controversial subject of women's right to vote, the Addams family was divided. Jane described her father as pro-suffrage. Weber and Mary were opposed. Alice's views are unknown. Anna also was opposed. The issue was the subject of one of the first letters Anna and John exchanged after their marriage. Anna, writing to him in early January, 1869, when he was in Springfield, summed up the supporting view dismissively in language typically used by the press. She wrote heatedly, " 'Women's rights' would . . . do away with *baby* and *cradle,* and ape instead a *statesmanship* or *professorship.*" Not coincidentally, the newspapers just then were full of the arguments for and against women's suffrage and women's rights. In Washington, Congress was debating the bill proposing the Fifteenth Amendment, which was intended to protect the right of all men to vote regardless of race and which some women's rights advocates wished amended to include the word "sex." And in Chicago, Mary Livermore and other women were organizing the state's first women's suffrage convention.[16]

On February 19, Livermore and Stanton, who had attended the Chicago suffrage convention, addressed a gathering of Illinois state legislators and others on the subject of women's suffrage at the Opera House in Springfield, drawing a fashionable crowd that included John Addams. He described the event to Anna. "The Strong Minded Women are in the City, Woman's Suffrage in the Advance," he wrote, imitating the style of a newspaper headline. He praised Livermore, who, he proudly noted, was from Chicago, for her "well-organized, . . . strong and convincing arguments" while declaring the short and stout Stanton "abominable [*sic*] ugly" and declared her remarks to be "rambling and bordering on the *egotistical,* which you know is no fancy of mine."[17] His remarks carried two implications. First, he liked women orators to possess the traditional female virtues of beauty and gentle graciousness. Second, he supported at least some women's rights, since he praised Livermore's arguments as "convincing" and did not convey, as Anna did, a general disgust with the movement.

There is almost no evidence of just what Jane Addams thought of the women's rights movement in high school. The single clue that she was following its progress appreciatively is an intriguing statement she made when she was in her seventies that the woman she most admired was Lucy Stone (Blackwell), a reformer whose last regular public appearances were made when Addams was in her teens. Stone, a skilled public speaker and one of the nation's first and most prominent supporters of women's suffrage and women's rights generally, traveled a good deal in the 1870s to lobby various state legislatures as they voted on women's suffrage bills. Although there is no record that she spoke in northern Illinois, her speeches were among those Addams could have read or read about in the *New York Tribune.* Stone's personality was an intriguing blend of velvet and steel. Her friend Mary Livermore described her in the words that would later often be used to describe Jane Addams as a speaker: "gentle, sweet-voiced, winning, persuasive." Mary Livermore herself was also often described similarly.[18] Jane Addams's public persona as an orator was one that would have pleased her father.

Aside from John Addams's support for women's rights, he had other progressive ideas about women. According to his grandson, he was "constitutionally opposed to all forms of tyranny, even the tyranny of men over women, of husbands over wives."[19] The few available facts bear this out. He did not choose a docile woman for his second wife but feisty, determined Anna, who, even if she believed she should submit to her husband's authority, regularly rebelled under the regime. And, although John had opposed Mary's and Alice's choice of husbands, he had not blocked their marriages; neither one had been forced to elope. He clearly expected to be obeyed, but he did not insist on enforcing his will. He preferred obedience inspired by a sense of duty.

He also respected his daughter's ability to think and to make up her own mind. *Twenty Years* reveals that by the time she was fifty Jane Addams's most treasured childhood memories of her father were the conversations with him in which he encouraged her to trust her own judgment. As she grew older, he reinforced the lesson more explicitly. Once, when she was in her teens and her father was away, Jane "bungled" the plans for a large family party. Apologizing to him afterwards, she explained that she had only tried to do what he would have done if he had been there. She tells the story not in *Twenty Years* but in a 1912 essay.

> His expression of amused bewilderment changed to one of understanding as he replied: "That probably accounts for your confusion of mind. You fell into the easy mistake of substituting loyalty and dependence on another's judgment for the best use of your own faculties. I should be sorry to think that you were always going to complicate moral situations, already sufficiently difficult, by trying to work out another's point of view. You will do much better if you look the situation fairly in the face with the best light you have."[20]

It was his usual Hicksite, individualistic lesson. Trust yourself; use your own judgment.

John Addams was the kind of parent who stretched a daughter's expectations of herself. Appreciating this about him, Jane closed the chapter in *Twenty Years* that deals with her memories of her father with a line of poetry from Elizabeth Barrett Browning's epic poem "Aurora Leigh," a poem

partly about a father and a motherless daughter, that she said always made
her think of him:

> He wrapt me in his large
> Man's doublet, careless did it fit or no.[21]

The poet's image suggests a devoted father who at once flattered his daugh
ter with his high expectations and protected her. Like so many adoring and
adored fathers, Jane Addams's father did both these things for her.

She met two more heroes—metaphorically, of course—in the pages of
the leading literary publication of the day and a symbol of sophistication,
the *Atlantic Monthly*. Every month Anna's subscription brought a crisp
new magazine to the house full of news, literature, and essays to feed a
curious mind. The short stories and poetry showed women in the usual
ways: as sweetly sympathetic, coyly flirtatious, obsessed with their appearance, falling in love, high-mindedly moral, devoted to the home, or desiring
vaguely to have adventures. But what drew Jane Addams's interest in these
years were two long series of articles, each about a famous male radical social reformer. One, published in 1873, was about Robert Owen; the other,
published in 1875, was about John Brown.[22]

Robert Owen was a broad-minded Scots cotton industrialist and former
laborer who was considered the founder of the cooperative movement in
Great Britain and the United States. He offered his idea of cooperative industry, in which profits were shared among all workers, as an alternative to
the capitalist model of competitive labor. His vision of cooperation was inspired by his desire to end the unhappiness spawned by the individualism
that capitalism nurtured. "The happiness of the self clearly understood,"
he wrote, "can only be attained by a direct and conscious service [to] the
community." Determined to test his ideas against reality, he lost his wealth
in the failed social experiment he founded in New Harmony, Indiana, a
classless utopian community that lasted from 1825 to 1827.[23]

John Brown was a stubborn prophet on the urgency of abolishing slavery. He instigated a guerrilla attack against pro-slavery sympathizers in
Kansas in 1856 and three years later, as part of his effort to lead an armed
slave insurrection, led twenty-one men as they seized the federal arsenal at
Harper's Ferry, Virginia, and took citizens as hostages. The two-day battle
ended with his capture and led to his execution.

Jane Addams was not put off by the more radical tenets of these men's
ideas; she was intrigued. She found Robert Owens's vision for cooperation

"thrilling" and John Brown's passion for direct action, though presumably not his violence, inspiring. "I always had a secret sympathy," she would later write a friend, "with [Brown's] impatience and his determination that something should . . . happen." [24] These youthful enthusiasms would be sustained. Her interest in Owen's ideas about cooperation would evolve into a lifelong devotion to the cooperative movement, which in the 1870s had already spawned the labor movement and the socialist movement in England and the United States. Reading about John Brown, she was introduced to direct action as a political method, a method that in its less violent form she would also eventually embrace. Thus did Anna's subscription to a magazine of high culture inadvertently plant seeds of revolutionary thinking in her stepdaughter's mind.

Did Jane discuss these heroes with her father? Or did she decide not to, fearing that he would not approve? John Addams might have respected Owen's devotion to service to the community and Brown's hatred of slavery and tyranny, but it seems likely he would have disapproved of Owen's rejection of the ethic of individualism and Brown's apparent abandonment of the electoral process. Nor would he have liked Owen's cooperative approach to business. By the mid-1870s, the cooperative movement had reached Stephenson County and, from a banker's point of view, was stirring up trouble. In August 1875, in response to the economic pressures generated by the Panic of 1873, local farmers organized the Stephenson County Farmers' Cooperative. This retail store, located in Freeport, was soon undercutting the competition by selling farm supplies and equipment at cost plus a small markup. Financed by shares purchased by members, the store had no need for a banker's capital and threatened the profitability of the farm supply stores that did. John Addams could not have been pleased by the development. [25]

The Panic of 1873, which took place when Jane was twelve, was upsetting to employers and employees alike. As the economy worsened, there was a surge in the number of unemployed men walking the countryside looking for work, food, and shelter. Wandering men with dirty clothes and faces and gaunt bodies, the tramps, as they were called, brought the presence of poverty and the threat of crime to the backdoors of rural middle-class homes. The Addams homestead, with its look of solid prosperity, must have often attracted such visitors. In these years Jane Addams thought such men were moral failures because they had no work. Writing on the subject in an 1878 college essay she titled "Tramps," Jane asserted that such men disregard "the principle set down from the foundation of the earth, that a man must give a full equivalent for everything he receives. . . . [T]hey render themselves abject and mean and merit . . . universal contempt." She called it "absurd" for a tramping man to expect people to help him. [26]

Since John Addams placed a high value on self-reliance as a test of one's morality, it seems likely that he agreed with Jane's assessment. The scant information we have about his conversations with her about poverty imply that he viewed it as solely an individual responsibility. When Jane, at six, asked him why some people lived in "horrid houses," he answered that they lacked money. Two years later, when his requirement that she wear her old cloak prompted her to ask him what could be done about material inequality, he told her that nothing could be done. He was, of course, kind to the poor. After he died, the author of an obituary described his heart as "always full of love and sympathy for the poor." Believing in the benefits of moral reform, he expressed his compassion through his Sunday school teaching, on which, as a minister observed, "he labored so long and earnestly." [27]

Such views—in particular, the belief that any able-bodied man who was poor was morally deficient—were typical of the Whig and Republican upper middle class. As Horace Bushnell argued in his much-reprinted 1844 sermon "Prosperity Is Duty," the poor were lazy and shiftless and lacking in virtue. If a man was poor and unemployed, Republicans held, the solution was for him to relocate to the west, where he could acquire land cheap through the Homestead Act and work his way to prosperity and moral redemption. [28]

But these ideas about poverty were not the only ones Jane absorbed. In Dickens's novels, "the poor" as a class stand for a shifting kaleidoscope of human qualities. Vividly portrayed characters in every book, Dickens's poor people possess both generosity and selfishness, wisdom and ignorance, great joyousness and beaten-down despair, courageous industriousness and slovenly turpitude. The novelist humanized the poor for her even as he deepened her faith in certain stereotypes.

The Addams household's view of immigrants—who were sometimes equated with the poor—was ambivalent. In 1870, of the 28 percent of the people of Stephenson County who were foreign-born, 70 percent were German immigrants. These immigrants held a special place in the family's affections because of its own German ancestry. Many of John's hired hands came from Germany, including the miller who ran the flour mill. [29] Sarah Addams had done much charity work within the German community.

But John Addams disdained immigrants from other nations, whom he called "Dutchmen," which was American slang for ignorant foreigners. Addams reported on a particular encounter in which he, Sarah, and George Weber were traveling from Chicago to Freeport in August 1844. He wrote in his diary, "Father and Self visited a Dutchman. [We thought at first] by the house and barn that he was a German but we found him to be a foreigner and very ignorant and at first unwilling to speak to us, suspecting us to be Yankees, as he first termed us[,] but we told him we were descendants of Pennsylvania Germans." His views were those of his party. In the 1850s, the Republican Party, having absorbed portions of the Know-Nothing Party, fought with some success for anti-immigrant laws and blamed political corruption on the Democratic Party, devoted as it was to immigrant voters.[30]

In sharp contrast to her later views, Jane Addams's beliefs as a teen were, like her father's, disdainful of immigrants. In college she would write about the "foreigners" who had come to work in the mills of New England as contemptible, not, in this case, because they did not work, but because their "low grade of intelligence" made them a likely source of "vice." The foreigners she had in mind were in fact, though she does not mention it, mostly Irish and French Canadians, who were Catholic and therefore more likely to arouse Protestant America's (and her own) nativist prejudices.[31] In a word, the Addams family was typically Republican in their views of foreigners and atypical only in their assumption that German immigrants did not belong in that category.

In Cedarville as elsewhere in the United States, these prejudices had somehow to be made compatible with the ethic of social equality that dominated daily life. While silent in *Twenty Years* about her family's views concerning foreigners, Jane Addams proudly describes the village's egalitarian ethic: "[I]n a rural community . . . the early pioneer life made social distinctions impossible."[32] The story of her new Sunday school cloak illustrates the same point but also highlights the limited scope of that equality. It suggests that social equality was about practicing politeness, about paying attention to people's feelings. In other words, it was acceptable to disdain the poor and foreigners as the Addams family did; the important thing was not to convey this attitude to their faces.

To be sure, these real-world concerns occupied only a part of Jane's attention. Most of the time when she was not in school, she was lost in her imagination, her head in a book. When she was fifteen she read Thomas Carlyle's best-selling work *On Heroes, Hero-Worship and the Heroic in History,* which was in her father's library. Carlyle enchanted her with his "sonorous sentences" and "exaltation of the man who 'can.' " In essays on Napoleon, Cromwell, Mohammed, Luther, Rousseau, and Shakespeare, among others, Carlyle laid out the archetype of the Victorian hero.[33] Sometimes a poet, sometimes a warrior, sometimes a religious leader, the hero was distinguished by his defiant independence, his originality of thought, his intuitive grasp of what Carlyle referred to as "the times," and perhaps most of all by his vast superiority to the average man.

She had not yet finished reading *On Heroes*, she reports in *Twenty Years*, when she was jolted out of Carlyle's rarified world. John Addams gave a speech to the "old settlers" of Stephenson County at an annual gathering, held in his front yard, in which he recalled his difficulty selling railroad shares in one town until a woman had set an example by buying a $200 share with her egg and butter money. As he praised her courage, a voice called out, "I'm here today, Mr. Addams, and I'd do it again if you asked me." Invited to the platform, the woman, a seventy-year-old German immigrant, stood before the crowd, her body bent from a lifetime of hard work, as John Addams praised her again for her "heroic fortitude" in helping build the country. Suddenly Jane felt her admiration for Carlyle's heroes dissolve; she wondered whether this ordinary person was the more convincing hero. She did not comment on the other aspects of the immigrant's appeal to her: that she was a woman and, like Addams's family, of German descent.[34]

Books supplied a few more female heroes. The one that captured Jane's heart at fifteen was Louisa May Alcott's *Little Women*. She wrote her Iowa cousin Vallie Beck that she kept reading *Little Women* over and over. Its pages offered two kinds of rather opposite heroes—the devoted, self-sacrificing mother and the ambitious and independent girl—making the book seductive no matter which direction a girl's sympathies lay, and doubly so when they lay, as they did for Jane and for most girls, in both directions. Marmie was the serene and selfless mother who kept the family together. Her daughter Jo wanted to be a writer. Jo dreamed, Alcott writes, of "do[ing] something . . . heroic or wonderful that won't be forgotten after I'm dead. I think I shall write books." Jane could admire Napoleon and the woman railroad investor, but Jo was the hero who was the most like herself, a girl with heroic ambitions and a love of the written word.[35]

Finally, there was Emerson. Jane developed a great admiration for him. She began reading him at age fifteen, when a new edition of his essays was published in the United States. His ideas would often surface in her college writing. It may have been Emerson's essay "Man the Reformer" that first set her dreaming of a career in social reform. There he characterized the reformer in classic heroic mode as a "brave and upright man" who calls "the institutions of society to account."[36] Robert Owen and John Brown were the obvious cases in point.

Given all that Jane Addams was reading, it is clear that her adolescence was dominated by adventures of the mind and that reading was the magic carpet for her journeys. Entirely private, it linked her through her imagination to the world. Its effects, as future developments will show, were various. Sometimes reading flooded her mind like a tide that swept into a shallow inlet and set swirling eddies of confusion in motion; sometimes reading exploded in her mind like a bomb, perhaps when an idea was first met, perhaps later, when it collided with another idea and there was a double explosion; sometimes reading corroded her mind with a steady drip of acidic doubts, tiny "what ifs" that, over the years, would eat away the iron framework of surety built by her parents, church, and school; eventually, reading would transform her mind from a sponge that absorbed to an engine of initiating, discriminating energy, from a receiver to a transmitter, from an organ of her body to an instrument of her soul. In the 1870s, reading was changing Jane Addams. From then on, because she wished it to, but even when she did not, it would never stop changing her.

Books, of course, could not suffice forever. The wider world beckoned as Jane's dissatisfaction with mundane Cedarville grew. We hear the distant echoes of her youthful frustration in a statement from 1909: "We can all recall our own moments of revolt against life's actualities, our reluctance to admit that all of life was to be as unheroic and uneventful as that which we saw about us, it was too unbearable that 'this was all there was' and we tried every possible avenue of escape."[37]

Escape on a grand scale came during the summer Jane was fifteen in the form of a trip to the first world's fair held in the United States. Leaving Weber at home to manage the businesses, John, Anna, George, and Jane left in May to attend the Centennial Exhibition in Philadelphia. Organized to commemorate the hundredth anniversary of the Declaration of Independence and to prove to the world that the United States had arrived as an industrial power, the fair sprawled over seventy-five acres. With 170 buildings and thirty-seven countries represented, the exhibition offered a panoply of new sights to the millions of American and foreign visitors. Ralph Waldo

Jane Addams, Anna Haldeman Addams, and George Haldeman, Philadelphia, 1876.
Jane Addams Memorial Collection (JAMC neg. 502), Special Collections, The
University Library, University of Illinois at Chicago.

Emerson, ever the enthusiast, was "dazzled and astounded" by the "glories" he saw; grumpy, worldly Henry Adams found it "bigger, noisier, more crowded . . . than any of its predecessors." Among the many fascinating sights was the Woman's Pavilion, where there was a photo exhibit of institutions founded or led by women, an exhibit about the Woman's Medical College of Philadelphia, and a display asserting that there should be "no taxation without representation" created by the American Woman's Suffrage Association, Lucy Stone's organization.[38]

In addition to attending the fair, the Addams family explored Philadelphia. They visited Independence Hall, where they saw the desk at which the Declaration of Independence was signed. Another day Anna took Jane to the hairdresser's.[39] Anna emerged with a bouffant effect in her bangs;

Jane's hair remained in its usual demure bun but gained a wavier aspect. Then, with George, but not John, they went to sit for a family photograph. George and Anna look stoically alert, but Jane's expression suggests a hint of grumpy defiance.

The fall found Jane back at Cedarville Public School, working on a translation from Latin to English of Julius Caesar's *Commentaries*. Looking around for excitement to match what she had experienced in Philadelphia, she found it in politics. That autumn, Rutherford B. Hayes was running as the Republican candidate for president in an intensely close race against Democrat Samuel J. Tilden. The newspapers were full of the campaign and its contested aftermath. By March Hayes, who lost the popular vote but won the electoral vote, was in office, leaving Jane a bit wistful. She wrote Vallie, "I enjoy politics very much and was especially interested last fall and winter. It seems rather tame now when the excitement has stopped."[40]

There had been excitement of a grimmer sort earlier that winter. It had been nearly nine years since Martha died, nine years since death had intruded on the Addams family. Abruptly—and death seemed to always come abruptly in Jane's life—it returned to take a person who was nearly family, Polly, the elderly housekeeper. In *Twenty Years* Jane writes that Polly's passing, which she witnessed, was her "first direct contact with death."[41] Whether she was referring to seeing a person die or only to seeing a dead body is unclear. In any case, she penned the words in 1910, three years before her trip to Egypt, when she would suddenly remember attending her schoolmate's mother's burial.

On January 7, 1877, Polly unexpectedly fell ill while visiting cousins at a nearby farm. When it became clear that she was dying, her cousins sent word to the Addams family and it was decided that Jane should go. Traveling four miles through a blinding snowstorm, Jane felt she had been charged with "a fateful errand." She joined the cousins at Polly's bedside, but after they went down to supper, she was left alone with Polly in the cold room with the storm swirling outside. Suddenly, Polly stirred. In *Twenty Years*, Jane remembers, "I heard a feeble call of 'Sarah,' my mother's name, as the dying eyes were turned upon me." In a moment, she was dead. The face "familiar from my earliest childhood," Addams writes, now held "strange, august features, stern and withdrawn from all the small affairs of life." At that moment, Addams was "irresistibly seized" by "that sense of solitude, of being unsheltered in a wide world of relentless and elemental forces."[42] Her eloquent words capture what she felt at sixteen and at six, and in more primitive forms at four and two. She had been given too soon the existential knowledge of the solitude and mortality of the self: that she was alone in a vast, dangerous place, exposed to the raw will of an apparently cruel God. The consequences of her premature knowledge would ramify as she grew older. One was that she would find it difficult to feel herself to be in a loving, personal relationship with God. The other was that her greatest spiritual longing would be for human connection.

The religion that suited Addams in these years was deism, the faith that lacked a personal God. In *Twenty Years* she credits Emerson's essays with inspiring her to embrace it. The deist held that God was immanent in the entire world, a spirit present in nature, in men, and wherever beauty was found. According to Emerson, "The divine circulations never rest nor linger. Nature is the incarnation of a thought[;] . . . the world is mind precipitated[;] . . . wisdom is infused in every form."[43]

Now in her teens, Addams was of an age to consider converting to Christianity but, thus fortified, she resisted. She attended church weekly with her father but remained unbaptized. She felt, we may presume, that she did not understand Christianity, did not understand how Christ could be her savior, did not understand that God loved her, and therefore, as her father agreed, she could not be a believer. Alice, on the other hand, had joined the Christian fold. Shortly after Martha's death, she had converted.[44]

Deism was the religion of the idealist, and Addams embraced idealism, too. In Emerson's essay "Idealism," he set forth its basic tenets: that the most profound reality is not nature, not the world, but the spirit, that which occupies the human mind in its search for beauty and the eternal. The material—nature, the body, the physical, the temporal, all that decays— "is degraded [in the presence of] the spiritual." The best place to find the spiritual and the eternal, he claims, is culture. Poetry, religion, music, art, history, literature—all of these bring the mind closer to the truer, immortal reality. "[S]een in the light of thought, . . . virtue subordinates [the world] to the mind."[45] Addams made these views her own. Loving books, she loved the vision of culture's power that Emerson, among others, set forth.

Her idealism shaped her attitude toward romantic love. When Vallie Beck mentioned such love in a letter, Addams rejected the possibility on two grounds. First she did not think the promised mutuality of such love likely. She wrote Vallie pessimistically, "When love does not beget love, it is apt to produce dislike or what is worse hatred, rarely indifference." It was a warning often sounded in forward-thinking novels of the day. Second, she preferred its alternative. "I am a great admirer of Platonic love or rather sacred friendship," she observed to Vallie. "I think it is much higher than what is generally implied in the word love."[46]

Plato was arguably the founder, at least in Emerson's eyes, of idealism, and Platonic love, the love between two souls without reference to the body or sex, constituted the idealist view of love. According to a women's advice book of the period, Platonic love existed when the imagination "exalted the soul, instead of flaming the senses." Much praised for promoting mutual respect and self-control, Platonic love was also the sort of out-of-body experience likely to appeal to a girl like Jane, a "dreamy" and "highly introspective" girl with "strong feelings," as her childhood friend Flora Guiteau described her. Jane wanted her affectionate relations fed from spiritual or intellectual springs. And Platonic love had another appeal. It did not depend for its inspiration on an asset Jane thought she lacked: physical beauty. If at sixteen she did not still think herself ugly, she remained dissatisfied with her appearance. She was obsessed with her nose. "I could cover *pages* trying to vindicate my *nose*," she wailed to Vallie in a letter in which she enclosed her photograph. "[It] is simply a piece of flesh, expressing no character whatever and contains eight freckles! Horrible to relate (I counted them this morning)."[47]

Anna, lover of beauty, did her best to enhance Jane's looks. The Philadelphia photograph shows Jane dressed in a lovely outfit. Her stepmother may have lost the battle of the cloak with John, but she had won the clothing war. She did not win the war of the hair, however. Anna could only have found Jane's bun old-fashioned. Still, Jane had other assets. The steady gaze in her luminescent eyes and the determined tilt to her chin captured in the Philadelphia photo conveyed more character than she gave her nose credit for revealing. She had grown to a height of five feet four inches, neither short nor tall, and remained slender, the kind of young lady referred to in novels as "a slip of a girl." Though her back still bothered her, it did not keep her from playing hopscotch or sledding with George. To strengthen it, Anna insisted that she ride horseback often. The riding was painful but she loved the freedom and energy she felt on the back of a horse. Once she went for a twenty-two-mile ride with her stepbrother and brother-in-law Harry "over the boundless prairie." It was "perfectly glorious," she wrote Vallie.[48]

Jane's longing for a nose that had "character" and for a soulful, Platonic friendship expressed her interest in the forces that shaped a person's unique inner self. Pursuing that interest, in the winter of 1876–77, in what was possibly her earliest effort to bring people of like mind together, Jane organized a club, the Capenic Society of the West. Her enthusiasm for the renowned phrenologist John L. Capen had been inspired by a visit she and Anna had paid to his practice while they were in Philadelphia the previous summer. Phrenology, invented in the 1830s by a Frenchman, Franz Gall, was all the rage in America and in Europe in the 1870s. According to a handbill that Jane brought home, Gall argued that the shape of each person's head, when measured and interpreted according to a complex map of the skull, revealed his or her "natural disposition, character, talent, tastes, affections, powers and weaknesses."[49]

At Capen's office she and Anna had talked with Capen as he measured their heads. Capen gave them written diagnoses to take home. Copies of both assessments were in Addams's papers when she died. They are remarkably perspicacious:

> Anna: Vigorous constitution, suffers intensely, . . . sensitive to everything, great deal of personal dignity and pride, very affectionate, strong attachments to home and children, excitability great, . . . obdurate, . . . cannot bear direction, . . . a sharp critic and comments mercilessly, often hurting. . . . Nothing constrains her . . . intensity of feeling and domination, . . . strong imagination, . . . intuitive and penetrating.

> Jane: Evenness of temperament . . . marked traits of character . . . if she thinks a thing is true, she thinks it with all her might. Great sensitiveness, . . . lack of confidence in herself . . . thinks a great deal of her friends . . . inclined to be serious and earnest . . . obstinate. Strong reasoning powers, dislikes to be overpersuaded. Not enthusiastic in any project, will become slowly interested and by reason, but when interested will be . . . persevering and loath to abandon it. Large originality, dislikes to imitate others. Moral faculties very much larger than religious. Inclined to be skeptical. Will do anything from principle, believe nothing without a reason. . . . If subject to mortifications, great disappointment or anxiety in the next five years [this] would be apt to stunt the growth of her mind and injure its strength; inclin[ed] then to become melancholy.[50]

Capen's conversations with his subjects were undoubtedly helpful to him in making his assessments; for the rest, like a gypsy telling fortunes by reading palms, he relied on his intuition. He had a real gift. His words are full of insight about both women. Most amazingly, even his prediction about Jane Addams's growth being stunted in response to deeply unsettling events within the next five years would turn out to be true.

———————————

At sixteen Jane was a senior in high school (somewhere along the way she apparently skipped a year). The question of her further education now loomed. Her father wanted her to earn a collegiate certificate at the all-female Rockford Seminary, where Mary, Martha, and Alice had gone and where he had been named a member of the board of trustees in June 1876. This plan was not to Jane's liking. In her daydreams about her future she had concocted a different plan—to do as Lucy Stone famously did and attend a college where she could earn a real bachelor of arts degree. Smith College in Northampton, Massachusetts, which had just started enrolling students, was offering women that opportunity. "I was very ambitious to go to Smith College," she recalls in *Twenty Years*.[51] She and her father were thus at loggerheads on the question of where she should pursue her higher education.

John Addams's lack of enthusiasm for Jane's desire to earn a B.A. was not surprising. College graduates were a distinct and tiny elite in American society, and women college graduates, that is, those who had earned B.A.s and not simply collegiate certificates, were the tiniest elite of all. In the early 1870s, about two of every thousand college-aged women (.24 percent) were attending B.A.-granting institutions, as compared to between one and two of every hundred of college-aged men (1.5 percent). There were also widespread fears that a college education (as distinct from a less arduous seminary one) would damage women's mental and physical health.[52]

Rockford Seminary appealed to John Addams for many reasons. The one Jane Addams stresses in *Twenty Years* was its proximity. "My father's theory in regard to the education of his daughters implied a school as near home as possible." He intended that afterwards his daughters would travel in Europe, as Alice had done in 1875. John Addams thought that such travel, Jane explains, could substitute for "the wider advantages which an eastern college is supposed to afford."[53] One hears the echoes of a family discussion in her summary. Rockford appealed to John for another reason. Although Jane does not mention it, the school was an evangelical Christian institution. Its principal, Anna Sill, was devoted to encouraging her "unsaved" students to convert while under her care.

If John Addams had been willing to allow Jane to attend Smith, would she have been admitted? The college's admission requirements were difficult for someone educated in a small town in northern Illinois to meet. They included basic Greek and algebra through quadratic equations and some geometry, all of which Addams lacked. (Rockford Seminary required neither Greek nor geometry.) But this did not mean she could not go to Smith. The college also enrolled special students, who were not matriculating. Such students took selected courses and received tutoring in the other subjects they needed to pass the entrance exams. Jane could have been a special student at first.[54]

She wanted to go to Smith because she was ambitious. As she formulated her ambition at the time, it was not about fame or accomplishment but about two things: her moral aspirations and her desire to become a medical doctor. Her moral goal was one of vague self-improvement. People go to college, she would later write, to find the "wider life," the "nobler life." Smith's B.A., being a higher standard, seemed to offer that. Smith also offered women unusually solid training in science. An article in *Scribner's Monthly* in May 1877 emphasized the splendid quality of Smith's laboratories.[55] (In those days a student was not required to have a B.A. in order to go to medical school.)

She had wanted a career of some sort for a long time. Anna, no enthusiast for female ambition, remembered later that as a child Jane "was anxious to have a career." Perhaps Jane found her inspiration in Carlyle and Emerson, both of whom stressed that the great man, that is, the hero, should choose his life's work carefully. Jane may have settled on medicine because of the doctors she knew. Samuel Bucher, the doctor who had tried to save her mother's life and who was a beloved citizen of Cedarville, died when Jane was fourteen. Her stepbrother and brother-in-law, Harry Haldeman, was also a doctor.[56] Then again, doctors were society's warriors in the fight against death. Addams had deeply personal reasons to want to enlist in that army.

Somewhere along the way, she made the link between being a doctor and helping the poor, the task she had vaguely embraced at six: "Long before the end of my school days it was quite settled in my mind," she writes in *Twenty Years*, "that I should study medicine and 'live with the poor.'" Why the quotation marks around the last phrase? Writing in 1910, she seemed to be suggesting that her idea of "the poor" at sixteen was a creation of her imagination, something gained from books, not firsthand experience. It probably was. This would explain how she could have wanted to serve the poor and yet disdain the tramps who knocked at the back door. Two books in particular may have fed her idealism: Charles Dickens's *Bleak House* and John Habberton's *Jericho Road*. She read the latter in the spring of 1877.[57] Allan Woodcourt in the first and an unnamed doctor in the second were compassionate medical men who made the poor their particular concern.

In choosing medicine, Addams was being moderately daring. Strangely enough, the possibility of a woman becoming a doctor in those years was less radical than that of a woman earning a B.A. By 1878, six medical colleges for women had been founded in the United States, and the idea of women becoming doctors was much discussed in the popular press and explored in novels. The idea that women's work in medicine was an extension of their philanthropic work was part of the appeal. Many male doctors, to be sure, were fiercely opposed. In 1872 Alfred Stillé, the president of the American Medical Association, declared that women doctors were "monstrous productions." He continued, "Woman is characterized by uncertainty of rational judgment, capriciousness of sentiment, fickleness of purpose, and indecision of action which totally unfit her for professional pursuits."[58] It is difficult to imagine a more sweeping case for banning women from the medical profession.

What John Addams thought of Jane's life plan, if she told him of it, is difficult to say. The historical record provides only frustratingly vague hints of his expectations of her. Intriguingly, it is not a subject that she addresses in *Twenty Years*. No doubt he approved of her interest in poor people, given Sarah's interest and society's assumption that charity was women's work. Certainly, as an evangelical Christian, he felt a broad compassion for humanity. The best evidence we have of his expectations is a single observation his son-in-law made in a letter to Jane after John died. Mary Addams Linn's husband, the Reverend John M. Linn, wrote that her father had desired her "to live" not only "for herself" but also "for . . . humanity and for Christ."[59] Clearly, he hoped she would give others selfless, Christian service.

In any case, his rejection of the Smith College plan was clear. Addams writes in *Twenty Years*, "I was greatly disappointed."[60] It is one of the few sentences in the book that directly expresses her unhappiness with something someone else did. Her father's decision was a difficult one for her to accept. She had been a good student of her father's teachings and of the books she had read. She had made up her own mind and trusted her own judgment, and was ready to take her own bold action, to be as heroic as she could be within her limited circumstances. But just as she stood on the brink of launching herself into the wider world—the world of Lincoln and Mazzini, of Carlyle and Emerson, of Owen and Brown, of Lucy Stone— her father had blocked her path. She complied with his wishes but she did not change her mind about Smith. John L. Capen had described her as "persevering and loath to abandon" any project in which she had become interested. In this assessment Capen would again prove astute.

CHAPTER 4

AMBITION

1877–81

In September 1877, as he had long intended, John Addams drove his youngest daughter to Rockford Seminary. In *Twenty Years* Jane Addams recalls, "I was greatly disappointed at the moment of starting to humdrum Rockford." This feeling mingled with another that she had not forgotten when she was seventy-four years old and, hesitantly, was willing to name. She confessed to her nephew Weber Linn, "I was . . . resentful, I suppose you might call it."[1]

The seminary was "humdrum" in part because it offered no B.A. but also for other reasons. For one thing, it was entirely familiar. She knew some of the teachers—Sarah Blaisdell, who had taught Latin to Alice and Martha and now would teach her; Sarah Anderson, who had been a student with Alice and now taught art and gymnastics; and the principal, Anna Sill, whom she had first met when she was a child.[2] For another thing, the seminary was in Illinois and therefore enrolled "western" students, not the sophisticated "eastern" students likely to attend Smith College.

But life at the seminary would be a greater adventure for Addams than she realized. For the first time she would be living in a place organized not around family but around learning and gender. Rockford Seminary was something entirely new to her—a community led by women that encouraged young women to have large dreams. She would thrive under such nurturing conditions. These conditions were artificial, to be sure, when compared to the worlds of Cedarville and Freeport, not to mention the wider world. Eventually, as Addams thought about her future, she would sense that her dreams clashed with expectations outside the seminary's walls and that this fact would have consequences. As her first year began, however, she was thinking only of the present and that she did not want be at Rockford Female Seminary.

Rockford was a community defined by the personality and vision of its sixty-one-year-old founder and principal, Anna Sill, a woman of unrelenting moral purpose, deeply Christian evangelical faith, and great organizational skill. Although Congregational and Presbyterian ministers founded the school in 1849 to prepare the young women of the community to be charming and useful daughters, wives, and mothers, to make them "as cornerstones polished after the similitude of a palace," as the school's motto put it, Anna Sill intended them to be Christian missionaries serving God and she therefore gave religion prominence in the school's routines. At chapel every morning she delivered a sermon on the day's scripture passage, which students were required to memorize and were expected to recite, on request, at any point in the day. Her goal was to inspire what she called the "missionary spirit, or a spirit of self-denying benevolence toward all." Sunday morning church attendance was required. On Sunday evenings there was a prayer meeting, with teachers and students praying on their knees, followed by a religious talk. Every month the students fasted on a designated day. Every January, as was the tradition at many evangelical institutions, the school hosted a weeklong revival.[3]

As Jane took up residence in this community, she complied unhappily with the required rituals. Her outer compliance satisfied no one. Once faculty and students discovered that she was "unsaved," they tried to persuade her to convert and be baptized. She was prayed for at chapel and prayer meetings and urged to join a church. Addams resisted conversion but also worried about whether she was doing the right thing. On a carriage drive with her father during a weekend visit home, she and he had an "earnest" conversation about religious doctrine. What denominational label did he claim for himself? He was reluctant to give an answer at first, presumably for the same reason he had not joined a church: a desire not to be pigeon-holed. When she pressed him, he told her with a twinkle in his eye, knowing it was not the expected answer, that he was a Hicksite Quaker. Probably unsure just what he meant by that, Jane stayed focused on her own dilemma. Should she agree to convert when she had no faith? He "testified again," she remembered, "in favor of mental integrity above everything else."[4] Converted Christian though he was, John Addams continued to train Jane in the rare quality of rigorous intellectual fortitude that, in his resistance to denominational dogma, he also practiced. She understood that, first and foremost, her father required her to be honest with herself about what she believed.

Thus encouraged, Addams decided to keep up her resistance at seminary, even though it was not a good way to begin her life there. Looking back, she felt that this was "why I got off on the wrong foot with Miss Sill." But she also decided, at least in retrospect, that her resistance had its benefits. Writing in *Twenty Years* with her tongue in her cheek, she noted that the experience of "clinging to individual conviction" at Rockford was "the best moral training" she received there. The fact that she was rebelling against authority did not bother her. In fact, it suited her. In 1881 she would acknowledge this in a letter to her father, informing him, although he surely already knew it, "I am naturally perverse."[5]

At first she cared no more for Rockford's social life than for its religious life. The girls at Rockford Seminary, like girls at other boarding schools, often formed intense romantic friendships. Jane wrote her cousin Vallie Beck, who was encountering such friendships at another boarding school and who had asked Jane for her opinion on them, that she thought them demeaning and that she admired cold people. Vallie agreed, replying that she, too, was drawn to "a dignified (rather haughty) proud—not vain— . . . *cold* person," adding, "(this describes you!)."[6] Apparently Jane was like her father, emotionally cool, even a bit stiff. Vallie's comment suggests that such a manner was not only desirable but admired in their social circles.

Jane Addams's first weeks at Rockford were not easy. She was unhappy that she was not at Smith, at odds with Anna Sill on the question of her religion, alienated from the easy, affectionate intimacy of her fellow students, and lonely for her father's strengthening presence. It was obedience that kept her there, not her own desire.

"I have always liked to write," Addams told a newspaper reporter in 1910, "even as a girl in school."[7] At Rockford, her pen produced essay after essay, each written in her careful, round schoolgirl hand. Her prolixity and the fact that she saved so many seminary papers hint at what a lifetime of writing would prove: that writing was her chosen art. Words, sentences, and paragraphs were the tools she would use to discover and refine her ideas and put them before the world. At seminary, if not before, Jane Addams discovered she was a writer.

Rockford demanded a good deal of writing. In her rhetorical composition course, required of all first-year students and taught by the school's leading teacher, Caroline Potter, Jane wrote an essay every two weeks on a topic of her choice, exploring in each one a different literary form. Many of her pieces bristled with opinions about political and economic issues that, presumably, echoed her father's views. She endorsed Horace Greeley's theory of how the poor "live off" the rich and condemned mechanical inventions that forced skilled workers to migrate to cities and take demeaning, unskilled industrial jobs. Her most complex and creative essay of the year, "Plated Ware," however, abandoned economics for philosophy. Potter arranged for it to be published in the *Rockford Seminary Magazine* that spring, making it Jane's first published work. Using electricity as her metaphor, Jane argued, in Emersonian style, that one mind can affect another without knowing it: "[O]ur words strike a *negative* mind, and go forth into the universe of electric thought."[8] The piece, although obscure in meaning, has a certain aplomb. Jane Addams was fearless of, even enchanted by, abstraction and mystery. While others sought the concrete, she luxuriated in the abstruse, the vague, and the philosophical.

She made some friends. Two were a year ahead of her: Eva Campbell, from Durand, Illinois, who would become her second-year roommate, and Katie Hitchcock, from Des Moines, Iowa, with whom she would later study Greek. Sarah Anderson, the young art teacher, became another friend. Years later, her friends gave their impressions of Jane at seminary. Sarah remembered her as "so delicate looking yet so brim full of energy and determination." Jane was petite, weighing a little less than 114 pounds. Another recalled her "direct, earnest eyes." In time, students were drawn to her. One remembered, "We liked to go to her room. . . . [W]e just knew there was always something 'doing' where she was . . . , that there was intellectual ozone in her vicinity."[9]

Another new friend was one of the seven girls in her own class, the class of 1881, Ellen Gates Starr. They met the first day of school but their friendship was cemented in Potter's rhetorical composition course. They shared a love of writing and literature, particularly Dickens, a passion for ideas, and a determination to earn a good education.[10] Ellen Gates Starr was Jane Addams's first intellectual friend.

Temperamentally, they were quite different. Ellen, the second daughter of New Englanders who had migrated to northern Illinois, shared Jane's serious-mindedness and idealism but not her emotional coolness. Cheerful and vivacious, she loved to talk and to laugh; melancholy was alien to her. A friend of Ellen's once wrote her, "I have seen you *fearfully* cross, but I cannot remember your being very sad ever." Nor, when she was angry,

Ellen Gates Starr. Ellen Gates Starr Papers, Sophia Smith Collection, Smith College, Northampton, MA.

did the mood last for long. Her explosions passed like summer storms, leaving her as cheerful as before. On the other hand, she did not hesitate to sit in judgment of others. During the summer after their first year she wrote Jane that "Miss Sill's crochets [are] despicable," a phrase that might well have described Jane's feelings but would never have escaped her pen or passed her lips.[11]

Such differences attracted each to the other. Addams particularly admired Starr's passionate high-mindedness. "I want you to know, my friend," Jane would later tell Ellen, "that my view of things is always a little higher and more vigorous when I take a standpoint beside you."[12] Starr, who would spend a lifetime struggling to control her anger and often longed for a peaceful soul, must have found Addams's unexcitable temperament, her "coldness," ballast by which to steady herself. In the early years of their friendship, they admired each other, inspired each other, and balanced each other.

During her first year, Jane was not challenged academically. She may have been underqualified for Smith College but she was overqualified for the seminary. Her required courses were in Latin with Sarah Blaisdell (Virgil's *Aeneid*, *Bucolics*, and *Georgics* and writings by Caesar), Bible Gospel, mathematics (algebra), natural science (physiology and botany), and history and literature (rhetorical composition) with Caroline Potter. To these she added German and music. Her grade point average at the end of the year was an impressive 9.3 out of a possible 10.0.[13]

Her performance gave her bragging rights and perhaps a case for transferring to Smith. In June 1878 she wrote a letter to her parents summing up her year's accomplishments, her satisfaction with her schoolwork, and her good health. The actual letter does not survive but its contents can be surmised from her parents' replies. Anna and John Addams's letters, both of which she uncharacteristically saved, were different in revealing ways. Her stepmother encouraged her: "[I] am glad my child . . . feels happy . . . that her school work has been *well-done* and gives her content." She told Jane to leave her bedding at Rockford in shape "to send for . . . in case you do not go back next year." Was she thinking that Jane might transfer to Smith? John Addams, on the other hand, was cool and businesslike. He said nothing about Jane's academic success, her sense of achievement, or her plans but merely thanked her for her letter, said he was pleased to hear of her good health, and shared some local news. He had, he explained, "no time to say more."[14]

That summer Jane tried again to persuade her father to send her to Smith. Aware of her intentions, a friend from Rockford, Hattie Smith, wrote at the end of August, "What does your father say of Smith College by this time?" He said no. More unexpectedly, Ellen wrote in the same month that she would not be returning to the seminary in the fall. Because her family was having financial difficulties, she would spend the next year teaching at a local school. Wistfully, she promised Jane that she would keep up with the reading for "Miss Potter's class."[15]

Caroline Potter had become Jane Addams's favorite teacher. In her second year, Jane took her required ancient history and modern history courses. Potter met with each student individually to discuss her essays. Fifty years later Addams recalled that "[t]he hours spent with her . . . are still surrounded with a sort of enchantment." She admired Potter's gifts as a teacher. She also found in her someone whose ideas about women's potential stretched her own. Potter, a graduate of the seminary's first collegiate class in 1855, was the jewel in the school's pedagogical crown. Her place in the collegiate department, which ranged in size from forty to seventy students, was central. Her literature and history classes were required regardless of which track—scientific, classical, or literary—a student chose, with the result that all the students in every collegiate class, first year through senior year, had her each year for at least one and often two semesters.[16]

Although Potter's job was to teach history, literature, and composition, her real responsibility, as she understood it, was to teach character, the force that, to her mind, shaped history and supplied the central theme in the study of Western civilization. Character was an expansive concept. A man of character was decisive, bold, creative, original, engaged with his times, able to withstand pressures to compromise his integrity, responsible, courageous, and determined.[17] Potter's entire curriculum was an intense and lengthy seminar on the heroic. Jane was entranced.

More fascinating still, Potter embraced the heroic as a virtue for women. Women are "grasping an enormous new power," she wrote a friend. Her words echo Margaret Fuller's ideas. In her influential book *Woman in the Nineteenth Century* (1845), Fuller expressed confidence that a woman's power was every bit as forceful as a man's and rejected the idea that real men and women fit the abstract ideals of masculinity and femininity put forth by, among other people, her influential friend Ralph Waldo Emerson. Potter's ideas matched Fuller's so exactly that one suspects that Fuller was as crucial an influence on Potter as she was on many others of Potter's generation. Furthermore, the topics about which Jane wrote some of her papers, discussed below, suggest that Potter assigned her book in class.[18]

As a teacher, Potter was looking for students who were most likely to fulfill women's grand potential. Teachers should prepare girls, she wrote, to "direct . . . this splendid accession of power." She watched for those whose minds were susceptible to discipline and who were willing, if she found the right course of study for them, to "exhaust [their] strength in [study's] pursuit." She also looked for originality and for the willingness to act "upon the demand of the occasion." Aware of the temptation faced by all students, but particularly women, to fall in love with learning and fail to carry the ideas back into the world, she warned that learning was not for its own sake. "If the mind of woman becomes chiefly a repository of learning," she told a group of alumnae in 1883, "then she will lose her vital power."[19]

Potter's influence was exercised over her students outside as well as inside the classroom. She was the founder, faculty advisor, and spiritual governor of the school's main student organizations, the Vesperian and the Castalian literary societies, and their joint publication, the *Rockford Seminary Magazine*. Every collegiate student was required to join one society or the other. The magazine was the sole seminary publication, serving as a combined campus newspaper and alumnae magazine. These three organizations constituted a sort of intellectual free zone where Potter and her students could study whatever interested them. Potter's extracurricular kingdom was the capital of fun and independent challenge for Rockford's students, and Jane was drawn in. In the middle of her sophomore year she would become editor of the magazine's "Home Items" department and then rise steadily through its ranks. In her first year, she joined the Castalian Society.[20]

Literary societies in the nineteenth century, whether attached to colleges or free-standing in communities, were considered a kind of boot camp for citizenship. John Addams understood this when he founded one as a young man in Sinking Spring. At the weekly meetings members practiced different methods of public presentation: declamation (memorizing and delivering a speech that someone else had written), essay delivery, oratory (extemporaneous or prepared speeches of persuasion), recitation, and debate. During the business portion of the meetings, they practiced parliamentary procedures, which were understood to be an essential skill for people aspiring to civic responsibilities. In 1876 these had been simplified and formalized into Robert's Rules of Order, and literary societies were eager to master them.[21]

During Jane's first two years at seminary the school's literary societies did no oratory, but Potter did have the women debate. Although their debates were written down and read rather than delivered extemporaneously, as was the practice at men's colleges, the fact that they debated at all was groundbreaking.[22] Potter set the debate topics. In the fall of Jane's sophomore year, Jane was assigned to argue the affirmative side of the proposition that French women (the reference was to George Sand and Madame de Staël) "have had more influence through literature than politics." Jane wrote a passionate debate essay, in which she used George Sand as her representative case, to argue for women's rights. "This splendid . . . woman . . . declares the social independence and equality of woman [in] her relations to man, society and destiny." Like Sand, she continued, today's woman "wishes not to be a man or like a man but she claims the same right to independent thought and action."[23] The defiant passage leaves no doubt that Jane Addams recognized at eighteen that there was a gap between what she wanted for herself and what some thought she ought to seek. It also captures her confidence in the power of ideas to change the world.

While Jane was testing out a new, radically self-assertive vision, she also kept in mind her practical goal of gaining an education in science as preparation for medical school. Because Rockford offered no laboratory work with its science courses, she and Ellen Gates Starr started a science club during their first year. During the summers she and George, now an aspiring scientist attending Beloit College, caught, killed, and stuffed birds, pounded rocks, and examined earthworms under a microscope. After visiting Harry and Alice in Iowa one summer, Jane borrowed Harry's copies of Darwin's *On the Origin of the Species* and *The Descent of Man*. Her enthusiasm for science as an "intellectual adventure," she writes in *Twenty Years*, was high. It was also socially acceptable. Science was thought an excellent new area of study for women because it did not encourage them to pursue civic action and was understood to be an amateur's pursuit, without professional opportunity (outside of medicine).[24]

Unfortunately, Addams did not find science heroic. Although she bravely wrote to Ellen that she would rather get her inspiration from "a dodecahedral crystal" than from "a Genius," the opposite was closer to the truth. She came up with an interesting theory to explain to herself what was missing. "Science demands from its devotees," she wrote in a sophomore paper, "only an exertion of the brain, and not a complete surrender of life and all its pleasures." Her point was not true, of course; science could demand such sacrifices. She was really speaking about her own feelings. For her, studying science was solely an intellectual enterprise. Equally discouraging, her summer research with George showed her that she had "no aptitude."[25]

Evidently Jane wanted a career that demanded larger self-sacrifice, even martyrdom, a close cousin of, but different from, heroism. Martyrs embraced suffering as destiny, whereas heroes passed through suffering on their way to victory; martyrs consistently denied the self, whereas heroes celebrated the self; martyrs did not seek power, but heroes did. The martyr was the aborted hero. Martyrdom was also the Christian's and the woman's greatest crown. Jane Addams, trained from childhood in Christianity, familiar with the female duties of self-sacrifice and with personal suffering, felt martyrdom's appeal.

———————

No list survives of all the books that Jane Addams read at Rockford Seminary, but she undoubtedly read a great many. In a sense, she had come to seminary, and had wanted to go to Smith, simply to read as widely and as fruitfully as possible, that is, to pursue culture, as Emerson had urged. The aspiration was not solely Emerson's, of course; it pervaded the age, and the British intellectual Matthew Arnold was one of its most articulate spokespersons. His 1869 essay *Culture and Anarchy*, which Addams read at seminary, was required reading for English speakers who aspired to sophistication. Famously, he defined culture as "the pursuit of total perfection by means of getting to know . . . the best which has been thought and said in the world." In particular, absorbing culture would strengthen a person's commitment to improving society. Culture, he wrote, inspires a "moral and social passion for doing good." Emerson sounded the same theme of service, observing that the secret of culture was "the wish to serve, to add somewhat to the well-being of man." In effect, culture was being conceived as Christianity's replacement, as the faith by which to redeem oneself and others. Culture offered secular salvation. [26]

Because it promised moral transformation, however, culture was also elitist. Jane and her friends were proud that they were becoming those rare things—educated women. On the wall of the Chess Club they posted a quotation from Aristotle that delighted them: "There is the same difference between the learned and the unlearned as there is between the living and the dead." [27] Culture, then, was a tool for making class distinctions. In nineteenth-century America, where social status was often unmoored from tradition and place, people in the Victorian upper and middle classes used culture to set themselves apart from the uncouth lower, or working, class.

Rockford Seminary promoted both of culture's contradictory goals— selfish self-improvement and selfless service—but Sill was always looking for ways to stress the latter. In June 1879 she invited an Iowa minister with an enthusiasm for overseas missionary work, James Griswold Merrill, to speak at commencement weekend. Jane ran through his arguments, which made a strong impression on her, in a letter to her roommate Eva Campbell, who had gone home early owing to illness. She was struck by Merrill's understanding of the morality of culture. He claimed, she wrote, that most students were aiming for "self-culture." This goal, Jane said, quoting Merrill, merely "impales a man on his personal pronouns." She thought the metaphor delightful. "Think of your soul," she wrote Eva, "spinning around on a great I."

By comparison, Merrill argued, those who possessed true culture (missionaries, for example) would escape the self and "throw [them]selves into the tide of affairs." The truly cultured were those who had gained a "breadth

and sweep" in understanding the world. He pressed his point by inviting his audience to imagine praying, as a missionary would, for a "South
African." (By "South African" he meant a non-Christian black South
African who lived in a tribe.) Jane had mixed reactions. On one hand, she
thought Merrill's vision "splendid." "Just think, Eva," she rhapsodized, "of
having expansiveness of soul enough to pray, actually pray[,] for a South
African, a man barbarous & brutal[,] . . . coarse and uncouth, . . . like an
animal." On the other, she could not imagine herself doing it. "I am
doomed to reach on toward self-culture," she wrote with morose self-
mockery.[28] Addams felt herself to be so high above the "brutal" black African that she could not imagine caring for the fate of his soul, or even,
apparently, believing that he had one."breadgivers

For Addams, as for so many, culture was a double-edged sword. It both
challenged her to escape her class and racial biases and reinforced their
claim on her. After she graduated from seminary, she would wrestle with
the two faces of culture. In time she would take offense at culture's selfish
pleasures, yet she would also rely on culture for the encouragement to resist
them. In time she would see that culture distanced her from those who
seemed to lack it, yet she would also rely on culture to inspire her to draw
closer to them. Eventually her desire to bring culture as she understood it
to those whom she perceived to be without it would cause her to reshape
her life. And then that new life would change her ideas about culture again.
A good way to trace the larger shifts in Jane Addams's thought is to trace
the changes in her definition of, and feelings about, culture.

At seminary, however, Addams was intent on pursuing self-improvement; in the language of the day, she was seeking to develop her "higher"
faculties. It was thought that humans had four: the lower ones of the passions and the affections and the higher ones of reason and morality. The
faculties were not innate talents but human capacities that training could
strengthen. In the spring of her sophomore year Addams was worried that
this training of her higher faculties was not going well. In an allegorical
essay, "Follow Thou Thy Star," which she wrote for Potter's class, she described a hero who could not perceive his life's purpose because "his faculties are locked up, . . . his powers are paralyzed." The language is vague;
it seems to suggest that the hero fears using all of his talents to pursue his
dreams but the reason why is not explained. In any case, the result was
both definite and fatal. Now he would never act out "the happiest, noblest
and best part of his life." Desiring fiercely to become a hero, she was pre-

dicting, sensing, fearing that she would fail. The same pessimism can be found in other essays she wrote in college about the hero.[29] And was it not the same pessimism found in her wheel dream? It appears she had brought the unconscious pattern of her childhood nightmares and dreams into the conscious, imaginary world of her seminary essays.

In late May or early June, while the dangers of inaccessible faculties were much on her mind, there was a major crisis at the school. The details are unclear, but one student badly burned her hands and two others were suspended and sent home. Jane wrote an editorial about it for the magazine's July issue. Obscure on its face, her piece shows her borrowing heavily from Emerson's essay "Experience" in order to work through the problem of inaccessible capacities. After calling the crisis a "tempest" and referring to the "locked up faculties" of the students, she adopts Emerson's conclusion—that it is dangerous to spend all one's time in routine and in preparation for the future—and his solution—that it is important to focus on the present, to engage in the world around one. To avoid locked-up faculties, each individual must take up his duties as a citizen in the community where he finds himself; whether that be "in the wide world or a school, with its own laws and regulations, his responsibility is the same."[30]

Although her advice was for her readers, she was talking to herself. After watching the unfolding crisis without getting involved, she realized that her obsession with the future, that is, with Smith College, had prevented her from becoming fully engaged with the "humdrum" world in which she found herself; she had failed to enter enthusiastically into the times. The consequences of this new understanding were evident in a letter she sent Eva in June. She had decided, she wrote, that she would return to Rockford the following year.[31] It was the first time she made such a statement. Realizing that she had "locked up" her faculties herself, she decided, heroically, to commit herself fully to Rockford. It was a turning point.

That summer Jane made the first change stemming from her new outlook. In previous summers, judging from her letters, she had ignored the books she was assigned for the fall semester, apparently hoping that she might not be returning to the seminary. Now she devoted herself to reading them, including those for Potter's English literature course: Shakespeare's *Merchant of Venice* and *Macbeth*, Motley's *Rise of the Dutch Republic* and three novels, Walter Scott's *Guy Mannering* and *Monastery* and Edward Bulwer-Lytton's *Last Days of Pompeii*. Although she was often interrupted by relatives visiting from the east, George falling ill for a time, and a trip with Sarah Anderson to Iowa, it is clear from her correspondence that she found time to do much reading. Sometimes reading as many as five books at once, she read for hours, day after day, week after week. She read on the back porch, in the family parlor, sitting on Pine Hill, or in the rowboat as it floated on the meandering creek. When she went for a walk, she took a book. The character of the White Lady in *Monastery* held "peculiar attraction" for her; some scenes from *Last Days of Pompeii* were so vivid in her memory that she felt as if she had seen them. [32]

Perhaps she read too much. By mid-August, her mood was becoming restless. She felt contempt for well-read people, she told Ellen in a letter, because "they had to read to find out" what they wanted to know. News from Ellen reinforced her impatience. Starr wrote that she was giving up on returning to Rockford Seminary in the near future and instead was moving to Chicago in the fall to teach at a preparatory school for girls. Jane was envious. She wrote Ellen, "Being in a city [will give] you an education a good deal better than a boarding school will." She foresaw Ellen gaining in "self-reliance" and the ability "not to move in ruts." [33] Compared to Ellen's new life in Chicago, Jane's life at school seemed impossibly tame.

Both friends knew that Ellen's move would make it more difficult for them to see each other. Jane considered the possibility that their friendship was over but felt no regret. With the brutal frankness of youth she explained her feelings to Ellen. "It is queer . . . but a fact," she wrote, "that I am glad when I know some people just so much and then stop." Friends are a bit like books, she noted. If one friendship ended, then another could begin. She liked the "variety." Ellen may have been hurt by Jane's detachment. Certainly Starr's approach to friendship was quite the opposite. She would shortly become close friends with a fellow teacher at her school and would write Jane that she was "just on the verge of falling in love with her." [34] Ellen was a bit like Anna Addams—she enjoyed living on the emotional edge, sought out experiences that stirred her passions, and was always pressing for greater intimacy with others.

Jane Addams's emotional coolness was probably partly temperamental and partly inspired by her father's example, but it also reflected her beliefs about emotions, beliefs that shaped her expectations of herself as a woman in crucial ways. At seminary, these ideas were becoming more confused. Some of the books she was reading instructed her that affection was a lower faculty than reason or morality. Matthew Arnold made that case in his poem "Self-Dependence," which she copied into her commonplace book and quoted in a letter to Ellen. The stars, Arnold notes, do not ask that anything outside of themselves "[y]ield them love, amusement, sympathy."[35] But other books, in particular those by popular male Romantic authors such as Carlyle, Ruskin, and Emerson, valorized "spontaneity" and "intuition," as characteristic of the man of character and urged their readers to avoid overrationality. Their message was the secular Romantic version of the Hicksite inner light: trust yourself; trust your feelings.[36]

These authors intended all this advice first and foremost for men. For women, however, the advice on the role of emotions was equally confusing. The books and magazines that Addams read and the sermons she listened to instructed her that woman's loving, sentimental nature was her greatest asset within the home but was also her greatest handicap outside the home. "Woman's intuition," a phrase cultural commentators used to mean emotional capriciousness and irrationality, disqualified her, they argued, from entering the professions or assuming a civic role, including voting.

Could woman's intuition be redeemed as a respectable public asset? Addams was drawn to passages in her reading that suggested this possibility. Usually they involved goddesses, that is, female entities with distinctly public powers. In her sophomore year she was drawn to the nature goddess described in George Eliot's *Romola* and copied the passage into her commonplace book: "[A] loving awe in the presence of noble womanhood . . . is . . . something like the worship paid of old to a great nature goddess, who was not all knowing but whose life and power were something deeper and more primordial than knowledge." The phrase "deeper and more primordial than knowledge" was evidently deeply appealing. It appears in four of her seminary essays and one letter, including, in one case, as a description of the Egyptian goddess Isis. She read in Margaret Fuller's *Woman in the Nineteenth Century* that Cassandra, the prophetess of Troy, used "her intuitive powers" to foresee the future.[37] She would find a way to use that idea, too, in her graduation essay.

The profound appeal to Jane of the goddess-prophetess's power can be felt in an observation she made to Ellen during the summer of 1879, when they were writing about religion. "Christ," she admitted, "don't help me in the least" to come closer to "the Deity." (She was using Midwestern vernacular grammar.) What drew her was the idea of a female god. "Lately," she wrote, she had been getting "back to a great Primal Cause, not Nature exactly, but a fostering mother, a necessity, brooding and watching over all things, not passive, the mystery of creation[;] . . . the idea has been lots of comfort to me." [38] There was a hole in her heart where her mother's love should have been. She felt the void.

Was intuition male or female, good or bad? Should one express one's spontaneous feelings or keep them under strict control? Did women's feelings give them public power or only public embarrassment? To someone like Addams, serious-minded and ambitious, these issues were not theoretical but highly personal and perplexing. If she was determined to pursue perfection as culture defined it, then she would have to decide the place of feelings in the ideal cultured person that she was aiming to become.

Jane returned to campus in the fall of 1879 as a junior. Her required courses included Latin (Cicero and Horace), mathematics (geometry), science (astronomy), Bible history (monarchy), and English literature. Instead of taking the usual one elective, Addams took two, Greek and German, and, in her second semester, a special tutorial with Potter on medieval history. Carrying six courses the first semester and seven the second, she earned a grade point average both semesters of 9.8. [39] Pushing against Rockford's modest academic aspirations, she was extracting all she could from the institution.

She also returned, as usual, to a regular diet of Christian ritual but she now was less compliant in her response. She still looked as if she were praying, but her mind was elsewhere. She had decided to abandon the internal act. "[I am] shocked to find," she confessed to Ellen, "that I feel no worse for it." In fact, she admitted, she was happier. At the same time, on Sunday mornings she began reading the New Testament in the original Greek (a different Greek from the classical Greek she was studying in language class) with Sarah Blaisdell. Afterwards, Addams would "always feel sort of solemn." With her literary sensibility, religion as story appealed to her far more than religion as dogma, worship, or precept. She admitted to Ellen that her religion amounted to little but a love of heroes and acknowledged it as "shallow." She was seeking the "Perfect or Ideal man," she wrote, and intended to "yield myself to all nobility wherever I can find it." For the moment she was observing Caroline Potter. Meanwhile Ellen's Christian faith was strengthening daily, and she was becoming eager to bring Jane to the same depth of faith. Perceiving that they were going in different directions in their religious journeys, Jane told Ellen that she thought it would be better if they did not talk about religion anymore. [40] In all this, Jane seemed freshly determined to honor her true feelings.

The biggest change that took place Jane's junior year was that, desiring to engage in the present, she jumped into extracurricular activities with new enthusiasm. After being elected in the fall as the Castalian Society's new president, she orchestrated an evening of essays and recitations about gypsies, whom she and her friends perceived as passionate and spontaneous, for the literary society's first meeting. In the spring, inspired by the story of the witches' orgy on Walpurgis Mountain in Goethe's *Faust*, certainly a passionate affair, she and her friends organized the seminary's first Walpurgis Night, at which they read essays and poems on the theme. But of all the special events concocted by Addams's fertile brain that year, her greatest triumph was to persuade her class, the Class of '81, of which she had also been elected president, to launch another new tradition: a junior exhibition of oratory.[41]

At nineteen, Jane Addams was fully entranced by oratory and by the ideal of the heroic orator. As a teen, she had been influenced by her father's example and the writings of Emerson and Carlyle, both of whom equated the orator with the hero, the poet, the genius. At Rockford, her study of Cicero, Horace, and Tacitus in Latin class reinforced her fascination. In the fall of 1879, she was studying Cicero's much-admired orations. The following spring, in her literature and composition class, Caroline Potter would teach Addams rhetoric, that is, the art of persuasion, relying on Alexander Bain's *English Composition and Rhetoric* for the text. A psychologist as well as a rhetorician, Bain stressed the importance of establishing an emotional connection with the audience. Men follow "the lead of others," he wrote, "through imitation or sympathy." This approach had many adherents. If you wish to be a master orator, another expert observed, you must possess the "art of . . . identifying yourself with the feelings of your hearers . . . [and] the power . . . of making their thoughts your thoughts, or your thoughts theirs."[42]

Because Rockford's literary societies performed no oratory, the junior exhibition constituted an assertion by Addams and her classmates that oratory was not reserved for men. On April 20, 1880, the junior class, now numbering seventeen, presented the school's first oratorical exhibition in the chapel. The event drew a crowd of students, faculty, family, and interested Rockford citizens. The class decorated the chapel stage with evergreen boughs and stands of flowering plants; tiny scarlet flags that read "81" hung from the gas chandeliers. In imitation of the exhibitions at men's colleges, the class planned to present five orations—Latin, scientific,

Jane Addams (holding parasol) and eight other members of the class of 1881, Rockford Seminary (photo taken in their junior or senior year). Rockford College Archives, Rockford, IL.

ethical, Greek, and philosophical—several recitations and essays, and a "historical dissertation."[43]

Jane Addams had a prominent role. As class president, she opened the evening with the class address, and as the only member of her class who had studied Greek, she gave the Greek oration. In both speeches she explored her ideas, framed as general truths, about who she ought to become. Each was, in a different way, a personal manifesto.

"Breadgivers," the class address, was the first speech she had ever given to a general audience and her first attempt to be an orator. Her topic was what educated women of her generation wanted for their future. Work, she explained, is the answer, because it is central to happiness. But what kind of work? She structured her remarks around the metaphor that women should be breadgivers. She opened her speech skillfully by connecting the present moment to the larger theme she wished to address. The exhibition, she explained, was part of the change taking place in the "aspirations of women." Woman was developing both her "intellectual force" and her capacity for "direct labor." Turning to the question of what kind of work women should do, she introduced the metaphor: "[W]e have planned [to be] bread-givers." She explained that this was the literal translation of the Saxon word for "lady." She gave no more details about the kind of work she had in mind. She claimed vaguely, "[B]elieving that in labor alone is happiness . . . we have planned to idealize our labor, and thus happily fulfill woman's noblest mission."[44]

But her classmates knew exactly what she meant. They had recently adopted the word "breadgivers" as their class motto. It came from John Ruskin's *Sesame and Lilies*, which they must have been reading in Potter's English literature class. Ruskin writes, " 'Breadgivers' . . . refers not to the bread which is given to the household but to the bread broken among the multitude." To readers of the Bible and Ruskin the phrase "broken bread" invoked the miracle of the loaves and fishes performed by Jesus and, more broadly, feeding the poor. Building on that familiar story, Emerson, in his "Man the Reformer," invokes bread not only as embodying the necessity of work but also the commitment of man to aiding mankind. Bread, according to Emerson, is "the symbol of the power of kindness." Caroline Potter, artful spokesperson for women's influence, used bread in just this way—to signify all forms of good works. Bread, she told a group of alumnae in 1883, represented "that power which nourishes and sustains every conceivable phase of life." To the Class of '81, therefore, "breadgivers" meant their work of charity for the poor, or to use the grander term, philanthropy. (Whether it was called charity work, philanthropy, or social reform was not important; the terms were thought interchangeable.) The class song, which Addams co-wrote, conveyed the same message. It describes their hope "to inspire the world . . . to noble deeds and [to] labor to lighten its honest needs, breadgivers of '81." In "Breadgivers" Addams challenged the tradition of narrow domesticity for women and publicly declared her commitment to a career of service to the poor.[45]

To be sure, she could have made her meaning clearer. Why did she never mention the poor explicitly? Why did she not say that women should work outside the home? One explanation is the nature of her mind. Her literary sensibility and love of the mysterious made her disinclined to think in polarized fashion. In this case, she preferred to ignore the familiar poles of poor versus rich and of women's place in the private sphere and man's in the public sphere. She did not avoid choosing sides so much as fail to acknowledge that sides existed. The appeal of the breadgivers metaphor was exactly this: it allowed her to keep shifting her perspective. Another explanation is that she intended to be vague. Her rhetorical training and the examples of Potter's and Emerson's artful impenetrability taught her how to skillfully imbed controversial ideas in a soft cushion of conventionality. In "Breadgivers" Addams was making a case for a wider role for women without specifying what exactly she had in mind.[46]

For the rest of her life Jane Addams would often use this allusive and elusive rhetorical style. It would prove both a strength and a liability. Because she could present radical ideas gently, she often drew the politically cautious into new ways of thinking. Because she found it difficult to argue forcefully for the righteousness of a cause, she was not particularly effective in stirring people to action, although her skill would improve with age. As prone to amalgamation in her thinking as she would later prove to be in her methods of social reform, she was, from her first speech to her last, a woman at home with ambiguity.

In her second speech, the Greek oration, she took up the question of social reform more explicitly, using the Greek myth of Bellerophon as an allegory to probe the question of what methods a social reformer should use to accomplish her goals. In the story, Bellerophon, aided by the advice of the goddess Pallas Athena and by the winged horse Pegasus, which she gives him, slays the monster Chimera, but when he tries to ride Pegasus into heaven, the god Zeus throws him down to earth to wander melancholy and alone. Thus Addams claimed that "social reformers" (symbolized by Bellerophon) should employ their "idealism" (Pegasus) to slay the delusions of "prejudice and fanaticism" (the Chimera) abroad in the land. Idealism, it is clear, is a synonym for intuition and the opposite of reason. In Addams's version of the story, Athena, whom Addams called the "idealist," not only loans Pegasus to Bellerophon but also advises the youth to put his faith in that which is "deeper and truer" than reason, that is, in intuition, in feeling. Bellerophon's failed attempt to ride Pegasus to heaven, Addams explained, demonstrates that reason will not work as a reform method.[47] Aside from confirming her choice of social reform for her career, her Greek oration had as its subtext Addams's continuing fascination with intuitive women who wielded public power. The addition of Athena to the pantheon that already contained Eliot's nature goddess and Isis showed that she was edging her way to a new sense of whom she could become.

The junior class oratorical exhibition was a general triumph, receiving generous coverage in the Rockford city newspaper. Meanwhile Jane already had her eye on the next such opportunity, the Illinois intercollegiate oratorical contest that would take place the following fall at Knox College in Galesburg. The contests were relatively new on the scene and a source of much competitive excitement. Each October, the Illinois Intercollegiate Oratorical Association (IIOA), consisting of eight coed colleges and one men's college, held a contest at which the best orator from each institution competed for the state title. He or she then represented Illinois at the interstate contest in the spring, competing with the winners from five or six midwestern states for regional honors. Caroline Potter called the founding of the IIOA in 1874 a movement "in just the right direction." She was an enthusiast for the collegiate practice of oratory and likely encouraged Jane and her classmates to organize the oratorical exhibition and participate in the IIOA. Women had competed in the Illinois state contests, but their participation recently had been controversial. In 1878 and 1879, when women placed first and second, some male students had fiercely objected and, in the second case, schemed to have the final scores changed. [48] In Illinois, collegiate oratory was shaping up as a battleground for establishing women's equal rights. Although Rockford Seminary was not an IIOA member, it would find a way at the fall competition to join in the fray.

Jane Addams's junior year was remarkable in every way. Beyond her excellent grades and her achievements as a leader of her class and her literary society, she had flourished by opening her mind to unorthodox possibilities. Encouraged by Potter's woman-affirming curriculum and the creative freedom offered by extracurricular organizations, Jane had explored the appeal of female power, formulated her own hero-worshipping religion, performed the role of orator, and begun to see women's feelings as useful in the world of public action. No letter survives in which she expresses the joy that her courageous, bold, engaged junior year must have given her, but there can be little doubt that she felt it.

Addams began her senior year as editor-in-chief of the *Rockford Seminary Magazine,* but when the school year began it was oratory that was most on her mind. Her classmates had chosen her to compete at the IIOA contest in Galesburg in early October. Since none of the coed schools in the association had chosen a woman to compete, Jane was being sent, she was told, to represent college women generally. At Galesburg, Addams did not sweep triumphantly into first place. She placed fifth, while a student from

Participants in oratorical competition, including William Jennings Bryan (back row,
third from the right) and Jane Addams. William Jennings Bryan and Mary
Baird Bryan, The Memoirs of William Jennings Bryan
(Chicago: Winston Co., 1925), facing page 85.

Illinois College named William Jennings Bryan, who was also enamored
with the heroic possibilities of oratory, placed second. Afterwards, a photograph of the orators was taken. In it Jane can be seen seated in the front
row, the only woman among numerous young men. Back at Rockford, her
friends scolded her for having "dealt the cause of woman's advancement a
staggering blow."[49]

Setting aside this first disappointment of her oratorical career, Addams
turned her attention that fall to undertaking a thorough overhaul of the
now-monthly magazine. The improvements included adding a masthead
to the front of each issue, expanding the editorial department, replacing the
Alumnae Department with a more flexible Contributors' Department and,
after a fundraising fair, achieving a balanced budget. Pleased with her financial success, Jane teased in an editorial, "So why not become a capitalist?"[50]

One of the pleasures of being editor was that she had a small office
of her own in which to write. In her first editorial of her senior year she
praised it as "a cozy little retreat." Even the pen, ink, and paper enchanted
her. "Materials for writing stand so delightfully that to seize the pen and
write will be the very essence of happiness," she rhapsodized. Free to write
about whatever she chose in her editorials, she often settled on politics.

Her sympathies for women's suffrage were evident in three editorials, one of them inspired by Rockford's city election. Jane commented with spirit on the municipality's strange plan that the women vote but that their votes not be counted. "We suppose . . . this is a step toward eventual suffrage and as such ought to be applauded," she observed with tart courtesy, "but at present it seems but a mockery."[51]

As for the great political idea of the age, democracy, she mentions it only once, in a January 1881 editorial. Apparently, over the Christmas holiday she and her father had been discussing the dangers of the Republican Party's current dominance nationally and the threat the situation posed to democracy. "The two parties must be equally powerful" in a democracy, she wrote, or "national individualism, competition and independence" would come to an end.[52] She was using the word "democracy" as Republicans did—as a synonym for individual freedom and economic opportunity.

Meanwhile, Jane was pushing to complete the demanding curriculum she had laid out to prepare herself for Smith, which she now planned to attend the following fall. "This year is a solid dig," she wrote Ellen, "to make up all the odds and ends for Smiths [*sic*]; such little things as spherical trigonometry and the *Memorabilia* [of Xenophon]." Because of her heavy course load, her health sometimes suffered. In the middle of the senior year, she experienced eyestrain and wrote to Alice that she felt "run down." She dropped Greek and tried to rest her eyes.[53]

Her goal remained to earn a B.A. at Smith and then an M.D. and become, as she put it in one of her magazine musings, a "heroic physician." After finishing at Smith, she planned to travel in Europe, then enroll in the medical school at the University of Edinburgh. "My former vague dream," she wrote Ellen in February, "is growing into a settled passion."[54]

But if her plans had not changed, something else had. During her senior year a new note of hesitation and fearfulness crept into her writing. For one thing, despite her continued determination to study medicine, she felt a new distaste for life plans of any kind. In several essays she praised King Arthur, Leonardo da Vinci, and others for *not* having a purpose in life since this prevented them from having to "sink under disappointment" when they failed to achieve it. Then there was her new assumption that an outside agent was in charge of decisions about a person's future. The challenge, she wrote in a November editorial, is to "know . . . what niche in the world has been left for us to fill." And in another she stated, in regard to the class of 1881, "We can only hope that each in her 'small corner' will accomplish that where-unto she may be sent."[55] Who was leaving Jane a niche to fill? Who was sending her to her "small corner"? To whose authority was she submitting? She wrote as if she expected the future to have an absence of freedom, a lack of choice. Even her sentences were tied in knots. These were strange assumptions for someone aspiring to independence and courageous deeds.

In yet another peculiar shift, she began to praise the virtue of obedience. She had hardly mentioned it in her earlier Rockford writings, but now the topic arose often. It is too easy for a schoolgirl to acquire the habit of "shirking" her duty, she admonished in one editorial. The hero she admired most, she wrote in another, was the Roman soldier who guarded the gates of Pompeii as Mount Vesuvius erupted and who refused to move from his post because he had received no orders to go. "Submission to rightful authority . . . is one of the most useful habits of life," she sternly advised.[56]

And she began to praise the ethic of duty to family. Helpfully, George Eliot laid it all before her in *The Mill on the Floss*, which she read during Christmas vacation. In the novel the heroine, Maggie, commits suicide rather than pursue a love affair that would force her to betray her responsibility to her family. She justifies her act with the words, "[P]ity and faithfulness and memory are natural. . . . [They] live in me and [would] punish me if I did not obey them." Struck by the passage, Jane wrote it in her commonplace book. Eliot knew her audience. No virtue ranked higher in the Victorian ethical universe than the duty of love and obedience that a child, especially a daughter, owed a parent. The passage resonated with meaning for Addams. In the same letter in which she tells Alice she has just finished reading *Mill on the Floss*, she urges her sister to repair the hurt feelings Anna had because of an unappreciated Christmas present Alice gave to Harry, saying that such "faithfulness" would please their father.[57]

These changes in the ideals that Jane was putting first and the fact that they suddenly erupted in her senior year all point to one explanation. She was worried about the future and thinking about what her family would expect of her. Perhaps her father had told her directly that he did not want her going to Smith the following year. More likely, however, he had said nothing but she had divined that he wanted her home. It is not hard to imagine, doting father that he was, that he wanted her to be there to greet him every morning at his breakfast table, that he wanted her to be reading in late afternoon on the back porch, where he might join her after finishing his work. He wanted her to be his daughter again. Faced with his desire and her own, she was caught between what she longed for and her duty, between ambition and love, between desire and faithfulness. Her dreams of independence had hit the wall of her reality. She was a woman and a daughter.

Sensing she was about to lose her freedom, she seized it one last time. In the spring of 1881, she disobeyed her father. That May, the interstate oratorical contest was being held at Illinois College in Jacksonville. Anna Sill decided that Jane and associate editor Hattie Wells, of the Class of '82, should attend, ostensibly to represent Rockford at a concomitant interstate student editors' meeting but actually to press the case for Rockford to be admitted to the IIOA, whose leadership would be in Jacksonville for the big event. Jane knew she should ask her father's permission to go; instead she simply went. Perhaps she thought—eternal rationalization of the college student—that he would not find out. But in Jacksonville she bumped into Rollin Salisbury, a friend of George Haldeman's from Beloit College who was the orator representing the state of Wisconsin at the competition. Rollin, she knew, would tell George that he had seen her, and George would tell Anna, and Anna would tell John. The day after she returned from Jacksonville, she sat down and wrote two letters. To George she wrote, "You have probably heard from the Beloit delegation of my journey southward" and told him briefly about the trip. To her father she wrote, "I have been on a journey and have a long story to tell," adding, "I hope [my going] won't seem to you sudden and erratic." She explained what happened and acknowledged that she should have consulted her stepmother and him before going but added, "there wasn't time." Her letter is not quite persuasive. Mail service between Rockford and Cedarville only took a day. The more probable explanation is that she very much wanted to go and, fearful her parents would say no, had done what any determined college senior would have done in the same situation: she decided not to ask.[58]

For Addams, academics had always been a focus of her time at Rockford. Although she would only receive a collegiate certificate on graduation she had earned a B.A. in all but name. During her four years, she had taken ten to fifteen more courses than Rockford students were required to take, gathering extra credits in German, Latin, Greek, and math. And she had excelled. She would graduate with a grade average of 9.8.[59] Academically, by the end of her senior year, she had left her fellow Rockford students far behind.

Anna Sill was aware of what Addams had achieved. Eager for the seminary to offer a degree, Sill seized the opportunity to advance the cause. In early May she met with Jane to ask her whether she would like to receive a B.A. degree at commencement, should the trustees approve it. The offer caught Jane by surprise. It was the degree she had long wanted but it was from the wrong institution. She said she would think about it. Meanwhile Sill's offer turned out to be premature. By June the trustees had decided to postpone awarding the first B.A.s until curricular reforms were in place. Jane was first in line, but she would have to wait.[60]

Jane was unsure she wanted a B.A. from Rockford because she believed that it was a lesser institution than Smith. Was she right? The evidence suggests not. At Smith she would have been able to take only three courses in her favorite subjects of history and literature, but at Rockford she had dined on a rich smorgasbord of such courses over seven required semesters, all taught by the talented Potter.[61] At Smith the literary society and the student publication were new and very limited in scope; at Rockford, these were well-established organizations that enriched her education beyond measure, sharpening her writing, speaking, fundraising, and organizational skills—skills that she would take with her to Hull House and use in ways that would dazzle the world. Finally, at Rockford Jane Addams experienced something she would not have experienced at Smith and that was, in fact, truly rare in the United States of the 1870s and 1880s: a female-led institution. John Addams's insistence that Jane go to the nearby seminary may well have been a blessing in disguise.

At her meeting with Sill, Jane also learned that she had been named valedictorian of her class. She struggled to stifle her pride. "I do not feel puffed up," she wrote George firmly; "in short it appears of less consequence to me now than it ever did[;] it was never a passionate ambition." Her friends, however, recognized her drive and were not surprised by her accomplishments. One recalled, "She was of course the outstanding girl of the school. . . . We all felt that she would do great things some day." In a playful magazine profile published in 1881, another teased that "her brain is larger than her body." A third friend wrote, "Your prospects are bright . . . and you, I am very sure, will do nothing to mar and much to bring them into great brilliancy."[62] Everyone had high expectations of her.

Nonetheless, as a group, Jane and her friends faced the outside world

Jane Addams, graduation photo, 1881. Jane Addams Memorial Collection (JAMC neg. 5), Special Collections, The University Library, University of Illinois at Chicago.

with some trepidation and not a little disdain. Jane's scorn for the uncultivated was evident in her senior-year editorials, in which she wrote that appreciating the beauty of the campus signaled that one possessed "that culture so many people lack" and referred to the "stupid people" whom she and her fellow students would meet after they graduated. They feared that they would find it difficult to maintain the basis for their superiority, that is, their high ideals, once they were out in the world. They believed, she writes in *Twenty Years*, that "the difficulty of life would lie solely in the direction of losing these precious ideals of ours, of failing to follow the way of martyrdom and high purpose we had marked out for ourselves." They did not see themselves as snobs, of course, but when she was in her forties, she decided they had been. In 1901 she declared that "[a] society of young people held together by [a sense of special privilege] is a society of moral prigs." In *Twenty Years*, she condemns her "priggish tendencies" at Rockford.[63] It was an accurate if somewhat brutal assessment.

The day of commencement arrived. Alice and Harry came from Iowa and George came from Beloit along with Rollin Salisbury, who had become a friend of Jane's. John Addams was the beaming father. A friend of his who was also there later told Jane, "I shall never forget the hearty handshake which [your father] gave me and the contented, happy smile on his face as he talked of you." The juniors had decorated the chapel with flowers and evergreen boughs and every seat was filled. Although Jane and her classmates had lobbied for a college-style commencement—one that eliminated the reading of the senior class essays and added a prominent speaker—tradition had prevailed. Students would read their essays, all seventeen of them. The entire ceremony would take three hours.[64]

Finally, Jane stood on the podium, the last to speak before the certificates were awarded. To a friend she looked "slight and pale." In fact, during her last semester she had continued to push herself physically. She confessed to George in late May, "I am tired and rather worn out."[65] She had used up her body in her intense desire to achieve.

Her valedictory speech was short. She thanked the citizens of Rockford for welcoming her classmates to their "brave city" and the "gentlemen of the board of trustees" for providing the "basis and authority" for their education. Turning to the seminary community, she extended her class's thanks to Anna Sill for providing them with the example of "a life of noble purpose steadily fulfilled." To Sarah Blaisdell, who, at sixty-four, was resigning from Rockford owing to ill health, Addams gave her strongest words of praise. If any of them stood by principle in future years, she said, "to you will redound the glory of [our achievement] of character." To her classmates, she stressed again, as she had in her editorials, the importance of holding on to their ideals, reminding them of their shared belief that "beauty, genius and courage . . . can transform the world."[66] It was a polished and poised performance of rhetorical etiquette, a classic demonstration of how to suit a speech to the audience and the occasion.

Her senior essay was something else, something more personal and risk-taking. Blending the ideas from "Breadgivers" and "Bellerophon" together, she called for the educated woman to apply her gift of intuition to seek social reforms and to not restrict herself and her sympathies to the home, and childrearing. But the differences between this and the earlier speeches spoke volumes about her conflicted frame of mind as she stood that day on the brink of departure from seminary.

She opened the essay "Cassandra" by describing a famous scene from Greek mythology. The Greeks are at the city of Troy's gates. Cassandra, the daughter of the King of Troy and a priestess at Athena's temple to whom Apollo had given the gift of prophecy, addresses her father's soldiers and predicts their defeat and the destruction of the city. Addams told how the soldiers laughed, calling Cassandra mad, and how she soon became mad, driven so by her people's disregard for the truth she spoke.

Jane called Cassandra "a frail girl" who "knew the truth" but had "no logic
to convince the . . . warriors and no facts to gain their confidence." It was
her "tragic fate always to be in the right and always to be disbelieved and
rejected." Cassandra failed, she explained, because she made the mistake
that women in this century continued to make: she relied on her intuition.
Addams praised female intuition as a "mighty . . . perception of Truth,"
whose "highest use" was to apply it to "social ills and social problems." The
difficulty, she acknowledged, was that women's intuition, though honored
as the source of her love within the family, lacked authority as a source
of truth in the public arena. In the "busy, active world," she said, it was
dismissed as "a prejudice or a fancy."[67]

To achieve authority, she argued, woman should add reason, logic, and
facts to her resources and study science. Such study would make her a
more accurate thinker and more independent. It would also teach her silence and self-denial (revealingly, her logic here is obscure). Most of all,
it would allow her "to attain what the ancients called, in Latin, *auctoritas*, the right of the speaker to make [himself] heard." Auctoritas, Addams
knew from having read Cicero, was the word ancient Romans used to refer to the respect given to civic leaders. The woman trained in science
is at last ready for civic life. Equipped with "broadened sympathies" and
"trained intelligence," as well as auctoritas, she can "test" her intuition in
the wide world. "By extending those sympathies to the individual man or
woman who crosses our path," she can establish "justice." In the process,
she can also "prove to the world" that woman's intuition "is not a prejudice or fancy" but "one of the holy means given to mankind in [its] search
for truth." Dismissing Cassandra's example of failure, which she said it
would be better to forget, she ended by invoking her favorite Greek goddess, Athena, whom she described, using her favorite phrase, as being "not
all knowing but [with] a power deeper and more primordial than knowledge." She recommended her as the kind of woman one should aspire
to be.[68]

The essay was Addams's best effort to date to set forth her theory of
how to "do" social reform. In addition to implicitly endorsing her plans to
attend Smith and earn an M.D., the speech affirmed science and reason as
the keys to public respect. But it also affirmed the importance of respecting
(female) intuition. In "Bellerophon" the allegorical form had forced her to
polarize the choice between reason and intuition; here she urged women
of her generation to embrace both methods.

But her solution did not eliminate the contradictions. Addams was clearly worried about how her sex would affect her ability to fulfill her ambition. She believed that women should claim a place for themselves in the "busy, active world" but she also worried that being a woman was a liability in that effort. Part of the appeal of the medical degree, it now became clear, was that it would allow her to acquire auctoritas. Without an M.D. she feared she would be like Cassandra, disbelieved and laughed at.[69] The speech was permeated with her realization that femininity itself was limiting as perceived by others because it brought with it the "female" quality of powerlessness. Still, in the end, she resisted that loss of power. In "Cassandra" she asked why female intuition could have authority, that is, why women could not be respected and active in public life. It was an important question.

Behind the theoretical ambivalences of the speech there lurked a personal one. While Addams clung stubbornly to her original plan to gain a B.A. and an M.D., she knew it was on a collision course with her duty and desire to be an obedient daughter. With her future unknown, these were the troubles that absorbed her as she parted from her friends and teachers and climbed into her father's carriage for the journey home.

CHAPTER 5

FAILURE

1881–83

Other than her worry that her father might refuse to send her to Smith College in the fall, Jane Addams had reason to assume that the summer of 1881 would be like most summers, a quiet time in which nothing in particular happened. Instead, as the summer unfolded, she found herself caught up in a series of epochal events, each of which plunged her deeper into crisis and confusion. Indeed, the summer's shocks were only the beginning. The next two years would be the most difficult of her young life.

The first event was the one she had feared. Her father decided that she would not go to Smith in September. She wrote her friends the news within a few weeks of graduation and, although her letters do not survive, her friends' replies mirror the gist of what she had written: that her "family"— she did not choose to single out her father—thought she had overworked herself at Rockford, though she did not think so, and that to protect her health she should wait a year to attend Smith.[1]

Jane Addams presents her father's decision as simply a practical one involving her health, but John Addams also believed that each question of behavior had a moral dimension. In addressing the subject of how Jane ought to spend the coming year, he had available to him the most powerful argument a father could make to a daughter against pursuing something she desired—that to do so would be selfish, would be caring more for her own happiness than for her family's. Did her father make this second argument?

It appears that he did. In the 1890s, after Jane Addams moved to Chicago, she gave a series of speeches at women's colleges about the woman graduate whose family opposed her future plans and who charged her with selfishness for wanting to pursue her dreams. These speeches, searing in their frank portrayal of the graduate's and her family's pain, are too vivid to leave much doubt that she was speaking from first-hand experience. The story she tells in all of them is more or less the same. The daughter, freshly graduated, is full of eagerness to begin her adult life of "independent action," to be of some use to the world. Her parents, however, dismiss her ambition as "a foolish enthusiasm," arguing that "she is restless and does not know what she wants." When the daughter insists, the family is "injured and unhappy" and charges her with "setting up her will against [its will] for selfish ends."[2]

The daughter does not become angry or rebellious; instead she acquiesces. Long trained to believe that her obligation to her family is "sacred," she supposes that she *is* being selfish. She "hides her hurt. [H]er zeal and emotions turn inward, and the result is an unhappy woman, whose vitality is consumed by vain regrets and desires."[3] Caught in a conflict between her longing to set her own course and her desire to please, obey, and do her duty to her parents, the daughter yields to their authority at the very moment she expected to exercise her own.

In the summer of 1881 Addams accepted her situation. She did not rebel. She understood that she had a duty to sacrifice her happiness for the sake of the family. She knew from her reading of George Eliot that "pity and faithfulness and memory are natural ties." She wished to make this sacrifice lovingly, for her father's sake. Addams would later write, "[T]he path we all like when we first set out in our youth is the path of martyrdom and endurance."[4] Meanwhile, her anger, as Addams relates in her story of the daughter, turned inward, upon herself.

She was not the only member of the Class of 1881 whose plans were disturbed by a parent. In the coming year several of her classmates would cope unhappily but obediently with the same restrictions, their anger, judging from their letters, equally buried. Helen Harrington wrote Jane that her father wanted her to "rest, not go away to work or study for a while. It is hard to be patient." Emma Briggs wanted to continue her education by going to Smith or to medical school, but her father refused to pay for either. Eleanor Frothingham wanted to do further studies to earn her B.A. but she wrote Jane that she would teach school in the fall instead, to help her brother through medical school. Addams would later observe that "many a young woman of [the 1880s] . . . had [a] great ambition in which she was thwarted." In her 1909 book *The Spirit of Youth and City Streets*, she explored the effects on young people when adults, believing they know best, prevent them from pursuing life ambitions. She regretted, she wrote, that older people often insist that "young people shall forecast their rose-colored future only in a house of dreams."[5] Beginning in 1881 and for much of the next seven years, first because of her father's decision but later for other reasons, she would inhabit that ethereal house, often unsure what her future would be and always sure she was dreaming.

Addams's absorption in her own troubles was interrupted by the second event of the summer, one that was at once a national catastrophe and a family tragedy. On the morning of July 2 a "frustrated office seeker," as the newspapers characterized him, shot and seriously wounded President James A. Garfield. The would-be assassin was Charles Julius Guiteau of Freeport, the forty-year-old son of John Addams's friend Luther Guiteau. The elder Guiteau had, until his death the previous year, been one of John's closest business associates; he had served as the manager of John's bank, the Second National Bank of Freeport. And there were other ties. A younger half-brother of Charles Julius's, also named Luther, was working for John in the bank that summer, and a half-sister, Flora, who was a few years older than Jane and had just graduated from a female seminary in New York State, was one of Jane's good friends.[6] Fate had determined that the Addams family would be deeply intimate with the now notorious Guiteau family.

The friendship of John Addams and Luther Guiteau was woven of many strands of commonality, not the least of which was their shared evangelical Christian perfectionism, but in the light of all that would follow, one strand stands out. The world would soon learn what both families already knew: that Charles Julius, whom the family called Julius, had a history of mental instability. While Luther Guiteau was still alive, he and John Addams had shared the heavy burden of having flawed sons whose "nervous condition" was a source of perplexity, sorrow, and humiliation.

When word of Guiteau's attack on Garfield came over the telegraph wire in Freeport, a local reporter hurried to the Second National Bank seeking the scoop of his life. John Addams listened to the reporter tell the news of Julius's crime calmly, then told him that "he felt no particular surprise as he had known him to be a very erratic man from his youth and just the person to execute some sensational act." After the reporter left, John called Anna on his private telephone line and told her the news and his plans. Determined to protect the Guiteau family from the questions of reporters and the heartlessly curious, he brought young Luther, Flora, and their mother home to Cedarville.[7]

News of the assassination attempt spread quickly that day via telegraph and word of mouth. By noon, the streets of downtown Chicago were jammed as people poured out of buildings to discuss the horrifying event. One paper called the crime "a sacrilege, . . . a national desolation." President Lincoln's assassination by a Confederate loyalist only sixteen years earlier was on everyone's minds. Passions were high; men who expressed sympathy for Guiteau were reportedly beaten by mobs. In the next few days, papers editorialized that Guiteau was a traitor to his country.[8]

The Guiteaus were also shocked by Julius's action, but not completely. Julius had long led a troubled life checkered with failure, frustration, and minor crime. He had enrolled briefly at the University of Michigan but dropped out; he had joined John Noyes's Christian perfectionist community Oneida, in New York State, but was expelled. Over the years, unable to settle down in a city or a profession, he had lived in New York, Chicago, and Washington, D.C., working as a clerk, a journalist, a lawyer, a bill collector, an itinerant preacher, and a Garfield presidential campaign worker. Always broke, he repeatedly pestered his father for loans he never repaid, argued violently with him and others, and generally left family and associates feeling offended and angry. He was described as being irascible, egotistical, and hungry for fame and wealth. Eventually Luther senior concluded that his son was a "fit subject for an insane asylum" and "possessed with a devil." The two assessments fit together logically in his mind. In Luther's judgment, because Julius had failed to submit his life to God, the devil now possessed him and had rendered him insane. Thus Luther held his son responsible for his insanity and his actions. Sometime in the 1870s, Luther Guiteau, refusing to commit Julius to an institution, instead disowned him.[9] Now Julius had committed this heinous crime.

As the weeks passed and a sultry heat wave settled over the Midwest, newspapers ran frequent reports about the president's uneven recovery. He would linger for more than two months before dying in mid-September. Meanwhile the discussion in the press and among the citizenry focused on the nature of Julius's guilt. Most shared Luther Guiteau's assessment of his troubled son: that he was evil, insane, and responsible for his actions.[10]

Science, however, had a different theory to propose: hereditary insanity. The theory was part of a new field, neurology, that had emerged in the 1870s for the treatment of psychoses and neuroses of all kinds. Although the Addams's family doctor had rejected this diagnosis for Weber Addams in 1872, state law had required him to consider the possibility. By 1881, hereditary insanity was understood to be a subset of a broader category of disease called neurasthenia. The new term, roughly translated, meant nervous exhaustion. Symptoms included not only depression, fatigue, muscle spasms, nervous ticks, inability to concentrate, interrupted sleep, irritability, and back pain but also, in the worst cases, the "complete alienation of reason," that is, insanity. The causes of neurasthenia were thought to be physical and mental overwork, emotional distress, moral confusion, and, in the specific case of insanity, heredity.[11] Thus when the Stephenson County Court had ruled in 1872 that Weber Addams's attack of insanity was brought on by physical and mental exhaustion, it was implicitly diagnosing neurasthenia.

Because Guiteau had been arrested with a pistol in his hand and had freely admitted to shooting the president, his legal guilt was not in question. His lawyers, hired by his brother, John Wilson Guiteau, decided to try to prevent his execution by arguing that he suffered from inheritable insanity. If the court agreed with the defense, Guiteau would be institutionalized for treatment. The Guiteau trial was one of the first in the United States to attempt this argument.[12]

As it happened, there was evidence in the Guiteau family that Julius *had* inherited his insanity. In the trial the defense brought forward the evidence that in 1876 Luther Guiteau's nephew, Julius's first cousin, had been institutionalized in the Elgin insane asylum after suffering an insanity attack. The jury rejected the argument. Its verdict was that Guiteau should die— unjustly, it would appear. Historians now believe that Julius Guiteau was a paranoid schizophrenic.[13]

John Addams was fully caught up in the unfolding Guiteau family crisis. As a former employer of Julius's father and a close family friend, he would be expected to testify at the trial in Washington. The idea of associating his name with a man who had viciously betrayed his country must have mortified him. Furthermore, discussions about sons and insanity undoubtedly stirred painful memories of Weber's case that he preferred to forget.

Jane Addams was equally caught up in the crisis because of Weber's history as well as her friendship with Flora. Furthermore, if insanity was inheritable, then she and Flora were candidates for the disease because they both had brothers deemed insane (in Flora's case, a half-brother). They were also candidates because they had had recently been exhausting themselves unwisely in academic study. In 1881 the theory that college study had bad effects on young women was recirculating in a new book, *American Nervousness*, by the neurasthenia expert Dr. George M. Beard. An article about the book in the *Freeport Budget* that summer cited the author as believing that competitive exams in college were a cause of nervous strain in girls.[14] John Addams may well have believed that Jane risked neurasthenia, and even its worst manifestation, insanity, if she physically exhausted herself by attending Smith in the fall.

In early August, John Addams decided to take his family on a short vacation, perhaps to give himself and his family a break from the grim reality of the summer's tragedy. (Apparently the Guiteau family was no longer staying with them.) As part of the trip, he planned to inspect some iron and copper ore mines in northwestern Michigan as possible investments. The traveling party of Anna, John, Jane, and George set out by train on August 4, their route taking them north through the woods of Wisconsin into Michigan. At Marquette, on Lake Superior, they rented rooms in a hotel. Jane would later savor her memories of buying raspberries from local children, watching fishing boats sail the lake, studying the ramshackle miners' shacks that perched precariously on the sides of the old mining diggings, and enjoying her father's company.[15]

The family had only been gone a week when John Addams suddenly fell ill while climbing in a copper mine. Although they may not have realized it at the time, his appendix was inflamed and would soon rupture. Deciding to hurry home, the family, traveling by train, reached Green Bay, Wisconsin. Too ill to go further, John Addams died of appendicitis in a hotel room six days after falling ill, on August 17. He was fifty-nine years old.[16]

No death could have been more unexpected. Jane was devastated. Once more she had lost a parent abruptly. Years later she would describe the feeling: "In the heart-breaking . . . death of our well-beloved, nothing is harder to understand and nothing is harder to bear than the sense of disappearance, so sudden, so irrevocable, so mysterious." Still in shock two weeks later, she wrote Ellen that she had experienced "the greatest sorrow that can ever come to me."[17]

George left Green Bay immediately for Cedarville to arrange for the funeral while Anna and Jane made plans to bring the body home. Traveling by train, they arrived at Freeport with the black velvet–covered casket the evening of August 18. They were greeted by a large, solemn crowd. John Addams's obituary had run on the front page of the *Freeport Journal* that morning, along with the time of the train's arrival. News of his death also made the Chicago papers.[18]

Tributes poured in to the family from friends and acquaintances. They praised John Addams for his industry, honesty, determination, moral dignity, and gentle courtesy and celebrated him as "an affectionate husband and a kind and indulgent parent."[19] A former pastor of the Cedarville Presbyterian Church wrote Jane of his memories of "your gentle and strong father. . . . [I]n the most diversified relations, [he was] . . . always true to the best that was in him." Perhaps the most touching was the resolution that the board of directors at his bank adopted, which appeared in the Freeport paper. They noted his "indomitable perseverance, . . . solid judgment and transparent truthfulness." These qualities, they stated, as well as his "genial cordiality [and] genuine kindness of heart won our love and bound us to him with hooks of steel."[20]

On the day of the funeral, a crowd of fifteen hundred mourners gathered in the front yard of the Addams homestead. The pastor of the Cedarville Presbyterian Church, John C. Irvine, gave the funeral sermon from the front porch, choosing for his themes John Addams's broad civic-mindedness and moral righteousness. "The world was his field; of humanity he thought; for humanity he acted. . . . The guiding principle of his life [was] love of right and hatred of evil." He closed with a challenging question: "Who is there to take up this controlling principle in his life and embody it in their character and follow it as he did?"[21] Then the funeral procession, led by the casket bearers, traveled the short distance around the back of Pine Hill to the Cedarville cemetery. With family, friends, and neighbors gathered around, John Addams's body was lowered into the plot where he had buried five of his nine children and his beloved Sarah.

The minister's question, a favorite one of the age, would linger in Jane Addams's mind. She would return to it again and again in her later writings: How can one make the excellence embodied in a frail and mortal human being permanent?[22] To take up the task of carrying her father's greatness forward when she was only twenty years old was a great honor but also a terrible burden; she thought his excellence far beyond her reach.

As the bleak days passed, Jane felt that the meaning had gone out of her life. "How purposeless and without ambition I am," she wrote Ellen two weeks after the funeral. People tried to comfort her. Ellen wrote, "You are too much like your father, I think, for your 'moral purposes' to be permanently shaken by anything, even the greatest sorrow." Her friend Eva Campbell Goodrich (she had recently married) suggested some soul-searching. "You will have to take [your sorrow] to your heart and make it a part of you and it will nourish you until you are strong again."[23]

Jane's brother-in-law John Manning Linn offered supportive words framed by his understanding of what John Addams expected of his daughter. Because Jane Addams does not discuss those expectations in *Twenty Years*, Linn's words provide the best evidence we have for them. Apparently her father wanted Jane to achieve noble Christian selflessness but not to direct it into any specific channel. Linn notes revealingly, "Your life aims were high enough and your plans broad enough so that he could take an interest in them and it was his great delight to prepare you for your mission." Linn continued, "He did not desire you to live for him, but for the world, for humanity, for yourself and for Christ."[24] Had she ever told her father about her plan to be a medical doctor? If Linn's assessment was correct, perhaps not.

All of the advice Jane's friends and relations gave to her was good, but she could not follow it. Her grief was too raw and too overwhelming. Her father had been the basis of her self-confidence all her life. Even in seminary, as she had begun to develop her own ideas and to act independently, his moral views had guided her and his reliable, if rarely expressed, affection for her had strengthened her. Now, it was as if the sun had expired and the planets of her universe—her moral purpose, her plans for a career in medicine, her dreams of accomplishing social reforms—having been released from the gravitational pull of her father's influence, were spinning off into the wider chaos of empty space.

His absence also left a psychological void. Her father had died at the exact moment when she, as a fledgling adult, needed to test her capacity to resist him. Earlier that summer she had buried her strong desire to be in charge of her own life in order to obey him, but the desire would have pushed up again sooner or later. Now his sudden death, occurring before she could work her way through to an adult relationship with him, had aborted the process.[25] How could a daughter fight the will of a father in the grave when her heart was full of grief for him and her desire to do what would have pleased him was overwhelming? Future events would confirm that after her father died, Jane Addams renewed her determination to be an obedient, sympathetic, and self-sacrificing daughter, to put the family first, as he would have wished her to and as her own mother had once done. Martyrdom's claim on her, already strong, only deepened in the aftermath of her father's death.

Anna Haldeman Addams did not withdraw into her darkened Cedarville bedroom in her grief. She quickly embraced a plan that Alice and Harry Haldeman, who had come from Iowa for the funeral, may have been the first to propose: that the family move that fall, temporarily, to Philadelphia. The plan suited many purposes. Anna had family in the city and so did the Addams siblings. Furthermore, Harry, who wanted to undertake further medical studies, could now use the money from Alice's inheritance to enroll at the University of Pennsylvania Medical School, and Alice, who wanted to be better trained to assist Harry in his medical practice, could take courses at the Woman's Medical College in the city. The plan did not benefit George, who, having entered college a year after Jane, had one more year of study at Beloit, but on the face of it, the plan suited Jane. She had always intended to go to medical school. The family meant to stay two years, to allow everyone enough time to earn their degrees. [26]

But there is reason to suspect that Jane was not entirely pleased with the plan. She had wanted to attend Smith College before entering medical school in order to gain a better grounding in science. Still, she agreed to honor the family's wishes and take care of Anna, as her father would have wanted and perhaps as he asked her on his deathbed to do. The idea of refusing may not have crossed her mind, but, at least in theory, she could have chosen not to go. Her inheritance gave her, for the first time, the financial resources to send herself to Smith College without family approval. It was not a freedom she was used to. She would spend much of her twenties testing her willingness to claim it.

Addams's inheritance was what might be called modestly comfortable. Its size was determined by the fact that John Addams left no will. His plan was for his death to trigger the application of the Illinois inheritance law, of which he was a co-author. The law provided that his wife would inherit one-third of his estate during her lifetime and that his four children would divide equally the remaining two-thirds and share what remained of the wife's inheritance after her death. If he had written a will Anna most likely would have pressed him to leave something to her two sons. As it was, he avoided the issue, the law being silent on the matter of stepchildren. An initial estimate placed the estate's value at $250,000 ($4.53 million in 2005 dollars). Two-fifths was invested in real estate. He owned 2,600 acres of land, mostly in Stephenson County, but also in Canada, the Dakota Territory, and Iowa. The remainder of his estate was personal property—bank and railroad stock, outstanding bank loans, and government and railroad bonds. [27]

With John Addams's death the estate was divided. Although Weber asked the court to name him executor, it refused and named the Addams family lawyer, Edward P. Barton, instead. In the settlement, each of the

Anna Haldeman Addams. The Jane Addams Papers, Stephenson County Historical Society, Freeport, IL.

four children received a farm plus other tangible assets. Jane's share was a 247-acre farm south of Cedarville, 60 acres of local timberland, 80 acres in Dakota Territory, 52 shares of the Second National Bank of Chicago, and 42 shares of Northern Pacific railroad stock (the old Galena and Union stock).[28] Assuming that her father's estate was worth $250,000, her one-sixth share came to $41,666. However, the final value was apparently higher. Addams recalled in 1935 that her inheritance was worth $65,000 to $70,000 and that her income from it was $4,000 (this is a 6 percent return on $65,000), or $75,000 in 2005 dollars.[29] Such an income placed her firmly in the upper middle class.

Barton served the Addams family in a second way in the fall of 1881. As John Addams would have been, he was called to testify in the Guiteau trial. The testimony he gave was the testimony John Addams would have likely given: that the assassin's father was a "reliable, honest businessman" and that there was no insanity in the Guiteau family.[30]

In early October the Addams-Haldeman family began its new life. Jane and her stepmother closed up the house in Cedarville and took the train to Philadelphia, where they rented lodgings with Alice and Harry. Immediately, Harry began his studies at the University of Pennsylvania and Jane and Alice enrolled in the first year of medical school, called "winter term," at the Woman's Medical College. Jane, still grieving for her father, must have hoped that studying at one of the leading women's medical schools in the country would restore her spirits. She wrote friends that she took satisfaction in her studies and felt that they were moving her closer to her life's work.[31]

But being in school so soon after her father's death turned out to be difficult. She wrote Sarah Anderson that she felt an emotional numbness that made it hard to concentrate. And there were other problems. Her back hurt continually and her energies were low. She was also feeling guilty trying to split her attention between medical school and Anna, whose happiness she felt to be her first responsibility. Later she would remember that "my experience in Philadelphia of trying to fulfill too many objects at once [left me with] . . . an uneasy consciousness that I had not done what I came purposely to do, because I tried to do something else and failed in that." By early December she was exhausted and a doctor advised rest.[32]

Her illness was both physical and psychological. Her bad back would not have taken well to the physical demands of long hours of medical lectures, dissecting demonstrations, and study. But her back, as she was learning, was also part of her nervous system and responsive to her moods. And her moods were increasingly blue. In January, despairing of the way her resentment toward Anna was showing, she wrote in her commonplace book, which she had begun to use as a diary, "Am growing more sullen and less sympathetic every day" and noted, "Must learn to reverence others' feelings"; other people "deserve respect." Filled with revulsion at her own moral weakness, she called herself "an utter failure." She was in fact depressed. The condition was prompted by her father's death, an enormous loss for anyone, but for her, because of her earlier experiences with death, a particularly devastating trauma.[33]

Things did not get better. Jane was still under a physician's care in February 1882, when Anna became seriously ill. Her neuralgia, a nerve disease from which she had suffered in the 1870s, apparently had returned. Anna underwent surgery—its nature is not clear—and the family decided that, for the sake of Anna's health, they would go home at the end of the winter term at Woman's Medical School instead of staying in Philadelphia for the full two years. Jane, weak and in pain, doggedly completed her first-year exams the first week in March. Then, the pain in her back unbearable and her exhaustion complete, she gave up the struggle and entered a hospital.[34]

The hospital was the highly specialized Orthopaedic Hospital and Infirmary for Nervous Diseases. There her physician, the famous doctor S. Weir Mitchell, had built up one of the nation's largest practices in the field of neurasthenia.[35] Given her back troubles, fatigue and depression, inability to concentrate, and student status, Jane Addams fit perfectly his profile of a typical female neurasthenic patient. At last, Jane had "caught" the disease she had long been expected to catch, the same disease that, according to nineteenth-century medicine, had led to Weber's psychotic break and Julius Guiteau's murderous act. She entered the hospital an invalid, without strength.

No records survive of the hospital treatment she received but it was likely to have followed the guidelines Mitchell laid out in his popular book *Lectures on Diseases of the Nervous System, Especially in Women*, written for the suffering public and published the previous year. The best treatment, he wrote, was four to six weeks of seclusion, rest, full feeding, massage, and electric shocks. Because Addams was in his care at the hospital for less than three weeks (she and her family left Philadelphia on March 22), she did not undergo the complete Mitchell regime. Still, she must have experienced the substance of it. Mitchell's intention was to treat the patient's mind. He hoped to make being ill so unpleasant that his female patients would abandon what he believed was the cause of their disease, their selfishness, and declare themselves well by the end. Visitors, books, and other pleasures such as good food and letter writing were banned from the patient's sickroom.[36] The coup de grâce consisted of his lectures about being less selfish in the future.

Jane Addams did not need him to remind her. She saw her illness as he did, as a moral defeat, a sign of her inability to lead the life of sacrifice to family that she had chosen and that was her duty. Later that year she recorded in her commonplace book a warning from a sermon: "Strength to begin a life of self-sacrifice without strength enough to carry on, makes one lead a life of duplicity and falsehood." Her duplicity lay in trying to appear selfless when she lacked the strength of character to truly be so. Believing she had failed, she foresaw a lifetime of failure. "The sensitiveness which one always feels after an illness," she said sixteen years later, "the fear that because you have failed, you are going to fail again, . . . can scarcely be overestimated."[37] She had, of course, expected to fail long before she became ill, as her childhood dreams and her seminary essays about the hero made clear. But in Philadelphia she had actually done it.

Back in Cedarville, she poured all the mental energy she had once invested into earning a B.A. into self-criticism. She disapproved of her flaws and then, instructed by Emerson, whom she was rereading, she disapproved of her obsession with them. Emerson condemns self-preoccupation, she wrote in her commonplace book; it is "another form . . . of selfishness." "Talk too much of myself and motives, am in danger of self-pity." She repeatedly hammered home the need to be more sympathetic. She must try, she told herself, "to be for others and [take] an interest in other people." She must "[s]trive to be the highest, gentlest and kindliest spirit." She sought out ways to make sacrifices. Despite her poor health, she flung herself into doing the housekeeping at the Addams homestead and worried that she was not a cheerful enough influence on Anna.[38]

Addams's primary ambition now, it is clear, was to be the ideal woman of gracious selflessness that she had been raised to be. A typical book of ladies' etiquette from the 1870s laid out the requirements. "Christian politeness will always be the result of an unselfish regard for the feelings of others. . . . [T]o be truly a lady one must carry the[se] principles into every circumstance of life . . . and never forget to extend the gentle courtesies of life to every one."[39] It was an impossibly difficult ideal and she could not meet it. She *was* self-absorbed, and for good reasons. She was young, with a future ahead of her whose shape she longed to know. She fiercely desired to make a difference in the wider world. Such ambition would have been much praised if she had been a young man; because she was a young woman, it was labeled "selfish" and seen as a source of shame.

In June her luck turned, for a time. Rockford Seminary, which had given her so much, propped up her self-confidence again. At commencement she, along with a few other alumnae and two seniors, formally received the B.A.; the chairman of the board even announced that the seminary was now a college, although the trustees would not rename the school to reflect this fact until 1892.[40] Jane's mood improved. Reconnected to the community where she had had her greatest success, bolstered by the affection and respect she received at the ceremony and by being awarded the long-sought B.A., empowered by her recent inheritance, she began again to plan to attend Smith College. In late June she took a trip to Massachusetts with Flora Guiteau to distract her friend from Julius's scheduled execution and, after visiting Nantucket Island, they stopped in Northampton to see the college.

Jane's plan at the time was to be tutored by a Rockford teacher and enroll as a special student at Smith for the second semester. By August, however, she had decided to enroll in September, perhaps because of encouragement she had received at Smith.[41]

She felt some guilt about her plan. To dispel it, she told herself that she owed it to her father, who had given her so many advantages, and to society, to do something meritorious. "People with wealth and a start of right ideas from their father," she admonished herself in her common-place book, "have no right not to make the very highest use of life, [hav-ing gained] the . . . higher intellectual things of life." She had redefined selfishness. Now it was selfish to stay in Cedarville and unselfish to go to Smith. Her mood continued to improve. "Going to Smith College to start fresh," she wrote optimistically in the commonplace book in August. She pondered her intention to transform herself into a sophisticated young lady. She vowed to be "courteous and elegant" at Smith and always "to be truthful, accurate and careful in statements."[42] At last, she was only weeks away from achieving the goal she had set her heart on at sixteen. This time her plans were derailed by a letter she received in September from Alice.

"I write you, Jane," her sister's letter began, "to have you come out to see us. Harry has something to relieve your back." He had devised a new operation for her back problem, Alice reported, and had already tried it successfully on another patient. "So come on Jane. . . . Harry wants you to come *before* you go to Smith's as he feels sure[,] and so do I[,] that he can help you. . . . Now Jane don't disappoint us as we must help your back when we can and we can *now*." With what must have been great reluctance, Jane agreed, postponing her plans for Smith once more. Perhaps she feared a repeat of her experience in Philadelphia if she became a student again.[43] In late October she took the train west to Mitchellville, the opposite direction in several senses from that in which she wanted to go.

Harry's plan, which he now implemented, was to restore strength and straightness to Jane's spine by using heated wires to fuse together the spinal disks damaged by the tubercular virus. She later wrote about it in a poem. "My spine had got a twist so queer / It called for red hot searing." It was a daring and novel operation. Afterwards, she lay strapped to her bed in the Haldeman house for all of November and December while her back healed.[44]

During this time, her mood was black again. The surgery, the physical

Alice Addams Haldeman. The Jane Addams Papers, Stephenson County Historical Society, Freeport, IL.

immobilization, her crooked back itself, all thrust her once more into the pit of despair out of which she had only recently climbed. The burden of failure settled again on her shoulders. She wrote no letters that fall, she later explained, because she was "ashamed" to show her friends "against what lassitude, melancholy and general crookedness I was struggling." It was only in January that she could bring herself to inform Ellen of her surgery. She tried to sound upbeat in her letter, noting that she now had "a fresh hold of life" and that she had found a renewed pleasure in reading.[45]

The operation was an apparent success, but it had one important side effect of which Harry now informed her: her back would probably never be strong enough for her to bear children. Weber Linn reports that this news was a blow to Jane. Was it? Had she wanted to marry? She had had one boyfriend in college (at least from his point of view): Rollin Salisbury, the orator from Beloit College. Like her, he was the editor of his college paper, his college's best orator, and valedictorian. Salisbury thought his courting of Jane was progressing nicely as their senior year drew to a close. After his class and Jane's took a steamboat trip on the Rock River together, he sent her roses. Years later, when he was a prominent and respected professor of geology at the University of Chicago, he told Weber Linn, who taught English at the university, how he "fell in love with Jane Addams" as he listened to her speak at her Rockford commencement, "and never got over it." According to Linn, Rollin proposed marriage soon afterward but she turned him down.[46]

Her reasons for refusing him may be guessed from a family story, told later by Weber Linn's daughter. Addams was playing a game of Ouija at the Linn house in Hyde Park (which, as it happened, was within blocks of Rollin Salisbury's house) when the Ouija board prompted her to spell out an old beau's name. After she had done as instructed, her hands spelled out on the board: "Woman's place is in the home!"[47] Apparently, Salisbury was conventional in his views about marriage and did not approve of women having careers.

The attitude was common among men of Jane Addams's generation, as she would note in 1930. Women, she explained, had to choose between marriage and a career because men either "did not want . . . to marry women of the new type" or thought that women could not do both. But she could not resist making a further observation. Early career women, she noted revealingly, possessed "pioneer qualities of character and sometimes the divine urge of intellectual hunger." In other words, in retrospect, Addams believed that her ambition in the broadest sense—a desire to test herself against large challenges, to explore and understand complicated realities and ideas—was the overriding obstacle. She had her own priorities.[48] In any case, nothing in her early life suggests that she had a romantic interest in men. At a time when many women of her age were pining for romance, she did not pine. Of course, many women married out of economic necessity. Jane Addams's family wealth and her financial independence after her father's death shielded her from that pressure.

Jane's convalescence from the surgery was slow. In January, her torso encased in a heavy plaster cast, she was able to leave her bed for a few hours each day. She weighed less than one hundred pounds and the cast must have weighed at least twenty-five. Later that summer, she would replace it with a distinctly uncomfortable leather corset with ribs of steel and whalebone that Harry had made for her in Chicago. She was to wear it every day until her back was strong.[49]

Plaster-bound, Jane returned from Alice and Harry's house in Iowa to Cedarville in mid-March to stay with Weber and Laura in their new house. Anna was away in Florida with George, where she was recovering from

*John Weber Addams, ca. the 1880s.
The Jane Addams Papers, Stephenson
County Historical Society, Freeport, IL.*

an illness that had befallen her in November. Feeling better, Jane was once more making plans. Harry thought a return to medical school unwise while her back was healing, which meant that Smith College was out of the question. He prescribed a trip to Europe to reduce the stress on her nerves. According to a strange logic only the Victorians could have concocted, physically exhausted and ill people were often urged to take arduous journeys in order to recover their health. Jane, having discovered—or rediscovered— her lack of aptitude in science in Philadelphia, liked Harry's prescription: "I was very glad to have a physician's sanction for giving up clinics and dissecting rooms," she writes in *Twenty Years*.[50] She does not say how she felt about not going to Smith. And so she arrived in Cedarville expecting to spend a serene summer floating in a boat on the creek and planning the sights she would see on a trip she intended to take in the fall.

But fate was not done with her. Two weeks after she returned, Weber Addams's mind gave way for the second time in his life, and for a week Jane and Laura tried by themselves to cope. His behavior was probably similar to his behavior during a subsequent collapse, when he was observed to be "unusually excited and violent, . . . [displaying] confused speaking, . . . very excitable . . . [showing] complete loss of self-control." For Jane to see her brother sink into madness again must have been horrifying. Writing to Ellen, she could not broach the pain of it but simply wrote that she was "in the midst of perplexity and 'a peculiar kind of trouble.'" Alice hurried from Iowa and they asked the court to commit Weber. He was declared insane (the cause, as before, "undue mental exertion, disease not hereditary") and transported to the Illinois State Hospital for the Insane in Jacksonville. Later they moved him to the Hospital for the Insane at Elgin.[51]

Weber's attack was a shock. It had been eleven years since his first episode and, on the surface, his life during that time had appeared to be as successful as any son of John Addams might have wished. He had run the cattle stock farm, was a director of his father's bank in Freeport, was a supervisor for Buckeye Township, and was active in local Republican politics. After his father's death he had taken over the two mills. But they were soon failing, and his debts mounted.[52] When the family discovered the state of his businesses, it must have thought that the court's theory—that his illness was brought on by "undue mental exertion"—made sense.

For Jane, Weber's collapse came at a dangerous moment. During the past two years she had lost her father, failed in her pursuit of a medical degree, been hospitalized for neurasthenia, undergone back surgery, and been repeatedly frustrated in her desire to earn a B.A. at Smith. Weber's neurasthenia attack might well have threatened her own psychic health and even triggered a breakdown. But her response was the opposite. Instead of collapsing, she took charge. She and Laura met with the millwright, toured the mill and the dam, and found out what repairs were needed. "I find myself quite absorbed in business affairs," she wrote Ellen. She was also gaining weight and thought that being outdoors agreed with her.[53] Her reaction revealed that the foundation of her psyche was sound; real challenges did not defeat her—they grounded her. Work, not leisure, was what she needed.

Her satisfying sense of usefulness, however, did not last. When Anna and George returned to Cedarville in the last part of May, Jane moved back to the homestead and to a life less absorbed in her brother's business. She told Alice that this was a relief because she had begun to feel that the work was "beyond my powers and comprehension."[54] But it is interesting that the note of self-doubt arrived with Anna, who may well have thought, given her opposition to women's rights, that it was unladylike for women to handle business affairs.

Jane turned her attention back to planning the trip to Europe. In a sense, she had been preparing to visit it all of her life. Her father had always intended that she make the trip after graduation, and she had originally planned to go, albeit after attending Smith and before entering medical school.[55] Harry and Alice, who had both been there, had told her stories.[56] For years she had been reading magazine articles that were rhapsodic in their praise of the charms of sightseeing in Europe and illustrated with enticing engravings. But most of all she had been prepared by the books she read. Dickens's London, Eliot's England, Scott's Scotland, Sand's Paris, Goethe's Germany, Cicero's Rome, and Plato's Athens were all fabled places she had often visited in her imagination. Europe was also the place to go if she wished to continue her pursuit of self-development. Americans thought of travel in Europe, like academic study, as a means to acquire culture, and those who could afford the cost flocked there in the post–Civil War years. Addams, too, assumed that she would become a nobler person by going to the place where noble ideas had originated. She intended to search "for those mountain tops upon which" she might "stand and dream [of] righteousness." By "righteousness" she meant the "nobler life."[57] Now Europe would redeem her.

Still, she sometimes doubted that the pursuit of culture was a good idea. Caroline Potter, as always, had started her thinking. She listened as Potter gave a speech about the woman of the future at the annual Alumnae Association meeting at Rockford Seminary that June; she heard Potter warn of the dangers of pursuing learning for its own sake, detached from action. That summer Jane wrote to Ellen that she suspected she was "not following the call of my genius" as she headed to Europe "in search of . . . this general idea of culture," which, she pointedly added, had never "commanded my full respect." She feared that it would be hard to "hold to full earnestness of purpose" while abroad.[58] In this mood, she saw Europe as possibly corrupting, a seductress drawing her away from the serious-minded work she had intended to pursue.

These conflicting feelings surfaced in a speech Addams gave at the same Alumnae Association meeting at which Potter spoke. In "The Uncomfortableness of Transition" she set out to portray her alma mater's unstable sense of self but ended up inadvertently revealing something about the nature of her own uncomfortable transition. "Freighted with the responsibilities and historic demands of the word College, depressed and drawn back by her long Seminary ideas and associations," she wrote, "[Rockford Seminary] has vainly striven to adjust herself to her new standards.

She has pressed forward with every step attended by . . . perplexing disappointments."[59] It was an odd speech to give to an alumnae association, its oddness perhaps the best evidence that Addams was speaking of the condition of her own soul.

Regarding the Christian religion, Anna Sill's solution to all perplexity, Addams was equally confused. She remained unbaptized, but after the experiences of the past two years, Christianity's message of comfort to the troubled had a new appeal. During the summer of 1883 she read Matthew Arnold's *Literature and Dogma*, where she encountered his explanation of the Bible's real meaning, a meaning that emphasized Christ but ignored Christ's divinity and stressed the Hicksite-Emersonian message—the importance of trusting one's own moral judgment. Christ's "method" of repentance, he wrote, means attending to what "passes within you" as you live your life and means "listening to your conscience." If a person did this he would discover Christ's "secret" of peace, which was the true "intuition of God" and the meaning of "righteousness." Addams wrote Ellen, "My experience of late has shown me the absolute necessity of the protection and dependence on Christ [and on] his 'method and secret,' as Matthew Arnold put it."[60] It was not a statement of new faith but an acknowledgment that she saw the need for one.

That summer Jane put together her traveling party for Europe. She decided that Anna should go with her. There was a strong element of family duty in this but also an element of practicality. Jane would need Anna as a chaperone if she was to stay in Europe to study German and French in the winter, which had become her plan. Anna's niece Sarah Hostetter would join them for the first year. The rest of the group, along only for the summer, would consist of a classmate from Rockford, Mary Ellwood, and Mary's sister Harriet (called "Pussy"), their aunt, Alida Ellwood Young, and Mary Hodges Penfield, whose daughter would join them later. They would depart from New York City in August. Meanwhile, Weber returned from the hospital in early July. Jane felt sad to realize the extent to which his self-confidence had been undermined by the experience. "I feel as though he must necessarily be very uncertain of himself all summer," she wrote to Alice. She knew how painful self-doubt could be.[61]

In early August she and Anna went east separately. Anna visited George on Cape Cod. Having graduated from Beloit College in May, he was spending the summer in Massachusetts doing biological research and planned to pursue a Ph.D. in biology at Johns Hopkins University in Baltimore in the fall.[62] Jane stopped by Philadelphia to visit relatives. She and Anna and the rest of the party all met in New York City, where they boarded the *Servia* for the trip across the Atlantic. On deck, Jane Addams watched the American shore sink below the horizon feeling more hopeful, we may imagine, than she had in several years. Pushing aside her doubts about the wisdom of cultural pursuits, she was contemplating its pleasures. Soon she would be standing in the places where great men had stood, connecting through her senses with those who had built Western civilization. Her mind had long been pointed toward Europe. Now the steamer was bearing her toward her mind's home.

CHAPTER 6

CULTURE

1883–86

Favored with good weather, the *Servia* arrived off Queenstown, Ireland, a week after leaving New York Harbor. The crossing had produced some seasickness among the traveling party but nothing unpleasant enough to dampen their high spirits. Jane wrote to her sister Alice in mid-ocean, "I hope you are feeling as cheerful as we do. . . . The party is jolly and good-natured." Her health was also improving. "The salt breeze acts on me like magic," she reported. "I feel quite rested."[1]

The trip was a great adventure for Addams and, although she did not know it, the beginning of a new phase of existence. Plunged into the meaning-laden world of Europe, she would be once more drawn into the life of ideas she had enjoyed at Rockford, but this time she would have no like-minded people with whom to share it. She would become a kind of intellectual hermit, posing questions to herself that only she could answer. From the outside, as the trip began, she seemed the quiescent tourist and agreeable daughter. In truth she had entered a period of incubation from which she would emerge transformed.

As the steamer crossed the Atlantic, the travelers, consulting maps and guidebooks, sketched out their journey for the first year. After visiting Ireland, Scotland, and northern England, they would spend three weeks in London, then travel to Holland before settling in Dresden, Germany, for the winter. In the spring they would travel to Italy, Austria, Switzerland, and France. The party's size would shrink in time. Mary Penfield and her daughter would split off quite soon. The Ellwoods and Alida Young would return home in April 1884. Then, for a few months, it would be only Jane, Anna, and Sarah Hostetter. In June George Haldeman, on vacation from Johns Hopkins University, would join them. The group planned to spend the summer in Great Britain, after which George and Sarah would depart for the United States and Anna and Jane, if their stamina held, would spend another winter in Europe before heading home.[2]

The question of Jane's health remained. "The long illness" is the phrase she uses in *Twenty Years* to describe the health problems she had from 1881 to 1883. Her illness left her, she writes, "in a state of nervous exhaustion with which I struggled for years. . . . At best it allowed me but a limited amount of energy." Although she was able after the first few weeks of travel to stop wearing the heavy leather corset, fatigue continued as her periodic companion, a regular reminder that she was not well.[3]

And so the trip began. After an unexpectedly long stay in Dublin, where Anna had a serious attack of neuralgia, the party traveled to Scotland. They explored Edinburgh and made a special trip to visit the monument to Anna's favorite poet, John Burns. Heading south to England's Lake District, they paused respectfully at Wordsworth's grave, then traveled on, arriving in London on October 3.[4]

Jane was dazzled by the city. Enormous, noisy, crowded with people of many nationalities, it, like "old Rome," she wrote Ellen, was "the world in itself and possessing the best of all nations, times and peoples." The comparison was obvious and apt. London was not only the capital of a world empire; it was, with a population of 4.7 million people, by far the largest city in the world. Paris was second at 2.2 million, and New York City was third with 1.2 million.[5] As compelling for Addams, London was the capital of the Anglo-American literary world, home of William Shakespeare, Thomas Carlyle, George Eliot, and of Westminster Abbey, whose glorious roof sheltered so many literary graves. In London the culture that Addams believed was the key to acquiring the "higher" life was thick on the ground, figured in brick, stone, and marble.

As a tourist, Addams's attention was focused mostly on manifestations of the past, but one facet of the present caught her interest. As she notes in *Twenty Years*, the issue of working-class poverty was stirring controversy in London in October 1883. The immediate cause of the debate was the publication of an anonymous pamphlet, *The Bitter Cry of Outcast London*, about the living and working conditions among the poor. Articles about the pamphlet and excerpts from it immediately appeared in two London papers, the *Pall Mall Gazette* and the *Daily News*.[6]

If Addams read the pamphlet or the articles—and she implies that she did—she would have been left with a troubled conscience. The pamphlet's author, a city missionary and clergyman named Andrew Mearns, vividly described buildings in miserable repair, severe overcrowding in housing, child neglect, starvation, and criminally low wages. For years Addams had been reading about the poor in fiction and in the Bible and been preached

The traveling party, London, 1883. Back row, left to right: *Harriet Ellwood, Jane Addams, Mary Ellwood, Sarah Hostetter;* front row, left to right: *Alida Ellwood Young, Anna Haldeman Addams. Jane Addams Memorial Collection (JAMC neg. 921), Special Collections, The University Library, University of Illinois at Chicago.*

to about the poor in sermons, but *Bitter Cry* presented the issue of poverty not as a subject of historic remoteness or condescending sentimentality but as a compelling reality in what Jane thought of as the world's most famous and cultured city. Mearns wrote as an eyewitness. He spoke of the people's "emaciated, starved bodies" and "staring eyes." And he wrote as a reporter who had inquired into the facts. One woman he and his colleagues spoke with worked seventeen-hour days doing finishing work on trousers to earn a shilling a day. They often found families of eight or more living in one room. Having little money to buy food, they scrounged, always hungry. One woman whom Mearns met had retrieved from a refuse can a rotten turkey that she planned to cook for dinner.[7]

At the end of his pamphlet, Mearns put a provocative question to his readers: "Will you venture to come with us and see for yourselves the ghastly reality?" Addams's answer was yes. An outing was arranged. The woman who ran the boarding house where she and her party were staying, a city missionary named Miss Warner, offered to take her and other boarders to the East End to observe the poor buying food at midnight at the Mile

End Road Market, where decaying meat, fruit, and vegetables that were too far gone to sell when the market reopened Monday were sold cheaply at auction to those willing to buy.[8]

Writing to Weber two days later, Addams reported that she and the others had taken the underground railway to the East End, then rode on top of a double-decker omnibus the entire five-mile length of the market, "through rows of booths and stalls, and swarming thousands of people." She gives other details in *Twenty Years*. The bus stopped "at the end of a dingy street." Beneath a sputtering gas street lamp she saw "two huge masses of ill-clad people" gathered around two hucksters' carts, clamoring to buy the rotten food. Their clothing was "ragged" and "tawdry," their faces "pinched and sallow." As she looked down from the top of the bus, she saw "a myriad of hands, empty, pathetic, nerveless and workworn, showing white in the uncertain light of the street." They were "clutching forward for food that was already unfit to eat."[9]

The sight upset her. Here, indeed, was the grim, suffering world of the Mearns pamphlet come to life. She wrote Weber that her "outside superficial survey of the misery and wretchedness" of the East End had left her feeling "thoroughly sad and perplexed." In *Twenty Years*, speaking more frankly, she writes that she felt "despair and resentment." Resentment towards whom? She does not say. The experience disturbed her so much that she dreaded a reoccurrence. While they remained in London, she recalls, "I went about . . . almost furtively, afraid to look down narrow streets and alleys lest they disclose again this hideous human need and suffering." Her visit to the East End left her in a "deep depression" and "overwhelmed by a sense of failure."[10]

Her unusually despairing response to what she had witnessed was accompanied by an equally striking reaction. As she had sat on the top of the bus horrified by the sight of the flailing hands, she had suddenly thought of a piece of literature: Thomas De Quincey's essay "The Vision of Sudden Death." In it he tells how, while riding on top of a fast-moving mail coach, he was unable to warn two young lovers in the road to get out of the way until he recalled, as Addams put it, the "exact lines from the 'Iliad' which describe the great cry with which Achilles alarmed all Asia militant." Finally, once he remembered the lines, De Quincy shouted and saved the lovers from being trampled. Mortified at his near failure to prevent disaster, he decided that his years of study of the classics had made him dangerous in the real world.[11]

Thinking about her East End visit afterwards, Addams decided that the layers of literary reference were piling up dangerously in her own mind as well. "It seemed to me too preposterous," she writes in *Twenty Years*, that "I should have recalled De Quincey's literary description." Culture had forced itself into her consciousness when a dire reality should have had center stage. Suddenly, she felt revolted by culture. She decided that De Quincey was right, that she and her friends at Rockford had been "lumbering our minds with literature that only served to cloud the really vital situation spread before our eyes."[12] Of course, there was irony in the way she arrived at the insight. Her revulsion against culture was prompted by her memory of De Quincey's essay; she needed culture to instruct her on the dangerous effects of culture.

De Quincey's realization that he should have acted sooner struck Addams as the essential thing. Sitting at the top of the bus, she was compelled by the same feeling. Why? One might point to the writings of those advocates of the deed, Carlyle, Emerson, Arnold, and Ruskin, as well the instruction of Caroline Potter, to explain it, but two clues in the story of her East End crisis hint at a less literary reason. The first is the title of De Quincey's piece, "The Vision of Sudden Death." Did Addams think of his literary analogy because she felt she was seeing death from the top of *her* high conveyance? The second is the analogy she herself uses in *Twenty Years* to describe how she felt after the encounter, apparently not realizing the underlying meaning of what she wrote: "I carried with me for days . . . that curious surprise we experience when we first come back into the streets after days given over to sorrow and death; we are bewildered that the world should be going on as usual and unable to determine which is real, the inner pang or the outward seeming. In time all huge London came to seem unreal save the poverty in its East End."[13] Addams felt she had seen death. In wishing she had acted, she was responding to death as she always did, with a feeling that she urgently needed to do something and a sense of deep inadequacy about whether she could.

No private mood, of course, could stop the inexorable progress of the American traveler in Europe. Within a week, the party was in Holland, discovering the pleasures of Rembrandt. After a brief stay in Berlin, where they attended concerts and the opera, in early December they reached Dresden, where Jane applied herself to improving her fluency in German, the native

tongue of the ancestors with which her father and mother proudly identified and the language she had studied for four years at Rockford Seminary. During that winter, she read *The History of Art*, visited art galleries,
and again attended the opera. In the moment, these pleasures charmed
her and confirmed her image of herself as cultured and sophisticated, but
afterwards she often felt revulsion again.[14]

During this time, Jane kept her letters to her family and friends light and
chatty; she did not mention her perplexity about the value of acquiring culture or her depression, even to Ellen. Her silence was a matter of good manners. She and her sisters had been taught, as she would later note with frustration, to write cheerful letters regardless of what they were really feeling.
Admiration may have also stopped her pen. In this period of their friendship, Ellen, who was still teaching art and literature at Miss Kirkland's
School in Chicago, seemed to Jane to be all that Jane was not: a woman
of action with real work to do, improving lives. When Ellen wrote Jane that
she sometimes felt "blue," Jane expressed surprise. How could she, Jane
asked, "when you possess the faculty of so spiritedly giving out, which after
all is the only assurance and confirmation we have of our powers[?]"[15]

Jane's mood of sadness was made worse by her loneliness. It is likely
she had been lonely for a long time. Since leaving Rockford, she had spent
most of her time among people who found her vague ambition to do "social
reform" a foolish fancy. The situation was no better on her trip. Although
she and Anna shared a love of culture, these were exactly the pleasures she
sometimes felt guilty enjoying. She was not close to the Ellwood sisters or
Sarah Hostetter, whose interests lay in different directions from her own.
Her ambitious dreams, once nourished by her coursework and friends at
seminary, languished in a secret corner of her mind. Marcus Aurelius, the
Roman emperor-philosopher who was a favorite of hers and whose famous
Meditations she had therefore certainly read, captured her mood when he
wrote, "How great a weariness there is in living with those who are out of
tune with you, . . . [who do not] share your principles."[16]

But she was beginning to formulate a solution to her dilemma, and it
reflected the wisdom behind Aurelius's insight. It emerges in some advice
she sent to George from Dresden. Intending her words to shake him out
of his natural inclination to be, as she put it, "an anchorite," she observed,
"I am more convinced all the time of the value of social life, of its necessity
for the development of some of our best traits. There are certain feelings
and conclusions which can never be reached except in an atmosphere of

affection and congeniality." To Ellen she wrote something similar. "I am more convinced every day that friendship . . . is after all the main thing in life, and friendship and affections must be guarded and taken care of just as other valuable things."[17]

"I am more convinced every day" was her admission that in the past she had not valued friendship highly. With her good mind, large imagination, self-discipline, and ability to inspire the trust of others, she had sailed through Rockford an outstanding student and a respected leader, possessing many friends but not needing to rely on anyone. She had viewed friendships as she viewed books: as resources to feed her curiosity. But in the two years since leaving Rockford, she had failed to act on her ambition by herself. The experience taught her a lesson. As she would write in 1894, "Isolation is a great blunder. . . . [I]t results in dreariness and apathy." She decided that she needed the affection and idealism of like-minded people if she was to become a better person.[18] It was a major revolution in her personal philosophy of life, one that would provide a foundation for decisions that were to follow.

She and Anna stayed in Dresden for three months except for one side trip to the city of Saxe-Coburg-Gotha. There Jane's attention was caught again by the difficult lives of working-class people. Looking out the window of their hotel as she sat eating breakfast one morning, she saw a line of women with heavy wooden tanks on their backs moving across the town square in single file. Snow was falling. The tanks were open at the top and filled with a steaming, sloshing liquid. She would later learn that the women were carrying freshly brewed beer to a building where it would be cooled. She writes in *Twenty Years* that they "were bent forward, not only under the weight they were bearing, but because the tanks were so high [they could not] lift their heads. Their faces and hands, reddened in the cold morning air, showed clearly the white scars where they had previously been scalded by the hot stuff which splashed if they stumbled ever so little on their way." Indignant at these "cruel conditions," she sought out the innkeeper and persuaded him to take her to speak to the owner of the brewery, apparently hoping that she could somehow talk the employer into making the situation safer for the women. The brewer, however, showed "an exasperating indifference," and Addams returned to breakfast.[19] She tells about the event without comment. Yet her point is clear: she had acted. She had pursued conduct instead of culture.

The story also reveals that a shift had taken place in her mind. After her visit to London's East End, she had been terrified that she might glimpse urban poverty again. Now, only a few months later, she had had the opposite reaction: she had left her hotel to insert herself into the workers' suffering world. In *Twenty Years* she describes this new feeling without noting how different it was from her previous one. "During the following two years on the continent . . . I was irresistibly drawn to the poorer quarters of each city."[20]

She tries to explain to her readers what drew her. "The poverty had become to me the 'Weltschmerz.'"[21] The German word means "world pain," the pain of human existence. Addams now perceived the suffering of the poor as part of a wider human suffering in which she shared. They suffered; she suffered. It was all connected somehow and the idea was comforting. Believing it did not make her see herself as less of a personal failure or be less disappointed with herself, but it relieved her feeling of isolation. Carrying her own pain from death, failure, and illness on her back, she had discovered that the urban poor of Europe carried similar burdens. Across the barrier of class, with all the material and educational differences that barrier implied, she felt at one with people whose misery was more obvious than her own.

The travelers moved on. After staying for a time in Munich and Vienna, they arrived in Florence in time to enjoy the spring. In a sunny land of great beauty and ancient history, Jane found her mood lifting. As she immersed herself in the Catholic art of the Italian cathedrals, hints of her old spiritual longing for a female god began to creep into her letters home. She was particularly moved by Giotto's frescos of the Virgin Mary in the Church of the Arena in nearby Padua. These "affect[ed] me," she wrote Ellen solemnly, "with a tremor and a corresponding desire for the power arising from mere goodness."[22] Here was culture's deepest appeal: its ability to awaken her profoundest longings and desires. Her ambition was stirring.

In Rome, ever the diligent tourist, Jane turned her energies to learning the history of the "eternal city" and studying the early Christian church. She was most impressed by the catacombs, where the spirit of the early Christians seemed almost literally present. In these underground burial grounds, a true place of death, Addams was startled and enchanted to see images of cheerful spring flowers, shepherds, and lambs on the low ceilings and dank walls. It seemed to her, she later wrote, that the Christians had "deliberately written down that the Christian message was one of expressible joy."[23]

It was the joy that drew her. Fascinated, Addams read more about the early Christians and formed a new impression of the religion she already knew so well. Now she saw it in simpler terms—as a faith founded by a community of people from all walks of life who wished to help each other, even at great personal cost. The early Christians, she would later write, "longed to share the common lot" and were willing to "sacrifice themselves for the weak, for children and the aged." For the rest of her life this would be how she interpreted Christianity—as a religion grounded in human brotherhood and sacrifice and drained of its traditional tenets of human sinfulness, the need for confession and personal redemption, belief in Jesus Christ as the Son of God, and even a personal faith in God. Having gained this vision in Rome, she did not immediately become a Christian, but the idea was no longer impossible for her to imagine. Perhaps she had this new understanding in mind when she wrote somewhat elliptically in *Twenty Years*, "Before I returned to America I had discovered that there were other genuine reasons for living among the poor than that of practicing medicine upon them."[24]

The spring was a whirlwind of traveling. After a quick round-trip boat ride to Greece and a donkey ride up Mount Vesuvius near Pompeii, the party headed to Switzerland, where George joined them. Then it was on to France, Germany, and Belgium. In early July the Addams-Haldeman family and Sarah Hostetter arrived in Great Britain, where they planned to spend the summer.

During this time Jane's letters to Ellen Gates Starr became increasingly frank. Writing from Geneva that June, she finally spoke of the sense of failure that was haunting her. Her pen was freed by a desire to give advice. Having received the news from Sarah Anderson that Ellen was tired and ill, Jane fired off a warning to Ellen to avoid her own fate. "I wish everybody were as thoroughly convinced as I that failure through ill health is just as culpable and miserable as failure through any other cause and if you do not recuperate through this summer, my friend, you are [heading] . . . towards that failure." Continuing in her mood of self-critical introspection, she sorrowfully summed up how she felt about what she had accomplished since her winter in Philadelphia. "I have been idle for two years," she wrote, "just because I had not enough vitality to be anything else, and the consequence is that while I may not have lost any positive ground I have constantly lost confidence in myself and have gained nothing and improved nothing. A sad record, isn't it[?]"[25]

Still the travelers pressed on. At the end of the summer, George and Sarah left for the United States. Jane hoped that she and Anna might head for Spain, but Anna, fearing the cholera epidemic in that country, decided they would return to Germany for the winter, this time to Berlin. In the German capital through Christmas, Jane attended lectures at a women's university, enjoyed the opera, and worked on her German. In January she and Anna moved to Paris to work on their French. They visited the French legislature, attended an organ concert, and read French romances to each other. On Palm Sunday in late March, Jane attended services at the magnificent Notre Dame Cathedral. The event brought Christ to the center of her attention, although, as always, she resisted his divinity. "I believe more and more," she told Ellen, "in keeping the events and facts of Christ's life before me and letting the philosophy go."[26]

As spring drew to a close and their remaining days in Europe dwindled, Jane's thoughts turned with pleasure to seeing Ellen, whom she admired more than ever. "I have profound respect for the work you are doing," she wrote, adding, "I am very impatient to see you and am haunted by a fear that I [will] not know you."[27] After almost two solid years of Anna's company, Jane was eager for the companionship of someone who understood her and who would not expect her to be happy with the privileges of culture and wealth.

Ellen understood Jane's frustration that she had not fulfilled her career ambitions, but she had a different theory from Jane's as to why. While Jane blamed herself, Ellen blamed fate. One of her students had read an old essay of Jane's that was in Ellen's possession and asked why such a talented writer was not writing books. Ellen wrote Jane that she had explained to the student, "If my friend's body had been equal to her mind and if a great many demands on the strength of both hadn't come to her which do not come to most people, she would have done a good many remarkable things which the Lord doesn't seem to have intended her to do."[28] Ellen's explanation was comforting but also limiting; Jane's version, though a torturous burden, also suggested that she had the responsibility and ability to heal herself.

By mid-June 1885, the weary travelers were in Cedarville. Alice and Harry Haldeman were there to greet them, having come to visit for a month. They had traveled from Girard, Kansas, where they had moved in 1884.[29] With Alice's money they had purchased a part ownership in a bank in Girard, a small mining and farming community in the southeastern part of the state. Also there to greet the European travelers were Weber Addams and his wife Laura, but events would soon reveal that all was not well with Weber. On August 1, a few days after Alice and Harry left for Kansas, he had another breakdown, his third. It had been only two years since his last psychotic break. Instead of getting better, he appeared to be getting worse. This time Jane did not wait for Alice to arrive. After she petitioned the court on August 3, it ordered him committed to the Elgin State Mental Hospital. She would spend the rest of the summer and much of the fall worrying about him. Laura Forbes, a family friend, wrote to Jane sympathetically, "Verily, you are being called upon to pass through the 'dark waters' early in life."[30] It appeared that the steady stream of unpredictable troubles that had burdened Jane before she had left for Europe would recommence now that she had returned. Perhaps Ellen's theory that fate was to blame for Jane's failure was correct after all.

In Europe Addams had decided she needed to find a way to spend more time with like-minded people, but back in Cedarville no obvious strategy suggested itself. Instead, she continued to live with Anna. This could not have been particularly easy, given Anna's demanding nature and firm opinions. One trace of the tensions survives in a letter Jane sent to Alice to explain Anna's and her plans for the winter. Anna had decided that she and Jane would spend it in Baltimore, where George was continuing in graduate school in biology at Johns Hopkins University, and by early October she had departed. Jane, however, stayed in northern Illinois in order to spend a week with Weber at home after he left the hospital. While she waited for him to be released, she visited with Mary Addams Linn, who now lived in Harvard, Illinois, where her husband had a new ministry. Jane wrote Alice, "Ma understands my motives in going to Harvard and approves, I think," adding, "It is not a break or anything of the sort."[31] She meant that she and Anna still intended to live together. But it was a break, in a sense. Subsequent events would reveal that this small act of autonomy marked the beginning of the end of Anna's governance over her.

At Harvard Jane helped her often-exhausted sister and a hired girl run the household and care for the five children: John (thirteen), Weber (nine), Esther (five), Stanley (two), and Mary (four months). The children delighted her, and she found she had unexpected strength when required to do things for them. Feeling more relaxed, she began to gain weight and declared herself to be in better shape physically than she had been since her senior year at Rockford.[32]

Another pleasure she enjoyed there was reading George Eliot's 1876 novel *Daniel Deronda*. What she gained from it, she informed Alice, was "motive power." The hero's situation nicely summarized her own. Though Deronda, in Eliot's words, "longed to be . . . an organic part of social life," his "early awakened sensibility and reflectiveness had developed into a many-sided sympathy, which threatened to hinder any persistent course of action." Only "fellowship," Eliot claimed, would spur him to action— that is, the company of like-minded people and a strong feeling of connection with general humanity.[33] Henceforth, for Addams, whose inclinations were already moving in this direction, the word "fellowship" would resonate with these meanings.

Soon after Jane finished *Daniel Deronda*, Ellen Gates Starr paid her a long visit at Harvard. Here was fellowship indeed. Afterwards, their letters were more openly affectionate than before. Ellen wrote that she "felt forlorn" without Jane, and Jane replied that she had been thinking of Ellen all day. During her visit they had had long talks about religion. Ellen had converted to Episcopalianism while Jane was in Europe. Jane was full of admiration for Ellen's faith and freshly burdened by a sense of her own religious inadequacies. After Ellen returned to Chicago, she wrote Jane that her faith was more unsettled than it appeared. Jane replied with a startling confession. "[M]y religious life has been so small;—for many years it was my ambition to reach my father's moral requirements and now . . . I . . . [need] something more [and] find myself approaching a crisis."[34]

She does not say what her father's moral requirements were or why she equated them with her religious life, but what she meant can be surmised. At Rockford she had decided that her religion, as she told Ellen, consisted of admiring her heroes. Her father had certainly been one, perhaps the main one. Among other things, he embodied, and expected his daughters to embody, moral perfection and self-reliance. Jane had failed to meet these standards, which was no doubt one reason for her crisis. But she was also saying that she no longer aspired or, perhaps, felt able to aspire to meet these standards; she needed a religious life that was not centered on the heroic, one that included space for failure and interdependence. The shift was subtle. Her father's memory remained enormously influential on her; it was his authority as a parent that was slipping. She was beginning to trust her own judgment more in moral matters as, of course, he himself had taught her. Her intentional journey away from moral perfection and individualism had begun.

Her first step was to abandon her efforts at complete self-sufficiency and acknowledge her need for a close friend's support. She wrote Ellen a week or so after the visit, "[I am] looking wistfully to my friends for help. Your letter, dear friend, was such a help." Too shy, perhaps, to express her affection more directly, Jane enlisted literature's aid. When Ellen sent Jane a gift of a book of Robert Browning's poetry soon after the visit, Jane wrote that her favorite poem in the book was "My Star" and quoted a line of it to explain why: "Mine opened its soul to me; therefore I love it." Spontaneous and affectionate, Ellen offered a companionship that was healing to Jane's troubled spirit. "Your letter," Jane added, "made me feel that friendship is a very precious thing." [35]

Once in Baltimore, Jane again spent her days in Anna's company. They paid and received social calls and attended and hosted parties and teas, all of which Jane found exhausting. They took a short trip to Pennsylvania to visit Jane's Addams and Weber aunts and uncles. Jane also pursued culture, studying French literature with a tutor, reading art history, and attending two public lecture series at Johns Hopkins University, one on archeology and one on the United Italy movement. The latter reintroduced her to the leader of that movement, Giuseppe Mazzini, who had been her father's hero. It was probably then that she read Mazzini's *Duties of Man*. [36]

Reading the book was an unsettling, even shocking, experience for Addams. In *Duties of Man* Mazzini is critical of the family's excessive demands on a man's loyalty and interest. Those who limit morality's "obligations to duties towards family," he writes, "teach . . . a more or less narrow egoism." He had reversed the usual case; now it was selfish to serve the family and unselfish to serve humanity. To stress that humanity was the greatest duty, Mazzini used an image of circles: Duty to "Country and family are like two circles drawn within a greater circle of [duty to humanity] which contains them both." [37]

In another essay in the book, "Thoughts upon Democracy in Europe," Mazzini argues that this duty to humanity was both Christian and democratic. Addams read this essay, too. In 1894 she would use a passage from it in writing about democracy. Serving humanity, he observed, was a Christian duty because love of mankind was Christ's love. It was a democratic duty because democracy was about helping each person become "better than he is." Mazzini had some practical ideas as to how to help. Education was an important means but so was social mingling, which allowed people from different walks of life to come to know each other. "[I]f you wish to attain [Democracy]," he writes, "let man commune as intimately as possible with the greatest possible number of his fellows." Addams gives no summary of Mazzini's thought in *Twenty Years* but conveys his importance to her. His influence, she writes, was "a source of great comfort to me" that winter.[38] His ideas would become building blocks in the new life she was constructing in her mind.

Meanwhile, Jane's general mood was bleak. Now that her trip to Europe was over, the depression that had haunted her for years gripped her with new intensity. It seemed to her that she was feeling the same way she felt at the end of her sophomore year at Rockford, seven years earlier. Writing Ellen, she invoked the Emersonian metaphor she had found so compelling then. "Since I have been in Baltimore, I have found my faculties . . . perfectly inaccessible, locked up away from me." The similarity between her sophomore year and her current life was obvious. She was living a detached life again, thinking—or worrying—about the future and uncommitted to the present. She condemned herself for her uselessness. "I am filled with shame that with all my apparent leisure I do nothing at all," she wrote Ellen glumly. Addams was trapped that winter in a life she did not want and she did not know what to do about it. She once described a frustrated young woman in words that seem to capture her feelings at this time: "Her life is full of contradictions, she looks out into the world, longing that some demand be made upon her powers, for they are untrained to furnish the initiative." Looking back years later, she felt that it was the winter of 1885–86 when she reached "the nadir" of her "nervous depression."[39]

Adding to Jane Addams's unhappiness were the intensifying emotions swirling in her immediate family circle. George, who was living in a student boarding house nearby, was dependent on Jane for friendship. Shy, eccentric, and sensitive, he knew that few people liked him. That year he told Anna, "I am queer and everybody thinks so."[40] Anna was determined that her son and stepdaughter should marry. It was a solution to George's moodiness, which she worried about, and it would place Jane's portion of the family inheritance under George's control, just as Harry's marriage to Alice had allowed Harry to gain control of Alice's wealth. Jane, however, was not that fond of George. As early as 1882 she had admitted guiltily in a diary entry in her commonplace book that the reason she had not visited

Jane Addams in Baltimore, 1885–87.
Jane Addams Collection, Swarthmore
College Peace Collection.

George at Beloit was her "want of affection" for him. She thought George was reclusive, an "anchorite." Furthermore, he had no sympathy for Jane's murky visions of social justice.[41] On the matter of George, Jane and Anna were at loggerheads.

Jane did make various small attempts to accomplish something. One was to write and submit an article about her European travels to *Rockford Seminary Magazine*; it was published in January. She also pursued her interest in working-class people by paying charity visits. The children at a sewing school struck her as "very interesting" as well as "patient and sick-looking." She visited a home for elderly African American women and vowed to return often. She would do so during her second winter in the city, and she would also visit a mission school and an orphanage for African American girls who were being trained to be servants. Oblivious to the racial and class bias involved in training the orphans in low-income work, she thought the idea excellent. As she made her visits the first winter she was intrigued to discover that they did not tire her. Charity work, like playing with Mary's children, appeared to be good for her health.[42]

And she continued to read. Her new interest in Christianity led her to a new book, Leo Tolstoy's *My Religion*, which was published in the United States in 1885. In her state of spiritual hunger, it touched her as no other book had; in 1927 she would identify it as "the book that changed my life."[43] Although most of *My Religion* is about Tolstoy's fresh interpretation of Christ's teachings regarding love and how far removed these were from those of the Russian church, what struck Addams most, as she remembered it years later, was that Tolstoy, at fifty, felt himself a failure and became a Christian, that he managed to transform his life rather than despair that it could not be done. "The reading of that book," she writes in *Twenty Years*, "made clear [to me] that men's poor little efforts to do right are put forth for the most part in the chill of self-distrust." Tolstoy was the ultimate anti-hero, the opposite of her father in his imperfection, a man whose example she could follow if she still wanted to try to become, as she had dreamed at Rockford, a social reformer. "I became convinced," she writes, "that if the new social order ever came, it would come by gathering to itself all . . . pathetic human endeavor."[44] She could now imagine failure as an acceptable place for her to start from.

The book also introduced Addams to a new idea: nonviolence, or "nonresistance." In *My Religion* Tolstoy endorses Christ's teaching "to resist not evil," to meet evil with love, not hatred. He interprets this to mean that a person should avoid both physical violence (most notably, by refusing to participate in war) and anger. Anger, Tolstoy wrote, "is an abnormal, pernicious, and morbid state." Physical violence was alien to Jane Addams's experience, but anger was familiar. Living with the willful and relentless Anna meant living with both Anna's anger and her own. It is quite likely she abhorred it, hated herself when she succumbed to it, and longed to gain mastery over it. The practice of nonresistance also required a psychological willingness to embrace suffering, and this, too, appealed to Addams.[45] She had long been drawn to the idea of self-sacrifice on a heroic scale. The ethic of Christian nonviolence strongly appealed to her. By the time she arrived at Hull House in 1889, but possibly as early as 1886, it had become a shaping force in her life.

The balance scales in Addams's mind were now tilting in one direction: toward conversion to Christianity. When she returned to Cedarville that summer, she was baptized at, and joined, the Cedarville Presbyterian Church. As she observes in *Twenty Years*, the minister did not require her to "assent to dogma or miracle"; the kind of faith required "was almost early Christian in its simplicity."[46] Her new understanding of Christianity and the Presbyterian Church's new willingness to accept members who did not profess to the entire dogma allowed her to embrace her father's faith minus his personal God and redeeming Christ.

Why did she convert? Explaining her decision in *Twenty Years*, she gives four reasons. First, her efforts "to be good in [her] own right" had not succeeded. Her claims to "self-dependence" had been "broken into" by "many piteous failures." Second, she wished to identify herself with the "simple"—she might have added, joyous—faith of the early Christians. Third, she felt "growing within me an almost passionate devotion to the ideals of democracy." Drawing on Mazzini's ideas, she now thought Christianity gave "thrilling" expression to democratic ideals. These were her intellectual reasons. The fourth was an emotional one: she did not want to feel so at odds with the world. "At this moment," she remembered, "something . . . made me long for an outward symbol of fellowship, some bond of peace, some blessed spot where unity of spirit" reigned. In her mind, Christianity was "the institutional statement . . . of universal fellowship."[47] Thus it was that at twenty-five Jane Addams surrendered, albeit on her own terms, to the faith that had been pressing her to yield to it since the day she was born. Hers was not a spiritual conversion but a decision to move her life in a positive direction.

On the surface that decision changed little. In the fall of 1886 and throughout most of 1887, her life continued to flow in the familiar channels of culture, charity visiting, and family duty. Beneath the surface, however, feelings and ideas now started to coalesce, drawing new energy and direction from her commitment to Christianity. Her emergence from five years of depression began in the summer of 1886. Within three years this new trajectory of optimism would carry her into an entirely new world. The journey, however, would not be without bumps along the way. Some old ideas still stood as obstacles and, as before, it would be books, ever her true friends, that helped her remove them.

The first sign of change was in her relations with Anna and George. After Jane visited with Ellen, Sarah Anderson, and the Linns the following fall, she belatedly joined Anna in Baltimore. Soon, however, she was off to visit her father's and mother's relatives in Pennsylvania, this time without

Anna. Her independent act had predictable results. She was only gone a week, but when she returned, she wrote Alice, she found Anna and George "dreadfully depressed." Jane told her sister that George had grown "suspicious and doubtful of everybody" but, she added, he was getting better now and "we are all in good spirits and happy again." The change was not only that she had gone without Anna but that she felt no guilt for doing so. Instead of accepting the blame for Anna and George's misery, she shook it off. She wrote Alice in the same letter, "I am feeling so well this fall . . . vigorous [and] happy . . . in a way [that] I had imagined I should never feel again."[48] She had broken free not of family responsibilities generally but of the excessive ones that had tied her too much to Anna and George.

Her independence from her stepmother and stepbrother continued throughout much of 1887 as she gave herself over to Addams family duties. Mary Addams Linn, now living in Genesco, Illinois, where her husband had yet another new parish, was expecting the birth of her sixth child in March. When the baby came in February, Jane, who was again visiting her Pennsylvania relatives, hurried to her. She stayed with her for the months that followed, as the premature child struggled for life. In May, little Charles Hodge Linn died. Meanwhile, Alice Addams Haldeman was expecting in June. Jane was in Girard on June 18 when Alice delivered a daughter, Marcet.[49]

There was still one last tie to Anna and George that Jane needed to remove from her future. It is impossible to date exactly when she formally refused George's marriage proposal, but it appears to have been May 1887, before she left Cedarville to visit Alice and Harry in Kansas. According to the version of family history told to Marcet (her source was Anna), George was devastated. Thereafter, his mental health began to deteriorate even more seriously. Anna, furious at Jane's refusal, was convinced that George's worsening condition was Jane's fault. Over the coming months and years she would repeatedly criticize her stepdaughter for turning George down, charging her, we may assume, with selfishness.[50] The confrontations must have been painful. But there is no evidence that by 1887 Jane was susceptible to her stepmother's angry accusations. Far from thrashing around in agonies of guilt, she simply walked away.

The shift in Jane's relations with Anna and George opened up a new possibility—that she might redesign her life. The boldest plan would have been for her to use her inheritance to strike out on her own, perhaps by moving to Chicago or some other large city. But she continued to keep her home in Cedarville and to live partly with Anna and George and to visit her relations. Why? Apparently, she still believed that her first duty as a woman was to her family. Equally problematic, she was finding it difficult to justify pursuing something more than a little charity visiting when on every side she was told that she ought not concern herself with the "lower classes." "This then was the difficulty," she writes in *Twenty Years* about her life in the 1880s, "the assumption that the sheltered, educated girl has nothing to do with the bitter poverty and the social maladjustment which is all about her, and which, after all[,] cannot be concealed."[51]

Addams's ideas were inspiring her but also blocking her. When she thought of herself as a human being, as the individual whom Mazzini and Tolstoy urged should put "humanity" first, she felt eager to pursue her dreams. But when she thought of herself as a woman, the iron curtain of convention closed off her horizon. She needed to understand how convention—her gender role—was holding her back before she could act. There are people who can act instinctively, impulsively, without a rationale, solely on the basis of strong feeling, but Jane Addams was not one of them or, at least, not when she was young. She lacked the strong feelings, for one thing. She needed her mind to motivate her. But she also had a particular relation to ideas. To her they were major forces, either obstacles that stood in her path or resources that fueled her courage.

Two books challenged her thinking about women. They were John Stuart Mill's *The Subjection of Women* and another book by Leo Tolstoy, *What Shall We Do?* Each in its own way powerfully undercut the beliefs about gender she had held since childhood, although one of them was not about women at all. As she read them, her mind, which had earlier been sabotaging her with self-criticism, became her ally.

Addams probably read Mill's hard-hitting *Subjection of Women* soon after returning from her first trip to Europe. Reissued, along with *On Liberty*, in a new combined American edition in 1885, the book likely reached her hands in 1886. Mill wrote movingly of a prosperous woman's despair at her lack of needed work to do. In a speech four years later Addams would borrow a key sentence from the book, without giving the source, to make that point: "There is nothing, after disease, indigence and guilt, so fatal to life itself as the want of a proper outlet for active faculties." Women, Mill argued, should be free to choose their work on the basis of their experience and their gifts. The idea that women were only fit to be wives and mothers is "an eminently artificial thing," he noted, produced by "forced repression" and "unnatural stimulation."[52] Mill both invited Addams to live the life of "independent action" she had long aspired to and reassured her that the social rules about excessive duty to family she would therefore be breaking were unworthy of her respect.

Tolstoy's book helped Addams rethink her assumption that an upper-middle-class, educated young woman could ignore the social problem of poverty. First published in the United States in 1887, *What To Do?* was ostensibly about his first encounter with urban poverty, which took place when he assisted with the census of Moscow in 1881. The book's philosophical message was that if a Christian abhorred the people's suffering, then he must be careful that he did not increase their suffering in any way, even indirectly. He must take his responsibility for the poverty of the world very seriously. Tolstoy believed that poverty was caused by capitalism, that is, by one man employing others and then "keeping" some of the value of their work by paying low wages. His solution was to abandon money and cease to employ others. Tolstoy therefore renounced his private wealth (turning it over to his family), abandoned his novel writing, and began to live like the peasants on his estate, working in his own fields, wearing peasant clothes, and eating peasant food.[53]

Addams wrote that reading *What to Do?* "profoundly modified my religious convictions." She meant that she now believed that a Christian, even a sheltered, educated female Christian, must have "something to do" with poverty. She took Tolstoy's message of economic guilt to heart, too. For the next two years she "had an awful time," she later remembered, accepting her farmer's rent. Now possessed of a "conscience that craved economic peace," she notes in *Twenty Years*, she tried to invest some of her money less exploitatively. In a decision that signaled a reawakening of her old enthusiasm for Robert Owen's ideas of cooperation, she and a young man eager to learn sheep farming became partners in a "cooperative" sheep farm. But her partner cared for the sheep ineptly, causing their hooves to rot; much discouraged, she sold the sheep farm.[54]

Addams does not comment in any letters or in *Twenty Years* on the obvious fact that Tolstoy's critique of capitalism was not one that John Huy Addams, who had been happy to prosper from the labor of others, would have agreed with. Did she realize this? It is difficult to believe she did not. She never wrote about it, but to interpret her silence as a lack of awareness is risky. Letters in which she addressed the subject may have been lost or destroyed or never written. As for her silence in *Twenty Years*, Addams was a skilled rhetorician and writer, always aware of audience, and temperamentally and rhetorically inclined to emphasize commonalities and ignore differences. In the case of any differences with her father, she had an additional reason to prefer to not to discuss them in her memoir—her daughterly desire to perceive and present her own life as an extension of his.

Tolstoy's opinion that capitalism was a morally flawed enterprise was not a commonly held view in Jane Addams's middle class, but it did exist. A radical portion of the middle class, deeply troubled by the suffering of those at the low end of the income scale, was expressing such views in print in the late 1870s and the 1880s, though it is unknown whether Addams read any of their works at the time. The books included Henry George's *Progress and Poverty* (1879), which argued for a land tax in order to recycle into government hands some of the wealth accruing from excessive land accumulation; Richard Ely's somewhat timid *The Labor Movement in America* (1886), which at least praised the labor movement as a potential source of gradual social reform; Henry Demarest Lloyd's eloquent speech "The New Conscience," which savaged the capitalists for their selfishness and called for public cooperation for the public welfare (published in the *North American Review* in 1888); and Edward Bellamy's compelling anticapitalist novel *Looking Backward* (1888), about a future United States in which all the productive property was owned and run by the state. Meanwhile, the mainstream portion of the middle class favored individual moral redemption or the power of the free market as the solution to poverty. They were reading Josiah Strong's nativist call for urban missionary work, *Our Country* (1885), and William Graham Sumner's *What the Social Classes Owe Each Other* (1883). Sumner makes the case that the "social problem" would be solved by means of economic improvements.[55] In the 1880s the country was engaged in an intense debate about the causes of and solutions to poverty.

For working-class people, the debate was hardly theoretical. Their complaints were not only about low pay but also about long hours (workdays were generally ten or twelve hours) and dangerous working conditions. As their frustrations intensified in the mid-1880s, strikes proliferated.

Employers, like workers, had much at stake. Fearing for their profits and believing in their absolute right to control their businesses, they strenuously opposed unions. They bolstered their case by arguing that the "foreign element" among the workforce was inherently dangerous and un-American. Most of all, they feared workers (many of whom were indeed immigrants) who were socialists or anarchists. The socialists sought government ownership of production; the anarchists were radical libertarians who opposed government's authority altogether. The atmosphere was so heated that social gospel minister Washington Gladden could plausibly claim in 1886, "The state of industrial society is a state of war." The labor press spoke of the "class struggle."[56] Addams certainly knew about this debate, being a reader of newspapers and magazines, even though she does not mention it in her letters or in *Twenty Years*.

Then, suddenly, events crescendoed. On May 1, 1886, a series of frequent strikes across the country culminated in a nationwide work stoppage involving 340,000 union members. It was the first general strike in the history of the international labor movement. Tensions were high in Chicago, where thousands of strikers marched in the streets. On May 3 a policeman killed a striker on a picket line; the next day a group of mostly foreign-born anarchists convened a protest meeting at Haymarket Square. Police were sent in, a bomb was thrown—no one ever knew by whom—and seven policemen and an uncounted number of protesters were killed. Eventually eight men, all self-described anarchists, were arrested, tried, and convicted. All but one were sentenced to death; the eighth received life imprisonment. The evening before the execution, two of those sentenced to death had their sentences commuted to life imprisonment, with a third cheating the hangman's noose by committing suicide. On November 17, 1887, the remaining four were hanged.

The events of Haymarket and their aftermath, deeply unnerving to a country already on edge, would dominate the nation's thinking about labor and immigration for the next decade. As the historian John Higham notes, "For years, the memory of Haymarket and the dread of imported anarchy haunted the American consciousness." Unions, in particular, tried to distance themselves from labor militancy, aware of the distrust Haymarket had aroused. Jane Addams recognized the impact of the Haymarket Affair on her contemporaries. Writing in 1935, she recalled that it had a "profound influence" on "the social outlook of thousands of people." But she inadvertently revealed how distant she felt from it when she claimed she was abroad at the time. In fact, she was in Philadelphia.[57]

Addams may not have been in Europe in May 1886, but she was thinking about going overseas again. The idea was irresistible, and by January 1887 she and Ellen had begun planning a yearlong trip for the following fall. Ellen would take a leave from her job at the Kirkland School; she planned to finance half the costs of the trip by chaperoning several of her students at various interludes, and she agreed to let Jane pay for the other half. For Jane, of course, money was no obstacle.[58]

Jane had set herself two projects. In order to deepen her newfound Christian faith, she wanted to undertake a study of the catacombs in Rome. She also wanted to visit the cathedrals of Europe. This second project grew out of some reading she had been doing about the ideas of the French positivist Auguste Comte. Apparently, Comte, or one of his interpreters, believed that the cathedrals of Europe, having been built by the people, nicely embodied the Comtean "Religion of Humanity." Judging from Addams's later writings, Comte's vision of "unity"—that is, the belief that most men desired to feel a universal affection for other human beings (he called this his "Religion of Humanity")—strongly appealed to her. His progressive expectation that history was leading to the development of a human race that would be entirely unselfish, or, to use the word he invented, "altruistic," must have enchanted her. Comte was the compleat idealist, a man who had absolute confidence that great, abstract truths conquered all. His motto, "Live for others," might well have been the motto of the early Christians whom Addams aspired to emulate.[59]

In wishing to travel again in Europe, Jane was being entirely conventional. Such trips were expected of a prosperous, educated young woman. But her plan camouflaged the fact that her mind was now moving in less orthodox directions. As her depression lifted and as she removed, timber by timber, the structure of old assumptions that blocked her path, she was beginning to think creatively about her future. Sometime in 1887, she conceived of a vague plan. She writes in *Twenty Years*, "It is hard to tell just when the very simple plan which afterward developed into the Settlement began to form itself in my mind. It may have been even before I went to Europe for the second time, but I gradually became convinced that it would be a good thing to rent a house in a part of the city where many primitive and actual needs [were] found . . . [and live there with other] young women who[se time] had been given over too exclusively to study."[60] The two sentences are the pivot point of the book, marking as they do the moment when she makes the biggest decision of her life. But the sentences slip by the reader quietly, perhaps because of the tentative phrases in which the decision is wrapped: "It is hard to tell . . . It may have been . . . I gradually became convinced . . ."

Although Addams does not say so, her plan was not entirely new. By her own account she had intended to live among the poor since she was six. But that claim aside, she had been committed while at seminary to being a doctor who served the poor. Although she had since abandoned medicine as a career, her latest plan reflected her continuing interest in poor people's daily lives, her desire to achieve cross-class social mingling, her growing humanitarian, Christian faith, her need to work in fellowship, and her conviction that, even as a woman, she had a duty to humanity that she could not ignore.

Addams mentions none of these motives, however, in noting her decision in *Twenty Years*. Indeed, she supplies no motives at all beyond the comment that she thought "it would be a good thing." Possible motives are strewn across earlier pages of the book but she gives no summary of them. It is a strange omission, and yet it implies the point she makes elsewhere in the book—that it was natural for her to go live among the poor, that no special reason was required.[61] She was writing as the reformer she was, making an argument about how society should be.

But living among the poor was not the obvious thing for a woman of twenty-six of Addams's class to do. She had available to her only one motive that was both socially acceptable and morally compelling: benevolence, the duty of the privileged to help and care for the underprivileged. Did Addams intend to be benevolent?

She does not exclude this motive from the pages of *Twenty Years* but she certainly underplays it, probably because of her distaste for benevolence in 1910. But in 1887 she did not feel the same distaste. That fall, speaking to a group of Rockford alumnae in Chicago on the assigned toast theme, "Our Debts and How We Shall Repay Them," she stressed the need for women to undertake "beneficent action" to advance "the progress of the human race." She justified benevolence to her classmates in two ways, in each case sounding a striking note of self-doubt. First, she said, benevolence was their birthright, a duty placed on them by their families' class position. "[W]e are taught subtle theories of heredity, that . . . [we] have inherited tendencies, [a] predisposition for benevolence." But she does not therefore feel confident that she can live up to this inheritance. "This view of ourselves is rather overwhelming," she adds. Second, benevolence was their duty as educated women. Such a woman "demand[s] from herself high purposes, active and beneficent conduct, because she has had opportuni-

ties desired by the women of all other ages." Again Addams feels daunted
at the thought. "We may at last be . . . paralyzed by the enormity of our
debt if we continue so to cultivate our sense of responsibility."[62] Her self-
doubt reveals the most basic reason for her years of paralysis. She feared
she would fail to live up to the high expectations that others had of her and
that she had of herself.

Addams's plan was vague, but her imagination now received some help.
Sometime in the summer or fall of 1887 she picked up a copy of *Century*
magazine and came upon an article about a new kind of philanthropic organization called a settlement house. It told how some fifteen young men,
most of them graduates of Oxford University, were living in a house in the
East End of London called Toynbee Hall, named in memory of the recently
deceased economic historian and social critic (and uncle of the later famous
historian of the same name) Arnold Toynbee. The residents were spending
their time trying to make "the lives of the East End poor more wholesome
and beautiful than they could be without such help."[63] The hall offered lectures, clubs such as the Shakespeare Club, the Adam Smith Club, and the
Natural History Society, and classes in singing, drawing, and reading—the
list seemed never to end.

The rough similarity between her plan and Toynbee Hall—they both involved living among one's own class while also living among the poor—is
not surprising. The suffering of the poor and the social gap between them
and the rich in major cities in England and the United States, as Mearns's
pamphlet had conveyed, were real, and growing, and much on people's
minds on both sides of the Atlantic. Also, Toynbee Hall's British founders,
the Reverend Samuel and Henrietta Barnett, were reading the same books
and being influenced by the same ideas as Addams was. Ruskin, Kingsley,
Arnold, Mazzini, Carlyle, and Eliot had been pounding away for years on
the tragedy of the economic gap between the classes, the redeeming power
of culture, and the dangers of social isolation. Finally, the settlement concept, though novel in purpose, was conventional in method. Throughout
the century, missionaries had been going forth from Great Britain and the
United States, including some from tiny Rockford Seminary, to convert
"pagans" to their faith by living and teaching among them. Toynbee Hall
was praised as highly innovative, but it was also an entirely predictable
invention: a middle-class outpost in "uncivilized" territory whose mission
was conversion of the "natives," not to Christianity, but to culture. Fascinated by the *Century* article, Addams decided to visit Toynbee Hall on her

European trip and wrote down its address. Still, she told no one about her plan, not even Ellen. Like many a dreamer in the early stages of a project's conception, she feared, she admits in *Twenty Years*, that she would be mocked.[64]

In considering the settlement house idea, she apparently was confident that encouraging the poor to discover culture's pleasures was a good thing. But might it not damage them as it had damaged her? What about the revulsion for culture she had felt so strongly in recent years? Apparently, she did not see the problem. Her literary, Romantic mind, drawn as it was to feelings, not conceptual categories, inhabited each feeling at a separate moment. She saw culture, alternatively and depending on the context, as a savior, an enemy, or a gift.

———————

Meanwhile, the Haldeman family's situation took a new turn in the summer and fall of 1887. George, having put the crisis of Jane's rejection of his marriage proposal behind him, left Johns Hopkins for Leipzig, Germany, in August to pursue further biological studies. But by November he was home again. He wrote Harry on November 12, "I hope [my return] may prove advantageous to Mother. I did not realize how deeply she seemed to feel my absence. . . . I will stay with her as long as she says." Three weeks later, he had settled back into life in Cedarville. He told Harry, "[Mother] seems to have use for me here as a companion and consequently I have no present intention of seeking employment."[65] Now Anna was his responsibility, not Jane's.

George's servility to his mother was no accident. Anna had carefully nurtured in him an appreciation for the great closeness she felt they had and for the crucial role she had played in his life. In a letter written in 1885, George mirrored back this understanding: "There is something more than a natural relationship between us, . . . a similarity of disposition and mind also, which is one reason [you understand me so well]. . . . My destiny has been placed in your hands, . . . you [have] directed . . . the development of my character. . . . I see it now as you have often told me I would."[66] It appeared that Anna had succeeded in tying the apron strings around George very tightly.

Jane's own plans to visit Europe had also shifted somewhat. She had intended to leave in the fall but when Sarah Anderson, her friend from Rockford days, decided to join her, this delayed their departure until December.

Ellen Gates Starr was already in Europe, chaperoning some young ladies from her school. She would meet Jane and Sarah in Germany. Meanwhile, Jane remained in Cedarville through November, except for Thanksgiving, when, freed by George's return from having to spend the holiday with Anna, she went to the Linns'.[67] On December 14, 1887, Jane and Sarah Anderson boarded a steamer at Hoboken, New Jersey, for Southampton, England.

Jane watched the American shore disappear from view with a greater sense of selfless purpose than she had had on her first European trip. That trip's goal had been to make her a more cultured person for her own sake; on this one she was to prepare herself to lead the new philanthropic life she was secretly planning. What the two trips had in common was her persistent faith, despite her moments of revulsion, in culture's transformational powers, a faith justified not only by the confident assertions of Matthew Arnold and others but also by her own experience. During the seven years since she had graduated from seminary, culture in the form of books—that is, the humanities—had continued to change her. Books had freed her from a too narrowly defined duty to family, shown her that society's restrictions on women's responsibilities were artificial and cruel, allowed her to examine the responsibilities that accompanied her inherited wealth, deepened her ideas about class, capitalism, and poverty, revised her understanding of Christianity, and helped her reinterpret the meaning of her interest in the poor. These were large gifts. In her childhood, culture—in the broader sense of society's teachings—had placed her in a necessary prison of unexamined assumptions. But as she grew older, culture—in the sense of "higher" learning—also gave her the key to unlock the door. From culture she received the ability to stand back and examine those assumptions and consciously and selectively reject them.

Addams was aware of her debt to books; her gratitude is captured in a tender passage she wrote years later. When a person "finds himself morally isolated among those hostile to his immediate aims," she observed, "his reading assures him that other people in the world have thought as he does. . . . He has become conscious of a cloud of witnesses torn out of literature and warmed into living comradeship."[68] Given what culture had meant to her, it is not surprising that she was still pursuing it in December 1887.

But her doubts about the moral benefits of culture's pursuit, doubts felt before she left for her first trip to Europe, had also been strengthening. In

1883 she had confessed to Ellen her fear that she would find it difficult to "hold to full earnestness of purpose" while traveling abroad. In her mind, Europe, with its enchanting enticements, was the choice of the morally weak, those without character. Now she was making the same choice again. Beneath her delight at the trip's prospects lay a gnawing apprehension that she was permanently caught in what she would later call "the snare of preparation," unable or unwilling to break free.[69]

Three days after the ship docked at Southampton, Jane and Sarah were in Paris celebrating Christmas. The novelty added pleasure to the start of their adventure. But their fellowship was short; plans soon required them to separate for a time. While Sarah stayed in the French capital on personal business, Jane left for Munich to meet Ellen and her students. On her way to Munich, she visited Ulm Cathedral, the first station on her Comtean pilgrimage.[1]

The church delighted her. Though a Christian house of prayer, it openly celebrated humanism. Reflecting Renaissance and Reformation influences, the formerly Catholic, now Protestant, place of worship was decorated with carved wooden figures of Christian saints and pagan philosophers. Saint Paul was on equal footing here with Plato, Aristotle, and Cicero. "Matthew Arnold's idea of culture came to me so often," Jane wrote her friend Flora Guiteau. She left Ulm Cathedral filled with the longing to be part of something larger and finer than herself—the same desire that had fueled her pursuit of culture and her conversion to Christianity. That night, with Comte's idea of a Religion of Humanity and his motto "live to serve" on her mind, she scribbled in a notebook about her hope for a Cathedral of Humanity. She wanted it to be "capacious enough to house a fellowship of common purpose" for all and to be "beautiful enough to persuade men to hold fast to the vision of human solidarity."[2] The cathedral was an appealing metaphor for a shared undertaking because it was large and beautiful, but perhaps also because it was a building, something tangible that made her dreams manifest.

She met Ellen in Munich, where they stayed for a week. In the mornings they visited art galleries looking for prints for the Kirkland School and in the afternoons they talked for hours, studied Italian, and paid visits to people they had met. Jane's contentment was complete. She wrote her sister

Alice that she had "seldom in my life had a happier week than [this week Ellen and I] have had together."[3]

Each was finding in each other the quality she most wished to possess: the strength of will to make herself a better person. Jane wrote Flora Guiteau that she admired Ellen's "persistent efforts to get the *best* in the world, the highest and truest" and her "patience to work out [the best] in her own character." A few weeks later Ellen wrote Anna Addams praising Jane's "beautiful character" and expressing regret that she herself was unwilling to invest "the moral effort and self-discipline . . . required to develop a character like hers."[4]

The road to a better character, already difficult, was complicated by Addams's and Starr's confusion about the kind they aspired to possess. According to their Christian views, they ought to have compassion for the flawed. Yet culture loved perfection. Did a well-read, well-traveled Christian scorn the uncultured or treat them courteously? On their trip, Addams and Starr wobbled between the two standards of behavior, perpetually dissatisfied with themselves.

An event that epitomized their dilemma was an encounter with a stranger at their pension in Florence, where they traveled after leaving Munich. An elderly Missouri farmer dressed in a flannel shirt and a paper collar sat at their table in the dining room spearing his bread with his fork and picking his teeth as they all discussed Florence's artistic sights. Ellen, reporting this in a letter to Anna, added that she disdained the farmer for his ignorance of Ruskin but Jane did not. Jane talked with him "as she would have done to a man of the world. I never admired her more." She takes a "beautiful[,] unpretentious interest in everybody. . . . I wish I could be like her." But Addams, too, could succumb to the temptation to mock. One night, she and Ellen observed at dinner a nearly bald man who had carefully combed his few remaining hairs over his otherwise naked pate. Ellen drew a sketch of him and Jane sent it to Anna. Jane reassured her stepmother that they had been careful not to laugh in the man's presence. "We were perfectly proper and didn't giggle until we got to our rooms."[5]

On the whole, however, Jane's efforts to rein in her dislike of the uncultured, at least while writing letters, were relatively successful. Though she was Anna's own stepdaughter in her disapproval of the "uncivilized," her letters home contained no nasty remarks. When she wrote Anna about meeting the Missourian, for example, she kept her disdain within factual bounds, noting that he "only knows what he has read in Hare's guide."

Ellen's letters, on the other hand, were sprinkled with passionate eruptions. At one point, writing to a friend about a distinctly "inferior" boardinghouse where she was staying with a student, she observed condescendingly of its owners, "They are such fools, too. They don't know an earthly thing and are so bumptious!"[6]

Nor did Ellen hesitate to criticize friends, in some cases directly. She felt it was her job to improve them. At Kirkland School, she often subjected her friend Miss Runyan to her helpfulness. She reported to Jane in 1882, "Have been brow-beating [Miss Runyan] terribly tonight about her lack of confidence in herself." No doubt Ellen criticized Jane for the same lack. Perhaps this was what Addams had in mind when she described Ellen as "my critical and literary friend."[7]

Sarah rejoined them in Florence, and the three friends' acquisition of culture proceeded apace. For several weeks they luxuriated in the city's cultural riches, practicing their Italian, attending the opera, and visiting art museums. In early February they moved on to Rome, where Jane planned to undertake her study of the catacombs.[8] Only pleasure was on her horizon. But, once again, fate had other plans.

The visit in Rome began splendidly. In the catacombs, Jane's attention was seized this time by the Chi-Rho symbol that decorated the ceilings and walls. *Chi* and *rho* are the Greek letters *X* and *P*, the first two letters of the word for "Christ" in Greek. The early Christians used the two letters, one overlaid on the other, as their religion's symbol. (The cross would not become widely popular until several centuries later.) After her conversion, Jane bought a Chi-Rho pin, probably in Rome on this visit, to wear on her dress collar.[9]

Then, on February 16, only days into her study, she received two letters from home with shattering news: her sister Mary had lost her two-year-old daughter Mary to whooping cough. "[She] has gone into the better world," Jane's fifteen-year-old nephew John Addams Linn wrote tenderly. The grieving mother wrote, too. With characteristic unselfishness, Mary was worried about how Jane, whose intense reactions to death she understood perhaps better than anyone, would take the news. "I know how you will suffer," Mary wrote. "I hope you will not grieve unduly. . . . Do take care of your health."[10]

Mary was right to worry. Within days of receiving the news, Jane suffered a severe attack of sciatica and was unable to get out of bed because of the pain shooting down her leg. Though everyone agreed that it was the

Jane Addams, wearing the Chi Rho pin, 1892, from a sketch by Alice Kellogg Tyler, a Hull House resident. Twenty Years at Hull-House, *114.*

unusually cold weather that had triggered her attack, she may have had her own theories. Her immobilization no doubt brought her sharply and unexpectedly back to her old conviction that, as she had written Ellen four years earlier, "failure through ill health is just as culpable and miserable as failure through any other cause." This new illness, arising abruptly in the midst of an enjoyable trip, served to remind her that she was still responsible for the failed direction of her life. A letter Jane sent to Alice at the time suggests her self-condemning mood. "I have been self-absorbed and priggish in my life," she writes, "and pray every day for redemption and beneficent goodness."[11] In fact, her niece's death was a deep blow. The seismic vibrations it triggered below the level of her consciousness would require time to surface.

Thanks to Ellen's devoted nursing, Jane eventually recovered enough to rejoin the group as they continued their Italian travels. They returned to Florence, where Jane's classmate Helen Harrington and an older woman, Amelia Collins Rowell, joined them. After the Easter celebrations they moved on to Madrid, where a friend of a friend of Ellen's, an American woman who had married a Spaniard, offered to take those who were interested to attend a bullfight. Helen and Mrs. Rowell refused to go.[12]

A bullfight was exactly what Jane wanted to see. She thought of it, she writes in *Twenty Years*, as "the last survival of all the glories of the [Roman] amphitheater." While recuperating in Rome, she had spent two weeks reading Spanish history, including the history of the bullfight, which was thought to have evolved from the Roman practice of forcing the "pagan" Christians to face raging bulls in the Coliseum, among whose crumbling ruins she had recently walked. She had read how, at the bullfight, the mata-dor was like "the slightly armed gladiator facing his martyrdom" at the hands of the Roman emperor. And there were medieval references as well. The riders on "the caparisoned horses," she had read, created the illusion that they "might have been knights of a tournament."[13] In short, it would be history come to life. She expected that watching a bullfight would be like visiting Ulm Cathedral. To her, both were beautiful objects worthy of con-templation because of their many points of reference to the past. She was proud that she could perceive them as laden with cultural meaning; doing so affirmed her sense of herself as a sophisticated, well-educated person.

She and her friends took their seats in time to watch the first grand procession around the ring. The amphitheater was immense; the crowd of ten thousand people roared its delight. Jane sent Sarah Hostetter a vivid description of what followed. "[T]he bull came rushing in, . . . lithe and ac-tive as a cat," she wrote, followed by the picadors, ten men on horseback "who irritate the bull with long wooden lances." They and their mounts soon became the target of the bull's ire. The first bull killed four horses right from under the picadors, she reported. Then six men in red cloaks, the banderilleros, tried to weaken the bull by stabbing "gaily decorated little swords" into his back. Finally, when the bull was exhausted, the matador killed him "with one clever stroke into his spinal cord." Six bulls and many more horses were killed that day, she wrote in another letter, this one to her sister-in-law Laura Shoemaker Addams.[14]

It was intensely gory, yet Jane hardly noticed the bloodshed. Her imag-ination was busy, she writes in Twenty Years, conjuring up all the "vivid associations" with early Christian Roman history that the sight inspired. She thought it magnificent. As the afternoon wore on, however, Ellen and Sarah became increasingly disgusted by all the blood. They told Jane they wanted to leave and she agreed but remained glued to her seat as they walked out. They waited for her in the foyer of the amphitheater, and when she finally appeared she found them "stern . . . with disapproval for my brutal endurance."[15]

At first she did not regret her fascination, but that evening, mulling things over, she felt herself "tried and condemned" by "the entire moral situation . . . which [the experience] revealed." She became upset that she had been fascinated by something so revolting. Absorbed in recalling the struggles of the early Christians against the Roman bulls, she had watched the horses and bulls die horribly without a twinge of sympathy. As she noted in her letter to Laura, "The interest was so great as to throw the cruelty and brutality into the background." She added, "We were rather ashamed and surprised to find that we were brutal enough to take a great interest in it." The inclusive "we" suggested that her friends fully shared her fascination, as they may well have at first. But in her letter to Sarah Hostetter she spoke more personally of her own feelings of "shame" and "wonder at my brutality in enduring it so well."[16]

Why had she cared so little for the animals' suffering? Turning her powers of interpretation on herself, she once more felt ashamed by her love of culture. Her behavior at the bullfight struck her the way her behavior in the East End visit had—as compelling proof that culture cut her off from feeling compassion for suffering. Or, as she would write years later, that "an armour of erudition" protected a person from "hideousness."[17]

That night, Addams questioned why she had returned to Europe at all. Her theory that she needed to study the catacombs in Rome and the cathedrals of Europe before she could start her plan now struck her as foolish. She was in Europe not to advance her plan but to feed her own love of culture. "It was suddenly made quite clear to me," she writes in *Twenty Years*, "that I was lulling my conscience by a dreamer's scheme, . . . that I had fallen into the meanest type of self-deception, . . . that, so far from following in the wake of a chariot of philanthropic fire, I had been tied to the tail of the veriest ox-cart of self-seeking."[18] In a word, she was selfish, betraying her conscience instead of listening to it. Would she be nothing but a moral failure her whole life?

Action was the only solution, which meant that, as a first step, she had to talk about her plan. Still she hesitated, fearing that if she told anyone she would "suddenly feel that there [was] nothing there to talk about and . . . the golden dream [would] slip through [my] fingers." But she plunged on. The next day, "stumbling" and "uncertain" but determined, she told Ellen that she wanted to live among the poor in the spirit of the early Christians, providing neighborly kindnesses and culture. To her surprise, Ellen liked the idea. Five years earlier, she had written to Jane of her longing to find a way to combine work and friendship. "If all the good things in the way of work and friends could be gotten together in one time and place," she wrote, "what happy people we might be." Now Jane was proposing just such a plan. Ellen's enthusiasm, Addams later recalled, was hugely important.

It helped her feel that the scheme, though "still most hazy in detail," was "convincing and tangible." She had found a partner for her project. She and Starr would do this daring thing together.[19]

In *Twenty Years* Addams writes about this crisis with a fair amount of drama. No reader can doubt that she believed it to be a crucial turning point in her life. Some have wondered, however, whether she exaggerated what had happened. How could her reaction to watching a bullfight be so hugely consequential? But such skepticism neglects the deeply Romantic way the twenty-seven-year-old Jane Addams looked at the world. Her college essays are permeated with the belief evident in the bullfight story: that in order for a person without character to acquire character (that is, become a hero), she must have a crisis of conscience and resolve the crisis with an anguished decision to embody her better self, her ideals, in action. This secular model of personal transformation, sometimes called conversion, came directly from her evangelical Christian upbringing, her father's emphasis on trusting one's conscience, and her reading of the British and American Romantic literature (itself shaped by evangelical influences).[20] Though no Romantic, the philosopher Immanuel Kant articulated the dynamics of this sort of conversion experience brilliantly. "[T]he establishment of character," he writes, "is similar to a kind of rebirth, a certain solemn resolution which the person himself makes." He almost seems to be describing Addams's experience when he adds: "The transformation . . . can only be done by an explosion which suddenly occurs as a consequence of our disgust at the unsteady condition of [an inclination]. . . . Wishing to become a better person in a fragmentary manner is a vain endeavor because one impression fades away while we labor on another. . . . Perhaps there will be only a few who have attempted this revolution before their thirtieth year."[21] His point was psychological—it is difficult for a person to know that he has begun to change unless he can pinpoint that change, symbolically and emotionally, in time. The bullfight crisis served exactly that purpose in Jane Addams's life. Until that day she had not felt herself to be a person of moral integrity, that is, someone whose practice aligned with her theory, whose deeds matched her conscience. The day after the bullfight, she chose to believe that she had started to become that person and began to act accordingly.

But why was a *bullfight* the trigger for her conversion? The answer seems to lie in the nature of the event itself. It was thick not only with the cultural meanings that Addams found compelling but also with religious and psychological ones. The historic analogy to the early Christians' suffering was

no doubt more potent than Addams admitted in *Twenty Years*. Equally important, the Spanish arena had been full of death, with bulls killing horses
and matadors killing bulls. Death affected Jane Addams that day as it always
did, by arousing shame at her own inaction. Yet it also triggered something
new. In the past, Jane's response to the deaths of her mother, sister, and
father, to the vision of death in the East End market and perhaps to her
niece Mary's recent death, had been to succumb—to suffer nightmares
that reenacted her powerlessness or to sink with a feeling of helplessness
into depression. This time, she acted constructively. It was a sign of health.

Soon afterwards Addams apparently wrote her stepbrother George and
her sister Alice about her bullfight crisis. The letters do not survive, but
her replies to *their* replies do. These suggest that she was not proud of
the messy way things had unfolded. She wrote George somewhat elliptically in early June, "I regret the imperfect hatching" of "the scheme." In
an exchange with Alice later that summer she may have echoed the point.
Her sister replied by praising her for "always doing right." Jane quickly
corrected her. "Don't say I always do right[;] it is only the narrowest escape
from great wrong and weakness all the time with me." [22] As usual, she was
full of self-blame.

But beneath her habitual sense of failure, a more profound self-under-
standing was stirring. By some process that left only a few traces in her
letters, she was coming to the realization that the scheme could serve her
ambition to succeed and that she had been foolish in trying to suppress
that ambition. She explained to George that her plan's "imperfect hatching"
was "most of all, the sad [fate] . . . of ungratified ambition[. I]t is said to be
the only absorbing passion which does not ennoble its victim." [23] She was
beginning to see her effort to lead a submissive, obscure, private life as
ill-advised.

She would make the same point more clearly to Alice in another letter
written in early 1889. After congratulating Alice on her recent appointment as a trustee of her church, Jane quoted a passage from a poem she
had been reading, Robert Browning's "Bishop Blougram's Apology," introducing it with the observation that the passage "seems to . . . appl[y] in a
modified sense to us both." She copied it into the letter. "There's power in
me and will to dominate which I must exercise, they hurt me else / In many
ways I need mankind's respect, obedience." To Browning's insights she
added an explanation of the source of Alice's and her own drive to power,
even as she elaborated on the difficulty of ignoring it. "It seems almost impossible . . . to express inherited power and tendencies [while] constantly

try[ing] to exercise another set [of behaviors]." [24] Her language, as always, was impersonal, but her point was not: she and Alice had inherited their ambition and desire for wide public reputation from their father, and when they tried to tamp it down to fit the small scope allotted to women, they could not do it.

Embracing her father's ambition as her own also undercut Jane's intense identification with the female ideal of duty to family that she had spent most of the 1880s trying to honor. Events would show that she still believed she should practice other tenets of the female ideal, particularly self-sacrifice and sympathy, but she would never again force herself to put her ambition in a box and deny its existence. Drawing on her sister's example and with Browning's help, she used the fact that her father was ambitious to reclaim the desire for power and fame that Caroline Potter so carefully nurtured at Rockford. In accepting this longing in herself, she was declaring her gender irrelevant to her ambition, although perhaps in a narrower sense than Potter would have liked. She had decided not that women could be legitimately powerful but that the daughters of John Huy Addams could.

The group toured more of Spain and then went to France to visit cathedrals. Next was England, but without Ellen. Starr and Addams had wanted to visit Toynbee Hall in London together in June as the first step in executing their plan, but Ellen had to chaperone the students again in Italy and could not reach London until the end of July. They decided that Jane would visit Toynbee Hall first; then, she would visit it again with Ellen when she arrived. [25]

Addams approached her visit to Toynbee Hall with mixed feelings. She describes herself in *Twenty Years* as full of "high expectations" as well as a sense that "perplexities and discouragement" might well lie ahead. At the same time, she remembered feeling glad that she would "at least know something at first hand" and have "the solace of daily activity." She did not consider changing her mind. She was convinced she had arrived at a new phase. "I had confidence," she writes, "that . . . I had at last finished with the ever-lasting 'preparation for life.' " [26]

Toynbee Hall stood (and still stands) on Commercial Street, a major East End thoroughfare not far from Five Mile Road and the market Addams had visited. The crowded East End embraced several districts and each district was divided into several parishes. Toynbee was in Whitechapel District and in the parish of St. Jude's, which was the parish of Toynbee Hall's co-founder, Samuel Barnett. About eight thousand people of English, Irish,

Toynbee Hall, London. Jane Addams Memorial Collection (JAMC neg. 848),
Special Collections, The University Library, University of Illinois at Chicago.

Welsh, and eastern European Jewish backgrounds lived there, in the space
of a few square acres, often crowded six to eight in a room. The Whitechapel
District was adjacent to the London docks, where jobs were particularly
sporadic and low-paying. Overall, the district housed a high percentage of
people in the struggling segment of London's working class.[27]

In such a down-and-out neighborhood Toynbee Hall was an elegant outpost. Built in 1884 with funds raised by students, alumni, and faculty of Oxford and Cambridge Universities, the hall was set well back from Commercial Road and consisted of three interconnected brick buildings encircling
a quadrangle. As intended, it looked like and, to a degree, functioned like, a
college at a British university. It had a large drawing room, a lecture hall, a
library, a dining room, classrooms, and bedrooms for twenty men. There
were no women residents, nor would there be any for many decades. The
new settlement was named for Arnold Toynbee, a friend of the Barnetts
and an Oxford graduate who, before his untimely death 1883 from nervous
exhaustion (he was thirty-one), had sometimes lived in the East End as a
way to get to know workingmen.[28]

When the house opened on Christmas Eve, 1884, two extraordinary people were at its helm: the forty-four-year-old Samuel Barnett, its new warden,

Reverend Samuel Barnett. Henrietta Barnett, Canon Barnett: His Life, Work and Friends *(Boston: Houghton Mifflin, 1919), vol. 1: frontispiece.*

and thirty-seven-year-old Henrietta Barnett, his wife, who was as essential to the project's success as her husband but without official title. Samuel was the son of a wealthy Bristol manufacturer and a graduate of Oxford, a short man with a scruffy beard and loose-fitting clothes. Gentle to a fault, he was described by his wife as blessed with "humility" and a "restless, ruthless energy for reform." Henrietta was in some ways his opposite. Like him, she was from a wealthy family, but, unlike him, she dressed elegantly, had a forceful manner, and lacked humility. A neighbor in Whitechapel once said of her that she was "the only person I've ever known who could recite the Ten Commandments as if she had just made them up." Behind her authoritative manner, however, was a kind and practical heart. One friend remembered that she was "full . . . of ingenuity for [finding] new ways of helping everybody."[29] Unceremonious and unflaggingly honest, she offended the pompous and won the affection of the down-to-earth.

The Barnetts had been running Toynbee Hall for three years when Jane Addams met them. Toward the end of her life Henrietta recorded Samuel's and her first impressions. "[W]e realized," she wrote, "that she was a great soul, and took pains to show her much and tell her more." For Addams, the conversations with the Barnetts amounted to a graduate education in the settlement house idea condensed into a period of days. A hint of her delight comes through in a letter she wrote Alice shortly after her visit. Toynbee Hall "is a community of University men who live there, have their recreation clubs and society all among the poor people yet in the same style in which they would live in their own circle. It is so free from 'professional doing good,' so unaffectedly sincere and so productive of good results in its classes and libraries that it seems perfectly ideal."[30]

The settlement house concept had grown directly out of the Barnetts' eleven years of work heading the parish church of St. Jude. By the early 1880s they were already bringing friends from different social classes together for receptions at the vicarage in the conviction, Henrietta wrote, that "people must talk together if they are to break down the class barriers built by mutual ignorance." Matthew Arnold was one source of inspiration. He wrote in *Culture and Anarchy*, "We habitually live in our ordinary selves, which do not carry us beyond the ideas and wishes of the class to which we happen to belong." Arnold advocated spreading the benefits of culture as widely as possible. Samuel Barnett liked to carry a small book of Arnold's essays in his pocket.[31]

At the same time, many young Oxford students, including Toynbee, had been inspired by the lectures of their professor, the philosopher and social Christian T. H. Green, to visit the East End. Green urged them to be of service to society by establishing social ties with working-class men and pursuing civic engagement concerning working-class issues. He thought it would do them good to work toward the "common good." Citizenship "makes the moral man," Green wrote. "Morality consists in the disinterested performance of self-imposed duties." He also thought that working men would benefit from association with cultured, educated young men. Samuel Barnett, a Green admirer himself, later described Green's theory as "education by permeation."[32] The phrase neatly summed up the classical Greek idea that people learned best from example. In the modern Victorian version, the Oxford graduate was expected to enrich the life of the worker by his presence and friendship.

From all these influences, as well as frustration regarding low attendance at their parish church, the Barnetts forged a new mission and a new method for their work in the parish. College men would come to live together, or "settle," for a few months or years in the East End, form friendships with East Enders, and introduce them to "the higher life." Instead of saving souls from sin by leading them to God's forgiveness, the Barnetts and their friends would build character and bring joy by sharing knowledge and beauty. They would proselytize the humanities. The young men would live in a house called a "settlement house" and other educated young men living elsewhere in London would join them in their free time to help offer education, recreation, and conversation to working-class men (and soon afterward, women and children) via clubs, billiards, classes, lectures, concerts, and other gatherings. Aside from the Barnetts and the servants, everyone was to work on a volunteer basis. The cross-class relationships would be ones of "mutual benefit." The settlement residents would work with their working-class neighbors on shared projects, rather than doing things for them.[33]

And the vision did not end there. The Barnetts also intended the settlement to improve the lives of working people in material ways. This was what Samuel Barnett called the "socialistic" part of the scheme, and it, too, derived from the ideas of Green, who favored the expansion of state services. Barnett wanted settlement residents to sit on the town councils of working-class districts and other government bodies of London and to push for a variety of reforms, some cultural (neighborhood libraries, art galleries, and playgrounds), and some material (low-income housing, public baths, job training, shelters for the homeless, and public health services). Barnett was committed to these reforms for their own sake, but he also believed that workingmen, who had only gained the vote in 1884, would learn from watching settlement residents seek such reforms. East Enders, he wrote, would see how the college men "bring the light and strength of intelligence to bear on their government."[34]

In sum, the settlement idea was democratic, but only in part. The Barnetts were sincerely committed to an egalitarian ethic, but just beneath their rhetoric of mutual benefit lay the assumption that educated men were essentially and broadly superior to poor, uneducated men. Nothing in Barnett's writings suggests that he respected the class- or ethnicity-based cultures of working people or expected them to teach settlement residents about the virtues of courage, sacrifice, generosity, compassion, equality, and loyalty commonly found among the working class. Nor, in the early years, did he expect workingmen to represent their own interests on the town councils.[35] The settlement idea as the Barnetts first conceived it was, like most reforms that prove popular, both egalitarian and hierarchical. It challenged and reinforced the status quo; it moved society forward but did so comfortably.

And this was its appeal to Jane Addams. The settlement was quite daring in its cross-class mingling but, aside from the uniqueness of its neighborhood, traditional in the mode of living it offered residents. It showed Addams a way to live among the poor "in the same style," as she put it, as her "circle." Settlement life reinforced her familiar sense of herself even as it stretched her social horizons. It offered her a way to cross over into a new world while keeping a foot in the old one.

The aspect of Toynbee Hall that likely startled Addams the most was the third element of its work: its involvement with the trade union movement and its materialistic reform agenda of higher wages and improved working conditions. The Barnetts believed that there was a connection between ending a man's poverty and developing his human potential. As Henrietta Barnett put it in 1884, "Can a man live the highest life when the preservation of his . . . body occupies all his thoughts—from whose life pleasure is crushed out by ever-wearying work . . . ?"[36]

Addams knew little about trade unions and strikes before visiting Toynbee Hall, her main source of information being the generally antistrike stories in newspapers and magazines. That summer she experienced union organizing firsthand when a major strike erupted in the East End. In an interview for a social reform magazine, three "match girls" criticized their employer, the Bryant and May Factory, for low pay and dangerous working conditions and subsequently were fired. Afterwards, the rest of the matchworkers—fifteen hundred women—walked out. Toynbee Hall residents investigated and reported on their findings in letters to the *London Times*; some labor union men helped the matchworkers hold their first strike meeting and organize a union.[37]

Addams attended the meeting and was shocked to hear the young women describe their lives of misery. They told about their low pay and grim working conditions and how daily contact with phosphorous gave many of them phossy jaw, a disease that massively disfigured their faces as it slowly killed them. She felt quite "wretched" about their suffering; however, she entirely missed the union-organizing dimension of what was going on. "I did not . . . connect [this meeting]," she writes in *Twenty Years*, "with what was called the labor movement, nor did I understand the efforts of the London trade unionists." Addams ascribes her obliviousness to her innocence. At the time she assumed that employers did not intend to expose their workers to dangerous working conditions and would not be so selfish as to do so merely in order to increase their profits. "Such a young person [as myself] . . . believe[d] that . . . redeeming magnanimity [could solve] . . . all suffering." It never occurred to her that the world might be "contemptible or . . . self-seeking."[38]

She must have expressed these views to someone at Toynbee Hall. A copy of Karl Marx's *Capital* was thrust into her hands. She found reading it distasteful: "I cared . . . more for Mazzini," she later wrote, "than for Carl [*sic*] Marx."[39] Her dislike was understandable. *Capital* exposed her to serious economic theory for the first time. Furthermore, because of her upbringing, she felt a strong prima facie loyalty to employers. And there were other points of tension. Addams, like Mazzini, was a moralist who argued from duty; Marx was a philosopher who argued from economic and historic necessity. Also, Marx's solution to the problems created by capitalism was different from that of the other thinker who was an important influence on Addams's economic thinking at the time, Tolstoy. Marx sought to abolish private property and to establish state control over the means of production. He wanted to restructure the world's economy. Tolstoy's (and Addams's) solution to capitalist oppression, in keeping with their Christian focus on the health of the individual soul, was entirely individualistic: each person should change his or her own behavior.

And Addams possessed a second blindness watching the match girls' strike rally. The union and Marx sought concrete, physical changes; Addams thought that ideas were the crucial reality. This perspective is evident both in her essay "Bellerophon" and in writings dating from her early years at Hull House. It is mirrored in her fascination with Comte's thought. Her deeply felt idealism clashed painfully with Marx's materialism. Thus, although she felt wretched at the match girls' suffering, these feelings did not shake her conviction that the spirit's, not the body's, condition was the crucial object of reform. Nor did she see the two as linked. She did not believe, as Henrietta Barnett did, that the problem of poverty had to be solved before workers could pursue the highest life. A passage from Carlyle's *Sartor Resartus*, a book Addams read in 1879, captures a view that was common among idealists, particularly those from evangelical backgrounds: "I do not lament for the poor that they must toil . . . but what I do mourn over is that the lamp of [a poor man's] soul should go out; that no ray of heavenly or even earthly knowledge should visit him but only . . . Fear and Indignation[,] . . . [t]he soul. . . . blinded, dwarfed. . . . [It is a] tragedy."[40]

Addams was drawn to the Barnetts and their ideas not because of their concern regarding the material state of society but because of their desire to nurture the spiritual, or thinking, life of the workingman. This dual vision had its roots in the left-leaning branch of the British Christian socialist movement, to which the Barnetts were devoted. Their first book, published the year Addams visited Toynbee Hall, was titled *Practical Socialism: Essays in Social Reform.*[41]

The movement began in the 1840s as a fringe critique of Protestantism's single-minded determination to save individual souls and as a religious response to the secular cooperative, or socialist, movement launched by Robert Owen in the 1820s.[42] By the 1880s social Christianity had split into near left, far left, and mainstream branches. The mainstream branch, embraced by the leadership of the Anglican Church, retained the critique of individualism that was the core idea of the cooperative movement but abandoned the socialist economic vision and was almost completely spiritualized. Concern for the poor and the suffering was primarily expressed in sympathy.

Two books reflected and spread these moderate views. One was by a former mentor of Samuel Barnett's who was the canon of Canterbury Cathedral, W. H. Fremantle. In *The World as the Subject of Redemption* (1885) he wrote that the "main object of effort is not . . . either . . . the saving of individual souls out of a ruined world, or . . . the organization of a separate society destined always to be held aloof from the world, but . . . the saving of the world itself." This would be accomplished, he advised, by abandoning selfishness and "imbu[ing] all human relations with the spirit of Christ's self-renouncing love." The result would be the kingdom of God on earth: social harmony and the brotherhood of man instead of the present class hostilities.[43] The other book, by another Anglican leader, Brooke Foss Westcott, the canon of Westminster, put forward similar ideas. In *The Social Aspects of Christianity* (1883) he noted the suffering caused by "tyrannical individualism" and called for his readers to find fellowship with those in the household, the factory, and the warehouse and to discover the lesson of duty: that "the end of labor is not material well-being but that larger, deeper, more abiding delight which comes from successfully administering to the good of others."[44]

This middlebrow version of social Christianity was dissatisfying to the left. To those on the near left, among whom were numbered the Barnetts, it was too completely spiritual because it ignored the material side of the question, including the labor union movement. To the far left, that is, the secular, or scientific, socialists, it looked like so much status-quo-justifying foolishness. Marx and Engels dismissed the movement bitingly as "the holy water with which the priest consecrates the heart-burnings of the aristocrat."[45]

For Addams, however, the mainstream version was an excellent fit. Already persuaded of the moral urgency of sympathy and the moral imperatives of unselfishness and duty, she found Fremantle's and Westcott's ideas consistent with her own. And their desire to transform the world, a desire that was evangelical at its core, echoed the ambition she had absorbed from her father's Christian perfectionism and Anna Sill's missionary zeal. Furthermore, their rejection of Christian conversion as their method completely suited her. She had hated being its target and would never be its instigator.

But Addams did absorb something of the left's version of social Christianity from the Barnetts: their method of cooperation, which they saw as being the day-to-day act that embodied "Christ's self-renouncing love." Taking "with, not for" as their motto, they helped organize a cooperative hotel for shoeblacks and undertook school reform by seeking cooperation among parents, teachers, administrators, and students. The many clubs for children and adults at Toynbee Hall were self-governing. They also put in place a structure that allowed the settlement residents to be self-governing. Each week Samuel Barnett chaired "the Grand," as the residents' meeting was mockingly called, to settle policy questions relating to the residential life at the house.[46] For Addams, who was already an enthusiast for Owen's ideas and more recently had been drawn to Tolstoy's nonresistance theory, which was not very far removed from cooperative theory, the Barnetts' methods seemed essentially right.

Soon after meeting the Barnetts, Addams began to perceive her settlement work as part of the social Christian movement. She became well-versed in the writings of some of its important American thinkers, such as Richard T. Ely and Henry Demarest Lloyd, who would also become friends.[47] In a letter to George Haldeman of December 1889 she predicted approvingly that Christian socialism would spread as people realized the extent of the misery of the poor. In 1892 she would write of the settlement movement as part of a "renaissance of the early Christian humanitarianism" and of its desire to express "the spirit of Christ" through social service.[48]

Jane Addams's friendship with the Barnetts fed her mind and heart. To a greater degree than any other settlement house leader in the United States or Great Britain, she would adopt their methods and articulate them to the world. Though she would do some things differently, Hull House's success would be grounded in Toynbee Hall's.[49] The Barnetts also introduced her to issues such as urban political citizenship, material reforms, and trade unions, regarding which she would need years to sort out her views. With their heads in the same books she had been reading and their feet in the mud of Commercial Road, the Barnetts were the perfect guides for Addams as she began her new work.

Jane Addams's second European tour was nearly over. For their last few weeks in Great Britain she, Sarah Anderson, and Helen Harrington planned to continue visiting cathedrals. Joining them was Flora Guiteau, who arrived in early July. They were to tour London and the countryside; then Sarah and Helen would leave for home on July 19, and, soon after, Jane and with Flora would meet Ellen Gates Starr in London for one last month of sightseeing.[50] This would be Ellen's opportunity to visit Toynbee Hall. Once more, pure pleasure was the only thing on Jane Addams's agenda—and, once more, fate intervened.

Flora brought letters from home that contained disturbing news. Jane's sister-in-law Laura wrote that George Haldeman had disappeared from Cedarville in mid-June. When last seen he had been walking west toward Dubuque, Iowa. He had left behind no letter, nor had he written to anyone since. Jane sensed that his flight arose from deep personal anguish. She wrote Alice, "The touch of the melodramatic is so unlike George that the poor fellow must have suffered desperately before he would do it. . . . I fairly weep when I think of his . . . distress of mind" and asked her sister whether she should come home with Sarah and Helen, instead of staying in England. The cable must have come. She and Flora left England on the nineteenth, though it meant that she missed reconnecting with Ellen.[51]

Eventually, Jane would learn George's story. After an argument with Anna, he had snuck out of the house. When she discovered that he was gone, she was frantic as well as mystified as to why he left. As she explained to the *Freeport Weekly Democrat*, which sent a reporter to cover the story, she had given her son "every advantage." Weeks went by. Finally there was a report from Nora, Iowa, that he had been spotted. Anna persuaded the sheriff of Stephenson County and Harry, who had come up from Kansas, to look for George and, after searching for a week, they found him just east of Waterloo, Iowa, walking along the road, his body gaunt, his clothes ragged and dirty. The sheriff reported to the newspaper that George said he had left because he had a "little 'tiff' with his mother."[52]

George's strange behavior of mindlessly walking in a straight line in one direction for days had a name—"fuguing"—though the family was probably unaware of the term. It was common among men in Europe in the 1880s and 1890s. A man who fugued was understood to be having a kind of mental breakdown; he had lost his sanity temporarily, despite the fact that he appeared sensible in conversation. Ian Hacking, who has researched this phenomenon, has defined the fugue as "a body language of male powerlessness." The definition certainly fits George's case.[53]

After this episode, aside from a few trips to Europe and several long stays in Colorado and in Kansas between 1889 and 1893, George stayed at the homestead for the rest of his life, lost in his books and rarely speaking. He was always pleasant to others, patient and kind, but withdrawn. Some days he would not come downstairs at all. His niece, Alice and Harry's daughter Marcet Haldeman-Julius, who knew George well from her summers with Anna and understood the nature of his sacrifice, later wrote that "in [the house in Cedarville] Uncle George spent the slow years of his crucifixion."[54]

Was Jane, in choosing to have an independent life, responsible for this tragedy? Not unless she could have been held responsible for Anna's tyranny and George's weakness. In the months that followed, after she had moved to Chicago, she visited Cedarville. She found George and Anna unhappy, but, as she wrote Alice, she knew that it was "useless and purposeless" for her to try to do anything about it; their misery was "self-inflicted."[55] It was an eminently sane, psychologically healthy conclusion, and if she had not reached it, her entire life would have been different.

Home again in Cedarville in July 1888, Jane Addams was ready to continue her pursuit of character using new methods. She intended, she writes in *Twenty Years*, "to live in a really living world" rather than in "a shadowy intellectual or aesthetic reflection of it."[56] And she had a new hope—that if she gave her ambition for public achievement a constructive outlet, she could escape the "snare of preparation" that she now believed had made her twenties such a trial. Most important, by August 1888 the other obstacles in her path to a new life—her ideas about women's first duty being to family, her doubts about whether someone who had failed could accomplish anything, and her loneliness in having a secret dream—were all gone. They had not fallen away or been dissolved by fate; they had been removed by Jane herself. Her given life was ending and her chosen life was about to begin.

PART TWO

THE CHOSEN LIFE

1889–99

In those [first] ten years Jane Addams grew . . . as a citizen.
Beginning with little but the hope of somehow "socializing" a part
of what Carlyle had called "this huge black Democracy of ours," she
had given much, but she had got much more. . . . She had given . . .
sympathy, . . . time, . . . energy, and money; she had got an
understanding.

JAMES WEBER LINN, Jane Addams

CHAPTER 8

CHICAGO

1889

In February 1889 Jane came to Chicago to join Ellen, who was again teaching at the Kirkland School. The previous April they had discussed starting a settlement house; now, ten months later, they were doing it. Addams's mood may be gauged from the letters she was sending her sisters, Alice and Mary. She did not step back to comment on the momentous nature of the new undertaking or share her fears or doubts. Instead she filled her correspondence with news of past and future meetings and the names of people she met and the organizations she visited. Already she was fully absorbed in the work.

The plan had become more specific. She and Ellen wanted Toynbee Hall, with its classes and clubs, to be their model, and they had embraced the Barnetts' theory that the classes could benefit each other. But they had also decided that their settlement would be "very unlike its English prototype" in certain ways.[1] Three differences were already obvious, all of them adaptations due to circumstance.

First, their settlement would specialize in working with immigrants. As Addams later put it, she "found no precedent at Toynbee Hall for dealing with foreign life." Toynbee had immigrant neighbors, to be sure, but in modest proportions. In 1888 about 24 percent of the people of Whitechapel were immigrants. By contrast, Chicago's one million people were, remarkably, 78 percent foreign-born or the children of the foreign-born. More than half of Chicago's immigrants, who tended to concentrate in certain neighborhoods, came from northern and central Europe (Germany, Ireland, England, Scotland, and Sweden), but a rising proportion came from eastern and southern Europe (Poland, Bohemia, Italy, and Russia). The immigrants of greatest interest to Addams and Starr were the Germans and Italians because Jane and Ellen spoke those languages, had visited those countries, and had studied their cultures, both as tourists and as students of literature. Addams had read Goethe's *Faust* and Virgil's *Aeneid*, Carlyle's *Frederick the Great* and George Eliot's *Romola*. She had wintered in Berlin one year and in Rome another.[2]

Second, Addams and Starr were women, and they expected other women to join them. Indeed, Addams would soon make the case in recruiting speeches that women were particularly suited to improving cross-class social ties since they had traditionally taken responsibility for social matters.[3] The argument, which was historical, not essentialist, was one a skilled rhetorician would make but, given Addams's difficulties in finding a life that did not violate what was expected of her as a woman, it seems likely that she believed it.

Third, the new settlement would embrace what Addams thought of as the "western American" approach to class. While visiting Toynbee Hall she had been unimpressed, she writes in *Twenty Years*, by the "involved and roundabout" way that "class-conscious Englishmen" stressed the necessity of reconnecting with "the people." This argument struck her as "artificial."[4] She felt distinctly superior to the British in the matter of social equality.

Other differences with Toynbee Hall were still murky. "I've been writing a good deal about the scheme this week," Addams wrote Mary Addams Linn on February 26, "to clarify my own mind." Starr was comfortable with Addams serving as the project's conceptualizer. Jane "has done the thinking," she wrote her sister Mary Starr Blaisdell the same week, "although she resents my putting myself out of it in any . . . way. Still I am unwilling to let people suppose that I would ever have worked it out."[5]

Ellen's letter to her sister was no ordinary missive, but a long explanation about the friends' plans that they asked Blaisdell to circulate among members of both their families.[6] Ellen wrote it because, as she explained in the letter, she wanted to save Jane from the tiring effort, but she stressed repeatedly that the ideas were Jane's. The result was a document that approximately captured Addams's frame of mind in the months before she and Starr launched their experiment.

Ellen reviewed the basics. They would rent a house or a flat in a neighborhood with a good many German, Italian, and French immigrants, "furnish it prettily, . . . put [up] all our pictures, . . . and live there." They hoped, she added, that eventually as many as six young women might stay with them "for a season," paying for their bed and board. Jane would rent the house, provide the furnishings, and underwrite her own costs of living and part of Ellen's; Ellen would earn some income by teaching at the Kirkland School part-time. (The plan would soon change. In the fall Ellen would find her new life so absorbing that she would quit Kirkland; for the rest of her working life she would live on a tight budget, scrambling to piece together enough income by tutoring, lecturing, and teaching part-time.)[7]

The letter went on to explain what they were trying to accomplish. At the settlement, Ellen wrote, they and other residents were "to learn to know the people and understand them and their way of life; to give them what [we] have to give out of [our] culture and leisure and over-indulgence and to receive the culture that comes of self-denial and poverty and failure, which these people have always known." It was not exactly the Toynbee Hall approach. The Barnetts did not admire working people for their culture of self-denial and failure. Where did these ideas come from? The words did not describe objective reality. People living in or near poverty endured scarcity; they were not like monks, practicing self-denial. Nor, with some exceptions, did they see their lives as full of failure; rather, as Addams would later learn, they saw them as full of adversity.[8] These ideas, in fact, came from her own imagination; they reflected her inner reality. It was Addams who would be practicing self-denial at the settlement, and it was Addams who saw her life as full of failure.

Ellen's letter is silent on interesting points. Their Christian faith was certainly an important motive for both of them, but Ellen mentions it only to say that Jane was wary of the temptation it offered to feel benevolently superior. "Jane feels," Ellen noted, "that it is not the Christian spirit to go among these people as if you were bringing them a great boon." The words resonate with the Barnetts' teachings. The Barnetts' influence can also be seen in Jane and Ellen's decision to meet right away with the city's leading social Christian Protestant ministers. In her letter, Ellen names several of them and notes with pride that one thought their scheme "distinctly Christian."[9]

Ellen was also silent about their desire to do good. This, like their underplaying of the Christian motive, was a studied effect. Addams and Starr believed that it was a fine thing to bring culture and sociability to working people's lives, but they avoided claiming the moral high ground. As Ellen explained, the men at Toynbee Hall dismissed the idea that they were being noble or making any sacrifice. The extent to which this silence was a camouflage was revealed a few months later, when Addams gave a speech to Rockford alumnae. As she described the aspirations of the rising generation, her old devotion to selflessness leaked through. Young people, she said, yearn to "confirm by the deed those dreams of sacrifice and un-selfish devotion of which [their] heads are full."[10]

Also missing from the letter was any intention to provide charity to neighbors who needed it, that is, to aid the weak and suffering. The pro-vision of charity also was too embarrassing to admit, because it implied moral goodness on their part. Instead, Starr and Addams preferred to em-phasize not only that both classes would gain from mutual relations—the Barnetts' message—but that those of the upper middle class would gain more. "Jane's idea," Ellen wrote, "which she . . . on no account will give up, is that [the settlement house] is more for the benefit of the people who do it than for the other class." Her goal, Starr continued, was "simply to make life more worth living" for herself and for other frustrated young people.[11] Behind Addams's intensity on this point lay both the pain of her recent experiences and a desire to avoid the charge of arrogance.

The most personal part of Ellen's letter deals with her own desire to help her former students find meaningful activity. She felt "pity" for girls, she wrote, especially rich girls, who had "nothing in the world to do." She had seen their mothers discourage them from doing something to help the "less fortunate." She and Jane hoped that if they could offer a "safe" place, at least a few mothers would relent and allow their daughters to come.

The letter casts only a small amount of light on perhaps the most well-thought-out and defining aspect of their plan: the three ethical principles that were explicit in Addams's early writings about the settlement and were part of the philosophy of Toynbee Hall. These were to teach by example, to practice cooperation, and to practice social democracy, that is, egalitarian, or democratic, social relations across class lines. All were grounded in the need to respect every human being, and none was individually new to Starr or Addams, but when adopted in systematic and conscious fashion they amounted to a new ethic of human relations for them. This settlement ethic was meant to guide not only their plans but also the ways they related to people at every moment of their day. In time they hoped other residents of the settlement also would practice this ethic. In adopting it, Addams and Starr were setting the bar high.

Starr attended most directly to the principle of teaching by example, that is, the conscious use of personal influence. She endorsed it emphati-cally: "[A] personality is the only thing that touches anybody." Because the residents at Toynbee Hall came to know people, she explained, "the thing

Ellen Gates Starr. Jane Addams
Memorial Collection (JAMC neg.
3566), Special Collections, The
University Library, University of
Illinois at Chicago.

spreads; it's an influence." Addams echoed the point when she told an in-terested reporter that they intended to "teach by example."[12]

As to the kind of example Addams wished to embody, around this time she settled on the ideal of the grandmother. Why? She had not known either of her own grandmothers. Nor did she have an interest in the stereotypical grandmother's skills at being a housekeeper, wife, and mother. Instead, she was drawn to the grandmother's quality of emotional engagement. "I gradually reached a conviction," she writes in *Twenty Years*, "that the first generation of college women had . . . departed too suddenly from the ac-tive, emotional life led by their grandmothers and great-grandmothers."[13]

Addams's choice of the grandmother as her new hero seems peculiar at first glance. Her earlier female heroes, Isis, Athena, and Cassandra, were women with world-shaping powers; the grandmother was a kitchen god-dess. She governed only the family and the neighborhood, traditional fe-male territory. And the timing of Addams's change in tastes was also pecu-liar. Why did she embrace this small-scale female hero just when she was making peace with her drive to power and feeling a greater willingness to unleash it, just when she was acknowledging her desire for public influ-ence instead of denying it? One answer is that the grandmother embodied the quality of intuition that she had found so appealing in college. Although the scope of the grandmother's influence was easy for Addams to accomplish, the intuitiveness—the warm, spontaneous affection—was not. For the cerebral Addams, being a grandmother type was a challenge. Another aspect of the grandmother's appeal was that hers was an old-fashioned female role. She gave Addams's bold deed of starting a settlement house acceptable cover, in her own eyes if no one else's. Addams's admiration for the grandmother was one more sign that her gender identity was a continuing conundrum.

The second principle of their settlement philosophy was the easily blended ethics of cooperation and nonresistance. Addams would write in 1892 that the first residents began with the conviction that "it would be a foolish and unwarranted expenditure of force to oppose or to antagonize any individual or set of people in the neighborhood." They intended to "live with opposition to no man, with recognition of the good in every man, even the meanest." In order to do this, she explained, the residents "must be emptied of . . . all self-assertion and be ready to arouse and interpret the public opinion of their neighborhood. They must be content to . . . grow into a sense of relationship and mutual interests." A few years later she would write, "The design of the settlement is . . . co-operation with all good which it finds in its neighborhood."[14] This ethic involved a daily discipline of working on other people's needs, agendas, and projects. A key tenet of Christian socialism and of the Barnetts' method, cooperation was idealism in action, because it implicitly denied the salience or power of material forms of selfishness. It forebore. Addams would find many ways to practice it. Teaching by example was one way, but there would be others.

The third ethical principle was egalitarian or democratic social relations with all classes. Starr and Addams intended to treat everyone with equal courtesy, regardless of their wealth, poverty, influence, state of cleanliness, English skills, mental acumen, skin color, ethnicity, social status, or level of education. This etiquette, in addition to being that of their "western American" childhoods, was the etiquette of the early Christians and of the Barnetts. It was grounded in the belief, as Matthew Arnold put it, that "men are made equal . . . by the humanity of their manners."[15] Of course, their education had also supplied them with an inner sense of entitlement and superiority. Did a cultured social Christian love the flawed human being or consider the imperfect inferior? This familiar dilemma would continue to haunt Starr and Addams in their new settlement life.

It is crucial to understand the depth of Addams's commitment to these three principles. In 1888–89 she made a conscious decision to embrace them; henceforth they defined what having integrity, or character, would mean to her. She would not always live up to them, but she would always come back to them as the standards against which she measured herself. She thought when she moved to Chicago that she understood what "teaching by example," "cooperation," and "social democracy" meant. Words are like that—easily invoked before their meaning is fully fathomed.

Beyond theories, Addams and Starr brought other resources to the project. Ellen knew "girls," both as a type and in the sense that she knew particular girls who might join them. In previous years she also had visited most of the leading Protestant churches and was therefore in touch with the social Christian movement in the city.[16] Jane brought administrative talent, which was first evident at seminary when she ran the campus magazine and had been president of her class and of her literary society. Her gift for execution would blossom when she had a whole settlement house to run.

She also brought the most obviously crucial resource: money. It is difficult to imagine Jane Addams starting a settlement house without it. To live in Chicago, she would have needed a job, which would have filled much of her time. Indeed, at first work was forcing Starr to miss some of their appointments. Addams, thanks to her inheritance, was able to invest all her resources—her energy, time, money, and considerable creativity—to advancing the settlement plan. Also, Addams's independent income freed them from having to fundraise immediately and from the economic pressure to affiliate their project with another organization. Although they explored collaborating with several churches, they eventually decided the project would be freestanding. This in turn allowed them to choose a neighborhood rather than have the decision made for them by a sponsoring group.[17]

Although Ellen's resources were helpful, by the early months of 1889 it was clear that Jane, because of her theoretical and financial contributions and her ability to concentrate all her time on the project, was the leader in their uneven partnership. At first she was uncomfortable in the role and tried to keep up the fiction that things were equal, as is evident in Ellen's remark that Jane resented her taking lesser credit for conceiving the project. Jane also tried to share the administrative tasks. In June she wrote Ellen apologizing that she had written a letter to someone "after entrusting the affair to you." But it is not likely that Ellen minded. As her niece later remembered, "While an enlivener and an inspirer, Ellen Gates Starr had no slightest capacity for administration." Jane and others close to the settlement would always describe Ellen as the co-founder of Hull House, but from the beginning Ellen saw her theoretical and administrative roles, accurately and without resentment, as secondary.[18]

Chicago was the obvious location for the new settlement because Ellen was well-established there and it was the largest city in their native state. Still, the decision was crucial. In 1889 Chicago was no ordinary metropolis but the second largest city in the United States and sixth largest in the world.[19] Economically, socially, and politically, it was a dynamo. Starr and Addams had seized a roaring bull by the tail.

The most striking dimensions of the city were its vibrant economy and the intense forces that were shaping it. Chicago in 1889 was a major manufacturing and agricultural business center. Its meatpacking, liquor, steel and iron, clothing, railroad car, and agricultural machinery industries were thriving. In addition, massive amounts of wheat and lumber passed through its markets. Its economy depended on the twenty-one railway lines (the most in the nation) that converged on its six major railroad stations. It was also one of nation's the largest ports. In 1888 the Port of Chicago had more arrivals and clearances (twenty-two thousand) than the ports of Baltimore, Boston, Philadelphia, New Orleans, Portland, Falmouth, and San Francisco combined. For all these reasons, the city was rich with jobs. In 1890 there were 360,000 census-counted wage-earners (and probably many more were missed by government tabulators).[20]

Not surprisingly, Chicago's personality as a city was dominated by its economic ambition. The streets were full of people rushing about making and spending money, as foreign visitors were quick to notice. The famous Polish pianist Stanislaw Paderewski recalled that Chicago's atmosphere in 1891 was one of "intense competition, of continuous effort, and of speed— speed, speed, speed." British men of letters were offended. Matthew Arnold, visiting in 1884, thought the city "too beastly prosperous." Rudyard Kipling declared after his 1889 visit, "I urgently desire never to see it again. It is inhabited by savages." The comment of H. G. Wells was the most insightful. Chicago, he wrote, "is the most perfect presentation of nineteenth-century individualist industrialism I have ever seen."[21]

As Chicago produced jobs, it attracted workers, including immigrants in large numbers. This led to an oversupply of labor, which led to cutthroat wage and employment practices and great poverty, especially among the 29 percent of the city's workforce that was unskilled. Whereas unskilled workers were difficult to organize, those with skills, about 39 percent of the workforce, increasingly turned to unions to improve their situation, despite employer resistance. The labor movement also contained workers drawn to the anticapitalist ideologies of Marxian socialism and of anarchism; societies promoting these ideas had proliferated in Chicago in the 1880s.[22] The city's intense materiality and divisive labor situation would present Addams and Starr with many challenges.

Perhaps the circumstance—it was not really a choice—that would shape their work the most was their settlement's location in a nation that, by the 1880s, defined itself proudly as a democracy. This was new. Earlier in the century, democracy had been the workingman's cry; the propertied classes and upper middle classes considered the word a synonym for "mob rule" and rule by "faction." But as the categories of men who could vote kept broadening, a wider range of public opinion began to pay democracy homage. Although even in the 1870s "universal" (that is, male) suffrage seemed a doubtful proposition to many "mugwump" intellectuals and politicians, by 1889, influential northeastern magazines were writing of democracy as a central American value.[23] Jane Addams's own turn toward democracy as an inspiring ideal in the mid-1880s no doubt owed something to this wider cultural shift.

The belief that the nation was unified in its commitment to democracy was actually a charming conceit. The idea of democracy in 1889 was hotly contested ideological territory, a chameleon whose colors shifted easily according to its placement in an argument. Ideas about democracy were used both to justify and to undercut the status quo. By the late 1880s, democracy had become the battleground on which other disputes were being fought.

Democracy's first meaning was political power bestowed by the right to vote. In the north in 1889 the franchise was restricted to men, including, in most states, male immigrants who generally could vote after being in residence six months, or less if they had declared their intention to become citizens. In the south, where suffrage had been extended to African American men in the 1860s and 1870s, poll taxes, literacy tests, and targeted violence were beginning to narrow the franchise to white men again. In the north, resistance to voting by male immigrants was also mounting. They were thought too ignorant, too corruptible, or too non-Christian to be good voting citizens.[24] And women were excluded from participating in this first meaning of democracy altogether.

Democracy's second meaning was economic. Among individualists of the sort that John Addams had been, it meant the freedom of the individual to act in his own best interest, to compete, to obey no one but himself. As Abraham Lincoln famously put it, "As I would not be a slave, so I would not be a master. This expresses my idea of democracy." It was on these grounds that employers called labor unions antidemocratic, because they restricted the employer's competitive freedom. But this meaning was contested. Although most Marxists and anarchists rejected democracy altogether, socialists were ambivalent. Some, like Edward Bellamy, liked to define democracy as public control over the means of production. Trade unionists and their supporters believed that the idea gave workers a mandate to gain a voice in the workplace. Some workers and their supporters thought democracy meant eventual equality of resources. One was a young, radical, pro-labor philosophy professor at the University of Michigan, John Dewey, who would soon come to teach at the University of Chicago. He argued in an 1888 essay for the necessity of a "democracy of wealth."[25]

Democracy's third meaning was social. In the 1870s and 1880s, social commentators promoted democracy as a "sentiment," a feeling, of equality among people from all walks of life. Henry Carter Adams, a colleague and friend of John Dewey's at the University of Michigan, observed in 1881, "Harsh class relations are out of harmony with democratic conceptions." Dewey worked Adams's point into a grander theory in the same 1888 essay, writing, "Democracy is a social, that is to say, an ethical conception." When Jane Addams and Ellen Starr embraced egalitarian social relations as a key ethic of their new settlement, they were situating themselves within a familiar American cultural map. This is not to say that everyone liked the idea of social democracy. Lydia White, the author of *Success in Society*, an 1889 etiquette book, was a reluctant practitioner. She complained in its pages, "We are all forced, in spite of individual objections and protests, to put into practice the national theory of equality. We must mix together, and it therefore behooves us . . . to make the mixture as smooth and as agreeable as possible."[26]

In sum, democracy's contradictions were fully present in Chicago in 1889. Social democracy was fervently believed in but virtually absent in social life; economic democracy was either thriving or thwarted, depending on one's point of view; political democracy was already achieved or sadly lacking, again depending on one's point of view. Henceforth, Chicago would be Jane Addams's city, and she would become deeply engaged in its tempestuous public life. Unavoidably, its social tensions and confused democratic aspirations would determine her obstacles and shape her agenda.

Addams and Starr undertook their first few months' appointments, conversations, teas, interviews, and presentations in Chicago with confidence. This confidence was grounded in their theory that actions springing from an unselfish commitment to ideals would inevitably draw support. They believed, Addams writes in *Twenty Years*, that the "disinterested action" of starting a settlement was "like truth or beauty" in its attractiveness. Addams called this belief her "theory of universal goodwill," but it was really another manifestation of her belief in the theory of idealism.[27] She had endorsed it somewhat schematically in "Bellerophon" and in her valedictory speech; later she had seen its theoretical implications in the positivists' prediction of mankind's shining future and seen its practical implications in the work of the Barnetts at Toynbee Hall. A trust in the power of ideals was the faith of the age; it provided the bedrock for middle- and upper-class Victorian moral confidence in progress and the concomitant view that those with the advantage of education—presumed to be the source of ideals—could do no wrong.

At first, the theory seemed well proved by the response Addams and Starr received from Chicago's Protestant philanthropic and social reform communities, who warmly welcomed them and their new project. But this reception was not because, as the theory held, the two women's purposes were thought to be selfless but because their project was familiar. Organizations in Chicago similar to settlement houses were already attempting to address the "social problem" of the wide gap between rich and poor by similar means. These organizations were the independent nondenominational missions and the institutional churches. Like Toynbee Hall, they were located in working-class neighborhoods and devoted to the needs of working people; they also provided places where middle-class volunteers or paid staff could live. They offered kindergartens, boys' clubs, reading rooms, vocational training, free medical dispensaries, and gymnasiums.[28]

Two features set Toynbee Hall and Addams's and Starr's new settlement apart from these organizations: the focus on offering "high" culture—literature and the arts—to workers and their families and the refusal to offer religious instruction.[29] To those involved in the mission and institutional church movements, the first was merely innocuous; the second was shocking.

Sometime in the spring of 1889, if not earlier, Addams and Starr decided not to offer Protestant Christian education or seek to convert people who came to the settlement. Beyond the influence of Toynbee Hall's example, Addams was determined that they not set themselves in opposition to the Catholic and Jewish families likely to be their neighbors. At bottom, however, the decision reflected both Addams's dislike for proselytization and her view of Jesus Christ as a model to imitate, not a personal savior. In the coming years, her devotion to Christ as a teacher would never flag. (She would, however, be careful to mention him only to appropriate audiences.)[30]

In their letters, Jane and Ellen gave no inkling that they were worried about the possible consequences of their decision not to be missionaries for Christ. If they were not, they should have been. Many in Chicago's conservative evangelical community, though initially intrigued, would eventually prove severe critics of the new settlement once they understood its nonproselytizing nature. Addams wrote in 1934 that when the settlement house opened, "it encountered much criticism on the . . . ground that it was not a mission," although she and Starr were at pains to explain that they "were trying to serve God." At one point, a perplexed writer for an evangelical Christian paper would observe of Addams, "I don't quite understand her religious position. She seems to be a Christian without religion."[31]

By contrast, the reception of the settlement proposal among nonevangelical Protestant women was warm and remained so. The Chicago Woman's Club, in particular, was happy to take the two young women under its wing.[32] Founded in 1876, the club had four hundred members in 1889 and was committed to "the general good and progress of the community."[33] Its agenda included not only encouraging the pursuit of cultural enrichment and domestic skills but also philanthropy and social reform. In 1889 the members of the club were all white and, aside from a few Jewish members, Christian. The classes mingled to a degree. Members included the extremely rich, such as Bertha Honoré Palmer, doctors such as Sarah Hackett Stevenson, lawyers, and teachers.[34] Addams and Starr made a presentation to the Philanthropy Committee in February that was a great success and opened many doors. On April 10, 1889, they were elected to club membership and were soon giving recruitment speeches at various receptions organized by members. Addams titled her speech "Toynbee Hall and Its Offshoots." It was the first of many versions.[35]

But attracting women was not enough. Addams also wanted men to join as residents and volunteers. (It is not clear that Starr was as committed as Addams was to this aspect of the plan.) After one reception, Addams wrote her sister Mary, "More than half [of those attending] were men so our whilom [former] fear re [becoming a] home for single women [is] allayed."[36] Addams had apparently been impressed with the Barnetts' belief that men as volunteers and residents could model political citizenship to voters in the neighborhood. Of course, male volunteers could also lead the boys' and men's clubs. In time, men would take on all these roles at the new settlement.

In the campaign to spread the word, Addams and Starr attended carefully to the newspapers. The first article about the scheme was published in the *Chicago Tribune* on March 8, 1889, after Addams had been in town only a month. "A Project to Bring the Rich and Poor Closer Together," the small headline on page 8 announced. The reporter ignored the settlement's educational and social purposes, calling the proposed settlement "an interesting departure in humanitarian work . . . proposed by a young lady of independent means and generous culture."[37] Jane Addams received the credit for conceiving of it, as Starr wished.

This first piece was typical of the flood that would soon follow. In the years to come, reporters would generally stress Hull House's benevolent or charitable aspects, perhaps because these fit their middle-class readership's expectations of why two upper-middle-class women would have anything to do with those "beneath" them in social rank. News stories also tended to sentimentalize the women, emphasizing their noble sacrifices for the sake of others. This emphasis had more to do with the changing culture of newspaper reporting and developing tastes of readers than with how Addams and Starr represented their work. Newspapers had just discovered their role as popular entertainers in the early 1890s, and the result was a flood of sensationalist and overly dramatic reporting. Addams, Starr, and their settlement house were good copy.[38]

Addams and Starr may have thought they were founding the first settlement house in the United States, but as early as February 1889 they learned that other young American women had similar plans. Someone gave them a printed circular about a group of alumnae from the seven sister colleges in the east (Smith, Wellesley, Vassar, Bryn Mawr, Mount Holyoke, Radcliffe,

Jane Addams, ca. 1890. Jane Addams Memorial Collection (JAMC neg. 518), Special Collections, The University Library, University of Illinois at Chicago.

and Barnard) who had formed the College Settlement Association (CSA), which was planning to open a settlement house in New York City.[39]

Addams tried to deal with the news in a spirit of cooperative Christian fellowship. She sent a letter to Jane Fine, the person organizing the New York City settlement, describing the Chicago effort and asking how Fine's was progressing. Still, Addams could not entirely suppress her feelings of competitiveness. She sent the CSA circular to her sister Mary with the comment, "We are modest enough to think ours is better, is more distinctively Christian and less social science." The College Settlement would open on New York's lower east side two weeks after Addams and Starr opened theirs, and Fine would visit the Chicago settlement the following year.[40]

Ellen, writing about the New York settlement in her February letter and feeling equally competitive, identified two other key differences. The New York settlement was to take only college women as residents (Addams and Starr had decided not to restrict eligibility by education). Second, it "intended to be an 'organization.'" She and Jane had no such intentions for their settlement. This was the flipside of the point Ellen had made more directly elsewhere in the letter: that they would seek to achieve influence through their personalities. Not being an organization would become a kind of mantra to them, signifying the informal, creative, spontaneous, natural life they wished to lead and the centrality of human relationships to their work. In the early years, they would refuse to own buildings or land, believing that it would lead to "rigidity of method." Even after Addams had responsibility for running a thirteen-building institution, her friend Frances Perkins recalled her as being "uninterested in organization for its own sake." For years she refused to raise money for an endowment for the settlement, seeing the lack of one as a strength.[41] What interested her always was the power of personality.

Of course, they knew that from the world's point of view their settlement would look like (and, indeed, be) an organization and that it would need to establish ties with other organizations in the city. Addams put in much time that spring building such ties. In addition to reaching out to Christian groups, she sought out secular ones. In March she gave a talk about the scheme to the Illinois Woman's Alliance, the most politically ambitious women's organization in the city. Six months old, it was a cross-class coalition of twenty-five organizations, most run by and for women, ranging from labor unions to temperance and suffrage societies. Men's organizations such as the Chicago Trade Labor Assembly could join by sending women delegates. Founded and led by the union organizer Elizabeth Morgan and the educator Corrine S. Brown, it brought together working-class, middle-class, and upper-class women, including African American women, to address a broad list of women workers' concerns, from proper working conditions for women and children to city sanitation, health standards, teacher salaries, compulsory education, free public baths, homelessness, and child truancy.[42] Addams left no record of her impressions of this remarkable group. Her path would cross the IWA's again.

During the same month Addams arranged to attend an anarchist Sunday school where two hundred children, mainly those of German immigrant parents, were instructed in the importance of thinking freely, without the influence "of either religion or politics," as she explained in a letter to Mary Addams Linn. The anarchists she visited were "individualists" who, unlike the "communistic" type, were passionate about personal freedom. Ellen, perhaps puzzled by this radical enthusiasm, wrote dryly to Mary Starr Blaisdell, "Jane . . . thirsts very much for the Anarchists."[43]

In pursuing them, Addams was apparently untroubled by the fact that they and the evangelical Christians in the city viewed each other with deep suspicion, if not hatred. She had been teaching Sunday school on Wednesday nights to a group of boys at the evangelical Moody Institute since arriving in Chicago; now she was discussing teaching a Sunday school class for the anarchists.[44] Presumably she did not tell the anarchists of her ties to Moody Institute. Her simultaneous embrace of both groups is early evidence of her eclectic, nonbinary intellect and her determination to be cooperative, not oppositional. Each group would have been horrified to be associated with the other, but Addams was happy having a foot in each camp.

Choosing a neighborhood to live in was the most pressing task Addams and Starr faced. Almost from the moment Addams had arrived in Chicago, she had been visiting possible " 'slums,' " as she wrote in a letter to Mary. She put the word in quotation marks to acknowledge it as a slang expression for a "low and dangerous neighborhood."[45] Their intention to live in such a neighborhood, also mentioned in Ellen's circulating letter, was perhaps the thing about their plan that most worried their friends and family. People had warned them that they would become ill from the unsanitary conditions and be the targets of criminals. Addams and Starr staunchly dismissed such fears as ridiculous. Once we are there, Ellen wrote, "people [will] see that we don't catch diseases and that vicious people do not destroy us or our property."[46]

Throughout March and April they searched out the immigrant neighborhoods with many Germans and Italians, those on the North and South Sides. The neighborhood they finally chose, however, was on the West Side, in the city's Nineteenth Ward. The 527-acre ward, which lay just west of the city's downtown and was divided by Halsted Street and bordered on the west by Throop Street and on the east by the Chicago River, was home to 44,380 people. The inhabitants east of Halsted Street were nearly all immigrants: southern Italians and Germans but also Irish, Polish and Russian Jews, Bohemians, French Canadians, English, and others; eighteen nationalities altogether were represented. Scattered across the ward were 120 "colored," the catch-all term the U.S. Bureau of the Census used for "Negroes, Chinese, Japanese, and civilized Indians." The number of "Negroes" living in the ward is not broken out; however, an 1893 residential pattern map of the half of the ward east of Halsted Street reveals that two were living in that section at the time. According to the bureau, about 13 percent of the ward's population was "native-born" (by which was meant "noncolored") with "native-born" parents.[47] (At the time most of Chicago's African Americans, who made up 1.8 percent of the city's population, lived on the South Side.) On the ward's southern edge of Twelfth Street was the large Bohemian (Czech) community of Pilsen.[48]

The choice of the Nineteenth Ward was daring. People of Starr and Addams's class lived mostly on the North and South Sides and viewed the West Side as the exotic other, an unexplored, darkly threatening place, indeed, as a slum. In fact, the ward *was* exotic to the upper middle class, although perhaps not in the way they supposed. Manufacturing establishments of every size and description, with their accompanying smells, waste products, and noise, were scattered among the ward's small houses, apartment buildings, and tenements. The leather, metalworking, paper box, cigar, garment, printing, woodworking, glass, and candy industries were the most numerous.[49] This was a working neighborhood, where people's jobs were close to where they lived.

With the neighborhood chosen, Addams and Starr searched for a house or apartment to rent. Addams, riding in a carriage down Halsted Street one day with a new friend, Allen Pond, the assistant superintendent at the Armour Mission (and later a successful architect), saw what looked like the ideal house: a two-story red brick structure standing between a saloon and an undertaker's parlor. Addams described it in *Twenty Years* as "a fine old house standing well back from the street, surrounded on three sides by a broad piazza [that] was supported by wooden pillars of exceptionally pure Corinthian design and proportion."[50]

The elegant house had a misplaced look. Built in 1856 as a country residence on the edge of the city, its gracious Italianate style did not match the ugly industrial neighborhood that had grown up around it. The house had been constructed, Addams soon learned, by Charles J. Hull, a real estate developer and philanthropist. For decades his first cousin, the businesswoman Helen Culver, had managed his extensive real estate holdings, worth $3 million, in Chicago and around the country, including much land in the Nineteenth Ward. When Addams discovered the house, Hull had just died and Culver had just inherited his estate.[51] Investigating, Addams and Starr learned that the house was not empty. A school furniture factory was renting half of the first floor for storage space. But the second floor was available, as was the first-floor drawing room. Culver told them that the factory's lease would end in March 1890, at which time Starr and Addams could rent the rest of the first floor.[52]

The house had many features to delight the cultured. It had a wide double front door, tall first-floor windows, and high ceilings. The drawing room was large, running the length of the house. A handsome curved and cantilevered staircase dominated the front hall. There were ornate cornices over the doorways, rope pattern casings for the doorframes, and marble fireplaces, several of which were sculpted in the same rope pattern. Delighted to have found such a beautiful house, Addams signed an agreement with Helen Culver on May 16 to rent three-quarters of the house for $60 a month, beginning in September.[53]

That summer Addams paid $1,000 to have the second floor, which had five rooms, and drawing room spruced up under Allen Pond's supervision. New doors and windows were installed, the floors were repaired and polished, and the halls and rooms painted—upstairs in terra cotta tints, downstairs in ivory and gold. Addams also paid for a new roof for the piazza. In exchange, Helen Culver promised a new furnace.[54] Jane and Ellen now had not only an address and a neighborhood but a home that, like Toynbee Hall, embodied the love of culture they hoped to inspire in their new neighbors.

Leaving Pond to supervise, the friends departed Chicago to see family. Jane visited Anna, George, Weber, and Laura in Cedarville and the Linns in Genesco, where Alice was also visiting. In all these visits, she sought her family's support for her startling project. The response was mixed. Her two sisters stood by her. Weber's views are unknown. George was doubtful, and Harry Haldeman thought the plan "sentimental and futile." Anna did not like the plan. She was still furious with Jane and in coming years would refuse to make donations to the settlement. She was angry that Jane had refused to marry George, angry that Jane had moved to Chicago and a new life, and, worst of all, she continued to blame Jane for George's collapse into invalidism, his care being the cross of her old age.[55]

In other ways, too, the gap between Jane and Anna was widening. As of 1889, Jane considered her home to be with Mary in Genesco. Letters between Anna and her would become less frequent; in the summer of 1889 or soon afterward, she began staying with Weber and Laura on her visits to Cedarville and spending her Christmases in Chicago. At first Addams tried to bridge the divide with letters that received no response and invitations to visit that were ignored. Eventually she accepted the situation,

Hull House, interior view, first floor. The Jane Addams Papers Project, Fayetteville, NC.

seeing Anna when she came to Cedarville but not otherwise trying to stay in touch. Anna's estrangement from her stepdaughter would last more than a decade.[56]

On June 18, while Addams was in northern Illinois, the other Anna in her life, Anna Sill, died. She had retired as principal of Rockford Seminary in 1884 but still lived on campus. The Alumnae Association, already on campus for commencement and its annual meeting, quickly organized a memorial service. Addams, who had been named a trustee of the seminary the previous year, not because of her postgraduate accomplishments, which were nil, but because of her wealth, was asked to speak.[57] She delivered her remarks in the familiar space of seminary chapel.

As she had done so often before, she spoke on the subject then absorbing her thoughts, presenting it as if it were of general interest. Everyone studies institutions, she claimed. "We are all . . . constantly looking for . . . the meaning of an institution." It is supplied, she argued, by a "moral purpose" that "represent[s] the strong convictions of at least one person[.]"

When an institution is young, it will "always . . . struggle with doubt and self-distrust before its friends learn to believe in it and allow it to assert itself."[58] Apparently Addams was drawing courage from Anna Sill's example in her efforts to fend off skeptics and her own self-doubts.

On September 19 Addams and Starr, along with a housekeeper, a young woman named Mary Keyser who had worked for Jane's sister Mary in Genesco, moved into the splendidly restored Hull mansion.[59] Addams remembered their excitement: "Probably no young matron ever placed her own things in her own house with more pleasure than that with which we first furnished" Hull House.[60] Their "things" included chairs, a bookcase, and a writing desk Jane had brought from Cedarville, a piano, a sideboard given by a Chicago friend, and a new oak dining room table and chairs Jane had bought.[61] On the freshly painted walls they hung framed photographs, lithographs, drawings of the cathedrals of Europe, a copy of Jean François Millet's painting *Woman Feeding Her Children*, and portraits of Addams's intellectual mentors, George Eliot, Ralph Waldo Emerson, and Thomas Carlyle.[62]

They also felt ready intellectually. Addams would later explain that to undertake life in a settlement house, you must "provide yourself with the necessary ideas."[63] This preparation had been the work of her late teens and twenties. She had embraced idealism, equipped herself with a knowledge of culture, trained her imagination, and decided to teach by example, to work cooperatively, and to practice egalitarian etiquette. She was ready to do as she later advised others to do: "[H]ook yourself fast with your whole mind to your neighborhood, [as you] live in social relations with the people among whom your life is cast."[64] Her aspirations to warm grandmotherliness notwithstanding, her intellect, as usual, was in charge.

CHAPTER 9

HALSTED STREET

1889–91

Addams and Starr awoke the morning after moving in—it was a Thursday—to the workaday sounds of Halsted Street. These started early; the street was, in Addams's words, "one of the great thoroughfares of Chicago." Straight as a rod and thirty-two miles long, it was a major north-south artery and, in the six-mile section closest to downtown, the business district for the West Side. The sounds of commerce filled the street, which was lined with butcher shops, clothing and grocery stores, and numerous saloons. Peddlers and newsboys shouted, shoppers' feet drummed on boardwalks, and streetcar bells clanged. A steady stream of wagons and carriages rumbled and rattled up and down the street to the clatter of horses' hooves hitting wooden pavement, for unlike some streets in the neighborhood, Halsted Street was paved.[1]

If the windows were open, then the smells of Halsted Street also came wafting in, intensely pungent in the warm weather of mid-September. Those smells—of rotting food, animal carcasses, spilled beer, and human and animal waste—mingled in an indescribable mélange of aromas. Stinking refuse was a serious problem in the Nineteenth Ward. Garbage piled up because the city emptied the ward's large wooden garbage boxes too infrequently. When the boxes were full, the garbage went into the streets, where, pressed down over time, it became part of the pavement. The Sanitation Department was supposed to remove the animal bodies and waste but often did not. The human waste was in the streets because the usual systems were not working. Most houses were not connected to the city sewer system. Outhouses were used during the day, but chamber pots were popular at night; their contents were dumped in the streets every morning. At night, big black rats scurried about, dining out in the dark streets and alleys.[2]

And then there were the dirt (omnipresent because most of the streets and alleys were unpaved) and the soot. The latter was a problem all over the city. "The [factories] vomit dense clouds of bituminous coal smoke," one visitor to Chicago reported, "so that one can scarcely see across the streets on a damp day."[3] The air was particularly freighted on the industrial West Side. Keeping a house clean in the Nineteenth Ward was an hourly enterprise.

These things any casual visitor to Halsted Street could notice; other conditions were less obvious without inspection. The housing stock, neglected by its absentee landlords, was inadequate in every way. In most of the neighborhood's numerous small wooden cottages, each built to house a single family, several families lived together to make the rent affordable. Families also lived above the stables at the rears of these lots. Generally everyone on the lot shared the faucet and the outhouse in the backyard. The few tenement buildings in the ward offered tenants plumbing but also the added unpleasantness of dingy courtyards, poor airflow, and greater darkness. Disease spread across the ward easily because of the overcrowding, lack of plumbing, lack of ventilation, and rotting waste. Tuberculosis, typhoid fever, and other illnesses were common, and the death rate among babies and children was high.[4]

These were dismal living conditions. What did Addams and Starr, as new residents of the ward, think of them? A glimmer of their response appears in a letter Jane wrote to George Haldeman two months after moving in: "One is so overpowered by the misery . . . of so large a number of city people that the wonder is that conscientious people can let it alone."[5] But this is one of the few references either she or Ellen made in an early letter regarding the suffering around them.

Part of their silence may be chalked up to discretion. Given their families' fears about life in a "slum," why alarm them with reports of rats and dead horse carcasses? But part reflected their convictions about what mattered and what did not. In a letter to George in 1890, Jane explained that she and Ellen were not living on Halsted Street to "stem poverty" but to "fortify" their neighbors' spirits. The statement is startling because eventually, the settlement would seek to do both and become more famous for the former, but this was not true in the early years. Far from wishing to reduce poverty, Starr and Addams dismissed the importance of the physical. Having never experienced physical want, having been raised in a Christian church that emphasized the spirit rather than the body, and having been enriched intellectually by their extensive idealistic educations, they believed that the material was the animal, the low, and that the primary human need was to nourish the life of the mind, the soul, and that any one interested in the physical side of life was spiritually impoverished.[6]

Addams's distaste for materialism was usually a subtle subtext in her speeches, but it sometimes erupted in uncharacteristically passionate jeremiads. One occurred in 1903, when she declared materialism to be "a great menace" to the nation and urged others to "arouse high-minded youth of this country against this spirit of materialism." She penned another in 1904, when she wrote that Chicago's materialism "sometimes makes one obsessed. . . . One is almost driven to go out upon the street fairly shouting that, after all, life does not consist in wealth, . . . in enterprise, . . . in success."[7] Mostly, however, these feelings operated below the surface, shaping her positions but not her explicit arguments.

Antimaterialism taken to its logical conclusion requires a life of poverty. Were Starr and Addams hypocrites to live in a lovely mansion, eat regularly, and wear attractive clothes? If the test was that they practice Tolstoyan self-denial, then they failed the test. But their refusal to embrace the extreme should not obscure the extent of their voluntary renunciation of the physical. Although they did not live in a derelict house, they spent a good deal of time in such houses, sometimes coming home with vermin in their hair and clothes. They shared the garbage-strewn streets and endured the noxious odors with others in the neighborhood. They also lived on reduced incomes. Starr was continually broke for the rest of her life. Addams, too, was generally strapped for money. She would spend most of her inherited wealth on Hull House and friends' emergencies in the 1890s, with the result that she was soon living primarily on the income she earned from lecture fees. After 1900, she added income from magazine articles and book royalties.[8] Later the two women would move in wealthy circles and, because of their well-off friends' generosity, take some fine vacations; they would never be evicted or freeze for lack of money for heat or starve for lack of food. But their disinterest in material things was reflected in the way they lived their new lives.

Being focused on the human spirit, Addams and Starr were not particularly curious about or interested in the forces that shaped their neighborhood and produced its obvious state of deprivation. They did not suspect that the city's economy and the practices of employers had produced the scarcity around them or that city politics influenced the number of jobs in the ward. They were not alert to the grinding nature of industrial work, the

South Halsted Street, *by Norah Hamilton, a Hull House resident.*
Twenty Years at Hull-House, *401.*

reasons for the neighborhood children's intense material aspirations, and, most important, the impact that poverty had on souls and minds. They did not understand what the Barnetts did: that physical suffering affected the spirit. All of these things were part of the layered reality of Halsted Street that they had yet to fathom. Life in the Nineteenth Ward was a bit like the garbage that "paved" its alleys—it had to be uncovered one layer at a time.

Eager to create social ties, Addams and Starr made getting to know people the first order of the day. They invited those they met in the street to visit, and they were invited to visit in return. Addams called this "the neighborly aspect of settlement work." At first they visited with a feeling of unease, although they did not admit it in letters to family and friends. The "first settlers," Addams later recalled, in her third-party fashion, "felt as if they were going into a strange country, [where they would] . . . encounter people more or less unlike themselves." They also found the crowded nature of that country a bit overwhelming. "[W]hen you go and live in [such] a neighborhood," she wrote, "you feel a little swallowed up." [9]

Their new neighbors, although usually friendly, were often puzzled. Why did these two prosperous young women want to live in the Nineteenth Ward when they could afford to live elsewhere? One man, Addams writes in *Twenty Years*, "used to shake his head and say it was 'the strangest thing he had met in his experience.'" Some suspected that the women had some trick up their sleeve, or as Addams put it in the slang of the day, they thought she and Starr "had 'got a dodge somewhere.'" Enacting their parents' distrust, small boys threw stones at the Hull mansion and broke windows. The most common assumption was that the two women intended to convert people to Protestantism. It would be several years, Addams recalled, before neighbors began to understand that they were not there to "proselyte them" and began to become comfortable discussing "religious problems and differences" frankly. [10]

They spent a great deal of time listening as people told them their stories. "We hear about experiences," Addams wrote in 1890, "sad and amusing, humbling and inspiring, but always genuine and never wearisome." She called such conversations "the part of the life . . . which the [settlement] residents care most for." She was delighted to discover, she wrote George Haldeman, that "people diverse in circumstance but alike in feeling [can] form warm friendships." [11] Her new life was confirming her idealistic hopes about the fellowship of humanity.

Although some children threw stones, others, curious, were also among the settlers' first visitors. This made it easy for Addams and Starr and other volunteers to organize children's clubs. Jane wrote Alice on October 8, "We have two boys clubs every Tues. eve. Miss Starr has hers downstairs and mine are in the dining room. I have twenty. . . . They are so anxious to come and very respectful. The little ragamuffins downstairs are harder to manage." By November, a couple of men were helping out with a third boys' club, teaching the children to remove their hats in the house and not to spit tobacco juice. Another started a children's drawing class. A kindergarten was an early success. Less than a month after Starr and Addams moved in, three volunteers, including two former students of Ellen's, Jennie Dow and Mary Rozet Smith, had organized twenty-four children six years of age and older into a weekday morning kindergarten in the drawing room, and seventy more were on a waiting list.[12]

For adults there were weekly receptions organized by ethnicity. On Saturday nights the Greeks were upstairs in the dining room while the Italians were downstairs in the drawing room. The German reception on Monday evenings was for women only. These gatherings, led by various middle-class (that is, "cultured") volunteers of the same nationalities, offered conversation, refreshments, singing, and dancing. The Nineteenth Ward was full of ethnic societies and religious organizations, but many were not primarily social in function and many excluded women. There were relief societies, loan societies, burial societies, literary societies, and religious schools. The Russian, Polish, German Jewish, and Greek immigrants had many organizations; the Italians had fewer.[13]

Perhaps the most unusual club the house hosted was the Working People's Social Science Club. This was both a club for its members and a free weekly series of public lectures about economic and social issues of interest to working people. The club, Addams wrote, helped give Hull House its "early reputation for radicalism"; it also launched her political and economic education.[14]

The idea for the club came from Toynbee Hall, which had a weekly series of lectures and discussions for men on labor and reform issues. Addams suggested the idea of a "Social Science Club" for men to a couple of male volunteers in the fall of 1889. They agreed to try to organize it, but the effort fizzled out. The following spring, a small group of socialists approached the settlement about giving them a room in which to meet. Happy to cooperate, Addams laid out the idea of the social science club and offered to finance the lecture fees, and the club was reborn, this time with no gender restrictions and with its new, more welcoming name: the Working People's Social Science Club.[15]

The lectures were held at 8 P.M. so that workers on eleven-hour shifts could attend. Early topics included strikes, socialism, trade unions, progressive taxation, unemployment, Christian socialism, and "The Negro Problem."[16] There was no lecture series like it anywhere in the city. All sorts of people—working-class people generally but especially Russian Jewish socialists and German anarchists, settlement volunteers and young professional men, and women of leisure—flocked to the Wednesday night gatherings.[17] In a city whose social life was rigidly structured around class and where many middle-class citizens only knew about socialism or unionism from sketchy newspaper reports and magazine articles, the club broke barriers.

The evening's format never varied. The lecturer had one hour to speak, and the audience had a second hour to question the speaker. Questioners were limited to five minutes (timed by the chair, who usually borrowed Jane Addams's watch) in order to prevent long harangues and allow more people a chance to speak. Not surprisingly, the exchange was often heated, since all views were welcome. This tolerance was firm club policy and reflected club members' and Addams's conviction that free speech was, as Addams told a reporter in 1894, "the elemental principle of democracy."[18]

For Addams and Starr, who, like most of their middle-class guests, knew virtually nothing about the topics of the club's lectures, the weekly sessions were the best education possible on working people's reform agendas. During these evenings, dry, abstract social theories were transformed by personal stories and articulate arguments into vital questions. Addams recalled being "often baffled" by the club's radicalism but, given her insatiable curiosity, she must have also found the lectures and discussions an enticing intellectual feast.[19]

The settlement's formal educational effort was also quickly launched. The subjects offered—initially all in the humanities—were academically substantive. The students who took them tended to be the factory workers, teachers, bank tellers, clerks, and others who, in Addams's words, had "some education" and had "kept up an intellectual life and are keen for books" in spite of "adverse circumstances." Starr taught George Eliot's novel *Romola* and the history of art. Addams taught Mazzini's *Duties of Man* in English translation to a group of Italian men (was this because they wanted to improve their English?). Many of them had fought in Italy's nationalist struggle. Afterwards, they presented Hull House with a bust of Mazzini. As more volunteer teachers joined them, offerings in French and painting, Latin and Greek were added, and the effort was christened "College Extension Classes." These were the first adult college extension courses in Chicago.[20]

Addams and Starr were simply teaching what they knew and loved, but they were also teaching the classics of their students' own former national cultures or, in the case of Italian immigrants who may have studied *Romola*, a foreigner's version of their history. Future courses would repeat the pattern of offering courses on the "best" of European civilization to European immigrants. The curriculum was not so much cross-cultural as defiant of the usual class barriers.

Philanthropic or charity work was the settlement's third undertaking; Addams sometimes called it the humanitarian function, or "being neighborly." Their question was, What can we do to help? This work, mostly undocumented except by the stories Addams tells in *Twenty Years*, grieved and delighted them in equal measure and taught them more than anything else they did about the lives of the working-class people among whom they now lived. Addams and Starr spent a great deal of time minding children and nursing the sick. In time, as they learned more about other organizations in the city, they also tracked down aid for women whose husbands had deserted them, government insurance payments for widows, child support owed by husbands who had abandoned their wives and children, and damages for injured employees.[21]

For Addams, perhaps the most difficult of her neighborly tasks was attending the dying. During her first year at Halsted Street she spent many long hours with a young man suffering from tuberculosis who was drunk most of the time, thanks to the gifts of whiskey his friends had given him. The liquor sent him into "wild periods of exultation," she recalled, and during one of these he died. At a second deathbed, an embittered, elderly Scotch woman treated her to "gibes and taunts" as she tried to keep her warm and fed. The woman was cursing her "damned charity hot-water bottles" when her "harsh, gasping voice" was suddenly "stilled by death." Addams waited, "shaken and horrified," for the doctor to come to issue the death certificate.[22] In such moments she who greatly feared death touched it again and again. Her new life required much personal courage.

Another searing moment involved a birth. A young unmarried woman went into labor and when her neighbors refused to help her because her baby was illegitimate, someone ran to the Hull mansion for help. At the time, Julia Lathrop, a Vassar graduate and a niece of Caroline Potter's whom Addams had gotten to know while at the seminary, was visiting from Rockford. After calling a doctor, she and Jane hurried over and, when no doctor appeared, they delivered the baby themselves. The grateful mother named her son Julius John in their honor. Addams had an ambivalent reaction to the experience. As they walked home she told Lathrop that she felt awed by the "mystery of birth" but dismayed that they had tried to practice a profession in which they had no training. "Why," she asked, "did we let ourselves be rushed into midwifery?" The question reflected not only Addams's usual desire to be well-prepared but also her usual worry that she might fail. Lathrop's answer—that it would hardly have been kind to refuse—put Addams's self-absorbed fears gently in their place.[23]

Addams and Starr discovered to their surprise that their neighbors, whose resources were generally scarce, were often inordinately helpful to each other. Addams marveled when an Irish woman whose husband was unemployed and who worked to support the family took in a homeless widow and her five children "without a moment's reflection upon the physical discomforts involved." And she was touched when a young woman who badly needed a job and had finally found one with Addams's help chose not to show up for work the first day although, the young woman later told Addams, "it broke me heart." A friend had fallen ill, she explained, and she had gone to take care of the children. Jane and Ellen compared these acts of generosity with the way they knew people of their own class, though possessing "greater economic advantages," would have responded. They did not think upper-middle-class people would have been as kind.[24] The contrast suggested a startling, troubling thought: might the uncultured possess a higher morality than the cultured?

The opposite seemed the case enough of the time, however, to leave Starr's and Addams's class-based moral map intact. They were often dismayed at their neighbors' apparent cruelty. A mother did not want to take her baby home from the hospital because it was born with a cleft palate. It had had a corrective operation immediately, probably at Addams's and Starr's instigation and expense, but the mother still refused to take her child. The two women took the baby in and kept it until Addams persuaded the reluctant mother to bring her child home but, soon afterward, the baby died of neglect.[25]

Another abandoned newborn had been attending the settlement's new crèche. This small day nursery, or day care program, opened in February 1890; working mothers could leave children under six there all day for a fee of five cents.[26] One day a mother did not come for her ten-day old infant, and after several weeks, during which Addams was trying to find her, the baby died. Because the family could not be found to pay for the burial, Starr and Addams asked Cook County officials to handle the arrangements. Six neighborhood women, learning of this plan, formed a committee to express their disapproval. In what must have been a tense confrontation, they told Starr and Addams that the mother would have been ashamed to have her baby given a pauper's burial by the state and that there must be a private one or the family would be condemned for its lack of respectability. Jane and Ellen, no doubt puzzled that abandoning one's child was not the greater shame, refused at first, arguing in legalistic fashion that because they had been taking care of the baby, it was now their decision who should bury it. But when the women offered to take up a collection to pay for the expense of a proper private funeral, Starr and Addams agreed.[27]

Gradually they understood that their plan to involve the county was a terrible blunder. "It is doubtful," Addams wrote in 1898, recalling the event, "whether Hull House has ever done anything which injured it so deeply in the minds of some of its neighbors." Addams and Starr realized they were ignorant outsiders. "No one born and reared in that community," she added, "could possibly have made a mistake like that." Their plan had challenged "a genuine moral [feeling]" in the neighborhood. The lesson that working-class people had their own ethical principles was one they would have to learn repeatedly. Meanwhile, after some rocky relations, some of "the most indulgent" of the neighbors forgave them "on the ground," Addams wrote, "that we were spinsters and could not know a mother's heart."[28]

Although busy enough with receptions, clubs, visits, and emergency aid, Addams also took an interest in the labor movement. She had arrived on Halsted Street committed to cooperation and, schooled by Toynbee Hall, willing to view unions in a positive light. Still, she did not see, she later wrote, "organizing for working people [as] a necessity." Her belief in unions lacked "the driving force of conviction."[29] Reading between the lines, one senses that she held the common middle-class assumption that reasonable conversation and discussion ought to make confrontations over power unnecessary. Her enthusiasm for cooperation would have reinforced such a view.

Addams became interested in labor issues in response to many pressures. Chicago was in turmoil in 1890. That year there were roughly eighty-three strikes by carpenters, plumbers, railroad workers, and others in the trades seeking the eight-hour day and union recognition. In the neighborhood, workers began to come to her for help resolving their labor disputes. She was attending the weekly lectures and discussions of the Working People's Social Science Club. And she was reading. One particularly influential book was Arnold Toynbee's *Lectures on the Industrial Revolution of the 18th Century in England*, which she read just before or after moving to Halsted Street.[30] Under all these influences, Addams was drawn into labor reform, with consequences that would be crucial to her development as a social theorist, a social reformer, and a citizen.

Her education in industrial working conditions began at the settlement's first Christmas party. She was shocked when a group of little girls turned down an offer of candy because, as one explained to her, they worked in a candy factory and could not "bear the sight of it." The children, Addams discovered, had been working fourteen-hour days and eighty-two-hour weeks during the six-week Christmas rush. And it was not only children whose labor conditions were difficult and it was not only at Christmas. Many older workers had similar hours on and off throughout the year. Addams asked one man what it was like to work so many hours every day. He said that after three or four weeks he did not "feel [anything] at all." She watched exhausted workers attending Hull House events fall asleep in their chairs. She was impressed by their determination. "I am touched every night in the week," she wrote in 1893, "by the fact that the people think it worthwhile to eat their suppers and change their clothes and come to Hull House—and perhaps they do not get there until eight or nine o'clock—for the sake of the very meagre feast we are able to spread for them—so very meagre I am ashamed of it."[31] If nothing else, she was seeing the educational benefits of labor's call for the eight-hour day.

Living on Halsted Street, Addams and Starr quickly learned about the sweatshop system. It was particularly popular in the garment industry, which dominated the Nineteenth Ward. In the sweatshop, or sweating, system, a factory owner contracted with a subcontractor (the "sweater") to do finishing work, usually on garments such as coats, cloaks, trousers, and shirts. The sweater then hired short-term workers, skilled and unskilled, to do the finishing work during ten-to-fourteen-hour days, often in a cheap apartment rented for the purpose or at home. The practice was only possible in crowded labor markets and in hand trades requiring no heavy machinery. Wages were, on average, low, because much of the work, such as the needle, thread, and pressing work, was unskilled. As a result, the largest proportion of workers consisted of women and children. In 1892, twenty thousand to twenty-three thousand women and children and five thousand men worked in the sweatshops of Chicago, according to one estimate. Wives and children worked to keep the family from starving because many men, in the sweatshops and elsewhere, earned too little to support a family.[32]

Addams and Starr also quickly learned that in most industries job instability was rampant. Factories and sweatshops operated according to seasonal sales rhythms, which meant that most workers were laid off four times a year. Statewide, only 20 percent of all industrial workers worked full-time in 1886. In Chicago in 1892, women at the lowest end of the wage scale were laid off for an average of 115.5 days, or almost a third of the year. Because there was no government unemployment system— this was a twentieth-century invention—many workers and their families barely managed to subsist when unemployed.[33]

At first Addams tried to solve labor problems by her own efforts. An early case involved three boys who worked at a nearby factory and were all members of an evening club at Hull House. One after the other, they were injured at the same machine because it did not have a guard on it. The third one died from his injuries. Horrified, Addams paid a visit to the owners of the factory, confident, she writes in *Twenty Years,* that they would "do everything possible to prevent the recurrence of such a tragedy." To her surprise, they did nothing. Her shock was a measure of her limited knowledge of the way some businessmen operated. Having only known them socially—as fathers of friends, as friends of her father, as her father—she was not familiar with the "profit-at-any-cost" side to economic enterprise. Small wonder, then, that early on she felt some "perplexity over the problems of an industrial neighborhood."[34]

Addams dealt with the next labor dispute by turning to voluntary arbitration, that is, the use of a neutral third party to settle disputes. When twelve girls from a nearby factory approached her in 1890 about a disagreement they were having with their foreman over a wage cut, she asked Judge Murray Tuley of the Cook County District Court to arbitrate the disagreement. The employer agreed to participate, and the matter was resolved.[35] From then on, she urged voluntary arbitration whenever possible.

In her small way, Addams was catching the wave of a much older and wider trend. Voluntary labor arbitration first gained popularity in England and the United States in the 1880s. Pennsylvania, Massachusetts, New York, Ohio, and California adopted laws creating state boards of labor arbitration in the 1880s, and Congress passed an act in 1888 authorizing the creation of arbitration boards for settling differences between railroad corporations and their employees. Trade union advocacy, particularly that led by unions affiliated with the Knights of Labor, was the main reason such laws had passed, although the effort had failed in Illinois. Compulsory arbitration, on the other hand, was distrusted by strong unions, although weak unions were happy to have any type of arbitration at all.[36]

Addams's embrace of voluntary arbitration may have been prompted by her reading of Arnold Toynbee's writings. Toynbee argued that workers needed a fair procedure to use in negotiating with employers and rejected the idea of the harmony of class interests. Workers and employers, he wrote, have antagonistic interests in the setting of wages, and power was not equal between them. One party possessed the power of capital and the other did not, and the party with capital also had the law on its side. Workers needed to combine, to form unions, to negotiate, and to participate in arbitration.[37]

At first, Addams's contributions to labor issues were merely reactive and centered on the resolution of specific disputes. But sometime during the spring of 1890 she sought out a woman bindery worker, Mary Kenney, as someone with whom she could cooperate. Kenney was not only a worker; she was also a union organizer for the bindery industry, another industry well-represented in the Nineteenth Ward. Addams likely learned of Kenney from a new friend, Henry Demarest Lloyd, the journalist, author, socialist, and reformer from Winnetka, a Chicago suburb. Lloyd was friends with the socialist labor organizer Thomas Morgan, whose wife Elizabeth was working closely with Kenney in union organizing efforts.[38] Addams's choice of Kenney as a person with whom to build ties, possibly coached by Lloyd, was astute. The resulting friendship would open up new worlds for them both.

Mary Kenney was the twenty-six-year-old daughter of Irish immigrants. She had grown up in Missouri in a modestly prosperous family that had been plunged into economic crisis on the death of her father when Kenney was fourteen. With her mother an invalid, Kenney had to go to work. She dropped out of school and took a job in a bookbindery, working eleven-hour days Monday through Friday and a ten-hour day on Saturday.[39] By the late

1880s, Kenney and her mother had moved to Chicago, where Kenney's efforts to demand a raise got her fired and led her to seek out the help of the founder and guiding spirit of Ladies' Federation Labor Union (LFLU) No. 2073, Elizabeth Morgan.

In 1890 the LFLU was, only two years after its founding, the most important trade women's unionizing effort in the nation, organizing typists, clerks, and cloakmakers, among others. Reflecting Morgan's Knights of Labor origins, it was a cross-class reform organization that desired to improve conditions for female wage workers in the city by using investigations and lobbying to prod the government to act. The similarity with the Illinois Woman's Alliance was intentional; the same people who founded the Alliance in 1888, Elizabeth Morgan and Corinne Brown, had also founded the LFLU. The alliance was in fact a nonunion statewide version of the LFLU in its role as a cross-class reform organization. But the LFLU was also a labor union, or rather, a mini-federation of trade unions and a member of the American Federation of Labor. Elizabeth Morgan and Mary Kenney were LFLU's delegates to the city's federated trade union organization, the Chicago Trades and Labor Assembly (CTLA), headed by Thomas Morgan, which represented more than a thousand skilled trade unions.[40]

Addams sent Kenney a letter inviting her to dinner at Hull House and explaining that she wanted her to meet some people from England who were interested in the labor movement. Kenney was skeptical. Assuming Addams to be a wealthy woman, she expected her to hold working girls and women in contempt and was inclined to refuse the invitation. Her mother urged her to be open-minded, however, so she went.[41] Later, Kenney and Addams both enjoyed telling the story of their first meeting. Addams remembered that Kenney arrived late for dinner in a "recalcitrant mood." Kenney remembered that Addams rose respectfully from her chair to greet her, gave her a seat of honor beside her, and asked her, "What can we do with each other for the girls in your trade?" They agreed that Kenney's new bindery union could meet at Hull House, and Addams took the assignment of paying for the printing of flyers announcing the meeting and distributing them to bindery workers in the neighborhood. In the face of Addams's courtesy and helpfulness, Kenney's resistance melted. "When I saw there was someone who cared enough to help us and to help us in our way, it was like having a new world opened up." Addams would eventually persuade Kenney to become a guest at Hull House for several weeks to find out more about the settlement.[42] In the next few years Kenney would become a friend, a sometime resident of Hull House, and a strong supporter of the settlement's pro-labor work.

In welcoming Kenney and her union organizing to Hull House, Addams was being unorthodox. Proper society thought unions to be troublemaking organizations controlled by anarchists and prone to violence. Stanton Coit, founder of the Neighborhood Guild in New York City, an organization similar in purpose to a settlement, observed of Addams's union support, "It [is] a plucky thing to do, and perhaps a stroke of moral genius, [because] the prevailing sentiment of 'cultivated Americans' is at the present juncture strongly opposed to trades-unionism." Addams was mindful of this attitude. She would write a bit defensively to a professor at Wellesley College in late 1891, "We find ourselves almost forced into trades unions. . . . [T]here are very few for women in Chicago and we hope to help form them on a conservative basis."[43] But she did not cease her efforts.

The friendship that grew between Kenney and Addams benefited both. Kenney would go on to organize other unions at Hull House, making use of its meeting space, the extra hands it offered for publicity, and its connections in the city.[44] And Kenney helped Addams understand why working women needed unions and the challenges involved in organizing. Together, they launched Hull House's long, controversial engagement with the labor union movement.

———————

All of this work of the settlement was launched with lightening speed. In a few months, the two friends had filled up every available corner and hour with activities and Addams still had more ideas. "So many things are constantly opening up that we might do," she wrote her sister Alice in November, "if we had the room and the people." The pace was hectic. "I have been interrupted so many times," she explained to Alice in March, "that I think I will give up trying to write more." Later she would recall "my wild activity in the early days of Hull House." People remembered how she appeared in these early years—"slender," "quick moving," fond of "frequent, brisk encounters," "keen, alert and alive in every fiber." The invalid of the 1880s was gone; the bustling, efficient Rockford student of her junior year had returned. The contrast with her former life was abrupt. She felt some discomfort at first. Unused to the "unending activity," she was "confused," she writes in *Twenty Years,* by the way the house was "constantly filling and refilling" with people. She had to abandon some former "habits of living," in particular her "student's tendency to sit with a book by the fire."[45] Peaceful, contemplative solitude had disappeared.

What were the sources of Addams's new energy? One was the deeply felt sense of duty to her fellow human beings, carefully hidden in Starr's circulating letter. In 1892 she described that sense among educated young people, without confessing that she felt it. "I think," she wrote, "it is hard for us to realize how seriously many of them are taking to the notion of human brotherhood." In 1894 she brought the feeling closer to home. "People living in settlements," she observed, "live for the good of those around them."[46]

But there was also something simply enjoyable about it all. She recalled later the "excitement," "pleasure," and "delight" she felt in these years. She loved plunging into the unknown and finding out what would happen. She called it "gratif[ying my] spirit of adventure."[47] Addams does not reveal this side of herself in *Twenty Years*, but we can feel its presence in her life. Excitement was to her taste; danger appealed to her. This was part of what made her want to go east to Smith College; it drew her to oratory at the seminary; it was, no doubt, an aspect of the secret appeal of the bullfight. It attracted her to the idea of living on Halsted Street, the "dangerous slum," and it was a source of her great courage in later years. Jane Addams had wrestled with her fears in the 1880s, when she felt pulled in conflicting directions, but when she had her feet solidly under her she was a bold risk-taker.

In the early years, to be sure, she sometimes wore herself out. She often pushed herself beyond her strength, as she had done at Rockford and in medical school. Ellen sometimes thought she was overdoing it. She once complained to her cousin Mary Allen, "There is no moderation where Jane is—can't be." Looking back in her forties, Addams admitted that her memories of the first few years were "blurred with fatigue." Nor was her mood always happy or content. At times she felt "overwhelmed" with " 'grief of things as they are' " and had "many moments of depression."[48] These brief phrases, which she offered not in *Twenty Years* but when she was almost seventy, confirm that her life on Halsted Street brought great sorrow as well as delight.

Jane Addams's deepening friendship with Ellen Gates Starr was another reason for her pleasure and energy. Jane hinted at the intimate and personal nature of their commitment in a letter to Ellen in early 1889. Writing just before arriving in Chicago, she seemed to be reminding Starr of a

Jane Addams, ca. 1891. The Jane Addams Papers Project, Fayetteville, NC.

promise they had made to each other: "Let us love each other through thick and thin and work out a salvation."[49] The goal of salvation, a touchstone for them both, expressed their desire as social Christians to improve society but it also implied a personal hope: that each friend could improve herself by knowing the other. Ellen continued to see in Jane an effortless spiritual strength and serenity that she longed to achieve in herself. In a lyrical passage in a letter she wrote her cousin Mary Allen just before she and Jane moved to Halsted Street, Ellen tried to describe what she admired. "I always feel her rare . . . character, which simply means obeying God, rather than man. . . . She 'strengthens the weak knees and upholds the feeble hands,' and has no sense of strength herself. It is a strange and beautiful thing for me to see." She marveled at how everybody who came near Jane felt it. "It is as if she simply diffuse[s] something which comes from outside herself, of which she is the luminous medium." She added, "I don't know how, just at this point, I should live my life without her."[50]

What Addams appreciated in Starr was another kind of strength: her ebullient and impatient zeal. "Ellen always makes everything so graphic and dramatic," Jane observed to Mary Linn with a trace of envy. She thought of herself, on the other hand, as "a little insipid."[51] Ellen bolstered Jane's tentative spirits and provided the antidote to Jane's corroding, enervating self-doubt. Jane was grateful. In the summer of 1889, when they were apart, she wrote Ellen about how important she was to her, though, as was typical, she spoke of her in the third person: "I think [often] . . . of the . . . soul without whom I get on so badly." Jane also relied on Ellen to scold her for her failings. In the same letter she confessed her latest one. Earlier she and Ellen had discussed how important it was that Jane marshal her money for the scheme. Now Jane admitted she had sent a $25 gift to Beloit College. "I don't know why I am so weak and need you to help me from my weaknesses. My greatest self-denial [is to] refus[e] to give to other things and you must make yourself a big bear for that."[52] Addams needed Starr to be her conscience and her prod.

Happy to oblige, Starr was nonetheless mindful that at times she was not an easy friend to live with. She wrote her cousin Mary in 1889 that in her friendship with Addams she was "subject to attacks of obstinacy, peevishness [and] conceit." Her admiration for Jane did not still her critical tongue or quiet her combative nature. "I scold and oppose her," she confessed. But Addams knew how to pacify her. When family duties delayed her arrival in Chicago in January 1889, she wrote Ellen, "I know you disapprove, dear heart, and I appreciate your disapproval. . . . Have patience for a few days longer and don't scold me, dear. I am awfully sorry about the delay."[53]

Full of affection for each other, Starr and Addams had formed a devoted partnership. They may have thought of their commitment as permanent. In the United States in the nineteenth century, life partnerships, sometimes called "Boston marriages," were not unusual between women who had or could earn money to support themselves. A Boston marriage usually involved two women living together in a long-term, romantic, devoted relationship. These "marriages" were understood to be as emotionally sustaining and as respectable as marriages between men and women.[54]

The theoretical or ideal place (not to be confused with the actual place) of sex in such arrangements was, approximately, the theoretical place of sex in the idealized heterosexual marriages of the period. For both kinds of marriages, sexuality was equated with "mere" animal sensuality and therefore judged to belong to the lower orders of morality. The only difference was that in heterosexual marriages, limited sex was thought appropriate because it was essential for procreation. In Boston marriages, procreation being impossible, sex was assumed to be irrelevant, while sensuality was understood to be a temptation to be resisted in favor of spiritualized love. To achieve it, the parties were expected to elevate their sexual urges and sensual feelings to a higher plane, to pursue the beautiful not in one person's body but in the beauty of the individual soul and of the wider world.[55]

Jane and Ellen's frame of mind as they began their partnership was innocent. Although they were now sharing a bed as an affectionate couple, they had not even considered the physical temptations of sensuality or, at least, Ellen had not. Her cousin Mary wrote Ellen in September 1889 warning her that resisting those temptations might not be easy. Ellen replied: "About the weakness of the flesh, which you think I have not considered— probably I haven't. I don't quite know how to. Perhaps it's as well not to. I do know, however, the strength of the beautiful spiritual life beside me[.] . . . I couldn't do this [start a settlement house] without her."[56]

Jane Addams, of course, had long found the ideal of spiritualized, or Platonic, love, appealing. Her adolescent inclinations had been reinforced at Rockford Seminary or sometime afterwards by reading Diotima's famous speech about love in Plato's *Symposium*. In 1909, in discussing the nature of ideal love, she cited the dialogue as the "classical expression" of the subject. If sensuality is avoided, she explained, then "the sex impulse [can] awaken the imagination [and] the heart[; it can] . . . overflow into neighboring fields of consciousness." The sex impulse would be "diffused" instead of "concentrated." A person in love, she explained, concentrates her sexual feelings on that one person and sees in the other all her "newly found values" and a solution to "eternal melancholy." But when there is no lover, that is, when a person chooses to sublimate her sensuality, then she will see those values "dispensed over the world" and she may become "a lover" of poetry or nature or may be filled with "religious devotion" or "philanthropic zeal." [57]

Was Addams thinking of her experiences with Starr? Certainly, her new-found values were mirrored in Starr, and their friendship provided Addams with a solution to her "eternal melancholy." She was, to that extent, like the lover she described. At the same time, she may well have viewed the spiritualized affection she felt for Ellen as a gateway to her own higher aspirations and may have seen herself as redirecting her love, and her sexual desire, into an intensified philanthropic zeal. In the same passage, Addams comments on the challenges of achieving such a state as if she knew them from experience. "It is neither a short nor an easy undertaking to substitute the love of beauty for mere desire, to place the mind about the senses." [58] If nothing else, Addams aspired to controlling physical desire through spiritual discipline.

It is impossible to know whether Jane Addams was celibate (or perhaps the better term is "not consciously sexual") all of her life since she did not write or speak explicitly about it, but she appears to have spent the years between 1889 and 1909 believing in the redeeming value of celibacy. [59] Given her distaste for self-indulgence and her belief in self-discipline, she may have also achieved it. The letters between herself and her closest friend of her later years, Mary Rozet Smith—at least those written during the period covered in this book—appear to confirm this. They reveal that the two friends experienced moments of emotional and physical intimacy together, but nothing is said that could be interpreted as explicitly sexual. Such letters, of course, may have been destroyed or never written. [60] As far as one can tell for this period, any erotic pleasure Addams and Starr (or later, Addams and Smith) had in their relationship appears to have remained unconscious. [61]

When Addams and Starr first rented the Hull mansion, they had been able to occupy only the second floor and half of the first floor. In March 1890 the furniture factory moved out; delighted, they took possession of the rest of the house after Addams spent $500 for more repairs and fresh paint. To balance this extravagance, they economized in other ways. They put off hiring staff to assist housekeeper Mary Keyser, and Addams tried to cut back on her personal expenses. In *Twenty Years* she recalls, "We cooked the meals and kept the books and washed the windows without a thought of hardship if we thereby saved money for the consummation of some ardently desired undertaking." As she explained to Alice in January, she wanted her money to go "to the house and its plans" as much as possible.[62]

Other donors to the settlement helped. Within weeks of the house's opening, a woman pledged to contribute $50 per month. She would give $5 herself, ask nine other friends to do the same, and then go around every four weeks and collect all the gifts. The method, known as Ten Account fundraising, was popular at the time. Within three years, thirty people would be contributing a total of $150 a month, or $1,800 a year, to the settlement's Ten Account. In May 1890 the settlement received its most significant gift to date, an enormous in-kind donation. Helen Culver agreed to give them the use of the house rent-free for four years. In return, with Culver's permission, Addams and Starr gratefully named the settlement Hull House, after Culver's uncle, Charles Hull, the original owner.[63] Finally, the scheme had a name.

On this happy note, the settlement closed for the summer at the end of June. With the hot weather settling in, Starr and Addams took advantage of their middle-class resources to depart. Starr visited her sister in western Massachusetts, and Addams visited a new Chicago friend's summer house in western New York State.[64]

When the settlement reopened in October there was another improvement: a third resident, Anna Farnsworth, moved in. Although her father did not approve, Farnsworth would remain at Hull House for three years. (Mary Keyser was not yet technically considered a resident, although she was as neighborly as they in her relations. Eventually, however, she would be declared one.)[65] The house needed more residents. To escalate her recruitment campaign, Addams decided to give a major talk to the members of the Chicago Woman's Club about the settlement and about why people should volunteer. She delivered the speech, titled "Outgrowths of Toynbee Hall," on December 3, 1890. No doubt she spoke as she usually did, in a quiet, earnest manner, her warm, cordial voice carrying easily and clearly thanks to her oratorical training.[66]

In this speech, which is the earliest version of her recruitment talk that has survived, she put forth the best arguments she could muster to draw others into engagement with the Nineteenth Ward. She spent most of it describing Toynbee Hall and Hull House, but her subtle recurring theme was the need for women to be good citizens in new ways. She began by critiquing the narrowness of the meaning of democracy in the United States as she perceived it. Democracy ought to involve not only "political freedom and equality" but also "social affairs" and a democratic "theory [of] the social order."[67] Weaving women into her analysis, she suggested that women should take up the practice of democracy in social affairs as a duty of "good citizenship." Her justification was not biological but historical: "[S]ocial matters have always been largely under the control of women." Then she made a claim that was probably startling to her audience: that the quality of their charity depended on getting to know those they were helping. "We need the thrust in the side," she said, "the lateral pressure which comes from living next door to poverty to make our humanitarianism of highest avail," that is, to make it most useful.[68] The metaphor made her practical point, but it also captured what life on Halsted Street must have sometimes felt like to Addams—like a painful jab in the ribs.

Addams's expectations for middle-class women were moderate. She called for them to broaden their social role as citizens in a democracy but did not suggest they take up a political role. In fact, there are various clues in the speech and elsewhere that Addams was having difficulty imagining a place for women in democratic political theory and practice. The first social science club she proposed had been for men only. In "Outgrowths" she described approvingly the way the boys in Hull House clubs learned parliamentary procedure while the girls socialized.[69] Addams was also silent about women's lack of the vote. This does not mean that she did not support women's suffrage—she had probably not changed her mind since her college years—but her failure to call for it in "Outgrowths" when discussing the partialities of democracy suggests that in December 1890, woman's suffrage did not compel her interest.

Beneath the structure of Addams's logical arguments, two longings permeated the speech. One was her desire to supply working people with the benefits of education, of "culture." She noted that the "intellectual faculties" of poor people were "undeveloped"; they were "untrained and unused."[70] She praised Mazzini's vision of education as "a Holy Communion with generations dead and living" that all men should receive. This belief in the transformational power of education was, judging from her writings and actions, her deepest passion in the 1890s. She was convinced that every human being had gifts to be nurtured. Her other longing was for young people to find something meaningful to do. Girls who were just out of school, she said, faced particular difficulties. "There is nothing, after disease, indigence, and guilt," she observed, taking a phrase from Mill's *Subjection of Women*, "so fatal to life itself as the want of a proper outlet for active faculties."[71] These two longings stemmed, of course, from her own delight in culture and her own pain at feeling useless. She could readily suppose her listeners had felt them, too.

More difficult for her audience to imagine was the city life of formerly rural working-class immigrants. Addams, herself a migrant from country to city, took up the subject with tender care, mindful of the prejudices she would encounter. She spoke respectfully of the "European peasants" who had come to live in the Nineteenth Ward "direct from the soil" and told how they maintained their traditions of hospitality, visiting cousins on Sunday in their brightly colored holiday clothes. She assured her skeptical listeners that Italian homes were full of "gaiety, family affection and gentle courtesy." They and the settlement residents respected each other's national loyalties. "They do not renounce their country, nor we ours."[72]

To further undermine her audience's nativist biases, she told a story intended to put club members in an immigrant's shoes. A southern Italian who fought with Giuseppe Garibaldi in the 1860 campaign to regain Naples, she said, was attending the weekly Italian reception at the settlement one Saturday evening when a statue of Garibaldi, a gift to the house, was being unveiled. The man had been wearing a "hang-dog look" when he arrived, but when he saw the familiar face of his leader, his demeanor changed. Suddenly standing tall and looking dignified, he broke into a campaign song they had sung as they marched into Naples. "He had come into the house," Addams said, knowing that "in the opinion of the Americans . . . he was a 'dago' . . . fit only to sweep the streets and dig with a shovel." He came out "straightened by the memory that he had been a soldier under the most remarkable leader of modern revolutions," proud that "Americans had taken his hand, not with condescension, but honor," and inspired that he might again "become a valuable citizen."[73] Immigrants were worthy citizens, and their nations had proud histories.

At the same time, even as she respected the immigrants and their cultures, she was confident of her own cultural, class, and national superiority. Hull House intended "to conserve and keep for [immigrants] whatever of value their past life contained and to bring them in contact with a better class of American." She spoke repeatedly of her own class's training in culture and of her neighbors' ignorance and asserted several times that poor people lacked "social organization of any kind." She took particular pride in her inherited American spirit of "improvement," describing those in her own class (and by implication herself and her audience) as "the people who embody the traditions and energy that make for progress."[74]

There were obvious tensions between Addams's respect for immigrants and her condescension toward them. Her theory of human progress, however, provided an intellectual framework that resolved or at least rationalized the tensions. Implicit for the most part in her writings, it was the advanced thinking of her day, drawn from Mazzini, from idealists such as Comte and Emerson, and from many other secondary writers. Human society, it was argued, developed in stages from the "primitive" to the civilized. Those who had read the best literature and acquired a higher, universal, selfless ethic were superior to those who had not. Thus immigrants from peasant or primitive backgrounds, because they lacked education, were inferior to people from civilized classes or societies. On a continuum of human development that was aiming for perfection, European peasants were thought to be "stunted," "dwarfed," and "underdeveloped" and educated Anglo-Saxon Americans, with their gracious manners and distaste for things uncouth, were believed to be closer to fulfilling the universal human ideal. Addams and Starr held this view, but with one difference. They were convinced that a peasant could benefit from education, while many clubwomen were happy to abandon the peasant to his ignorance.

This theory of evolutionary progress, which might be called cultural Comteanism, was not the same as that other dominant evolutionary theory of the nineteenth century: social Darwinism. The British thinker Herbert Spencer coined the phrase that best summed up this second theory, "survival of the fittest." (Spencer was also an influential proponent of cultural Comteanism. He embraced both theories, impervious to their contradictions.) For the cultural Comteans, the engine of progress was culture and the meaningful manifestations of progress—increased sociability and sympathy, less selfishness, and a wider knowledge of the world—were also cultural. For the social Darwinists, the engine of progress was each individual's economic behavior, that is, his competitiveness and (necessary) selfishness, and the meaningful manifestations of progress were technological advancement and a society's increased wealth.[75] Addams used the language of progress from her first years at Hull House, but this should not be understood to signal an embrace of social Darwinism, whose materialism and rejection of cooperation were deeply antithetical to her beliefs.

Addams's new life on Halsted Street was most different from her old life in that it immersed her in the reality of urban poverty. She was walking the garbage-strewn alleys, visiting neighbors in their cramped homes, hearing their stories, and witnessing their suffering and deaths. In December 1890, the pain of those around her weighed on her heavily. As before, it was to George that she was most willing to mention suffering, perhaps because she knew he suffered, too. In a letter she sent a few weeks after her Chicago Woman's Club speech, she wrote, "We have seen a great deal of suffering and want this winter."

The letter also suggests that she was finding comfort in her religious faith. "It seems as if [this] dark side [of life]," she told George, "would be quite unendurable if it were not for [the] central fact . . . of Christ's mission to the world." Christ's mission, of course, was to save the world from sin by His death, as the son of God, on the cross. Did her statement suggest that she believed in Christ's divinity? If so, it was apparently a fleeting conviction. Christ as the redeemer does not make its way into any other of her surviving written references to Christ, private or public. Still, it is interesting that in 1891 she joined the evangelical Congregational church, the Ewing Street Church, in the neighborhood.[76] In 1890–91, her Christian faith may have been closest to traditional dogma.

The misery of that winter had many causes. Very cold weather had forced people to spend more on fuel. This, when combined with the seasonal unemployment cycle of many industries, had pushed more families than usual into starvation and homelessness. Addams gave money to people she knew to help with their rent, food, and heating bills and was soon low on funds herself. She explained apologetically to George that she could only afford to send him candy for Christmas.[77]

A more cheerful reason for Addams's tight budget in the second year was that Hull House was continuing to grow. In the spring of 1891, the settlement's college extension classes included Roman history, music, German, Shakespeare, rhetoric, drawing, and mathematics. There were more clubs. Someone, probably Addams, worked out a system for counting how many people came to Hull House, allowing one newspaper to report that the settlement drew about nine hundred men, women, and children to its clubs and classes that spring. Seventy-five people were volunteering each week to lead various activities and help in other ways.[78]

The year 1890–91 also saw the settlement gain its first new building: a combination art gallery, reading room, and art studio. Helen Culver allowed it to be built lease-free on land she owned just south of the Hull mansion. Edward Butler, a trustee of the Art Institute, gave $5,000 to construct it; hence it was called the Butler Art Gallery. There was a gala opening in June 1891, with the Reverend Samuel Barnett, who was visiting from England with Henrietta, giving remarks for the occasion. The gallery's first exhibit, curated and hung by Starr, attracted 4,079 visitors in its first ten days. One reason was that the gallery's hours were tailored to working people's schedules. It, along with the new reading room, which was operating as a branch of the Chicago Public Library, stayed open late every night so that people could visit after work.[79]

While Starr focused on art, Addams remained the generalist. That spring, she led a girls' club on Monday nights and a travel club on Tuesday nights whose study topic was a favorite city, London. The following fall, she would teach a course about her other favorite city, Rome, using Hawthorne's *Marble Faun*. She and Starr, joined by Farnsworth, continued making neighborly visits and answering calls for help, although Farnsworth refused to care for the very sick.[80]

Addams, however, unlike Starr and Farnsworth, also wore an administrative hat. Facilities were often on her mind. In June 1891 she renovated the drawing room to add an alcove with a raised stage, making the space more useful for lectures, concerts, and union meetings. The following fall, the settlement opened a gymnasium in a rented building just to the north that had previously housed a saloon. Soon afterward, volunteers set up a "diet kitchen" in a rented cottage around the corner where nutritious broths, gruels, and custards for the sick were sold for a small fee.[81] In response to the community's needs and interests, Hull House was providing more and more of the charitable and recreational services that missions and institutional churches typically provided.

The settlement's financial records for 1890–91 confirm that Addams's enthusiasm for new projects was outrunning the settlement's ability to pay for them. In that fiscal year, expenses, including those for furniture and general repairs, were $9,123, while income from donors' gifts, resident fees, and student fees for college extension courses totaled $6,758. When

*Hull House and the Butler Gallery, ca. 1891. Jane Addams Collection,
Swarthmore College Peace Collection.*

Addams invited Helen Culver to review the books midway through the year,
Culver astutely sized up Addams's financial management practices. The
books, she reported to a friend, showed "a great mingling of economy and
lavish expenditure." The fiscal year would end in September with a shortfall
of $2,365, 26 percent of the year's budget; Addams paid for the shortfall out
of her own pocket. It is doubtful that she could afford it. In the settlement's
first year, she paid 58 percent of its total expenses of $8,634, while living
on an annual income of $4,000. In the second year she paid the $2,365
overage, additional capital expenses such as furniture and repairs, and her
own living expenses.[82] How did she finance these early costs? She may
have spent some savings or she may have sold some of her assets. The
latter would have permanently reduced her annual income, independent
of economic fluctuations. Her income was roughly $4,000 in the 1880s;
by late 1891, it may not have been as high.

Addams's most ambitious effort in 1891, predictably, was educational.
She launched a working people's summer school. Held for four weeks
in July 1891 on the leafy campus of Rockford Seminary, the school offered a liberal arts college curriculum and residential learning experience
to the same working-class women who took the college extension classes

at the settlement: factory workers, public school teachers, seamstresses, and others. Rockford Seminary donated the use of its buildings, and Addams fundraised among Rockford's citizens to cover part of the expenses. About ninety women, most of them first- or second-generation Chicagoans of Irish, German, Jewish, or English descent, attended the summer school in the first year, staying for two weeks or a month, paying $2 a week. The collegiate curriculum had heft. Taught by Starr, Addams, and volunteers, the course offerings included Browning, Emerson, Victor Hugo, Ruskin, and botany; gymnastics, tennis, singing, and German conversation were available for recreation.[83] Jane and Ellen were giving working women the same pleasures they had themselves enjoyed at the very place where they had enjoyed them. The summer school was a formula that worked. Possibly the first institution in the nation to offer the residential liberal arts college experience to working women, the school would flourish for ten years.

In the fall of 1891, after two full years of operation, Hull House received its first real influx of new residents. Three arrived, bringing the total to six. The first addition was a young woman named Mary McDowell, a graduate of the National Kindergarten College in Evanston, who had begun volunteering in the kindergarten in the fall of 1890. The second was a young man named Edward Burchard, the settlement's first male resident. Burchard, a recent graduate of Beloit College, would stay only for a year, but his presence amounted to a quiet revolution.[84] When he moved in, Hull House became the first coed settlement in the world and, if one ignored the male volunteers involved in the clubs and classes from the beginning, technically ended its status as a community of women. Of course, that community remained intact in spirit. Throughout much of Addams's lifetime, female residents would have a two-to-one majority in the house. More intangibly, Hull House would remain a women's community because it was led by women and because the women tended to stay longer than the men. Some of the women lived there for decades; few of the men stayed for more than a year or two.[85]

The third new resident that fall was Julia Lathrop, the friend who, on one of her earlier visits, had joined Jane in the adventure of delivering a baby. Vassar-educated, Lathrop had trained as a lawyer in her father's Rockford law office and was admitted to the bar. She was a stellar addition to the residents' circle and would become a close friend of Addams's.[86]

Lathrop's primary interest in her more than twenty years at Hull House was improving private and government (city and state) charity. She was an enthusiast for the latest thinking in private charity—the modern and increasingly popular principles of "organized charity" set out by the Charity Organization Society (COS) in Great Britain. This type of society had quickly spread to the United States. The aim was to systematize what was usually a random process. Under Lathrop's influence, Hull House began using COS methods in a loose sense in its relief work in 1892, while still making sure that every charity visit was undertaken for a social reason. At Hull House relief was understood to be an incidental aspect of the work, not part of its mission; they felt that helping one's neighbors in crisis was simply humane in the economically struggling Nineteenth Ward. Judging from her writings in this period, Addams remained relatively uninterested in issues of poverty, but she was willing, because she wished to be cooperative, to help Lathrop seek the application of COS methods citywide. In 1891–92, Lathrop, Addams, and others from the Chicago Woman's Club would try without success to persuade the Chicago Relief and Aid Society (CRAS), the city's oldest and largest private relief organization, to adopt COS methods.[87]

Two years apart in age, Addams and Lathrop had much in common— childhoods in northern Illinois, fathers who were Republican politicians (Lathrop's father had served in Congress), a passion for higher education, and a similar experience of confusion in their twenties about what to do with their lives. They also shared a strong sense of moral purposefulness. But Lathrop was different in some ways. Unlike Addams but like Starr, she possessed a sparkling sense of humor. Unlike Starr, whose cleverness was sometimes barbed, Lathrop used her humor to make educational points. Weber Linn called her humor "informational." Addams, impressed by the way Lathrop avoided using "her wit to the disadvantage of another person," thought it was due to her affection for people. And their minds were different. While Addams's intellect was subtle, connecting, and interpretive, Lathrop's was analytical, incisive, and practical. Addams was struck by her ability to sum up a discussion and lay out the best way to proceed. "Such clear thinking," Addams once wrote, "has an enormous liberating power and taps new sources of energy in others."[88]

Mary Rozet Smith would have been the seventh resident that fall if it had been her choice. The tall, slender kindergarten volunteer and former student of Ellen's often stayed at the house for a week or two and wanted to move in permanently but felt it was her duty to live with her elderly parents.[89] By early 1891 she and Addams had become close friends; Addams

Mary Rozet Smith, ca. the 1880s.
Ellen Gates Starr Papers, Sophia Smith
Collection, Smith College,
Northampton, MA.

wrote to her affectionately that their friendship had "come to mean a great deal to" her.[90] Smith, who was nine years younger than Addams, charmed everyone with her beauty, clever wit, and generously sympathetic nature. Another almost-resident was Mary Kenney. A guest in the house for part of 1891, she was often at the settlement.[91]

By the fall of 1891, a lively friendship circle was forming at Hull House. It was what Starr and Addams had hoped for. But the benefits they each gained from friendship were different. Starr, intensely emotional, needed friends to sustain her sense of well-being. Addams, hungry for fresh thinking and often suffering from self-doubt, relied on friends to stimulate her mind and bolster her courage. She had not forgotten the lesson she had learned in the 1880s about how difficult it was to work out her ideas in isolation. She invoked it in her speech to the Chicago Woman's Club. "[I]ntellectual life requires for its expansion the influence of the affection of others." Now, with more friends around her, she was finding the intellectual stimulation and courage she wanted and needed and was feeling more affection daily for her settlement home. She wrote Alice at one point in 1891, "I grow fonder of this place all of the time."[92] Hull House was becoming a locus of human energy, creativity, and affection that, as she had hoped, fed her as much as she fed it. She was thriving in her chosen life.

CHAPTER 10

FELLOWSHIP

1892

One snowy morning soon after Christmas 1891, Jane Addams, with the cook's baby on her hip and a neighbor's child at her skirts, answered a knock at the front door. On the other side she found Florence Kelley, who, it would emerge, was thirty-two years old and had just come from New York City with her three children to escape an abusive marriage and start a new life. At the moment she knocked at Hull House's door, her two sons and a daughter, aged six, three, and five, were at the Woman's Christian Temperance Union nursery for working mothers. To prevent their father from reclaiming them, Kelley planned to hide them with a friend's brother in a suburb until she could get her divorce and gain legal custody under Illinois law. Then she planned to set up her own household in Chicago.[1] Meanwhile, she needed a place to stay and a way to earn a living.

Jane Addams was happy to assist. She offered Kelley a bed at Hull House and went with her the next day to Henry Demarest Lloyd's house in Winnetka to make arrangements for the children. Lloyd, the socialist pro-labor journalist who was a friend of Addams's, was also the brother of Kelley's friend Caro Lloyd—altogether a splendid friend-in-arms for Kelley, who sorely needed friends just then. Soon afterward, Addams created a job for Kelley as the head of a new Hull House project, a labor bureau to help unemployed girls and women find employment. Kelley's salary was to be funded partly by Addams and partly by the Chicago Woman's Club.[2] Kelley intended to find more challenging work eventually, but for the moment she was grateful for the income.

Florence Kelley was a rare being in Jane Addams and Ellen Starr's world. She was a career social reformer, a Marxist socialist, and, most impressively, a successful author. She had published twenty-five articles and two pamphlets in national and international publications, mostly on labor issues, and translated one book, Friedrich Engels's landmark investigation

The Condition of the Working Class in England in 1844 (1887), into English. Kelley's arrival at Hull House was a landmark event in the settlement's modest history. From her first day there, Weber Linn observed, she was "a power." In 1935 Addams assessed her impact with precision. Florence Kelley "galvanized us all into [a] more intelligent interest in the industrial conditions around us."[3] As usual, Addams minimized the personal aspect, but "we" contains "I" and "she galvanized me" would have been equally accurate.

In some ways, Kelley's activism on labor issues was surprising. As a child and young woman she had led a comfortable, protected life. Her father, William Darrah Kelley, was, like John Huy Addams, an early Republican and abolitionist and had served as a legislator (in his case as a Congressman representing a portion of the city of Philadelphia) for almost thirty years, until his death in 1890. Kelley had also, like Addams, gone to college, in her case Cornell University and had aspired but failed to earn a professional degree, in her case, law. Thwarted, she, too, had spent time in her early twenties traveling in Europe and becoming fluent in French and German.[4]

But there were differences. Kelley's father had been thrust into poverty as a child by his own father's death, had worked as a child laborer, had belonged to a union, and had participated in a strike—experiences that led him to become a lawyer, a judge, a legislator, and an advocate for ending child labor. He taught young Florence about the issue. She later recalled her father's "years of effort to enlist me permanently in [the struggle on] behalf of less fortunate children." He gave her children's books about the suffering of child workers, and when she was twelve he took her to see children working in a fiery steel factory, carrying heavy pails of water. The lessons stuck. At Cornell University, Kelley's undergraduate thesis was on the history of the legal status of the child.[5]

Her father was also responsible for Kelley's sophisticated knowledge of and fearless attitude toward legislative reform. When she was younger he had written her letters about political news and strategies; when she lived with him in Washington, D.C., in her twenties, their boarding house was within blocks of the Capitol, making it easy for her to watch her father in legislative debate. He had even helped her read law with him, to prepare for law school. The young Jane Addams could only eavesdrop on her father's political reminiscences, but the young Florence Kelley observed her father's politics firsthand. And her father educated her about women

Florence Kelley, ca. the 1880s. Nicholas Kelley Papers, Manuscripts and Archives Division, The New York Public Library, Astor, Lenox, and Tilden Foundations.

as political leaders. He and Florence's mother were friends with Lucretia Mott, Elizabeth Cady Stanton, and Susan B. Anthony, women who were skilled lobbyists and orators. The young Jane Addams did not know a single woman engaged in politics; the young Florence Kelley knew many. Kelley wrote in an autobiographical essay, "My father's daughter could never[,] from early childhood[,] be . . . unaware of the developing struggle for women's political rights."[6]

There were other large differences between Addams and Kelley. Two were that Kelley had taken a husband and was a mother. While studying in Europe in 1884, she had married a Russian medical student and socialist named Lazare Wischnewetsky and had a child. They had two more children after returning in 1886 to the United States, where they settled in New York City and Lazare struggled to establish a medical practice. Kelley, also unlike Addams, was a Marxist. She had joined the German socialist party in Europe and the Socialist Labor Party in New York City. In an 1887 speech, she boldly told a room full of middle-class college alumnae that she had joined the "proletariat" in its struggle "to end [the capitalist] system" and hoped that they would join her. In the "great strife of classes . . . that is rending society to its foundations," she charged, "[the question] 'where do I belong?' [is] the imperative question for women of our generation."[7]

But, daughter of a legislator that she was, she had a practical side. Even as she called for the overthrow of capitalism, she began using the law to modify it. In 1889 she joined with Knights of Labor leader Leonora Barry to organize the Philadelphia Working Women's Society, a cross-class group similar to the Illinois Woman's Alliance (founded the previous year) to press for legislation to benefit the working class. The result was a law passed in the same year that regulated the employment of women and children and required the state to hire two women factory inspectors. Kelley organized a similar society in New York, and the result was an 1890 state law that more strictly limited workingwomen's hours, limited the working day for minors to eight hours, and added eight new factory inspectors to the state's roster.[8]

Kelley would build on these efforts in her new life in Illinois. By moving to Chicago, whether intentionally or by sheer good luck she had located herself in a major industrialized state ripe for labor reform. Illinois had no labor protection laws for industries other than mining. Furthermore, Hull House's location in the heavily industrial Nineteenth Ward offered Kelley a splendid chance to learn about working people's lives. She wrote Friedrich Engels that spring that by living at Hull House "I am . . . learning more in a week of actual conditions of proletarian life in America than in any previous year." Kelley moved out of Hull House the following year to set up her own apartment with her children and her mother. By the winter of 1893–94, however, her mother had returned east, and Kelley had moved with her children back into Hull House. It was then that she became officially a "resident."[9] For Florence Kelley, Hull House would prove the ideal place to take her commitment to labor reform to a new level.

That said, Kelley and Hull House were, in some ways, a mismatch. There was a gap between Kelley's bold visions for social change and the settlement's short-term horizons. Kelley and Starr had a conversation one day that made this difference clear. Starr was heading out the door to wash a corpse in preparation for its burial when Kelley admonished her, "[I]f we [are to] bring about a change in this country *peaceably* we've got to hustle. I believe it's a solemn duty to wash the dead but it's mighty incidental!" A year or so earlier Kelley had written a friend, "The futility of palliative work . . . impresses me more from year to year."[10] Caring for the sick, the dying, and those in crisis was not high on her priority list.

Behind her impatience was her fear that the frustrated and suffering working class would rise up violently. She wanted the Marxist revolution to take place, but peacefully. Her Marxism was an even larger difference between Kelley and her new Hull House friends. Though Addams had read *Capital*, she had not liked it. Kelley distrusted capitalism and felt that workers needed to undertake a class-based struggle; Addams, Starr, and Lathrop disagreed.[11]

Such intellectual differences created tensions. Kelley's feisty temperament created others. Kelley was outgoing and genial but also uncompromising and hot-tempered. Sometimes she scared or even offended people. "Foolish questions, half-baked opinions, sentimental attitudes, are met with no mercy at [Kelley's] hands," one resident later wrote. Her moral map was as definite as her temperament. One friend commented that she saw "life and people in black and white" and that she could love or hate "with an almost equal ardor."[12]

The result was a debating style that, as another friend remembered, was one of "direct assault." Kelley "hurled the spears of her thought with . . . apparent carelessness of what breast they pierced," Weber Linn wrote; he called her "a rough and tumble fighter." The Chicago cloakmaker and union organizer Abraham Bisno, who became a friend of Kelley's soon after she came to Halsted Street, remembered that her "criticism of the present order was sharp, bitter [and] vigorous." Kelley knew she sometimes went too far. She described herself in 1890 as possessing "an inborn brusqueness which has brought me much trouble."[13]

The scene was set for sparks to fly and they did—not between Addams and Kelley but between Kelley and Lathrop. Both daughters of lawyers with legal training, rapier wits, and substantial debating skills, they loved to spar. Weber Linn, a frequent witness to these conversations when he lived at the house, described their talks as "a firework." Addams, painting the same dynamic in more pastel shades, recalled "their long and scintillating discussions."[14] Linn sketched the scene:

> Mrs. Kelley was a fighter; Miss Lathrop was a diplomat. Both were brilliant, imaginative, humorous, and troubled by injustice; both had great powers of persistence. . . . But Miss Lathrop had endless patience[,] Mrs. Kelley, a kind of fiercely joyous impatience. Miss Lathrop glowed with determination, Mrs. Kelley burnt with eagerness. Miss Lathrop could bide her time, Mrs. Kelley must [move] on. . . . When both were at Hull

House together, arguing [about] . . . correcting a social injustice and dis-
agreeing as they often did on the best [way to proceed], it is doubtful if
any better talk was to be heard anywhere.[15]

Alexander Bruce, a lawyer and a friend of the Lathrop family who would
join the house in 1893 as a resident, drew a similar comparison. "Mrs.
Kelley was brilliant and impulsive; Miss Lathrop was brilliant, yet self-
contained." He called Kelley "a lioness at bay." He thought Lathrop's force
came from her "reasonableness and her calm judgment."[16]

Discussions between Kelley and Lathrop would become one of the most
appealing features of house life. Wrote one resident, "Hull-House . . . was
the most interesting place in the world when Julia Lathrop and Mrs. Kelley
were both there." Ellen Starr, who thrived on confrontation herself, was especially intrigued with Kelley, whom she thought "very brilliant." She wrote
her cousin about listening to Kelley talk: "I roar [with laughter], meditate
profoundly, and do everything in between over her remarks."[17]

Jane Addams, too, delighted in the fireworks, whether between Lathrop
and Kelley or anyone else. She would laugh, a resident remembered, "as
verbal shots were fired." Her pleasure was intellectual. The exchange of
ideas remained for her, as it had been at seminary, a favorite method of connecting with others. "We go," she observed in 1897, "to social gatherings,
hoping that somehow, with somebody, we can have the real intercourse of
mind with mind, and when we do get it in the midst of all our toil and
trouble, it is the most refreshing thing which life offers." Decades later she
would write that friends meet "in the kingdom of the mind."[18]

In her appreciation for this kind of friendship, Addams was similar to
the rest of her college-educated circle. An outsider to this world was able
to discern the pattern easily. Union organizer Abraham Bisno astutely described the difference between the friendships the Hull House women
had with each other and the friendships he had with fellow workers. The
women's friendships, he wrote, involved "an intellectual mutual understanding and need for each other's company, a joy in each other's efforts, a
reverence and respect for each other, . . . but it was intellectual[;] . . . it was
not personal, it was not intimate." His friendship with them was also like
this; he called it a "touch-me-not friendship." His workers' friendships, he
thought, contained more of "the meat of human life." They told each other
about their "troubles and personal problems," their "worries and passions,"
their "enjoyments and happiness." In other words, their relations were

Julia C. Lathrop, ca. the 1890s. Twenty Years at Hull-House, *facing page 310.*

based on what he called "normal human affection." Bisno was not privy, of course, to all the women's conversations, but he thought it strange that private topics did not come up in the conversations in which he took part. Seeking to understand the reasons for this, Bisno arrived at two theories, both of them based on class differences and both insightful. One was that their cultural training was the problem: he hypothesized that "culture in itself chills intimate friendship." The second was that their economic security freed them from needing to depend on each other for life-sustaining help. [19]

Addams's delight in the intellectual side of her new friendships was fed by her own mental sharpness. Her niece Marcet Haldeman-Julius recalled her "eager, sensitive mind." Another person praised "the quickness of her perception, the keenness of her mind, [and] her ability to grasp the crux of an argument or statement almost before it had fully escaped . . . a speaker's [lips]." She was every bit Lathrop's and Kelley's mental equal as a sparring partner. Still, she did not spar. Instead of grappling with an opponent, she encircled the battle. Rather than take a side, she would probe the topic as if, a friend once said, she had "completely suspended judgment." She was

Jane Addams in the 1890s. Jane Addams Memorial Collection (JAMC neg. 494),
Special Collections, The University Library, University of Illinois at Chicago.

seeking to see the issue, as Weber Linn put it, "from everybody's point of view." This was not simply her intentionally nonresistant approach to conversation, though it was probably that; it was also characteristic of her mind. "One cannot talk to her for five minutes," a later resident recalled, "without realizing that hers is the great gift of synthesis, of bringing things to unity, by 'patience, subtlety, and breadth.'" Addams's refusal to be a conversational partisan was part of what lay behind the affectionate sobriquet that Kelley and Lathrop, and then other residents, adopted for her: "the gentle Jane."[20]

Given these differences, Addams and Kelley might well have found each other exasperating, even irritating, but instead they became good friends. Addams found Kelley immensely appealing. She recalled, "During that first winter . . . we all felt the stimulus of her magnetic personality." Part of Kelley's appeal was her bold decisiveness. While Addams was sometimes immobilized by her tendency to sympathize with everyone and with all points of view and her compulsion to be fully prepared, Kelley simply plunged ahead. One friend remembered of Kelley that "[e]veryone was brave the moment she came into the room."[21] She gave Jane Addams courage.

And Kelley admired and loved Addams. Kelley's son Nicholas wrote, "[F]rom the time my mother first went to Hull House . . . she approved of [Jane Addams] unreservedly." She particularly admired Addams for a quality that Kelley felt she distinctly lacked: her steady, generous-spirited unflappability. Kelley wondered how Addams had become such a person. One day, according Nicholas, Florence put the question to Addams. Addams told her that "she had had a great struggle to master her temper when she was young."[22] Florence Kelley never achieved that mastery.

The Hull House that Kelley joined was now in its third year and a thriving institution. The crèche and the diet kitchen shared inadequate space in a rented cottage. The kindergarten was cramped in the main drawing room. The five public bathrooms recently constructed at the rear of the mansion were in constant use. The settlement had started a relief fund to help families in financial crisis. The winter quarter of the college extension classes was offering thirty-one courses to 182 students, with Starr teaching the history of Greek art and Shakespeare's *Hamlet*, Addams teaching George Eliot's *Felix Holt*, and Lathrop teaching English literature. Kelley joined in, teaching elementary German on Friday nights. The Thursday night free lecture and concert series, a new project that had been started the previous year, was particularly erudite that winter, with three university professors, including a young philosophy professor from the University of Michigan named John Dewey, giving talks. The Butler Art Gallery attracted roughly three hundred people per day. On Sunday afternoons, there were free concerts that showcased musicians and music clubs in the city. Altogether, about one thousand visitors and ninety volunteers were coming to the house every week.[23]

Kelley was drawn like a magnet to the Working People's Social Science Club, which continued to hammer away at solutions to the "industrial problem." In February she gave a talk titled "Child Labor." Others on the roster that spring included Sigmund Zeisler, a lawyer for the Haymarket Anarchists, who spoke about the jury system, and Samuel Gompers, president of the American Federation of Labor, speaking about labor organizations.

The other clubs were also prospering. Among the fourteen listed in the Hull House Program were the Pansy Club, which Addams led, and the new Hull House Woman's Club, founded by Mary McDowell. There were too many girls' clubs to list them all, the program apologetically explained. Addams, while teaching and doing club work, managed everything. Starr, worried about her friend's habit of pushing herself too hard, accused her that spring of "working yourself to death."[24] But she also knew what everyone knew: that Hull House's remarkable growth was due mainly to the indefatigable Addams.

That growth was still strapping Addams's finances. During fiscal year 1891–92, the combined operating and capital budget grew by 30 percent, to $12,140. Since the residents' fees only generated $738, Addams needed to raise $11,402 to balance the books by September 30, when the fiscal year ended. She raised only $8,985, which left a deficit of $2,417. As she had before, Addams quietly paid the shortfall, possibly by selling off more of her inherited assets. The bulk of the loss was the result of a gap between the income from the far-too-low residents' fees and the burgeoning operating expenses of $2,000.[25] One suspects that Addams was keeping the fee low to help the cash-strapped Starr and Kelley.

———————————

John Dewey used his visit in January to educate himself about the settlement; he stayed for a week. Although only thirty-three, Dewey was already well known in his discipline, having published a popular textbook of psychology, then a subfield of philosophy, in 1887. But he had yet to write any of the many philosophical works that would bring him a national following. Dewey was interested in the role of ethics in everyday life. His essay on the ethics of democracy was published as an occasional paper by his university in 1888. More recently he had written a second textbook, *Outlines of a Critical Theory of Ethics* (1891).[26]

During his week at Hull House Dewey and Addams had long talks. They connected immediately. Dewey, like Addams and so many of their generation, was disenchanted by institutionalized religion, enthusiastic about the power of Christ's teachings to transform the world, attracted to the ideas of T. H. Green, and in favor of cooperative action. In other words, he was a social Christian. When Addams explained that Hull House intended to build cross-class human connections by embodying the Christian spirit and practicing cooperation, Dewey understood the vision instantly. "I am

John Dewey, 1894. Bentley Historical Library, University of Michigan.

confident that twenty-five years from now," he wrote her after his visit, "the forces now turned in upon themselves in various church[es] or agencies will be finding [an] outlet very largely through just such channels as you have opened."[27]

Dewey and Addams also shared a deeply philosophical way of thinking. Some of this was temperamental. When confronted with a dilemma, their minds shifted naturally to an abstract plane. But some of it was intellectual. Dewey, like Addams, was an idealist, or, in philosophical terms, a Hegelian idealist. At this stage of his life, he believed that ideas were the most powerful reality. Dewey wrote in *Outlines*, "[A] new perception of [the social world's] scope and bearings is, perforce, a change of that world." But he had also just read William James's *Principles of Psychology* (1891) and was beginning to be drawn more toward the world of experience. Dewey met Addams—or perhaps sought her out—at just the right time.[28]

Dewey was the more complete intellectual, of course, the truer philosopher. He would remain a professor all his life and organize his life around
scholarly pursuits. And Addams was on her way to becoming the more
complete social activist, the truer experimenter; having started a settlement
house, she would remain "in the trenches" and organize her life around
her commitment to social reform. But this difference in career choice was
almost incidental, since each was powerfully drawn to what the other pursued most intently.

Dewey was fascinated with Hull House and Addams's ideas and grateful
for the visit. "I cannot tell you," he wrote afterwards, "how much good I
got from my stay at Hull House. My indebtedness to you for giving me
an insight into matters there is great. I think I got a pretty good idea of
the general spirit and methods. Every day I stayed there only added to my
conviction that you [have] taken the right way."[29]

Within two years, their budding friendship would be blessed by the gift
of proximity. In 1894 Dewey would take a position at the brand-new University of Chicago, after which he and Addams would see each other often.
During the decade Dewey lived in the city, they no doubt held some of the
most fascinating conversations ever conducted in the history of American
social ethics. Sadly for posterity, most of what was said has vanished into
the air. The respect and affection they had for each other, however, speaks
through their actions. Addams helped Dewey start an innovative school for
children at the University of Chicago; Dewey gave lectures at and visited
Hull House often; Addams invited Dewey to join its Board of Trustees in
1897; Dewey and his wife named a daughter after Addams. The influence
of the two friends on each other was profound, and, in many of its various
parts, untraceable to one party or the other. As the years passed, it was
not Dewey who influenced Addams or Addams who influenced Dewey so
much as the friendship that influenced them both.[30] With John Dewey as
much as with any friend she ever had, Jane Addams truly connected "in
the kingdom of the mind."

The winter Addams and Dewey met was, like the previous winter, a harsh
one in Chicago; people in the prosperous classes were again worried about
the working classes. In early 1892 a left-leaning men's club in the city, the
Sunset Club, chose for its February meeting the topic "How Would You
Uplift the Masses?" The club, a cross-class organization of businessmen,
professional men, academics, journalists, and trade union leaders, also de-

cided to make the meeting a Lady's Night—that is, to allow wives to attend and women to address the gathering. Four speakers were invited to give remarks: a labor union man who was also an immigrant, two women, and a rabbi. Jane Addams was one of the women. The other speakers were Lucy Flower, a leader of the Chicago Woman's Club, Emil Hirsch, a reform rabbi active in the labor movement, and George Schilling, an immigrant and a socialist-anarchist trade union leader.[31] Three of the speakers would criticize the current industrial system as unjust and call for government or union action to rectify the conditions that the system had produced. Only Addams would not. The evening at the Sunset Club sets Jane Addams in context among other progressive reformers in the city. Her lack of interest in the material side of the industrial situation and her unwillingness to judge the status quo as unjust stand out.

Lady's Night produced a huge crowd. On February 4, 1892, six hundred men and women were in attendance at the Grand Pacific Hotel for the two-hour, nine-course dinner, brass band serenade, and speeches. Chairing the session was Frances Willard, the fifty-two-year-old founder and president of the Woman's Christian Temperance Union. In recent years the famous temperance and women's rights reformer had joined the Knights of Labor and begun speaking out against the injustices of the capitalist system. She therefore did not like the question posed for the evening, especially its assumption that the masses would not and could not "uplift" themselves. After the last coffee was poured, Willard took up the gavel. "I wonder," she began with pointed humor, "if the question will not some day be inverted and we [will] ask how the masses will uplift us. I hope they will not hoist us by our own petard." She then offered a bold prediction. "I am glad to say that the masses send us word that they are rising, and ten years from now I don't think [tonight's] question . . . will be germane."[32] The evening was off to a lively start.

Lucy Flower's speech, which came next, was also hard-hitting. She had been orphaned as a child, and the experience had apparently opened her eyes to the needs of those with few resources. Wealthy by marriage, she had helped found a series of institutions through her activism in the Chicago Woman's Club, including an industrial school to give orphaned and troubled boys the skills to make them employable and a legal services clinic to give the poor access to lawyers. She had also joined others to lobby the state to reform its compulsory education laws and the city to improve its sweatshop laws. Flowers called the audience's attention to the problem that, in her mind, defined the current societal dilemma: the failure of middle-class people to understand the physical suffering of the poorest working people. "[T]he mental, moral, and spiritual are largely dependent on the physical," she warned. "The best mind can be stunted if not destroyed by insufficient bodily nourishment." Her proposed solutions, all requiring government action, included stricter landlord-tenant ordinances, a legal ban on child labor, jobs for the unemployed, and more public schools to relieve overcrowding. "We must legislate," she said. These reforms would come "as soon as you, the people and voters, . . . act instead of talking; when you [take] time from your selfish struggle [to] accumulate wealth, and [make] an earnest effort [to advance] your neighbor."[33]

Then the two men spoke, hitting many of the same themes. Emil Hirsch criticized the "industrial system" for forcing its workers to live ten or twelve people to a room and giving them no chance to develop their individual gifts. George Schilling, the only worker to address the crowd, blamed the workers' exploitation on the principle of "legalized privilege" as embodied in monopolies and, like the others, called for "justice in the realm of economics."[34]

Jane Addams, who spoke last, was greeted, according to press reports, by enormous applause. By 1892 her popularity among Chicago reform enthusiasts was apparently huge. She delivered her usual message—that cultured people had a responsibility as citizens to help immigrants and other working people seek a fuller social and intellectual life—but there is a hint in the speech that she was feeling a twinge of interest in politics. She noted almost wistfully the limits that had been placed on women's citizenship. A settlement of women could provide a neighborhood center to "keep intellectual and social activity alive," she said, but there are "certain activities of citizenship which society thus far has insisted on thrusting upon men and which a women's settlement must perforce leave unperformed."[35] But if she was wistful, she saw no solution. Focused on what women could not do in the political realm, namely, vote and hold political office, she did not speak of what they could do. It was as if she saw the shaping of public policy as beyond her reach as a woman, as if she felt unauthorized without the vote.

Kelley was one of Jane Addams's guests at the Sunset Club that night. Raised for a life in politics, she did not suffer from such qualms. With her work at the new labor bureau paying her bills, she resumed her activist political work in her spare time. That spring she took up three issues: the overcrowded elementary schools in the Nineteenth Ward, the city's failure to provide the ward with adequate garbage removal services, and sweatshop reform. Addams knew about all three problems—she had mentioned the overcrowded schools in "Outgrowths," she lived daily with the garbage problem, and she spoke often with sweatshop workers—but she had not tackled them in any practical way.[36] The story of Jane Addams's education in politics begins here, in the spring of 1892, as she watched the gifted and skillful Florence Kelley, in cooperation with the Chicago Woman's Club (CWC) and the Illinois Woman's Alliance (IWA), launch herself into persistent and strategic political action.

At that time the situation in the public schools of the Nineteenth Ward, like that in many other crowded working-class wards in the city, was dire. Only 2,957 seats were available for the 6,976 school-aged children (ages six to fourteen) living in the ward. Under such conditions, Illinois's newly improved compulsory education law, passed in 1889 thanks to the lobbying efforts of the IWA and the CWC, was a dead letter. Furthermore, seeking a statewide ban on child labor did not make sense when the unemployed children would find no places waiting for them in school.[37]

In order for a new school to be built in the Nineteenth Ward the City Council would need to appropriate funds and the Chicago Board of Education would need to expend them. Thus both public bodies required persuading. Kelley began by marshaling her facts. She dug up the census figures for school-aged children in the ward and compared them with the enrollment capacities of the schools. Then she and the IWA, whose help she had enlisted, sought press coverage to publicize the gap and circulated a petition, which they then presented to the Board of Education. The board voted its support. Now the only obstacle was the City Council. One evening in May 1892, Kelley and a large number of IWA supporters showed up at a council meeting to present the petition. By rights, Alderman John Powers, one of the Nineteenth Ward's two aldermen and one of the most powerful aldermen in the council, should have presented it and led the fight for funding the school. But Powers, an Irish Catholic, was opposed to public education, preferring that parochial schools meet the need. He made sure that the petition was referred to a committee that Powers's good friend William J. O'Brien chaired, in effect killing it. But Kelley and the IWA were undaunted. The following fall they would issue a report titled "The Condition of Public Schools in Chicago." It created so much public pressure that the City Council was forced to address the problem. Over Powers's opposition and much to his fury, a new school would be built in the Nineteenth Ward in 1893.[38] The struggle to improve the public schools in the ward was not over, but a start had been made.

Just as the problem of crowded schools was not unique to the Nineteenth Ward, neither was the problem of inadequate garbage removal. Indeed, both problems were part of a broader national crisis: the inadequate funding of public services in rapidly growing cities. In the spring of 1892, members of the CWC, working with the IWA, announced the formation of a new organization, the Municipal Order League, to enlist the citizens of the city in a volunteer-driven street inspection campaign. In a well-publicized speech, the league's president, Ada Sweet, laid the blame for the streets' bad state squarely on the political patronage system. The city contracted with "scavengers," men with wagons for hire, to remove the garbage. Scavenger contracts, she charged, were awarded as political spoils in return for kickbacks. Aldermen would ensure that city contracts were awarded to the contractors, who promised them cash bribes or votes in return. The practice was called "boodling." Few in the council cared whether the scavengers actually did the work. Though contracted to collect the garbage three times per week, scavengers sometimes collected as seldom as twice a month.[39] The Nineteenth Ward's condition, in other words, was the direct result of John Powers's boodling skills.

Sweet saw women as key to creating public pressure on City Hall to clean up the garbage. "Under the present system of party government," she declared, "the rage for accumulating money [is] drowning out public spirit among men. Women must take the initiative." The plan was for women citizens, organized into ward clubs, to collect written complaints about poor garbage removal services during the summer and forward them to the city health department. Florence Kelley, assisted by Hull House resident Edward Burchard, coordinated the complaint-filing effort in the Nineteenth Ward. Altogether Hull House collected and reported 1,037 complaints in the summer of 1892. Feeling the political pressure, the mayor appointed a series of new inspectors for the ward, but each was quickly removed, no doubt thanks to the behind-the-scene maneuverings of John Powers, who preferred his scavenger friends to operate without harassment.[40] Hull House was beginning to look like a troublemaking organization to Powers. And Powers was beginning to look like a troublemaking politician to Hull House residents. Meanwhile, the garbage continued to pile up.

The third reform Kelley tackled that spring was the reform in which she possessed the greatest expertise: improving the industrial working conditions of women and girls. In Chicago, Kelley, already skilled in legislative reform, found other women with the same knowledge and skills: Elizabeth Morgan, Mary Kenney, members of the IWA, Lucy Flower, Ellen Henrotin, and the members of the CWC. Between 1889 and 1891 these women had used factual research, petitions, newspaper publicity, mass rallies, and personal lobbying of legislators to reform the state's compulsory education law and the city's sweatshop laws.[41]

The phrase "sweatshop reform" stood for two distinct issues, both of which were prevalent in sweatshops but not restricted to them. The first problem was the long workday of young children and women. Many were working eleven-hour shifts with few breaks. The second problem was that they faced unsanitary and unhealthy working conditions. Sweatshops were typically small, filthy rooms without light or ventilation. Workers ill with such diseases as tuberculosis and typhoid fever were forced by poverty and the absence of health insurance to go to work when they should have been in bed. They contaminated the clothing they handled, which was then sold to middle-class and upper-class people, spreading the disease across class lines.[42]

Sweatshop reform had made some progress in the east, thanks to the efforts of trade unions and their supporters. The Massachusetts legislature had passed the nation's first factory inspection law in 1866. Subsequent laws had limited women and children to working ten hours per day and mandated the hiring of women factory inspectors, who were thought to be more effective in monitoring working conditions for women and children. Between 1885 and 1889, ten more states passed laws regulating child workers. In the late 1880s and early 1890s, nudged by Kelley and her colleagues, New York and Pennsylvania had joined in the movement.[43]

Illinois, on the other hand, had no state legislation, despite the fact that the Chicago Trades and Labor Assembly (CTLA) had begun seeking a law prohibiting labor by children in 1879.[44] In 1884 the CTLA put forward a new proposal to require factory and workshop inspections. In October 1888, in the wake of a series of articles in the *Chicago Times* that aroused the concerns of middle-class readers about the terrible working conditions in the sweatshops, Elizabeth Morgan, Corinne Brown, Ellen Henrotin, and Ada Sweet had founded the IWA; its first meeting was spent criticizing sweatshop bosses, in particular, their cruelty to children.[45]

With the IWA's forming, the initiative in sweatshop reform passed from trade union men to trade union women. Instead of seeking state legislation, the IWA sought reforms through passage of city ordinances. Between 1889 and 1891 the Chicago City Council, under steady pressure from the IWA, passed a series of laws that appointed five female factory inspectors, banned child labor for those younger than fourteen, and limited the hours that older children and women worked in a day to eight. One alderman observed with some disgust that the City Council "was succumbing to the influence of female lobbyists."[46]

The problem was that the laws had no enforcement mechanism—that is, the factory inspectors had no legal power to enforce the law. Manufacturers ignored them. Frustrated, in 1891 Elizabeth Morgan persuaded the CTLA to appoint a committee, headed by her husband Thomas Morgan, to investigate the sweatshops. The resulting report, "The New Slavery: Investigation into the Sweating System," was published by the CTLA in October 1891 with notable local and national press coverage.[47] Thus it was that by early 1892, just as Florence Kelley was settling in at Hull House, Chicago reformers from across a spectrum of organizations and classes were ready to begin a campaign for state legislation to regulate sweatshops and were equipped with the skills and experience to accomplish it.

Meanwhile, interest in sweatshop reform was also percolating at the federal level. That spring the chair of the House Committee on Manufactures, Sherman Hoar of Massachusetts, decided to investigate the sweatshop problem in several large cities. Hoar and his committee arrived in Chicago in April to find themselves the target of a well-organized campaign. Kelley, Elizabeth Morgan, and garment workers all testified before his committee; Mary Kenney helped organize massive public rallies of working people at which she, Henry Demarest Lloyd, Elizabeth Morgan, and Kelley spoke, and the IWA orchestrated a massive newspaper publicity campaign about sweatshop abuses, both in Chicago and nationwide.[48]

Did Jane Addams help in this anti-sweatshop campaign? No evidence survives in newspaper articles that she did. And in *Twenty Years* she does not mention being involved. But whatever else she was doing, she was watching closely as Kelley, Kenney, and Morgan spoke to mass rallies, testified before the House committee, and personally lobbied elected officials, all things she herself had never done. She saw the care with which they planned their strategies and the unflagging persistence with which they pursued them.

Kelley knew that to make a strong case for Illinois labor reform on behalf of women and girls, she, the CWC members, and female trade union members would need more systematic data than Morgan's report contained. In the spring of 1892 she persuaded the Illinois Bureau of Labor Statistics to undertake two investigations in Chicago, one of the wages and working conditions for women and girls in all areas of employment, including factories and offices as well as sweatshops, and one of the sweating system. She was then hired to collect the data in the Nineteenth Ward and to write the two reports. Published in the bureau's *Seventh Biennial Report* in early 1893, these reports would provide sweatshop reformers with exactly the factual ammunition they needed to make the case for legislation to the state legislature.[49]

While Kelley was joyously entering the political fray, Addams was working on women's labor issues in the same way she had been working on them since 1889: through private means and on a neighborhood scale. Her newest project, perhaps inspired in part by Toynbee Hall's shoeblacks' cooperative hotel, was something she and Mary Kenney concocted: a "working girls'" cooperative boarding club. It was intended to provide female workers with secure housing in case of a need to strike. Kenney found a few women to join her, and Addams led a little seminar in which she and the other women all read aloud together Beatrice Potter's new book *The Cooperative Movement in Great Britain* and discussed "all the difficulties and fascinations" of a "cooperative residential club." Addams paid the first month's rent for two apartments and provided the furnishings, and on May 1, 1892, five young women (two bookbinders, two shoemakers, and one shirtmaker) moved into one of them. It was in a building around the corner from Hull House that Helen Culver owned and managed. They drew up bylaws, elected a president and treasurer, voted to tax themselves $3 a week for food, rent, and domestic service, and named their club the Jane Club, in honor of their mentor. Possibly the first working girls' cooperative boarding club in the United States, the Jane Club would soon inspire the founding of others, in Chicago and elsewhere.[50]

Summer, as usual, marked a change of pace for Addams. She spent part of it at the Hull House Summer School and part of it at her desk writing. The previous November she had received an invitation to give two lectures in late July at a large conference in the east. The request, which included the offer of lecture fees and paid expenses, came from Henry Carter Adams of the University of Michigan, Henry Demarest Lloyd's friend and John Dewey's close colleague. The conference to which Adams, who was a political economist with socialist leanings, invited her was actually a summer school. Called the School of Applied Ethics, it was an offshoot of the Ethical Culture Societies movement and had been held for the first time the previous year. Meeting at Plymouth, Massachusetts, for six weeks, it had quickly established a luminous reputation, having attracted as lecturers some of the country's most prominent Protestants in the fields of applied ethics.[51]

Addams's inclusion in such a group was an accomplishment and evidence that both she and Hull House had become nationally famous in social reform circles. Publicity had been key. Since 1889 a steady stream of articles on Chicago's first settlement had been appearing in national religious and secular magazines, including the WCTU's *Union Signal*, the *Review of Reviews*, the *Chautauquan*, the *Altruistic Review*, the *Charities Review*, and the widely read *Scribner's Magazine*. In addition there had been an untold number of newspaper articles.[52]

Part of this remarkable editorial attention may be chalked up to the public's fascination with the burgeoning American settlement house movement as a whole. In 1891 and 1892, ten new settlements had opened in New York City, Boston, Philadelphia, and Chicago. East Coast publications, which almost all of these were, found news about the movement from the progressive west especially enticing. As one Massachusetts newspaper noted in writing about Addams and Hull House that summer, "It is good to see Chicago instructing the wise men and wise women of the East."[53]

But Addams's talented guiding hand can also be sensed behind the scenes. None of these articles was by Addams herself, but they were often by settlement residents or friends of hers. Hull House would continue to receive the most publicity of any settlement house throughout the 1890s.[54] Clearly, this was no accident. Her motives were no doubt professional and personal. On one hand, it was her job, as Hull House's leader and co-founder, to promote the settlement, which, because it depended on volunteers and donors for its survival, needed fame to thrive. And as a co-founder of one of the nation's first settlements, she had a responsibility to spread the word about the movement as well. On the other hand, her old desire to have a respected public reputation surely played a part. In this, as she had realized in 1889, she was much like her father.

Hull House's rising fame impressed many, but not Ellen Gates Starr.

Ever the skeptic, she worried that fame might go to their heads. "The success of Hull House outwardly and visibly is something of a snare," she wrote her cousin Mary Allen that summer. The praise "serves as an excuse for [our not doing and being] the things we ought to do and be." It was characteristic of Starr to insist on achieving the ideal, the excellent, but there was also a more personal reason for her dissatisfaction. That summer she was frustrated with herself, disappointed in the gap between her vague ambitions and her modest achievements. So far her work at Hull House, aside from curating shows at the Butler Art Gallery, had consisted mainly of volunteer teaching in the college extension classes and earning money by tutoring, teaching, and lecturing about art history around the city. She had not yet found the vocational focus that some around her, most notably Kelley, had. Restless, she traveled to England in April, where she joined up with the Barnetts and went to Italy for an art tour, her expenses presumably paid for by a friend, possibly Jane Addams or Mary Wilmarth, but when she returned to Chicago in July, she had no more answers.[55]

Miserable, she bore down on her most human failing: her bad temper, which she seemed unable to control. "I have been very bad," she wrote her cousin Mary Allen soon after her return, "and it has come to a sort of crisis. . . . [Please] pray for me." Throughout the following fall she would send her cousin and her sister bulletins about her battles with her temper, sometimes reporting success, sometimes failure. "My temper is improving," she wrote her sister at one point. At another she reported to her cousin, "I've . . . lost my temper out and out" and called it "humiliating."[56]

Perhaps also contributing to her bleak, dissatisfied mood was the fact that Ellen's intense feelings for Jane had begun to cool by the summer of 1892. The friendship had long been important to her. Begun in 1877, it had become close in 1885 and was a deeply devoted partnership by 1888. It had allowed Ellen, like Jane, to turn her back on her old life and to launch a new one. Troubled that her feelings for Jane were changing, Ellen tried in August to analyze her situation in a letter to Mary Allen. She thought the affection she had felt for Addams when they lived apart, an affection she had felt again when she was away in Europe, was different than what she felt when she was at Hull House. "They are two kinds of affection," she observed, "and they interfere with each other almost." She did not explain further but simply wrote wistfully of the first kind, "I find that I miss it."[57]

And there were other issues. Ellen liked her friendships to be intense, to involve a "special affection." But if she ever felt she had that with Jane, she did not feel she had it in 1892. She complained to Kelley with wry humor that Addams's affection for her also "includes the 19th ward." And her former admiration for Addams's patience with flawed humanity had turned into irritation. She once told her in exasperation, "Jane, if the devil himself came riding down Halsted Street with his tail waving out behind him, you'd say, 'What a beautiful curve he has in his tail.' "[58] To the zealous Ellen, Jane's open-mindedness now seemed morally compromising. Clearly, Starr no longer felt as she had in 1889, when she had treasured the "beautiful spiritual life" beside her. It appears that she was finding it difficult to idealize her friend now that she was living with her.

Ellen could not enjoy life if she was not "in love" with someone. Sometime in 1891 or 1892, she, in her own words, "fell in love" with her cousin Mary Allen during one of her annual late summer visits to Deerfield, Massachusetts. She began to write long letters to her addressed "Dearly Beloved" and to speak freely of her strong feelings.[59] Mary's distance from Chicago posed no obstacle; rather, it was an advantage. Corresponding with her, Starr was able to enjoy again the kind of affection she preferred—the kind that she could only feel when the object of her affections was far away and that could be expressed in the letters she so enjoyed writing.

Although disorienting, Starr's change in love objects suited her restless, passionate nature. In truth, she enjoyed finding new people to be enchanted by; she liked the adventure, the excitement, the drama of it all. At Hull House, as at Kirkland School, she was open to the experience of falling in love. She tried to be honest with Mary Allen about this; no doubt she tried to be honest with Jane about it, too. In 1891 she wrote Mary Allen that she had "sometimes been fickle." A few years later, when she had "fallen in love" with an unnamed person at Hull House, she wrote Mary, "I am more in love with you than the other person, but you know the lengths and depths of my fickleness so don't be deceived. The other person has innings in October [when residents returned to Hull House]—first ups pick."[60] Ellen's playful tone showed the pleasure she took in the game and her unwillingness to be devotedly monogamous.

Just when Jane Addams's admiration for and dependence on Starr began to dwindle is not clear, but she, too, experienced a shift in her affections. Ellen felt it. Many decades later, in a letter she sent to Jane in 1935 just a month before Jane died, Ellen, who had been rereading Jane's letters to her from the 1880s, wrote, "I can see by the way you overrate me in these letters that it was inevitable that I should disappoint you." One source of irritation for Jane was an aspect of Ellen's temperament that she had once appreci-ated: her relentless and critical frankness, her willingness to scold. This had worn Addams down, leaving her to wonder whether Ellen approved of her as she was. She once said as much to Ellen. In the same 1935 letter, Starr reminded Jane that, years earlier, she had heard her say about some-one else that she "liked and respected her but did not love her." And then, according to Ellen, Addams had turned to Starr and said, "[Y]ou respect me and love me but you don't like me." And Addams's needs were also changing. In 1889 she had needed Ellen's enthusiasm to give her the con-fidence to act. By 1892 she had a wealth of friends, including Julia Lathrop and Florence Kelley, to provide that stimulus. Now she needed a different kind of friend, one who would provide a quiet, affectionate refuge for her from her increasingly demanding, hectic life. She was finding that friend in Mary Rozet Smith. In July, Addams wrote Smith, "I am very grateful to my sweet nurse for all her good letters. . . . [I] will feel dreadfully if I don't see you [this weekend]."[61]

Like Starr, Smith had a lively sense of humor and was a scintillating conversationalist, but the similarities ended there. Where Ellen pushed, Mary sheltered; where Ellen scolded, Mary was tender; where Ellen lost her temper, Mary was serene. Weber Linn remembered "the look and the love, the brightness and the patience in [Mary's] eyes." Alice Hamilton, a later resident at Hull House, was struck by Mary's gift for listening, for draw-ing another person out, for giving comfort. A long-time friend of Mary's, Eleanor Smith (no relation), who was teaching music classes at Hull House in 1892 and would later become a resident, thought Mary combined "the rarest human traits— . . . great nobility and tolerance, boundless generos-ity and sweetness." Where the combative Ellen found it easy to make ene-mies, Mary made only friends. Alice Hamilton thought her "the most uni-versally beloved person" she had ever known.[62]

But there was more to Mary Rozet Smith than a loving heart. Jane Ad-dams's niece Marcet Haldeman-Julius, Alice's daughter, who would spend much time with Addams and Smith in later years, thought that her aunt "drew upon Mary Smith mentally as well as emotionally." When Mary thought she needed "straightening out," Marcet recalled, she offered Jane "a tender, tonic criticism that she found no where else." Weber Linn found Smith a "decisive thinker" who could not "abide social injustice . . . to the poor, the unaccepted." And it is clear from Addams's letters to her over the years—their close friendship would last until Mary's death in 1934—

that Smith shared Addams's passion for Hull House and its never-ending new projects in a way that Starr, so skeptical of its success, did not. Smith, using her large family wealth, would fund those projects generously. She and Addams spent many happy hours talking and strategizing about the settlement.[63]

———————

Jane Addams left for the conference in Plymouth toward the end of July, accompanied by Julia Lathrop and two Hull House volunteers. In her absence, friends would take up her administrative duties. Florence Kelley would cover Hull House while Starr, up at Rockford, would manage the last weeks of the summer school.[64]

Her two lectures were in her traveling trunk. They amounted to the most ambitious writing project she had ever undertaken. She had organized them around the Kantian-Comtean distinction also favored by the author of her seminary rhetoric textbook, Alexander Bain, between the subjective and the objective. In "The Subjective Necessity of a Social Settlement" she described why she wanted to start a settlement house. In "The Objective Value of a Social Settlement" she treated the facts of the case: what the neighborhood was like and what the settlement did. Although the titles were cumbersome, the distinction they made brought a useful structure to the ideas in "Outgrowths" and her Sunset Club remarks, both of which she borrowed from in writing the new speeches.[65]

She was to be one of several lecturers in a weeklong course on philanthropy and social progress. As its organizer, Henry Carter Adams had chosen lecturers from across the Protestant social reform spectrum. The conservative Bernard Bonsanquet from London believed that poverty was a sign of character failure. The secular radical Franklin Henry Giddings, a political economist at Bryn Mawr College, held that practical socialism should rein in unrestrained individualism. The Christian radical James O. S. Huntington, an Episcopalian priest and Christian socialist who had worked among the poor in New York City, criticized middle-class people for practicing condescension in their charity work. Addams and another settlement house founder, Robert Woods of Boston, occupied the comfortable middle. Unwilling to criticize anyone, be they the poor, the capitalists, individualists, or charity volunteers, they endorsed the Toynbee Hall vision of cross-class social relations as the best means to achieve social progress.[66]

The audience, admitted at no charge, consisted of members of the general reading public, in particular, those interested in social Christian reforms. Most exciting to Addams was the presence of her colleagues in the nascent American settlement house movement: about twenty people, mostly from Boston and New York who were working to establish more settlements on the East Coast. One afternoon later that week, the "settlers" would meet separately, holding, in effect, the nation's first tiny settlement house conference. Addams recalled later how proud she felt to be associated with such a gathering.[67]

Addams kicked off the series of lectures on philanthropy and social progress on Thursday night, July 28, 1892, with her speech "Subjective Necessity." Henry C. Adams was astute to put her first. Her name on the program, one reporter noted, was enough to attract an unusually large crowd. The next morning the audience for her second talk was even larger. Reporters found her "modest," "sensible," and "inspiring" and her delivery one of "invincible energy" and "convincing."[68]

"Subjective Necessity" was the more powerful of the two speeches she gave that week because she wrote it from the heart. She did not say "my" and used the word "I" rarely but she had a great personal stake in what she was saying, as she obliquely admitted. "[T]his paper," she said, "is an attempt to . . . analyze . . . motives based upon conviction [and] genuine emotion."[69] It covered the familiar ground of "Outgrowths"—her desire to bring democracy to social affairs, share culture with working people, and be a part of the human experience—but whether because her audience now included reformers, or because she could speak at greater length in the educational setting of the School of Applied Ethics, or because her thinking had deepened and shifted in the year and a half since she had delivered "Outgrowths," she had new things to say on these matters at Plymouth. And there was a new theme. Mindful of the presence of her settlement colleagues, she also addressed the settlement method.

Of the three "subjective," that is to say, personal, motives she gave for co-founding a settlement house, the one she invested with special passion was the example of the early Christians' love for humanity and its connection to nonresistance (nonviolence), a subject to which she had allotted only a sentence in "Outgrowths." To Christ and to the early Christians, she said, "nonresistance" was a belief "in love as a cosmic force." Crediting Tolstoy for "reminding us" of this, she asserted that opposition is futile and that "evil can be overcome only with good and cannot be opposed." If "love is the creative force of the universe, the principle which binds men together and, by their interdependence on each other makes them human," she observed, then "just so surely is anger and the spirit of opposition the destructive principle of the universe, that which tears down, thrusts men apart, and makes them isolated and brutal." The passage stands as the most cogent statement Addams ever made of her philosophy of Christian nonresistant, loving cooperation. Generally when she mentioned Christ in her speeches or writings—and she did this only to distinctly Christian audiences—she invoked him as an example of someone who lived among the common people and knew how to combine thought and action.[70] "Subjective Necessity" marked a high point in her willingness to explain Christian love.

In this speech Addams also linked democracy to Christianity. When Christians revealed their love for humanity through their actions, she said, a "wonderful fellowship, that true democracy of the early Church," arose. She had not connected the two in "Outgrowths," but the idea was no doubt familiar to her. In the mid-1880s, reading Mazzini had reminded her about the connection, and he was hardly original in his insight. American Protestant reformers and social thinkers had been pointing out the close ties between them throughout the nineteenth century.[71]

But there was a more proximate source of inspiration for Addams on this point: John Dewey. In March he had delivered a paper titled "Christianity and Democracy" to the Christian Student Association at the University of Michigan in which he argued that "democracy [is] . . . the means by which the revelation of [God's] truth is carried on, ... [is] brought down to life." Dewey must have sent Addams a copy because, as the historian Neil Coughlan was the first to note, Addams used some of Dewey's phrases in "Subjective Necessity." None is about democracy per se—three are about the nature of truth and one about social relations motivating action—but it is immediately after she used these phrases that she described the early church as a "true democracy."[72] It is hard not to suspect that Addams and Dewey had spent time in January talking about Christianity and democracy. Indeed, Dewey's paper, written soon after his Hull House visit, may have been partly inspired by their conversations.

In "Subjective Necessity" Addams also and for the first time connected democracy with the political power of working people. In a "democratic country," she observed, "nothing can be permanently achieved save through the masses of the people." She added: "The people themselves . . . crave a higher political life." Her new awareness of the centrality of politics is also reflected in "Objective Value," where, in describing the settlement's "lines of activity," she added "civic" to her usual categories of "social," "educational," and "humanitarian." She felt a bit self-conscious about the addition. "I have added civic," she said, "if indeed a Settlement of women can be said to perform civic duties." Once more she was hesitant because women could not vote. Working-class women, she pointed out, are unfortunately of "little political value" to (male) unions since "they possess no votes." And she was unsure what she thought about women's participation in campaigns to shape public policy. She mentioned the public school and garbage clean-up campaigns as "civic" activities of the house but, interestingly, not the sweatshop legislation campaign. At the same time—more qualms—she found her list too short. After reviewing the settlement's civic work, she apologized. "I am sorry we have not more to present in the line of civic activities."[73]

With ambivalence dogging her every step, Jane Addams was beginning to see this as an important category of Hull House's work. She had spoken of women serving as citizens in "Outgrowths," but that was about their socializing efforts. Now, under the influence of Mary Kenney, Florence Kelley, Lucy Flower, and others, her old fascination with politics, policy, and power, forced into dormancy in the 1880s by her attempt to be an obedient, self-sacrificing daughter, was reawakening. Still, her mind balked. Absent women voting, she needed a theory to justify women's civic engagement but was not yet able to formulate it.

Finally, she advanced in "Subjective Necessity" her thinking about a daughter's responsibility to embrace the humanitarian motive. In "Outgrowths" she had ignored the problem of family disapproval as a cause of a young person's frustration and inaction and had solely blamed overeducation. She had spoken of young women's frustration and even quoted Mill's *Subjection of Women* but she had framed the issue as including young men, too. At Plymouth she made a gendered argument for the first time and, in the process, put forth a more complete theory of moral responsibilities in relation to the family. Daughters, she said, are raised to be "altruistic, . . . self-forgetting . . . and self-sacrificing." They then become torn between two sets of duties: "the family claim," the responsibility the daughter feels to subdue her dreams in favor of serving the family, and "the social claim," the duty to society that she longs to fulfill. When these duties clash because the family refuses to let the daughter honor the "social claim," it is "a tragedy."[74]

This framework of the two claims was new for Addams; it was also new for her audience. Throughout much of the nineteenth century, American cultural leaders, ministers, essayists, public intellectuals, and citizens generally spoke of the world as divided into public and private "spheres." Influenced by the thinking of the Greeks and the Romans and many other subsequent Western philosophers, they perceived the public sphere as being for political matters and the private sphere for domestic and personal ones, that is, as being the one where women belonged. Arguments about women's role in society took this metaphor as a given. Women's rights advocates, while challenging its gendered aspect, used it as much as anyone else.[75] When Addams avoided it, this was no accident but a deliberate act.

The words she chose to use instead suggest why she rejected the usual labels. The neutral word "claim" permitted Addams to demasculinize the "territory" of the public sphere that women were hesitant to enter. It also signaled her desire to frame women's choices as moral ones. Mazzini had done that for men's choices, but he used the word "duty," a word generally popular in nineteenth-century American moral discussions but freighted with meaning for women in relation to their duties to family. Addams used the word "duty" rarely and never when she was speaking of a person's family and social responsibilities. The words "family" and "social" were also strategically chosen. "Social," unlike "public" or "nation," was feminine in its associations; using the word encouraged women to believe that they had a responsibility to society. Addams understood that her message about the family and social claims was potent for women. Throughout the rest of the 1890s, she would write and speak often about the daughter's dilemma and the claims she felt had been made upon her.[76] The family-and-social-claims framework is one of Addams's most original, if too long neglected, contributions to social, as well as feminist, thought.

But why did she formulate this theory about the two claims on daughters in 1892? Had she read a book or had a conversation that changed or clarified her thinking? Her new friend Florence Kelley had broken with her own family in 1886—in Addams's vocabulary, disregarded "family ties"— because she disapproved of her father's loyalty to capitalism in the face of the suffering of workers. By then she was a socialist determined to define herself against the man who had so greatly shaped her. Had the two friends been talking about their dilemmas as daughters and the conflicting loyalties they felt after college? In 1897, Kelley would explain to a visitor to Hull House that when young women enlisted in settlement life their choice amounted to "the revolt of the daughters."[77] Addams would never have gone so far as to *say* that. But she may have begun to be willing to think it and to believe that daughters were caught in an uniquely difficult situation.

Finally, "Subjective Necessity" addressed the settlement method. A few months earlier, in her Sunset Club remarks, Addams had described settlement house founders as "experimenters" who had been "forced" to undertake a project for which they had "inadequate" preparation—her usual concern. But at Plymouth, her anxiety was gone and she advocated the desirability of learning from experience. The settlement was "experimental," she said; it must be ready to "change its methods as its environment may demand." She expressed this idea even more poetically in "Objective Value" when she warned that when a successful institution "lace[s] itself up in certain formulas, [it] is in danger of forgetting the mystery and complexity of life, of repressing the promptings that spring from growing insight." From this new understanding, other conclusions followed. A person who comes to live at a settlement house confident that she or he knows all about working-class people, Addams noted, is making a mistake. Residents need to be "emptied of all conceit of opinion and all self-assertion." They "must come . . . assuming that the best teacher of life is life itself."[78]

She was describing something she herself had had to learn, although she did not admit it in the speech. She had arrived on Halsted Street convinced that her high ideals guaranteed success, that in knowing culture, she knew what she needed to know, but she had been learning otherwise during the previous three years. Indeed, the evidence is strong that by August 1892, Addams's philosophy of truth was under siege. In 1889, as a thorough idealist, she had had no space in her mental system for truth that was contingent. Now she did. This valuing of experience, also evident in her choice of "subjective" for her title, had important implications for her work at Hull House. She could be less focused than before on what she thought and more attentive to the situation and the people involved. She could also be freer of her old guilt about inadequate training. And she could question the assumption that her education made her intellectually, morally, and culturally superior to people in the "lower" classes. Her respect for experience as a teacher did not rebut this assumption, but it marginalized it, tamed it. By embracing experience as a means to discover truth, she took her first step toward the moral philosophy called pragmatism. Ahead lay further dangers. She did not realize it yet, but she was opening up a Pandora's box of moral complexities.

Was John Dewey was an influence in these developments? In 1892 Dewey, later to be the nation's most famous pragmatist philosopher, was not yet a pragmatist but was beginning to move in that direction. We necessarily date changes in thought to publications, but these lag behind the work of the mind in conversation and unpublished writing.[79] Perhaps Addams nudged Dewey's thinking or Dewey nudged Addams's thinking. Or, more likely, their conversations nudged them both.

Jane Addams hoped that the two speeches she gave at the Plymouth School contained material worthy of a national readership. Julia Lathrop was confident that they did. She also thought it crucial, Addams later recalled, that Hull House's approach to the settlement movement be "put before the country" while the public mind was still a relatively blank slate on the subject. They formed a plan to visit New York City while they were in the east and ask the editor of the *Forum* to publish Addams's speeches. Accordingly, after the conference the two friends took the train from Boston to New York, where they went to see the magazine's editor, Walter Hines Page.

At the meeting, Lathrop was firmly confident while Addams was, as she later put it, "embarrassed and weak-kneed." Addams's trepidation was a function of the writerly heights at which she was aiming. The *Forum* was a prestigious national monthly magazine, widely read by people of broad intellectual interests, especially those drawn to social reform. The likelihood that the editor would accept one of her pieces, let alone two, seemed slim to her. In her biography of Lathrop, Addams tells how Julia tried to stiffen her resolve as they sat in the outer office. "Don't cave in, J.A.," Lathrop told her, "this is our chance to give the public the pure milk of the word!" Once in Page's office, Lathrop marshaled her considerable forensic skills to argue the case for the speeches' "immediate publication," and to their "astonishment" he not only accepted them but offered to pay their author a fee.[80]

Page did as he promised with remarkable alacrity. In October 1892 the *Forum* published Addams's speech on the social settlement's objective value under a new title, "Hull House, Chicago: An Effort Toward Social Democracy." The speech on the subjective necessity for the social settlement appeared in November, also with a new title, "A New Impulse to an Old Gospel."[81]

The Plymouth conference, the two speeches, and their publication were high-water marks for Addams in several ways. First, she, the former editor of the *Rockford Seminary Magazine*, was back in print—and for pay. Her professional career as a writer was finally launched and there would be many published pieces to follow. Second, her long and distinguished career as a paid traveling lecturer had begun. Addams had become the orator she had dreamed of becoming at Rockford. Third, her youthful longing to be a social reformer had reached a symbolic pinnacle of accomplishment. She had admired that exotic being in her senior essay, "Cassandra"; at Plymouth, more than a decade later, she had become one.

But there was a problem, and it, too, was foreshadowed in "Cassandra." There she had struggled to reconcile her desire for woman to have *auctoritas* in public speech with her instinctive sense that men would doubt her. That dilemma had its echoes in her Plymouth remarks. When she added "civic" to the other categories of settlements' responsibilities, she had doubted her decision in the same breath. Apparently, despite her brave words about the family and the social claims, she continued to feel that her civic authority was undermined by her gender. Although Jane Addams's education as a citizen had in one sense been under way since childhood, in another sense it had only just begun.

CHAPTER II

BAPTISM

1893

Between 1892, when she first emerged on the national stage, and 1898, Jane Addams would become increasingly engaged in shaping governmental policy. In retrospect, Addams saw this broadening of her agenda as an inevitable consequence of the times. In *Twenty Years at Hull-House* she presents herself as "the personality upon whom various social and industrial movements in Chicago reacted." When she was sixty-nine she recalled the urgency she and others felt. "There was something in [those years]," she wrote, "that was very overwhelming. I am sure if it caught us again it would make us do what we could moment by moment because we felt under pressure to do something."[1]

But Addams did not only react. She also made choices. And in late 1892 she faced a choice. During her first three years on Halsted Street she had been busy living the settlement life—conducting clubs, teaching classes, making neighborly visits, responding to the neighbors' immediate difficulties, managing the settlement, and fundraising. At the same time, the issue of sweatshops had been moving gradually to the center of her attention. She could see clearly now the ways in which the unregulated system created terrible conditions—particularly the long hours that left the adults with no time or energy to learn and prevented the children from going to school. Still, her settlement house methods were not intended to change those conditions. The methods adopted by Kelley, the trade unions, the Illinois Woman's Alliance, and the Chicago Woman's Club, on the other hand, were. What should she do? Should she cooperate with them in sweatshop reform? Should she enter the policy arena?

Returning from New York City to Chicago in September 1892, Addams and Lathrop found the city swept up in a governor's race whose outcome would influence hopes for statewide sweatshop reform. The Democrats had nominated a progressive "populist" reformer, German-born John Peter Altgeld, to run against the incumbent Republican governor. Altgeld was a wealthy lawyer, real estate mogul, and former judge who had not forgotten his immigrant and working-class roots. He supported an improved system of compulsory education, state civil service reform, and sweatshop reform, including the end of child labor. These views earned him the votes of working-class men, male farmers, immigrants, and union members, as well as of liberal and left-leaning middle-class men. National politics further boosted his competitive position. That fall, the newly formed People's Party ran James Weaver as its presidential candidate on a radical platform of "free silver," government ownership and operation of all transportation and communication services, and a shorter workday. In Illinois in November, farmers and laborers turned out in droves to vote for the People's Party national ticket as well as for Democratic populist Altgeld. Altgeld won the race, and there was celebration on Halsted Street.[2] His triumph was an earthquake in the state's political landscape. After electing Republican governors for twenty-two years, the men of Illinois had elected a Democrat and the state's first foreign-born governor, to boot.

The new governor wasted no time. At his inauguration he called for "more thorough legislation" to regulate the employment of children and to improve sanitary conditions in factories and sweatshops. The legislature, also under Democratic leadership for the first time in decades, had already received Florence Kelley's reports from the Illinois Bureau of Labor Statistics; it immediately appointed a joint House and Senate committee to undertake an investigation of sweatshops in Chicago.[3]

As they had with the U.S. Senate committee's investigation, Chicago's various labor reform communities swung into action, using the same arsenal of strategies. Kelley, Morgan, Bisno, and others testified before the committee at hearings held in the city, gave the joint committee members a sweatshop tour, and stirred up publicity. The tour brought two worlds into collision. People in the neighborhood watched as the well-dressed men of the committee—had their crisp suits been made somewhere in the neighborhood?—moved up and down the dingy, garbage-strewn streets and alleys and in and out of murky stairwells. The details of what the legislators and the accompanying reporters found (workers crowded into dark, dirty, cramped spaces that stank of human waste; people, some of them ill, laboring for long hours; small, pale children working long days for pennies) were published in the Chicago press, sometimes in front-page stories.[4] The need for reform was obvious. Addams recalls in *Twenty Years* the upbeat mood, writing, "[O]ur hopes ran high."[5]

To further arouse public opinion, Mary Kenney, with the help of the Chicago Trades and Labor Assembly and Bisno's Cloakmakers Union, organized a large anti-sweatshop rally. On February 19 an enthusiastic crowd of more than two thousand working people packed Central Music Hall at State and Randolph Streets. After rousing speeches by Henry Demarest Lloyd, Florence Kelley, and others, the meeting adopted a resolution, proposed by Lloyd, appointing a committee of twenty-five called the Anti-Sweatshop League to push for the needed legislative reforms, particularly the eight-hour-day for women and a ban on employing children under the age of fourteen. The league members named that day included Kelley, Kenney, Lloyd, and Morgan, as well as Mary Wilmarth, a leader from the Chicago Woman's Club with an interest in labor reform, Ellen Gates Starr, and, representing the CTLA, Abraham Bisno and Maggie V. Toomey, a bookbinder and friend of Kenney's. Jane Addams was also named.[6]

On the day of the rally, Addams was in the east on a lecture tour.[7] Since at least half of the members of the league, including Wilmarth, were personal friends of hers, it is not surprising that she was named to the committee, but given that she apparently had not participated in the earlier anti-sweatshop campaign and that she was out of town at the time the league was formed, it seems possible that her friends recruited her involuntarily. One clue that they may have was the distaste Addams felt for lobbying, the league's main assignment. In early 1893, as she admitted in *Twenty Years*, she "very much disliked the word, and still more the prospect of the lobbying itself."[8]

Her dislike stemmed from two beliefs. One, tattered but still intact, was that politics was for people, that is, men, who could vote. The other was that politics in general, and lobbying in particular, was a dirty, messy, corrupt affair that women could not undertake with dignity. In 1893 the latter belief still had wide currency among Americans, although, as with so many social myths, reality had been contradicting it for decades. In 1838 an abolitionist, Angelina Grimké, had been the first woman to testify before an American legislative body, and since then, hundreds if not thousands of women had personally lobbied legislators and spoken to legislative bodies on behalf of numerous social reforms—women who were leaders, such as Grimké, Clara Barton, Dorothea Dix, Lucy Stone, Susan B. Anthony, Elizabeth Cady

A Sweatshop, *artist unknown*. Scribner's Magazine *24 (1898), 109.*

Stanton, and Mary Livermore, but also many less famous women. In Chicago, the CWC and the IWA had been lobbying the city council and the mayor on education issues for years. In Springfield in 1869, Stanton and Livermore had lobbied the Illinois state legislature for women's rights with John Huy Addams in the audience.[9]

Since the Civil War, the issue on which women had lobbied most intensively was suffrage. As women pressured state legislatures and Congress for other reforms, they could see that their disenfranchisement undercut their political influence. In the words of Illinois suffrage leader Elizabeth Harbert, "Every measure proposed for progressive action, industrial, educational, political, philanthropic or moral [has been] thwarted because of woman's inability to crystallize her opinions into law. . . . [Only] political power [will] give weight and dignity to [women's] words and wishes."

Harbert was writing in 1882. Nine years later, in 1891, she and Catherine Waugh McCulloch, a Chicago lawyer who had graduated from Rockford Seminary a year behind Jane Addams, were co-leading the Illinois Equal Suffrage Association, which Mary Livermore had founded decades earlier. The first successful bill, which authorized women to vote for elective school offices, passed in 1891 after an intense lobbying effort.[10]

By 1893, then, Addams might have felt that it was acceptable for women to lobby. That she did not reveals how removed she was from the suffrage campaign and from the political scene generally. But her doubts appear to have also had a second, more personal source: her father's dislike for being lobbied, revealed in his determination to legislate according to his own conscience. This was evident in the letter Lincoln had sent her father. When Lincoln had inquired about John Addams's political support for him, he had done so gingerly, hoping not to offend the new state senator by appearing to pressure him. If Jane Addams took up lobbying, she would do so knowing that her father would not have approved.

She took it up. Along with Kelley, Lloyd, and representatives of the CTLA, the IWA, and the CWC, Addams went to Springfield in the spring of 1893 to lobby for the Anti-Sweatshop League's legislation.[11] She remained worried, however, about whether she was doing the right thing in entering the political arena, and her ambivalence surfaced in a peculiar and revealing way. Two clothing manufacturers, acting on behalf of a larger group, offered her a bribe to withdraw Hull House's support from the sweatshop legislation over lunch in the women's dining room at the Union League Club in Chicago. William Colvin, an upright, socially conscientious businessman who was a major donor to Hull House and who apparently did not realize the tawdry scheme his associates were about to propose, had arranged the lunch. The gentlemen told Addams that if the residents of Hull House would drop "this nonsense about a sweatshop bill," they were prepared to give $50,000 to the settlement house to use however it wished. It was an enormous sum. Hull House was in the process of constructing a new building, the Gymnasium Building. Partially funded by Colvin, it cost $15,000.[12] The manufacturers' "gift" would have paid for constructing three more buildings of equal size.

Addams turned the bribe down. She told them she was not trying to make Hull House "the largest institution on the West Side." With a touch of youthful "heroics," as she describes it in *Twenty Years*, she said that if the destruction of Hull House was necessary to help its neighbors be protected from bad working conditions, so be it. Her response was principled and firm. But instead of feeling satisfied with her rejection of the bribe or shocked that the manufacturers had fallen so low as to offer her one, Addams had a different, rather self-absorbed reaction: she was ashamed that they had offered one to *her*. She wrote in 1910, "I feel now the shame [I felt then] . . . as the fact broke upon me that I was being offered a bribe." She believed that the businessmen's offer reflected poorly on her moral state. "What had befallen the daughter of my father," she remembers asking herself in the stilted, third party voice her father often used, "that such a thing could happen to her?"[13]

Addams describes only her discomfort at lobbying in *Twenty Years*, but one suspects that part of her was drawn to the idea of shaping legislation. Had she not been fascinated by politics when growing up? Had she not long admired those who, like Lucy Stone, had fought for reform through the legislative process? For what purpose had she striven so fiercely to gain the skills of oratory if not for this purpose? And how could she, a politician's daughter, not find delight in becoming more like him?

Helping to take the edge off of her doubts was the participation of the Chicago Woman's Club in the campaign. Experienced in applying political pressure, its members backed the sweatshop reform effort all the way. Apparently in preparation, the club had organized its first Committee on Legislation more than a month before the Anti-Sweatshop League was formed. Fifteen women strong, its members included Ada Sweet and Lucy Flower. After the club voted to endorse the league's bill, it sent delegates to Springfield to lobby for it.[14]

In the narrow world of female club life, the CWC's willingness to lobby was bold. Many middle- and upper-class women were as ambivalent as Addams was about women engaging in direct political action. When Addams approached the General Federation of Women's Clubs that year for its endorsement of sweatshop reform, it refused. The problem, she writes in *Twenty Years*, was that the federation was "timid in regard to all legislation," fearing to "frighten . . . its membership."[15]

In Chicago, the Anti-Sweatshop League poured its considerable energies into arousing the widest possible support for the bill, believing that, in Addams's words, the bill could not pass until it had found support from "all elements of the community." Addams was fully caught up in the campaign. Throughout March, April, and May, she and other members of the league exhausted themselves speaking "literally every evening" to open meetings of trades unions and benefits societies, church groups, and social clubs. The trade unions were the backbone of the effort. Addams was impressed with the "well-conducted campaign" of the Chicago Trades and Labor Assembly and thought it provided the "most energetic help" and the most "intelligent understanding."[16]

Her 1893 sweatshop legislation speeches do not survive, but an observation she made in "Objective Value" captures their likely flavor. She condemned the conditions in which workers were forced to labor. In search of low rental costs, she wrote, the "unscrupulous contractor regards no basement as too dark, no stable loft too foul, no rear shanty too provisional, no tenement room too small for his workroom." She felt a great sympathy for the workers, particularly the children. She later recalled seeing "a little girl of four who pulled out basting threads hour after hour, sitting on a stool at the feet of her Bohemian mother, a little bunch of human misery."[17] It tore at her heart to see that the younger children were not playing and that the older children were not in school.

At the same time, walking around the issue and looking at it from another angle, she knew that families needed the income they received from their children's earnings to survive and that they would pay a real price for sweatshop reform. It assuaged her feelings of guilt for supporting the legislation when she met working mothers who supported compulsory education and the end of child labor. "There was always a willingness," she recalls somewhat sweepingly in *Twenty Years*, "even among the poorest women, to keep on with the hard night scrubbing or long days of washing for the children's sake."[18]

The sweatshop legislation, formally titled the Workshop and Factory Act, sailed through the General Assembly that spring. With reformers across all the classes pressing hard for the legislature to pass the bill, the governor supporting it, and the manufacturers using such ham-handed lobbying methods as bribery of the incorruptible to try to defeat it, the bill easily passed the Senate by a vote of 40 to 0 and the House by a vote of 106 to 8. On July 1, 1893, Altgeld signed it into law.[19]

In a sense, the new law was nothing new for Chicago's manufacturers. Its provisions were essentially the same as those of the poorly enforced provisions the IWA had persuaded the Chicago City Council to adopt in 1889, 1890, and 1891. Under the terms of the new state law, children under fourteen were banned from working in manufacturing establishments,

Sweatshop Workers, *by Norah Hamilton, a Hull House resident.*
Twenty Years at Hull-House, *198.*

women and older children were limited to working an eight-hour day and a forty-eight-hour week, and factory inspector positions were created. But the new law had more teeth than the council's ordinance because it authorized the state board of health to search for and confiscate goods found in tenement workshops that violated the sanitary code and because it gave strong enforcement powers to the new office of state factory inspector. It would be a powerful law if a hard-working, conscientious inspector could be named. To the surprise of no one, the governor appointed Florence Kelley to the position.[20] Another significant accomplishment of the law was its eight-hour provision. Ohio, Minnesota, and Massachusetts laws limited women to working ten hours; Illinois, the nation's third-largest manufacturing state, was the first state in the country to adopt as policy the long-sought number of eight.[21]

The Illinois law's swift passage was a stunning demonstration of the power of what has been variously called extraparty, ad hoc, direct, grassroots, or collective political action, that is, political efforts using investigation into the facts, publicity, lobbying, cross-class and cross-organization coalitions, and mass meetings. The CTLA, the IWA, and the CWC had used such strategies before in Illinois, and Kelley and others had used them in other states, but for those inexperienced in such methods, the bill's rapid success dramatically demonstrated that voteless women of various classes, working cooperatively with men in trade unions, could change state policy.

Jane Addams absorbed these lessons from the 1893 sweatshop campaign. As she worked alongside others, giving speeches and lobbying elected officials, she saw a new kind of female citizenship in action and learned what she herself could do. For the first time she ignored the implicit message of the nation's voting laws that politics was for men and, inspired by the political courage of Mary Kenney, Elizabeth Morgan, Florence Kelley, Lucy Flower, Mary Wilmarth, and others, she crossed over the gender line into politics, or, more precisely, she concluded that it did not exist, that her femaleness did not, after all, banish her from that precinct.

And she learned two other lessons. She discovered that grassroots politics, unlike the politics of representative governance, set no limits on who could participate, that it welcomed the nonvoter and the inexperienced, and that it could operate outside party structures. And she learned that grassroots politics was real politics—that is, it redistributed political power and resources. The political philosopher Mary Dietz has observed, "[C]itizenship as the people's power . . . transform[s] the individual . . . into a political being . . . endowed with the capacity to speak, act, organize, and potentially change the world."[22] In working for the passage of the sweat-shop bill, Jane Addams took crucial steps toward full citizenship by finding her political identity and her political voice.

A city, like an individual, discovers its ability to influence the wider world in stages. The early 1890s was a pivotal moment in the history of the city of Chicago. Its star had been rising since the railroad revolution had transformed it into a major urban center, but its fresh prominence had yet to be officially recognized by the country and the world. That, however, was about to change. Even as the labor reform legislation was moving forward in the spring of 1893, construction on Chicago's first world's fair was nearing completion. The fair would bring twenty-seven million visitors to the city. For her part, Jane Addams would seize the opportunity the fair offered to put the settlement house movement and its issues on the national and world maps and to showcase the accomplishments of Hull House.

The fair was a public-private project. Chicago's energetic business community, led by such men as the banker Lyman Gage, the meatpacker Philip Armour, and the railroad car magnate George Pullman, using money from the U.S. Congress, the City of Chicago, and their own pockets, were building a huge fair on the southern edge of the city, next to Lake Michigan and just east and south of the newly opened University of Chicago. Called the World's Columbian Exposition to celebrate the four hundredth anniversary of Christopher Columbus's arrival in the Americas in 1492, it kept its title and theme even after the organizers missed the 1892 deadline.

In addition to the fair itself, an ambitious series of world conferences, or congresses, were planned. These were to cover nearly every topic of interest to mankind, from religion to labor, medicine, manual education (crafts), temperance, higher education, household economics, philology, suffrage, and stenography. To provide a space for the congresses to meet, the fair's board of directors personally financed the construction of an off-site building, the Art Palace, on Michigan Avenue in downtown Chicago. Between May and October, many of the 210 congresses would be held there.[23]

The congresses gave Addams her opportunity. In January she proposed to a planning committee that she organize a Congress on Social Settlements as one of the educational congresses to take place in July. The committee approved. In February, Addams, accompanied by Mary Rozet Smith, traveled in the east giving lectures on the settlement movement at various women's colleges and using the opportunity to visit settlement houses in New York, Philadelphia, and Boston to discuss with their leaders the idea of a congress and to plan it. [24]

The fair opened on May 1, 1893, to huge and enthusiastic crowds. Railroad tracks build especially for the occasion deposited travelers from around the world right onto the fair's central plaza. Wide-eyed, the visitors gazed in every direction upon a stunning view of enormous white Beaux Arts classical buildings encircling manmade lagoons. The scene, rising up from the mundane prairies of Illinois, evoked Venice and the cultural sophistication of Europe. Although the two hundred buildings were temporary—constructed of frames of wood or iron wrapped in a plaster made partly of hemp—their apparent elegance was all that the fair's visitors, hungry for splendor, could have hoped for. [25]

Jane Addams's sisters Mary and Alice came with their children. Even Anna H. Addams, unable to resist the draw of a glittering world's fair less than two hundred miles from her Cedarville front door, came, paying her first visit to Hull House. The conversations between Anna and Jane and Anna's impressions of Hull House went unrecorded. But apparently Anna's visit did nothing to modify her general stance of disapproval. Their cool relations would continue throughout the 1890s. [26]

The month of May was hectic for Addams. She was speaking almost nightly about the sweatshop legislation, overseeing the completion of the new gymnasium building, working with other residents on launching two new neighborhood projects, public baths and a playground, and chairing a committee of the Chicago Woman's Club to investigate whether it should start a consumer's league similar to the one recently organized in New York City. For the congresses, she chaired a meeting of the local committee of the Peace Congress, which was to be held in August (apparently a new interest, although it left no other early trace), hosted a meeting of the national advisory committee of the Congress on Social Settlements planned for July, and gave a speech at the World's Congress of Representative Women. [27]

The Congress of Representative Women, an unprecedented event in the history of the world, was the brainchild of Ellen Henrotin, Mary Wilmarth, and Lucy Flower. Held in the third week in May, it had the grand goal of demonstrating the progress women around the globe had made in education, industry, literature, art, moral and social reform, government, and religion. Wildly popular, its eighty-one sessions drew more than 150,000 people, most of them women. Chicago citizens and fair visitors flocked to hear important speeches such as Susan B. Anthony's "Women's Influence and Political Power," Elizabeth Cady Stanton's "The Ethics of Suffrage," and Lucy Stone's "The Progress of Fifty Years." Among the Chicago women who spoke were Fannie Barrier Williams, an African American civic leader who gave a powerful address on the intellectual progress of African American women, and labor leader Mary Kenney, who spoke with equal passion on the organization of working women. [28]

Jane Addams spoke on domestic service, a topic particularly close to the hearts of those in her audience. In 1893 almost all middle- and upper-class American women employed at least one domestic and often more. Although this was Addams's first speech on the subject, women reformers had been urging fresh thinking about the "servant problem" for several years, and magazines often ran articles on the issue. The problem was that servants, many of whom were single young women, worked only for a short time and then quit. Women employers, frustrated, concluded that the "girls" considered hard work beneath them and that they should have been more grateful for the chance to live in pleasant surroundings. Nearly everyone in Addams's prosperous audience had a strong opinion about the "servant problem." [29]

Addams's views on servants before moving to Halsted Street are unknown, but, like every woman of her class, she had lived among them all of her life, given them orders, been served by them, and been part of conversations with family and friends about the difficulty of finding "good help" and keeping it. Furthermore, since moving to Halsted Street, she had become an employer herself. Mary Keyser was their first servant and, by 1893, she was supervising two other household staff. But Addams also gained a new perspective on servants. At Hull House she talked with many "working girls," including some of those whom Kelley tried to recruit for the Hull House Labor Bureau. (The term referred to single women, regardless of age, although most were in their teens and twenties.) What she had learned was evident in her speech, which she called, cagily, "Domestic Service and the Family Claim." [30]

Unskilled working girls had two choices of employment, she observed: factory labor and household labor. Factory work struck them as the better choice because, although those jobs might not pay as well, they offered, at least in theory, the tantalizing promise of increased wages in the future. It also introduced them to people their own age. The advantage of household

labor was that it was potentially more permanent than industrial employment, which could be sporadic; the disadvantage was that domestic employers required girls to live away from home and to work evenings and
part of Sundays. "It is well to remember," Addams admonished her audience in carefully class-neutral language, that young women, "as a rule, are
devoted to their families; they want to live with their parents, their brothers and sisters, and their kinsfolk."[31] In other words, what young women
wanted was the same, regardless of class.

For the most part, "Domestic Service" conveyed the capacious quality
of Addams's mind that her friends admired. Because she was inclined to
see a subject from many sides and was committed to nonresistance and
cooperation, she did not attack employers—that is, her audience—with an
advocate's passion. Instead she invited them to stand outside themselves
and see the world from their servants' viewpoint. Using language that was
empty of judgment, she kept their attention on working people's feelings
and implied at every opportunity that those feelings were simply human.
She sought to catch the audience members off-guard, to arouse in them
feelings of sympathy by connecting them with her own.

Cannily, Addams detailed the employer's assumptions as if the members of her audience were unfamiliar with them. The domestic employer,
she noted, being devoted to her own family and its ritual of the family meal,
restricts her cook to seeing her family no more than once or twice a week.
But Addams did not leave it there. Taking an ironic stance, she drove her
point home with a series of stinging metaphors. The female employer, Addams observed, is so "imbued with the sanctity of her own family life" that
she thinks the "sacrifice of the cook's family life . . . perfectly justifiable."
The male employer was also implicated. To him, the cook is "a burnt offering, and the kitchen range [is] the patriarchal altar."[32] In this passage Addams dropped the veil of impartiality and flashed out with polemical fire.
No doubt it shocked her audience as she intended. The biting metaphors
proved what her college essays at rare moments had also hinted: that Addams could be a powerful oratorical combatant and that she sometimes
felt fierce emotions. Here it is clear that what stirred her passion was the
selfishness of her own class. In these years she experienced social reform
as first and foremost a project of self-critique.

Scholars have not thought of "Domestic Service" as a particularly important speech, but for the biographer it stands out for two reasons. First, Addams further developed in it her theory of moral responsibility. When she

spoke about the "family" and the "social" claims in "Subjective Necessity" at Plymouth, she had had prosperous daughters in mind. In "Domestic Service" she argued that "the family claim" fell on young working women as well. Still, she did not argue they should honor the social claim. That idea was not relevant to her topic, to be sure, but its application to working women also may not have occurred to her yet.

Second, "Domestic Service" was the first speech entirely shaped by Addams's desire to act as a cross-class interpreter.[33] Speaking to a prosperous audience, she set out the choices, values, and desires of working people. She was doing something that perhaps only someone of her background could do: reporting back to those of her own kind what she had learned from living on Halsted Street. She spoke in the accents of the upper middle class, dressed in its style, used its vocabulary, understood how its members thought, and yet she had seen and experienced things that its members had not. Beginning with this speech Addams would serve as a cross-class interpreter often, using her knowledge of her own class's motives and misconceptions and her story-telling gifts to build a bridge of human connection across the class divide.

The stance of interpreter was inherently one of authority. Addams was comfortable in this role. She conveyed no hesitation in "Domestic Service"; she believed that her interpretation was objective. Her confidence seems to have been grounded in the fact she had earned a B.A. Like others of her generation, Addams thought her advanced education allowed her to step outside her own class's perspective and gain a universal view.

In fact Addams achieves a fair degree of objectivity in "Domestic Service," but her class bias leaks through in one sentence, although it does so in a way that is complicated for the modern ear to correctly discern. The sentence, "There are few women so dull that . . . they cannot do some form of factory work," jars. By "dull," however, she did not mean that they were not intelligent in the modern sense. She makes clear in the previous sentence that she means they are "untrained," that is, they lack skills, including the skill of literacy. Elsewhere, she uses the words "primitive" and "less intellectual" and "less intelligent" the same way, as synonyms for "untrained" or "uneducated," in keeping with the primary meaning of these words in the nineteenth century.[34]

That said, however, the words convey condescension. Although they hint at a person's potential, they also emphasize his or her current limits. Furthermore, Addams nowhere speaks of wealthy or upper-middle-class women as "less intelligent" even though most of them had no college education. She assumed that, given their possession of "culture" and literacy, women of her class had trained their faculties somehow. Consciously, Addams felt superior to working-class people because of her education; unconsciously, she felt superior because of her class.

———————

Throughout the summer, the magnificent congresses proceeded. The Congress on Social Settlements took place from July 19 to 21. Held at Hull House, it was the first conference the settlements had organized for themselves, and it marked a new highpoint in the "world" (Anglo-American) movement. It was a movement in which the Americans were pulling ahead in the race to found settlements. There were now fourteen in Great Britain and nineteen in the United States, where eight were founded in the year 1893 alone. Most of the American settlements were concentrated in New York, Boston, and Philadelphia. Chicago, with four, was an aberrant outpost.[35]

Inevitably, the congress, co-chaired by Addams, showcased the achievements of Chicago's first settlement. By virtually every measure, those achievements were impressive. First, the expertise of its accomplished residents was on full display. Florence Kelley gave a speech titled "The Settlement in Its Relations to Municipal Reform." She had just assumed her position as state factory inspector and started hiring her eleven deputies. In only seven months, she had gone from an unemployed gadfly to a state employee with a staff and a budget dedicated to social justice work. Julia Lathrop's speech was titled "The Settlement in Its Relations to Charitable Institutions." Earlier in the month, she had begun serving as the first woman member of the State Board of Charities, a volunteer position to which Governor Altgeld had appointed her. She would soon become an expert on the publicly funded orphanages, asylums, and poorhouses of Illinois. Ellen Gates Starr's speech was "The Social Settlement and Its Relation to the Arts Movement." She had recently organized a project with the Chicago Woman's Club to place art in the city's public schools and was now president of the Chicago Public School Art Society. That spring she was chairing the planning committee for a congress to take place later in the summer on manual and art education.[36]

Equally impressive was the size and nature of the Hull House resident group. In the previous year and a half, the number of residents had grown to twelve, making Hull House the largest American settlement. It was also still the only coed house in the country. By the summer of 1893 there were seven male residents, including Addams's nephew John Linn. In fact, for the first and only time in the settlement's early history, there were now more men living there than women. As the number of male residents had burgeoned in the spring of 1893, the settlement had rented additional resident space across the street from the Hull mansion.[37]

Then there was Hull House as a physical space. Throughout the settlement congress, volunteers gave tours of the Hull mansion, the Butler Building, and the sparkling new Gymnasium Building. The latter, which opened officially that month, was connected to the mansion at the rear but faced Polk Street. It housed a coffee house (which sold nutritious food to the public and was open from 6 A.M. to 11 P.M. every day), a diet kitchen (which sold nutritious food for the sick), a gym (which had a stage so that the space could double as a three-hundred-seat theatre), twelve public showers, and a clubroom for the Men's Club, another new project. No other settlement had such a large physical plant. Addams, always inclined to spiritualize the material, saw in the buildings an expression of the settlement's conviction that "education and recreation ought to be extended to the immigrants." She would also write, "The first buildings were very precious to us, [they gave] . . . the greatest . . . pleasure."[38]

The numbers of visitors and volunteers, which Addams shrewdly continued to track, were equally impressive. In May 1893, one thousand people, one hundred of whom were volunteers, were coming weekly to participate in the house's activities.[39] The numbers had stayed roughly the same for several years given the constraints of available space, but with the addition of the Gymnasium Building, they would once more begin to grow.

Perhaps most remarkable of all, the residents were writing a book, or at least they were discussing the idea. Kelley, aided by four government investigators, had been collecting data all spring for a new study of the part of the Nineteenth Ward that was east of Halsted Street, funded by the federal Department of Labor. The focus was on workers' and families' places of residence, nationalities, and wages. It was part of a larger national study of slum conditions in four major U.S. cities. The residents had decided to create and publish two brightly colored maps that would correlate nationalities and wages with housing patterns in the ward. But nothing else had been decided. At a Residents' Meeting in August, the minutes plaintively recorded the question, "What is to go with the maps?"[40]

The Residents' Meeting was itself one of Hull House's more interest-ing practices, although its existence was not readily apparent to visitors. In January 1893, or possibly earlier (records may have been lost or destroyed) Jane Addams and the other residents began using the meeting as a way to settle policy questions concerning household life and shared projects such as the map book.[41] Toynbee Hall had such a self-governing committee, but as best can be determined, Hull House was the only American settlement house that had one in 1893.[42]

The Residents' Meeting at Hull House merits close attention. It is key to understanding Jane Addams's methods as a leader of the settlement be-cause it set limits on the power she could wield. The meeting took place, or was supposed to take place, (reliability was elusive), weekly. All the resi-dents, or all who were available, attended and, duly elected, Addams chaired. At the meeting residents decided by vote which projects the house would undertake as a whole (individuals also had their own projects), who could be a resident (after the required six months probationary period), and which house tasks were mandatory.

As of the spring of 1893, the tasks were few. All residents were required to sign up for times to answer the door and give tours, called "toting." In Oc-tober, they would vote to exempt Starr, Brockway, and Addams from the re-quirement, presumably because of their other responsibilities. People vol-unteered for other tasks (Addams did not assign them) depending on their weekly schedules. These tasks included supervising the playground and the gymnasium. For example, one Monday in July Addams supervised the playground from 6 P.M. to 9 P.M. but the following week someone else took that time slot. In September, residents also began serving on four standing committees created by the Residents' Meeting to oversee the house's most complex enterprises: the college extension program, the coffee house, the gymnasium, and the settlement household.[43]

The residents elected Jane Addams as chairman of the meeting every year but, because the group complied with Robert's Rules of Order, her powers were constrained. While chairing the meeting she could not con-trol the agenda (motions were in order from the floor and she could not offer motions); nor could she advocate or vote for a motion under debate, although her opinions were undoubtedly known. Most important, since decisions were made by vote, the view she favored sometimes lost. One of her new projects would squeak by the Residents' Meeting in the fall of 1893; two others would not.[44] As the October 1893 vote indicated, she could not even exempt herself from door duty without the approval of a majority of the residents.

Addams wielded a good deal of power outside the Residents' Meeting. She managed the day-to-day operations, shaped the settlement's future through her fundraising and willingness to subsidize its debt, shaped its reputation via her public roles, and probably—the facts cannot always be documented—proposed many of its new projects. Because of the affection in which she was held, she also had great personal influence over residents; her opinion mattered. Still, the limits she imposed on her power by turning over certain decisions to the meeting were substantial.

Given that the Residents' Meeting restricted a settlement leader's power, it is easy to see why such self-governing groups were not popular among settlement houses. Most head residents, despite their expressed enthusiasm for the Toynbee Hall model, viewed the residents, even if they were volunteers (which, initially, all of them were), as the equivalent of paid staff available for assignment. The heads organized their settlements hierarchically, with power distributed from the top down.[45] Addams might have taken the same approach. Certainly she shared her colleagues' instinct to control. She had admitted as much to her sister Alice in 1889 when she told her that Robert Browning's phrase about the "will to dominate which I must exercise" could justly be applied to herself. But while her desire for power pulled her toward an authoritarian style of leadership, her commitment to the theory of cooperation and the idea of democracy pushed her away from it. The evidence suggests that she disciplined herself to relinquish some power at Hull House.

And it was good that she did. One of the persistent questions that historians ask about Hull House is why so many remarkable people remained there as residents for years. Florence Kelley would stay for eight, Julia Lathrop for roughly twenty. Dr. Alice Hamilton, a subsequent leader in the field of industrial toxicology, came in 1897 and stayed for more than twenty years, and a nationally prominent music educator, Eleanor Smith, came at the same time and stayed, with one break, for thirty-six years. Part of the answer lay in the fact that policy decisions about residential life and joint projects were made by the residents as a collective body, not by Addams.

The other part lay in Addams's refusal to treat residents as unpaid staff. The required tasks at Hull House were few and not onerous. Nor did Addams assign residents to projects, as did other head residents; rather, following Samuel Barnett's example and the theory of cooperation, she encouraged them to decide what they wanted to do. Many chose to lead a club or teach a class; others started projects (a music school, in one case) or simply helped with requests from neighbors or assisted another resident in her or his project. One reporter who took an interest in this aspect of the house wrote in 1893, "Each elects that for which she thinks herself best fitted, finding her own field and inaugurating and carrying out her own work." Nor did Addams ever try to rein in a resident whose activities reflected dangerously on the House's reputation.[46] Thus talented, independent women flourished at Hull House. Given the freedom to pursue their own projects, left unburdened by house responsibilities, never asked to feel that in their decisions or public statements they in any way officially represented Hull House, they were happy to live in the lively, interesting community that the settlement had become.

Jane Addams's commitment to the theory of cooperation was also evident in the governance structure of the clubs. The Jane Club and the Working People's Social Science Club were self-governing, as was the new Men's Club, which adopted a constitution that established its members' responsibilities. The children's and other clubs were also self-governing; they chose their own members, elected their own officers, and made their own choices, using proper parliamentary procedure, about what they wanted to do.[47]

Addams applied the cooperative principle to economic projects as well. What compelled her was the ideal that had compelled Robert Owen—in her words, "the dream that men shall cease to waste their strength in competition and shall come to pool their powers of production." When Mary Kenney decided in late 1892 to try to eliminate capitalism from the bookbinding business, Addams helped her raise the $500 that she and her friend Maggie Toomey needed to buy a perforator and a stitcher for their bookbinding cooperative by soliciting wealthy friends for loans and making a loan herself. Another cooperative project Addams pursued was the public, or cooperative, kitchen. Stanton Coit, the founder of the Neighborhood Guild in New York City, thought that every neighborhood should have one, and the idea was gaining popularity in reform circles. The Coffee House, which opened in the Gymnasium Building in the summer of 1893, was a public kitchen of the sort he had in mind. At the Labor Congress held in August, Addams endorsed public kitchens as the way of the future and the solution to the "servant problem." Domestic service is a "belated" industry, she said. It ought to be replaced by kitchens where skilled cooks could serve hundreds instead of handfuls. The Cooperative Congress of the Columbian Exposition was held at Hull House. Later, there would be other cooperative economic experiments. Addams was always looking for ways to apply her beloved cooperative theory.[48]

There was one very obvious opportunity, however, that she was missing. For at least the two years since the house had gained its first residents other than herself and Starr, Addams had kept residents in the dark about the budget deficits and the contributions she was making each year to erase them. Finance was the single area of settlement management that, although economic, was distinctly uncooperative; it was the one aspect in regard to which Addams determinedly flew solo. The practice was leading her into increasingly dangerous waters.

The current year was the worst yet in financial terms. During the fiscal year that was to end September 30, 1893, the budget jumped 70 percent, to $20,768. The deficit, despite Addams's efforts at fundraising and Helen Culver's recent decision to waive rent charges through 1910, jumped to $3,738, 54 percent higher than the previous year's.[49] About half of it was due to one-time capital costs related to opening of the new men's residence across Halsted Street from the mansion and the construction costs for the playground. But the rest was due to operating expenses, including a $1,000 deficit in the household account.[50] Addams paid the debt of nearly $4,000. Could she afford this? Assuming that her income in 1893 was roughly $3,000, or even if it was still $4,000, she would again have had to sell some of her assets to cover the debt. She and Hull House were both heading for a financial crisis; indeed, they were already in one. The settlement's finances were a house of cards propped up by the dwindling resources of Jane Addams's checkbook and her willingness to cash in her inheritance.

She took some steps to correct the situation. In August 1893, after reviewing the books, Addams told the residents about the deficit and announced that the resident fee for the next year would need to be raised. In her capacity as chair of the Residents' Meeting, she named an ad hoc committee, the House Committee, to set a new fee and named herself to serve on it. In early October the residents approved a fee of $20 per month (the amount of the previous fee is unknown). The committee also recommended that a sinking fund (a fund to extinguish indebtedness) be set up. Finally, as chair, Addams proposed that the financial accounts be read to the residents once a month. The settlement entered its new fiscal year on

October 1 debt-free. The residents were told that the house had a surplus at the next meeting.[51]

Still, they did not know that Addams was writing checks behind the scenes. Why did she not tell them? She had several likely reasons. An astute fundraiser, she understood the damage that continual insolvency inflicted on an organization's reputation. By quietly covering the deficit at the end of the fiscal year, she could make sure that the books were always balanced by that crucial date and that no rumors circulated to the contrary. Equally important, writing checks gave her the freedom to proceed with new projects without having the funds on hand. No one could tell her, "We can't afford it," because no one knew what the house could afford. Finally, she apparently felt comfortable in her role as secret financier of the settlement. When it came to money, Addams found it hard to shake the habits of an old-fashioned benevolent—albeit anonymous—philanthropist.

In the summer of 1893 Hull House, its financial troubles hidden from view, appeared to those attending the Congress of Social Settlements and to its Chicago friends and donors as if it were successful in every way. Not surprisingly, its remarkable accomplishments translated into generous praise for its head resident. Robert Woods, head of Andover House in Boston, wrote Addams after his visit, "You are doing the best piece of social work anywhere in the country and the future of Hull House seems to me to be filled with great promise." *Harper's Magazine* complimented her on her "gentle character" and invoked the well-meaning but dehumanizing moniker that would prove so popular with the press: "Saint Jane." Writing in the same year, Henry C. Adams, the organizer of the Plymouth sessions, characterized Hull House as "the most influential Settlement in the country" and Jane Addams as its "guiding spirit." *Unity*, writing about the settlement congress, called her Hull House's "justly beloved head."[52]

Addams was ambivalent about the praise. When compliments were paid to her at the settlement congress, one observer thought she found them "a trying ordeal."[53] Her reaction, of course, reflected her family's stern training in the duty of humility. Furthermore, for someone as desirous of moral perfection and as conscious of her moral failures as she was, praise—which was, by its nature, exaggerated—may have held a distinctly mocking quality. Throughout her life, there are hints in descriptions of her reactions to praise that part of her did not like it. But part of her did. In "Subjective Necessity" she mentions in passing that another of her motives for starting Hull House was a "love of approbation." Praise, fame, public honor—these were forms of love and signs of power that bolstered her. A close friend of hers from the peace movement, Emily Balch, who knew her well in later years, once observed, "Jane Addams enjoyed approbation and love even more than most people." The summer of the world's fair, with Hull House's accomplishments on public display, Jane Addams received a bounty of respect and affection. In her long climb out of the despair of the 1880s, she reached a new peak of contentment and pride in July 1893.[54]

CHAPTER 12

COOPERATION

1893–94

Nothing could have been more triumphant for Chicago and the nation than the spectacle of the world's fair as it sparkled all summer. And nothing could have been more tragic—and grimly ironic—than the economic depression that struck Chicago and the nation in those same months.

The depression's origins lay in Europe, which, after a long decline in agricultural prices, began to experience severe business contractions in 1889 and 1890. Meanwhile, agricultural prices had also been falling in the United States, triggering intense debate about monetary policy. Following the passage of the Silver Purchase Act in 1890, the nation's financial interests, borrowing heavily from banks, had speculated on whether the country would remain on the gold standard or switch to silver. In December 1892, as the economy continued its long-term trend of contraction, banks began calling in their loans and speculators began selling their stocks and bonds. A surge of bankruptcies began in February; the New York Stock Exchange crashed in May.[1]

The extent of the devastation was clear by the end of 1893. About six hundred banks and fifteen thousand businesses, with liabilities totaling $550 million, had failed, and one-fourth of the railway capital of the country had been placed in the hands of receivers. As a result, a great many workers were laid off—estimates ranged from one million to three million. In New York, the largest city in the United States, the unemployment rate in the fall of 1893 was thought to be 40 percent. Other workers kept their jobs but suffered massive cuts in their wages.[2]

In Chicago the impact was equally severe. One-third of the factories closed their doors, and many others laid off most of their employees; wage cuts were widespread. At the Pullman Factory in Pullman, a private community within Chicago's southern boundary, the normal industrial workforce of forty-five hundred was reduced between July and November to eleven hundred. Illinois Steel laid off 94 percent of its thirty-six hundred employees, and 80 percent of McCormick Reaper's twenty-two hundred employees were let go. In Chicago, as in New York City, there was 40 percent unemployment by September.[3] The Panic of 1893, the most severe economic crisis in the nation's history, had begun.

The panic was aptly named. It stunned the nation. The historian Henry Adams, himself protected from homelessness and starvation by his family's inherited wealth, observed of businessmen in his usual sardonic way, "Everyone is in a blue fit of terror, and each individual thinks himself more ruined than his neighbor."[4] The mood was black among laid-off workers and those whose wages had been cut. Many sank quickly into desperate poverty. In a matter of months Chicago, one of the nation's largest, most prosperous cities, had become a place of scarcity, despair, and fear—for how long, no one knew. Capitalism, that reliable servant, had become a thief.

Who would alleviate the suffering? City governments did not think it was their responsibility. In New York State and New York City the authorities resisted pressure from trade union leaders to create public works jobs. Believers in laissez-faire economic theory, these government officials held that job creation should be left to the market and individual initiative. "It is not the province of the government," the governor said, "to support the people." If the government gave charity, he warned, it would lead only to "corruption." (He meant that the individual's work ethic would be corrupted.) Most working people, being practical when it came to their own survival, thought the government ought to help. They distrusted the proffered rationales for inaction. Their views were well expressed in a statement made by a group of economists sympathetic to the workers' situation: "Laissez-faire [is] an excuse for doing nothing while people starve."[5]

As the economists' skepticism revealed, the panic raised the stakes in society's ongoing discussion about how best to organize the economy. The underlying question had not changed. Was poverty generally caused by individual failure, and was it best met with charitable giving to "worthy cases," or was there such a thing as structural, or class, poverty that needed to be addressed by reform or even revolution? The depression now added a new element to the debate. The proponents of laissez-faire, who believed that poverty was the deserved price paid by lazy or sinful individuals in a prosperous, capitalist economy, now argued that the economic crisis proved their case. Those who believed in the necessity of regulating capitalism's markets in a healthy economy now claimed that the depression was conclusive evidence for the need to restrain the markets. Most people had arrived at their answers long before this and did not wish to reexamine their conclusions.

Those who already had doubts, however, found the panic's implications unsettling. Jane Addams was one of these. She was suffering from divided loyalties. The daughter of a successful capitalist, the inheritor of his wealth, and a believer in Emersonian self-reliance, she was also a social Christian, a cooperator, and an antimaterialist, as well as a tentative supporter of labor unions and a friend of socialists, most notably of Florence Kelley.[6] Complicating her dilemma was her essential lack of interest in economic matters. She had read Marx, to be sure, but she had never really applied her good mind to the subject. Now that was about to change.

The depression hit Chicago hard. Business owners and management faced business failures and debt; wage employees faced homelessness, starvation, and even death. To buy food and pay the rent, people pawned or sold their furniture and clothes, borrowed money from or moved in with friends and family, and arranged extensions of credit from landlords and storekeepers. Many had few resources to sustain them. According to one estimate, roughly one-tenth of the city's population faced starvation that winter.[7] An untold number would die.

Organizations in the city tried to help. About half of the city's six thousand saloons, many owned by or with close ties to aldermen, combined compassion with political savvy by giving away sixty thousand free meals per day during the first winter. Trade unions helped members with relief. Urban missions provided penny meals and free lodgings. Churches passed the plate to support private charities. The Chicago branch of the Catholic Women's National League opened free soup kitchens, and hundreds of ethnic mutual benefit societies stretched their resources to help their members. Cook County's relief office struggled to cope with the huge number of requests for in-kind relief such as shoes and coal.[8]

For many, none of this was enough. When the rent went unpaid, eviction followed, and thousands became homeless. Soon the floors of City Hall, police stations, and churches were filled every night with gaunt, sleeping bodies. The Cook County poorhouse at Dunning, called the Infirmary and located nine miles northwest of downtown Chicago, was also overwhelmed.[9]

Aside from letting the homeless sleep on the floors of City Hall, the city government did nothing. For weeks union leaders called for authorities to create public work jobs for the able-bodied and to provide meal tickets to help fend off starvation. The city saw matters the same way as officials in New York did. As one Chicago alderman put it, "[C]ity officials [have no legal] obligation . . . to . . . furnish employment to . . . citizens."[10]

On August 26 the frustration of Chicago's unemployed came to a head. In a demonstration organized by trade union leaders, thousands of unemployed men marched past City Hall calling for work. Fearing violence, the city sent out policemen armed with clubs to line the route. Middle-class citizens stood behind the police lines, some sympathetic, some curious, some hostile and there to taunt. Suddenly, a government mail truck determined to keep to its route cut across the parade, and a few of the marchers attacked it. The peaceful scene exploded into a violent melee. Police moved in. Nine men, police officers and demonstrators, were injured; arrests were made. Soon afterward, Mayor Carter Harrison arrived to calm the crowd. People must be patient, he said; businessmen and city officials would do "all they can." His words could not touch the despair that some felt. One of the arrested men told a reporter, "I will get a razor and slit my throat. I have had nothing to eat . . . and now I get clubbed. I don't want to live."[11]

The violence proved a turning point for the city. The fear of lower-class anarchy that it aroused prompted the government to act when calls for compassion and arguments about its responsibilities had not. The following Saturday Mayor Carter Harrison convened an emergency Relief and Public Safety Committee, one of whose members was Jane Addams, and it was decided that public works jobs and meal tickets were the solution. Booths were immediately set up at Lake Front Park to process requests, and in just two days nine hundred men registered for work. Most of those who were able-bodied were sent to dig on the Chicago Sanitary and Ship Canal, the city's biggest construction project, already under way.[12] These relief jobs would help many survive. Thousands would sign up for them in the coming months.

Meanwhile, Hull House struggled to respond to the crisis. The settlement felt the impact as early as August. "We are sunk under a mass of the unemployed morning, noon, and night," Ellen Starr wrote a friend. On August 26, the day that the unemployed marched on city hall, Jane Addams wrote Mary Rozet Smith, who was traveling in England with her parents, "Our neighbors are . . . forlorn and literally flock to the house for work." Some, already desperate, asked for money for rent and food. Hull House's total monthly relief expenses doubled in August from the usual $100 to $200. The sadness Addams felt in seeing the physical and mental suffering stole its way into her letter to Mary. "It takes something . . . in these hard times," she wrote, "to keep up one's spirits." Shifting to the first person, she ended the letter wistfully, "I miss you very much."[13]

Like everyone else, Addams was shocked by the gravity of the depression. The Panic of 1893, she later wrote, was "our first [contact] with dire poverty." The first-person plural hints at the possibility of the first-person singular that she preferred to avoid. She paid many relief visits and found herself, she recalled, "dealing directly with the simplest human wants." She and the residents felt overwhelmed yet determined. "We all worked under a sense of desperate need," Addams remembered, "and a paralyzing consciousness that our best efforts were most inadequate."[14]

Characteristically, her attention was caught by the spiritual and mental effects of the panic. Addams watched with sorrow as formerly self-sufficient and proud workers from the neighborhood sank into mental confusion or severe depression. The worst problem the unemployed faced, she told the Sunset Club at another Ladies' Night, in December 1893, was fear. Their "mental suffering," she said, "sticks to you most closely." They feared three things the most: debt, the shame of appearing as paupers to their children, and dying of hunger. "You can bear everything better when you have enough to eat," she explained. "[W]hen to all your mental trouble is added the fear of starvation, you go under very quickly."[15]

When she said "go under," she was referring to going insane. Since August, the Infirmary had become overcrowded with people who had lost their minds. Insanity, temporary or otherwise, was a form of suffering Addams knew intimately. Weber Addams had had another attack only a year earlier, in November 1892, his fourth. But Weber was relatively lucky; he could afford to pay the fees that the Elgin Hospital for the Insane charged; this allowed him to receive care from experts in relatively spacious and comfortable surroundings. The Dunning Infirmary was a grim, crowded, foul place.[16] For working people whose minds gave way, the economic crisis triggered a journey into hell.

The workers' misery troubled Addams profoundly and deeply unsettled her ideas. Life on Halsted Street had already been corroding her belief that the human spirit was unaffected by poverty; now the depression completed the process. In that crucible she forged a new sensitivity to the material

Out of Work, *from a drawing by Alice Kellogg Tyler, a Hull House volunteer.* Twenty Years at Hull-House, *220.*

essentials of life. Never again would she take economic matters lightly. The panic also cast her own prosperity in a new light. She wondered, perhaps for the first time, about whether she deserved her material security. "I was constantly shadowed" during visits to neighbors, she writes in *Twenty Years,* "by a certain sense of shame that I should be comfortable in the midst of such distress." Her work at Hull House now struck her as "futile and superficial"; the settlement seemed to her "a mere pretense and travesty." [17] She decided to devote her energies that winter to the distinctly material agenda of helping the unemployed.

Of course, she intended to do this cooperatively. To the Sunset Club audience that met in December to address the question "What Shall We Do for Our Unemployed?" she put another question: Why not consult unemployed people about what to do? "They have practical ideas," she said; "they would be glad to do their share to remove this trouble, of which they are the chief victims. . . . [W]e should consider not what shall we do [for] the unemployed, but what shall we and the unemployed do together." Such cooperation, she claimed, may help the people of Chicago "grow . . . into a wider and better citizenship." [18]

Did she follow her own advice? It seems likely that of the plethora of cooperative projects that Addams pursued that fall, some grew out of suggestions from neighbors. At a Residents' Meeting Addams, having vacated the chair, moved that Hull House cooperate with Alderman John Powers, who annually gave away turkeys at Christmas to his faithful political supporters, by providing names for his distribution list and by serving as the distribution point. Powers liked the idea, she reported, but some of the residents did not want to be associated in any way with the boodling alderman. Ellen Gates Starr, Clifford Barnes, and Julia Lathrop made a substitute motion to defeat Addams's proposal. When their motion was defeated, two other residents moved, as an amendment to Addams's motion, that Hull House provide Powers with lists but not distribute turkeys, and the motion passed as amended.[19] Addams's willingness to cooperate with Powers had not been blocked entirely, but it had been firmly reined in.

Addams proposed another cooperative project with more success. The settlement residents had first discussed starting a coal cooperative in July, around the time of the cooperative congress. Members of the co-op would buy a large supply of coal at the wholesale price at the beginning of winter, when the price was low, and sell it to its members throughout the season at a price lower than the usual seasonal price. With the approval of the Residents' Meeting, a group of neighbors and residents met in October, formed the cooperative, and elected officers. Addams was elected treasurer—a clue, perhaps, that she was a moving force behind the venture. The co-op hired an English workingman who had experience with cooperative societies as manager, and the ever-faithful William Colvin, who had donated funds for the Gymnasium Building, agreed to advance the money to buy the coal. By December 2 Addams had collected $115 from a growing number of members. Soon several tons of black coal nuggets were delivered to the playground, which was serving as the temporary coalyard, and the co-op was in business. It was one of the first projects of a new club, the Nineteenth Ward Improvement Club, whose officers were the cooperative's officers. The cooperative was later renamed the Hull House Cooperative Association.[20]

The relief problem was also tackled cooperatively. By September the settlement's monthly relief expenses had burgeoned to $565. Julia Lathrop proposed to the residents on September 24 that Hull House cooperate with David Swing's Central Church in doing "systemized charitable work." The proposal sparked a debate. Some residents argued that "systematized charitable work was not the province of the house." Lathrop presumably argued for the urgency of the need. With Lathrop pushing, the proposal passed, but only because, as the minutes carefully noted, "of the emergency of the present season." The project quickly evolved into an "organized" relief bureau to screen relief applicants from across the city for private charities. In late November the Hull House Bureau of Labor and Charity Registration, a revamped version of Kelley's short-lived Labor Bureau, had opened in a small cottage at 247 West Polk Street, next door to the Gymnasium Building. Addams favored Lathrop's proposal, although as chair she could not speak in its favor at the meeting. She, Lathrop, and their friends from the CWC had been working since 1892 to encourage charities to systematize their relief efforts. [21]

Another cooperative project that Hull House launched that fall was a public dispensary, or free health clinic. It had first been discussed at a Residents' Meeting in August. Hull House literature described it as being run on a "mutual benefit plan." Three women, a physician with a general practice in the neighborhood, a nurse from the Visiting Nurses Association, and a newly arrived Hull House resident with a medical degree, Harriet Rice, staffed it. Rice, an African American, was the settlement's first black resident. [22]

As winter, cold and blustery, settled in, the lines of people desperate for jobs, food, and shelter grew long outside the Bureau of Labor and Registration. "[A] solid, pressing crowd of hundreds of shabby men and shawled or hooded women [came] from all parts of a great city," Julia Lathrop remembered. "[They stood,] held in check by policemen, hour after hour, . . . polyglot, but having the common language of their persistency, their weariness, their chill and hunger." [23]

In early December Addams came to the residents with a project designed to help unemployed, unattached women and their children, whose needs were being neglected by the charities and other relief efforts. Only men could take the canal jobs offered by the Mayor's Relief Committee. Only men could chop wood at the Chicago Relief and Aid Society (CRAS) woodyard in exchange for food, clothing, and shelter. For reasons of modesty, only homeless men could sleep on the closely packed police station and city hall floors. Women were assumed to be the responsibility of their fathers or husbands, although the truth was that many were widows or had been abandoned by their husbands or had no father to turn to. There were no public works jobs for women, and the only public space homeless women could sleep in was the crowded, dark, and filthy Infirmary in Dunning. At the Residents' Meeting of December 10, Addams proposed from the floor, another resident having been elected chairman pro tem, that the settlement organize a temporary sewing workshop and "lodging house" for homeless women. The idea was not greeted with enthusiasm. Presumably—the minutes give no details—residents objected that the project was "charity" and not appropriate for a settlement house. A motion in favor of the proposal passed only after it was amended to read that the workshop and lodging house "should be organized and supported in every respect by some other person or organization."[24]

Undeterred, Addams turned to the Chicago Woman's Club as a potential partner; she had probably planned to approach them in any case, or perhaps club leaders had been the first to make the proposal to her. At a club meeting on December 13, Henrotin urged the members to help destitute women and children and announced that Lucy Flower had already donated $1,000. Other donations soon followed. Six days later, a sewing workshop and a women's lodging house opened near Hull House. Other women's clubs started similar projects. During the winter of 1893–94, forty clubs throughout the city raised $20,000 to support nine workrooms and 3,092 families, or 15,406 persons.[25] The hugely cooperative venture no doubt saved many lives and salvaged much self-respect among unemployed women that winter.

So far, the citywide response to the relief crisis had consisted of establishing a privately funded program to provide meal tickets and jobs to build the canal. Hull House's Relief Bureau was attempting to fill the gap, but it was obviously insufficient. The private relief agencies badly needed to coordinate their emergency relief work. In December, Julia Lathrop, Jane Addams, Lucy Flower, and others were named to a body called the Committee of 50 to set up a new temporary emergency relief organization, the Central Relief Association (CRA), to do the coordination. In keeping with Charity Organization Society (COS) procedures, the city was divided into districts, Hull House's citywide office became CRA's main office and was moved downtown, and Hull House began operating a branch office for the west side. By the time the CRA disbanded in the spring, it had handled twenty-three thousand cases. The existing charities provided most of the relief dollars; CRA gave a small amount when necessary.[26]

The COS system was unyielding in its discipline. Trained "visitors" (sometimes volunteer, sometimes paid) called on families who applied for charity to assess "scientifically" the facts of the case. If an able-bodied man was part of the family, the family received no relief, on the theory that to provide it caused the man to become dependent on charity, which in turn would ruin his character. Jane Addams's involvement with the Committee of 50, as well as her prior work on relief reform, suggests she agreed with the COS philosophy and system. But did she? The settlement method of personal ties and compassionate neighborliness sometimes led settlement residents to help the families of able-bodied men. On that point, the COS system and the settlement philosophy disagreed. Addams was finally forced to face that fact by what she describes as the "most painful episode of the winter for me."[27]

The incident took place at the Hull House's CRA branch office, where Addams volunteered. Her task was to apply COS rules, in which she had been carefully instructed, when individuals came to the office seeking relief.[28] In addition to being forbidden to give relief to able-bodied men, she was required to send such men to do public relief work. This was in order to teach them the value of work and self-sufficiency, something that, according to COS principles, the unemployed badly needed to learn.

One day a man she had known for years, a neighbor who had lost his job as a shipping clerk because of the depression, came to seek relief for himself and his family. The clerk was clearly not sick or disabled, yet, according to the branch office's records, he had received relief four times.[29] It was obvious why, as Addams notes later in telling the story in *Twenty Years*. He was thin and unfit for demanding manual labor, especially in cold weather. Because he was technically able-bodied, however, Addams dutifully told him to seek a job digging the Sanitary and Shipping Canal. The clerk, doubtful, replied that he had always worked indoors and he did not think he could "endure outside work in winter," but Addams did not relent. "I was too uncertain to be severe," she recalls, "but I held to my instructions." The man did as he was told. After signing up for relief work, he labored on the canal for two days, pushing heavy wheelbarrows full of dirt up the steep inclines of the canal walls in freezing weather. Then he caught pneumonia, and a week later he died.

Addams does not describe further how she felt about the clerk's death. Yet she implies that she felt responsible when she relates how she helped the clerk's family (a widow and two children) in every way she could; it is possible she made them her personal financial responsibility. Fifteen years later, she would still be in touch with them.[30]

Why had Addams obeyed the COS rules? Did she still believe, as she had when young, that the poor needed to be taught the ethic of work? Was she

thinking in 1902 of her earlier self when she described the typical "charitable visitor" as "blam[ing] the individual for his poverty"? Or perhaps she
disagreed with the COS rules but obeyed them because of her commitment
to cooperation? Both theories are possible, but the most likely explanation
was that she was confused about just what she believed and, being inclined
to see all sides of the question, had not fully thought through her own position.[31] Adding to her confusion was the fact that she had a close friend on
each side of the theoretical debate. Lathrop believed in the COS rules and
Kelley thought that economics, not character development, was the crux of
the problem.

Indeed, Jane Addams's dilemma soon became even more perplexing.
The Committee of 50 took up the problem of the scarcity of public works
jobs for the unemployed men and the need for less arduous work than
ditch-digging. The committee thought that street-cleaning jobs would be
a good idea and persuaded the city to use private charitable funds to offer
such jobs for wages. But what should the wage rate be? The matter was
referred to a subcommittee.

Addams, a member of the subcommittee, now found herself wrestling
with the intricacies of wage policy. Some of her fellow subcommittee members, determined to employ as many men as possible to do as much street-
cleaning as possible, thought the wages should be $1.00 per day. Addams
urged that the pay be $.75 per half-day, that is, a rate equivalent to the $1.50
per day normally paid for such labor, an amount understood to be the minimum livable wage at the time. Paying too low a wage, she told the subcommittee, might "permanently lower wages," that is, might restructure
the unskilled wages sector of the economy. But the committee approved
the $1.00 wage. Frustrated, Addams resigned from the subcommittee. It
was an uncharacteristically uncooperative act for her.[32] Perhaps Kelley not
only supplied her argument but stiffened her resolve.

What *did* Jane Addams believe about the forces that produced poverty?
In cooperating with Lathrop and her COS methods, she apparently felt a
vestigial loyalty to teaching the work ethic through coercion. In cooperating
with Kelley, she was willing to embrace the structural analysis that poverty
was inevitable when a capitalist system was free to set wages as low as the
labor market would bear.

Addams realized after the wage-setting discussion that she was ignorant
of economic theory. "The discussion," she writes in *Twenty Years*, "carried
me far afield in perhaps the most serious economic reading I have ever

done." Capitalism's failure to explain why the depression happened or to offer a constructive solution troubled her. "I longed," she remembered, "for the comfort of a definite social creed" that could explain "the social chaos" all around her and provide "the logical steps towards its better ordering."[33] That is, she wanted to know the causes of poverty and the way to prevent it in the future. In the fall of 1893 a major debate opened up in Jane Addams's mind about why poor people were poor.

She was familiar with the usual range of explanations; she had listened to them for years. That fall, at a meeting of Working People's Social Science Club, she heard the familiar liberal, laissez-faire argument again. Charles Henderson, university chaplain and professor of sociology at the University of Chicago, made the case to a deeply skeptical audience, many of its members listening as hunger gnawed at their bellies. In his talk, titled "The Unemployed," Henderson excused capitalism from any responsibility for the crisis. No one, he said, was responsible for the economy's collapse; the depression was caused by "the advance of trade." Workers must be patient and live economically until the "panic" passed. During the discussion, the audience rebutted. An elderly, unemployed Bohemian shoemaker scorned Henderson's claim that "we should blame nobody" and argued that the rich man driving by in his carriage was the most useless member of society. A German immigrant was even more hostile. "A nice thing it is for professors and ministers and indolents to instruct those who are killing themselves with work!" He called such people "cowards and thieves." Another mocked the professor's suggestion that those with nothing practice economy.[34]

A second explanation for poverty, embraced by some of the less strict proponents of COS, viewed individual responsibility and circumstances as its causes. In late 1894 Addams read a book that took that approach: the newly published *American Charities: A Study in Philanthropy and Economics* by Amos Warner, a COS administrator who would later become a professor at Stanford University. Addams, summing up Warner's views in a letter to Mary Rozet Smith, noted that he thought poverty was caused by sickness and old age, intermittent work, and drinking. She found his book "very interesting."[35]

Another author Addams was already familiar with, the industrial economist Arnold Toynbee, gave a purely economic explanation for poverty. In his lecture "Wages and Natural Law," included in the book of his essays that Addams owned, he rejected the laissez-faire theory that natural law determined wages. Wages were shaped, he explained, by the amount of product produced, the efficiency of its production, and the proportion of earnings that were allocated back to labor. He endorsed the role of trade unions in adjusting the balance among these factors.[36]

Addams was particularly interested in the Christian socialist explanation. She no doubt read Richard Ely's book *Socialism and Social Reform* soon after it came out in the spring of 1894. Ely, a prominent economist at the University of Wisconsin, a Christian socialist, and a friend of Florence Kelley's, rejected the economic theory of laissez-faire and favored the "soft" socialism preferred by mainstream labor unions, which accepted capitalism but wished it to be regulated, as the best way to prevent poverty.[37] Another "soft" socialist, Edward Bellamy, pressed for similar progressive solutions in his highly popular novel *Looking Backward* (1888), which Addams quite likely read.

Surrounded by Marxists as she was, Addams gave serious thought to Marxian socialism, and in particular to Marx's explanation for poverty. She probably reread Marx's *Capital* and either reread or read for the first time Florence Kelley's translation of Engel's *The Condition of the Working Class in England*. Other socialists she knew, although not explicitly Marxist, shared his hope that the government would own the means of production. She read the new book by her good friend the radical anticapitalist socialist Henry Demarest Lloyd, published late in 1984, *Wealth against Commonwealth*, in which he rejected government regulation as bound to fail and called for the abolishment of private property. The British socialist Herbert Burrows made the same argument when speaking in September 1893 before the Working People's Social Science Club. When he put forth his anticapitalist conclusion that "ownership and control of [production] should be lodged in society, or the people as a whole," the crowded settlement gymnasium rang with cheers of delight.[38]

Addams heard the same strict socialist arguments in conversation with the many German and Russian Jewish working-class socialists who visited Hull House. Some of them trained their persuasive armaments on her in relentless fashion. They saw her, a woman of inherited wealth, she writes in *Twenty Years*, as "an awful example" of someone who "had been caught in the toils of capitalism." Addams recollects that she was sometimes "reasoned with" for "hours at a time" and that they "constantly forced [me] to defend . . . the poverty in the midst of which I was living." The British editor William Stead, visiting Chicago in the fall of 1893, witnessed some of these exchanges. He was more blunt than she about the intensity of their

The Socialist Meeting, *artist unknown.* Scribner's Magazine 24 (1898): 95.

attacks. Jane Addams, he wrote, "was the subject of considerable criticism, not to say denunciation, among the stricter devotees of cast-iron creeds."[39]

Addams seriously considered embracing Marxist socialism. The idea no longer offended her. "[I] conscientiously made my effort," she writes in *Twenty Years*, "both by reading and by many discussions with comrades." She continued a few pages later, "I should have been most grateful at that time to accept the tenets of [Marxist] socialism." She wanted to be a Marxist partly because of a feeling of human fellowship, a desire to be cooperative. "I should have been glad to have had the comradeship of that gallant company" of socialists, she writes.[40]

But she did not become one. She could not accept Marx's theory that "commercial crises" were caused by the willingness of capitalist class ("the bourgeoisie") to pursue overproduction. This seemed to her a severe charge to lay at the feet of capitalists. A second stumbling block was Marx's class theory. She had difficulty, she writes in *Twenty Years*, "accepting . . . economic determinism [since it was] so baldly dependent on the theory of class consciousness." Marx, in his most famous formulation of that theory, writes, "It is not the consciousness of men that determines their being, but, on the contrary, their social being [class] that determines their consciousness."[41] In other words, a wealthy woman, for example, must inevitably hold the views of her own class. Marxism denied the possibility of cross-class (or, as Addams might have thought of it, universalist) consciousness on which the settlement movement was based; it denied the possibility that someone like Addams could go beyond her own class perspective and understand the worker's point of view. Marxism declared universalism impossible.

Addams's response, not surprisingly, was passionate and personal. She felt, rightly, that Marx was charging her with an inability to determine her judgments independent of her class origins or, to state the same point differently, independent of what others might think. The accusation made her angry. These feelings surfaced in a "hot discussion" she had one day. A group of "radicals," as she described them, had invited her to speak to their club, which met regularly on a street corner a few blocks north of Hull House, at Halsted and Madison Streets. Standing on the speaker's box, she was holding forth on a working-class issue when someone interrupted, shouting, "You are all right now, but mark my words, when you are subsidized by millionaires, you will be afraid to talk like this." The prediction that she would lose the freedom to speak her mind offended her. "The defense of free speech was a sensitive point with me," she writes, "and I quickly replied that while I did not intend to be subsidized by millionaires neither did I propose to be bullied by workmen, and that I should state my honest opinion without consulting either of them." To her surprise, the crowd burst into applause and began to discuss "the need to resist tyranny wherever [it was] found."[42]

Addams, who tells this story in *Twenty Years*, goes on to say that her response to the radicals grew out of her "desire to bear independent witness to social righteousness."[43] The words, like her conviction, carry the traces of her evangelical Protestant heritage. The need to bear "independent witness," to listen to her conscience, as her father had taught her, was one of the few principles on which she refused to compromise. At Hull House, as at Rockford Seminary, she was ferociously determined to think through matters on her own. There was intellectual hubris in this position—she was clearly confident of her ability to reason things out for herself and reluctant to consider that her class origins blinded her in any way—but there was moral courage in it, too. Many of the most difficult and defining moments in Jane Addams's life would arise because she insisted on speaking the truth as she saw it. This was one tenet of individualism that she would never abandon.

Addams's self-education in economic theory in 1893–94 did not result in any immediate intellectual revolutions, or at least she does not admit to any in *Twenty Years*. But her intellectual map had been redrawn to include new frontiers. Although economics still held no appeal to her literary sensibility, circumstances had forced her to think more systematically about it. Essential groundwork was being laid for the changes in her thinking that were to come.

Like unemployment, the issue of municipal political corruption was cast in a new light by the depression. The extreme economic conditions created a greater sense of urgency about the problem and a greater willingness among Chicago's citizens to take bold steps. Perhaps the boldest step taken that winter was to create a citywide volunteer organization, the Civic Federation of Chicago, to guide and channel the city's burgeoning municipal reform energies. Jane Addams would be present at its founding and have a place at its leadership table. The stories of its emergence and of her development as citizen are deeply intertwined.

The need for municipal reform in the United States had its origins in rampant urban economic growth. During the 1880s, as industrialism intensified and immigration exploded, the nation's largest cities grew very fast, creating opportunities for boodling. Private contractors who delivered votes to aldermanic candidates on Election Day made easy money providing (or at least promising to provide) city services; entrepreneurs purchased illegally discounted utility licenses to run transportation and energy monopolies in exchange for paying bribes to aldermen. City services were of low quality, and city revenues shrank as dollars owed to the government slid into private pockets. By the early 1890s, the nation's large cities were in trouble. A professor of the new field of municipal government, Andrew D. White, opined in 1890 that "the city governments of the United States are the worst in Christendom, the most expensive, the most inefficient, the most corrupt." Chicago had had serious problems for years.

The streets were filthy; utility companies had the city council under their thumbs. Adding to the general sense of moral dissipation were the corrupt alliances between the Police Department and the illegal gambling houses and brothels.[44]

Behind the scenes was the machine. In Chicago, this referred to a group of mostly Irish American, increasingly though not exclusively Democratic, politicians whose personal wealth derived from boodling and whose political careers depended on the support of unskilled, illiterate, mostly immigrant voters who needed work. These voters reelected their aldermen year after year to the city council in return for jobs, citizenship papers, and other personal favors. The pattern of Irish American political dominance had begun in Chicago in the 1860s. By 1893, the machine had a firm grip on the levers of political power in the city.[45]

Businessmen had been trying to end Chicago's political corruption for decades without much success. Two men were leaders in the campaign. Franklin MacVeagh was a wholesale grocer, millionaire, and self-made man without much formal education. Lyman Gage was the president of the First National Bank of Chicago and a graduate of Yale University and Columbia University Law School. Both had been active in the Citizens Association in the 1870s when it tried to clean up City Hall but became frustrated by the group's narrow focus on serving only business interests. After the Haymarket tragedy in 1888, they sought to broaden their own education by inviting working people, anarchists, socialists, businessmen, and middle-class women to participate in a series of conferences to discuss economic conditions and solutions. Jane Addams went to several sessions in the spring of 1889.[46]

The freewheeling discussions changed Gage's and MacVeagh's minds about some things. They decided that capitalists had no right to operate monopolies and that unions were needed in order to restrain them. They also learned that not all workers had close ties to the Democratic Party or were pro-machine and that some of their fellow businessmen secretly favored machine politics. One experienced reformer warned MacVeagh that some of those "with their hands in the till" were "the well-to-do of your acquaintances; some of them are men of influence and standing, men who are pious church members and good fathers." These are "the enemies . . . of your own house."[47]

Gage and MacVeagh decided they needed to create anticorruption coalitions between business and labor to accomplish civic reform. The first such coalition, formed in 1889, successfully elected a nonpartisan Sanitary Commission, which was the new taxing body created to finance the sanitary canal. In the spring of 1893, they formed a second coalition to put forward an antimachine candidate for mayor, but Carter Harrison, a former mayor with close ties to the Democratic machine and a devotion to the spoils system, was elected. What was needed, Gage and MacVeagh decided, was a larger, broad-based, nonpartisan, permanent organization to bring maximum political pressure to bear.[48]

Conversations about launching such an organization were under way when the depression hit. The people's mood shifted to a combustible mixture of fear, anger, and a longing for action. By the fall of 1893, all that was missing was the right person to strike a match. In October 1893, that person arrived in the city: William T. Stead. Stead, a minister and journalist, had come to Chicago to see the fair just before it closed its doors forever and to investigate living conditions in the poorest neighborhoods of the city. Famous as the editor of two reform magazines, the English and American editions of the *Review of Reviews*, he often campaigned in his editorials against the problems of "vice" in large cities (gambling, prostitution, and political graft) and called for government to address the needs of poor people. Like MacVeagh and Gage, Stead believed that if the city government failed to act, then citizens ought to create a single coordinating organization to serve as a general watchdog over city government and press for reforms.[49]

Arriving in Chicago, Stead visited the fair and met with local religious, reform, and labor leaders. At the end of October, he addressed the Working People's Social Science Club at Hull House and stayed for a time at the settlement. Addams later remembered how he would return at midnight cold and wet from his visits to the vice district and deliver "brilliant monologues" to the gathered residents while drinking hot chocolate by the open fire. Stead, for his part, remembered Addams as being "pale and weary, but indomitable to the last, answering with ready helpfulness to every appeal that came from without," whether it was a sick child who needed a doctor or someone in danger of eviction.[50]

After two weeks, satisfied that he had taken the pulse of the city, Stead rented Central Music Hall, which seated two thousand, and, under the auspices of various trade unions, invited Chicago's citizens to a mass meeting on November 12 to "discuss" the present crisis. Whether by coincidence or by intent, the date was auspicious. November 12, 1893, was the day after the seventh anniversary of the execution of four of the Haymarket anarchists. Only a few months earlier Governor Altgeld had pardoned the three remaining anarchists, the eighth having committed suicide. Stead's meeting was haunted by the ghost of Haymarket, that is, the threat of class warfare. The meeting itself, a turbulent affair, highlighted the tautness of class tensions in the city and the general, urgent feeling that action was needed.

Chicagoans responded with enthusiasm to Stead's and the trade unions' invitation. Businessmen, workers, clerks, clergymen, the unemployed, city councilmen, labor leaders, prostitutes, saloonkeepers, members of the Woman's Christian Temperance Union and the Chicago Woman's Club, socialists, and matrons of distinguished families all attended. On the stage, the millionaire Bertha Palmer sat beside Samuel Fielden, one of the pardoned anarchists, and the socialist labor leader Thomas J. Morgan took his chair near representatives of the WCTU. Addams, sitting somewhere in the hall, thought the crowd "huge."[51]

Stead opened the afternoon session in his best revivalist style. "If Christ came to Chicago," he proposed, "what would He think of it?" The audience hissed and cheered, reflecting its divergent opinions of the answers to the question. Some were ashamed of Chicago's condition but others remained defiantly proud of the city. Morgan, who then took the floor, was even more provocative than Stead. He ripped into the prosperous class. "If . . . this infernal desire of the well-to-do to crush out of sight this awful suffering [continues], do not think you will rest in security," he roared. "If the pleadings of Editor Stead in the name of Christ and for justice cannot shake you out of your false security, someone may use dynamite to blow you out!" There were more hisses and shouts of "No!" Offended, some people left.[52]

Morgan's polemical words deepened the feeling of class antagonism already present in the hall. From the stage, William C. Pomeroy, president of the Waiters' Union and chair of a committee of the Chicago Trades Labor Assembly, added to the tension by denouncing the preachers who ate and dressed well with untroubled consciences. The son of a prominent preacher, feeling defensive, rose from his seat in the audience to assure the massive crowd that his father and others were looking for "practical solutions." Then a laborer broke in. Coming to his feet, he asked the minister's son the underlying question of the afternoon: "What will become of the working man if he is unable . . . to . . . get work?" The auditorium fell silent. The minister's son, having no answer, reverted to the safer topic of the immorality of violence. The situation, he replied, is "deplorable, but I say no man, unemployed or otherwise, who believes in a republic, who believes in republican institutions, ever . . . thought to . . . use dynamite!" Portions of the crowd erupted. The first session ended.[53]

That evening, the atmosphere at the second session was, according to the *Chicago Tribune*, one of "repressed excitement." After more debate, Stead finally closed the proceedings by calling on Chicago to organize an alliance of church leaders and reformers of all classes, to be called "the Civic Church." Apparently, however, this idea did not appeal. Regrouping, Stead asked for suggestions. A union leader moved from the floor that a "civic federation" be established and the crowd roared its approval. On the spot, someone announced the names of a "Committee of Five" to organize the "confederation" and the tumultuous session adjourned.[54]

Those named to the committee had been chosen—by whom is unclear—with strategic care. They were Turlington Harvey, a prominent businessman who was president of the Chicago Relief and Aid Society board, E. I. Thomas, minister of the social Christian People's Church, Edward Bemis, an economics professor at the new University of Chicago, L. T. O'Brien, president of the retail clerks' union, and Jane Addams. As the *Chicago Tribune* noted the next day, the group was meant to represent business, church, educational, labor, and women's interests.[55]

Was the committee, as some later implied, the result of a flash of spontaneous activism at Stead's meeting? It made a good story. Stead was the first to tell it, in an appendix of his book *If Christ Came to Chicago*, published in 1894; Addams, trusting the printed word rather than her memory, repeats his version in *Twenty Years*. Stead's story even became the official version that the Civic Federation promulgated decades later.[56] But Stead did not deserve the credit. In fact, Gage, MacVeagh, and a handful of their reform-minded colleagues in business, labor, religious institutions, and clubs, working behind the scenes, had seized the opportunity Stead provided, apparently without his knowledge, to launch their new organization, which they called the Civic Federation of Chicago.

After Stead's book was published, Lyman Gage did his best to clarify that the publicity-hungry Brit played no key role in the federation's founding. In his address at its first annual meeting in February 1895, Gage told the members somewhat pointedly, "Your association was not an invention, the result of an ingenious mind studying to provide some new form of public activity for restless persons hungry for notoriety. It was a crystallization of sentiment slowly forming through long periods against civic and social abuse no longer bearable."[57]

Gage might have also said that Stead's vision and that of the federation's organizers were not the same. Stead, the moralist, wished to bring Christ to Chicago, that is, to end sin, corruption, and suffering by reforming local government. The federation's leaders were more concerned about strengthening democracy. Their goal, as stated in the organization's first annual report a year later, was to influence the "public spirit" and nurture "a wise and tolerant citizenship." President Lyman Gage stated that he was proud that the federation had, "reawakened the city's slumbering civic life."[58]

The founding of the Civic Federation of Chicago marked the maturing of the city's twenty-year-old anticorruption movement. Its purpose, formulated by the Committee of Five, captured the breadth of the movement as of 1893: to concentrate "in one . . . nonpolitical nonsectarian center all the forces that are now laboring to advance our municipal, philanthropic, industrial and moral interests, and to . . . energiz[e] . . . the conscience of Chicago." The federation also intended to be fully inclusive in its membership. The committee announced that the new organization would bring together people "who reside in different parts of the city, . . . pursue different vocations, who are by birth of different nationalities, who profess different creeds or no creed, [but] . . . have similar interests in the well-being of Chicago."[59] It would be a kind of shadow government, a civic conscience equipped, via its network of concerned citizens, with the means to act.

The high-flown rhetoric produced a remarkably diverse group of leaders. Businessmen held key positions but were not numerically dominant. Lyman Gage was elected the federation's first president and Franklin Mac-Veagh served on the board, and two of the five officers were businessmen, but only three of the remaining ten board members were businessmen.[60] Women were strongly represented in the leadership. Nine women were on the forty-member organizing committee, and four women were on the fifteen-member board of directors. First vice president Bertha Palmer and board members Lucy Flower and Sarah Hackett Stevenson were stalwarts of the Chicago Woman's Club's previous municipal reform campaigns. The fourth woman board member, Jane Addams was a fast-learning political neophyte. Women would chair committees as well. Of the first one hundred members of the federation, 16 percent were women. Visitors to Chicago in 1893 had noted that the city's women seemed to have more power and influence than women elsewhere; their role in the Civic Federation confirmed it.[61]

Trade union men were also at the table, all of them active in the Chicago Trades Labor Assembly. Four were named to the organizing committee: the president of the CTLA, the president of the Retail Clerks Association, the president of the State Federation of Labor, and the president of the Building Trades Council. The first of these, John J. McGrath, also served as second vice president of the board.[62] Two more trade union men, J. J. Linehan and M. J. Carroll, were board members. Trade unionists made up one-sixth of the federation's initial membership. Their inclusion was controversial, especially among conservative churches. A Presbyterian group refused to support the federation because it included workers as social equals. In fact, the federation was not cooperating with all of labor but only with the trade unionists, the "labor aristocracy," some of whom were essentially middle-class.[63]

Trade union women were glaringly absent from the organizing committee and the board. Elizabeth Morgan, as head of the Ladies' Federal Labor Union, was the most obvious choice, but the leadership of the CTLA, who had wrested power from Thomas Morgan two years earlier, apparently blocked her appointment. This may also have been why her associate Mary Kenney was also not named to any position. Still, other women trade unionists were active in the city. Their categorical exclusion from Civic Federation leadership bodies was the likely result of trade union men's well-documented sexism. It was a great loss. Women unionists had been a key force in progressive politics in the city in the 1880s and early 1890s. Roughly 12.5 percent of the workforce in Chicago's leading industries and a higher percentage of the general workforce was composed of women.[64]

The federation's leadership was religiously diverse. Although Protestants dominated the organizing committee, Emil Hirsch, the rabbi of Sinai Congregation, was a member; he also served on the committee to draft the plan of the organization, and was named to the board of directors the following year. Chicago's leading Roman Catholic layman, William J. Onahan, was also on the board. There was, however, little other racial or ethnic diversity. There were plenty of Irish names but no Italian ones in the initial membership list. As best can be determined, no African American, Hispanic American, or Asian American was a member, either. Of course, each of the latter groups still amounted to less than 1.5 percent of the city's population.[65]

The organization's structure, at least on paper, was boldly representative and democratic. Members belonged to their local federation precinct council, each of which sent an elected representative to sit on one of the federation's thirty-four ward councils, each of which sent an elected representative to a citywide body called the Council of 100, or Central Council. The mayor of the city was also a council member. At the top was the board of directors, which oversaw the council and was elected from the council's membership.[66] The entire hierarchical structure, grand, systematic, and rational, captured the way these early progressives thought an urban political system ought to work.

But the federation did not intend to be merely the embodiment of the principle of democratic representation. As its founding statement of purpose demonstrated, it meant to accomplish real reform on every possible civic front. Initially, five departments—municipal, philanthropic, industrial, educational and social, and moral reform—were organized. Each department had its own standing committee to guide it, its members drawn from the Central Council and named by the board. There was no political committee in the original structure, not because the founders had lost interest in politics but because the board was perplexed as to how to organize that part of the federation's work. Initially, the board named a committee to ponder the question of what "non-partisan action" the federation should take.[67]

Citizen-organized municipal reform was hardly unique to Chicago. By 1894 there were more than eighty such organizations (city, state, and national), sixty of them formed since 1890, and thirty, including the Civic Federation of Chicago, founded in 1894 alone. Women were not as welcome in some of these organizations, however, as they were in the early years of the Civic Federation. As of 1895, twenty-one of the fifty-two municipal reform organizations banned women from membership.[68]

In January 1894, when New York's and Philadelphia's civic organizations convened a national planning conference in Philadelphia, these groups formally coalesced as a national movement. Delegates, including Franklin MacVeagh, came from twenty-one cities in thirteen states. MacVeagh was named to a Committee of Seven to organize a National Municipal League. Later that year, the Civic Federation of Chicago sent a delegate to the league's first national convention in Minneapolis. With the speed of lightning, progressive municipal reform suddenly became an unmistakable presence on the national stage. In launching the league when they did, a large number of activist American citizens expressed their renewed optimism in an extrapartisan, citizen-initiated democracy during the nation's most serious economic crisis. Progressivism was born in the depression of the 1890s. The founding of the Civic Federation was also nationally significant.[69] Cross-class and cross-gendered at its birth, the organization's democratic vision was particularly ambitious. It was the proud child of a western city that delighted in breaking with eastern traditions.

Jane Addams benefited greatly from the creation of the federation. She threw herself into its work. In 1894 she sat on the Central Council representing the Nineteenth Ward, served on the board of directors, and, intriguingly, served on the Industrial Committee.[70] She also served on a new committee that was quickly organized, the Special Committee on the Lake Front Park.[71] The Civic Federation suited her perfectly because it was welcoming to women of her class, hugely cooperative in its methods, and eager to bring to life the American ideal of a democratic, unified citizenry. For all these reasons, Addams was deeply drawn to it. Immediately immersed in its many-faceted undertakings, she would find in the organization the opportunity to transform herself into a leader of social reform in Chicago and in the nation.

CHAPTER 13

CLAIMS

1894

During the difficult winter of 1893–94, Addams pushed herself hard. More than one visitor to Hull House noticed her paleness. At the urging of her doctor, in January she took a brief vacation to Green Bay, Wisconsin, with Mary Rozet Smith. The opportunity for a longer rest came a few weeks later when she left for California on her second paid lecture tour. Her traveling companion was her sister Alice, who joined her train as it passed through Kansas.[1]

Addams found the train ride across the western states startling. As she peered out the train window she saw something quite different from the gray, suffering world of Chicago's West Side. "I found myself amazed," she writes in *Twenty Years*, "at the large stretches of open country and prosperous towns . . . whose existence I had quite forgotten." In sunny Los Angeles she and Alice spent time with Mary's oldest son, John Weber Linn; Jane had sent him there to recover from tuberculosis. It was a restful time. She reported to Mary Smith, "I am lounging 'considerable' to live up to the climate." Traveling north with Alice, she then spoke about the settlement house movement at Stanford University in Palo Alto and the University of California at Berkeley. She also gave three talks in San Francisco: one to workingmen under the auspices of the Socialist Labor Party, one to the Intercollegiate Alumnae Association, and one to the Congress of Women.[2]

The audiences were appreciative and the conversations interesting, but by mid-February Addams was beginning to find her trip tame. She wrote Sarah Anderson, "I [am] eager for the fray,—in other words quite homesick for Hull House."[3] She invoked the metaphor of battle playfully. She could not know that the most fearsome labor battle of the nineteenth century was about to explode in Chicago and that she would soon find herself at its volatile center.

Once back at Hull House Addams was not pleased to find that the machinery of residential governance had collapsed in her absence. Florence Kelley had convened one Residents' Meeting but had left in the middle of it. "The meeting gradually dissolved," the minutes blithely reported. Ellen Starr chaired the next and it became a party, with punch and fruitcake provided by Julia Lathrop. Again, the minutes were cheerfully self-incriminating: "The meeting disappeared."[4]

The failed attempts showed just who was pushing for self-governance and who was not. Addams, determined that she and her colleagues would do things cooperatively, now whipped the Residents' Meeting into shape. After convening the group, she turned the chair over to another resident and made motions from the floor that the residents sheepishly passed: that the standing committees would report weekly, that the roll would be called, and that a "reasonable excuse" was needed to miss a meeting.[5]

Another domestic difficulty Addams faced on her return was more expected. The previous fall her sister Mary Addams Linn had fallen ill (the nature of her illness is not clear), and by March her condition had worsened. Addams decided to bring her from Storm Lake, Iowa, where the Linns were now living, to Chicago for medical treatment. But who would pay for it? The Linns could not. John Linn had proved a poor breadwinner over the years. Except for some land, Mary's inheritance had been spent and the family was in debt. Jane proposed to Alice that they share Mary's medical costs, but Alice sent no money. After Jane had moved Mary to a sanitarium in Kenosha, Wisconsin, about fifty miles north of Chicago, and after Alice still had sent no funds despite Jane's repeated requests, Jane took out a bank loan of $200 to help pay Mary's bills. Throughout April Jane visited Mary and sent updates to Alice. "The family claim is strong this spring, isn't it?" she wrote.[6]

Addams took out the loan because by the spring of 1894 she was facing a serious financial crisis regarding paying her own bills and Hull House's. Although she still owned the farm outside of Cedarville, most of the rest of her wealth was gone. Four years of spending her money on Hull House— the total now came to $13,437—had been the first drain; the economy's collapse, which had further increased the need for relief on Halsted Street, had destroyed what had remained of her already tenuous financial equilibrium. "Our leak this year," she wrote Sarah Anderson in June, apparently speaking of both herself and Hull House, "has been the huge amount given in relief to our neighbors. . . . The suffering has been and is fearful and it is absolutely impossible to live in the midst of it and not do something about it. . . . [I]t is a pull on one's personal loyalty and affection." She confessed to Sarah the reality of her situation. "I probably won't ever be flush again." By 1894 Addams's earned income was her financial mainstay, and it would remain so until she died. As a working woman, she would live on a tight budget for the rest of her life.[7]

In theory, Hull House's debt could be addressed by raising more money from donors. Unfortunately, most of them had also been hit by the economic collapse, a problem Addams was embarrassed not to have anticipated. She admitted to Sarah, "It was of course stupid—one ought to have seen that the same thing that made the poor poorer, made our donors poorer too, not to mention one's friends and relations."[8] Not to mention herself. Beyond these immediate crises there loomed another: Addams's fear of being personally liable for the settlement's debts. In 1889 she had refused to incorporate the settlement as a separate legal entity, not wanting it to be "an institution." She was still not ready to take that step in the spring of 1894. But the pressures to do so were increasing.

Meanwhile, despite the fact she and Hull House were struggling, she remained a true daughter of prosperity and a true daughter of a successful entrepreneur by recklessly—or courageously, depending on one's point of view—plunging ahead with plans for a third building. The nursery and the kindergarten needed their own space, and by April Addams had devised a plan to construct a children's building on Culver land just north of the Hull mansion. She approached Culver about the idea and found her interested, as Jane reported to Mary Rozet Smith, who was considering funding the building.[9]

The source of Addams's boldness—her large ambition—surfaced a week later, when she wrote Smith again. She had even bigger plans—plans, she frankly confessed, that were inspired in part by her feelings of competition with a new settlement that the University of Chicago was launching. To be headed by Mary McDowell, a former Hull House resident whom Addams had recommended for the job, the University of Chicago Settlement was scheduled to open the following fall in the Stock Yard district and looked as if it had the potential to become as big and successful as Hull House. "I want to talk to you of many things," she wrote Mary. "Perhaps my ambition has been stirred by the undertaking of the settlement at the Stock Yards."[10] Addams would sometimes claim in later years that Hull House merely grew in response to the needs of the neighborhood, but the truth was that she drove its growth. Responding to the power in her that, as Robert Browning's Bishop Blougram had observed, "will hurt me else," she repeatedly created opportunities, often in the face of crisis, to lead and to succeed.

———————

On May 11 Addams, after giving a talk at the University of Wisconsin and visiting Mary Addams Linn in Kenosha, wrote Alice that their sister's health was improving. The same day, a major strike erupted at the Pullman Car Works, in the southernmost part of Chicago. The immediate cause of the strike was a series of wage cuts the company had made in response to the economic crisis. Since September the company had hired back most of the workers it had laid off at the beginning of the depression, but during the same period workers' wages had also fallen an average of 30 percent. Meanwhile, the company, feeling pinched, was determined to increase its profits from rents. In addition to the company's refusing to lower the rent rate to match the wage cuts, its foremen threatened to fire workers living outside of Pullman who did not relocate to the company town. The result was that two-thirds of the workforce was soon living in Pullman. By April, many families were struggling to pay the rents and in desperate straits; some were starving. The company's stance was firm. "We just cannot afford in the present state of commercial depression to pay higher wages," Vice President Thomas H. Wickes said. At the same time, the company continued to pay its stockholders dividends at the rate of 8 percent per annum, the same rate it had paid before the depression hit.[11]

The workers had tried to negotiate. After threatening on May 5 to strike if necessary, leaders of the forty-six-member workers' grievance committee met twice with several company officials, including, at the second meeting, George Pullman, the company's founder and chief executive, to demand that the company reverse the wage cuts and reduce the rents. The company refused, and on May 11, after three of the leaders of the grievance committee had been fired and a rumor had spread that the company would lock out all employees at noon, twenty-five hundred of the thirty-one hundred workers walked out. Later that day, the company laid off the remaining six hundred. The strike had begun. "We struck at Pullman," one worker said, "because we were without hope."[12]

For Addams, the coincidental timing of the strike and Mary's illness, both of which would soon worsen, made each tragedy, if possible, a greater sorrow. The strike was a public crisis. Its eruption raised difficult questions for Addams about the ethics of the industrial relationship. What were George Pullman's obligations to his employees? And what were his employees' to him? Was it disloyal of him to treat his workers as cogs in his economic machine? Or was it disloyal of his workers to strike against an employer who supplied them with jobs and a fine town to live in? Who had betrayed whom? Where did the moral responsibility lie? Mary's illness was Addams's private crisis. Mary was the faithful and loving sister whose affection Addams had always relied on and whose life embodied the sacrifices a good woman made for the sake of family. Mary had given up her chance for further higher education for her family's sake and had been a devoted wife to a husband who had repeatedly failed to support her and their children. The threat of her death stirred feelings of great affection and fears of desperate loss in Addams.

As events unfolded, the two crises would increasingly compete for Addams's loyalty and time. She would find herself torn, unsure whether she should give her closest attention to her sister's struggle against death or to labor's struggle against the capitalist George Pullman. It was a poignant and unusual dilemma; still, it could be stated in the framework she had formulated in "Subjective Necessity": What balance should she seek between the family and the social claim?

The causes of the Pullman Strike went deeper than the company's reaction to the depression. For the workers who lived in Pullman, the cuts in wages and the high rents of 1893–94 were merely short-term manifestations of long-term grievances, all of them tied to company president George Pullman's philosophy of industrial paternalism. These included the rules regarding life in Pullman, a privately owned community located within the city of Chicago. Pullman had built the town in 1880 to test his theory that if the company's workers lived in a beautiful, clean, liquor- and sin-free environment, the company would prosper. Reformers, social commentators, and journalists around the world were fascinated by Pullman's "socially responsible" experiment. Addams would later recall how he was "dined and feted throughout Europe . . . as a friend and benefactor of workingmen." The workers, however, thought the Pullman Company exercised too much control. Its appointees settled community issues that elsewhere would have been dealt with by an elected government, company policy forbade anyone to buy a house, the town newspaper was a company organ, labor meetings were banned, and company spies were everywhere. Frustrated by this as well as by various employment practices, workers organized into unions

Mary Addams Linn, Jane Addams's sister. The Jane Addams Papers Project, Fayetteville, NC.

according to their particular trades (the usual practice), and these various unions repeatedly struck Pullman Company in the late 1880s and early 1890s. The May 1894 strike was the first that was companywide.[13]

Behind that accomplishment lay the organizing skills of George Howard, vice president of the American Railway Union (ARU), the new cross-trades railroad union that Eugene Debs, its president, had founded the previous year. To organize across trades was a bold idea. Howard had been in Chicago since March signing up members, and by early May he was guiding the workers in their attempted negotiations with the company. The ARU's stated purpose was to give railroad employees "a voice in fixing wages and in determining conditions of employment." Only one month earlier it had led railroad workers at the Great Northern Railroad through a successful strike. Thanks to the ARU as well as to the mediating efforts of some businessmen from St. Paul, Minnesota, voluntary arbitration had resolved the strike, and three-fourths of the wage cut of 30 percent had been restored. Impressed, 35 percent of Pullman's workers joined the ARU in the weeks that followed, hoping that the new union could work the same magic on their behalf.[14]

At first, the prospects for a similar solution at Pullman did not look promising. After the walkout, George Pullman locked out all employees and, using a business trip to New York as his excuse, removed himself from the scene. Meanwhile, a few days after the strike began, Debs, a powerful orator, addressed the strikers to give them courage. He had the rare ability to elevate a controversy about wages into a great moral struggle. The arguments he used that day, familiar ones in the labor movement, would be echoed in Jane Addams's eventual interpretation of the Pullman Strike. "I do not like the paternalism of Pullman," he said. "He is everlastingly saying, what can we do for the poor workingmen? . . . The question," he thundered, "is what can we do for ourselves?"[15]

At this point, the Civic Federation of Chicago decided to get involved. Its president, Lyman Gage, an enthusiast for arbitration, appointed a prestigious and diverse body, called the Conciliation Board, to serve as a neutral third party to bring the disputing sides before a separate arbitration panel. Made up partly of members of the federation's Industrial Committee, on which Addams sat, it was designed to be representative of various interests, particularly those of capital, labor, academia, and reform. It included bank presidents, merchants, a stockbroker, an attorney, presidents of labor federations, labor newspaper editors, professors, and three women civic activists: Jane Addams, Ellen Henrotin, and Bertha Palmer.[16]

The board divided itself into five committees. In the early phase of the strike it would meet nightly, in Addams's words, to "compare notes and adopt new tactics." Having had some success in arranging arbitrations in the Nineteenth Ward, Addams was eager to see the method tried in the Pullman case.[17] She would soon emerge as the driving force and the leading actor in the initiative.

The first question the board discussed was whether the Pullman workers wanted the strike to be arbitrated. Addams investigated the question by visiting the striking workers in Pullman, eating supper with some of the women workers, touring the tenement housing, and asking questions. Afterwards, she asked the president of the local ARU chapter, Thomas Heathcoate, and ARU organizer George Howard to allow the Conciliation Board to meet with the Strike Committee. Refusing her request, Howard told her that the ARU was willing to have the committee meet with the board but that first the Pullman Company would have to state its willingness to go to arbitration.[18]

Meanwhile, three men from the Conciliation Board were supposed to try to meet with the Pullman Company. The board's president, A. C. Bartlett, a businessman, was to arrange the meeting but, as of May 30, two weeks into the strike, he had done nothing. Frustrated, Addams stepped in. On June 1 she arranged for Bartlett, Ralph Easley (the Civic Federation's secretary), and herself to meet with Vice President Wickes and General Superintendent Brown. At the meeting, which Bartlett failed to attend, Wickes merely repeated the company's well-known position: that it had "nothing to arbitrate."[19]

Thwarted, Addams decided, with the board's support, to try again to arrange for the board to meet with the Strike Committee. At a Conciliation Board meeting, Lyman Gage suggested that she propose that rent be the first issue to be arbitrated. Agreeing, Addams decided that, instead of taking the idea to the uncooperative Howard, she would take it over his head to Debs. Persuaded by Addams, Debs immediately arranged for members of the board to speak that night to the Strike Committee about the proposal.[20] Once again, however, Addams's colleagues failed to follow through. She was the only board member to turn up.

At the meeting, the strike leaders were suspicious, believing that arbitration was the company's idea. No report survives of how Addams made her case to them, but one can glean impressions from a description of Addams that a reporter published in a newspaper article in June 1894. She described Addams as a "person of marked individuality[;] she strikes one at first as lacking in suavity and graciousness of manner but the impression soon wears away before [her] earnestness and honesty." She was struck, too, by Addams's paleness, her "deep" eyes, her "low and well-trained voice," and how her face was "a window behind which stands her soul."[21]

Addams must have made a powerful presentation to the Strike Committee. After she spoke, it voted to arbitrate not only the rents but any point. It was the breakthrough Addams had been hoping for. "Feeling that we had made a beginning toward conciliation," Addams remembered, she reported her news to the board.[22]

Meanwhile, with the workers and their families' hunger and desperation increasing, tensions were mounting. Wishing to increase the pressure on the company, Debs had declared on June 1 that the ARU was willing to organize a nationwide sympathy boycott of Pullman cars among railroad employees generally if the company did not negotiate. The Pullman Company's cars, though owned and operated by the company, were pulled by various railroads. A national boycott of Pullman cars could bring the nation's already devastated economy to a new low point. Meanwhile, the ARU opened its national convention in Chicago on June 12. Chicago was nervous. Even before the convention began, Addams commented to William Stead, in town again for a visit, that "all classes of people" were feeling "unrest, discontent, and fear. We seem," she added, "to be on the edge of some great upheaval but one can never tell whether it will turn out a tragedy or a farce."[23]

Several late efforts at negotiation were made. On June 15 an ARU committee of twelve, six of them Pullman workers, met with Wickes to ask again whether the company would arbitrate. His answer was the same: there was nothing to arbitrate and the company would not deal with a union. Soon afterward George Pullman returned to town. He agreed to meet with the Conciliation Board but, perhaps sensing the danger that the sincere and persuasive Jane Addams posed, only with its male members. At the meeting he restated his position: no arbitration. At this point, Addams recalled, the board's effort collapsed in "failure."[24] The strike was now more than a month old. Addams had done everything she could to bring about arbitration. Resourceful, persistent, even wily, she had almost single-handedly brought the workers to the table, but because she was denied access to George Pullman on the pretext of her gender, she had failed to persuade the company. Her efforts, however, had made something very clear to herself and many others—that George Pullman's refusal to submit the dispute to arbitration was the reason the strike was continuing.

The situation now became graver. At the ARU convention, the delegates voted on June 22 to begin a national boycott of Pullman cars on June 26 if no settlement were reached. Abruptly, on the same day as the vote, a powerful new player, the General Managers Association (GMA), announced its support for the company. The GMA had been founded in 1886 as a cartel to consider "problems of management" shared by the twenty-four railroad companies serving Chicago; it had dabbled in wage-fixing and had long been opposed to unions. George Pullman's refusal to arbitrate had been, among other things, an act of solidarity with these railroad companies, his business partners. Disgusted with the outcome of the Great Northern Strike, they were determined to break the upstart ARU, which threatened to shrink the profits of the entire industry. Pullman departed the city again in late June for his vacation home in New Jersey, leaving the GMA in charge of the antistrike strategy. It announced that any railroad worker who refused to handle Pullman cars would be fired.[25]

The ARU was undaunted. On June 26 the boycott began. Within three days, one hundred thousand men had stopped working and twenty railroads were frozen. Debs did not mince words in his message to ARU members and their supporters. This struggle, he said, "has developed into a contest between the producing classes and the money power of this country."[26] Class warfare was at hand.

Jane Addams was not in the city when the ARU voted for the boycott. She had gone to Cleveland to give a commencement speech on June 19 at the College for Women of Western Reserve University.[27] But she was in Chicago when the boycott began. Chicago felt its impact immediately. There was no railroad service into or out of the city, and public transportation within the city also ceased as the streetcar workers joined the boycott. With normal life having ground to a halt, the city's mood, which had been initially sympathetic to the workers, began to polarize along class lines. Working people's sympathies for the railroad workers and hostility toward capitalists rose to a fever pitch while many people in the middle classes felt equally hostile toward the workers; some thought that the strikers should be shot. In *Twenty Years* Addams writes, "During all those dark days of the Pullman strike, the growth of class bitterness was most obvious." It shocked her. Before the strike, she writes, "there had been nothing in my experience [that had] reveal[ed] that distinct cleavage of society which a general strike at least momentarily affords."[28]

The boycott quickly spread, eventually reaching twenty-seven states and territories and involving more than two hundred thousand workers. It had become the largest coordinated work stoppage in the nation's history and the most significant exercise of union strength the nation had ever witnessed. The workers were winning through the exercise of raw economic power. Virtually the only railcars moving were the federal mail cars, which the boycotting railroad workers continued to handle, as required by federal law and as Debs had carefully instructed them. The railroad yards in the city of Chicago were full of striking workers and boycotters determined to make sure that other railroad cars did not move and to protect them from vandalism.[29]

Now the GMA took aggressive steps that would change the outcome of the strike. On June 30 it used its influence in Washington to arrange for its own lawyer, Edwin Walker, to be named a U.S. Special Attorney. Walker then hired four hundred unemployed men, deputized them as U.S. Marshals, armed them, and sent them to guard the federal mail cars in the railroad yards to be sure the mail got through.[30] In the yards, the strikers and marshals eyed each other nervously.

Meanwhile, on June 29, Jane Addams's family crisis worsened. Jane had visited Mary on June 28 but returned to Chicago the same day. That night she received word that her sister's condition suddenly had become serious, and the following day she rushed back to Kenosha accompanied by Mary's son Weber Linn (apparently they traveled in a mail car thanks to Addams's ties to the strikers). She deeply regretted having been gone so much. "My sister is so pleased to have me with her," she wrote Mary Rozet Smith, "that I feel like a brute when I think of the days I haven't been here." As Addams sat by Mary's bed in Kenosha, the situation in Chicago remained relatively calm. Nevertheless, the GMA now took two more steps that further drew the federal government into the crisis. Claiming that the strikers were blocking the movement of the federal mails (although the subsequent federal investigation produced no evidence that this was true), the GMA asked the U.S. attorney general to ask President Grover Cleveland to send federal troops to shut down the strike. Cleveland agreed, and on July 3 the first troops entered the city. The same day the attorney general ordered Special Attorney Walker to seek an injunction in federal court against the ARU in order to block the union from preventing workers from doing their work duties. The injunction was immediately issued.[31]

By July 1 it was clear that Mary Addams Linn was dying. Addams wired her brother-in-law John and the two younger children, Esther, thirteen, and Stanley, who had recently turned eleven, to come from Iowa to Kenosha.

By July 3 they had somehow reached Chicago but, because of the boycott, they could not find a train for the last leg of their trip. At last John signed a document relieving the railroad of liability; then he, Esther, and Stanley boarded a train (probably a mail train) and within hours had arrived in Kenosha, protected, or so Esther later believed, by the fact that they were relatives of Jane Addams, "who was working for the strikers." Mary's family was now all gathered around her except for her oldest son, John, who was still in California. Unconscious by the time they arrived, she died on July 6.[32]

While Jane Addams's private world was crumbling, so was Chicago's civic order. On July 4, one thousand federal troops set up camp around the Post Office and across the city, including the Pullman headquarters. On July 5 and 6 thousands of unarmed strikers and boycotters crowded the railroad yards, joined by various hangers-on—hungry, angry, unemployed boys and men. Many were increasingly outraged by the armed marshals and the troops' presence. Suddenly a railroad agent shot one of them, and they erupted into violence. Hundreds of railroad cars burned as the troops moved in. Now the strikers were fighting not only the GMA but also the federal government. This had been the GMA's aim all along. In the days to come, thousands more federal troops poured into the city.[33]

After attending Mary's funeral in Cedarville Jane Addams returned on July 9 to find Chicago an armed camp and class warfare on everyone's minds. In working-class neighborhoods such as the Nineteenth Ward, people wore white ribbons in support of the strike and the boycott. Across town, middle-class people were greeted at their breakfast tables by sensational newspaper headlines claiming that the strikers were out to destroy the nation. One *Tribune* headline read, "Dictator Debs versus the Federal Government." The national press echoed the theme of uncontrolled disorder. *Harper's Weekly* called the strikers "anarchists." And the nation remained in economic gridlock. Farmers and producers were upset that they could not move their produce to market. Passengers were stranded. Telegrams poured into the White House.[34]

Like the strikers' reputation, Hull House's was worsening daily. Until the strike took place, Addams later recalled, the settlement, despite its radical Working People's Social Science Club, had been seen as "a kindly philanthropic undertaking whose new form gave us a certain idealistic glamour." During and after the strike, the situation "changed markedly." Although Addams had tried to "maintain avenues of intercourse with both

Illinois National Guard troops in front of the Arcade Building in Pullman during the Pullman Strike. Neg. i21195aa.tif, Chicago Historical Society.

sides," Hull House was now seen as pro-worker and was condemned for being so. Some of the residents were clearly pro-worker. Florence Kelley and one of her assistant factory inspectors, Alzina Stevens, befriended Debs during the strike and its aftermath. Stevens sheltered him for a time in her suburban home when authorities were trying to arrest him; Kelley tried to raise money for his bail after he was arrested later in July.[35]

Addams and Hull House began to be severely criticized. Donors refused to give. Addams told John Dewey, who had come to town to take up his new position at the University of Chicago, that she had gone to meet with Edward Everett Ayer, a Chicago businessman with railroad industry clients who had often supported Hull House's relief work, to ask him for another gift. Dewey wrote his wife, "[Ayer] turned on her and told her that she had a great thing and now she had thrown it away; that she had been a trustee for the interests of the poor, and had betrayed it [*sic*]—that like an idiot she had mixed herself in something which was none of her business and about which she knew nothing, the labor movement and especially Pullman, and had thrown down her own work, etc., etc." That autumn Addams had "a hard time financing Hull-House," a wealthy friend later recalled. "Many people felt she was too much in sympathy with the laboring people." Addams merely notes in *Twenty Years* that "[in] the public excitement following the Pullman Strike Hull House lost many friends."[36]

And there were public criticisms as well. Some middle- and upper-class people attacked Addams, one resident remembered, as a "traitor to her class." When Eugene Debs observed that "[e]pithets, calumny, denunciation . . . have been poured forth in a vitriolic tirade to scathe those who advocated and practiced . . . sympathy," one suspects that he had in mind the treatment Jane Addams received.[37] Meanwhile, the workers were angry that Addams would not more clearly align herself with their cause. Her stance—that she would take no side—guaranteed that nearly everyone in the intensely polarized city would be angry with her.

Standing apart in this way was extremely painful. She was "very dependent on a sense of warm comradeship and harmony with the mass of her fellowmen," a friend, Alice Hamilton, recalled. "The famous Pullman strike" was "for her the most painful of experiences, because . . . she was forced by conviction to work against the stream, to separate herself from the great mass of her countrymen." The result was that Addams "suffered from . . . spiritual loneliness."[38] In these circumstances, no one could mistake Addams's neutrality for wishy-washiness. Practicing neutrality during the Pullman Strike required integrity and courage. In being true to her conscience, she paid a tremendous price.

Of course, the strike was not the only reason she was lonely. Mary's death was the other. And if, as we may suspect, Mary's passing evoked the old trauma for Jane of her mother Sarah's passing, not to mention the later losses of her sister Martha and her father, then the loneliness Addams felt in the last days of the strike and the boycott was truly profound.

She does not describe these feelings when she writes about the strike and Mary's death in *Twenty Years*, but in the chapter about Abraham Lincoln, she conveys her feelings well enough. She tells about a walk she took in the worst days of the strike. In that "time of great perplexity," she writes, she decided to seek out Lincoln's "magnanimous counsel." In the sweltering heat, dressed in the long skirt and long-sleeved shirtwaist that were then the fashion, Addams walked—because the streetcars were on strike—four and a half "wearisome" miles to St. Gaudens's fine new statue of Lincoln, placed at the entrance to Lincoln Park just two years earlier, and read the words cut in stone at the slain president's feet: "With charity towards all."[39] And then, still bearing on her shoulders the burden of public hatred that Lincoln had also borne, she walked the four and a half miles home.

Although the deployment of troops had broken the strike's momentum, the government needed to put the strike's leader behind bars to bring the strike to an end. On July 10 Debs was indicted by a grand jury for violating the injunction and arrested. Bailed out two days later, he was arrested again on July 17 to await trial in jail. However, when the government prosecutor, the ubiquitous Edwin Walker, became ill, the trial was postponed, and Debs went home to Indiana, where he collapsed gratefully into bed. The trial was held in November 1894; Debs would begin serving his six-month sentence in January 1895.[40]

With Debs removed from leadership and fourteen thousand armed troops, police, and guardsmen bivouacked in Chicago, the strike and the boycott soon collapsed. On August 2 the ARU called off the strike, and on the same day the Pullman Company partially reopened. The railroads were soon running again. The anti-labor forces had won. Private industry and the federal government had shown that, united and with the power of the law on their side, no one, not even the hundreds of thousands of workers who ran the nation's most crucial industry, could defeat them. If the strike had been successful, it would have turned the ARU into the nation's most powerful union. Given that the strike failed, the opposite result took place. As the GMA had intended, the ARU died. After Debs was released from jail, he did not resurrect the union.[41]

Although the strike was over, innumerable questions remained unanswered. For the country as a whole, whose only sources of information had been sensational news stories and magazine articles, the first question was: What were the facts? To sort these out, President Grover Cleveland appointed a three-person fact-finding commission to investigate and issue a report. Jane Addams would testify before the United States Strike Commission in August, as would George Pullman.[42]

Meanwhile, for Addams and other labor and middle-class reformers in Chicago, the question was how to prevent or resolve future strikes. The failure of the Conciliation Board's effort to promote voluntary arbitration revealed, Addams believed, certain "weaknesses in the legal structure," that is, in state and federal laws. On July 19, two days after Debs' second arrest, as the troops began slowly to withdraw from the city, the Central Council of the Civic Federation met at the Commerce Club. At the meeting, M. C. Carroll, editor of a labor magazine and a member of the Conciliation Board, proposed that the federation host a conference "on arbitration or conciliation" to seek ideas about ways to avert "strikes and boycotts in the future." The Central Council "enthusiastically endorsed" the proposal and appointed a committee to devise a plan. The hope was to do something immediately, while interest was high, to increase public support for arbitration legislation in Illinois and across the nation.[43]

Addams missed the meeting because she was assisting at the Hull House Summer School at Rockford College, which began on July 10. But she was back in Chicago by the second week in August and had soon joined the arbitration conference committee. It devised a three-part strategy. First, it would convene "capital and labor" at a national conference titled "Industrial Conciliation and Arbitration" in Chicago in November to provide a forum for "calm discussion" of the questions raised by the strike and bring together information about methods of arbitration and conciliation. Second, conference participants from Illinois would press the Illinois General Assembly to pass a law creating a state board of arbitration. Third, a national commission would be named at the end of the conference to press for federal legislation. Elected as secretary to the committee, Jane Addams threw herself into organizing the event.[44]

At the same time, she took on new family responsibilities. With Mary's death, Jane Addams, at thirty-three, became the guardian and mother of the two younger Linn children. Their father had decided he could not afford to keep them. For the fall, she and Alice agreed that Stanley would live at Hull House and Esther would attend the preparatory boarding school that was affiliated with Rockford College. Weber, nineteen, was still a student at the University of Chicago. He would spend his vacations at Hull House. The oldest son, John, twenty-two, having returned from California, was once again a resident at Hull House and studying for the Episcopalian priesthood.[45] Esther remembered Addams as taking "me and my brothers in as her own children. . . . [She] was a wonderful mother to us all." Addams was particularly close to Stanley, who, according to Alice's daughter Marcet, "became . . . Aunt Jane's very own little boy[;] . . . he was always like a son to her."[46]

Jane Addams would honor this family claim for the rest of her life. Her niece and nephews, later joined by their children, would gather with her for

Jane Addams and her nephew, Stanley Linn, ca. 1894. Jane Addams Memorial Collection (JAMC neg. 1703), Special Collections, The University Library, University of Illinois at Chicago.

holidays, live with her at Hull House at various times in their lives, and rely on her for advice, as well as for a steady supply of the somewhat shapeless sweaters that she would knit for them.[47] Because few letters between Addams and the Linn children have survived, the historical record is mostly silent about the affectionate bonds that linked them and the faithfulness with which she fulfilled the maternal role. Her devotion arose from a deep understanding of what it felt like for a child to lose its mother and from a deep gratitude that she could give to Mary's children the gift Mary had given her.

———————————

The Pullman Strike was a national tragedy that aroused fierce passions and left many scars. For many in the middle classes, including Jane Addams, some of the most painful were the memories of the intense hatred the strike had evoked between the business community and the workers. Was such class antagonism inevitable? Many were saying so, but Addams, committed as she was to Tolstoyan and Christian nonviolence, social Christian cooperation, and Comtean societal unity, found it impossible to accept the prevailing view. That fall she and John Dewey, now the first chair of the Department of Philosophy at the University of Chicago, discussed this question.[48] In a letter to his wife, Alice, Dewey reported telling Addams that conflict was not only inevitable but possibly a good thing. Addams disagreed. She "had always believed and still believed," he wrote, that "antagonism was not only useless and harmful, but entirely unnecessary." She based her claim on her view that antagonisms were caused, in Dewey's words, not by "objective differences" but by "a person's mixing in his own personal reactions." A person was antagonistic because he expected to be. This was either because he took pleasure in opposing others, because he desired not to be a "moral coward," or because he felt hurt or insulted. These were all avoidable and unnecessary reactions. Only evil, Addams said, echoing Tolstoy, could come from antagonism.[49]

During their conversation, she asked Dewey repeatedly what he thought. Dewey admitted that he was uncomfortable with Addams's theory. He agreed that personal reactions often created antagonism, but not that the expectation of antagonism played a key role. As for history, he was enough of a social Darwinist and a Hegelian to believe that society progressed via struggle and opposition. He questioned her. Did she not think that, in addition to conflict between individuals, there were conflicts between ideas and between institutions, for example, between Christianity and Judaism and between "Labor and Capital"? And was not the "realization of . . ·. antagonism necessary to an appreciation of the truth and to a consciousness of growth"?

Again she disagreed. To support her case Addams gave two examples of apparently inevitable conflicts involving ideas or institutions that she interpreted differently. When Jesus angrily drove the moneychangers out of the temple, she argued, his anger was personal and avoidable. He had "lost his faith," she said, "and reacted." Or consider the Civil War. Through the antagonism of war, we freed the slaves, she observed, but they were still not free individually, and in addition we have had to "pay the costs of war and reckon with the added bitterness of the Southerner besides." The "antagonisms of institutions," Dewey told Alice, summarizing Addams's response, "were always" due to the "injection of the personal attitude and reaction."

Dewey was stunned and impressed. Addams's belief struck him as "the most magnificent exhibition of intellectual & moral faith" that he had ever seen. "[W]hen you think," he wrote Alice, "that Miss Addams does not think this as a philosophy, but believes it in all her senses & muscles—Great

God." Dewey, gripped by the power of Addams's grand vision, told Alice, "I never had anything take hold of me so."[50]

But his intellect lagged behind. Struggling to find a way to reconcile his and Addams's views, Dewey attempted a formulation that honored Addams's devotion to unity, which he shared, while retaining the principle of antagonistic development that Addams rejected but he could not abandon. "[T]he unity [is not] the reconciliation of opposites," he explained to his wife. Rather, "opposites [are] the unity in its growth." But he knew he had avoided a real point of disagreement between them. He admitted to Alice, "[M]y pride of intellect . . . revolts at thinking" that conflict between ideas or institutions "has no functional value."[51] His and Addams's disagreement—was *it* an antagonism?—was real, and in discovering it, the two had taken each other's measure. Addams's principled vision and spiritual charisma had met their match in the cool machinery of John Dewey's powerful mind.

Two days later Dewey sent Addams a short note in which he retracted part of what he had said. He was now willing to agree, he wrote, that a person's expectation of opposition was in and of itself not good and even that it caused antagonism to arise. "[T]he first antagonism always come[s] back to the assumption that there is or may be antagonism," he wrote, and this assumption is "bad." In other words, he was agreeing with Addams's points that antagonism was evil and that it always began in the feelings or ideas of the individual.[52] Dewey did not, however, retract his claim that conflict had its historical uses. These were, as he had said, to appreciate truth and to be conscious of its growth, that is, its spread. He was speaking as the Christian idealist he still was—someone who saw truth as God's revelation. Antagonism, in other words, helped bring man to see the truth.[53]

Why could not Addams, herself a Christian idealist, agree with Dewey? The answer may lie not in what her mind had been taught but in what her heart knew. For many years she had endured the antagonism sparked by Anna's temper without gaining much in the way of truth. When she argued that antagonism was always personal, was she generalizing from her own experience?

When Dewey agreed with Addams that opposition originated in individual feelings, he was joining her in rejecting the usual view that objective differences justified antagonism. This was the view that unions held. Workers believed that the antagonism between themselves and employers arose because workers lacked something real and necessary: sufficient negotiating power in the relationship. In denying this, Dewey and Addams were being, in the simplest sense, determinedly apolitical. Addams, despite her recent involvement with strikes and politics, still refused to believe that actual conditions could provide legitimate grounds for opposition. Her idealism, expressed in her fierce commitment to cooperation, Christian love, nonresistance, and unity, stood like a wall preventing her from seeing that power, as much as personal feelings, soured human relations. A strong mind is both an asset and a liability.

That fall, Hull House, returning to normalcy, resumed its rich schedule of classes, club meetings, lectures, and exhibits. As usual, Addams was seriously worried about the settlement's finances. The size of the total deficit for the year is unknown, but her awareness that the household operating account was $888 in arrears surfaced in a letter to Mary. As she had in previous years, Addams paid for part of the debt herself (how much is unclear; the documentation does not survive). Mary Rozet Smith, among others, sent a generous check. "It gives me a lump in my throat," Addams wrote her in appreciation, "to think of the dollars you have put . . . into the . . . prosaic debt when there are so many more interesting things you might have done and wanted to do." Aware of the delicacy of asking a close friend for donations, Addams sounded a note of regret. "It grieves me a little lest our friendship should be jarred by all these money transactions."[54]

As before, the residents were in the dark about Hull House's finances. Despite her intentions to keep them informed, Addams had convened no Residents' Meeting between April and October, perhaps because the strike and her sister's illness had absorbed so much of her attention. Finally, in early November she and the residents had "a long solemn talk," as she wrote Mary. She had laid "before folks" the full situation and asked them "for help and suggestions." And she had vowed that she would "never . . . let things get so bad again" before she consulted them. "I hope," she told Mary, "we are going to be more intimate and mutually responsible on the financial side."[55]

Addams was renewed in her determination for two reasons. First, there was the problem of her own worsening finances. Since July she had assumed the new financial burden, apparently without any help from Alice, of raising Mary's two younger children. Second, there was her increasing fear that her personal liability for Hull House's debts could literally put her in the Dunning poorhouse. Meanwhile, she pushed herself to speak as often as she could to earn lecture fees. In October she reported to Alice that she had given five talks in one week. In November, she gave lectures in three states—Illinois, Wisconsin, and Michigan.[56] It was all that she could think of to do: to work harder.

Hull House was doing well enough by other measures. The residents' group continued to grow. Despite the house's recently stained reputation and the risky state of its finances, five new residents arrived, all women, bringing the total to twenty. For 1894–95, the residents had decided, probably at Addams's urging, to limit the size of the residents' group to that number. There was now a good mix of old and new, with the majority, like Starr, Lathrop, and Kelley, having been there two years or more. The number of men had shrunk from seven to two, but in a few years it would be back to five. Addams, as always, took her greatest pleasure in the effervescent dailiness of it all. The settlement was first and foremost something "organic," a "way of life," she told an audience at the University of Chicago that fall.[57]

Furthermore, the residents' book of maps was moving toward completion. Conceived originally as a way to publicize some of the data about the neighborhood from the Department of Labor study, it had expanded to include a collection of essays on various related subjects and had acquired a sober New York publisher, Thomas Y. Crowell and Company, and a glorious title, *Hull-House Maps and Papers: A Presentation of Nationalities and Wages in a Congested District of Chicago, Together with Comments and Essays on Problems Growing Out of the Social Conditions*. The byline, it was agreed, would read "Residents of Hull-House." It would be published in March 1895. Five of the essays, those by Kelley, Lathrop, Starr, and Addams, were much-expanded versions of the presentations they had made at the Congress on Social Settlements the previous year. Five others rounded out the collection. These dealt with the Bohemians, the Italians, and the Jews of the neighborhood, the maps, and the wages and expenses of cloakmakers in Chicago and New York.[58] The maps were the book's original inspiration and its most extravagant feature. Printed on oiled paper, folded and tucked into special slots in the book's front and back covers, they displayed, block by block and in graphic, color-coded detail, where people of different nationalities lived in the ward and the range of wages they earned.

Addams, happy to be back in the editor's chair, wrote the prefatory note, edited essays, and wrote the meaty appendix that described the settlement's activities and programs. The book's title was likely also her handiwork. Descriptive, indeed, exhaustive, it was the sort of title in which she specialized. As she once admitted to Weber Linn, "I am very poor at titles." The book was very close to her heart. When she wrote Henry Demarest Lloyd on December 1 to thank him for sending the house a copy of his *Wealth against Commonwealth*, she observed, "I have a great deal of respect for anyone who writes a good book." After *Maps* was published she noted to those to whom she sent copies, "We are very proud of the appearance of the child."[59]

Jane Addams's contribution to *Maps* was her essay "The Settlement as a Factor in the Labor Movement." Her intention was to give a history of Hull House's relations with unions as a sort of case study and to examine why and how settlements should be engaged with the labor movement. The piece is straightforward in tone, nuanced, not polemical. In it she settles fully into the even-handed interpretive role she had first attempted in her speech on domestic servants eighteen months earlier.

But the essay also burns with the painful knowledge she gained from the Pullman Strike. She wrestles with the tension between the labor movement's loyalty to its class interests and her own vision of a classless, universalized, democratic society. And she probes the philosophical question she and Dewey had been debating: Are (class) antagonisms inevitable? Are antagonisms useful? The resulting essay was the most in-depth exploration of the subject of class that Addams would ever write. She was trying to find her way back from the edge of the cliff—class warfare—to which the Pullman Strike had brought her and the nation.

On the question of what the strike accomplished, her thoughts had shifted somewhat. Although she had told Dewey that antagonism was always useless, she argues in "The Settlement as a Factor" that strikes, which certainly were a form of antagonism, can be useful and necessary. Strikes are often "the only method of arresting attention to [the workers'] demands"; they also offer the permanent benefits of strengthening the ties of "brotherhood" among the strikers and producing (at least when successful) a more "democratic" relation between workers and their employer.[60] Perhaps Dewey had been more persuasive than he realized.

She still felt, however, that personal emotion was the main cause of antagonisms, including strikes. She admits that labor has a responsibility to fight for the interests of the working people (that is, more leisure and wealth) but only because achieving them would help the workingman *feel* less unjustly treated. She charges labor with storing up of "grudges" against "capitalists" and calls this "selfish."[61] She ignores the question of whether low wages and long hours are fair. Social justice is not a touchstone for her arguments in this essay.

Instead, Addams stresses the ideal she had emphasized since coming to Chicago: that of a society united by its sense of common humanity. She writes prophetically of "the larger solidarity which includes labor and capital" and that is based on a "notion of universal kinship" and "the common good."[62] One might read into her argument the conclusion of social justice, yet the principle remains uninvoked. Instead, Addams stays focused on feelings. She calls for sympathy for others' suffering, not for a change in workers' physical condition.

Addams disapproves of capitalism but not because of its effects on the workers. What troubles her are the moral failings of the individual capitalist. She slips in a rather radical quotation by an unnamed writer: "The crucial question of the time is, 'In what attitude stand ye toward the present industrial system? Are you content that greed . . . shall rule your business life, while in your family and social life you live so differently? Shall Christianity have no play in trade?' "[63] In one place, although only one place, she takes the workers' perspective and refers to capitalists as "the power-holding classes." Here at last was a glancing nod toward power. The closest she comes to making a social justice argument is in a sentence whose Marxist flavor, like the previous phrase, suggests Florence Kelley's influence, yet it, too, retains Addams's characteristic emphasis on feelings. She hopes there will come a time "when no factory child in Chicago can be overworked and underpaid without a protest from all good citizens, capitalist and proletarian."[64] While Debs had wanted to arouse middle-class sympathies as a way to improve the working conditions of the Pullman laborers, Addams wanted the labor movement to cause society to be more unified in its sympathies. Their means and ends were reversed.

Addams found the idea that labor's organizing efforts could benefit society compelling. "If we can accept" that possibility, she adds, then the labor movement is "an ethical movement."[65] The claim was a startling one for her to make. It seems the strike had shown her at least one moral dimension to the workers' struggle. The negative had become the potentially positive. Instead of seeing labor's union organizing as a symptom of society's moral decay, as she once had and many other middle-class people still did, she was considering the hypothesis that such organizing was a sign of society's moral redemption.

The Pullman Strike also cracked her moral absolutism. In "Cassandra," she had praised the prophetess's ability to be always right. In "The Settlement as a Factor" she argues for the first time that no person or group can be absolutely right or absolutely wrong. "Life teaches us," she writes, that there is "nothing more inevitable than that right and wrong are most confusingly mixed; that the blackest wrong [can be] within our own motives." When we triumph, she adds, we bear "the weight of self-righteousness."[66] In other words, no one—not unions and working-class people, not businesses and middle-class people, not settlement workers and other middle-class reformers—could claim to hold or ever could hold the highest moral ground. The absolute right did not exist.

For Addams, rejecting moral absolutism was a revolutionary act. She had long believed that a single true, moral way existed and that a person, in theory, could find it. This conviction was her paternal inheritance (one recalls her father's Christian perfectionism) and her social-cultural inheritance. Moral absolutism was the rock on which her confident upper-middle-class Anglo-American culture was grounded. Now she was abandoning that belief. In the territory of her mind, tectonic plates were shifting and a new land mass of moral complexity was arising.

In the fall of 1894, as she was writing "The Settlement as a Factor," this new perspective became her favorite theme. In October she warned the residents of another newly opened settlement, Chicago Commons, "not to be alarmed," one resident recalled, "if we found our ethical standards broadening as we became better acquainted with the real facts of the lives of our neighbors."[67] That same month, speaking to supporters of the University of Chicago Settlement, she hinted again at the dangers of moral absolutism. Do not, she said, seek "to do good." Instead, simply try to understand life.[68] And when a group of young men from the neighborhood told her they proposed to travel to New York City that fall to help end political corruption and spoke disdainfully of those who were corrupt, she admonished them against believing that they were purer than others and asked them if they knew what harm they did in assuming that they were right and others were wrong.[69]

What had she seen during the Pullman Strike that led to this new awareness? She had seen the destructive force of George Pullman's moral self-righteousness. It seemed to her that his lack of self-doubt, that is, his unwillingness to negotiate, had produced a national tragedy; his behavior and its consequences had revealed the evil inherent in moral absolutism. In *Twenty Years* she writes of how, in the midst of the strike's worst days, as she sat by her dying sister's bedside, she was thinking about "that touch of self-righteousness which makes the spirit of forgiveness well-nigh impossible."[70]

She grounded her rejection of absolute truth in her experience. "Life teaches us," she wrote. This was as revolutionary for her as the decision itself. In "Subjective Necessity" she had embraced experience as a positive teacher in a practical way. Here she was allowing experience to shape her ethics. The further implication was that ethics might evolve, but the point is not argued in "The Settlement as a Factor." Still, in her eyes ideas no longer had the authority to establish truth that they once had. Her pragmatism was strengthening, but it had not yet blossomed into a full-fledged theory of truth.

The Pullman Strike taught her in a compelling way that moral absolutism was dangerous, but she had been troubled by its dangers before. She had made her own mistakes and, apparently, a whole train of them related to self-righteousness. The details have gone unrecorded, but they made her ready to understand, and not afterwards forget, something James O. Huntington, the Episcopal priest who had shared the podium with her at the Plymouth conference, had said in a speech at Hull House the year before the strike. "I once heard Father Huntington say," she wrote in 1901, that it is "the essence of immorality to make an exception of one's self." She elaborated. "[T]o consider one's self as . . . unlike the rank and file is to walk straight into the pit of self-righteousness."[71] As Addams interpreted Huntington, he meant there was no moral justification for believing in one's superiority, not even a belief that one was right and the others wrong.

A deeply held, central moral belief is like a tent pole: it influences the shape of the entire tent that is a person's thought. A new central belief is like a taller or shorter tent pole; it requires the tent to take a new shape. The tent stakes must be moved. Jane Addams had decided there was no such thing as something or someone that was purely right or purely wrong, but the rest of her thought had yet to be adjusted. Among other things, she still believed that a person of high culture was superior to those who lacked it; that is, she still believed that cultural accomplishment could justify self-righteousness.

Some hints of this can be found in the adjectives Addams attaches to democracy in "The Settlement as a Factor." After proposing that the workers might lead the ethical movement of democracy, she anticipates the fear her readers might feel at this idea. "We must learn to trust our democracy," she writes, "giant-like and threatening as it may appear in its un-couth strength and untried applications."[72] Addams was edging toward trusting that working-class people, people without the cultural training in "the best," could set their own course. Such trust, should she embrace it, would require her to favor a democracy that went beyond her old ideas—her enthusiasm for egalitarian social etiquette, for the principle of cooper-ation, and for the ideal of a unified humanity. Not feeling such trust yet, she was unable to give working people's power a ringing endorsement. The essay is therefore full of warnings about the negative aspects of the labor movement.

These radical claims—that the labor movement was or could become ethical, that the movement was engaged in a struggle that advanced society morally, that capitalists were greedy and ethically compromised, and that there was no absolute right or wrong—opened up a number of complicated issues. Addams decided she needed to write a separate essay—would it be a speech?—to make these points more fully and to make them explicitly, as honesty compelled her to do, about the Pullman strike. Sometime in 1894, she began to write it. A page from the first draft, dated that year, survives with the title "A Modern Tragedy." In its first paragraph she writes that, because we think of ourselves as modern, "it is hard to remember that the same old human passions persist" and can often lead to "tragedy." She invited her readers to view "one of these great tragedies" from "the his-toric perspective," to seek an "attitude of mental detachment" and "stand aside from our personal prejudices."[73] Still grieving over what had hap-pened, Addams was hoping that the wisdom of culture, of the humanities, of Greek and Shakespearean tragedy, could give her the comfort of emo-tional distance. But she had pulled too far back. The opening was so blandly vague and philosophical that no one could tell what the essay was about. She set the piece aside.[74]

———————

Throughout the fall of 1894, as Addams coped with Hull House's shaky finances, edited *Maps*, polished her essay on the labor movement and tried to start an essay on the Pullman Strike, she and the rest of the Civic Feder-ation's Industrial Committee organized the arbitration conference. It con-vened on November 13 at the Woman's Temple Building as the Congress on Industrial Conciliation and Arbitration. The conference was a landmark in the history of the American arbitration movement.[75]

In her address to the conference, Addams expressed the same complex assessment of the labor movement, and by implication, the strike, that she had expressed in "The Settlement as a Factor." She both embraced the Pullman Strike as "a [working people's] revolution" and declared strikes a "belated method of warfare." Then, grasping the burr of the class divide, she eviscerated it with a bold rhetorical flourish. "We do not believe that the world can be divided into capitalists and laboring men. We are all bound together in a solidarity towards this larger movement which shall enfranchise all of us and give us all our place in the national existence."[76] This was Addams in her prophetic mode, as she had been with Dewey. In the wake of the Pullman crisis, she was stalwart in her belief in the possibility of unity.

The conference was a triumph in several regards. First, it had its desired impact in Illinois. Afterwards, trade union activists who were on the Industrial Committee drafted a bill creating a state arbitration board that would arbitrate if both parties requested it. In July 1895, after Addams joined others in lobbying for the bill, the Illinois legislature passed it, and in August Governor Altgeld signed it into law.[77] The hope to spur a movement for national legislation also bore fruit. At the end of the conference thirty people, including Addams, were named to a national commission to lobby Congress for federal arbitration legislation.[78] For the first time Jane Addams was at the center of a campaign to achieve a national progressive legislative reform. And in a limited way the campaign would succeed. Four years after the conference, Congress would pass the Erdman Mediation Act, which recognized the right of railroad workers to organize and authorized government boards to mediate disputes. The law would be in effect until 1908, when it was knocked down by the Supreme Court for violating contract and property rights guaranteed by the Fifth Amendment.[79]

The arbitration conference also marked Addams's emergence as a national opinion-maker. Her speeches at the Plymouth ethics school, their publication in the *Forum*, and her efforts to organize the Congress on Settlements at the World's Fair had established her as a leader of the American settlement house movement; her work in the Civic Federation of Chicago in the previous year had established her as a leader in the city. But it was at the Congress on Industrial Conciliation and Arbitration that she first took up the role of public intellectual by speaking from a national platform on a social reform issue. She had achieved such prominence in only five years; she would remain a national leader for the rest of her life. Many small steps had brought her to this point. Certainly she had developed an expertise in the issue that was the congress's theme, and she had persistently promoted arbitration as a method to solve labor disputes from her first year on Halsted Street. But it was the Pullman Strike and her role in attempting to promote its resolution while on a committee of the Civic Federation that had catapulted her into her new status. And behind her involvement with the federation lay the foundational influences: the stalwart companionship, organizational and political savvy, and reforming spirit of her colleagues at Hull House, in the labor unions, at the Chicago Woman's Club, and at the Civic Federation, in addition to her own skill, persistence, and vision.

By the end of November Addams was exhausted. Mary Rozet Smith, worried about her friend's health, invited her to take a trip to Florida and South Carolina with her and her parents. Addams, somewhat guiltily, accepted. "I have been fearfully run down," she wrote Alice in early December, by way of explaining the plan. "I am anticipating much relief from the change."[80] As the turbulent year of 1894 drew to a close, she looked forward to taking a vacation from the substantive actuality of Halsted Street, her astute but relentless teacher.

Returning on December 22 to Chicago from her trip south, Jane Addams found the settlement in good spirits. She wrote Mary Rozet Smith, who remained in South Carolina, "The House seems full of Christmas cheer. . . . [A]ll is merry as can be." A hundred and thirty turkeys had been given away, as well as many bushels of cranberries and apples. The four Linn children were all home, and their father had come for a visit. Addams's only disappointment was that Alice, Harry, and Marcet were not also there. She had tried but failed to persuade them to join them. Everyone was complimenting her on her "improved appearance," she informed Mary, and she felt "quite rested and fat." Affirming their bonds of devotion, Addams ended, "I bless you, dear, every time I think of you, which is all the time at present."[1]

During her travels Addams had not only enjoyed the balm of Mary's affection; she had also found time to ponder the ongoing problem of Hull House's finances, and in particular, her continuing and dangerous financial liability for the settlement's debts and contracts. Reluctantly she had decided the settlement needed to incorporate. Perhaps, too, she was seeing the wisdom of having a board to turn to for donations of a particularly large or urgent sort. She presented a list of possible directors at the Residents' Meeting in late January. In addition to herself, she proposed Helen Culver, William Colvin, Allen Pond, Mary Wilmarth, all friends and advisors and all already major donors to Hull House. Soon after the meeting, she added two more names: Mary Rozet Smith and Edward B. Butler. These seven became the first board of the new Hull House Association, whose incorporation papers were filed with the State of Illinois in March 1895. At the first meeting, Addams would be elected president of the board; she would be reelected every year until her death.[2]

Time would show that she had chosen loyal stewards. All of the directors except Colvin, who would die unexpectedly in 1896, would serve on the board for the next thirteen years, and all except Wilmarth and Culver would continue to serve well beyond that, until their deaths. These board members' financial generosity would also be remarkable. They would fund emergency repairs, new programs, deficits, and new buildings. Culver would continue to waive all rental charges for her buildings and land. They also raised funds diligently.[3]

And they found other ways to help. Mary Wilmarth "took upon herself many of the burdens of the House in the early days," her friend and later fellow Hull House trustee Louise deKoven Bowen wrote, "and through her speeches, her influence and her defense of its policies gained for it many supporters and friends." Addams remembered Wilmarth's "great tolerance of spirit" and the saying she liked to quote: "I will permit no man to make me to hate him." When Addams needed a quiet place to think and write, she would often go Mary Wilmarth's suite of rooms at the Congress Hotel (Wilmarth owned it). There, in the suite's storeroom, seated at a table and surrounded by trunks, boxes, and shelves full of books, she would write. Helen Culver also became a friend. In 1922 Addams would dedicate a book to her, noting that Culver's "understanding mind and magnanimous spirit have never failed the writer." Allen Pond, in addition to serving as the settlement's architect with his brother Irving, played a useful role when the settlement was caught in the "crossfire" between conservatives and radicals. He "had the ability to touch both points of view," Addams wrote, "to get the differing opinions, to reach his own conclusion and to stand by that conclusion with a great deal of courage." William Colvin was devoted to Addams and her work. A friend later said, "He carried Hull House on his heart."[4]

Addams now had a team of colleagues to think with her about the settlement's long-term future in a way that most of the residents, with their sometimes shorter horizons, did not. The board's faithful support became the rock on which she and Hull House relied. Although she created the board as a defensive move, she could only have been pleased with the results.

Something else new was prompted by the incorporation process: the mission statement required by the State of Illinois. Writing it caused Addams to grapple again with the question that had been on the table since the day she moved to Halsted Street: Did the settlement intend to solve the problem of poverty? The answer to that question had been evolving over the years. In 1890 Jane had told George Haldeman that she and Ellen were not trying to end poverty; in the years since, however, the needs of the community had compelled them to find ways to at least mitigate poverty's ill effects. Hence the creation of the public kitchen, the public dispensary, the public baths, the nursery, the relief fund, the coal cooperative, and the lodging house. The first resident to make efforts toward systemic reforms was Florence Kelley, when she began to document wages and working conditions and to work with the unions on sweatshop reform. Then Addams had joined her in lobbying for the sweatshop legislation and, once the depression occurred, had pressed for better wages for street cleaners. The residents as a group had become more interested in documenting conditions in the ward through Kelley's campaign to collect garbage complaints and through the *Maps* book, a project derived from her Department of Labor study.

With these developments in mind, Addams wrote a mission statement in March 1895 that set out a broader set of goals than she and Ellen had conceived six years earlier. The purpose of Hull House Association, she wrote, was "to provide a center for a higher civic and social life; to initiate and maintain education and philanthropic enterprises; and to investigate and improve the conditions in the industrial districts of Chicago."[5]

The relevance of the new mission statement to Jane Addams's own beliefs was subtle. Almost from the beginning, Hull House had sheltered projects that did not address her priorities. Addams, embracing the passions of others, had cooperated with those who sought to mitigate the effects of poverty, like Lathrop, and those who sought to solve the problem of poverty, like Kelley. But now their passions had become her own. The mission statement reflected well-established practice but it also signaled her own widening agenda.

At the same time, her preference for the nonphysical remained intact. She expressed it again in March 1895 in a speech in Cleveland. "It seems sometimes as if we ought to drop everything else and merely feed people, clothe people, [and] clean their houses[,] that they may live better; but that would be treating our enterprise merely on the animal side. The effort is to be directed as well to the other side of life." She could not dismiss the central importance of the spirit. One sign was the soulfulness others saw in her face. Often described by friends and strangers as "serene" and "sad," her face, another wrote, reveals "the sorrows of the world and the love which alone can master those sorrows." Her nephew recalled that though she often smiled, her eyes were sad.[6] She possessed depths few could fathom.

Jane Addams's continuing lack of interest in the problem of garbage—that omnipresent, omni-aromatic, unappealing material that filled the streets of the Nineteenth Ward—is as good evidence as any that in her first years at Hull House she disdained the purely physical. Although Kelley and Burchard had worked on the garbage issue in 1892 and several other Hull House residents had begun collecting and filing complaints with the city in 1893, Addams apparently was not centrally involved until June 1894, when, in the midst of the Pullman Strike, the president of the Civic Federation, Lyman Gage, named her to its new Sanitation Committee.[7] She accepted the assignment but her interest in the issue, she recalls in *Twenty Years*, remained lukewarm.

Then things changed. After Stanley Linn came to live with his aunt, she began to see the filthy streets of the Nineteenth Ward with a mother's protective eye and felt "ashamed" that she had not acted sooner on behalf of all the children in the neighborhood. A few weeks later, she reluctantly packed Stanley off to a boarding school, fearing that life on Halsted Street was too risky, given his delicate health.[8] Now committed and fully energized, Addams, in cooperation with the Civic Federation, would follow the garbage trail to its ultimate point of origin: the messy, contentious world of municipal government politics.

When Addams joined the Sanitation Committee, it was just beginning to line up volunteer garbage inspectors to report to the city on conditions in the wards. Addams became the Civic Federation's inspector for the Nineteenth Ward. The federation printed thousands of leaflets instructing citizens in how to complain if their garbage was not being collected properly. Addams turned to a new club, the Hull House Woman's Club, for help. Guided by its founder and president, resident Mary McDowell, its members, mostly women of the neighborhood, filed more than 700 complaints with the city during the strike summer of 1894 (fewer complaints, to be sure, than the 1,037 that residents and neighbors had filed under Kelley's leadership during the summer of 1892). Addams had her doubts about whether the effort could make a dent in the problem. She told a *Chicago*

Herald reporter glumly, "It will take ten times five years to leaven this lump."[9]

In early 1895, searching for a point of leverage over the city, the Sanitation Committee hit upon another strategy: to arrange for someone to submit a competent bid for the garbage removal contract for the Nineteenth Ward. Addams volunteered. Perhaps the quixotic scheme was her idea. In March she sought and was given the Hull House residents' approval to place a bid for the ward's contract.[10] If she received it, she would become the boss who subcontracted with the scavengers to remove the garbage.

Addams prepared the bid with characteristic thoroughness. She gathered information about new garbage collection methods and what they would cost to implement in the Nineteenth Ward. She learned how the garbage was handled in Boston, Massachusetts, Glasgow, Scotland, and Manchester, England, and consulted local experts in hauling. Her resulting plan, she told a reporter, represented the latest thinking in sanitary engineering. Among other things she proposed to recycle clean ashes, tin cans, bottles, paper, and rags, replace the wooden garbage boxes with washable metal cans, and use crematories to burn the "offensive" waste. Such innovative methods would cost money, and Addams's bid was high. In 1894 the ward's garbage removal contract was for $9,430; Addams's bid for the 1895 contract was 40 percent higher at $13,238.[11]

While she was working on the bid, Addams and the Sanitation Committee undertook a public campaign to generate interest in the ambitious scheme. She presented the plan to Mayor John Hopkins, who, although he was considered corrupt because of his ties to the political machine, approved of it. She persuaded the *Tribune* to editorialize on her project and the result was an endorsement in the March 21 edition of the paper, which appeared just after she had submitted the bid. "Miss Addams ought to be awarded the contract," the editors urged. "By all means let it be seen what she can do." They predicted that she would do a thorough job, in which case, "Johnny Powers has reason to feel uneasy." The scavengers, of course, were all Powers's friends, happy to serve his political interests in exchange for easy work. Just how easy it was is evident from a single statistic about the infrequency of garbage removal services in the Nineteenth Ward during the summer of 1894. Nine scavengers were supposed to collect garbage from the ward's 1,691 boxes three times a week, but in actuality they made their rounds only twice a month.[12]

It is not clear that the Sanitation Committee ever expected Addams's bid to be successful. Certainly Addams did not; she told the *Tribune* she thought her bid was too high to be chosen.[13] Instead the strategy was to educate the public about what a competent bid would look like and what it would cost. The committee may have chosen Addams in part because it hoped her fame, as well her media skills, would attract news coverage and put pressure on City Hall to take the problem of garbage more seriously.

Addams was not awarded the contract, but government officials rejected it cagily. Not wanting to bring the wrath of a good portion of the city down upon their heads for mistreating the popular Jane Addams, they threw her bid out on the technicality that it lacked a certain affidavit that Addams later explained she did not know she needed to submit. In reality, Powers had blocked her bid. The contract went to M. H. McGovern for $9,375, an amount less than previous year's contract, and Addams appeared to be out of the garbage business.[14]

Throughout the spring of 1895, while the Sanitation Committee pressed forward on the garbage question, the Civic Federation's leadership was focused on the underlying problems—the corrupt aldermen and mayor and the dominance of the patronage system—and the underlying solution: the mayoral and aldermanic elections on April 2. Addams was involved in the planning as a member of the Federation's Central Council, and Florence Kelley was the driving force in support of the federation's political efforts in the Nineteenth Ward.[15]

Of the sixty-eight aldermen in office in early 1895, fifty-seven were known to be corrupt. Mostly members of the "Irish machine," they used many methods to increase their vote count. In addition to bribes, boodling, and charity, they used political networks of precinct captains, social networks of saloon owners, many of whom were aldermen (conveniently, saloons often served as polling places), intimidation, ballot-box stuffing, and ballot-box discarding. The results in certain wards, especially those where the Irish were numerically in the minority but politically in charge, were impressive. In the early 1890s in the Tenth Ward, a mere 830 male Irish Americans elected one of their own as alderman in a ward where 2,285 Germans lived. A similar pattern was evident in the Fifteenth Ward. Italians, like the Germans, were unable to elect aldermen of their own nationality in various wards, but they were particularly frustrated about it in the Nineteenth, because more Italians lived there than in any other ward of the city.[16]

The federation, convinced that well-informed voters were essential to the workings of a democracy, decided to give the voters a great deal of information on the issues and the candidates and to run honest candidates in the wards where corrupt aldermen had sinecures. In each targeted ward, its members organized themselves into a "ward improvement club." Each club then found a "clean" candidate to run, held rallies, and leafleted the ward to urge support for their candidate. In addition, the federation convened two enormous citywide meetings in early March, each attended by more than five thousand people, to protest widespread aldermanic corruption and call for the machine's defeat at the polls. It also persuaded a "clean" Republican, George Bell Swift, to run for mayor. (The Civic Federation was ostensibly nonpartisan but really Republican, given that the boodling aldermen were mostly Democrats.)[17]

The fact that Irish Americans dominated the machine in Chicago politics also contributed to the support the Civic Federation received for its anti-corruption campaign. Many middle-class people were proudly anti-Irish; it was an entirely respectable view. No less a public figure than the president of Cornell University, Andrew White, the passionate advocate for municipal reform, observed that the work of the city (he was thinking of New York City) should not be managed by "a crowd of illiterate peasants, freshly raked in from the Irish bog."[18] The Civic Federation's leadership did not use that kind of language, but some of its foot soldiers undoubtedly shared the feeling.

Patronage, a key tool for machine control, was another target of the federation's reform efforts. The garbage collection contracts and the garbage inspectors' jobs in the city's thirty-four wards were part of the patronage system, and other jobs were equally for sale. Most of the city's street sweepers were "friends" of aldermen, as were many police and city clerks. Boodled utility contracts generated jobs with private companies that aldermen, because of their ties to the companies, distributed. The jobholders— mostly recent Irish and Italian immigrants, that is, former peasants without literacy or industrial skills and eager for work of any kind—felt bound with bands of steel to whatever local politician needed their vote. On the other hand, those who paid the most in city taxes—businessmen and other middle-class citizens, including the better-paid trade unionists—were angry that they received so few municipal services in return. Their anger also helped fuel the activism of the Civic Federation.[19]

To eliminate patronage, or at least to reduce it, the federation sought city laws requiring qualification standards for city jobs. The idea was not new. The Citizens Association had begun pushing for civil service reform in Chicago as early as 1881, in the wake of "frustrated office seeker" Julius Guiteau's assassination of President Garfield. The issue had also been gathering momentum around the country. After the National Civil Service Reform League held its national convention in Chicago in 1894, Gage and MacVeagh convened fifteen civic groups in the city to form the Joint Civil Service Reform Committee. Its charge was to lobby the state legislature to terminate its current authority over the city's hiring practices. That policy change occurred in early March 1895. With only weeks to spare, the civil service reform proposal was placed on the citywide ballot as a referendum and the federation launched a sophisticated citywide campaign. It sent five hundred speakers to address workers in factories at noon; the clergy hammered at the issue from the pulpits on Sunday, and the newspapers gave the issue blanket coverage.[20]

Meanwhile, in the neighborhoods, all eyes were on the aldermanic races. In the Nineteenth Ward, Powers was not up for reelection but the other alderman, a political crony of Powers, was. To run against him, the Nineteenth Ward Improvement Club, led by its president, Florence Kelley, and consisting mainly of 150 members of the Hull House Men's Club, put forward one of its own, Frank Lawler, as the Independent candidate. Lawler was a seasoned politician. He was a long-time Protestant Irish trade union leader (although not part of the Irish machine, which was Catholic) with close ties to the CTLA, a former Democratic alderman from the Near West Side, and a former Congressman; his name recognition alone promised success.[21] His election, it was hoped, would lay the groundwork to defeat "Johnny" Powers in 1896.

April 2 was a day of triumph for the one-year-old Civic Federation. In the sixty-eight-seat city council, thirty-four aldermen were up for reelection. Of these, twelve corrupt aldermen, mostly Democrats, lost their seats. Furthermore, the reform candidate, George Swift, won the mayoral election, and the municipal civil service law, endorsed by Swift, passed. In the Nineteenth Ward, there was more success. In a field of four aldermanic candidates that included two Republicans and one People's Party candidate, Lawler won by a mere 368 votes.[22] It was a triumph for Kelley, the Nineteenth Ward Improvement Council, and the forces of reform.

In the wake of these triumphs, garbage collection reform came back into Jane Addams's life. As hoped, the election benefited the Civic Federation's garbage campaign. Swift appointed a new commissioner of public works, who shortly thereafter replaced the garbage inspectors in seven

John "Johnny" Powers. Lawrence J. Gutter Collection of Chicagoana (GUT neg. 63), Special Collections, The University Library, University of Illinois at Chicago.

wards with new appointees. Two people he appointed in late April were recommended by the Civic Federation: A. A. Howard for the Thirty-second Ward and Jane Addams for the Nineteenth. Addams was now the city's first woman garbage inspector. Hull House and its friends were jubilant at Addams's appointment, but the machine politicians were outraged. The job, paying $1,000 per year, was a political plum.[23] The mayor, however, did not back down.

The day after she was appointed, Addams began work, joined very soon by a deputy inspector with experience in garbage inspection, a young woman from Philadelphia named Amanda Johnson, who became a Hull House resident.[24] The method of financing Johnson's position is unclear since the city did not employ deputy inspectors. Addams may have found a donor to subsidize the position, or she may have split her salary with her assistant. In any case, Jane Addams now had her first paying job.

The work was hard. Three mornings each week she and Johnson rose at 5 A.M. and put on special uniforms they had designed themselves: ankle-length blue serge outfits whose skirts did not touch the garbage-strewn ground. By 6 A.M. they were in their horse-drawn wagon, ready to follow the contractor's nine garbage wagons on their rounds. For more than four hours they watched as the scavengers shoveled out the garbage boxes and then followed them as they carted the stinking, rotten material all the way to the city dump at Thirty-Fifth Street and Western Avenue.[25]

But they did more than inspect. Addams and Johnson persuaded the contractor to increase the number of wagons to seventeen, arranged for the city to pay for eight emergency teams to remove the ashes, manure, and other refuse that was not garbage, took six negligent landlords who failed to remove manure or certain other refuse to court and won, and generally enforced the law. "The position was no sinecure," Addams noted dryly.[26]

She also acted on the other parts of her original plan to win the collection contract. Johnson and some other Hull House residents set up six incinerators to burn refuse, began bringing tin cans to a window weight factory, which used the tin to make the weights, and pestered the contractor to remove the bodies of dead horses and cows. It was a job he was paid to do but preferred to leave to the city ambulance service, which preferred not to do it at all.[27]

These were stellar accomplishments, but Addams thought her greatest triumph was the discovery on one street that beneath eight inches of garbage was that rarity of rarities, actual pavement. She brought the skeptical mayor to see it, had the garbage removed, and arranged for a reluctant street commissioner to restore the pavement. By early August 1895 Addams could report proudly to Mary Rozet Smith, "The Ward really is cleaner." When University of Michigan professor Henry C. Adams proposed a visit to Chicago, Addams replied, "It would . . . gratify my pride to take you for a drive through the Nineteenth Ward alleys."[28]

The two women's accomplishments quickly became well known. The press loved the story, particularly because the inspectors were female—and one of them was famous. Throughout May and June, the *Tribune*, the *Herald*, and other Chicago papers featured reports on Addams's and Johnson's garbage inspection efforts, while ignoring the work of the other new inspectors. In July, the *Chicago Journal*, the *Chicago Evening Post*, and the *Chicago Times-Herald* did additional in-depth reports. As newspapers across the country picked up the stories, Addams, Johnson, and Hull House received a small explosion of national publicity.[29]

People in the neighborhood were less impressed. Although they were delighted with the cleanliness of the streets and alleys, they had their doubts about the propriety of female garbage inspectors. Addams writes in *Twenty Years* that some of her female neighbors were "shocked by this abrupt departure into the ways of men." Addams would explain that it was just as "womanly" to prevent diseases at their source as it was to go about visiting tenement houses in order to nurse the sick, but many were not persuaded. Her point was not rhetorical. She knew that she had begun to care deeply about the garbage problem only because of her recently acquired maternal responsibility for Stanley's Linn's health.[30]

The neighbors also expected Addams, as a government official, to be as corrupt as the previous inspectors. Ever the enthusiast for teaching by example, Addams took pleasure in showing them a new type of government employee. "Such daily living" she writes in *Twenty Years*, referring to her garbage inspection work, "is of infinitely more value than many talks on civics. . . . We credit most easily that which we see."[31] She was not, of course, the only Hull House resident teaching that lesson. Even before Addams's appointment to inspect streets and alleys, Hull House was a regular hotbed of government inspectors, with Kelley and Alzina Stevens inspecting factories and sweatshops and Julia Lathrop inspecting state charitable institutions. But Addams's genius for attracting publicity soon made her the settlement's most famous government inspector.

By 1895, Hull House's reputation as a staunch advocate of civic reform had become well established in the Nineteenth Ward, the city, and the nation. Still, for many working people in the neighborhood and across the city, the settlement remained what it had always been: a delightful place for learning and socializing, a place to enrich the mind and feed the soul. A reporter from Nebraska, stopping by on a warm spring night in 1895, caught that aspect of the settlement in her news story. The front doors were wide open, she wrote. She could hear snatches of music and glimpse pictures, statuary, and "well-filled" bookcases. People of all ages came and went. Inside, she found the German reception under way in the library and the Italian reception under way in the dining room. A woman (it was Ellen Gates Starr) was teaching a class on Dante in the Octagon, a young man was giving a lecture in the drawing room on Bohemian history, and a young woman was teaching cooking in the kitchen. A girl's club was meeting in one of the halls, and in the Butler Art Gallery a French reading was going on in one room and a class in English and letter writing in another.[32]

This was the Hull House the neighbors later remembered with special fondness. Hilda Satt Polacheck, who worked in a knitting factory and spent nearly every night at the settlement as a teen, described it as an "oasis in a desert of boredom and monotony[; it was] the university, the opera house, the theatre, the concert and lecture hall, the gymnasium, the library, the clubhouse of the neighborhood. It was a place where one could become rejuvenated after a day of hard work in the factory." Hull House, another observed, "was the first house I had ever been in where books and magazines just lay around as if there were plenty of them in the world."[33]

Everyone came knocking at its door: policemen, novelists, union organizers, ministers, missionaries, socialists, club women, university professors, workers, mothers, people from Europe and people from around the corner, people aiming to change the world and people facing personal crises. William Kent, the local businessman who donated his land for the playground, was impressed that "[a]ll sorts of people feel at home there."[34]

During the day, the doorbell and the telephone rang constantly. Answering them had become a job in itself, albeit an unpaid one. From 8 A.M. to 1 P.M. a nonresident volunteer, Miss Holden, filled it. Another volunteer took the afternoon shift. Residents filled in as needed. John Dewey, observing the hectic atmosphere, wrote his wife, "I sh'd think the irritation of hearing the doorbell ring, and never doing one thing without being interrupted to tend to half a dozen others[,] would drive them crazy." The children of the neighborhood thought it looked like fun. At home they "played Hull House," as they called it, by pretending to go to the door, then to the telephone, then to the door again. The settlement's front door was locked at midnight, but those who came later could always rouse someone to help them.[35]

The house's welcoming atmosphere was consciously created and diligently maintained. Residents were careful to treat visitors not as people who must justify their presence with a request or a need, but as guests. The Nebraska reporter noted, "The residents do not pounce upon the newcomer or oftcomer and talk to him about his body or his soul. He having eyes and ears is allowed to [walk about] freely where he may see and hear and beyond a friendly greeting no more is said unless he desires it." A member of the British upper class who spent a few days at the settlement noticed the same thing and was shocked. Visitors, she remarked disapprovingly, "wander here, there and everywhere." A Greek child from the neighborhood remembered, "We would walk into Hull House as though [it were] . . . our own house[;] there was absolute freedom to enjoy the house [and] its nurturing warmth."[36]

For Addams the daily life of the house, the thing so effervescent to history but so palpably alive to her, remained what was most important. She wrote in 1896, "[More important than] the organized work . . . [are] the more neighborly and informal relationships." She hoped that the "mingling of well-to-do people with the poor" would soon become "natural and universal."[37]

Still, Dewey was right to suppose that life at Hull House had its drawbacks. In addition to residents' being constantly interrupted, solitude was unavailable. Alice Hamilton, a resident who would arrive in the fall of 1897, wrote her cousin that she was "never alone." And the noise could be overpowering. Florence Kelley described the house as being "as noisy as bedlam." Hamilton, who had an M.D. degree and worked in a research laboratory, thought her ability to escape the house during the workday was a blessing that helped make her life there somewhat less "intense and emotional."[38]

Most residents were like Hamilton in having day jobs that took them away from the settlement. A few residents held "fellowships" for which Addams raised money from wealthy donors. These might be for projects at Hull House or for projects that took place elsewhere. When Harriet Rice, the African American physician, staffed the public dispensary, for example, she had a fellowship. In their free time, residents did whatever interested them or responded to whatever need arose. Generally, everyone was extremely busy. Resident Agnes Holbrook admitted, "In the press of doing one cannot find time for understanding."[39]

Addams was as pressed by sudden requests as anyone, and she tolerated no assumption that she or the other more senior residents were exempt from the demands of the moment. Robert Woods, head resident of South End Settlement (formerly Andover House) in Boston, disapproved. He wrote Addams sternly after a visit in 1895, "It is my impression that there is too much activity and not enough repose, and that you and all the older residents are spending creative vitality upon mechanized detail." He suggested that she and the other "experienced" residents "give up the notion that [you] are members of an emergency corps subject to call or bound to guard duty."[40] But Addams did not follow his suggestion.

Hull House was the most relaxed and felt most like home to the residents late at night. They tended to gather in the kitchen for snacks. One resident remembered, on coming home at 1 A.M., that "[e]verybody in the House was eating in the pantry[;] . . . we had bread and jam and apples and crackers and cheese." In the winter, they made cocoa. At Sunday suppers, which they cooked for themselves because the cook was off, Julia Lathrop sometimes would make her famous omelets or, on special occasions, her brown buttered oysters.[41]

Jane Addams's sense of responsibility for the house was most apparent in these late hours. She was often the last person go to bed, after first making the rounds to confirm that all the lights were out and the doors locked. One night she found two pairs of shoes in the hall outside a bedroom door, placed there by a visiting British couple on the assumption that a servant would polish them overnight. She polished them.[42] Robert Woods would not have approved.

———————————

In the spring of 1895 the social clubs for children and adults remained among Hull House's most popular offerings. Many of the two thousand people who flocked to the house each week in 1894–95 were coming to a club meeting. They could choose from the Young Heroes Club, the Lincoln Club, the Longfellow Club, the Jolly Boys Club, the Cash Girls Club, the Mandolin Club, the Young Citizens Club, and the Italian Children's Clubs, among others. Each club planned its own programs; members might sing, play games, tell stories, read aloud together, or do crafts and other handwork. Young people and adults, whose clubs met in the evening, practiced debating, performed plays, studied topics in science or literature, played pool, held conversations, or danced (the perennial favorite). All club members learned parliamentary procedure to run their meetings.[43]

Criteria for membership were determined by club members, including whether a club would be coeducational or single-sex. They possessed this freedom despite the fact that Addams had a definite opinion on the subject. As she stated in 1897, "I believe very strongly in young men and women meeting together." Clubs, however, were not required to conform to her views. Racial and ethnic mixing was encouraged but also not required. It appears that in 1895 only two clubs, the Italian Children's Club and the adult Italian-American Club, restricted membership by nationality. Language was rarely a barrier in the children's clubs because club members generally spoke English, regardless of the languages their parents spoke.[44]

The membership criterion that mattered most to the young people, those in their teens and early twenties, was class, or, more precisely, class aspiration. This became particularly clear in a dispute that arose in July

1895 between two young people's clubs. The coed Lincoln Club attracted young men and women ambitious to better themselves; they performed plays and sought to gain skills in debating, the skill that Abraham Lincoln had used to escape the working class. The Men's Club enjoyed the pleasures of pool and athletics and took a lively interest in local politics.[45] The original dispute between the two clubs was triggered by hurt feelings; the second dispute, which arose from the first, was between the Lincoln Club and Hull House and involved club membership criteria. Jane Addams mentioned the second dispute in several letters to Mary Rozet Smith and recalls it in *Twenty Years*. It troubled her a good deal. Here was antagonism—that which she was so determined to avoid, tamp down, head off—lodged on her own hearth, erupting in her own settlement house.

The first dispute arose when the Executive Committee of the Lincoln Club, which was now devoted solely to the activity of debate, decided to expel three female members for being too "frivolous" at meetings. The women complained to friends in the Men's Club, and there was a confrontation. Someone from the Men's Club shot a gun at a Lincoln Club member, although, luckily, he missed his target. Afterwards both clubs regretted the fight. Addams talked with them separately about the need to avoid using force when a disagreement arose and about the benefits of cooperation. "Both sides," she wrote Mary Rozet Smith, who was out of town, "are thoroughly ashamed and it has been really a triumph for non-resistance, I think."[46]

But the Executive Committee of the Lincoln Club was not satisfied. They disapproved of Addams's tolerant treatment of the Men's Club. Seeing themselves as a "better class" of young people than the Men's Club "toughs," they wanted Hull House to register its moral disapproval of the miscreants, either by expelling those who had been involved in the quarrel from club membership or by expelling the club itself from Hull House. The settlement refused to do either. Offended, the Lincoln Club decided to break with the house. It began holding its meetings at a rented hall a mile west of Halsted Street.[47]

The break was not complete, however. The Executive Committee of the club invited Addams to its first meeting in the new quarters to discuss the situation. Accepting their invitation, Addams attempted to persuade them to change their personal feelings and stop feeling so superior. She told them, she writes in *Twenty Years*, that the settlement stood for inclusion and tolerance, not exclusion, even of "tough" young men. She also invoked the warning James Huntington had given about the moral dangers of self-righteousness. Desiring to avoid all that was tough, she said, leads "straight into the pit of self-righteousness and petty achievement." Life was not so black and white, she advised, sounding her other new theme. "Right and wrong are most confusingly confounded." Perhaps, she suggested, they were being too harsh in judging the young men.

The Executive Committee had an answer. The issue, they said, was one of class, *her* class. They told her that she and other Hull House residents did not need to avoid proximity to toughness, but they did. They could not risk being "tainted."[48] In other words, Addams and her colleagues, having plenty of social prestige, could not be tarnished by those with whom they associated. The ambitious Lincoln Club members believed they needed to be more careful.

Addams did not understand their point. Because she was convinced that all antagonism was caused by personal feelings, she could not see the relevance of the committee's class analysis to explaining the painful antagonism that now existed between the Executive Committee and herself. When she left the meeting, frustrated and discouraged, all she could think about was the committee's conviction that it was right and she was wrong. As she wrote Mary Smith in reference to the crisis, "I do think that self-righteousness is the hardest thing in the world to deal with. I am sure it is for me." A week later, she wrote Mary, "The Lincoln Club affair still perplexes my soul."[49]

Addams's unsuccessful attempt to change the club members' minds was deeply ironic. In trying to persuade the club to be more inclusive, she was herself practicing the self-righteousness she abhorred. Convinced she was right, she could not see that they were right, too. Her stance suggests that she was still seeing herself as the exception, the person whose moral truth ought properly to override another's. She preached that others should avoid self-righteousness but she was not yet practicing what she preached. She was in that awkward transitional stage of change when, able now to see self-righteousness everywhere, she was as yet unable to fully acknowledge its presence in herself.

Indeed, only a month before the Lincoln Club crisis, she had preached against self-righteousness in a commencement speech she gave at Rockford College. Her subject was her own sex's tendency to feel morally superior to men. "I have a warning to give the college graduate," she said. It is "a warning against self-righteousness. Perhaps the reason women have not . . . corrupted legislatures and wrecked railroads is because they have not had the opportunity to do so." In her view, the idea that women were the purer sex was a fallacy, as was its companion assumption that one sex could have a monopoly on moral righteousness. "The world," she said, is "not divided into two armies, the right and the wrong."[50] It was an unwavering declaration worthy of the prophetess Cassandra. Indeed, she gave it from the very podium where she had first invoked Cassandra's name. But there was irony here, too, for she was warning the young graduates not to believe in the quality of Cassandra's that Addams herself had once most admired: the ability to be "always right."

Addams went on to explain the cause for women's being "exempt from the temptations of life," as she further described it. Her striking theory was that women had been actively denied the freedom to operate in the world. Dipping her pen in fire, she unleashed a stunning, passionate indictment. Women have not participated in politics, or legislatures, or railroads, she said, because "they have been chained down by a military code whose penalty [for violation] is far worse than the court martial."[51] The metaphor was potent. Addams was not only proclaiming the restrictiveness of gender roles; she was also arguing that women could not violate them without severe punishment, that women were caught in a relentless and oppressive system of power. Women's rights advocates had made the point—which remains a core insight of what we today call feminism—throughout the nineteenth century, but for Addams it was a new insight. When she had argued in 1892 that daughters faced special difficulties in honoring the social claim, she had offered no such critique. By 1895, however, power and women's relation to it had at last moved to the center of her consciousness.

What caused this change? The Rockford speech gives no clues but its timing provides an answer. During much of 1894 and 1895, the unfinished Pullman essay lay on Addams's desk. Then, in May 1895, a month before she gave the speech at Rockford, she gave a speech at a conference in New York City on the settlement movement and included in it a brief discussion of the Pullman Strike. Pursuing her idea of its classically tragic aspect, she made the passing observation that George Pullman was in some ways like King Lear, the title character in Shakespeare's play. Two New York newspapers picked up on her analogy and put it in the headlines of their articles about her speech.[52] Interest in the strike was evidently still high. Encouraged, Addams began to work on what she now was certain would be a speech, pondering again the puzzling lessons of the strike. The *Lear* analogy proved to be key. Shakespeare's play was about power and authority and their effects on both the dominator and the dominated. And did not those categories fit the participants in the Pullman Strike? And did not King Lear's daughter Cordelia rebel, as the workers did, against his domination? Perhaps Addams wrote about women's lack of power in her Rockford speech because she was thinking about Cordelia's and the workers' struggles.

Addams spent the summer working on the Pullman speech. By late August she had finished it, and in early September she delivered it at a Chicago conference on social economics organized by the settlements in the city. Her speech "certainly excited great interest," she reported to Mary, to whom she had sent a copy. She added, "I think I will publish it[;] it is certainly a candid opinion."[53]

But she was not able to act on her intentions. Within days of delivering the talk, she fell ill with a high fever and a severe pain in her abdomen. "Jane is in bed," Ellen Starr wrote to Jane's stepmother. Resident Harriet Rice, as Addams's attending physician, thought she had typhoid fever, and her colleague Dr. Sarah Hackett Stevenson, whom Rice called in, agreed. Bayard Holmes, a physician friend of Addams's who coincidentally stopped by, insisted that Addams had appendicitis. Ellen, frustrated by the disputing experts, wrote Anna Haldeman Addams wryly, "The lay mind, as usual, is confused." Holmes took over the case and decided to operate immediately. Rather than risk moving Addams to the hospital, he and another colleague did the operation in her bedroom at Hull House.[54]

A telegraph was sent to Alice Addams Haldeman, who arrived a few days later. Together she and Ellen, along with a hired nurse, protected Jane from other visitors as she lay in bed recovering. But her high fever did not abate. Rice had been correct in her diagnosis of typhoid fever. Addams was an obvious candidate for the disease, which spread via contact with contaminated waste, food, or water.[55] Although the Nineteenth Ward was much cleaner than it had been thanks to Addams's and Johnson's industry, it remained an incubator for disease.

Once the danger was past, Alice went home, leaving Ellen at her station. Addams's illness had restored Starr to her old role as caretaker. But, in a strange coincidence of medical events, Ellen was needed just then to tend to her father, who was scheduled for surgery. Mary Rozet Smith, now back in town, took over from Ellen and brought Jane to stay with her and her parents at Walton Place on the much quieter Near North Side. Addams completed her recovery there.[56]

The change in nurses may have taken place for purely practical reasons, but it captures symbolically something of Jane's feelings for her two friends at the time of the surgery. Her deepest devotion was reserved for Mary, not Ellen. In a letter Ellen sent to Jane many years later, in 1935, she claimed to have eventually risen above feelings of jealousy, but not at first. "I think I have always, [or] at any rate for a great many years, been thankful that Mary came to supply you what you needed." But Ellen was no wallflower abandoned for another partner. She had been distancing herself from Jane for several years. Indeed, the same month Addams fell ill, Starr was writing her cousin Mary Allen about how she had "fallen in love" with someone at Hull House.[57]

Ellen's friendship with Jane continued. After receiving a warm birthday letter from Ellen in 1907, Jane replied that she agreed with Ellen's observation that "twenty years has knitted our futures indissolvably together." They would remain affectionate until Addams's death. In the 1920s, when Ellen's poor health made her unable to support herself or to continue living at Hull House, Addams sent her regular checks and in 1931 set up a pension fund for her in the case of Addams's own death.[58] They felt a deep loyalty to each other, and this did not change.

But in 1895 Starr was finding that friendship could no longer satisfy her need for deep intimacy and for spiritual grounding. More than ever before, what she longed for was a close relationship with God. Seeking peace for her dissatisfied spirit, she was spending increasing amounts of time in private devotions, in church, and on spiritual retreats. The previous summer she had been at an Anglican seminary in Kenosha, Wisconsin (coincidentally just down the road from the sanitarium where Mary Addams Linn was staying at the time), wrestling with her private demons—her temper and her inability to love her fellow man. As Jane Addams was turning outward and connecting even more powerfully with life, Ellen Gates Starr, in these years, was turning inward.[59]

Addams found her slow recovery from typhoid fever "tedious." But the convalescence offered one benefit: she had time to prepare her talk about the Pullman Strike for publication. The Pullman-Lear analogy she had tested earlier on the New York audience and fleshed out in her speech at the economics conference provided a stimulating framework.[60] For the Lear part, she drew primarily from the action in the first scene of the first act of Shakespeare's play, in which Cordelia, a devoted and loving daughter, refuses to tell her father what he has insisted she must: that he is first in her adult affections. She replies that she must speak the truth—that she owes half her love to her fiancé. King Lear, hurt and outraged, disowns her and banishes her from his kingdom. He cannot fathom why his youngest and best-beloved child, on whom he has showered every kindness, should thus betray him.[61]

The analogy had set Addams's mind spinning. The most obvious similarity that struck her was that Pullman's will, like Lear's, had played a major part in the unfolding tragedy. There was also the similarity between the employees' refusal to obey Pullman and Cordelia's refusal to obey her father, or, to put the matter in the terms in which she may have been thinking while writing her Rockford speech, a similarity between the workers' and women's rebellions against domination. Furthermore, Pullman was mystified by his workers' actions in the same way Lear was mystified by Cordelia's. Finally, Pullman, the "indulgent employer," was stung by his workers' ingratitude just as Lear, the "indulgent parent," was stung by Cordelia's.[62]

The richly layered speech that resulted from Addams's revisions is really three speeches in one. The first is on the economic relations between industrial employees and their employer. Addams had been speaking and writing about labor issues since 1893, but here she writes in detail for the first time about an industrial employer, his motives, his responsibilities, and his failures, and she makes the argument that Karl Marx, Arnold Toynbee, Eugene Debs, Henry Demarest Lloyd, Richard Ely, and Florence Kelley, among others, had long been making—that the traditional industrial employer-employee relationship was paternalistic or feudal; indeed, her literary analogy is grounded in both tropes. She also presents for the first time in her writings a radical vision of what working people deserve. Several sentences in particular stand out. "The aroused conscience of men," she writes, requires "the complete participation of the working classes in the spiritual, intellectual and material inheritance of the human race." This "doctrine of emancipation" is a matter of "social justice." It is the "social passion of the age."[63]

Her reference to justice leaps off the page. Fourteen years earlier, when she was twenty and full of dreams and fears, Addams had endorsed the broad ethic of justice in "Cassandra," but she had not done so since. The motives for action she urged during her early years on Halsted Street and laid out in "Subjective Necessity" were Christian love and a moral responsibility to humanity, the motives of a philanthropist. More recently, in "The Settlement as a Factor," she had hinted at the possibility that the workers' labor movement was ethical but had gone no further.[64] Her embrace of justice—of fairness—in "A Modern Lear" was new, and her willingness to apply it to the workers' cause was significant. What had happened?

She had changed her mind about two things. First, she had come to see that improving material conditions was a worthy reform agenda. In "The Settlement as a Factor" she had dismissed the workers' calls for better wages, better working conditions, and shorter hours as "narrow" or "selfish," but in "A Modern Lear" she affirms them as emancipatory and includes "material" in the types of "inheritance" to which workers have a right.[65] Given that she would advocate forcefully in the future for improvements in physical conditions (indeed, she would become famous for that advocacy), her embrace of such goals in the speech marked a critical step in her development as a reformer and a citizen.

Second, she had decided that capitalism's labor practices needed active restraining. She now believed that when labor struck, it was for dire reasons and that it was using organizing power because it had no choice—in other words, that this form of antagonism did not originate in personal feelings but in conditions of injustice. Her acknowledgment of the role of power in oppressing women in the Rockford speech was mirrored in her acknowledgment in "A Modern Lear" of the role of power in oppressing workers. This insight, too, had implications for her career as a reformer. In the future, she would recognize power as a resource that those fighting for justice sometimes needed to use. She would never endorse violence, the destructive form of power, but she would never again doubt that unions were essential now that she understood the negotiating leverage they gave to workers.

The second speech within "A Modern Lear" is about a topic in which Addams had long been interested but about which she had never written at length before: the ethics of the modern philanthropist. The strike, she admits, has caused an upheaval in her thinking about benevolence, the virtue by which Pullman justified his domination. "The magnitude of [Pullman's] . . . failure . . . forces" us, she writes, "to challenge the ideal [of benevolence] itself." She sets forth two criticisms of the virtue. One is that it is "self-righteous" or "egotistical"—the moral failing that was so much on her mind. The other is that benevolence is old-fashioned, a feudal virtue "too archaic . . . to accomplish anything now."[66]

Probing deeper into the heart of the philanthropist, which is to say, her own heart, she identifies the erroneous assumption that undergirds the ethic of benevolence, the assumption she held when she moved to Halsted Street. "It is so easy for the good and powerful," she writes, "to think they can [succeed] by following the dictates of conscience [and] pursuing their own ideals." They may intend to establish relations of "frank equality" with those they are helping, but when they perform "too many good deeds," this reinforces the message that they are superior.[67] Benevolence's failing is that it does not lead to success in forming egalitarian social relations.

To reject benevolence, of course, was to question the moral system of which it was one tenet: individualism. Addams had implicitly rejected individualism long before this, when she became a cooperator, but she had not faced the limitations of the individualist ethic squarely until now. In "The Settlement as a Factor," she had judged the workers selfish and the capitalists greedy but she had not critiqued the underlying ethic that justified their narrow self-interest. This became her task in "A Modern Lear," with Pullman as the case study. The "individual virtues" that Pullman "pleaded for," she writes, are self-control, sobriety, respect for property, and industriousness. Inadequate and out-of-date, they are the "virtues [we] received from our fathers." But the "virtues of one generation are not sufficient for the next."[68] She might have said "the virtues I received from my father."

She proposes to replace those virtues with a broader "social" ethic. Philanthropists "need to remind themselves," she notes, "of the old definition of greatness": that it consists of possessing "the largest share of the common human qualities and experiences," not "peculiarities and excessive virtues." Abandoning their loyalty to "absolute right" and their sense of moral superiority, philanthropists can then insist on "consent," "move with the people," and "discover what the people really want"—what Abraham Lincoln called the "best possible."[69]

Some have interpreted this passage as Addams's call for democracy. In a sense, it is. But the word "democracy" does not appear in the speech; rather, her interest is in the moral view that undergirds democracy and produces justice. She variously describes this view as "a sense of responsibility to the community," as a "mutual interest in a common cause," as an "affectionate interpretation," as "a new code of ethics" that cherishes "the social virtues," and as having a heart whose "rhythm" is in sync with "the common heart-beat of the rest of the world." "Our thoughts, at least for this generation," she writes, "cannot be too much directed [toward] mutual relationships and responsibilities. They will be warped unless we look all men in the face." First and foremost, "A Modern Lear" is about what humans feel they owe and do not owe each other, that is, ethics—which, she believes, is the force that drives history. "Deep human motives . . . determine events." [70]

The centrality of human sympathy to human progress was not a new idea for Addams or her contemporaries. It is a theme found in the writings of many social Christians, and it echoes throughout her own early writings. But she probes its meaning far more deeply in "A Modern Lear," and the source of her inspiration was Abraham Lincoln. She refers to him there only in passing, but in her Rockford commencement speech, written while she was working on "Lear," she is more explicit about his influence on her thinking about the social ethic, although, characteristically, she speaks in terms of a broader "we." There has been "a change in our idea of greatness," she notes. "It was Abraham Lincoln who caused [this] change. . . . He never forgot how the cracker of Kentucky thought and felt and he remembered how the Illinois backwoodsman was thinking. It was the effort of his life to serve the cause of all and help those whose need he knew. North and south, black and white, he sympathized with all their sufferings." [71] She saw that Lincoln, a workingman without much formal education, never intellectualized and never lost his abiding sense of unity and identification with other working people.

Writing in "Lear," Addams, although born to a different class, longed to feel as Lincoln felt. Since coming to Halsted Street she had spoken and written of her commitment to human unity many times, but her conversion to the ideal had not been complete. Some part of her—the educated part—had been looking down on the uneducated portion of humanity as the inferior other. In "A Modern Lear" it is clear she wants to leave that feeling behind, wants to stand *inside* the circle, to feel fully the human connection. She is painting a portrait of the kind of philanthropist, indeed, the kind of human being, she wants to become. This, then, was the purpose of her arduous pilgrimage to the Lincoln statue during the Pullman Strike—to draw strength from this idea of greatness that Lincoln embodied.

Addams's old habits of admiring and learning from great men and absorbing their lessons from books may be credited with helping her reach her deepened insight. During the strike she had apparently been reading or rereading, two pieces of literature—a book and a lecture. The book was

Carl Schurz's *Abraham Lincoln: A Portrait*, the one she had given away to various young people in the neighborhood during her third Christmas at Hull House. The lecture was a talk on Lincoln given at Toynbee Hall in 1893 by a British moral philosopher named Edward Caird in which he gives an interpretation also found in Schurz's book—that Lincoln was "content merely to dig the channels through which the moral life of his country men might flow." Addams quotes this observation of Caird's in *Twenty Years*. It is her new "idea of greatness" paraphrased.[72]

Writing in "Lear," Addams justifies her rejection of benevolence and individualism and her embrace of a new definition of greatness with an argument that leads her straight into issues of philosophy. She calls benevolence "archaic" and credits Lincoln with bringing forward the new definition. She points out that ethics changes as society changes; that what is ethical is what society finds ethical in the present, that an out-of-date ethics must be left behind because societal experience has rendered it irrelevant. It is not just that experience shapes ethics, the point she had made in "The Settlement as a Factor"; it is that ethics, that which is true, changes.

The idea was not original; it was in the air. Broadly, evolution was a central intellectual trope of the nineteenth century. What caused Addams to connect the idea of evolution to ethics was, predictably, another book, also by Edward Caird, titled *The Evolution of Religion*. Addams read it in 1895, the year she wrote "A Modern Lear." In it Caird argued that ethics, like everything else in the world, is subject to the "great reconciling principle of Development" and that "all knowledge comes . . . in and through experience." Her subject in "Lear" is the underside of Caird's theory: What happened if a person's ethics did not evolve with the times? But Caird's point was also about the direction of history. It was the larger point that Dewey had made to her soon after the strike ended—that, historically, antagonism was useful.[73] In the speech Addams recognizes that the strike was not only about George Pullman's personal failure but about a historic and appropriate clash of ethics and that this clash was part of the evolutionary process by which society's ethics moved forward.

Addams's conversion to a philosophy of pragmatism was now complete. The process had begun in 1888 with her embrace of the theory of cooperation; although cooperation offered no philosophical theory of truth, it unmoored her from exclusionary, polarized rigidity. Also essential were her ties to the progressive labor movement. On the whole, working-class reformers were far more willing to challenge society's inherited, absolutist ethics than were reformers of Addams's own class. Most of all, she had lived on Halsted Street, had experienced the Pullman Strike, had read many books, particularly Caird's and Schurz's, and had had many conversations, most notably with John Dewey, an ethical theorist whose own ideas were evolving under the pressure of experience. Finally, there was the crucial fact that she had a habit of dogged intellectual persistence. She did not change her mind easily, but neither did she easily abandon a new idea when it jarred with her other beliefs. Jane Addams's theory of pragmatism—her theory of truth—was born of a great deal of determined, soul-wrenching thinking. But it was not only her theory that changed. The obvious must be stated: Jane Addams's own ethics changed by way of the very process that pragmatism theorized. In "Lear" she traces her path to her new ethic, her new idea of greatness, speaking always in the voice of the collective first person, and so camouflaging the profoundly personal nature of her discovery.

The third speech within "Lear" is more obviously personal. It is about the relations between fathers and adult daughters, another subject she had been pondering for several years. She now takes her analysis of the family and the social claims to a new level by focusing on the father.[74] Compelled by the power of Shakespeare's story and inspired, perhaps, by the courage the Pullman workers had shown in resisting their "father," in "A Modern Lear" she completes the daughter's journey into the dark side of a doting father's love.

Carefully, she establishes Cordelia's motives for her treatment of her father. Cordelia, Addams explains, is an "untrained soul" who has conceived "a notion of justice" and wishes to become "a citizen of the world." (Addams revises Shakespeare here to suit her own purposes, and, it seems, to match her own experience.) But King Lear perceives Cordelia narrowly. In his egoism, he does not believe that his children "could have a worthy life apart from him." He also errs in believing that his beloved adult daughter is a possession he has a right to control. "His paternal expression," Addams writes, "was one of domination and indulgence."[75] The "dictatorial relation" between Lear and Cordelia, she observes, is "a typical example of the distinctively family tragedy, one will asserting its authority through all the entanglement of wounded affection, and insisting upon its selfish ends at all costs." Addams, her eyes freshly opened, sees the imbalance of power in this father-daughter relationship. At bottom, Lear's failure is a moral one. "The overmastering desire of being beloved . . . is selfish," she writes.[76]

Clearly, Addams's own experience as a daughter is on her mind. She even goes so far as to hint that she has decided to compare the events of the Pullman strike to Shakespeare's play rather than to her own family because of the emotional distance the play provides. "We have all had glimpses of what it might be to blaspheme against family ties," she writes. "It will probably be easier to [compare] Pullman to "the family tragedy of Lear[,] . . . which we [can] discuss without personal feeling." The personal aspect of the story seems to be confirmed by the kind of person her father was—an upright, benevolent, wealthy man whom the neighbors had called the "king-gentleman of Stephenson County" and who had wanted a great deal to be loved. She needed Lincoln's new idea of greatness to replace her father's, which had become insufficient for her times.[77]

Addams never publicly said that she and her times had outgrown her father's ethics, but in "A Modern Lear" she makes it clear enough. The process she had begun in 1885 of separating herself from her father's "moral requirements" was now complete, brought to closure by the process of writing the speech. And she understood this. One startlingly frank sentence provides the clue. Speaking of her decision to compare the father-daughter relationship to that of Pullman with his workers, she writes, "It is possible to make them illuminate each other."[78] Perhaps that had been her hope from the beginning; she certainly had achieved that at the end.

In "Lear" Addams executed her daring analogy superbly. And she was the first to benefit from what she accomplished. Writing the speech had focused her mind and helped her complete an intellectual revolution that had long been brewing. Cordelia, the daughter who defied her father, was the key. Able to identify fully with her, Addams was able to identify fully with the oppressed workers and to see that the ethic of benevolence, whether in its filial, philanthropic, or industrial form, was out-of-date.

Having gained a new perspective as one of the oppressed, Addams came to see power everywhere. In "A Modern Lear" she equates the power of the employer with the power of a king, calls the benevolent philanthropist powerful, and describes the father as a dictator. She who had been raised to trust power now saw power's cruel, unjust side. For Jane Addams, the Pullman Strike and the act of writing about it were major milestones on the road to becoming a citizen.

———————

Addams's period of convalescence was richly productive in another way. "I had time to review carefully many things in my mind during the long days," she writes in *Twenty Years*. One thing she reviewed was her friendship with

Mary Rozet Smith, now her daily companion. They had spent time in each other's company before, but perhaps they had never had as quiet and private a time together as they now had, nor one in which Addams was less distracted by her settlement work. Under these conditions, Jane realized more than ever before how important Mary was to her; she even wrote a poem while staying at Walton Place about her regret that she had not awakened sooner to the gift of Mary's affections. Crediting Charles Lamb with first teaching her "a sense" of the value of gentle, brotherly relations and Tolstoy for reinforcing the lesson, she recalled her fruitless search to find such love and how, once at Hull House, she abandoned it, pouring her affections instead into the settlement itself and never noticing the love that Mary was offering. Why had she not noticed sooner? The poem states wistfully, "And thus I lost unnumbered days / And all because I did not know." She called what Mary gave her "the miracle" of "delivering love."[79] Eighteen ninety-five was a transforming year for Addams in more ways than one.

In the following months Addams would submit "A Modern Lear" to four magazines—the *Review of Reviews,* the *Forum*, the *North American Review*, and the *Atlantic Monthly*—and receive rejections from all of them. Their reasons varied. Horace Scudder of the *Atlantic Monthly* replied that he was "profoundly impressed by the skill of this paper" but questioned her central assumption, namely, that Pullman had intended to be a philanthropist in creating his town. He also correctly discerned that she thought Pullman "in the wrong" and hinted that he disagreed with her assessment. The editor of the *Forum* thought her subject "somewhat belated."[80]

What he meant was that the strike had been thoroughly covered already. Between July 1894 and April 1895, eighteen of the country's most prominent opinion-making journals, including all of those to which Addams had submitted her piece, had published forty-one articles on the subject. Also, although no editor commented on it, her approach to the strike was somewhat peculiar. Addams's essay did not deal with the issues that most people believed were at stake and that previous articles had dealt with: property rights, the dangers posed by unions and their strikes to the nation's law and order, and the role of the government in settling labor disputes.[81] Her comparison of the motives and ethics of the two disputants was intriguing but a bit obscure.

Meanwhile, she continued to give the speech wherever she could and to ask friends to read it. She asked John Dewey for criticisms but he had

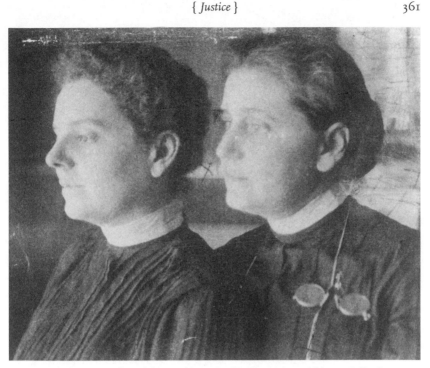

Mary Rozet Smith and Jane Addams in the 1890s. Jane Addams Collection,
Swarthmore College Peace Collection.

none to give, calling it "one of the greatest things I have ever read, as to its
form and its ethical philosophy." This was generous praise from the man
who would soon become one of the nation's leading ethical philosophers.
Addams's first major presentation of the speech in Chicago was before an
audience of five hundred women at the Chicago Woman's Club on March
4, 1896. The *Tribune* quoted from her remarks and declared the audience
"appreciative."[82]

But others did not like it. Eugene Debs's opinion, as summed up by
Weber Linn, was that it was "just another attempt to put out a fire with rose-
water." Not surprisingly, Pullman himself—he must have heard about the
lecture—"resented it bitterly," according to Linn. In *Twenty Years*, Addams
hints that Pullman made a nasty public comment about her speech, but she
discreetly forbears to share it. Henry Demarest Lloyd thought the piece too
much of a direct attack on Pullman and suggested that she "depersonalize"
it.[83] Addams may have had some doubts herself—she generally avoided

criticizing people—but she did not revise it, apparently believing there was something about the Pullman Strike that called for this treatment.

In the next few years, she gave the speech often. According to Weber Linn, it fully established her standing as a respected public intellectual. "More than [her speeches] . . . at the Plymouth Summer School . . . , more even than the found[ing] of Hull House itself, 'A Modern Lear' began to make Jane Addams a figure of national importance." He noted that it was widely discussed and attracted much attention. Yet it remained unpublished. As far as is known, Addams did not submit it to another magazine for sixteen years. Some have thought that it was out of regard for the feelings of the Pullman family. Certainly, by 1898, it was not to spare George Pullman, who died in late 1897. In 1912 "A Modern Lear" was finally published in a national social reform magazine, the *Survey*, on whose editorial board Jane Addams sat. The piece stirred up a storm of newspaper commentary across the United States, further evidence, if any was needed, of the strong feelings the Pullman Strike still aroused.[84] For Addams, the piece's publication was first and foremost a personal satisfaction. At last she had seen in print the speech whose writing had transformed her understanding of the Pullman Strike and her experience as a daughter. Having written it, she ever afterwards believed that ethics was pragmatic, that benevolence was oppressive, and that power was an inexorable influence in class relations.

CHAPTER 15

DEMOCRACY

1896–98

The place of democracy in Jane Addams's thought during her early years on Halsted Street was, in one sense, constant. She had been referring to the idea in her speeches since 1890—and had always done so in a way that showed it was centrally important to her. But this constancy was not the whole story. During the same period her thinking about democracy became more complex. At the beginning she had stressed its social side and called Christian fellowship the "true democracy"; in 1895, without abandoning her commitment to social democracy, she started to give equal stress to democracy's political side. Although she did not use the word in "A Modern Lear," she spoke there of the need for the leader to "insist upon consent" and "move with the people" and called for "the emancipation of the worker."[1] These observations confirm that her concept of democracy now included the workers' understanding of the meaning of social justice and their belief that their political power, both in the workplace and more broadly, was key to its achievement.

Still, there were two gaping holes in her political résumé and, concomitantly, in her understanding of political democracy. One was that she had not been deeply immersed in an election campaign. Although she may have had something to do with the Nineteenth Ward Improvement Club's effort to elect Frank Lawler in the aldermanic campaign of 1895, her efforts left no trace in the historical record.[2] The other was her silence about her own right to vote. She had not spoken a public word in favor of women's suffrage since writing her college editorials. She may have never lost her sympathy for the cause, but the feeling had not translated itself into advocacy.

Circumstances, what she liked to call "the spirit of the times," would now push her to become fully political. She was one among many who felt the pressure. Popular enthusiasm for broad-based, politically generated reform, which had been on the rise in the United States throughout the first half of the 1890s, surged in the decade's closing years. The American Federation of Labor's adoption of its first political program in 1893 and the rise and fall of the short-lived Populist Party between 1892 and 1896 were expressions of wage-earners' and farmers' increasing determination to shape national policy concerning issues that affected them. African Americans, the majority of whom lived in the South, were becoming increasingly politically organized even as Jim Crow laws thwarted their efforts. Likewise, women favoring suffrage, having regained their unified voice when the two national organizations reconsolidated into the National-American Woman's Suffrage Association in 1890, were now a much stronger political force. They had their first successes in converting states (as opposed to territories) to women's suffrage when they persuaded Colorado men in 1893 and Idaho men in 1896 to give women the vote.[3] In the mid-1890s, democracy's newest recruits—laborers, farmers, African Americans, and women—were becoming fully engaged in political action at the municipal and state levels.

As of early 1896, the Civic Federation of Chicago had done much to clean up Chicago politics, but much remained to be done. In 1895 certain aldermen on the City Council had, in essence, given away nine valuable franchises, including two to electric rail companies and one to a gas company, in exchange for kickbacks. When reform mayor George Swift vetoed one of the franchise ordinances, the city council overrode his veto. Determined to vanquish the remaining boodling aldermen, the federation spun off its political arm into a separate organization called the Municipal Voters League (MVL) to push for reform candidates to run in the targeted wards. The league was strictly nonpartisan, with an advisory committee that included two representatives from each ward, one Democrat and one Republican. It endorsed Democratic and Republican candidates.[4]

In the Nineteenth Ward, the boodler John Powers was up for reelection. Powers chaired the Finance Committee of the City Council and the caucus that distributed the chairmanships of committees. He was, in Florence Kelley's words, "the dominant man in the city government of Chicago." Forces for reform across the city urgently desired him out of office. The weighty responsibility of defeating Powers fell on the voters of the Nineteenth Ward. As before, Kelley and the Nineteenth Ward Improvement Club, guided by the Nineteenth Ward branch of the MVL, led the effort.[5]

This time Addams was centrally involved. Immediately, however, she and Kelley disagreed about who should be the reform candidate. Addams wanted a middle-class reformer named George Sikes, a newspaperman and Hull House resident, while Kelley favored a workingman named William Gleeson, a forty-two-year-old Irish immigrant who was a former bricklayer and a member of the Hull House Men's Club. When it was learned that Sikes could not run, the Nineteenth Ward Voters League selected Gleeson as its candidate.[6]

Defeating Powers promised to be difficult. "[Powers] isn't elected," Addams noted in a speech in February, "because he is dishonest but because he is . . . a friend of everybody[;] he takes the liveliest interest in their personal affairs." She detailed the variety of forms his kindliness took. He gave men jobs (he once boasted that he had placed twenty-six hundred people on the public payrolls, which was roughly one-third of the ward's voters). He paid funeral expenses, gave presents at weddings and christenings, and handed out free train passes. With a nod to the pleasures of recreation, he sponsored ward dances, parades, and picnics. He even bailed voters and their family members out of jail or arranged for the judge to drop charges. He was a one-man settlement house, with the difference that he specialized in material aid and helped mostly unskilled workers and their families. Given the extent of his largess, Kelley and Addams did not expect to defeat him, but as George Sikes explained to his fiancé in late February, "they want to make the fight anyway." The campaign would be, at the very least, a means to educate the voters.[7]

The anti-Powers effort was well launched by early March. Trade unions that had ties to the Civic Federation and to Hull House endorsed Gleeson. Hull House hosted a series of lectures on municipal administration issues. A new monthly publication, the *Hull-House Bulletin*, began appearing in January as part of the campaign strategy. One of its purposes, Addams explained in the first issue, was "to stimulate an interest in the public affairs of the Nineteenth Ward and secure more unity of action towards its improvement." That spring, alongside class schedules and news of the clubs, the *Bulletin* ran reports on the work of the Nineteenth Ward Voters League.[8]

Although Powers thought Gleeson's candidacy "a joke," Addams writes in *Twenty Years*, he mounted "the most determined and skillful opposition." He had the support of the Chicago Labor Congress, which represented unskilled workers, and its newspaper, the *Union Workman*, as well as that of the *Chicago Chronicle*, a firmly Democratic paper with close ties to the Irish machine. The city's most famous briber, the streetcar magnate Charles Yerkes, donated $5,000 toward Powers's $50,000 campaign.[9] The money was undoubtedly used to buy a staggering number of votes.

As Addams and Kelley expected, on Election Day Powers retained his seat handily. Gleeson received 2,703 votes and Powers 4,064. Powers was delighted. "Every man who voted for me," he crowed to the press the next day, "did so because he knew and felt I was his tried and proven friend. The cry of boodle, boodle, cut very little figure."[10]

Although Gleeson went down to defeat, across the city the league's anti-corruption campaign was once again a triumphant success. Of the twenty-four aldermen up for reelection that the league wanted to oust, eighteen lost their seats. Its candidates failed to win against boodlers in only four wards. The reformers now had the votes needed to uphold a mayoral veto.[11] The 1896 election was thus was a crucial turning point for municipal reform.

Florence Kelley learned several lessons from the campaign. Her theory that a working-class candidate would win, she later admitted, was wrong. Voters had explained to her that they wanted someone much grander and more important than themselves to represent them on the council. Powers, who lived in a fine house, drank champagne, and wore a diamond in his shirtfront, struck them as just the right sort. Also, Kelley reluctantly acknowledged that being female was an obstacle to political work. The Hull House residents "of longest standing," she noted, were all women, and this was "a serious disqualification for campaign work in a ward of foreign voters." Some of the voters told her they refused to support Gleeson because, she wrote, they "resent . . . attempts at political leadership" by women.[12]

No doubt Jane Addams agreed with Kelley on both points, but the main lesson she took away was something else. Her mind veered off politics and came to rest on morality. The experience of the anti-Powers campaign, like the Lincoln Club crisis, challenged her understanding of working-class morals. Perhaps she had both events in mind when she later wrote, "It is difficult . . . to interpret sympathetically the motives and ideals of those who have . . . rules of conduct . . . widely different from our own."[13]

That difficulty arose forcefully for her at a specific moment in the campaign. An MVL speaker, addressing an audience of working-class voters at Hull House, had disparaged the beloved memory of a deceased local alderman whose politics had been as corrupt as Powers's. As the speaker continued to criticize the man's unethical behavior, the audience, Addams writes, looked "puzzled, then astounded, and indignant." They were shocked, she realized, that the speaker did not share their values—first, that a man should be "good to the poor" and second, that one should always "speak gently of the dead." [14] In years past Addams would have thought that these voters' enthusiasm for a corrupt alderman was morally misguided and would have felt it her duty to help them see this. Now she thought differently. Determined to practice Lincoln's generous humanity, she began to look for the common moral ground that she and these Powers supporters could share.

She found her answer by rereading Edward Caird's *Evolution of Religion*. She was struck by Caird's conviction that religion is "subjected to a continuous process of development" leading to a "universal consciousness [that] transcends" people's objective and subjective experiences. Cocooned in his Anglo-Christian world, Caird thought Christianity was destined to evolve into this universal religion because of its universal message to humanity to abandon selfishness and embrace "wider interests." Addams, for whom selfishness was always the most important moral failing but who rejected Christian prosyletization, adapted Caird's theory. She wondered, she writes in *Twenty Years*, whether a shared "secular religion" of unselfishness might evolve in a neighborhood of "immigrant colonies" possessing a "labyrinth of differing ethical teachings and religious creeds." Caird's book gave her hope that such a common ethic, what she would later call a "wide humanitarianism," lay in the neighborhood's future. Reading the book gave her "unspeakable comfort." [15]

Addams rarely addresses her own ethical development in *Twenty Years*. Yet what she expected to happen to her neighbors was also happening to her. She, too, inhabited an "immigrant colony," Hull House, with its own "ethical teachings" (middle-class moral absolutism), and she, too, was broadening her ethical beliefs under the pressure of living in the neighborhood. Her most direct admission that life on Halsted Street was changing her ethics appears in some remarks she gave at a conference for charity workers in 1897. As usual she avoided the first person; nonetheless she was describing herself. "It is impossible," she said, "that you should live in a neighborhood and constantly meet people with certain ideas and notions without modifying your own." If, as she now understood, morality did not transcend history and culture but was of a piece with it, then her new challenge was to discern the direction in which morality in her time and place was evolving and to situate herself morally within that great and flowing river. [16]

Her methods were to read books, of course, but also to listen—carefully. People recalled her "questioning eyes" and her "gentle inquisitiveness." According to one, "She was always in that listening attitude of mind of 'What is it?'" A new young resident was struck by the way she tried "to understand and interpret [everyone] correctly and generously." Her "real eagerness," observed Weber Linn, "was always for understanding." [17] She had done as she had intended in 1889: she had "hooked" herself "fast" with her "whole mind" to her neighborhood. Complete and full attention, engaging the imagination and the heart, had taught her as much as any book, and that was saying a good deal. Behind the striking personal manner lay her beliefs that democracy was as much an inward process as an outer one and that if she was to learn from others, to reap the benefits of free speech, as it were, her mind would need to be open to being changed.

———————

Although Addams had returned in January 1896 to her hectic schedule of inspecting garbage, attending meetings, raising money, and giving speeches, she had not yet fully recovered her health after her bout with typhoid fever. In March, shortly before Election Day, Mary Rozet Smith generously invited Addams to take a four-and-a-half-month trip to Europe, all expenses paid, with her parents and herself, starting at the end of April. Playfully, in imitation of the ethics of Chicago's city council, she invoked her greatest leverage over Jane: her gifts to Hull House. "I will offer you bribes to the extent of my fortune," Mary wrote. "I'll even build a third floor on the Butler Gallery if you come. Otherwise I won't." [18]

Persuading Jane Addams to visit Europe was never difficult. Gratefully, she accepted the invitation. Unable to travel without a purpose, however, she set three goals for herself. One was to research social movements in Europe, in particular those in London; the second to meet Edward Caird, who was master of a college at Oxford University; the third to meet the man whose Christian conscience she had so long admired, Count Leo Tolstoy. She made the necessary arrangements to be gone from Hull House, which she was now describing as "the household I love best." Laura and Weber Addams in Cedarville agreed to take care of Stanley and Esther Linn. Addams resigned as garbage inspector and arranged for Amanda Johnson to be named to the post. Gertrude Barnum, a settlement resident since 1893, would take charge of running Hull House.[19]

On April 29, Addams, with Smith and her parents, Charles Mather and Sarah Rozet Smith, sailed from New York for Liverpool. The traveling party would be in England for two months, spending most of the time in London; then they would journey to France, Germany, and Switzerland. Mary and Jane hoped to make a side trip to Russia in August to see some sights and visit Tolstoy. They would then rejoin the Smiths and depart from London for home in mid-September.[20]

In London, though ostensibly resting, Addams was, as usual, energetic. She visited Toynbee Hall and other settlements. Sir John Gorst, a Member of Parliament, took her on a tour of the House of Commons, and she attended a meeting of the Fabian Society and the annual Cooperative Congress. She even had tea with Arnold Toynbee's sister.[21]

Her long-anticipated visit with Edward Caird was arranged by the Barnetts. She traveled to Oxford, where Caird, an eminent member of the British intellectual community and the author of six books in the fields of philosophy and religion, was master of the prestigious Balliol College. Addams went ready to ask him her question—whether a shared humanitarian ethos could evolve in a pluralistic neighborhood. No doubt she was hoping they would have what she most enjoyed—"real intercourse of mind with mind."[22]

By the time Addams made her way among the hallowed halls of Oxford University and arrived in the great man's drawing room, however, her confidence that she was his intellectual equal had dwindled considerably. At first embarrassed, she then became upset at her insecurity. Was she not a proud American who rejected the idea that the mother country was superior? Meeting Caird stirred conflicting feelings of intimidation and pride; this may be why she tells the story of their conversation somewhat murkily in *Twenty Years*. At first she tried to shore up her self-respect by bringing up her nation's great president, her own father's friend and the subject of the lecture by Caird that she had read. Cooperatively, Caird took up the topic, praising Lincoln (Addams quotes his words) as someone who was "content . . . to dig the channels through which the moral life of his countrymen might flow." The ready honor he gave to Lincoln, and the wisdom of his words, which echoed her own observation in "A Modern Lear" that a leader must move with the people and not ahead of them, touched her. Her insecurity evaporated. "Gradually," she writes, "a healing sense of well-

*Jane Addams in London, 1896. This photograph reveals the sadness in her face noted
by others. Jane Addams Memorial Collection (JAMC neg. 6), Special Collections,
The University Library, University of Illinois at Chicago.*

being enveloped me and [I felt] a quick remorse for my blindness."[23] One
result, however, was that her burning question was never discussed.

That she wanted to ask him the question at all is interesting. If it was
true, as she now believed, that experience guided the evolution of an individual's, as well as a society's, morality, then Caird's claims to wisdom,
which was the result of wide reading and deep thought in a book-lined
study, rested on a shallower foundation than her own. Yet she held him in
awe. Apparently some part of her continued to think that the philosopher,

the book writer, the theorist, the man of highest culture, knew more than someone like herself, who, though she had never written a book, had lived in an international community for almost seven years and daily faced the complicated moral issues raised by pluralism. Apparently, Addams had not completely lost the habit of respecting acquired culture more than experience. Her new tent pole was in place, but she was still adjusting the stakes.

From London the Smith party headed to France and to Germany. Then, Mary and Jane parted from Mary's parents to take the train to Russia and the hoped-for meeting with Tolstoy. Addams had a letter of introduction to Alymer Maude, the Englishman who was Tolstoy's authorized translator; she expected that he would be able to help. Addams's enthusiasm for Tolstoy had, if possible, increased since the 1880s. In 1894, when Tolstoy published a new book in English, *The Kingdom of God Is Within You*, she found it "a masterly exposition" of the "doctrine" of nonresistance. When, in an 1896 article about settlements for the WCTU's *Union Signal*, she described Christ as "the Man who sought . . . to be identified with [lowly men], not to be distinguished" from them, she labeled it Tolstoy's vision.[24]

She did not see his ideas as wholly perfect. In particular, she did not agree with him that one should live the same life of material discomfort as one's neighbors. She also doubted his theory that a Christian should support his needs wholly by his own labor. In 1895, when Mary Rozet Smith confessed to Addams that while reading Tolstoy's writings she felt guilty about her lack of economic self-sufficiency, Jane replied, "I am sorry that Tolstoi gives you such a hard time with your principles; I had an awful time the two years before I came to Hull House. I do not like it now when my farmer pays his rent but I do not believe that Tolstoi's position is tenable, a man cannot be a Christian by himself." Still, Addams came to Tolstoy as a disciple and with a great longing to lay the burdens that most troubled her at his feet. She hoped, she writes in *Twenty Years*, that seeing Tolstoy would help her "find a clew to the tangled affairs of city poverty."[25] She was longing once again for a real meeting of minds.

After visiting St. Petersburg, Addams and Smith arrived in Moscow, where they had some good luck. Maude was at home and, having just been invited to visit Tolstoy at his ancestral estate, Yasnaya Polyana, about 130 miles south of Moscow, he was willing to take the two American women along.[26] Traveling by train and carriage, they arrived at the estate in early afternoon. Tolstoy was away on an errand and Countess Tolstoy was enter-taining the usual mélange of foreign guests who showed up daily to pay court to the most famous man in Russia. Soon enough, Tolstoy returned. Having just ridden twenty miles on horseback, he was eager to take a swim. Content to follow him about, the group walked with him to the river.

At sixty-eight, Tolstoy was a striking figure, tall and fit in his loose peas-ant clothes. He had a long gray beard and "deep-set eyes," which, as Maude later remembered, "seemed to pierce one's soul." He was always a fervent man; after becoming a devout Christian his passions were for self-denial, integrity of thought and action, and telling the truth. He had also tried to discipline his moods. Once arrogant and quarrelsome, now he was more often, in Maude's words, "gentle" and "extremely kind" and exuded "a won-derful charm."[27] To many, including Addams, he was a fatherly figure. In-deed, at nearly twice her age, Tolstoy was a man of her father's generation. Though different in many ways from her father, perhaps especially in his anarchistic hatred of government as the oppressor of the people, he was quite like John Addams in his fiercely Christian absolutist morality.

On the walk to the river, Maude, speaking French, introduced Addams and Smith to Tolstoy and generously praised Hull House. Meanwhile, Tol-stoy was eyeing "distrustfully" the enormous puffy silk upper sleeves of Ad-dams's fashionable travel dress. Addams recalls the scene in *Twenty Years*. Taking hold of a sleeve, Tolstoy stretched it out, smiled, and asked, "And what is this for?" Before she could reply, he added that she could make a dress for a little girl from all that material and asked if she did not find wearing such a fashionable outfit a "barrier to the people." Ironically, it was the same criticism John Addams had made of Jane's new cloak. This time Addams gamely stood her ground. Working girls in Chicago, she ex-plained, wore the same stylish "leg o' mutton" sleeves. Furthermore, if she were to dress like a peasant, as he did, she would find it difficult to choose one national dress to wear from among the many nationalities in the ward. Countess Tolstoy now mercifully intervened. She had discussed this ques-tion of the sleeves with her husband many times before, she explained, and her attempts to make dresses for little girls from "superfluous" parts of her best gown had failed. She advised Addams to "take a firm stand" against her husband's opinions.[28]

Sensing the mood of female solidarity his criticism had aroused and desiring to not be excluded, Tolstoy changed the subject. He asked Addams whether women had the vote yet in the United States. When she told him they voted in only a few states, he called it "very queer" that suffrage came

Leo Tolstoy, *by Jack Coughlin.*
Courtesy of the artist.

so slowly. Equality for women, he opined, was a "fundamental teaching of Jesus."[29] Addams would remember his remark. No doubt she was pleased to find him in the pro-suffrage camp.

The mood of unity, however, did not last. As the group gathered for tea at five o'clock under the trees, Tolstoy asked Addams how she supported herself, and when she admitted that she was an absentee landlord and received part of her income from a farm outside Chicago, his next question, she remembered, was "scathing." "Do you think you will help the people more by adding yourself to the crowded city than you would by tilling your own soil?"[30] She must have expected his disapproval regarding this point. Nonetheless, it could only have been unnerving to hear it from his own lips.

The after-dinner conversation took up new topics, in particular, Tolstoy's commitment to nonresistance and his opposition to private property, both controversial views that he regularly and vehemently defended in public statements. Many Russians, a guest informed the international visitors, disapproved of Tolstoy. Then someone asked the famous novelist and Christian apologist why he was so combative in public debate. Was he not violating his principle of nonresistance in arguing his viewpoint so aggressively? Tolstoy denied it. He was using moral force, he pointed out, not physical force, and the two were different. Addams listened carefully. "Curiously enough," she writes in *Twenty Years*, "I was disappointed in Tolstoy's position. It seemed to me that he made too great a distinction between the use of physical force and that moral energy which can override another's differences and scruples with equal ruthlessness."[31] Addams thought both forms of force wrong, and she had thought Tolstoy did, too. Had she been misunderstanding his theory of nonresistance all of these years?

To keep to their schedule, Addams and Smith needed to return to Moscow that night. Alymer Maude, who was planning to stay on at Yasnaya Polyana, took them to the station to catch the midnight train. Once in Moscow, they immediately caught a train bound for Germany.[32] Addams used the time during the long trip westward to think. As her train passed through Russia and Poland, she writes, she was caught up in "a tumult of feeling" and "pursued relentlessly" by "a horde of perplexing questions."[33] On one hand she had been profoundly moved in meeting Leo Tolstoy. She was struck, as she wrote Maude a week later, by his "gentleness, the Christianity in the soul of him." (She did not comment on the fact that she had also repeatedly suffered from his blunt disapproval.) On the other hand, she did not agree with Tolstoy that moral force was acceptable. Was it not another name for self-righteousness? She explained to Maude that the non-resistant philosophy she had tried to practice at Hull House consisted of "selecting the good in the neighborhood and refraining from railing at the bad." This belief "has come to be part of my method of living, and I should have to start quite over again and admit the value of resistance if I gave it up."[34] Although she was too polite to say so, her implication was obvious: Tolstoy was betraying his own theory in exempting moral force from its jurisdiction.

Addams also doubted Tolstoy's wisdom in resisting those who disapproved of his views. She did not call Tolstoy a martyr, but she did discuss martyrdom in her letter to Maude. "I have come to believe," she wrote, that "the expectation of opposition and martyrdom, the holding oneself in readiness for it, [is] in itself a sort of resistance and work[s] evil."[35] Her former desire for martyrdom had been eradicated by her principled rejection of antagonism. Her mind had conquered a teaching of her upbringing.

Discovering her disagreement with Tolstoy deeply troubled Addams. She felt, she writes in *Twenty Years*, an "inner sense of mortification." Who was she to dispute the ideas of the great Tolstoy? Still, she did not change her mind. She who had relied on others—most notably great men—for ideas was now forging her own. The years she had spent on Halsted Street working with women such as Mary Kenney O'Sullivan, Florence Kelley, and Julia Lathrop, none of whom yielded male authority any quarter, had contributed to this change. So had her fresh grasp of George Pullman's limitations as a capitalist-philanthropist and of John Addams's limitations as a father. The understanding that there should be no gender hierarchy found its way into a pro-suffrage essay Addams wrote in 1913, in which she imagined a world where the roles were reversed and men, rather than women, lacked the vote. She discredited the weak points used to oppose suffrage, including the unfortunate "habit" some "women" had of regarding "men not as comrades and fellow citizens, but as a class by themselves."[36] When Addams stood her ground against Tolstoy, a leading male intellectual of the Western world, she was abandoning her own unfortunate habit of setting men apart. Able to see limitations in even the best of men, she was beginning to believe that a powerful person could be a woman.

Or nearly. At the very moment that she was refusing to abandon a central moral belief in the face of Tolstoy's disagreement, his former authority over her reasserted itself in a small but interesting way. She had told Mary she disagreed with Tolstoy about the need for people to support themselves through manual labor, but when Tolstoy found fault with her landlord status, she felt a "new sense of discomfort." As her train rumbled into Germany, Addams decided that when she returned to Hull House she would spend two hours every day baking bread in the bakery of the Coffee House. After all, she told herself, "What could be more in keeping with my training and tradition than baking bread?" Had not her father, she writes in *Twenty Years*, insisted that she be able to bake a perfect loaf? The invocation of her father in connection with the task made it irresistible. Back at Hull House in mid-September, however, reality soon intruded. She could not justify, she writes, pushing real needs aside while "I saved my soul by two hours' work at baking bread."[37] Self-sufficiency through manual labor was an ethic suited to a certain stage of economic development. The times had passed it by. It was the same conclusion she had reached in "A Modern Lear." Ethics must evolve. Again, in the end, she trusted her own judgment.

Despite the rocky aspects of her meeting with Tolstoy and her ultimate rejection of several of his key tenets, Addams was thrilled to have had the experience and found that afterwards she "could not stop talking about him." After her return to Chicago, she began to give talks about Tolstoy to audiences ranging from the Hull House residents to the Chicago Woman's Club, to large gatherings at the Chautauqua Assembly in western New

York. Although she made it clear in her speeches that she found his methods "blundering," she stressed again and again the characteristic that more than anything bound her loyally to him: his determination "to translate his theories into action." She saw him not "as a seer"—his message, she thought, was "much too confused and contradictory for that"—but as a man who knew how to "lift his life to the level of his conscience."[38] Her admiration for this aspect of Tolstoy is the surest proof that Addams's own moral integrity, perhaps her most stellar characteristic, was just as much the product of conscious effort as she believed Tolstoy's was.

Of the many tests Addams faced in her pursuit of integrity, one of the severest was the very thing she and Tolstoy disagreed about: the use of moral force. Her failures are mostly undocumented but include the conversation leading to the clerk's death and the Lincoln Club crisis. Another took place in 1897, in a conversation with a visiting British settlement worker named Helen Gow.

Gow was a single woman from a wealthy family who managed a Charitable Organization Society office at the Women's University Settlement in London. She arrived at Hull House in late April 1897, after a tour of East Coast settlements, for a month's visit, eager to observe everything and record it in her diary. Addams, however, had additional plans for Gow besides sightseeing. Mindful of her COS expertise, she arranged for her to advise Gertrude Gernon, the Hull House resident who was having some difficulty managing the Chicago Bureau of Charities office (the latest incarnation of Chicago's COS organization).[39] Addams wanted Gow to stay, become a Hull House resident herself, and take over the bureau.

She proposed the idea on Gow's last day. Addams invited her, Gow proudly wrote in her diary, to sit at her right hand at lunch, in the place where Florence Kelley usually sat. First Addams flattered Gow regarding her skills; then she pointed out Chicago's greater need for them. "There are so many people in London who both care very much and know how to work, while here we as yet are both few and ignorant," she told Gow. But Gow resisted. She felt that her family, by which she probably meant her parents, since she was unmarried, were her "nearest" duty. Her duty to the poor came second. Addams minced no words in rebutting that tired defense. The settlement work, she told Gow, was the "higher" claim. Later, as Addams was saying good-bye to Gow, she returned to the question of Gow's future, and this time she bore in mercilessly. "She said," Gow wrote, "perhaps I should find it on my conscience when I got away that I had not undertaken to help Chicago's poor." It was a full court press worthy of Count Tolstoy. Gow felt guilty. From New York City she wrote Addams a long letter reiterating her reasons for refusing the offer.[40]

Addams's response to Gow's resistance was revealing. Gow's loyalty to the family claim, the very morality Addams from which had struggled to free herself, aroused something fierce in Addams that she could not control—a desire to rescue Gow from making her own earlier mistake. There must have been many women who stirred this feeling. A few months later, in the summer of 1897, the person she tried to rescue was Mary Rozet Smith.

That summer Smith was wrestling with life's larger questions of purpose and personal commitment and leaning toward the same choice Addams had tried at first: the pursuit of self-improvement. She was twenty-seven years old, with her twenty-eighth birthday approaching in December—just the age Addams had been when she left for her second trip to Europe. Few besides Addams knew it, but Smith, too, suffered from depression, which she called "my melancholy." Whether as a side effect or as a cause of her sadness, Mary felt she had yet to find a purpose for her life in the way that Jane Addams had. Or, rather, the purpose she had been given, that of taking care of her parents, was not the deeply satisfying purpose for which she longed. She might have found a cause to serve, as many other residents had, by living at Hull House instead of only volunteering there, but the duty she felt toward her parents (or the duty they insisted that she honor) kept her living at home. Frustrated and depressed, with her own grand tour of Europe behind her, Mary was reaching a crisis point.[41]

She and Jane apparently had some long conversations about her morose restlessness and her plan to seek more education. To Addams, this plan bore all the signs of a major mistake, but when she tried to talk Mary out of it one night, Mary, struggling to assert herself in a relationship in which she felt herself the less accomplished person, refused to discuss it. Addams returned home frustrated. The next morning she sat down and wrote Mary a letter, unable to stop herself from insisting—even as she knew she should not—that her friend listen to her good advice.

July 22, 1897
Darling,
    I suppose that one of the hardest things one has to learn in life is that one's experiences (even the bitterest ones) are of no use to anyone else.

But I do find it hard that you insist upon repeating the self-same mistakes I made over and over again until I caught a clue at Hull House. The Medical College, the summer I did all the housework at Cedarville, my sheep farming, my studying languages and "art" in Europe . . . , would really seem less bitter to me to remember if I felt they had been of use to the person I love best. I really don't think you ought to put aside all my experience as of no avail—I could make a wild plea if you would only let me—and I don't think "withdrawing from [my] influence" is the most logical way of settling it.

Of course, "everybody approves" just as they would approve your staying at home or any other thing that was conventional or approximated it—but the heart knowest its own bitterness—and if you would just let me guide you and love you and cooperate with you I know I could be of use.

[What] I resist . . . is the fact that you are going [on] the wrong track— that one cannot go to school ever content—at 28 one begins to grapple with the thing itself or is unhappy. Do believe me, darling, and let me help you for once really and truly. I am not cross or anything but longing to do for you perhaps the one thing I am best able to do.

I am always and unchangingly yours,

J.A.

Why is it that the gift a person most longs to give another is never the gift that is wanted? Addams's letter captures fully the anguish she felt because the person she loved "best in the world" insisted on going her own way and learning her own lessons. Addams knew experience could not teach secondhand but she went down fighting, her heart refusing to listen to her mind.

Whether Mary kept to her plan is not known, but in the decades to come the broad outline of her life remained as it was. She lived at home, even after her parents' deaths, visited Hull House for days or weeks at a time, and remained Jane Addams's devoted life partner. She also would prove Hull House's truest friend. A fellow trustee of the Hull House Association, Louise deKoven Bowen, remembered on the association's fortieth birthday, "Without [Mary Rozet Smith], the settlement could never have prospered as it has. She has stood by it, worked in it, supported its causes and contributed to every department. She [rarely missed] a dramatic [or] musical performance. . . . [W]henever a 'down and out' in the neighborhood needed . . . [help], she was the one to respond."[42]

Mary's friendship with Jane would become her true vocation, at what sacrifice only Mary knew. Down the years she would help Jane stay in touch with her best self. In the opinion of Marcet Haldeman-Julius, Alice's daughter, Mary's "depths of sensitivity and consideration . . . brought [the same qualities] to the surface in Jane." And she thought it was Mary, more than anyone else, who kept Jane grounded with her gentle, constructive criticisms. "For this service Jane Addams was thoroughly grateful," Marcet noted, because "she [knew] the unreality that lurks along the highways of fame." Addams believed as early as 1896 that her friendship with Smith was essential to her happiness. "She is so good to me," she wrote Alice, "that I would find life a different thing without her." And Mary felt the same. She wrote Jane the same year, "You can never know what it is to me to have had you and to have you now."[43]

By 1896 Addams was an experienced political activist, having lobbied legislators and spoken in public on behalf of labor legislation and municipal reform, but she had not worked for women to gain the vote. Meanwhile, as her fame as a reformer had spread, the leaders of the revitalized suffrage movement had itched to recruit her to their cause. Susan B. Anthony, president of the National-American Woman's Suffrage Association, which had an upcoming convention, wrote Addams in December 1895, "I would love to hear you give the argument for woman's enfranchisement from the standpoint of your Hull House work."[44] If she could not come this year, Anthony wrote, perhaps she could come the next.

In 1897 suffrage supporters devised a new strategy to draw Addams into their camp. After learning that she would be giving her speech about the Pullman Strike in Boston in February, they decided to organize a large reception in her honor. Addams accepted the invitation. At the gathering, Mary Livermore, the seasoned suffrage campaigner who had impressed John Addams when she had addressed the Illinois General Assembly back in 1869, spoke for many there when she told the group, "I am glad [Jane Addams] is interested in suffrage."[45]

Why did Addams decide to join the suffrage campaign in 1897? Certainly the campaign against Powers in 1896 had shown her that women needed the vote to have credibility in politics and that reformers needed women's votes to defeat political opponents. Indeed, Anthony had made the second point to Addams in the same December 1895 letter. During the aldermanic campaign the previous spring, Anthony had visited Chicago and met with the anti-Powers Hull House Men's Club. She now wrote, "Have those men had the thought enter their noodles yet that women could . . . help . . . them provided they had the ballot in their hands?"[46] Addams's decision to fight for suffrage may also have been partly prompted by her new feminist consciousness, expressed to Rockford's graduates in 1895, that women were ruled by a code as harsh as a military court martial. And, finally, there was her newfound fortitude to resist the authority of at least certain great men.

Because Tolstoy had endorsed women's suffrage, resistance to his authority on that point, at least, was not necessary. In brief remarks at the Boston suffrage reception, Addams shared Tolstoy's observations that it was strange that most American women were not voting yet and that Christ would have favored women's suffrage. This was "impressive," she told the audience, "coming as it did from a great genius, and a man . . . determined on finding out . . . the thing that was right to be done."

In the rest of her remarks she argued the case for women's suffrage in the most pragmatic terms—that women needed civic experiences in order to develop as citizens. Women have civic duties, she argued; these cannot be "cast off." How can the nation expect women to recognize these duties if they have no real responsibility? "It is hard to hold to our ethics unless we can put them into practice. . . . If we do not act on" our civic duties, she said, they "tend to slip away and become intangible. . . . [W]e do not want the civic side of our nature to become intangible."[47] It was a good description of the process by which she had discovered her own civic side, not by pondering ethical duties in the abstract, as she was so inclined to do, but by engaging in the messy business of influencing policymaking. She who had once been deeply doubtful that a settlement of women could play a civic role was now fully persuaded that women of every class could be politically as well as socially active citizens.

Jane Addams's public embrace of women's suffrage was news. The organizers of the reception, delighted with her endorsement, placed an item in the national women's rights periodical, the *Woman's Journal*, and the *Boston Globe* also ran a story, which led, "Jane Addams has been lionized by the philanthropists and reformers of all kinds and degrees since she came to Boston. . . . Yesterday . . . the suffragists claimed her." Back in Cedarville, however, people were not as happy. A few weeks after her trip, she visited her family and reported back to Alice, without mentioning names, "The good folk seemed quite disturbed about the suffragist meeting."[48] Apparently they had read about it in the newspapers and felt as some of her neighbors on Halsted Street had felt when she took the garbage inspector's position—that women should not be doing the kinds of things generally reserved for men.

Addams's appearance at the Boston reception marked the beginning of her long involvement in the women's suffrage campaign. She would bring her cross-class perspective to a suffrage movement split over the question of whether poor, illiterate immigrants of either sex ought to have the vote. Many ardent supporters of suffrage, among them the chair of the National-American Woman's Suffrage Association's field work office, Carrie Chapman Catt, felt that women needed the vote to balance the "slum" influence. And some, including Elizabeth Cady Stanton, former president of NAWSA, were willing to endorse a literacy test for voters. Addams disassociated herself from the stance against immigrants and unskilled workers; she built her pro-suffrage argument on the need for all women to engage in reforming the nation. In 1904 she wrote, "[A]ll kinds of people [have] . . . reservoirs of moral power and civic ability . . . in themselves." She would not exclude any from the right to vote.[49]

Jane Addams would prove a wonderfully effective lobbyist and spokesperson for the suffrage cause. In the years to come, like many other women, she would move it to the top of her agenda, fighting for women's right to vote in Chicago, in Illinois, and across the nation and becoming a vice president of state and national suffrage associations. In 1912, as a member of the Progressive Party's platform committee, she pushed successfully for a women's suffrage plank, and in 1913 she addressed an international congress on women's suffrage in Budapest.[50] Afterwards her work on world peace drew her away from suffrage, but Addams celebrated as much as anyone when the Nineteenth Amendment became law in 1920.

A willingness to disagree was not an obvious part of the repertoire of a cooperator or of a well-bred Victorian woman, yet Addams was discovering that she could not lead a life of moral integrity without it. She had learned that when she differed from others about something important she had to do so firmly, that she could not just "go along," as she had done in the case of applying COS rules to the impoverished clerk. She might seek to understand George Pullman's morality, but she needed to criticize his labor relations; she might honor her father's memory, but she must express her disapproval of his benevolent ethic; she might appreciate John Powers's social ethic and that of his supporters, but she must oppose his reelection. More recently, she had admitted that she disagreed with Tolstoy regarding moral force and had actively insisted that women gain the vote. Experience had taught her that the practice of cooperation had to be constrained by her own developing ethical views and that at times she had to resist hiding those views and, for that matter, resist as well wanting only to sympathize and connect. Her responsibility to act in a way consistent with her beliefs demanded of her this difficult discipline.

Her actions also revealed that organized resistance was acceptable to her when absolutely necessary to achieve justice. Legislative reform, non-violent strikes meant to bring employers to the arbitration table, city politics, and suffrage politics were all oppositional methods she was willing to embrace. The philosophical interpretation of her actions was summed up in the two views Dewey had argued, the first of which was also Caird's: that sometimes opposition between ideas or between institutions produced progress and that the origins of such struggles could be objective conditions, not only personal feelings.

To be sure, she did not explicitly embrace the idea of antagonism. Other than a passing approving reference to "public agitation," one cannot find a passage in her writings of the 1890s that endorses it even though disagreement was an obvious and necessary part of social advancement.[51] Was she failing to endorse antagonism because it contradicted her other views, most notably her nonviolent principles? Perhaps not. She would have been right to draw a distinction between expressing her own beliefs in opposition to someone else's—that is, the practice of moral integrity—and using moral force, which involved trying through active means to influence another person's actions. Furthermore, it was possible to argue that although collective opposition using nonviolent means *did* seek to influence the actions of others, it was ethical because it was democratic.

But if there was no logical contradiction contained in her silence, it amounted to an intellectual and psychological blind spot. As a moral philosopher, her fascination was with the morality of the individual motive, not with the morality or the psychology of broad-based political action, even as her grasp of the latter deepened. In 1892 she probably had individuals in mind when she stated in "Subjective Necessity" that if love "is the principle which binds men together," so "anger and the spirit of opposition [are] the . . . principle[s] that . . . thrust[] men apart."[52] Six years later she had discovered that anger and opposition were not necessarily synony-mous and that the spirit of opposition could unify, but she did not choose to write about what she had learned.

In the years to come Jane Addams would cooperate when she could and strongly oppose when she felt she should and, in both cases, often stir up controversy. Combining firm advocacy with her awareness of the dangers of feeling superior was now the challenge. The sustained moral practice to which she was aspiring was enigmatic: to live out her beliefs firmly and at the same time to find the humility needed to avoid the pitfall of self-righteousness.

CHAPTER 16

ETHICS

1898–99

When the year 1898 opened, most of Jane Addams's efforts for women's suffrage still lay ahead of her. Indeed, she had yet to undertake nearly all of the reform work on which her later reputation as a leading reformer would be based. As of early 1898, she had never lobbied Congress or advised a president. Nor did she belong to any national organizations. Although she had acquired a widespread fame from her speeches and related news coverage, the nation's readers had access to only a few published writings by her. These were her two *Forum* articles (which had also been published in a book of essays), "The Settlement as a Factor" (her essay in *Maps*), one essay on domestic service in an academic journal, and a few odd printings of excerpts from speeches, mostly in religious publications.

But Addams was about to enter a new stage in her work and achieve a new level of national prominence. In part, this was a result of the changing mood of the times. Left-leaning urban reformers, encountering resistance from conservative state supreme courts and state legislatures and desiring to standardize reforms across state lines, saw the federal government as a possible solution. They were ready to seize the national stage.[1] Addams would join in the coming profusion of efforts to better coordinate state campaigns and to pass federal legislation.

Addams's increasing influence and prominence also grew out of her gift for addressing compelling social and moral questions and her developing talent for putting her ideas into national circulation. In 1898 and 1899 five major national journals and magazines would publish her articles about municipal corruption, labor unions, charity, and settlements, and she would begin to amalgamate her thinking into a series of integrated lectures that would become a book. In these years her devotion to a life of combined political action and writing and her profound commitment to moral integrity would shape her into an activist philosopher (or was it a philosophical activist?) of the first rank.

In 1898 John Powers was up for reelection. Doggedly, Hull House and the Nineteenth Ward Improvement Club, again under the guidance of the Nineteenth Ward Municipal Voters League, reentered the political lists, backing the Republican candidate, Simeon Armstrong. The club organized Armstrong supporters in every precinct of the ward. Nervous, Powers fought hard and dirty in the weeks leading up to the April election. He complained to the Civil Service Commission that garbage inspector Amanda Johnson was politicking against him, but the commission found Johnson innocent of the charge. Then he arranged to have Johnson's position reclassified as a political appointment and had one of his friends, a saloonkeeper in the ward, named to replace her. In an interview with a reporter from *Outlook* magazine in March, Powers promised, "Hull House will be driven from the ward and its leaders will be forced to shut up shop."[2]

Always interested in the ethical dimension, Addams had continued to ponder the morality of those in the pro-Powers camp. In January she made a major speech to the Chicago chapter of the Ethical Culture Society about the appeal of corrupt urban politicians to unskilled, low-income voters titled "Ethical Survivals in City Immorality: A Study of Aldermen"; it was published a few months later in the society's organ, the *International Journal of Ethics*. Some thought it the best thing she had ever written.[3]

The speech was an expanded version of the speech she gave about Powers in 1896, but the new version incorporated her theory that ethics could become out-of-date. The theory was proving to hold the key to all her moral puzzles. The ward voters who support Powers, she noted, are mostly immigrant men whose morals arise from their backgrounds as peasants in Ireland and Italy. They want protection and kindness, not justice, and are eager to admire a "good man." To such voters, she said, the argument that they should embrace the "notion of civic purity" is ineffective. "What headway can [such notions] . . . make against this big manifestation of human friendliness, this stalking survival of village kindness?" She called their morality "primitive," by which she meant "old-fashioned." It had lingered too long in times for which it was ill-suited.[4]

Addams also took seriously Powers's appeal as a supplier of material benefits. She knew a young man, she wrote, who had earned only twenty-eight dollars in nine months and was in debt for thirty-two dollars. When he told her he was disappointed that he had only been paid two dollars for his vote, she fell silent, gripped by the knowledge that the young man faced temptations she never had faced. And she told of the Italian day laborer who, wanting a job, must choose "between obeying the commands of a political boss [and] practical starvation." In "Ethical Survivals" Addams dealt frankly with the fact that democracy operated on the street as a distributor of crucial economic resources. She now thoroughly grasped, as she puts it in *Twenty Years*, "the interdependence of matter and spirit."[5]

Addams did not call in the speech for Powers or his voters to change their morality; rather, she asked her middle-class audience to learn a moral lesson from the man whose morality horrified them. Because we live in a democracy, she argued, we must imitate Powers in "obtain[ing] a like sense of identification" with the people. We must realize, she wrote, that we share a common human nature. It was the point she had made in "A Modern Lear," now explicitly linked to democracy. In a democracy, she was arguing, middle- and upper-class citizens had a responsibility not only to fathom the "primitive" views of working-class people and avoid sitting in judgment of them but also to somehow incorporate those views into their own evolving, shared, democratic ethic. A few years later, when she reworked parts of this speech into a new essay, she was blunter. "Perhaps a corrupt politician . . . is on a more ethical line of social development than the reformer," she observed, because the politician is "democratic in method," while the reformer believes that "the people must be made over by 'good citizens' and governed by 'experts.'" Reviewing the question in 1912, she called the valuing of the philanthropist's "smaller good" more highly than the politician's "larger good" a "subtle self-righteousness."[6]

The calm, contemplative tone of "Ethical Survivals" was also remarkable. Addams wrote the speech in the campaign headquarters on Halsted Street, yet it reads as if it were written in the quiet of a professor's study. One of the most striking aspects of Jane Addams's mature philosophy was that it was forged in the midst of an often brutal daily reality. This was certainly true during the 1898 campaign, as Powers's supporters turned vicious. Addams received many anonymous, vitriolic, and sometimes obscene letters from Powers's supporters. Looking at the situation from their point of view, she understood the source of their anger. Such letters, she writes in *Twenty*

Years, were examples of "that animosity which is evoked only when a man feels that his means of livelihood is threatened."[7]

For the final push before voting day, Tuesday, April 5, Hull House attempted its first political mailing. Rather inconveniently and no doubt intentionally, the city did not make the new voter registration lists public until Thursday, March 31. A new settlement resident, Alice Hamilton, wrote her cousin, "Between then and Saturday evening we must fold and put in envelopes and address and stamp twelve thousand appeals to voters! Imagine it! We expect to work until midnight every night."[8]

Despite this Herculean effort, Powers's triumph on Election Day was dramatic. He earned 5,450 votes to Armstrong's 2,219 and was returned to his seat on the City Council. Addams, according to Alice Hamilton, was "bitterly disappointed" at the result. During the campaign she had begun to hope that they might actually defeat Powers. Meanwhile, she and several other friends were in debt, having spent a total of $1,200 of their own money on campaign costs. Mary Rozet Smith insisted on paying $200 of the $325 Addams had spent, but Addams thought, according to Hamilton, that she would still need to "do a lot of lecturing to make both ends meet."[9]

Addams was not the only one pinching pennies at Hull House that year. Dr. Harriet Rice, the black physician who had been a resident at Hull House since 1893, was also struggling to support herself. An ambitious professional woman, Rice had no interest in the kinds of medical work that Addams and others at Hull House were in the best position to offer and thought the most important: providing health care to the poor. Rice's resistance made no sense to Addams. In her dealings with Rice, her sympathetic imagination failed her. The likely reasons why are revealing.

Rice's antipathy for serving the poor had first become apparent in 1893, when she was staffing the settlement's public dispensary and caring for its mostly immigrant clients. Addams wrote heatedly to Mary Rozet Smith, "[Rice] makes . . . us indignant by her utter refusal to do anything for the sick neighbors even when they are friends of the House." Nor did Rice want to practice medicine among poor black people living elsewhere in the city. In 1895, Addams and Lathrop suggested that she work at the new Provident Hospital, which had been founded to provide medical care to

African Americans, including those with severely limited means, but to their consternation, Rice refused.[10]

It seems likely that her reasons for not wanting to practice charity medicine related to her ambition. Born in Newport, Rhode Island, to an upper-working-class family with fierce aspirations, she attended Wellesley College and the best of the nation's medical schools that were open to women, the University of Michigan and the Woman's Medical College of the New York Infirmary for Women and Children, to qualify herself to compete with the best of the white professional middle class. She must have been eager to show what her race could do, both as a confirmation of her self-respect and as a way to dispel prejudicial treatment. Proud of her accomplishments, she may have felt distinctly uncomfortable when forced to associate with poor people. To Rice, working among the poor meant returning to that from which her family had only recently escaped. And in fact, economically, she had not moved up. She lived at Hull House, which was in a poor neighborhood, because she could not afford to live elsewhere.

Addams's reasons for not understanding how Rice felt can also be guessed. She apparently expected that, because Rice possessed a B.A. from a prestigious eastern women's college and an M.D.—the two accomplishments Addams had once eagerly sought herself but failed to achieve—she would want to work among the economically disadvantaged in the same helpful spirit as a white, economically secure settlement resident would. Addams's blindness about Rice was the same blindness that had hampered her understanding of the Lincoln Club members. She could not see that an ambitious young person from a working-class background might seek escape at all costs from lower-class associations. In addition, she could not see that when that person was an African American, the stakes were even higher. In sum, Addams did not recognize that her own upper-middle-class upbringing and whiteness gave her an unquestionable social security that no association she might enter into could trump.

This same class blindness also shaped Addams's initial response to an issue much on the minds of African Americans and others in 1898: lynching. It had become a national scandal by the time Addams gave her first speech about it in 1899. Two years later, she expanded her remarks in an article for the *Independent* in which she rejected the "hideous act" of lynching and blamed white people's racism (their "contempt" for those they supposed "inferior") for causing them to pursue illegal, violent means, but she erroneously assumed that the white men's charges—that the lynched black men had raped white women—were true. Her mistake was one that many northern middle-class people, white and black, made. In fact, as her friend the journalist and reformer Ida B. Wells carefully documented for the first time in 1892 and again in the 1901 article she published in the *Independent* in reply to Addams's piece, the southern white women whose cases led to lynchings had willingly entered into cross-race liaisons. The charge of "rape," Wells insisted, was an "old, thread bare lie" and, in any case, only a third of the lynching victims had even been charged with rape. Although Wells was too polite to say so (she was and remained an admirer of Addams's), Addams had uncharacteristically failed to do her homework before going public with her case. Another problem was that Addams, in her piece, seemed to express the belief that the issue of extralegal violence was at least as important as the issue of lynching, an assumption that Wells pointedly rejected.[11]

Although Addams did not fully grasp the complexities of racism in the 1890s, she had long understood racial prejudice to be a crucial social issue. In 1892, at the Plymouth Conference, she pointedly observed, "We are quite unmoved by the fact that [the Negro] lives among us in a practical social ostracism." The origins of her awareness of the issue seem to lie in her father's opposition to slavery and perhaps, in particular, to her brief encounter in her father's house when she was not yet four years old with a man who had escaped slavery. She had perhaps thought more about the social aspects of racism while doing volunteer work in Baltimore among elderly poor black women and young black women in training for domestic service. But the essential foundation of her thinking was her moral universalism. If all parts of human society should intermingle socially, then African Americans ought to socialize with people of other backgrounds.

Hull House had no real opportunity to serve African Americans in the 1890s given their small numbers in the neighborhood (the situation would change in the twentieth century), but Addams found other things to do. Between 1895 and 1902, she supported the nomination of the first African American woman, Fanny Barrier Williams, to the Chicago Woman's Club; she hosted, with Wells's help, the officers of the National Council of Colored Women at a luncheon at Hull House when it held its biennial meeting in Chicago (this was how Wells met Addams—Addams called her up to ask for her assistance); and she advocated, unsuccessfully, for the National Convention of Women's Clubs to admit African American clubs to their gatherings.[12]

In the twentieth century, as African Americans began to move to Chicago and, in particular, to the West Side in greater numbers, they found their way to Hull House. And Addams remained active in addressing issues of social racism. She was part of the campaign of the Illinois branch of the Niagara Movement to persuade drama critics to refuse to review a new play glorifying the Ku Klux Klan in 1906, was named to the executive committee of the newly formed National Association for the Advancement of Colored People in 1909, and was a member of the Chicago Urban League. In 1912, as a member of the platform committee for the Progressive Party, she vigorously protested Theodore Roosevelt's decision not to seat the African American delegates from several southern states. When the Marines occupied Haiti in 1916, she and others tried to arouse public opinion in support of self-government there.[13] Although she did not understand all the complexities of white privilege, she was committed to a vision of racial equality and was willing to fight for it.

Another resident who was struggling to make ends meet in 1898 was Florence Kelley. In early 1897, after Altgeld failed in his bid for reelection as governor, she lost her appointment as Illinois State Factory Inspector. At one point in the summer of 1898, she hoped to be named to a new federal commission created by Congress to investigate relations between capital and labor and to propose national and state legislation. She and Addams even met with President William McKinley in Washington to promote her candidacy, but nothing came of it. Kelley took an evening job at the John Crerar Library to support herself and her family until, in 1899, her employment requirements and reformer ambitions were fulfilled by a wonderful new job as the general secretary of the new National Consumers' League, located in New York City. In that position, which she would hold until her death in 1932, she marshaled consumers' buying practices to pressure industry to improve working conditions for employees and lobbied for pro-labor state and federal legislation.[14]

Although Kelley was no longer living at Hull House after 1899, she and Addams continued to cooperate on labor issues, and more specifically on raising the minimum age for child workers. Addams did not cease her efforts to improve the Illinois state law, but her interest, like Kelley's, was being increasingly drawn toward working at the national level. She and others had realized, she writes in *Twenty Years*, that local and state regulation of sweatshops could not work unless jurisdictions across the United States passed and enforced a uniform law. Addams, as chair of the Child Labor Committee of the General Federation of Women's Clubs, guided an ambitious study of child labor legislation in all the states to document the variety of laws. The findings were used by the National Child Labor Committee, a new organization that she and Florence Kelley helped found in 1904, to seek better state laws and a federal minimum age law. Despite the fierce opposition of industry, Congress eventually passed two federal laws and a constitutional amendment banning labor for children under sixteen but, each time, the accomplishment was short-lived. The U.S. Supreme Court declared both laws unconstitutional, and the constitutional amendment was never ratified by enough states. The labor of children under sixteen would not be banned nationally until the passage of the Fair Labor Standards Act in 1938, three years after Addams's death.[15] The urban democratic wing of the progressive movement waged one of its most difficult fights in the extended struggle for child labor reform.

Long interested in working people and in unions, Addams had been endorsing their concerns and their contributions to society for several years; she had not, however, previously spoken about what might be done to improve the situation of unskilled workers and those without unions. She took this next step in a speech she gave to the annual meeting of the General Federation of Women's Clubs in 1898, when she argued that the government should protect workers without unions from unfair working conditions and invoked her theory of the dangers of belated ethics to support her case. It was also her first observation on record about how to think philosophically about the government's responsibilities; her voice is that of a confident progressive. "We would not have the state remain motionless, enchained to the degree of civilization attained at the moment the state was founded," she admonished. Twelve years later, she set forth an even stronger argument for government action, one that derived from the old republican theory of government. "The very existence of the State depends on the character of its citizens," she wrote. Therefore, the state has a "right" to regulate "industrial conditions that are forcing . . . workers to live below the standard of decency."[16]

The work that Illinois women had done to support women's unions also went national in the early twentieth century. In 1903 Addams and Mary McDowell assisted their old friend, Mary Kenney O'Sullivan, in launching the Women's Trade Union League, the first national body dedicated to orga-

Jane Addams giving a speech, 1905. Neg. ICHi-29408, Chicago Historical Society.

nizing women workers. They were tired of trying to persuade male union leaders to take up the cause. The WTUL, with its headquarters in Chicago, was a cross-class organization in the tradition of the Illinois Woman's Alliance; its executive board was designed to ensure that working women always dominated the leadership. It quickly became a major force through its national office and its state branches. Addams became vice president of the Illinois WTUL.[17] She had come a long way since the day fifteen years earlier when she had attended the match girls' union organizing meeting in London and not quite understood what was going on.

In her national undertakings, as much as in her neighborhood-, municipal-, and state-level work, Addams practiced her theory of cooperation. To her this was as much about the frame of mind with which she approached a conversation as it was about joining groups or going to meetings. Cooperation meant, for example, being willing to work on issues of concern to those whose life circumstances made them experts on the problem. In

Twenty Years, Addams observes that "social change can only be inaugurated by those who feel the unrighteousness of the contemporary conditions."[18] Cooperation meant asking how she could help and believing that groups should make collective decisions about matters directly affecting their lives, whether those groups were residents, club members, union members, or citizens. Cooperation was about stepping back, creating space, but also about connecting with others' hopes and moving forward with a collectively determined agenda.

By necessity, the cooperative way of working included a willingness to set aside any desire for personal accomplishment. The point was mostly implicit in Addams's method, but it was explicit in a lyrical passage in "A Modern Lear" that, although it does not mention cooperation, both highlighted the need to sacrifice personal goals in working with others and summed up all that she understood the theory of cooperation to mean. What "the man who insists upon consent, who moves with the people" attains, she wrote, "is not the result of his individual striving" but something "upheld by the sentiments and aspirations of many others." She believed that this humility was required of a Christian and knew it was very hard to attain. "To give up the consciousness of one's own . . . achievements," she observed in 1901, "is perhaps the hardest demand which life can make upon us but certainly those who call themselves Christian . . . should be ready to meet the demand."[19] We may readily doubt that she achieved such obliviousness on a daily basis but not that she was aspiring in that direction.

Christianity certainly taught her this. Jesus Christ admonished that if a man follows him, "he who has found his own life will lose it, but the man who has lost it for my sake will find it." But the lesson had come to her repeatedly from all sides. Other great philosophers and spiritual leaders across time whose writings Addams had read had similarly urged men and women to suppress pride in self and to sense their deep unity with something larger of which they were a small part. Her favorite deist, Emerson, in his essay "The Over-Soul," warned that weakness and blindness begin "when the individual would be something of himself." Rather, he said, each should "let the soul have its way" through him. Here the passionate advocate of self-reliance was the spokesperson for the wisdom of corporate consciousness. And Emerson's and Addams's favorite Roman philosopher, Marcus Aurelius, taught the same: "Follow your nature and the common nature; and the way of both is one." The idea she was trying to describe went beyond the shallow confines of Victorian etiquette; it was something profound and mysterious, even eternal.[20]

———————

On April 28, 1898, Robert Woods, Jane Addams's settlement colleague in Boston, mused to her in a letter, "I wonder if you are managing to be patriotic about the War."[21] Nine days earlier, Congress, not having forgotten the destruction in February of the battleship *Maine* in Havana Harbor, had authorized military intervention to liberate Cuba from Spain's colonial rule. On April 23, Spain had declared war on the United States. A week later, just days after Woods wrote his letter, the United States Navy attacked and destroyed a Spanish naval fleet in Manila Bay, the Philippines. Ostensibly, by declaring war, the United States was merely supporting the Cuban and Philippine revolutions that had broken out earlier in the decade; in fact, its goal was to take control of the economic resources of Spain's nearby colonial islands. Thus did the United States, which had not fought an external enemy since the war with Mexico in 1846, join the European colonization movement then under way and become a colonial power.

Addams, like many Americans, was deeply troubled by the Spanish-American War. As someone committed to avoiding all use of force and to promoting cooperation, she could not have been otherwise. More profoundly, the war's outbreak made death, her lifelong nemesis, her government's official foreign policy. She could not stand by and do nothing. Opposing the national government's foreign policy, however, was not something she had ever done before. Troubled, she leaned on Tolstoy for strength. His view that government and force were synonymous, which she sometimes mentioned in her lectures about him, took on a new meaning for her in the spring and summer of 1898. As always, she found his fierce integrity a dauntingly high standard to match. In October, after attending a peace rally in Boston, Addams wrote Mary Rozet Smith that she was feeling "quite blue, not play blue but real depths," and concluded, "I will have to become more of a Tolstoyan or less of one right off."[22]

Addams took her first public stance against the war in a speech delivered in December 1898 on the settlement movement. She gave her first speech against the war the following April in Chicago at an anti-imperialism rally. She sat on the stage with several of her friends in the reform movement, including Judge Murray Tuley and Mary Wilmarth. A printed version of her speech, her first published writing about peace, appeared in *Unity Magazine* a few days later under the title "What Peace Means." Calling peace a "rising tide of moral feeling," she urged that it "engulf all pride of conquest and mak[e] war impossible." Workingmen, she said, were the first internationalists, and she cited their "growing conviction" that war leads to such antidemocratic developments as militarism and standing armies. Nor, she added, does imperialism advance civilization; rather, it undermines it. National events stemming from imperialism, she warned, "determine our ideals as much as our ideals determine national events."[23]

The grassroots anti-imperialist movement Addams had joined did not, like Addams, advocate nonviolence but rather self-government for all peoples and an end to militarism. A resolution adopted at the April meeting stated, "We insist that the forcible subjugation of a . . . people" amounts to "open disloyalty to the distinctive principles of our government[;] . . . that all men are entitled to life, liberty and the pursuit of happiness." The following fall the American Anti-Imperialist League was founded at a conference in Chicago. Addams continued to make speeches, and when World War I broke out in August 1914, she and twelve hundred other women marched down Fifth Avenue in New York City to demonstrate their opposition.[24]

From the march grew an effort to organize a women's peace conference and a new political party. In January 1915 members of a number of women's organizations gathered in Washington, D.C., to create the Women's Peace Party, and they elected Jane Addams chair. Notably, the party's platform was not limited to the war; it set forth a broadly feminist agenda. It demanded that women have a share in decisions about war and peace at home, in the industrial order, and within the state. The Women's Peace Party worked for peace behind the scenes during the war; when the war ended in 1918, the party and its work were absorbed into a new organization, the Women's International League for Peace and Freedom. Jane Addams was elected president. From then until her death, despite occasional severe persecution, she would do all she could through the WILPF to advance the cause of world peace and would be awarded the Nobel Peace Prize in 1931 in recognition of her efforts.[25]

In 1898, the explosion of national reform efforts lay in the future, but there were already signs of what was to come. The formation of the National Municipal League in 1894 had been one indicator of the reformers' widening angle of perception. In 1897, 1898, and 1899, new efforts constitutive of the nation's emerging progressive agenda were launched.

The first effort came from the labor movement. In Chicago in 1897 Eugene Debs tried to convert the old membership of the American Railway Union into a new, more politically oriented, equally radical organization called the Social Democracy of America whose goal was "a new cooperative order." Debs's hope was to lead a labor-based, third-party, populist political movement, but not enough workers were passionate about his approach and the effort was short-lived. [26]

The next was a purely educational effort with a Christian tinge. In August 1898 Dr. Josiah Strong organized a group of ministers, editors, writers, and others into the League for Social Service. Its purpose was to gather information about ways to achieve "the social betterment of humanity" from organizations guided by the Golden Rule (this is Jesus Christ's admonishment, "Do unto others as you would have them do unto you") and disseminate it via leaflets, a bureau of information, and a lecture bureau. Jane Addams was named to the advisory council, along with the Reverend Washington Gladden, the Reverend Edward Everett Hale, and Bishop John H. Vincent of Chautauqua, among many others. Strong was named president. [27] While the league had no political agenda, it was committed to local reform and to finding strength through coordination of knowledge at the national level.

A month later in San Francisco the social Christians organized their effort to unify and educate—the Union Reform League. In its membership and its agenda this league combined the socialist political tendencies of Debs's group and the Christian motive of Strong's. Its leadership included the Reverend George Herron, William Dean Howells, and the Reverend W. D. P. Bliss, who would shortly become its president. Its goals were to use educational and grassroots organizing methods to unite "the reform forces in the United States" in a "widespread movement" to achieve direct legislation, public ownership of utilities, and other reforms called for by the 1896 platform of the Populist Party as well as to oppose militarism. [28]

Meanwhile, plans for a national conference on social reform were brewing. Supporters of various reform movements, including those of the direct legislation movement, which had been pushing for much of the 1890s for states to adopt initiative and referendum laws, sought an opportunity to meet fellow radical reformers (their term) and discuss what to do next. They formed a general committee that eventually numbered 71 men and women, including W. D. P. Bliss, Henry Demarest Lloyd, and Jane Addams.[29] The National Conference on Social and Political Reform took place in late June 1899 in Buffalo, New York. Four hundred reformers came, from single-taxers, to prohibitionists, to direct legislation advocates, to socialists, to settlement house leaders, to trade unionists, to monometalists, to populists; those attending represented Judaism, Catholicism, and Protestantism. Addams signed the "call" to the conference and was hoping to attend but stayed in Chicago instead to work on the lectures for the University of Chicago extension course she would begin teaching on July 5.[30]

The conference had several results. The first was a statement of principles issued on the last day of the meeting that endorsed a number of specific reforms and, more broadly, "a free, just and progressive society." The second was a rebirth of Bliss's group, the Reform League Union, as the Social Reform Union. Ostensibly educational, its underlying agenda was political—to unify reform forces in order to apply political pressure on the democratic candidate for the presidency in 1900. Accordingly, the Social Reform Union adopted a five-plank progressive platform: (1) direct legislation and proportional representation, (2) public ownership of public utilities, (3) direct taxation of franchises, inheritances, and incomes, (4) issuance of money by government only and regulation of the quantity, and (5) antimilitarism. Serving as vice presidents and on the new national committee, which represented every state, were such people as Henry Demarest Lloyd, Eugene Debs, Florence Kelley, George Herron, John Altgeld, Booker T. Washington, and William Dean Howells.[31] The founding of the Social Reform Union was the strongest signal yet that left-wing progressives were determined to flex their collective political muscle on a national scale.

By 1898 Addams was ready, after nine years of intense education, to try to pull together her thoughts by writing something longer than a speech or an essay. Being an inveterate lover of books, she had probably also dreamed of writing one for a long time. She indirectly confessed to the ambition when she wrote Henry Demarest Lloyd in 1894 that she had "a great deal of respect for anyone who writes a good book." She took a step toward her goal when she accepted the invitation of George Herron, a Christian socialist minister and college professor, to give a lecture series at Iowa (later Grinnell) College in late February and early March.[32] The series proved to be the precipitating assignment she needed to undertake a larger intellectual project: to rework her speeches of the 1890s into a textbook for use in college and adult education courses. She would gather up the fragmented lessons of her years on Halsted Street, wrap her philosophical mind around them, and fit them into a common analytical framework. The result, which she would publish three years later, was a book that not only explored the ways morality was shaped but provided a testament to her own journey, missing only the ever-elusive "I."

For the Iowa College lecture series, she chose "ethical survivals" for her unifying theme. She was now seeing examples of out-of-date ethics everywhere and was more convinced than ever of the damage they did. "[O]bsolete" ideas, she explained in her introductory lecture, perpetuated "a great deal of wrong" because people held onto them for too long. She elaborated on the subject in four lectures whose topics were charitable organizations, municipal corruption, the Pullman Strike, and the labor movement. The fifth lecture was on Tolstoy's "social philosophy," a subject she found so irresistible that she included it even though it did not fit her theme. [33]

In the following months, she would continue to play with the theme. That summer she tried out "Legalized and Non-Legalized Social Ethics" when she and Florence Kelley did a joint lecture series using that title at the Chautauqua Institution, America's most popular summer educational venue. In the summer of 1899, when she gave a twelve-lecture course in the University of Chicago Extension Program, she essayed a third theme and title, calling the course "Democracy and Social Ethics." In the fall she gave a revised version in Davenport, Iowa. [34]

Democracy was the best choice yet. The theme of ethical survivals emphasized the human capacity to resist change; the theme of democracy emphasized the human capacity to change, or, to say the same thing differently, the first theme was about the past's lingering influence, the second about the untapped potential of the future. Democracy was also a good choice because the idea had long been important to her, even if she had been unsure when she first came to Halsted Street how to put it into action. Thinking of herself at that time, she later recalled how "literature and our own hopes . . . supply . . . hints . . . of a larger . . . democracy," but those hints "slip away from us and . . . leave us sadly . . . perplexed when we attempt to act on them." [35]

By 1899 she was less perplexed. For her the word "democracy" had become infused with memories of the blood, sweat, tears, and laughter of organized workers; of the delight of club women on discovering they could

Jane Addams, writing. Illinois State Historical Library, Springfield, IL.

have political influence; of hopeful train rides to Springfield to lobby for
sweatshop and child labor reform legislation; of the youthful idealism of
the members of the Lincoln Club and the Men's Club; of the fiery debates
of the Working People's Social Science Club; of Florence Kelley's skillful
political maneuvers; of grueling hours spent following garbage wagons; of
mass meetings of thousands of shouting Chicagoans calling for an end to
corruption in city government; of a reawakened passion for women's suffrage; and of long nights of folding, addressing, and stamping campaign
circulars. Now democracy meant not only citizens mingling socially but
also citizens working together to improve unjust conditions. She might
have written a book about those cooperative efforts, but instead, moral
philosopher that she was, she wrote about democracy's impact on morality.

Although *Democracy and Social Ethics* would not be published until
1902, it had essentially come together in structure, theme, and content
by 1899.[36] She organized the book around six pairs of human relation-

ships: those of the charity worker and the beneficiary, the parent and the adult daughter, the household employer and the servant, the industrial employer and the employee, the educator and the adult student, and the corrupt politician and the ward voter. Drawing on ideas from earlier speeches on these subjects, she traced for each relationship the ways that the old individualistic and out-of-date morality was evolving under the pressures of democracy into a new social humanitarian, or democratic, one. *Democracy and Social Ethics* is the most definitive examination Addams ever undertook of the process of moral formation.

The broad theme of democracy's impact on the individual's and society's morality is laid out in the book's gemlike introduction. It is gemlike not in the firmness of its argument, which, in fact, is Emersonian in its evocative, loose circularity, but in its sentences, which sparkle with condensed wisdom. Her most striking observation relates to finding a morality that is useful in life. High ideals or motives, she declares, are not enough; one must also undertake the work in the right way. "We slowly learn that life consists of processes . . . , and that failure may come quite as easily from ignoring the adequacy of one's method as from selfish or ignoble aims." Then she applies the insight to democracy. We are "brought to [understand] Democracy [as] not merely a sentiment which desires the well-being of all men, nor yet . . . a creed which believes in the essential dignity and equality of all men, but . . . [as] a rule of living . . . [and] a test of faith."[37] She spoke not as a historian but as a prophet, as one who sought to create a new reality by asserting her vision as truth.

Her former theme, which was that loyalty to old ethical ideas could block progress, remained as a subtext of each chapter. In the introduction, she boldly applies the idea to the ethical development of her own class, expanding on the criticism she had first made of George Pullman. Some people, she writes, share "the conviction that they are different from other men and women, that they need peculiar consideration because they are more sensitive or more refined." She is, of course, describing herself in 1889. In an essay written in 1901 she elaborates more boldly. The prosperous class's lingering out-of-date ethic, she declares, is an "aristocratic attitude" that is "founded upon a contempt for the inferior class" and a pervasive admiration for itself.[38]

Now the complete pragmatist, she asks herself what experiences might produce such an unlovely result. The crucial ones, she writes, are social. When people spend time only with those who love and admire them or only with those who agree with their political opinions or share their religious beliefs, they are likely to feel superior to those outside their small circle whom they do not know. When we "consciously limit our intercourse to certain kinds of people whom we have previously decided to respect," she explains, we grow "contemptuous" of our fellow human beings.[39] It was her old point, of course, that it was not good, that it was undemocratic, to live a life of isolation within one's own class, but her analysis of the reasons why had deepened since 1889. Such isolation, she argues, is not only a violation of the ideal of human unity; it does moral damage to the soul.

By what process, she asks, do people break free of this trap? Her answer is that they should practice social democracy. They should widen their "acquaintance with . . . the life around them," should have contact with "the moral experiences of the many," and should find in themselves "a new affinity for all men." She uses two extended metaphors. One is that of taking a journey by foot. A person, she writes, attains a social ethics not by "traveling a sequestered byway" but by "mixing on the thronged and common road, where all [can] . . . at least see the size of one another's burdens." The other metaphor, not surprisingly, is about reading. The task, she writes, is to undertake a "wide reading of human life."[40]

She also urges her readers to embrace cooperation as their method, for two reasons. First, it marshals the best human powers. "[A]ssociated effort towards social progress . . . enlist[s] deeper forces and evoke[s] higher social capacities . . . than efforts managed by a capable individual." Second, it is the best way to learn about people who are different from oneself. She is emphatic about the value of such experience. "[M]ost of the misunderstandings of life are due to partial intelligence, because our experiences have been so unlike that we cannot comprehend each other." With uncharacteristic firmness she admonishes readers: "We are under a moral obligation in choosing our experiences since the result of those experiences must ultimately determine our understanding of life."[41] The sentence states the book's core thesis and the main lesson she learned on Halsted Street.

Who then are the best bearers of democracy's banner? According to Addams, they are working-class union members. Her admiration for them is full-blown in *Democracy*. Union members are "the first class of men," she writes, "to organize an international association, and the constant talk at a modern labor meeting is of solidarity and of the identity of the interests of workingmen the world over." They want to see themselves "in connection and co-operation with the whole." They also revise their ethics to suit the times. Organized workers are the true democrats in the United States, she says, because it is they who are making the "actual attempts at [ethical] adjustment." She is not so impressed with the democratic contributions of the people of her own class. Describing them as "the educated and self-conscious members of the community," she judges them poor democrats indeed. Not only do they "feel perplexed" by the times; they take no action. And why are they so disengaged? The problem, as before, lies in their social isolation within their own class, their passion for individualism, and their snobbery. Addams observes, "[P]eople who are confident of their own inner integrity are often harsh in their judgments of other people." In another essay, also written in 1902, she similarly observes that democracy requires us to cooperate, but "we cannot [cooperate] so long as [one party] sets itself up as superior."[42]

Addams's own initial sense of superiority had been grounded partly in her rarified cultural accomplishments. Perhaps nothing so dramatically marked the significant transformation of her ideas on Halsted Street in the 1890s as her eventual abandonment of that attitude. She now sought to understand humanity as presented in the flesh in the way she had once sought to understand it as presented in literature and the arts. "The cultivated person," she observed in an 1898 speech at the Chautauqua Assembly, "is the one who [uses] his social faculties, his interpretative power, the one who . . . put[s himself] into the minds and experiences of other people." She had elaborated on the same theme earlier that year in Denver. Such a person does not "condemn without a hearing" and has the insight to "interpret aright [a fine] action." She wrote even more expressively in 1904. "What is the human?" she asks. "It is not the cultivated . . . [;] the human is the widespread, the ancient in speech or behavior, it is the deep, the emotional, the thing much loved by many men, the poetic, the organic, the vital." The same profound shift in perspective permeates *Twenty Years*, which she would write eight years after publishing *Democracy*, in 1910. There she again redefines what it means to be cultivated. "The uncultivated person," she writes, "is bounded by a narrow outlook on life, unable to overcome differences in dress and habit, and his interests are slowly contracting within a circumscribed area." The cultivated person is "a citizen of the world because of his growing understanding of all kinds of people and their varying experiences."[43] She was describing herself, of course, but also many of the working people of the Nineteenth Ward.

Perhaps most startling of all, she had come to believe that her condition as a highly cultured person in the earlier sense of the word was not due to her own merit but due to chance. "Intellectual and moral superiority [as some perceive it]," she writes in 1899, "rest upon economic props which are, after all, matters of accident." This was another lesson working-class people had taught her. One of John Powers's fellow machine aldermen, "Bathhouse Johnny" Coughlin, made the same point with more bite when he said, "It don't pay in this world to think you're better than th' next fellow just because you happen to be on top and he ain't."[44]

Addams's new grasp of the hollowness of upper-class claims to superiority recast her understanding of settlement houses as well. Writing in 1911, she recalled "the old phrase . . . we used to use so solemnly twenty-five years ago"—that the settlement was a "bridge across a 'gulf.' " Now, she notes, the settlement "more and more regards itself as a mere center . . . to which people from all parts of town and of all classes of beliefs and traditions may come and may consider together this incongruous life."[45]

Democracy and Social Ethics is written in the first-person plural. Ever the evader of the first-person singular, Addams does not write that she herself had traveled the narrow byway or had viewed her fellow human beings with contempt or that Halsted Street had been her thronged and common road and the Nineteenth Ward her book of life. But she said as much to friends and family. As Weber Linn once observed, she "died in the conviction that Hull House had made her, not that she had made Hull House."[46]

If Addams believed that she owed much to having lived on Halsted Street, this did not mean she took no credit at all for her education. Her contribution, as she saw it, was her determination to interpret her experiences. She repeated this point often in the form of a general principle about the process of moral development. She argues in *Democracy* that "[o]ur conceptions of morality, as all our ideas, pass through a course of adjustment; the difficulty comes in adjusting our conduct, which has become hardened into customs and habits, to these changing moral conceptions. When this adjustment is not made, we suffer from the strain and indecision of believing one hypothesis and acting upon another." A few years later, in *Newer Ideals of Peace* (1907), her second book about democracy, she discusses the dangers of failing to make the adjustment: "[I]t is so easy to commit irreparable blunders because we fail to correct our theories by our changing experience." Her determination to examine her experiences thoroughly was entirely self-conscious. "Our chief concern with the past," she writes in her 1916 book, *The Long Road of Woman's Memory*, "is not what we have done, nor the adventures we have met, but the moral reaction [we have to] bygone events." And perhaps most pungently, she writes in an 1899 work, "There is too much analysis in our thought and too much anarchy in our action."[47]

As Addams took steps in the 1890s that led her more deeply into the complicated, sometimes murky woods of democracy, she repeatedly tried to analyze and understand her often perplexing, sometimes exhilarating, sometimes deeply disturbing experiences. Aided by books, innumerable conversations, and her own writing, she studied those experiences not for an hour or an afternoon but for weeks and months and years, walking around them to see them from all sides, writing and revising her thoughts about them, and generally behaving more like an intellectual bulldog than a genteel lady who wore her learning lightly. It was this persistent rethinking, and not only the experiences, that produced her profoundest insights and taught her the most about her class, her gender, and herself. Addams's love of abstract theory, of sweeping generality, of uplifting philosophy had almost trapped her in her given life of reading, but it was that same passion for larger meaning that drove her to break free of that life, to struggle to integrate her experiences with her thought, and to change her mind.

To say that *Democracy* documents Addams's new understanding is not to say, of course, that she always succeeded afterwards in living by it. Moral, cultural, and class elitism is like white or masculine privilege. When a person is raised in an ethic that confers superiority, her psyche relinquishes it under protest and fitfully. Addams's later writings would contain traces of condescension and benevolence. But beginning in the late 1890s and for the rest of her life, the dominant themes of her work and thought were her abiding respect for working people's democratic political powers and the need for social justice.

Jane Addams's development into a full-fledged citizen was an achievement that she and the world accomplished together, and she would not have had it otherwise. Believing deeply in the ideals of cooperation and democracy, she had turned them into a way of life that brought many rewards. By joining in solidarity with other citizens of all classes, she gained the circle of friends she had longed for, a reform agenda that she worked to advance for the rest of her days, and a deep understanding of the nature of life and of her own humanity.

What many consider the most notable aspect of Jane Addams's life—that she worked not for the interests of her own class but, as it has been commonly put, "for the poor"—heightened her reputation in her own lifetime but has diminished it in ours. To a degree, this interesting shift in her public standing was simply a by-product of history. As American society lost its unexamined trust in white women of wealth and discerned the condescension implicit in their reform methods, it was inevitable that Addams would be transformed from "saint" to sinner. But the unthinking admiration with which she was treated in the decades immediately after her death in 1935 was unhelpful in any case. Addams deserved a closer analysis.

In the mid-1960s, she began to receive it. In essays and other forms of critical analysis, historians, literary critics, and others set aside the usual admiring framework to wrestle with the complicated issues, including those of class, race, ethnicity, gender, and sexuality, raised by Addams's life, work, and writings.

For biography, however, the situation has been different. There has been a smattering of popular biographies of Addams, including one published by her nephew James Weber Linn in 1935 (and a steady flow of juvenile ones). At the same time, scholarly biographies, that is, works that use original research to achieve new interpretations of a life, have been as scarce as hen's teeth. Until 2004 only one, Allen F. Davis's 1973 work, had been published.[1] By the opening years of the twenty-first century, a new scholarly biography of Jane Addams was long overdue.

Addams began her public life in 1889, and by 1910 her activism on behalf of workers, immigrants, women, children, and world peace and her public presence of gentle, inclusive civic-mindedness, conveyed in her many lectures, magazine articles, and books, had earned her the respect and affection of a wide portion of the American public. Although her pacifist stance during World War I and her continued progressivism in the conservative years of the early 1920s undercut that reputation for a time, it was restored in the 1930s, particularly after she received the Nobel Peace Prize in 1931. When she died in 1935, she was once more one of America's most admired women. As late as the centennial of her birth, in 1960, she was as widely admired as Eleanor Roosevelt, with whom she was often compared.[2]

It was the centennial that brought her to historians' attention.[3] In 1960 the left-liberal historian Henry Steele Commager wrote an essay in the *Saturday Review* praising Addams's genius for administration and moral philosophy, and another left-liberal historian, Merle Curti, gave an endowed lecture titled "Jane Addams on Human Nature" at Swarthmore College. These essays soon received wider circulation. Commager's became a short foreword for a new Signet inexpensive paperback edition of *Twenty Years at Hull House*, and Curti's was later published in the *Journal of the History of Ideas*. Also in 1960, the up-and-coming historians Anne Firor Scott and Allen F. Davis, the latter a former student of Curti's, both wrote about Addams's dealings with a Chicago ward boss, one in *American Heritage* and one in a state history journal.[4] All of these pieces took Addams and her work at face value and were written in a tone of warm appreciation.

The fresh interest in Addams also coincided, however, with the emergence of a group of radical, or New Left, historians.[5] The question of the day soon became whether Addams was a radical. Not surprisingly, historians differed regarding the meaning of the term. In 1961 Staughton Lynd tentatively claimed that she gradually became one because of her increasing alienation from society. The following year Daniel Levine, in the essay "Jane Addams: Romantic Radical, 1889–1912,"[6] said she was a radical because of her vision of "an all pervasive welfare state" and her commitment to a "social ethic." Levine was the first to raise the important question of class bias. Although he did not doubt Addams's commitment to the ideal of "social unity," he argued that, unknown to herself, Addams at times "looked with condescension on her neighbors." In an essay that was otherwise overwhelmingly positive in its assessment of Addams, Levine gently sounded the first note of skepticism on a subject that had long needed examination.[7]

Feminism was part of the radical agenda emerging in the early sixties, and it also had an influence on Addams scholarship. In 1963, Anne Firor Scott was the first to raise the important subject of gender in her introductory essay for a new edition of Addams's first book, *Democracy and Social Ethics*. In addition to stressing Addams's contributions as an intellectual, she analyzed Addams's ideas about women and briefly explored her relations with women and men. The following year, Jill Ker Conway, a young graduate student in history at Harvard University, took the gender theme in a different direction. In her essay "Jane Addams: American Heroine," Conway set forth two original theses. The first was that Addams's tremendous fame was the result of her determination to conform her personality to the American definition of "feminine excellence," by which Conway meant "activism and participation in a masculine world" and a determination to "redeem [that world] from the baser masculine passions." The second was that from childhood Addams had possessed an "extreme drive to power."[8] The latter point was a startling one to make about a woman whose modesty and selflessness were much celebrated.

Meanwhile, radical historians remained interested in Addams's radicalness. One was Christopher Lasch, Henry Steele Commager's son-in-law. Elaborating, perhaps, on arguments begun at the dining room table, Lasch entered the debate with a probing biographical essay published in 1965 in his *New Radicalism in America*. He called attention to the previously uncritical treatment the reformer had received at the hands of friends and essayists. "Her admirers," he wrote, without mentioning names, "fabricated . . . their own version of her life, pious and sentimental." Declaring Addams both an intellectual and a radical (which he defined as a person interested in "the reform of education, culture and sexual relations"), he also addressed the issue of class, writing, "[W]hat made the sons and daughters of the middle class so suddenly conscious of conditions they had previously ignored[?]"[9] The answer, he thought, was their desire to rebel against their class and, as in Addams's case, to reject their class's devotion to "the aesthetic principle." Grasping the complex nettle of gender in a second essay, "Woman as Alien," he argued provocatively that the "feminist impulse" was an aspect of that same class revolt. Somewhat contradictorily, he also posited that "feminists" such as Addams were "obsessed" with the idea that a woman who "pursued a masculine ideal . . . had betrayed her own femininity."[10]

Fresh insights about Addams were now plentiful, but there was still only one biography of her, the one by her nephew Weber Linn. The late 1960s, however, saw the publication of two appreciative assessments of her reform ideas wrapped in semibiographical packages. In 1965 John C. Farrell completed his dissertation, which was published two years later as *Beloved Lady: A History of Jane Addams's Ideas on Reform and Peace*. In 1971 Daniel Levine published his *Jane Addams and the Liberal Tradition*, which dealt mainly with Addams's involvement with progressive reforms and politics after 1900. Farrell did not address the question of whether Jane Addams was a radical, but Levine did. She was a radical, he argued, because she was impatient for change.[11]

Finally, in the early 1970s, the historian Allen F. Davis took up the biographical task. Denying that Addams was a "radical" without defining what he meant by the term, he built in other ways on all that had gone before, particularly on Conway's and Lasch's intriguing essays, as well as his own work on the history of settlement house leaders and progressive reform.[12] In 1973 he published the first scholarly biography of Addams, *American Heroine: The Life and Legend of Jane Addams.*[13]

Of necessity, his research was groundbreaking. He was the first to dig deep into the Jane Addams papers, which were scattered widely across the country. Among other things, he fully documented the origins of her "saintly reputation" in the early newspaper coverage Addams and Hull House received. Indeed, it was this material, as well as the copious words of praise her friends wrote about her in later years, that persuaded Davis to argue his main original thesis: Addams had gained fame not as a by-product of her pursuit of personal excellence and power, as Conway had said, but because she had sought the thing itself. His disapproval of what he saw as her desire and ability to manipulate her public reputation to feed her overweening ego became the underlying theme of the book.

Anne Firor Scott, reviewing Davis's book, thought Davis had badly misunderstood Addams. She questioned his theory that, in Scott's words, Addams "carefully nurtured an inaccurate view of herself as 'sage and priestess,' as a self-sacrificing leader." Scott believed that Addams deeply desired to be good and, although she did not disagree that Addams also wanted to be admired, she noted that she took unpopular stands when her beliefs demanded it.[14] Rosemarie Redlich Scherman, a graduate student at the City University of New York who was working on a dissertation on Addams in 1973, agreed, noting in another book review that in his effort to "shatter Addams's self-sacrificing image," Davis "loses sight" of two of the most important aspects of Addams: her "significance as a social thinker and the middle-class feminism that turned her into a leading social activist." These critiques had little effect. For three decades, Davis's book would stand as the definitive interpretation of Jane Addams. And for three decades, no new scholarly biography of Addams would be written.[15]

Meanwhile, however, scholarship in the fields of women's history, settlement history, immigrant history, ethnic history, psychohistory, labor history, the history of rhetoric, social history, the history of sociology, the history of education, reform history, political science, and urban history—all fields directly relevant to Addams's life and work—made striking progress, and scholarship concerning Addams herself reflected this.[16] The issues first raised by Curti, Lynd, Levine, Scott, Conway, and Lasch were further examined in various scholarly articles, and new issues regarding Addams's possible racism, ethnic prejudice, and lesbianism were also raised.[17]

Addams's ideas were also explored. Over the years, scholars in the fields of sociology, education, and, more recently, political science, religion, and philosophy have treated them in depth.[18] Jean Bethke Elshtain recently edited a selection of Addams's writings and published a study that examines some of the dominant ideas in several of Addams's books in a partially biographical context. The philosophers Marilyn Fischer and Judy Whipps have edited a masterly four-volume collection of Addams's writings on peace.[19] The indefatigable editor of Addams's papers, Mary Lynn McCree Bryan, has published them on microfilm, and has begun to publish a selection of the papers in book form.[20] The University of Illinois Press has reissued six of Addams's books.[21]

The publication of two scholarly biographies of Addams, Victoria Brown's *The Education of Jane Addams* (2004) and the present work, carry this renaissance of interest in Addams further. Both books cover the first four decades of her life, during which time she first emerged as a social reformer on the national stage. (This book concludes in 1899; Brown's study takes the story to 1895.) Brown's main argument is that in the decade after her graduation from Rockford Female Seminary in 1881, Addams "underwent" a "real ideological conversion . . . from Carlyle's ethic of heroic stewardship to an ethic of democratic humanitarianism."[22] She also highlights Addams's role as a mediator in the complicated dynamics of the Addams-Haldeman family. My book traces a more gradual process of change and examines the influences that lay behind it, particularly those of books, friendships, and experiences. I believe that it was only toward the end of the 1890s that she acquired the reform agenda and understanding of her own humanity that are now familiar to us all.

There are several reasons for doing a half-life. Perhaps the most compelling is the need to explore answers to the question that Lasch, Conway, and Davis were among the first to raise: Why did Addams, despite her birthright of privilege, become a reformer? Only a close examination of her life before Hull House and of her early years there can supply the answers. Another question is how her early experiences at Hull House shaped her moral philosophy and her reform theories, methods, and agenda. The field of Addams scholarship requires more clarity regarding this subject.

The early and later Addams are often blurred. Scholars have often quoted Addams's post-1900 writings, particularly her memoir, *Twenty Years at Hull House* (1910), to document her views in the 1890s, creating a misleading impression that she held mature theories about democracy and social ethics from the settlement's beginnings. I have made a particular effort in this book to restrict myself to contemporary sources as much as possible and to track shifts in her perspective, particularly as reflected in her speeches, carefully over time.

To understand Addams's early development as a citizen I have also relied on the rich contributions of scholarship of the past thirty years. The relevant subfields of social history—urban, labor, reform, education, cultural, immigrant, settlement, black, and gender—were modest in size in the 1960s; now they dominate the scholarly landscape. Intellectual history has also thrived. Three strands of studies have proved particularly relevant: those on ideas about women and culture,[23] those on American democracy beyond the borders of party, especially regarding women's engagement,[24] and those on the political activism of working-class people of both genders and its links to culture.[25]

One of the contributions of feminism, be it first- or second-wave, has been to take the ideas of women and their development as thinkers seriously. Scholars have long known that Addams was a voracious reader from childhood on; in this biography I connect her reading to her life choices and the early development of her thinking about society. Placed in this context, her decision to start a settlement house can for the first time be understood as marking an important intellectual breakthrough for her. In addition, the writing she did throughout the 1890s, when analyzed with strict respect for their chronology, the books she was reading, and the chronology of events, including her friendship with the philosopher John Dewey, tracks further fascinating developments in her thinking. In this light, her increasing doubts about her inherited ideology of individualism and her strengthening commitment to the ideas of social Christianity and its reform method of cooperation emerge as key to understanding her conscious transformation into a new kind of citizen.

Ideas about democracy and experiences in politics interweave both in life and in biography. Because Addams could not vote or run for office as a young woman, her rising desire to shape public policy had to find other outlets. She discovered them under the tutelage of female and male union organizers, politically active women's organizations in Chicago such as the

Illinois Woman's Alliance and the Chicago Woman's Club, her savvy friend Florence Kelley, and the grassroots Civic Federation of Chicago. The story of how these friendships and experiences prompted her to revise her understanding of the meaning of democracy and of politics has never before been adequately told.

More broadly, this book for the first time places Addams firmly in her times. If one breaks down Addams's civic contributions through the year 1899, they divide into three categories: her role as co-founder and head of Hull House, her role as a leader of reform, and her role as a public intellectual. In all these roles, scholars have tended to treat her ideas as sui generis, that is, they are not sufficiently compared to those of other settlement leaders, other leaders of reform, including union leaders, and other public intellectuals. One contribution of this work, I hope, is to situate her thoroughly in the thinking and events of her own period. For example, Addams's close work with labor unions in the 1890s can be put into proper context for the first time thanks to the excellent new work of labor historians.[26] When her interest in voluntary arbitration and the workers' reform agenda are understood in relation to the history of trade unionism in Chicago and its impressive record of political action, Addams's contribution emerges as far more cooperative than groundbreaking. Men and women workers, it now becomes clear, were her teachers in ways that we have not previously appreciated. This and other efforts to contextualize make it possible to see what she learned from others and what she contributed herself. These insights, I hope, will contribute to a deepened understanding of the progressive era when it was first emerging, before 1900, in the cities and the states.[27]

Citizen is intended to show how Jane Addams was born to one life and chose another and how she was transformed by that choice. Her self-expectations were strongly shaped by her femaleness and her upper-middle-class consciousness and status, yet she found a way to break with resulting social pressures even as she partly conformed to them. Her emerging feminism, though not fully robust in 1899, was one result. Her increased willingness to examine and selectively reject the dominant beliefs of her class was another. Her deepening humanity was a third.

Her story, compelling in itself, fascinates further because it intertwines with crucial social developments in nineteenth-century American society. In her first four decades, she went from a life of rural agriculturalism to urban industrialism, from accepting a narrow definition of "American" as native-born or northern European to embracing a broad definition that included all races, ethnicities, and nationalities, from a belief in an elite practice of democracy to a belief in a more inclusive one, from the assumption that women without the vote were excluded from shaping public policy to an understanding that voteless women could be deeply engaged, and from a belief in an ethic of individualistic benevolence to a belief in an ethic of cooperative justice. The story of Addams's early life reveals how democracy as an idea and as practice reshaped her ambition and gave her a new understanding of herself as a citizen.

ABBREVIATIONS

People

AAH   Alice Addams Haldeman, Jane Addams's sister; her full name was Sarah Alice Addams Haldeman

AHA   Anna Haldeman Addams, Jane Addams's stepmother; her full name was Anna Hostetter Haldeman Addams

EGS   Ellen Gates Starr, Jane Addams's close friend

FK   Florence Kelley

JA   Jane Addams

JHA   John Huy Addams, father of Jane Addams

MAL   Mary Catherine Addams [Linn], Jane Addams's sister

MRS   Mary Rozet Smith, Jane Addams's close friend

SWA   Sarah Weber Addams, Jane Addams's mother

MHJ   Marcet Haldeman-Julius, daughter of Alice Addams Haldeman and Harry Haldeman, wife of Emanuel Julius

Archives and Collections

CFMCR   Civic Federation Municipal Chicago Records, CHS

CHS   Chicago Historical Society

EGSP   Ellen Gates Starr Papers, Sophia Smith Collection, Smith College, Northampton, MA

FLHR   Freeport Local History Room, Freeport Public Library, Freeport, IL

HHA   Hull House Association

HHA Minutes
    Minutes, [Board of Trustees], Hull House Association Records, Special Collections, The University Library, University of Illinois at Chicago (*JAPM*, Reel 49)

HII Minutes
    Residents' Meeting, Hull House Association Records, Special Collections, The University Library, University of Illinois at Chicago

HJC   Haldeman-Julius Collection, Pittsburgh State University, Pittsburgh, KS

HJP   Haldeman-Julius Papers, Jane Addams Memorial Collection, Special Collections, The University Library, University of Illinois at Chicago

JA diary   Diary of Jane Addams, 1875[–1881], JAC, SCPC

JAC   Jane Addams Collection, Swarthmore College Peace Collection, Swarthmore, PA

JACR   Jane Addams Collection, Rockford College Archives, Rockford College, Rockford, IL

JAMC   Jane Addams Memorial Collection, Special Collections, The University Library, University of Illinois at Chicago

JDC   John Dewey Collection, Southern Illinois University

JHA diary
> Diary of John Huy Addams, father of Jane Addams, 1844, box 1, series 7, JAC

RCA   Rockford College Archives

SAAH   Sarah Alice [Addams] Haldeman Mss, Lilly Library, Indiana University

SCPC   Swarthmore College Peace Collection, Swarthmore, PA

SSC   Sophia Smith Collection, Smith College, Northampton, MA

"Two Mothers"
> Marcet Haldeman-Julius, "Two Mothers of Jane Addams," TS, n.d. [1920s], 1, JAC

Books and Other Items

Annals   Henriette Greenebaum Frank and Amalie Hofer Jerome, comps., *Annals of the Chicago Woman's Club*

Appendix
> JA, appendix to Residents of Hull-House, *Hull-House Maps and Papers*

Cedar Cliff
> "Cedar Cliff," *Chicago Record*, June 17, 1897, 4, col. 4

Emerson   Ralph Waldo Emerson, *Ralph Waldo Emerson: Essays and Lectures*

FK   Kathryn Kish Sklar, *Florence Kelley*

JA as I Knew
> Marcet Haldeman-Julius, *Jane Addams as I Knew Her*

JAPCG   Mary Lynn McCree Bryan, Nancy Slote, and Maree de Angury, eds., *Jane Addams Papers: A Comprehensive Guide*

JAPM   Mary Lynn McCree Bryan, ed., *Jane Addams Papers* (microfilm); in citations, the reel number precedes the colon and the frame number follows it

Maps   Residents of Hull House, *Hull-House Maps and Papers*

Scrapbooks
> Scrapbook 1
>> 1889–1894, Clippings, *JAPM*, Addendum 10
>
> Scrapbook 2
>> 1889–1894, Publications, *JAPM*, Addendum 10
>
> Scrapbook 3
>> 1894–1897, *JAPM*, Addendum 10 (1897–1907 missing)
>
> Scrapbook 4
>> 1907–1910, *JAPM*, Addendum 1A

Selected Papers
> Mary Lynn McCree Bryan, Barbara Bair, and Maree de Angury, eds., *Selected Papers of Jane Addams*, vol. 1, *Preparing to Lead, 1860–1881*

Addams Family Book Catalogues

1847 Catalogue

> Catalogue in *Cedar Creek Union Library Company Bylaws*, Cedar Creek
> Mills, IL: 1847, *JAPM*, 28:0852

Addams Family Library List

> "Addams Family Library" *JAPM*, 28:0857

JA's Hull House Library List

> JAMC, *JAPM*, 28:0851

Rockford Acquisition List

> Jane Addams Gifts of Books to the Rockford College Library, *JAPM*,
> 28:0951

Haldeman-Julius Book List

> "The Library of E[manuel] Haldeman" Haldeman-Addams Collection,
> Pittsburgh State University, Pittsburgh, KS

NOTES

All the letters to and from Jane Addams appear in *JAPM*. Books not consulted for this book but of interest to Jane Addams, Sarah Weber Addams, or John Huy Addams are cited in the notes but not in the bibliography.

INTRODUCTION

1 JA, *Democracy,* 9–10.

2 Ibid., 6.

3 Linn, *Jane Addams,* 34.

4 Re interpretation, see JA, "Trade Unions and Public Duty," 453; JA, *Twenty,* 144.

5 JA, *Democracy,* 6. The phrase "the essential dignity and equality of all men" is taken from the previous sentence to flesh out what she meant by "test of faith."

6 Ibid., 11.

7 JA, "Subtle Problems of Charity," 163.

CHAPTER ONE: SELF-RELIANCE

1 JA, *Opening Address* [1924], *JAPM,* 48:0635.

2 Keyssar, *Right to Vote,* 5, 52, xxiii; "Backsliding and Sideslipping," chap. 3 in ibid., 53–76; 87, 55, 60, 65–67.

3 Ibid., 65, 39, 41, 47.

4 JA, *Peace and Bread,* 76; JA, *Twenty,* 1.

5 The publication date preceded her fiftieth birthday in 1910. James Waldo Fawcett to JA, November 9, 1925. Fawcett quotes to JA her reply to his previous letter. JA to Flora Guiteau, quoted in an unidentified newspaper clipping, May 23, 1935, file "Jane Addams," FLHR.

6 JA, *Twenty,* 1, 8, 9.

7 Ibid., 12, 9, 8, 6.

8 Re JHA, see *Selected Papers,* 466–79.

9 JA, *Twenty,* 12; Howe, *Making the American Self,* 130, 149.

10 Swart, " 'Individualism,' " 1:86, 79.

11 It is thought that JHA was born in Sinking Spring (for example, see *Selected Papers,* 466), but according to JA's 1935 autopsy record, he was born in Millersville, Pennsylvania, a town southwest of Lancaster. For the autopsy record, see *JAPM,* Addendum 1A, 72:0227.

12 Tocqueville, *Democracy in America,* 2:621–22.

13 By 1839 Sinking Spring had only eighteen houses, two inns, a few stores and taverns, and one church. Miller and Miller, *Borough,* 9; "Ruth Family Assn of Ill," in box 1, "Addams Family," series 18, JAC. Re the Reitzels, see JHA diary,

August 11, 1844, JAC. See also JHA to George Weber, April 14, 1845, SAAH; *Selected Papers*, 4–5, 56n12. Two daughters of Samuel's brother Richard married Flickingers. Rupp, *History of Lancaster County*, 647. See also *Selected Papers*, 4–5, 56–57nn11, 12.

14 See Miller and Miller, *Borough*, 9; John Lowry Ruth, "Address to the Ruth Family Association of Illinois," in file "Addams Family," box 1, series 18, JAC; *JAPCG*, 39.

15 Re the uncles, see M. Montgomery, *Historical and Biographical Annals*, 1:546–47. Re apprenticeship, see *Selected Papers*, 467; JA, *Twenty*, 12–13. Re Reiff's being a Quaker, see JA to Weber Linn, February 2, 1935.

16 Re SWA, see *Selected Papers*, 56n13; 487–90. Re JHA, see Linn, *Addams*, 5; Wise, *Jane Addams*, 8. There were blood ties between the Reiff and the Weber families; George Weber's mother was a Reiff. *Selected Papers*, 57n15. Enos Reiff married Elizabeth Weber October 9, 1840. *Easton Sentinel* (Easton, PA), October 9, 1840, n.p.

17 "Two Mothers," 1–3, 7; Linn, *Addams*, 6; Asa K. McIlhaney, "Historical Notes from the Writings of Asa K. McIlhaney," TS (Easton, PA: Easton Public Library, 1956), 2:65. Re SWA's ethnic background see Beaver, *History*, 332; McIlhaney, "Historical Notes," 2:65; *Selected Papers*, 57n15. SWA's mother, also named Sarah, was a Beaver. The name Beaver was originally French Huguenot—Beavoir, later Bieber, later Beaver. Beaver, *History*, 9–13. Re JHA's Germanic background, see M. Montgomery, *Historical and Biographical Annals*, 1:1176; Miller and Miller, *Borough*, 8–9, 13. Weber Linn's claim that JHA came from English stock (*Addams*, 1) is merely a reference to his patrinominal line. Re SWA's religious upbringing, see McIlhaney, "Historical Notes," 2:1. Re JHA's religious upbringing, see Nein, "Alphabetized Compilation," 7; Miller and Miller, *Borough*, 21. John Addams owned a copy of John Calvin's classic of Protestant theology, *Institutes of the Christian Religion* (1838 edition). Addams Family Library List. Re the courtship, see JHA to Enos Reiff, January 26, 1843, box 1, JAC.

18 *Selected Papers*, 5–6; JHA diary, July 29, 1844 and passim.

19 JHA diary, August 8, 9, 1844.

20 Ibid., August 12, 1844; Tilden, *History of Stephenson County*, 247; Keister, *History of Stephenson County*, 64; *Selected Papers*, 11, 13, 469. JHA diary entries re needing father's approval for the price include those for September 3, 14, and 20, 1844.

21 JHA diary, August 12, 1844. I give the figure of $3,800 because John Addams bid on another mill for that price. JHA diary, August 21, 1844. On August 12, 1844, JHA writes, "[T]old Father I liked the property but [could not buy it unless] he would . . . go my halves." One scholar has supposed that this reference to "Father" refers to his father Samuel Addams back in Pennsylvania, but in the diary JHA also refers to George Weber as "Father." See August 9, 1844 entry. Re George Weber, see *Selected Papers*, 54.

22 Re the Como plan, see JHA diary, August 12, November 9, 1844; re interest

rates, see *Freeport Journal*, September 13, 1878. The information appears in a letter from a Mr. Meacham in which Meacham summarizes the remarks he had made at an old settlers' meeting on this subject. Clipping file, FLHR. Re views on debt, see JHA diary, December 18, 1844.

23 Re his impatience, see JHA diary entries for September, especially September 16, and early October. Quotations are from entries for October 8, October 1, November 30, and October 12, 1844. The October 12 diary entry reads, "Letter from Father [came,] giving me power to buy the property."

24 Ibid., October 15, 18, 1844; Fulwider, *History of Stephenson County*, 1:348; JHA diary, October 24, 1844. The quotation is from the October 25, 1844 entry. Re events in December, see entries for December 14, 15, 18, and 19, 1844.

25 Re the higher price, see JHA to Enos Reiff, January 12, 1845, box 1, JAC. Re each owning half in mid-1845, see Fenwick Property Abstract for the title of the land on which Cedar Creek Mills once stood; abstract in possession of Thomas and Moira Fenwick, owners of the property in the 1980s. Photocopy in the possession of the author. According to the abstract, in April 1851, Samuel Addams sold his son JHA the half of the property he owned (worth $2,200 at the original price) for $6,330; he then gave $3,150 to JHA and kept $3,150. Re Samuel buying more land, see SWA to George Weber; her letter appears at the end of a letter from JHA to George Weber, April 14/May 3, 1845. Both letters were transcribed by George Weber in a letter he sent to Enos Reiff, undated, SAAH; Fenwick Property Abstract. Re the second grinding stone, see Fulwider, *History*, 348. Re James Addams, see Tilden, *History*, 741. Re George Weber's last years, see *JAPCG*, 53; *Selected Papers*, 493; McIlhaney, "Historical Notes," 2:1.

26 U.S. Bureau of the Census, *1850 Census*, Buckeye Township, Stephenson County, microfilm. Calculations by the author. Strictly speaking, these statistics do not cover all of the wealth in the town because a small portion of Cedarville occupied two other townships, Harlem and Florence (the township in which most of Freeport was located). Such concentration of wealth in a frontier town was not unusual. See Faragher, *Sugar Creek*, 185. Re Cedarville's population of four hundred, see Beam, *Cedarville's Jane Addams*, 31.

27 SWA to Enos and Elizabeth Reiff; this letter is written at the end of JHA to Enos and Elizabeth Reiff, January 12, 1845, Weber-Reiff Family Correspondence, 1830–1863, box 1, JAC.

28 *JAPCG*, 46. Horace Addams lived two months. George Weber Addams lived two years. Re how SWA died, see George Weber to Elizabeth Reiff, January 17, 1863, box 1, JAC, and the end of this chapter.

29 Re JHA praying in the 1870s (Linn is drawing on childhood memories), see Linn, *Addams*, 51. A passage in JHA's diary has given at least one scholar the impression that he was determined not to be a Christian: "Spent the evening not becoming a Christian." Diary, November 24, 1844. The word "becoming" is being used as a synonym for "befitting." Among the historians who believe that John Addams was either not religious or only nominally so are Cavallo,

"Sexual Politics," 166; Crunden, *Ministers of Reform*, 18; Brown, *Education*, 19, 27, 304n35. Davis thought he had a "simple faith." Davis, *American Heroine*, 4. Elshtain calls him a "flexible" Hicksite Quaker. Elshtain, *Jane Addams*, 213, 40. The quotation is from John Manning Linn to JA, August 26, 1881. Re JHA weeping at Sunday school, see *Freeport Budget*, August 27, 1881; re tears as an evangelical trait, see McCloughlin, *Revivals*, 14. Jonathan Edwards endorsed tears as a meaningful spiritual register. Marsden, *Evangelical Mind*, 13. Edwards's book *A History of the Work of Redemption: Comprising an Outline of Church History* (New York: American Tract Society, n.d.) was in JHA's library. His library can be constructed from three lists: [1847] Catalogue, in *Cedar Creek Union Library Company Bylaws* (Cedar Creek Mills, Ill.: 1847), 7, *JAPM*, 28:0852 (hereafter cited as 1847 Catalogue); "Addams Family Library," *JAPM* 28:0857 (hereafter cited as Addams Family Library List); and "The Library of E[manuel] Haldeman," Emanuel Haldeman-Julius Collection, Pittsburgh State University, Pittsburgh, KS (hereafter cited as Haldeman-Julius Book List). The Edwards book is in the Addams Family Library List.

30 Noll, "Revolution and the Rise," 129.

31 Quoted in Block, *Nation of Agents*, 378.

32 SWA to Elizabeth and Enos Reiff, June 16, 1841, box 1, series 8, JAC. See also R. Brown, *Strength of the People*, 164. Confirming SWA's evangelicalism and giving a probable date for her conversion is the fact that she became a member of the German Reformed Church (the Stone Church) in Kreidersville when she was twenty-two. *Selected Papers*, 488.

33 The church was the German Reformed Church in Reading (later the First United Church of Christ), which is the church where they were married. Nein, "Alphabetized Compilation of Records," 7. The baptismal records are incomplete for the year JHA would have been baptized, but his older siblings were baptized there. (All baptisms performed between 1821 and 1829 are missing from the list.)

34 JA, *Twenty*, 14–15.

35 Mary Addams [Linn] (hereafter cited as MAL) to Alice Addams [Haldeman] (hereafter cited as AAH), January 26, 1867, file 253, HJP. Bryan states that an unidentified baby of John and Sarah Addams was baptized June 16, 1853, at the Presbyterian Church and suspects it was Alice, who had been born a few weeks earlier (*Selected Papers*, 63n57). The pressure on Alice to convert in 1867 indicates, however, that it is likely that she was not baptized. Another explanation is that the baby was Samuel Addams, the child of James Addams, John's brother, who was living in Cedarville as well. Samuel Addams the younger was also born in 1853, month unknown. See "Addams-Reiff Family Papers and Genealogy," box 1, JAC. Bryan does not indicate her source or whether it provides the first names of the parents.

36 All the books are listed in the Addams Family Library List. One of JHA's books was William Taylor, *The Model Preacher: Comprised in a Series of Letters Illustrating*

the Best Mode of Preaching, 7th ed. (1860). Taylor was an evangelical Methodist preacher who preached in the Midwest in the 1850s. T. Smith, *Revivalism*, 119. Other evangelical books in JHA's library are cited throughout this chapter. Elias Hicks, *Journal of the Life and Religious Labours of Elias Hicks*, 2nd ed. (New York: Isaac Hopper, 1832) is not listed in the 1847 Catalogue, suggesting that he did not want to lend it. Hicks preached in Pennsylvania during John Addams's childhood. Forbush, *Elias Hicks*, 87. Re JHA's self-identification as a Hicksite Quaker, see JA, *Twenty*, 16. Re Hicksite views, see Forbush, *Elias Hicks*, 43, 59; T. Smith, *Revivalism*, 31.

37 Re Hicksite views, see Hicks, *Journal*, 43, 58; Ingle, *Quakers*, 44; Barbour and Frost, *Quakers*, 181. The fit between JHA's Hicksite Quakerism and his modified Presbyterian evangelism was not ideal. Hicks did not believe that Christ saved anyone by his death on the cross or that man had fallen from grace through sinfulness (Ingle, *Quakers*, 44) and opposed "speculation" for wealth by investing in railroads (Barbour and Frost, *Quakers*, 329). Re mental integrity, see JA, *Twenty*, 15. In 1894, JA told John Dewey that her father was a Quaker. John Dewey to Alice Chipman Dewey, October 10, 1894, JDC. See also JA to Weber Linn, February 2, 1935. JHA's Quakerly manners when dealing with an Addams cousin are evident in a surviving letter. See Brandt, *Jane Addams Papers*, 4. Linn dismisses the idea that her father was a Hicksite Quaker as merely "tradition." Linn, *Addams*, 287. See also Brown, *Education*, 23, 305n46.

38 [Freeport] *Deutscher Anzeiger*, January 21, 1863, clipping, "Addams-Reiff Family Paper and Genealogy," box 1, series 8, JAC. Re her reputation, see Earle A. Berry, letter to the editor, *Kansas City Star*, May 29, 1935, file "About John Addams," box 1, series 7, JAC.

39 More, *Works of Hannah More*, 1:165–78. Re More's influence, see Mintz, *Prison of Expectations*, 54.

40 Re the evangelical focus on the individual, see Marty, *Protestantism in the United States*, 92. Re temperance in Addams family, see *Selected Papers*, 38; *JA as I Knew*, 21. Re Hull House and alcohol, see JA, *Twenty*, 131–32; Blanc, *Condition*, 75. Re JHA's Sunday school efforts, see *Selected Papers*, 85n10; *Freeport Budget*, August 27, 1881; MAL to JIIA, January 9, 1861, JAC.

41 Re JHA's apparent Presbyterianism, see Fulwider, *History*, 345–46. For JHA's obituary, see *Freeport Republican*, September 3, 1881; Tilden, *History*, 540. Jane Addams attended the Presbyterian Church with her family either every Sunday (Rev. Irvine, funeral sermon for JHA, *Freeport Budget*, August 27, 1881, 4, col. 4; JA, *Twenty*, 16) or every other Sunday ("Two Mothers," 8). They had a family pew. JA diary, January 10, 1875, JAC, *JAPM*, 28:1515. Mary Addams married a Presbyterian minister; in 1881 the minister of the Cedarville Presbyterian Church gave the sermon at JHA's funeral; and JA's cousin, Vallie Beck, thought of JA as a Presbyterian (Vallie Beck to JA, October 4, 1877). For additional information on the family's Presbyterian ties, see *Selected Papers*, 18, 62–63nn54–55.

42 Linn writes that JHA was not "inclined to profess Christianity." *Addams*, 3. His

source is JA, who wrote to him, "[M]y father was not a 'professing Christian,' he never belonged to any church." JA to Linn, February 2, 1935. As JA makes clear, a "professing Christian" is someone who joins a church. In the mid-nineteenth century, this involved formally swearing allegiance to a specific dogma. The Lincoln quotation is from Havlike, "Abraham Lincoln," 226.

43 Re Catherine Huy Addams's Quaker practices as a mother, see Wise, *Addams*, 10; Dunn, "Jane Addams," 20. Re JA's knowledge that she had "one Quaker grandmother," see JA to William I. Hull, January 16, *JAPM* 9:0801.

44 *Freeport Journal*, June 24, 1850, 2, col. 3; JA, *Twenty*, 35; Stennett, *Yesterday and Today*, 12; Wise, *Addams*, 7. Re the Mt. Carroll alternative route, see *Freeport Journal*, January 21, 1850, 2, col. 4; Tilden, *History*, 247; JHA obituary, unidentified newspaper clipping, Sill Scrapbook, 187, RCA; Linn, *Addams*, 23; Andreas, *History of Chicago*, 1:256. Re the Illinois Central alternative route and its defeat, see Sill Scrapbook, 187; Cronon, *Nature's Metropolis*, 67. Re "father of railroad enterprise," see Tilden, *History*, 271.

45 *Selected Papers*, 470; JHA to SWA, January 4, 1857. This letter and others from their 1857 correspondence are in the possession of the Cedarville historian Ronald Beam. They were found in the attic of the Addams home when renovations were undertaken.

46 Re JHA's property, see *Selected Papers*, 469. Re his bank business, see JHA obituary, *Freeport Daily Bulletin*, August 18, 1881; *Freeport Budget*, August 20, 1881, 4, col. 6. Re Guiteau's employment, see *Freeport Journal*, August 31, 1854, 2, col. 1; *Freeport Budget*, August 27, 1881, 4, col. 5. Re his presidency of the Farmers' Insurance Company, see *Combination Atlas Map*, 7. Re his second insurance company, see Tilden, *History*, 747. Re the Opera House, see Tilden, *History*, 433. Re his 1870 assets, see U.S. Bureau of the Census, *1870 Census* [series m593, roll 275, p. 16], Inhabitants in Township of Buckeye [Stephenson County, Illinois], September 21, 1870, page 31, schedule 1.

47 *Combination Atlas Map*, 26; Chernow, *Titan*, 217.

48 Fulwider, *History*, 344–47; Keister, *History*, 67, 70; Beam, *Jane Addams's Cedarville*, 26–27. Like Benjamin Franklin, whose autobiography was in JHA's library, JHA gave a donation each year to each church in town (Linn, *Addams*, 2–3).

49 Sill Scrapbook, 187, RCA; JA, *Twenty*, 24; *Combination Atlas Map*, 8.

50 Wise, *Addams*, 31; Linn, *Addams*, 17.

51 McPherson, *Battle Cry of Freedom*, 24–28. For the Carey quotation, see E. Foner, *Free Soil*, 19, 26; for the Colton quotation, see Hanson, *Democratic Imagination*, 139.

52 E. Foner, *Free Soil*, 31; Cole, *Social Ideas*, 169. For more on Bushnell, see McCloughlin, *Revivals*, 14–17.

53 Re the perfectionists, see McCloughlin, *Revivals*, 128; T. Smith, *Revivalism*, 114. The perfectionist evangelical authors and their books in the Addams Family Library List include Charles P. McIlvaine, *Selected Family and Parish Sermons: A Series of Evangelical Discourses, Selected for the Use of Families and Destitute Con-*

gregations (Columbus, OH: Isaac N. Whiting, 1838); Isabella Graham, *The Power of Faith Exemplified in the Life and Writings of the Late Mrs. Isabella Graham* (New York: American Tract Society, 1843); Taylor, *Model Preacher: Book of Public Worship for the Use of the New Church Signified by the New Jerusalem in the Revelation* (Boston: Otis Clapp, 1848); More, *Works of Hannuh More.* For Hicks's evangelical perfectionism, see Barbour and Frost, *Quakers,* 188; Smith, *Revivalism,* 31. Re Luther Guiteau, see JHA diary, October 20, 1844; Hayes, *Complete History,* 22; *Selected Papers,* 99n3.

54 The first quotation is from Isaac Carey to JA, August 21, 1881. The second is from Davis, *Heroine,* 26. (His source is an undated document he cites as "Jane Addams Notebooks and Note Fragments," JAMC. The archive cannot locate this document.) For the obituary quotations, see *Freeport Journal,* August 24, 1881, 8; *Freeport Daily Bulletin,* August 18, 1881, 1; unidentified news clipping, August 19, 1881, file "JHA Correspondence," box 1, JAC.

55 *Freeport Weekly Journal,* August 24, 1881; *Freeport Budget,* August 27, 1881, 4, col. 2; Fry, *Generous Spirit,* 22; Pierson, *Tocqueville in America,* 118.

56 *Freeport Republican,* September 3, 1881, 3; Linn, *Addams,* 17, 21.

57 For the remarks made at Sunday school, see *Freeport Budget,* August 27, 1881. For his son-in-law's observation, see John Manning Linn to JA, August 26, 1881; A. Smith, *Theory of Moral Sentiments,* vol. 1, pt. 2, sec. 1, chap. 1 and pt. 3, [no sec.], chap. 6.

58 JHA diary, September 20, 1844, November 4, 1844; JHA, "Speech," October 23, 1872, *Freeport Journal* [typed transcript, Marcet Haldeman-Julius notes], in file "John Addams's Public Life," box 1, JAC.

59 JHA diary, August 9, 1844; JHA to Enos and Elizabeth Reiff, January 12, 1845, SAAH. Illinois was one of only five states in this period that allowed aliens, that is, noncitizens, to vote. Keyssar, *Right to Vote,* 32 and table A.4.

60 For Isaac, see M. Montgomery, *Historical and Biographical Annals,* 546; Yeich, "Jane Addams," 13. For William see M. Montgomery, *Historical and Biographical Annals,* 546; Yeich, "Jane Addams," 13; *Biographical Dictionary,* 496. For Peter, see M. Montgomery, *Historical and Biographical Annals,* 547. William, who lived in Sinking Spring and was much respected for his "sterling integrity," had the most active public service career of the uncles and was possibly a hero to the young JHA. M. Montgomery, *Historical and Biographical Annals,* 505; *Biographical Dictionary,* 496. Samuel's brother Peter, having been a presidential elector for Jackson in 1824, ran as a Whig candidate for Congress in 1848. Re this and other Addams men's political affiliations, see M. Montgomery, *Historical and Biographical Annals,* 547. Their brother William served as a Democrat in Congress, 1825–1829. *Biographical Dictionary,* 496. Re John Weber, see Beaver, *History,* 332–33.

61 Re Whigs, see Carwardine, *Evangelicals,* 136. Re Hicksite Quakers, see Forbush, *Elias Hicks,* 89, 145–46. Re perfectionists and politics, see Strong, *Perfectionist Politics.* For JHA's opposition to expanding slavery, see his speech, October 23,

1872, *Freeport Journal*, TS, box 1, JAC. Re the escaped slave, see *My Friend*, 26; JA, *Opening Address* [1924], 3. Interestingly, Addams does not mention this memory in *Twenty Years*. JA mentions that she must have been less than four years old. She may have been thinking of the fact that Congress passed the law ending slavery in January 1865, when she was four. For more on the underground railroad through Freeport, see G. Turner, *Underground Railroad in Illinois*, 164.

62 Re JHA at Ripon, see Earle A. Berry, letter to the editor, *Kansas City Star*, May 29, 1935; *Freeport Journal*, August 17, 1854, 2, col. 1, August 31, 1854, 2, col. 4, August 27, 1881, 4, col. 4. It is likely that JHA knew by name the great majority of the men who voted for him in Stephenson County. In 1854, 750 Republicans voted in the county for the election for the House of Representatives. The total number of voters in the county that year was only 1,211. These facts underline the centrality of social etiquette to political success in these years. Allen and. Lacey, *Illinois Elections*, 134.

63 Linn, *Addams*, 17; Emerson, "Character," in *Emerson*, 496.

64 JA believed that JHA served together with Abraham Lincoln in the Illinois state senate. She does not claim this in *Twenty*, interestingly enough, but in a 1924 speech. *Opening Address*, [1924], 3. In fact, Lincoln's and JHA's terms did not overlap. Lincoln was elected to the state senate in the fall of 1854 but quickly resigned his seat to run for the U.S. Senate seat instead. It is plausible that they were not only acquaintances but friends: JHA attended a reception that Lincoln hosted in Springfield in 1857 (*Selected Papers*, 55n6), he was in Springfield for several months every two years between 1855 and 1860, when Lincoln left for Washington, and he became a prominent Republican leader in the state senate during the time Lincoln was also prominent in the Republican Party in Illinois. Re Washburne, see Donald, *Lincoln*, 183; Gienapp, *Origins*, 124.

65 Basler, *Complete Works of Abraham Lincoln*, 2:303; Mearns, *Lincoln Papers*, 1:200; JA, *Twenty*, 31. JA is quoting JHA's reply from memory. The letter does not survive in any publicly available collection. Since Lincoln did not serve in the state senate when Addams did, the only vote JHA could have cast for Lincoln in his career as a legislator in which his vote could have been in doubt is the vote for Lincoln's election to the U.S. Senate in 1855. Many Illinois Republicans had doubts about Lincoln's loyalty to the Republican Party's views at the time (he was still a Whig and married to a southerner). Holt, *Rise and Fall*, 870–71. Re the vote for Lincoln in the state senate, see White, *Life of Lyman Trumbull*, 43. Lincoln received the most votes on the first vote taken. White reports that only three state senators voted for Trumbull on that vote: Palmer, Judd, and Cook. Because JHA was anti-Nebraska, and Lincoln was the only other anti-Nebraska candidate besides Trumbull, this means that JHA voted for Lincoln on the first vote. It took nine more vote counts and Lincoln's withdrawal of his name in order for Trumbull to win. White, *Life*, 43–45.

66 JA, *Twenty*, 32–33. The friend, whom Addams describes further as editor of a "great Chicago daily," was Andrew Shuman of the *Chicago Evening Journal*.

67 *Selected Papers*, 471; JA, *Twenty*, 54. When JHA wrote Anna Haldeman Addams (hereafter cited as AHA) about hearing Elizabeth Cady Stanton, a known advocate for women's suffrage, speak, he did not express disapproval of her ideas. February 20, 1869, in box 1, JAC. Re JHA's leadership in the state senate, see *Illinois State Senate Journal* for the years 1867–1869. The *Chicago Evening Journal* contains coverage of his political record. Re his chairmanship, see Brown, *Education*, 48, 312n30.

68 For more on perfectionist liberalism, see D. McCabe, "Knowing about the Good," 311–38.

69 Horace Addams was born February 15, 1855; the senate adjourned on February 15 that year. George Weber Addams was born April 3, 1857. The senate was in session through February 19 that year.

70 This story is constructed from four sources: George Weber to Elizabeth Weber Reiff, January 17, 1863, in box 1, JAC; Linn, *Addams*, 22; MHJ's handwritten notes from a conversation with her mother, AAH, who was nine when SWA died, about SWA's death (file 39, HJP); and "Two Mothers." Because SWA collapsed at the neighbors' (all versions agree on this), it is clear that she fell on the way there, began bleeding internally, and then collapsed. Visitors to Cedarville today will find no steep hill between the Addams homestead and the rest of town. The State of Illinois rerouted and regraded Mill Street in the 1930s, flattening the hill that SWA climbed. Fry, *Generous Spirit*, 30; Keister, *History*, 69.

71 George Weber to Elizabeth Weber Reiff, January 17, 1863, box 1, JAC.

72 Ibid.

CHAPTER TWO: THREE MOTHERS

1 For a short discussion of the book's significance as a memoir, see Knight, "Jane Addams," *Encyclopedia*.

2 JA, *Twenty*, 39–40. Her observation was not meant as a personal reminiscence but as a metaphor for what immigrants from different countries experienced when thrown together in a neighborhood in a large American city and forced to rely on their own resources. In her seventies, Addams recalled knocking frantically on the door of the room where her mother lay dying and hearing her mother telling someone to let her in. Linn, *Addams*, 22.

3 Berry, letter to the editor, *Kansas City Star*, May 29, 1935, in file "About John Addams," JAC.

4 JA, *Excellent*; MAL to AAH, May 1866, file "1863–69," SAAH.

5 Linn, *Addams*, 25; *JA as I Knew*, 4. See also Sarah Uhl to JA, November 16, 1896; Jane Addams Linn Morse, pers. comm., March 19, 1994.

6 John Harrison Weber to JA, January 24, 1877; "Two Mothers," 10, 9, 16.

7 JA, *Twenty*, 11; JA, "Ethical Survivals," 276 (she recycles this observation in *Democracy*, 229); *Twenty*, 1; immediately after this passage, she tells us about confessing to her father that she had lied.

8 Re Alice's recollection, see *Kansas City Star* clippings from October 8, 1911, SAAH; JA, *Excellent*, 160.

9 JA, *Twenty*, 13, 2–3; Wise, *Addams*, 10; JA, *Twenty*, 14.

10 John Linn to JA, December 21, 1910; Linn, *Addams*, 34.

11 JA, *Twenty*, 8, 7; Wise, *Addams*, 17. See also Barker-Benfield, " 'Mother Emancipator,' " 395–420. Re being pigeon-toed, see Linn, *Addams*, 24.

12 JA, *Twenty*, 6–9. See also Lagemann, introduction to *Jane Addams on Education*, 21.

13 JA, *Twenty*, 9, 11; JA, *Peace and Bread*, 76; *Twenty*, 9.

14 JA, *Twenty*, 16. JA gives the height of the tallest cliffs in her essay "Address on Illinois Geography," May 26, [1878], *JAPM*, 45:1779.

15 See maps of Cedarville and Stephenson County and drawing of John Addams's property in *Combination Atlas Map*, 5, 51, 28. Re the orchard, see JA, *Long Road*, 156; MAL to AAH, May 17, 1869, file 253, HJP.

16 Beam, *Cedarville's Jane Addams*, 31–32; Fulwider, *History*, 345; Keister, *History*, 66–67.

17 This essay was published in three somewhat different versions: JA, "Unexpected Reactions" (1914): 178–86; *Long Road,* chap. 6, "A Personal Experience of Interpretative Memory" (1916); and *Excellent,* chap. 12, "Early Reactions to Death" (1932). In all versions, JA ignores the interesting question of why she had forgotten these memories. Freud's theory of repression provides one explanation. See Ervin, *Freud Encyclopedia,* s.v. "repression." Scholars have tended to interpret JA's memories as she does—as illustrations of the "development of her social conscience." Leibowitz, *Fabricating Lives*, 116; Elshtain, *Addams*, 119.

18 JA, "Unexpected Reactions," 182. She writes that she was "totally unprepared" to see the mother buried, implying that her severe reaction was caused by her ignorance of the normal practice. She may not have seen the burial of her own mother but she may also have been too young to remember consciously. In any case, she avoided the obvious explanation for her severe reaction—that it was connected in some way to her loss of her own mother.

19 Ibid.

20 I date this story about a year after the burial story because she was learning her letters in the first story and reading in the second; JA, *Long Road*, 150–52; *Excellence*, 150–51.

21 Martha Addams died March 23, 1867. *Selected Papers*, 28. In "Unexpected Reactions," Addams says only that a "relative" died; JA, "Unexpected Reactions," 180. Re her nightmare, see JA to AAH, August 20, 1880, and JA to AAH, August 1, 1890. Because she recalled it in 1880 and 1890, it appears not to have been repressed. In both letters she mentions that she had the dream after Martha died.

22 JA, *Twenty*, 5; Wise, *Addams*, 23; JA, *Twenty*, 5, 6.

23 The dream illustrates how a child's psyche responds to the trauma of a death of

a parent as it attempts to compensate for feelings of helplessness with feelings of mastery, influence, and power. Children often feel that the death of a parent is somehow their fault. M. Harris, *Loss That Is Forever*, 219–42. For various interpretations of the dream, see Leibowitz, *Fabricating Lives*, 122–23; Barker-Benfield, " 'Mother Emancipator,' " 406; Rudnick, "Feminist American Success Myth," 149; Davis, *Heroine*, 162, 314n14.

24 I establish the chronology of this event from the following evidence: JA writes that this trip to Freeport occurred before she was seven. *Twenty*, 3. All the evidence suggests that the mill they visited was the Haldeman mill, which was boarded up in August 1867, when JA was six. Wise says that the Freeport visit took place several weeks after her nightmares about the blacksmith shop occurred. *Addams*, 23. My source for JHA's response to Jane's question comes from ibid., 24. (Wise interviewed JA for the book.)

25 V. Brown, *Education*, 50, 313n41. Davis feels that it may have some factual basis but it is also a literary device. *Heroine*, 162, 314n14.

26 Berry remembered hearing the story from Addams's father in the late 1870s when he and his wife were guests in her father's house. E. Berry, letter to the editor, *Kansas City Star*, May 29, 1935. JA probably remembered the story because her father liked to repeat it. The two reporters were Clara Doty Bates ("Our Lady of the House," *Chicago Inter-Ocean*, March 20, 1892, Scrapbook 1, 19a) and Isabella Judd (["A Social Settlement"], [October 1892], Scrapbook 1, 25).

27 JA, *Twenty*, 11, 28; D. Levine, *Jane Addams*, 11; Davis, *Heroine*, 160; Crunden, *Ministers of Reform*, 19; Elshtain, *Addams*, 18, 276–7n28. SWA is referred to by name by Polly, the housekeeper, whose words JA quotes (*Twenty*, 19). No other family member's name is mentioned in the text.

28 "Two Mothers," 9; *JAPCG*, 69, 74.

29 For more on AHA, see *Selected Papers*, 442–66; for William Haldeman, see *Selected Papers*, 67n96; MHJ, "Grandmother" notes, file 39, HJP; "Two Mothers," 12. Re Swedenborgians, see Reid, *Concise Dictionary*, 81.

30 "Two Mothers," 18; Davis, *Heroine*, 7; "Two Mothers," 13, 12, 15.

31 AHA to JHA, January 2, 1869, JAC.

32 "Two Mothers," 11, 15–16.

33 John S. Hostetter to AHA, November 16, 1868, JAC; *JA as I Knew*, 4.

34 "Two Mothers," 12; *JAPCG*, 54. JHA and JA agreed that JA must read a certain amount of history first every day, after which she could read fiction the rest of the day. JA to Vallie Beck, March 30, 1876. Anna declined John's first proposal of marriage in June 1868 but changed her mind within months. *Selected Papers*, 452. Later she decided that it was wrong to marry in order to be a mother to motherless children. Fry, *Generous Spirit*, 55.

35 Executor's Report, Ann Haldeman, 1866–1868, box 81, Stephenson County Probate Court Records, Stephenson County, Illinois.

36 William Haldeman Estate Probate Papers, box 81, Stephenson County Probate

Records. The figure for his assets comes from U.S. Bureau of the Census, *1870 Census,* Carroll Township Census Records, Carroll County, 9. In October 1868, Nathaniel Haldeman notified AHA through his lawyer that he would apply to probate court to compel her to file a new bond and ask that he be released and discharged from "further liability as security upon your present bond." Document, box 81, Stephenson County Probate Court Records.

37 William Haldeman Will, box 81, Stephenson County Probate Court Records. Nathaniel failed to keep up the insurance payments, and when the mill burned to the ground in the spring of 1871, Harry and George Haldeman's inheritance went up in smoke, not to mention AHA's. The loss was valued at $13,516. Afterwards, the income from selling the land went to pay the taxes. Executor's Report, William Haldeman Estate, November 1868–June 1871, by Nathaniel Haldeman, box 32, Stephenson County Probate Court Records.

38 These items were listed in the initial estate records for the Haldeman estate. Box 81, Stephenson County Probate Court Records. MAL wrote JHA that she could hear Anna downstairs playing the guitar. MAL to JHA, January 13, [1869], file 252, HJP. At her death, Alice Addams Haldeman possessed a full series of bound volumes of *Harper's Monthly* from volume 1 in 1850. *Selected Papers,* 399n3. It seems more likely that these were Anna's than Sarah's.

39 AHA to JHA, January 2, 1869, JAC. Over the years, AHA's relations with people in Cedarville did not improve. See Linn, *Addams,* 29; Wise, *Addams,* 47.

40 JA, *Twenty,* 13, 14 (JA does not say that Anna bought the cloak for her but she must have because, clearly, her father did not). See also Brown, *Education,* 51.

41 Sarah C.T. Uhl to JA, November 15, 1896.

42 "Two Mothers," 16.

43 *JA as I Knew,* 4; for a brief biographical essay on George Haldeman, see *Selected Papers,* 494–507.

44 "Two Mothers," 14; JA diary, passim, 1875. Portions of this diary have been reprinted in *Selected Papers,* 103–34.

45 Fry, *Generous Spirit,* 48.

46 Wise, *Addams,* 35–36; Harry Haldeman to AHA, May 14, 1874, box 1, SAHP. Years later, a friend of AHA's refers to the event. See the letter from an unidentified person (living in Freeport) to AHA, May 23, 1886, SAAH; "The Girl of Cedar Cliff," *Chicago Record,* June 17, 1897 news clipping, SCPC.

47 JA, *Twenty,* 17; JA, "Subjective Necessity," 12.

48 JA, *Twenty,* 17–18; Wise, *Addams,* 39.

49 Terr, *Too Scared to Cry,* 200, 239, 300–301.

50 JA, *Twenty,* 26–27.

51 See Mosier, *Making the American Mind.*

52 JA, *Twenty,* 47, 13. See the 1847 Catalogue and the Addams Family Library List.

53 "Cedar Cliff," n.p.; JA to Vallie Beck, March 30, 1876; Davis, *Heroine,* 9.

54 Fry, *Generous Spirit,* 76; "Two Mothers," 18. Re Holmes, see [Annie Sidwell],

"Sage and Sibyl," *Rockford Seminary Magazine* 9 (July 1881): 193; JA diary, March 15, 1875.

55 AHA to Harry Haldeman, September 24, 1893, SAAH; JA diary, April 23, 1875, May 4, 1875.

56 JA to Vallie Beck, March 30, April 2, 1876; "Two Mothers," 13, 17; AHA to JHA, January 9, 1869, JAC. For the quotations, see "Two Mothers," 17; AHA to George Haldeman, February 27, 1885, HJP. Re Anna teaching sophistication, see "Two Mothers," 17

57 For the first quotation, see unidentified newspaper clipping dated January 13, 1932, file JA clippings, FLHR. MAL's strong sense of duty is evident in many of her letters to AAH, written while AAH was away at school at Rockford, from September 1866 through May 1872. See file 253, HJP. See also MAL's letters to JHA, JAC. Re her short attendance at Rockford, see MAL to AAH, November 19, 1869, File 253, HJP; AHA to JHA, January 11, 1869, JAC. Re Linn's personality and MAL, see *Selected Papers*, 533–44; *JAPCG*, 47; MAL to JHA, February 20, 1872, JAC. John Addams Linn was born September 9, 1872. *JAPCG*, 47. Re Alice and Harry's love affair and marriage, see Harry Haldeman to AHA, August 9, 1873, May 8, 1875, SAAH; Linn, *Addams*, 32. Re JHA's opposition, see ibid. Harry's drinking problem is well documented in AHA's letters to him in the 1880s, HJP. See especially AHA to Harry Haldeman, August 11, 1887. Anna understood Harry's struggle. In this letter she reminds him that she had stopped drinking by joining a temperance society.

58 Tilden, *History*, 741; MAL to AAH, August 21, 1871, file 253, HJP.

59 John Weber Addams Documents, box 283, Stephenson County Court Records, Stephenson County, IL.

60 Ibid.; Grob, *Mad among Us*, 58–60; Gamwell and Tomes, *Madness in America*, 105; John Weber Addams Documents, box 283, Stephenson County Court Records.

61 For characteristics of the schizophrenic patient, see Grob, *Mad among Us*, 8. For information about Weber's behavior, see box 240, July 1896 records for John Weber Addams, Stephenson County Court Records. He is described as "very excitable," "stammering at times," "unusually excited and violent," and possessing "delusions, hallucinations"; Watt and Nicholi, "Early Death," 472; Dennehy, "Childhood Bereavement," 1049–69. Weber lost his mother when he was ten. He also lost three siblings—a brother when he was three, another brother when he was seven, and a sister when he was fifteen.

62 Weber entered the hospital June 17, 1872. John Weber Addams Documents, box 283, Stephenson County Court Records. He was released November 11, 1872. *Selected Papers*, 480–81; *JAPCG*, 46; JA to Vallie Beck, March 16, 1876. For a biographical essay on Laura Shoemaker Addams, see *Selected Papers*, 483–86; for Weber's career in business and politics, see Tilden, *History*, 741; *Freeport Journal*, May 13, 1880, 2; *Portrait and Biographical Album*, 282.

63 Fry, *Generous Spirit*, 32–33.

64 "Two Mothers," 12; JA diary, April 3, 9, March 29, 1875. Re C. W. Moore, see *Selected Papers*, 66.

65 JA diary, February 25, April 9, April 26, 1875; Keister, *History*, 67.

66 JHA diary, October 5, 1844.

67 JHA to AAH, January 6, 1874, JAC.

CHAPTER THREE: DREAMS

1 JA, *Twenty*, 30, 24.

2 Ibid., 23, 30–32. JA thought her brother, Weber Addams, had lost the letters. JA to Gilbert A. Tracy, June 23, 1914; JA, *Spirit of Youth*, 140.

3 JA, *Twenty*, 31.

4 Re JHA subscribing to the *Tribune*, see "Speech," *Freeport Journal*, October 23, 1872, transcript, JAC; JA, *Twenty*, 21–22. Giuseppe Mazzini's obituary was published in the *New York Tribune* on March 12, 1872, 2, col. 1.

5 JA, *Twenty*, 30. Oglesby served as governor of Illinois from 1865 to 1869 and was reelected in 1872.

6 JA, *Twenty*, 30; MHJ, "Notes," in file "John Huy Addams, Public Life," JAC. In 1876 he was a delegate from Stephenson County at the district's Republican Congressional Convention at Freeport. *Freeport Journal*, September 20, 1876, 4. In 1880 he spoke at a "grand demonstration by the Republicans." *Freeport Journal*, October 20, 1880, 5, col. 1.

7 Re JHA's friendship with Trumbull, see JA, *Twenty*, 34.

8 JHA, "Speech," *Freeport Journal*, October 23, 1872, transcript, JAC; Allen and Lacey, *Illinois Elections*, 180; JA, *Twenty*, 54–56.

9 JA, *Twenty*, 276; Wise, *Addams*, 52.

10 MAL to AAH, October 10, 1867, HJP; Weber Addams described Mary playing with her friend Laura Gorham. Laura pretended to be "Pa" and Mary brought him his slippers. John Weber Addams to JHA, February 23, 1860, JAC.

11 *Freeport Journal*, March 27, 1878, 2, col. 4.

12 The first quotation is from JA, "Subjective Necessity," 14; Sarah W. Addams's books included Mrs. [Sarah Stickney] Ellis, *The Wives of England, Their Relative Duties, Domestic Influence, and Social Obligations* (New York: Appleton, 1843); Ellis, *The Women of England, Their Social Duties and Domestic Habits* (New York: D. Appleton, 1843); Ellis, *The Mothers of England, Their Influence and Responsibility* (New York: D. Appleton, 1844); Ellis, *The Daughters of England, Their Society, Character and Responsibilities* (New York: D. Appleton, 1843); Ellis, *Guide to Social Happiness* (New York: E. Walker, 1848). Addams Family Library List. Re the advice, see Ellis, *Women of England*, 131, 137–38; Margaret Coxe, *Claims of the Country on American Females*, quoted in Theriot, *Mothers and Daughters*, 27. Coxe's book is listed in the Addams Family Library List. The author of the second quotation is Elizabeth Oakes Smith, quoted in Theriot, *Mothers and Daughters*, 27. The Stowe quotations are found in Golden, *Slaying the Mermaid*, 94.

13 JA wrote to EGS that she reread *Little Dorrit* and *Dombey and Son* during the summer of 1879. JA to Ellen Gates Starr (hereafter cited as EGS), August 11, 1879. No documentation exists that she read *Bleak House* and *David Copperfield*, but given her enthusiasm for Dickens, it seems more than likely. The quotation is from JA diary, June 2, 1875.

14 AHA to AAH, July 6, 1871, SAHP. AHA writes that she has been reading *Prominent Women of the Age*, but she was probably reading *Eminent Women of the Age: Being Narratives of the Lives and Deeds of the Most Prominent Women of This Generation* (Hartford: Betts, 1868).

15 Elizabeth Cady Stanton, "Our Girls," reprinted in Waggenspack, *Search for Self-Sovereignty*, 141, 145. The speeches of Lucy Stone, Susan B. Anthony, Mary Livermore, and Elizabeth Cady Stanton were all published in the *Tribune*'s pages, as their biographies document.

16 JA, *Twenty*, 54; re Weber, see *Selected Papers*, 39–40. Mary was opposed to women giving speeches in public, which was a more conservative position than opposing suffrage. MAL to AAH, January 21, 1869, HJP; AHA to JHA, January 11, 1869, JAC; Buechler, *Transformation*, 68.

17 JHA to AHA, February 20, 1869, JAC. Livermore's remarks were indeed more conciliatory and more reasoned than Stanton's, which were quite pugnacious. *Illinois State Register*, February 20, 1869, 4, col. 2.

18 Re JA's admiration for Stone, see Linn, *Addams*, 404; *Time*, January 2, 1933, 24. Re Stone's career, see Blackwell, *Lucy Stone*; Kerr, *Lucy Stone*; Million, *Woman's Voice, Woman's Place*. Two speeches by Stone reprinted in the *New York Tribune* in these years are those of May 12, 1870, 2, col. 2, and May 11, 1871, 8, cols. 1 and 2. She was also featured in a news story September 28, 1872, 2. Re Stone as speaker, see Livermore, *Story*, 586; re Livermore, see *Notable American Women*, s.v. "Mary Livermore."

19 Linn, *Addams*, 262.

20 JA, "Progressive Party and the Negro," 30–31.

21 JA, *Twenty*, 22; Browning, "Aurora Leigh," bk. 1, lines 727–28. Addams slightly revised Browning's lines, which read: "He wrapt his little daughter in his large / Man's doublet, careless did it fit or no."

22 The evidence is strong that AHA subscribed to the *Atlantic Monthly*. She brought "bound magazine volumes" with her to Cedarville; JA read the writings of Mary Ann Holmes, who was serialized in the magazine; JA came to admire Owen and Brown in the 1870s, when the two men's ideas and accomplishments were featured at length in the magazine (see below). The three Owen articles were by Robert Dale Owen, the son of Robert Owen. "Robert Owen at New Lanark," *Atlantic Monthly*, March 1873, 310–21; "The Social Experiment at New Harmony," *Atlantic Monthly*, August 1873, 224–36; "My Experience of Community Life," *Atlantic Monthly*, September 1873, 336–48. "The Virginia Campaign of John Brown" was a six-part series by F. B. Sanborn published in the *Atlantic Monthly* throughout 1875.

23 Owen, "Social Experiment at New Harmony," 230; the quotation appears in Potter, *Cooperative*, 25–26. For Owen's role in the cooperative movement, see Webb,
Industrial Cooperation, 2.

24 JA, *Twenty*, 143; JA to MRS, August [4], 1904.

25 *Freeport Weekly Journal*, June 27, 1877, 6, col. 4. This advertisement for the cooperative gives the date of its founding. For more on the history of the cooperative movement in Illinois in these years, see Warne, *Consumer's Co-operative
Movement*. In 1877 the Stephenson County Farmers' Cooperative was advertis-
ing plows for $18 and reminding farmers that they used to have to pay $23 for
them. *Freeport Weekly Journal*, June 27, 1877, 6, col. 4. JHA did participate in a
cooperative, but it was in the noneconomic realm. The Union Library Company
of Cedar Creek Mills, which he co-founded, was a cooperative. Members bought
shares for $2 each. *Selected Papers*, 11. See *Bylaws, JAPM*, 28:0852. JHA and his
neighbors borrowed the idea from fellow Pennsylvanian Ben Franklin, whose
biography was one of the books in the library. 1847 Catalogue.

26 JA, "Tramps," April 4, 1878, *JAPM*, 45:1757. For more on JA's views concerning
the ethic of work in these years, see debate essay, "Resolved: That the Invention and Use of Machinery" [November 1877], *JAPM*, 45:1644–52, reprinted in
Selected Papers, 255–57.

27 *Freeport Budget*, August 27, 1881, 4, col. 4; letter of Rev. Isaac E. Carey, in which is
included the funeral sermon of Rev. Irvine, pastor of the Presbyterian Church
of Cedarville, letter printed in *Freeport Budget*, August 27, 1881, 4, col. 4. The
quotation is from the funeral sermon.

28 Cole, *Social Ideas*, 170; E. Foner, *Free Soil*, 27.

29 U.S. Bureau of the Census, *1870 Census*, "Selected Nativities by Counties, Table
VII—State of Illinois," 352; JA, *Twenty*, 12.

30 Re "Dutchman," see Lyman, *Civil War Wordbook*, 59; JA, *Democracy*, 238. The
quotation is from JHA diary, August 9, 1844. Re the Republican Party and anti-
immigration laws, see Keyssar, *Right to Vote*, 84–86.

31 JA, "Resolved: That the Invention and Use of Machinery," n.p. Re anti-
immigrant nativism, see Higham, *Strangers in the Land*, 15, 26; Jacobsen, *Whiteness of a Different Color*, 48; Sandel, *Democracy's Discontent*, 153.

32 JA, *Twenty*, 38.

33 Ibid., 35–36; 1847 Catalogue; L. Edwards, *Psyche as Hero*, 3, 285n1.

34 JA, *Twenty*, 36. She writes that she lost her enthusiasm for Carlyle that day. She
regained it in college. See JA to EGS, May 15, 1880.

35 JA to Vallie Beck, March 16, 1876. For more on Beck, see *Selected Papers*, 134–35.
The quotation is from Alcott, *Little Women*, pt. 1, chap. 13, "Castles in the Air."
Barbara Sicherman writes with insight about *Little Women*'s influence on ado-
lescents of JA's generation in "Reading and Ambition," 93. See also her "Sense
and Sensibility," 71–89.

36 Re JA's high school enthusiasm for Emerson, see Sidwell, "Sage and Sybil,"

193. The new edition she read was Ralph Waldo Emerson, *Essays, Second Series; Representative Men; and The Conduct of Life*, rev. ed. (New York: 1876). She refers to Emerson in "Claim on the College Woman," 60; "Unexpected Reactions," 178. The quoted words are from Emerson, "Man the Reformer," in *Emerson*, 135, 143.

37 JA, *Spirit*, 76–77.

38 JA to Vallie Beck, March 30–April 2, 1876; Wise, *Addams*, 57; Maas, *Glorious Enterprise*, 94, 113, 69; Ingram, *Centennial Exposition*, 115–16; *Concise Dictionary of American History*, 168. Re Emerson and Adams quotations, see Maas, *Glorious Enterprise*, 101–2; Paine, "Women's Pavilion of 1876," 6–9 (despite the article title, Paine uses "Woman's" in the text); McCabe, *Illustrated History*, 219.

39 Wise, *Addams*, 58.

40 JA to Vallie Beck, March 21, 1877.

41 JA *Twenty*, 19. Addams says she was fifteen, but, according to the Beer gravestone next to the Addams family plot in the Cedarville cemetery, Mary Beer died January 7, 1877, when Jane was sixteen.

42 *Selected Papers*, 154n1; JA, *Twenty*, 19–20.

43 JA, *Twenty*, 50; Emerson, "Nature," in *Emerson*, 555.

44 See MAL to AAH, May 18, 1867, HJP. She writes that she is glad that "you have been brought to accept Christ as your savior."

45 Emerson, "Idealism," in *Emerson*, 32–39.

46 JA to Vallie Beck, May 3, 1877, In her popular novel *The Woman Who Dared* (1869), Epes Sargent described the dangers of romantic love: "Passion is not Love; it may exist as Hate; too often [it] leads its victims blindfold into hateful bonds." Quoted in Leach, *True Love and Perfect Union*, 117.

47 Emerson, "Plato; or, the Philosopher" and "Plato: New Readings," in *Emerson*, 633–60. Re Platonic love, see Alger, *Friendships of Women*, 115, 120; Leach, *True Love*, 111–29; Flora Guiteau, "Notes for a Talk on Jane Addams," April 7, 1936, 2, in "Memorials," JACR; JA to Vallie Beck, March 21, 1877.

48 Most of JA's surviving passports give her height as five feet four inches. *JAPM*, 27:0492; JA diary, March 29, 1875, April 1, 1875; Wise, *Addams*, 50; Linn, *Addams*, 49, 77; JA to Vallie Beck, May 3, 1877.

49 JA to Vallie Beck, January 8, 1877. The Addams family library, which contained some of AHA's books, too, included George Combe's *Lectures on Phrenology*, 3rd ed. (New York: Edward Kearny, 1846). Addams Family Library List. Bryan provides details about the society in *Selected Papers*, 143–46. The handbill is titled "The Phrenological Office and Book Store," Est. 1843, Philadelphia. *JAPM*, 28:0729. See Kagan, *Unstable Ideas*, 109.

50 *JAPM*, 28:0730, 0736. The complete assessment for Jane Addams is reprinted in *Selected Papers*, 144–45.

51 *Rockford Catalogue, 1875–76*, RCA. Board meetings were held once a year, in June. John Addams never attended a meeting and, after the board made in-

quiries, he resigned on June 24, 1879. Rockford College Board of Trustees, Minutes, June 25, 1878, June 24, 1879, RCA. Re the collegiate certificate, see Townsend, *Best Helpers*, 150. Lucy Stone was famous for being one of the first women to earn a B.A.; she did so in 1847. Regarding the curricula at men's colleges, see Stevenson, *Victorian Homefront*, 104–5; Horowitz, *Alma Mater*, 70; Eschbach, *Higher Education*, 62–63; JA, *Twenty*, 43.

52 The figure of .24 percent was calculated as follows. In 1870, 7 percent of college students were women (Harris, "Educational Conference Address," 136). Harris makes it clear that he is applying a rigorous curriculum-based definition of college. According to Rudolph, 52,286 students were enrolled in college in the 1870s (Rudolph, *Curriculum*, 101). Seven percent of this number is 3,735, or .24 percent of the total number of women aged eighteen to twenty-one in the population in 1870 (1,537,823). The number of women enrolled in various sorts of postsecondary education in 1872 (to pick one year of the decade) was much higher—11,288. Woody, *History*, 1:396. Thus roughly a third of women pursuing advanced education in the early 1870s were attending a real college. Re seminaries that called themselves colleges, see Woody, *History*, 2:457, 147, 174. Re the percentage of college-aged men attending college, see Stevenson, *Victorian Homefront*, 101. The book most responsible for creating hysteria about women going to college was Edward H Clarke, *Sex in Education, or A Fair Chance for Girls* (Boston: Osgood, 1873).

53 JA, *Twenty*, 43. Re Alice's travels, see *Selected Papers*, 518.

54 *Smith College Official Circular, 1877–1878*, 2, SSC; "Smith College," *Scribner's Monthly*, May 1877, 9–17; *Rockford Female Seminary Catalogue, 1875–76*, RCA; *Smith College Official Circular, 1877–78*, 2, SSC. Eschbach reports that many of Smith's students were special students in its early years. *Higher Education*, 63. Linn is in error when he writes that she took the entrance exams at Smith in 1877. Linn, *Addams*, 40.

55 JA, *Twenty*, 60–61; re the "wider life," see JA, "Sunday Rest," 156. "Smith College," *Scribner's Monthly*, May 1877, 9–17. In *Twenty Years* Addams writes of her plan to go to medical school in the chapter about Rockford Seminary; I suspect that the goal was formed while she was in high school and that it shaped her interest in Smith.

56 Cedar Cliff; re Bucher, see *Selected Papers*, 115–16. JA recalls the day of Bucher's funeral in *Excellence*, 158–59. He died in late September 1874. *Freeport Bulletin*, October 1, 1874, 8. She visited the Haldemans in Iowa in 1877. JA to Vallie Beck, May 3, 1877.

57 JA, *Twenty*, 60–61; JA mentions reading *Jericho Road* in a letter to Vallie Beck, March 21, 1877. *Bleak House* is not mentioned in her correspondence or diary, but five other Dickens novels are. JA diary, February 13, 1875, June 2, 1875; JA to Vallie Beck, May 30, 1877; JA to EGS, August 11, 1879. In Charles Reade's *A Woman Hater*, a young American woman applies to the University of Edin-

burgh to study medicine. In college, this is precisely JA's plan. Reade's book was published in 1877, just when Addams was thinking about pursuing medicine.

58 "A Glimpse at Some of Our Charities, Part II," *Harper's Monthly* 61, no. 134 (March 1878): 601. Stillé is quoted in Lusk, "Monstrous Productions," 4.

59 John Manning Linn to JA, August 26, 1881.

60 JA, *Twenty*, 43.

CHAPTER FOUR: AMBITION

1 JA, *Twenty*, 43; Linn, *Addams*, 410–11.

2 Re Sarah Blaisdell, see *Selected Papers*, 184–85n45, 572, 174. Re Sarah Anderson, see MAL to AAH, March 9, 1867, box 1, SAAH; Wise, *Addams*, 77; Townsend, *Best Helpers*, 64. Re meeting Sill as a child, see AAH to JA, December 7, 1871.

3 Re Sill, see H. Goodwin, *Memorials*, 11; Cedarborg, "Early History of Rockford College," 82; Townsend, *Best Helpers*, 58, *Selected Papers*, 165, 178–79nn6, 10. Re the school's history, see Townsend, *Best Helpers*, 21, 32–41; H. Goodwin, *Memorials*, 19; *Selected Papers*, 162–63; *Rockford Female Seminary Catalogue*, 1871–72, 16, and 1874–75, 17, RCA. The motto is from Psalms 144:12. See also JA, *My Friend*, 13, and Townsend, *Best Helpers*, 81 (see 47 for the Sill quotation). Re religious requirements, see Townsend, *Best Helpers*, 167; Linn, *Addams*, 47; EGS to JA, December 25, 1879; *Twenty*, 49; Townsend, "Gender Effect," 74.

4 JA, *Twenty*, 15. For one reason she was refusing to convert, see JA, *Long Road*, 160–62.

5 JA, *Twenty*, 50, 49, 58; Linn, *Addams*, 411; *Twenty*, 56; JA to JHA, March 20, 1881.

6 The quotation is from Vallie Beck to JA, November 4, 1877. Re Vallie's inquiry of JA, see Vallie Beck to JA, December 1877. Re a friend's experience at another school, see Ida Carey to JA, December 5, 1877. JA's letters to her friends do not survive, but her friends' letters mirror what she had written to them.

7 *New York Sun*, April 30, 1910, quoted by Davis, introduction to *Spirit*, by JA, xxii.

8 The assignment pattern is evident from the dates, topics, and arguments of the first-year papers that survive. It was also common practice in higher education. See Berlin, *Writing Instruction*. Essays reflecting her father's views include "The Present Policy of Congress"; "Tramps"; "Resolved: That the Invention and Use of Machinery"; and "Plated Ware." I date this essay to November 1877 because the handwriting and frequent spelling mistakes suggest that it was written in her first year, and the first-year essay for the spring debate is dated and survives. The debates took place in November and February. Six of her debate essays survive, four of them dated. Because the essay by JA's opponent for this debate was published in the *Rockford Seminary Magazine* in April 1879, Bryan concludes that the debate took place that spring.

9 Sarah Anderson Ainsworth to JA, [April 1910]; Linn, *Addams*, 40, 46, 47. In October, 1885 JA wrote AAH she weighed 114 pounds, "more than I have weighed since I was seventeen." JA to AAH, October 23, 1885. Linn's statement that she

weighed 95 pounds in 1877 seems to be an error. "We liked going" is Corinne Williams Douglas's statement, quoted in Linn, *Addams*, 47.

10 For more on EGS, see Bosch, "Life of Ellen Gates Starr"; Stebner, *Women of Hull House*, 83–95; *Selected Papers*, 544–61.

11 Bedell, "Chicago Toynbee Hall," 1; Clark, "Ellen Gates Starr," 446; Josephine Starr, "Biographical Notes," 3, EGSP; "I have seen you," is from Frances Crane Lillie to EGS, quoted in Mary F. L. Barrows's memoir of Frances Crane Lillie (n.p., n.d.), 86, EGSP; EGS to JA, August 11, 1878.

12 JA to EGS, August 12, 1883; Linn, *Addams*, 45.

13 JA, seminary transcript, JAP, SCPC, *JAPM*, 27:0462. Some details are drawn from the seminary's catalogues for 1877–1881. JA's exam results for all four years are reprinted in Brandt, *Jane Addams Papers*, 4.

14 AHA to JA, June 11, 1878. Vallie Beck wrote to JA, February 5, 1878, "When do you expect to enter Vassar?" Beck may have been confused, or perhaps JA was actually considering Vassar. JHA to JA, June 17, 1878.

15 Hattie Smith to JA, August 28, 1878; Bosch, "Life of Ellen Gates Starr," 18; EGS to JA, August 11, 1878.

16 Re Jane's favorite teacher, see Linn, *Addams*, 59. See also JA, *Twenty*, 47. For JA's second-year courses, see *Selected Papers*, 231. The quotation is from JA, *My Friend*, 15–16. Potter was paid the highest salary of any female teacher. Minutes, Board of Trustees, Rockford Female Seminary, July 6, 1880, RCA. For more on Potter see Minutes, Board of Trustees, September 15, 1882; [Rockford] *Alumnae Notes* 1, no.1 (March 1915): 3–4; *Rockford College Bulletin of Information*, 1937, 3, RCA; and *Selected Papers*, 184n44.

17 In *On Heroes* Carlyle lays out the hero's characteristics. Biographies of Washington, Napoleon, Franklin, and others found in JHA's library also emphasized them.

18 The quotation is from C. Potter, "Dear Friend," 54. This undated letter from Potter was first printed in the *Auburn* [IL] *Daily Advocate*, n.d. See also C. Potter, "Madonna of the Future," 218–19. Re Fuller's ideas about woman's power see Fuller, *Woman in the Nineteenth Century*, 163, 171, 175, 115–16. See also Howe, *Making the American Self*, chap. 4. Re Emerson on masculinity and femininity, see Emerson, "Character," in *Emerson*, 499. As for Fuller's ideas appearing in JA's essays, Addams writes about Isis (Fuller, *Woman in the Nineteenth Century*, 51), Shakespeare's Portia (52–53), George Sand (75), Cassandra (105–6, 116), the female brooding soul (102), and woman's special intuitive genius (115). She also enacts Fuller's belief that women should speak in public (ibid., 110). I discuss these themes in this chapter. Re Portia, see JA to Eva Goodrich [Campbell], July 25, 1879. It appears that Margaret Fuller, one of the United States' early women intellectuals, was an important influence on Jane Addams.

19 C. Potter, "Dear Friend," 54; C. Potter, "Madonna of the Future," 218–19.

20 Re Potter's role in the magazine and the societies, see Townsend, *Best Helpers*,

174; *Rockford Seminary Magazine* (hereafter *RSM*) 11, no. 8 (July 1883): 222. Her role was so crucial that in 1883, when she left Rockford Seminary, the societies disbanded and the magazine published its last issue. Cedarborg, "Early History," 59. Re student participation, see Knight, "Authoritative Voice," 244n67. The lists of members of the two societies in the *Rockford Catalogues* match the lists of students in the collegiate classes. Re JA's involvement, see *Selected Papers*, 230n2, 241.

21 Re JHA's literary society, see JHA to Enos Reitt, January 26, 1843, box 1, JAC. Re literary societies, see Knight, "Authoritative Voice," 225–26. Henry M. Robert, *Pocket Manual of Rules of Order for Deliberative Assemblies* (Chicago: S. C. Griggs and Co., 1876).

22 Beloit's extemporaneous debates are described in "College Literary Societies," *RSM* 7, no. 8 (December 1879): 271. Re Wellesley, Smith, and Vassar Colleges, see Knight, "Authoritative Voice," 226, 245n71; Nanci Young, college archivist, Smith College, pers. comm., April 6, 2000.

23 JA, "Resolved: That French women" [first version, November 13, 1878], *JAPM*, 45:1797, reprinted in *Selected Papers*, 241–44. George Sand is featured in Fuller, *Woman*, 75–76.

24 Mary Downs, who had been at Rockford with Jane her sophomore year but did not return, referred in 1880 to Jane's plans to earn a B.A. at Smith, travel, then study medicine. Mary Downs to JA, May 23, 1880. See also Eva Pennell to JA, January 8, 1880. Re the Science Club, see *RSM* 6 (April 1878): 81–82. Re summers with George, see JA, *Twenty*, 62; Linn, *Addams*, 34; Wise, *Addams*, 72–74; JA to EGS, August 11, 1879; JA to George Haldeman, April 26, 1882. Re Darwin, see Wise, *Addams*, 74; JA, *Twenty*, 62. For botany class JA compiled an herbarium. This potentially scientifically useful collection survives, plants intact and names and locations labeled, at the Cedarville Historical Society. *Selected Papers*, 233–34n18; *JAPM*, 1A:0017. Re science as a field, see Townsend, *Best Helpers*, 107.

25 JA to EGS, February 13, 1881; JA, "Follow Thou Thy Star," 183–85; JA, *Twenty*, 62.

26 Arnold, *Culture and Anarchy*, 5, 34. JA quotes from *Culture and Anarchy* without identifying her source in "Resolved: The Civilization of the Nineteenth Century Tends." Re JA's enthusiasm for Arnold, see also JA to EGS, August 11, 1879; JA to EGS, February 13, 1881; JA to Flora Guiteau, January 7, 1888; Hackett, "Hull-House—A Souvenir," 279; JA, "Chicago Settlements and Social Unrest," 166. Emerson, "Considerations by the Way," in *Emerson*, 1096. Arnold understood the similarities between what he was advocating and religion, which he called "that other effort after perfection." *Culture and Anarchy*, 55.

27 JA, *Twenty*, 45.

28 JA to Eva Campbell [Goodrich], July 25, 1879; see also *Selected Papers*, 275n10. Re Merrill, see ibid., 273–74.

29 Re the four faculties, see Howe, *Making the American Self*, 130. JA, "Follow Thou Thy Star," 184; the phrase "follow thy star" is borrowed from Dante; it is quoted by Carlyle in *On Heroes*, 109. Bryan cites its source in Dante. *Selected Papers*, 285n3. The phrase "faculties are all locked up" is from Emerson's "Character," although Addams adapts its meaning. *Emerson*, 495. JA used the phrase again in "Savonarola," *JAPM*, 45:1654. Other essays by JA about the hero besides "Follow Thou Thy Star" include "Night Hath Stars" (45:1722), "We Miss the Abstract When We Comprehend" (45:1824), "High Trees Take the Wind" (45:1637), "Savonarola," "Bellerophon" (46:0090), "The Gipsies of Romance" (46:0049), "The Notion of Conscience" (46:0099), "Fear as a Conservative Element" (46:0141), all from *JAPM*, and "Self-Tradition," *RSM* 9 (April 1881): 97–100.

30 Re the crisis, see Eva Campbell [Goodrich] to JA, June 18, 1879; JA to Eva Campbell [Goodrich], July 25, 1879. Letters in *Selected Papers*, 258–60, 268–73, 260n2; [JA], "Editorial," *RSM* 7, no. 5 (June 1879) 5:166–67. Although the editorial is unsigned, there are clear similarities between it and her paper "Follow Thou Thy Star" (published in the same issue) as well as some direct borrowings. See Emerson, "Experience," in *Emerson*, 472, 479.

31 The woman who was her roommate during her sophomore year wrote her the following year, "Do you talk as strongly as you did last year of going east or do you think to graduate at RS first?" Eva Campbell [Goodrich] to JA, June 1, 1880; JA's letter about deciding to return to Rockford does not survive, but her decision is mirrored in Eva's reply. Eva Campbell [Goodrich] to JA, June 18, 1879: "So you are surely going back there next fall."

32 JA to Eva Campell [Goodrich], July 25, 1879; JA to EGS, August 11, 1879.

33 JA to EGS, August 11, 1879.

34 EGS to JA, October 12–19, 1879.

35 Quoted by JA in a letter to EGS, February 13, 1881. "Self-Dependence" is a poem in JA, commonplace book, n.p., box 1, "Rockford Notebooks," JAC, *JAPM*, 27:0147 (hereafter cited as commonplace book). JA quotes this stanza again in an editorial in *RSM* 9 (May 1881): 154. The commonplace book was actually two physical documents, each unpaginated. One is dated May 5, 1878 in the inside front cover. *JAPM*, 27:0147. The other is dated March 5, 1880. *JAPM*, 27:0352. She used it as late as 1882. Although Linn, Bryan, and others have called these her "notebooks," Addams calls them her commonplace books (*Twenty*, 36), by which she meant places to record favorite quotations. However, she often failed to record the author's name or include quotation marks. Some personal entries and some class notes are randomly scattered about.

36 See Carlyle, "Characteristics," in *Critical and Miscellaneous Essays* (New York: Appleton, 1865); K. Harris, *Carlyle and Emerson*, 19–21; Emerson, "Self-Reliance" (268–69) and "Intellect" (418–19), in *Emerson*; Arnold, *Culture and Anarchy*, 132.

37 JA, commonplace book, n.p; Eliot, *Romola*, 145. For more on Eliot's views of woman's nature and women's intuition, see *Romola*, 434, 363, 538. Re the description of Isis, see JA, "The Nebular Hypothesis" (January 28, 1880), which Bryan reprints with notes in *Selected Papers*, 324–33. For other uses of "deeper and more primordial," see "Bellerophon," "Darkness versus Nebulae," and "Cassandra." She also used it in a letter: "Friendship depends on something a good deal deeper and more primordial than conversation " JA to Clara Lutts, January 14–17, 1880, photocopy in possession of the author. She had first come across Isis in her reading in the summer of 1880. See Bulwer-Lytton, *Last Days of Pompeii*, 34, 52, 137; Fuller, *Woman*, 115–16.

38 JA to EGS, August 11, 1879.

39 JA, seminary transcript, *JAPM*, 27:0462; the grade point average is based on the grade points in her transcript.

40 Re abandoning mental prayer, see JA to EGS, January 29, 1880. For "I am shocked," see JA to EGS, February 29, 1880. Re reading Greek with Blaisdell, see JA, *Twenty*, 51. For "always feel," see JA to Clara Lutts, January 14–17, 1880, photocopy in author's possession. Re religion's appeal as story, see *Twenty*, 52. Re her shallow love of heroes, see JA to EGS, May 15, 1880. See also Carson, *Settlement Folk*, 45–46.

41 Re the Castalian Society meeting, see *RSM*, November 1879, 238, 243. Programme, *JAPM*, 27:0378–80; see also JA, "Gipsies of Romance"; JA, ["Tonight Is Walpurgis Night"]. The nearby men's college, Beloit College, held an oratorical exhibition; it was probably the inspiration. See [Beloit] *Roundtable* 25, no. 13 (April 23, 1879): 179; [Beloit] *Roundtable* 26, no. 1 (September 26, 1879): 25. See also *Selected Papers*, 350n4, 351n1. Addams is identified as class president in the program for the event. *JAPM*, 27:378–80. Although it is sometimes claimed that she was class president all four years or that she was president her senior year as well as her junior year, I have only been able to reliably document her junior-year presidency. One unreliable source claims that JA was class president three of her four years at seminary. "Jane Addams," [*Rockford College*] *Alumnae Notes* 1, no. 1 (March 1915): 2, RCA.

42 JA, transcript, *JAPM*, 27:0462. For details of her studies, see the report on the grades she received on her exams in Brandt, *Jane Addams Papers*, 44. JA wrote a college essay on Cicero and Caesar. See *JAPM*, 46:62. Alexander Bain, *English Composition and Rhetoric: A Manual*, 4th ed. (London: Longmans, Green, 1877), 171. For Potter's use of Bain, see *Rockford Catalogue, 1877–78*, 21, and *1880–81*, 22, RCA. For the other expert's quotation see Reed, introduction to *Modern Eloquence*, 1:vii.

43 Townsend, *Best Helpers*, 177–78; "Bread Givers," news clipping, April 20, 1880, Sill Scrapbook, 95, RCA. The class list appears in *Rockford Catalogue, 1879–80*, 7; [Junior Exhibition] Programme, *JAPM*, 27:0379.

44 Although the program titles Addams's first speech as "Opening Address," histo-

rians have referred to it as "Breadgivers" in recognition of its theme. The *Random House Unabridged Dictionary*, 2d ed., gives "hlafdige" as the Old English word of origin for "lady" and defines it to mean "loaf-kneader."

45 Re the class motto, see JA to AAH, January 23, 1880. At least one classmate interpreted the motto narrowly. Kate Tanner, "Too Many Gates to Swing On," *Essays of Graduating Class, Rockford Seminary, Thirtieth Commencement, Wednesday, June 22, 1881* (DeKalb, IL: News Steam Press, 1881), 19–20, *JAPM*, 27:0441–0442. The Ruskin quotation is from "Of Queen's Gardens," 89. Women as "breadgivers" forms an extended metaphor in "Of Queen's Gardens." In the Old Testament, the prophets instruct the people to provide bread to the poor. In the New Testament, Jesus gives bread to the poor who follow him and blesses it as a symbol of his body. The bread metaphor predominates throughout Emerson's essay "Man the Reformer." See *Emerson*, 145, 149. Re Potter on bread, see C. Potter, "Madonna of the Future." "Class Song," *RSM* 8 (April 1880): 109–10, *JAPM*, 46:0189.

46 As if to demonstrate the success of her rhetorical strategy, scholars have disagreed about whether to interpret "Breadgivers" as endorsing solely the traditional domestic role for women or as calling for women to move out into wider work. See Townsend and O'Neil, "Things Beyond Us," 37; Ross, "Gendered Social Knowledge, 237–39; Peaden, "Jane Addams," 194; Davis, *Heroine*, 20; Rudnick, "Feminist Success Myth," 150; Elshtain, *Addams*, 43–44, 157–58; V. Brown, *Education*, 69–70, 319n65.

47 Some have supposed that JA delivered this oration in Greek because she reports taking it to the Greek professor at Beloit (Sarah Blaisdell's brother) to make sure it contained "no mistakes." *Twenty*, 46. A news article about the Junior Exhibition, however, gives passages of the speech in English and makes no mention of her speech being delivered in Greek. "Bread Givers," *Rockford Register*, April 20, 1880, Sill Scrapbook, 95, RCA. The Greek version was undoubtedly for her Greek class. An English version with a Greek title survives in her college papers. *JAPM*, 46:90–94. See also *Selected Papers*, 352n2. JA, "Bellerophon." Emerson and Ruskin probably inspired her allegory. See Emerson, "The Poet," in *Emerson*, 452; Ruskin, in his *Queen of the Air*, mentions the Bellerophon myth twice in passing and stresses justice as one of Athena's virtues.

48 Anna Sill supported the junior oratorical exhibition and wanted Rockford to join the IIOA. See Anna Sill to Joseph Emerson, May 6, 1882, cited in Townsend, "Education," 239n21; *Selected Papers*, 400–1. Re IIOA procedures and JA's interest in elocution studies, see Knight, "Authoritative Voice," 231–37; C. Potter, "Intercollegiate Literary Contests," 37–40. Re the history of women competing in the IIOA contests, see Knight, "Authoritative Voice," 233, 245. Of the forty-two students from the coeducational schools in Illinois that competed in the intercollegiate contests between 1874 and 1879, only five were women. And they faced other forms of hostility. See ibid., 227, 245n72.

49 JA, *Twenty*, 55–56. Scholars have doubted whether Addams competed because she is not mentioned as competing in various relevant college newspapers or in the Galesburg newspaper. Reference to her participation was apparently omitted from these sources because of increasing opposition within the IIOA to women oratorical competitors. This opposition came to a head in the fall of 1880. See Knight, "Authoritative Voice," particularly 232–33 and 248–50nn114–123. Women have been omitted in this way from the printed record before. See Bacon, *Humblest*, 2. Re Bryan's competitive standing, see *Illinois College Rambler*, October 1880; the photograph is in Bryan and Bryan, *Memoirs*. For more about those in the photo, see Knight, "Authoritative Voice," 249n119 and passim. V. Brown believes that the story in *Twenty Years* about the oratorical contest "can easily be disproved." *Education*, 103. One scholar wonders whether the photograph is of the interstate competition. This is not possible because Bryan did not compete in Jacksonville. The quotation is from *Twenty* (56). Two pages later JA quotes from a speech she says she gave for "an oratorical contest" (58). The passage is from neither of her exhibition speeches, which were not for a contest, in any case. Was this speech the one she gave at Galesburg? The manuscript does not survive in her papers. She later lifted a sentence from the passage to use in her senior essay, "Cassandra." *Twenty*, 56.

50 JA, Editorial, *RSM* 8 (December 1880): 282; JA, Editorial, *RSM* 9 (March 1881): 86. See also JA to AAH, January 19, 1881.

51 The first quotation is from JA, Editorial, *RSM* 8 (November 1880): 256; JA, Editorial, *RSM* 8 (December 1880): 281. See also Flora Guiteau, "Notes for a Talk on Jane Addams," April 7, 1936, Rockford College Chapel, 4, JA Collection—Memorials, RCA; JA, *My Friend*, 23. The second quotation is from JA, Editorial, *RSM* 9 (May 1881): 155.

52 JA, Editorial, *RSM* 9 (January 1881): 24.

53 For the courses she took in her senior year, see JA transcript, *JAPM*, 27:0462. For "this year," see JA to EGS, February 13, 1881. The studies she mentions were both extra studies. Re her health suffering from hard study, see Sarah Anderson to JA, December 24, 1881 and January 11, 1882. Re dropping Greek see JA to AAH, January 19, 1881.

54 JA, "Home Items," *RSM* 7, no. 5 (June 1879): 158–63; Mary Downs to JA, May 23, 1880 (she describes JA's plans and asks her if they are still her plans); JA to EGS, February 13, 1881.

55 JA, "Magnificence of Character"; JA, Editorial, *RSM* 8 (November 1880): 256; JA, Editorial, *RSM* 9 (June 1881): 182.

56 JA, Editorial, *RSM* 9 (March 1881): 86; JA, Editorial, *RSM* 9 (June 1881): 180. She encountered the story of the Roman soldier in Bulwer-Lytton's *Last Days of Pompeii*.

57 JA to AAH, January 19, 1881. JA felt "cross and unsettled" during this Christmas vacation. JA to George Haldeman, April 26, 1881. She was apparently having

difficulty adjusting her expectations. Eliot, *Mill on the Floss*, 471. JA, common-place book, n.p. She replaced Eliot's word "natural" with the word "sacred." JA to AAH, January 19, 1881. See also JA, *Twenty*, 248.

58 JA to JHA, May 8, 1881; *Beloit Rambler* 3, no. 9 (January 1881): 100; JA to George Haldeman, May 8, 1881; JA to JHA, May 8, 1881. The timing of mail service to Cedarville is evident from the dates of the replies to letters in her seminary correspondence. Thirty years later, JA mixed up the sights she saw during her trip to Galesburg and to Jacksonville. *Twenty*, 55–56. This caused Linn to con-clude that she competed in the interstate contest in Jacksonville, not the in-tercollegiate contest in Galesburg. *Addams*, 53. This is despite the fact that her letters to George and her father make it clear that she was not competing at Jacksonville. Noting Linn's error, some scholars conclude that JA's confusion proves she never competed at Galesburg. See Davis, *Heroine*, 165–68; V. Brown, *Education*, 66–67. For further analysis, see Knight, "Authoritative Voice."

59 JA transcript, *JAPM*, 27:0462. JA took fifty single-semester courses, a very heavy academic load compared to Rockford's usual thirty-five to thirty-nine courses. See *Rockford Catalogue, 1877–1881*, RCA. Smith's course load in 1877, as best it can be calculated, was forty-five courses. *Smith College Circular*, 1877–78, SSC.

60 Sill was determined to bring the seminary up to the level of a college. For de-tails see Townsend, *Best Helpers*, 171; Linn, *Addams*, 411; V. Brown, *Education*, 100–101; *Selected Papers*, 161–64, 401, 412–14. Re Sill's offer, see JA to George Haldeman, May 8, 1881. Re the trustees' June decision, see Townsend, *Best Helpers*, 191.

61 JA still believed her seminary education was inferior in 1897. See JA to Ellen Hayes, May 22, 1897. *Smith College Circular 1877–78* (SSC) lists two history of-ferings and one English literature offering, all of them for juniors or seniors.

62 JA to George Haldeman, May 8, 1881; Emma Goodale Garvin to Hazel Cedar-borg, March 22, 1925, RCA. [Sidwell,] "Sage and Sibyl," 194; Vallie Beck to JA, February 5, 1878. For more on Garvin, see *Selected Papers*, 295–96n13.

63 JA, Editorial, *RSM* 8 (November 1880): 255; JA, *Twenty*, 63; JA, "College Woman and Christianity," 1853; JA, *Twenty*, 49.

64 Re Rollin Salisbury, see Linn, *Addams*, 63; JA to AAH, May 31, 1881. The quo-tation is from S. Kendall to JA, August 24, 1881; June 1881 news clippings, Sill Scrapbook; Minutes, Board of Trustees, Rockford College, June 1880; Anna Sill to Joseph Emerson, January, 1881, RCA.

65 *Thirtieth Commencement Program*, Rockford Seminary, *JAPM*, 27:0421; Linn, *Addams*, 63; JA to George Haldeman, May 29, 1881.

66 JA, "Valedictory," *RSM* 9 (July 1881): 219–22.

67 Addams knew Cassandra's story well; it was partially told in Homer's *Iliad* and told again in other Greek and Roman literature she had read: Aeschylus' "Agam-menon," Euripedes' "The Trojan Women" and "Alexander," Virgil's *Aeneid*, and Plutarch's *Moralia*. JA seems to have drawn her interpretation of Cassandra

from Plutarch's, Margaret Fuller's, and John Ruskin's observations. Plutarch writes in *Moralia*, in his "Rules for Politicians": "Cassandra had no reputation [for honor and justice] and that is why her prophecies did her people no good." Plutarch, *Selected Papers Essays*, 175. Fuller invokes Cassandra as a prophetess of intuitive power (*Woman in the Nineteenth Century*, 105–6, 116); in "Queen's Gardens," Ruskin writes that sympathy and justice are "woman's natural instincts" and recommends that woman "follow at least some one path of scientific attainment" in order to be "trained in habits of accurate thought" (77). The quotations in the text are from "Cassandra." Scholars have disagreed about how to interpret this speech. Several, e.g., Ross ("Gendered Social Knowledge, 239–40) and Westhoff (" 'A fatal drifting,' " 130–32) emphasize JA's gendered theory of knowledge. Davis (*Heroine*, 22–23) and V. Brown (*Education*, 92–97) affirm her desire to break with traditional female domestic roles, which S. Robbins ("Rereading," 42) sees her as endorsing.

68 JA, "Cassandra," 36–39. "Auctoritas" is misspelled "auethoritas" in the printed essay, which has other misspellings in it as well; a Roman citizen who had earned the respect of his fellow citizens and was attentively listened to in the Senate was said to possess auctoritas. J. Goodwin, "Forms of Authority," 276. Jane Addams would have encountered the idea of auctoritas in her junior-year course on Cicero but also in other Roman writings.

69 In 1910 Addams wrote that she chose medicine as a career because, as she expressed it in "Cassandra," she feared being always right but disbelieved. *Twenty*, 61.

CHAPTER FIVE: FAILURE

1 Sarah Anderson to JA, July 14, 1881; Helen Harrington to JA, July 23, 1881; Eleanor Frothingham to JA, September 22, 1881. The decision about Smith College was apparently made before the Garfield assassination attempt. When Alice left Illinois to return home to Kansas after attending JA's June 22 commencement ceremony, she knew that JA would not be going to Smith the following fall. Helen Harrington to JA, July 23, 1881. (The letter mentions that a mutual friend ran into Alice on the train and heard the news.). Even if Alice visited in Cedarville for a week after the ceremony, this would still date the decision before July 2. For the date of the ceremony, see *Selected Papers*, 422n1.

2 JA, "College Woman and the Family Claim," 4, 7.

3 Ibid., 4. For a list of Addams's speeches on this subject, see. Knight, "Biography's Window," 137n76.

4 Eliot, *Mill on the Floss*, 471; JA, "Settlement as a Factor," 200.

5 Helen Harrington to JA, July 23, 1881; Emma Briggs to JA, December 30, 1881; Helen Harrington to JA, July 25, 1882; Emma Briggs to JA, August 27, 1882; Eleanor Frothingham to JA, December 31, 1881. "Many a young woman" is from JA, *My Friend*, 25; JA, *Spirit*, 103. She used the phrase again in *Excellent*, 6.

6 For Luther Guiteau's obituary, see *Freeport Daily Bulletin*, July 21, 1880. Re Luther W. Guiteau Jr.'s employment at the Second National Bank, see *Chicago Inter-Ocean*, July 5, 1881, 2.

7 For JHA's interview with the reporter, see *Freeport Journal*, July 6, 1881, 5, col. 2, box 1, JAP. Re his activities to help the Guiteau family, see Fry, *Generous Spirit*, 39; *Freeport Daily Bulletin*, July 5, 1881. Re JHA's relationship with Julius Guiteau, see *Freeport Journal*, December 7, 1881, n.p., quoted in MHJ, "Notes, JHA Public Life," 22, box 1, series 7, JAC.

8 *Chicago Daily Inter-Ocean*, July 4, 1881, 12. Re the public reaction to Guiteau's deed, see Rosenberg, *Trial*, 51.

9 Hayes, *Complete History*, 120, 125, 503; Rosenberg, *Trial*, 31–32, 68, 129; Hayes, *Complete History*, 131; *Chicago Inter-Ocean*, July 4, 1881, 10. In 1882, Charles Julius Guiteau's sister Frances would be judged insane. Rosenberg, *Trial*, 256.

10 Editorial, *Freeport Budget*, July 9, 1881, 4, cols. 1 and 2.

11 Re symptoms, see Schiller, "Spinal Irritation and Osteopathy," 258–59; G. Beard, *Practical Treatise*, 7, 79. For a history of neurasthenia and the significance of the Guiteau trial, see Gosling, *Before Freud*, 21. Re insanity and neurasthenia, see Oppenheim, "*Shattered Nerves*," 7. Re causes of neurasthenia, see Hayes, *Complete History*, 185; Grob, *Mad among Us*, 135. Rosenberg, *Trial*, 60, 69.

12 Rosenberg, *Trial*, 248. Guiteau would be ruled "not insane" because he understood the consequences of his crime. The M'Naughten Rule, applied to Guiteau, held that a defendant was legally insane only if he did not understand the consequences of his actions. *American National Biography*, 1999, s.v. "Guiteau."

13 Hayes, *Complete History*, 131; Gosling, *Before Freud*, 21.

14 *Freeport Budget*, July 30, 1881, 3, col. 4.

15 Wise, *Addams*, 91.

16 *Freeport Weekly Journal*, August 24, 1881, 8.

17 JA, *Excellent*, 61; JA to EGS, September 3, 1881.

18 *Freeport Daily Bulletin*, August 18, 1881; JHA obituaries in box 1, series 7, JAC; *Freeport Weekly Journal*, August 24, 1881, 8, cols. 3 and 4; an editorial that appeared in the Chicago *Evening Journal* (n.d.) was reprinted in the *Freeport Budget*, August 27, 1881, 4, col. 2.

19 *Freeport Daily Bulletin*, August 18 , 1881, 1, in Sill Scrapbook, RCA.

20 L. H. Mitchell to JA, March 22, 1886; *Freeport Weekly Journal*, August 24, 1881, 8.

21 Re crowd size, see *Freeport Daily Bulletin*, August 20, 1881; *Freeport Weekly Journal*, August 24, 1881, 8. The minister's remarks are printed in *Freeport Budget*, August 27, 1881.

22 She titled a collection of memorial addresses *The Excellent Becomes the Permanent*.

23 JA to EGS, September 3, 1881; EGS to JA, September 10, 1881; Eva Campbell Goodrich to JA, March 4, 1882.

24 John Manning Linn to JA, August 26, 1881.

25 Rebecca Sherrick first put forward this interpretation. Sherrick, "Their Fathers' Daughters," 47.

26 Sarah Anderson to JA, December 19, 1881.

27 Re JHA leaving no will, see *JA as I Knew*, 5. Re Illinois inheritance law, see Linn, *Addams*, 66; *Freeport Budget*, August 27, 1881 box 1, series 7, JAC. Re the estimate of the estate's value, see John Weber Addams, petition to the court to administer the estate, August 23, 1881, Stephenson County Probate Court Records, *JAPM*, 27:0638. Re details about the land holdings, see *Selected Papers*, 469; Linn gives the erroneous value of $350,000 (*Addams*, 4). The 2005 dollar value was calculated by using the tables and methodology laid out in McCusker, *How Much Is That in Real Money?* and then adjusting for further inflation since 1991 by using the "inflation calculator" at www.bls.gov. The same formula has been used in all other applicable cases.

28 Documents filed with John Weber Addams, petition to administer the estate, August 23, 1881, Stephenson County Probate Court Records. For details of JA's inheritance, see Levine, *Addams*, 27, 248n; Davis, *American Heroine*, 31.

29 JA to Weber Linn, February 2, 1935. Linn, ignoring this letter, says that her inheritance's value was $50,000 to $60,000 and gives her annual income as $3,000, which assumes an average annual rate of return of 6 percent on $50,000. *Addams*, 84. I suspect that he is recalling her income in the early 1890s, when he was often at Hull House. Brown assumes a rate of return of 10 percent on $60,000, i.e., an income of $6,000. *Education*, 115–16.

30 Hayes, *Complete History*, 324.

31 Wise, *Addams*, 92; Helen Harrington to JA, March 9, 1882; JA, *Twenty*, 65.

32 Sarah Anderson to JA, October 26, 1881; Sarah Blaisdell to JA, December 24, 1881. Re guilt about Anna, Allen Davis was the first to put forward this interpretation. *Heroine*, 27–28. JA to EGS, October 23, 1885. The letter refers to a time when she lived in Philadelphia. The only time she lived there was the winter of 1881–82. Sarah Anderson to JA, January 11, 1882.

33 JA, commonplace book, entry dated April 27, 1882, SCPC. Anthony Storr writes, "Early bereavement . . . seems often to predispose the sufferer to react to any later losses with particular severity." *Solitude*, 124.

34 Re Anna's health, see JA diary, June 7, 1875. Re family plans, see George Haldeman to JA, February 12, 1882; Harry Haldeman to JA, March 9, 1882; George Haldeman to AHA, February 14, 1882; Sarah Anderson to JA, January 11, 1882. A key question is whether Addams completed her first-year of study or whether she dropped out. She writes that she entered the hospital after passing her medical school exams. *Twenty*, 65. According to school records, exams for the first-year students (i.e., those taking the winter term) were scheduled to begin March 2. Minutes of the Faculty, February 11, 1882, Woman's Medical College, Archives, Medical College of Pennsylvania. (See also Emma Briggs to JA, February 18, 1883.) Davis gives no source for his claim that she entered the hospital

in February. *Heroine*, 27. Addams writes that she was in the hospital "for the late spring" (*Twenty*, 65), though it was actually early spring. Her statement has led readers to suppose that she did not complete her exams, since American academic years now finish in May or June. Also confusing is that completing the winter term amounted to completing the first year of study. According to the Medical College catalogue, all first-year students were required to complete the winter term but the spring term was optional, offering additional enrichment courses. *Catalogue of the Woman's Medical College of Pennsylvania, 1881–82*, Woman's Medical College of Pennsylvania, Archives and Special Collections, Medical College of Pennsylvania, Philadelphia. See also Faculty Minutes for November 26, 1881, in ibid.

35 JA, *Twenty*, 65; Tucker, *S. Weir Mitchell*, 14–15.

36 S. Mitchell, *Lectures on Diseases of the Nervous System*, 217. Addams's exams began on March 2, and the family left Philadelphia on March 22. JA to EGS, March 19, 1882. Re Mitchell's regimen, see Poirier, "Weir Mitchell Rest Cure," 15–40.

37 JA, commonplace book, entries dated July 1882, Nantucket [MA], JAC; JA, "Comments to Open Discussion," 466.

38 JA, commonplace book, July 1882, April 1882, January 15, 1882, July 15, 1882, JAC. Re housekeeping, see Sarah Anderson to JA, August 13, 1882 and JA to MRS, July 22, 1897. Re Anna, see George to JA, June 1, 1882.

39 Quoted in N. Johnson, *Gender and Rhetorical Space*, 93. The quotation is from *The Ladies Book of Etiquette and the Manual of Politeness* by Florence Hartley (first ed. 1873; there were several editions through the 1880s).

40 *Twenty*, 63; Townsend, *Best Helpers*, 191–92, 207.

41 JA and Flora Guiteau spent the first two weeks of July on Nantucket. JA, commonplace book, July 1882 entries, JAC. Guiteau was executed June 30. Re the Northampton visit, see Sarah Blaisdell to JA, August 29, 1882. Re JA's plans for Smith, see Sarah Anderson to JA, June 6, 1882; Mary Ellwood to JA, July 30, 1882; Sarah Anderson to JA, August 13, 1882; Mary Ellwood to JA, September 1, 1882; Sarah Anderson to JA, September 9, 1882.

42 JA, commonplace book, August 1882, JAC.

43 AAH to JA, September 10, 1882. About JA's back in the summer of 1882, see JA to AAH, May 29, 1883; EGS to JA, October 22, 1882; AAH to JA, September 10, 1882; EGS to JA, October 22, 1882.

44 The first reported use of this method was in 1891. White and Schofferman, *Spine Care*, 2:779. JA writes in *Twenty* that she was "bound to a bed" for six months (65). Although it must have felt that long in retrospect, it was probably a bit less. See JA to EGS, January 7, 1883, and the date of Weber's attack (below), by which time she was home.

45 JA to EGS, January 7, 1883.

46 Re Harry's news, see Linn, *Addams*, 178. Rollin Salisbury to JA, January 15, 1881; JA to Rollin Salisbury, June 11, 1881. Re Salisbury's college career, see Linn, *Addams*, 50. Re roses, see Wise, *Addams*, 71. Re "fell in love," see Linn, *Addams*, 63,

50. Linn refers only to a "Beloit undergraduate," but his other references to Salisbury in the book make his identity clear. *Addams*, 49–50. V. Brown argues that Linn "concocted" the story of Salisbury falling in love with JA. *Education*, 320n6. For Bryan's view, see *Selected Papers*, 381n4. Linn, like Salisbury a professor at the University of Chicago, recirculates the university rumor that Salisbury was so hurt that he never visited Hull House, but this turns out to be apocryphal. Salisbury gave a lecture on the Arctic at Hull House in 1896. *Chicago Record*, March 3, 1896, *JAPM*, 55:0144.

47 Interview with Elizabeth Linn Allen, 1951 newspaper clipping, otherwise undated and unidentified, box 1, "Material About JA, 1936–1978," series 18, JAC.

48 JA, *Second Twenty*, 196; Linn, contradicting his earlier claim, notes toward the end of the biography that Addams never married because of her devotion to humanity. *Addams*, 433.

49 Re her weight and the plaster cast, see E. L. Hulbert, "Autobiography," 6, Hulbert Papers, SCPC; Linn, *Addams*, 69. Re the new corset, see Wise, *Addams*, 94. She wore it for about nine months to a year. Linn, *Addams*, 70; Wise, *Addams*, 98.

50 AHA to Harry Haldeman, November 30, 1882; JA, *Twenty*, 65.

51 ; Stephenson County Courthouse Records, box 240, July 1896; JA to EGS, April 24, 1883; Stephenson County Courthouse Records, box 94, April 4, 1883. These state that he had spent the past week suffering attacks. Re moving him to Elgin, see JA to EGS, April 24, 1883.

52 Tilden, *History*, 741; *Freeport Journal*, May 13, 1880, 2; *Freeport Weekly Journal*, May 19, 1880, 4, col. 4; *Portrait and Biographical Album of Stephenson County* (Chicago: 1888), 282. Tilden indicates that Weber was elected to represent the county convention at the state convention for the Republican Party. Re his business failing, and for a biographical essay, see *Selected Papers*, 479–84.

53 JA to AAH, May 1, 1883, May 7, 1883, April 24, 1883.

54 JA to AAH, May 22, 1883.

55 JA, *Twenty*, 43.

56 JA to AAH, October 23, 1883.

57 JA, *Twenty*, 432; JA, "Sunday Rest," 156.

58 Potter, "Madonna of the Future," 218; JA to EGS, August 12, 1883.

59 JA, "Uncomfortableness of Transition," 215.

60 Arnold, *Literature*, 193–97, 204; JA to EGS, July 11, 1883.

61 "On the Way to Europe" [passenger list, *Servia*], *New York Times*, August 23, 1883. "J.H. Addams" is listed; this is Mrs. J. H. Addams. The "Mrs." was accidentally omitted. JA to EGS, July 11, 1883; JA to AAH, July 2, 1883.

62 *Selected Papers*, 498.

CHAPTER SIX: CULTURE

1 JA to AAH, August 22, 1883.

2 This summary is drawn from their letters. For more on the trip, see Townsend, "Jane Addams Abroad," 185–206.

3 JA, *Twenty*, 66; Wise, *Addams*, 98.

4 JA, travel diary, inside cover, *JAPM*, 28:1674; JA, travel diary, September 28, 1883, *JAPM*, 28:1695. (The diary covers the period from August 29 to November 1, 1883). Re the Lake District and London, see JA to AAH, September 30, 1883; JA to MAL, October 3, 1883.

5 JA to EGS, November 3, 1883; B. Mitchell, *International Historical Statistics: Europe*, table A4, 74–76; B. Mitchell, *International Historical Statistics: The Americas*, table A4: North America, 48.

6 Briggs and Macartney, *Toynbee Hall*, 2, 182n10; Palmer, *East End*, 86–87; Wohl, introduction to *Bitter Cry*, by Mearns, 13. The pamphlet appeared in mid-October and the Gazette's articles appeared on October 16 and October 23, 1883. Its unnamed author, Andrew Mearns, was a Congregational minister, city missionary, and secretary of the London Congregational Union. Wohl, introduction to *Bitter Cry*, by Mearns, 13, 15.

7 Mearns, *Bitter Cry of Outcast London*, 69, 68, 73.

8 JA, *Twenty*, 67; JA to Weber Addams, October 29, 1883. Addams recalls visiting the East End in November but the Saturday night she refers to in her letter to Weber was October 27, 1883. *Twenty*, 69; JA to Weber Addams, October 29, 1883.

9 JA to Weber Addams, October 29, 1883. The letter documents well enough that it was a troubling experience. The frankness of the letter is surprising given that the Addams family expected that its members would write cheerful letters. (See JA to AAH, February 28, 1887.) Much less information about the East End visit is in JA's small travel diary, which was intended only to remind her what she had done on a given day. There she notes simply seeing "thousands of poor people marketing at the booths and market stalls." October 27, 1883 entry, JA travel diary, *JAPM*, 28:1722; *Twenty*, 68.

10 JA to Weber Addams, October 29, 1883; *Twenty*, 68–69, 66. JA knew the Bible well. Did she also recall the passage "She opens her hand to the poor, and reaches out to the needy"? Proverbs 31:20. JA writes that she went around London "for weeks" but she misremembered. She left London for Holland November 1, 1883, five days after she visited the East End. JA, travel diary, *JAPM*, 28:1723. Addams immediately follows this story with a discussion of how her generation of college women had absorbed their learning too quickly and lost their sympathetic response to life. *Twenty*, 71. The placement of the observation implies that she was fully persuaded by 1883 that the study of culture had damaged her; in fact, it took a bit longer. In *Twenty* she often includes ideas in her narrative that she gained later. I have tried to untangle these associations.

11 JA, *Twenty*, 70. De Quincey's piece, "The English Mail-Coach," actually consists of three essays. The second, titled "The Vision of Sudden Death," is the one JA has in mind. De Quincey, *Collected Writings*, 300–318.

12 JA, *Twenty*, 70–71.

13 Ibid., 68–69.

14 JA to EGS, November 3, 1883; JA to George Haldeman, November 30, 1883; JA to EGS, December 2, 1883; JA, *Twenty*, 75.

15 As already noted, the Addams family usually wrote cheerful letters. (See JA to AAH, February 28, 1887.) Linn confirms that JA kept her letters to the family upbeat during her first trip to Europe, not wishing to distress them by discussing her depression. *Addams*, 78–79. In 1882 and 1883, Addams was similarly polite with Ellen. For example, after JA's difficult winter in Philadelphia and her nervous collapse, she wrote, "I have had a profitable and pleasant winter." JA to EGS, March 19, 1882. For "when you possess," see JA to EGS, December 2, 1883.

16 Re the Ellwoods and Hostetter, see JA to EGS, July 11, 1883; JA to AAH, December 14, 1883; JA, *Excellent*, 21. The quotation is from Marcus Aurelius, *Meditations*, Book 9, #3.

17 JA to George Haldeman, January 4, 1884; JA to EGS, November 3, 1883.

18 JA, "Settlement as a Factor," 185, 184. This idea permeated the Romantic literature in which JA was so well read. See Holmes, *Coleridge*, 73.

19 JA, *Twenty*, 74. See also JA to AAH, January 17, 1884; JA to Weber Addams, January 27, 1884; JA travel diary, January 15, 1884.

20 JA, *Twenty*, 69. See also, Barker-Benfield, " 'Mother Emancipator,' " 413.

21 JA, *Twenty*, 71.

22 Ibid., 76; JA to EGS, March 9, 1884.

23 JA, *Twenty*, 76; JA, *Spirit*, 10.

24 JA, *Twenty*, 84; JA, "Subjective Necessity," 18, 8; *Twenty*, 66. I suspect that she read W. H. Withrow's *The Catacombs of Rome and Their Testimony Relative to Primitive Christianity* (New York: Nelson and Phillips, 1877); see, e.g., 453, 459.

25 JA to EGS, June 8, 1884.

26 JA to EGS, December 7, 1884; JA to AAH, December 28, 1884; JA to MAL, March 29, 1885; JA to AAH, April 9, 1885; JA to AAH, March 18, 1885. Re Christ, see JA to EGS, March 30, 1885.

27 JA to EGS, February 21, 1885.

28 EGS to JA, April 28, 1885.

29 *Selected Papers*, 511.

30 Box 94, Stephenson County Courthouse Records. For consistency's sake, I refer to it by its later name, the Elgin State Mental Hospital. In 1885 it was referred to as the Northern Illinois Hospital for the Insane. Laura Forbes to JA, August 20, 1885.

31 Linn, *Addams*, 79; JA to AAH, October 7, 1885, November 20, 1885.

32 JA to AAH, October 23, 1885; EGS to Mary Blaisdell, February 23, 1889; JA to AAH, Oct. 23, 1885; JA to AAH, November 20, 1885.

33 JA to AAH, October 23, 1885; Eliot, *Daniel Deronda*, 329, 328, 512, 157. For other references to fellowship in *Deronda*, see 434, 682, 727.

34 EGS to JA, [November 28, 1885]; JA to EGS, December 6, 1885. EGS writes that she was twenty-five when she converted to Episcopalianism. Since she was born March 19, 1859, this would have been between March 19, 1884, and March 18, 1885. EGS, "Bypath," 178.

35 For "looking rather wistfully," see JA to EGS, December 6, 1885; for the reference to "My Star," see December 9, 1885; for "Your letter made me feel," see December 6, 1885.

36 EGS to Mary Starr Blaisdell, February 23, 1889; JA to AAH, January 3, 1886; JA to AAH, January 25, 1886; JA, *Twenty*, 77; Linn, *Addams*, 79. She owned Venturi's *Joseph Mazzini*. JA's Hull House Library List, *JAPM*, 28:0932. Mazzini was a major influence on many of her generation. Handy, "Influence of Mazzini," 114–23.

37 Mazzini, *Duties of Man*, 41. See also JA, "Claim on the College Woman," 61; JA, *Opening Address* [1924], 2.

38 "Thoughts" is in the edition she owned: Venturi, *Joseph Mazzini*. The Mazzini quotations are from Mazzini, "Thoughts upon Democracy in Europe," *Life and Writings of Mazzini*, 110–11, 109. For "source of comfort" see JA, *Twenty*, 77. Mazzini hardly mentions democracy in *Duties of Man*, and then only to be critical of it (192). Addams quotes a passage from "Thoughts," crediting Mazzini but not mentioning the essay's title, in "Settlement as a Factor," 204. The passage begins "[W]e have torn the great and beautiful ensign of Democracy." See Mazzini, "Thoughts upon Democracy," 103.

39 JA to EGS, February 7, 1886; *Twenty*, 77. In 1895, JA would describe the experience of failing to live up to one's dreams as a "hellish torment" and blame her flounderings on her selfishness. "Claim on the College Woman," 61.

40 Linn, *Addams*, 79; *JA as I Knew*, 5; George Haldeman to AHA, December 22, 1883. The quotation is from AHA to Harry Haldeman, April 2, 1886. She is reporting what George said to her.

41 *Selected Papers*, 506; Linn, *Addams*, 33; AHA to Harry Haldeman, January 7, 1884; JA, commonplace book, April 1882 entry, n.p; Linn, *Addams*, 32.

42 JA to EGS, December 6, 1885. JA, "Three Days on the Mediterranean Subjectively Related," *RSM* 14 (January 1886): 11–17. Re charity visits, see JA to AAH, March 7, 1886, February 10, 1886. Re the following winter's visits, see JA to AAH, October 23, 1886, November 24, 1886, October 18, 1886, December 28, 2886. Re playing with Mary's children, see EGS to Mary Starr Blaisdell, February 23, 1889.

43 JA, "Book That Changed My Life." The American edition she most likely read was Leo Tolstoy, *My Religion* [*What I Believe*], trans. from the French by Huntington Smith (New York: Thomas Y. Crowell, 1885). There has been some confusion, created by JA, as to when she read the book. She could not have read it "immediately after I left college" (*Twenty*, 261) since it was first published in English in 1885. Another question is which two books by Tolstoy she had read as of November 1886, a claim she makes to Alice. JA to AAH November 24, 1886. The second book was probably Tolstoy's *The Gospel in Brief*, which

was first published in English in 1885. The only other candidate, Tolstoy's *My Confession*, was not published in English until 1887.

44 JA, *Twenty*, 261.

45 Tolstoi, *My Religion* [1899 Scribner's edition], 85, 263, 267. All citations regarding *My Religion* are from this edition. See Lerner, *Why History Matters*, 60.

46 JA, *Twenty*, 78. It is a matter of some disagreement when Jane Addams was baptized. A document in her papers titled "Certificate of Baptism" and dated October 14, 1888, appears to state that she was baptized on that date. *JAPM*, 28:0699. Scholars have generally used that date. JA states that her baptism took place before her second trip to Europe, during the summer she was twenty-five, which was the summer of 1886. *Twenty*, 78. Linn accepts this but does the math wrong and gives the year as 1885. *Addams*, 80. Farrell uses the 1886 date. *Beloved Lady*, 42. My theory about the baptism certificate stems from the design of the preprinted form. The form states the baptism happened on the date the document was signed. There is no second blank line to insert the date of the baptism. This is no doubt because people were expected to receive the certificate, it they requested one, at the time they were baptized. I think Addams did not bother to get a certificate when she was baptized in 1886 but in October 1888, as she prepared to move to Chicago and to join a church, she thought she needed proof of baptism and asked the minister of the Cedarville Presbyterian Church to provide her with a certificate. He used the form he had in his drawer, even though by dating it and signing it he was stating that the baptism had taken place in 1888. And what did it matter? The point was that she had been baptized and that was all that he or she wished to document. Confirming this hypothesis is much evidence, which I lay out in this chapter, that Addams reached a new conclusion about her relation to Christianity in the summer of 1886 and that her recovery of spirits dated from that time.

47 JA, *Twenty*, 78–79. It appears that she was thinking of herself when she wrote years later about how some people came "to the Church because they found they could not climb the steep and thorny road pointed out by life's noblest teachers." JA, introduction to *Religion in Social Action*, by Taylor, xvi.

48 JA to Laura Addams, October 18, 1886; JA to AAH, October 6, and October 23, 1886; the quotations are from JA to AAH, November 4, 1886.

49 Re baby Charles, see JA to AAH, February 28, 1887; the baby was born February 18. *JAPCG*, 47. In her letter to Alice, Jane refers to the baby as being eight months old but she meant eight (really ten) days. Re Marcet's birth, see Harry Haldeman to George Haldeman, May 28, 1887, SAAH; *JAPCG*, 48.

50 *JA as I Knew*, 5; Linn, *Addams*, 33. MHJ dates the refusal of the proposal as taking place in the spring of 1886, before George went south on a research trip (she says it was to Florida, but he went to Beaufort, N.C.). It seems suggestive, however, that throughout 1886 George continued his tradition of specifically sending Jane his love in his letters to Anna; when he wrote from Europe in

1887, he no longer did. In a June 23, 1887, letter to Harry Haldeman, George notes that he is unsure what to make of various unexpected events, which also seems suggestive. *Selected Papers*, 501.

51 JA, *Twenty*, 73. She makes this observation while telling about her first trip to Europe, giving the impression that she had reached this conclusion at that time, but I think she reached it after she returned.

52 The edition she likely read was John Stuart Mill, *The Subjection of Women and On Liberty* (New York: Henry Holt and Sons, 1885). This edition is not among those from her personal library that she gave to Rockford College, although an 1898 edition of *On Liberty* was. Jane Addams's Gift of Books to the Rockford College Library, hereafter cited as the Rockford Acquisition List; JA, "Outgrowths of Toynbee Hall"; Mill, *Subjection of Women* [MIT Press edition], 98, 27, 22. Later, in a greatly revised, published version of the speech, she added quotation marks to the Mill sentence. "Subjective Necessity," 12. The use of quotations without naming the author was a common nineteenth-century practice. She edited Mill's sentence slightly. His read, "There is nothing, after disease, indigence and guilt, so fatal to the pleasurable enjoyment of life as the want of a worthy outlet for active faculties."

53 JA, "Book That Changed My Life," 1196; *Twenty*, 260; Tolstoi, *What to Do?* 138–39. Addams wrote in 1895 that she read the book "two years before I came to Hull House." JA to MRS, September 4, 1895. This dates her reading of the book to 1887. My citations are from the first American edition, which is the one she likely read. The 1888 edition was in her Hull House library.

54 JA, "Book That Changed My Life," 1196; JA to MRS, September 4, 1895; JA, *Twenty*, 80–81.

55 Josiah Strong, *Our Country: Its Possible Future and Its Present Crisis* (New York: American Home Missionary Society, 1886); William Graham Sumner, *What Do the Social Classes Owe Each Other?* (New York: Harper and Brothers, 1883).

56 Gladden is quoted in Wiebe, *Search for Order*, 63; Higham, *Strangers*, 39–40.

57 Higham, *Strangers*, 55, 54. Hirsch, *Urban Revolt*, 76–77. Re being in Europe at the time, see JA, *My Friend*, 47. Re JA's location on May 4, 1886, see Mary Worrall to JA and AHA, June 5, 1886. This implies that they had only recently left Philadelphia.

58 Josephine Starr, "Notes," EGSP; EGS to Caleb and Susan Starr, February 19, 1888, EGSP; JA to EGS, January 10, 1887.

59 Re the reading she was doing, see JA, *Twenty*, 82–83. In this passage she refers to the positivists. These were likely Edward Caird, John Stuart Mill, and Frederick Harrison, all of whom wrote at length about Comte's ideas. Re JA's familiarity with these authors see *Twenty*, 40, 82, 189, 193; JA, "Subjective Necessity," 21. For more on Comte and his ideas and influence, see Wernick, *Auguste Comte*. She refers to Comte in "Outgrowths," 6–7, and *Newer Ideals*, 115. Re Comte's ideas, see Himmelfarb, *Poverty and Compassion*, 359; Wintle, *Makers of Nine-*

teenth Century Culture, s.v. "Auguste Comte"; Vogeler, *Frederick Harrison*, 30, 32; Wernick, *Comte*, 198. If she read any of Comte herself, which seems likely, she probably read his influential *Politique Positive*.

60 JA, *Twenty*, 85. See also Linn, *Addams*, 84; Lasch, *New Radicalism*, 25. A possible inspiration was Charles Kingsley's *Alton Locke* (1850), a British novel about an upper-middle-class person going to live among the poor. She had read Kingsley's *Hypatia* (1853). JA to George Haldeman, May 29, 1881. For other views about whether she had a plan before leaving for Europe, see Davis, *Heroine*, 49, 302n23; V. Brown, *Education*, 169, 186, 199–200. I do not quote Addams's famous phrase "learn about life from life itself" from this passage in *Twenty Years* because I am not persuaded that she had formulated her purposes quite so pragmatically in 1887 even if she had no doubt read Dante, whose phrase "learn from life" she was adapting, by then. She references that phrase in 1919. See JA, "Presidential Address [at the WILPF Congress, Zurich, 1919]," 4.

61 JA, *Twenty*, 109. See also JA, "Subjective Necessity," 25.

62 JA, "Our Debts and How We Shall Repay Them." One senses from reading this TS that it is a fragment of her complete remarks. Re the toast theme, see JA to AAH, October 9, 1887. About the event, see *RSM* 15 (October 1887): 220. For earlier signs of JA's enthusiasm for benevolence, see V. Brown, *Education*, 106.

63 Bowker, "Toynbee Hall, London," 158–59. John C. Farrell was the first to uncover evidence that she read the article and to identify the article. See *Beloved Lady*, 43n48. Robert Woods, who also visited Toynbee Hall and came back to the United States to found a settlement house, reports that JA told him about reading the article. Woods and Kennedy, *Settlement Horizon*, 46. She also told her juvenile biographer the same story. Wise, *Addams*, 125. The interesting question is why Addams does not mention reading the article in *Twenty Years*. I suspect she did not feel it was accurate to imply that the article influenced her when she felt she had worked through the basic idea first on her own. And her silence also reinforced the book's general message—that it was a natural thing to wish to live among the poor. The details of the settlement house method were not what she wished to stress. Indeed, the formal concept is distinctly absent from *Twenty Years*.

64 Carson, *Settlement Folk*, 1–9; Woods and Kennedy, *Settlement Horizon*, 46; JA, *Twenty*, 85, 87.

65 George Haldeman to Harry Haldeman, November 12, December 2, 1887.

66 George Haldeman to AHA, March 22, 1885. For an earlier example see George Haldeman to AHA, March 2, 1884.

67 JA to AAH, November 4, 1887.

68 JA, *Long Road*, 85. The phrase "cloud of witnesses" is borrowed from Hebrews 12:1. The reference is to having faith in things unseen.

69 This is the title of chapter 4 of *Twenty Years at Hull House*.

CHAPTER SEVEN: CRISIS

1 JA to AHA, December 22, 1887; JA to Flora Guiteau, January 7, 1888; JA to AAH, January 6, 1888; JA, *Twenty*, 82–83.

2 JA to Flora Guiteau, January 7, 1888; the motto is quoted in Himmelfarb, *Poverty and Compassion*, 359; JA, *Twenty*, 149, 82–83. Addams is quoting from her notebook, which is not the same as her travel diary. The notebook does not survive in her papers.

3 JA to AAH, January 6, 1888.

4 JA to Flora Guiteau, January 7, 1888; EGS to AHA, January 30, 1888, EGSP.

5 EGS to AHA, January 30, 1888; JA to AHA, January 28, 1888; "a man of the world" is from EGS to AAH, March 4, 1888, HJP; "we were perfectly proper" is from JA to AHA, February 5, 1888.

6 JA to AHA, January 28, 1888; EGS to Sarah Anderson [Ainsworth], July 29, [1888], Sarah Anderson Ainsworth Papers, RCA.

7 EGS to JA, January 1, 1882; JA to EGS, December 7, 1884.

8 JA to AAH, February 12, 1888. She mentions that they are reading Northcote's *Catacombs*. She is referring to Northcote and Brownlow, *Roma Sotteranea*.

9 Webber, *Church Symbolism*, 91–92; Withrow, *Catacombs*, 260–61, 164–66. Photographs in the JAMC show that Addams owned the pin by 1889 and wore it throughout the 1890s.

10 John Addams Linn to JA, January 31, 1888; MAL to JA, February 23, 1888, February 8, 1888.

11 Mary's letter arrived February 16, 1888. JA was in bed by February 19 or 20. EGS to AHA, February 23, 1888; JA to EGS, June 8, 1884; JA to AAH, March [3?], 1888. See also JA to AAH, March 22, 1888; Wise, *Addams*, 119; JA, *Twenty*, 83–84. According to Weber Linn, JA remembered the anniversary of his sister Mary's birth, May 21, for the rest of her life. Linn, *Addams*, 421–22. Addams herself would die on that date in 1935. However, Bryan gives the child Mary's birthdate as May 28. *JAPCG*, 47.

12 EGS to AHA, February 23, 1888; JA to AHA, March 27, 1888; JA to Sarah Hostetter, April 24, 1888; JA to Laura Shoemaker Addams, April 25, 1888. Linn erroneously states that they attended the bullfight on Easter. *Addams*, 87. Easter was April 1 that year.

13 JA, *Twenty*, 85–86; JA to AAH, March 22, 1888. Re the early Christians facing the bulls, see Pagels, *Gnostic Gospels*, 86.

14 JA to Laura Shoemaker Addams, April 25, 1888. In 1910 Addams mistakenly said that five bulls were killed. *Twenty*, 85.

15 JA, *Twenty*, 86; JA to Sarah Hostetter, April 24, 1888; JA to Laura Shoemaker Addams, April 25, 1888. She writes, "[W]e did not stay to the bitter end."

16 JA, *Twenty*, 86. JA to Laura Shoemaker Addams, April 25, 1888; see also her reference to her "mixed feelings." JA to Sarah Hostetter, April 24, 1888. Re "we were rather ashamed," see JA to Laura Shoemaker Addams, April 25, 1888. She

also refers to the "brutality" of the bullfight in a third letter. JA to AHA, April 27, 1888. Scholars have wrestled with the important question of whether the story she tells in *Twenty Years* accurately captures what she felt at the bullfight and immediately afterwards. Lasch has made the influential argument that she did not feel as guilty at the time as she claimed she did. His evidence consists of her use of the word "we" in her letter to Laura, which he interprets to mean that Starr and Anderson did not want to leave before JA did (and therefore that her story that they left before she did is untrue), and her omission of that story from her letters. Lasch, *Social Thought*, 8; Lasch, *New Radicalism*, 27n9. See also Davis, *Heroine*, 169; 47–48; V. Brown, *Education*, 198. On a related point, Davis argues that JA inflated the significance of her bullfight experience in *Twenty Years* to serve her literary need for drama. Davis, *Heroine*, 169; 47–48. See also Brown, V. *Education*, 197. There is much evidence, however, laid out in this and previous chapters, that Addams's literary imagination was vivid enough in the 1880s to have invested her bullfight experience with dramatic moral significance at the time that it happened. A piece of that significance, left unstated in *Twenty Years*, was her symbolic imperviousness to the suffering of the early Christians. I suspect that this meaning lay at the core of the crisis. Further back in her mind may have been Cicero's observation that the Roman games were excellent training for teaching spectators "to despise suffering and death." Quoted in E. Hamilton, *Echo of Greece*, 219.

17 The quotation is from JA, "Function of the Social Settlement," 42. Addams is describing feelings prompted by the contemplation of a bas-relief of a bull.

18 JA, *Twenty*, 86.

19 EGS to JA, January 12, 1883; JA, *Twenty*, 87; re JA's sudden determination to act, see Scott, introduction to *Democracy and Social Ethics*, lxxi; P. Abbott, "Reforming," 171–72; Lasch, *New Radicalism*, 26 -29. For more psychological interpretations involving JA's repressed aggression or sexuality, see Leibowitz, "Sheltering Self," 137; Rudnick, "Feminist American Success Myth," 151–52.

20 Much more could be said about the parallels between the classic Romantic conversion experience and the evangelical Christian experience, on one hand, and Addams's bullfight scenario, on the other. See "The Pattern of Conversion" in Buckley, *Victorian Temper*. For a cultural history of the idea of conversion in the United States, see King, *Iron of Melancholy*.

21 Quoted in Young-Bruehl, *Creative Characters*, 37.

22 JA to George Haldeman, June 9, 1888; JA to AAH, July 3, 1888.

23 JA to George Haldeman, June 9, 1888. An observation that Addams made to Starr in 1887 reveals more of what she had in mind. She wrote, "The sanction of success is such a powerful thing that without it a very noble action appears trivial and a trivial affair is simply no where." JA to EGS, April 3, 1887. In 1898 JA wrote with reference to Tolstoy, "It is the man who puts into actual practice what he believes who gains attention and influence." JA, "Tolstoi," *Chautauqua*

Assembly Herald 23, no. 21 (August 8, 1898): 7. Apparently, JA's brother-in-law recognized her desire for public praise in 1881. See John Manning Linn to JA, August 26, 1881.

24 JA to AAH, February 19, 1889; Robert Browning, "Bishop Blougram's Apology," lines 322–25. See Conway, "First Generation," 248.

25 JA to Laura Shoemaker Addams, July 14, 1888; EGS to Sarah Anderson [Ainsworth], July 29, 1888, EGSP; JA, *Twenty,* 87. By happenstance, JA met Canon W. H. Fremantle, a close friend of Samuel Barnett's, while she was in Canterbury, where she stopped on her way to London. Learning of her interest in Toynbee Hall, he gave her a letter of introduction to Barnett. JA to AAH, June 14, 1888; JA, *Twenty,* 87. H. Barnett, *Canon Barnett,* 1:13, 22, 27, 71. For other interpretations, see Davis, *Heroine,* 49; V. Brown, *Education,* 199.

26 JA, *Twenty,* 87–88.

27 H. Barnett, "Beginnings of Toynbee Hall," 111. See also Briggs and Macartney, *Toynbee Hall,* 17; the largest group of workers in the category Booth describes as "very poor" were dockworkers. Himmelfarb, *Poverty,* 109.

28 JA, "English and American Social Settlements," 6. In this speech Addams says that originally there were beds for thirty men, but Henrietta Barnett says the number was twenty men, and she seems the more reliable source for this. "Beginnings of Toynbee Hall," 118; Toynbee, prefatory note to *Lectures on the Industrial Revolution;* Kadish, *Apostle Arnold,* 215. Jane Addams owned the 1887 second edition of Toynbee's *Lectures.* JA's Hull House Library List.

29 H. Barnett, *Canon Barnett,* 1:37, viii; Briggs and Macartney, *Toynbee Hall,* 27; for "ten commandments," see Koven, "Henrietta Barnett," 97; for "full of ingenuity," see Jones and Muirhead, *Life and Philosophy,* 210.

30 EGS refers to the visit Jane and Sarah made to Toynbee Hall in a letter to Sarah Anderson. EGS to Sarah Anderson [Ainsworth], July 29, 1888. Apparently Helen Harrington did not go with them. For "we realized," see H. Barnett, *Canon Barnett,* 2:30. Henrietta Barnett writes that Jane Addams came twice to Toynbee Hall before founding Hull House, once in 1887 and again in 1889. Neither date is correct. For "a community of," see JA to AAH, June 14, 1888.

31 When Addams first met the Barnetts, Samuel was still the vicar of St. Jude's Parish and they were still living in the vicarage. Later they moved to an apartment at Toynbee Hall and Samuel resigned from his parish position. Meacham, *Toynbee Hall,* 35. For "people must talk," see H. Barnett, *Canon Barnett,* 1:153. Arnold, *Culture and Anarchy,* 77; H. Barnett, *Canon Barnett,* 2:210.

32 Green is quoted in Himmelfarb, *Poverty and Compassion,* 253–54; for the "common good," see 249. S. Barnett, "Education by Permeation," 5. Re Green, see Meacham, *Toynbee Hall,* 11–18, 32; F. Turner, *Greek Heritage,* 359, 365; Kloppenberg, *Uncertain Victory,* 129, 139. Re Green and social Christianity, see Phillips, *Kingdom,* 10–11; Meacham, *Toynbee Hall,* 12–13.

33 H. Barnett, *Canon Barnett,* 1:78–79; Carson, *Settlement Folk,* 1–9; S. Barnett,

"University Settlements," 98; Meacham, *Toynbee Hall*, 68. To establish the Barnetts' views as of 1888, I have tried in this discussion to draw primarily on their writings from that year or earlier; S. Barnett, "Town Councils and Social Reform," 181.

34 Meacham, *Toynbee Hall*, 13; S. Barnett, "University Settlements," 104. Re residents' service on boards, see S. Barnett, "University Men," *Practicable Socialism*, 101; Briggs and Macartney, *Toynbee Hall*, 33; Himmelfarb, *Poverty and Compassion*, 236. For "bring the light," see Barnett, "University Men," 103.

35 See S. Barnett, "University Settlements," 106. Re the condescension, see Phillips, *Kingdom*, 101; Meacham, *Toynbee Hall*, 41–43; and Koven, "Culture and Poverty." Barnett would soon modify his plan in a democratic direction. See H. Barnett, *Canon Barnett*, 1:340. See also Meacham, *Toynbee Hall*, chap. 6.

36 Re trade unions, see H. Barnett, "Charitable Efforts," 165. In 1888 Toynbee Hall sponsored a conference about the usefulness of strikes to which union members and management came. Meacham, *Toynbee Hall*, 67. "Can a man live" is from H. Barnett, "Charitable Effort," 159.

37 Addams left London in late June to meet Flora Guiteau at Southampton. They were back in London by mid-July, when the strike took place. JA to AAH, June 27, 1888; JA to Laura Shoemaker Addams, July 4, 1888. Re the strike, see Briggs and Macartney, *Toynbee Hall*, 46; H. Lynd, *England*, 277, 285; H. Barnett, *Canon Barnett*, 2:65; Fishman, *East End*, 284–86.

38 JA, *Twenty*, 81–82.

39 Linn, *Addams*, 195; JA, "Has Nationalism Become a Dogma?" 4. She had an 1890 edition of *Capital* in her library. JA's Hull House Library List.

40 Carlyle, *Sartor Resartus*, chap. 4, "Helotage." JA to EGS, August 11, 1879.

41 Re the Barnetts' social Christianity, see Pimlott, *Toynbee Hall*, 32.

42 Re the cooperative movement, see Knight, "Jane Addams's Early Theory."

43 Fremantle, *World as Subject*, 8, 1. H. Lynd, *England*, 323–24; Phillips, *Kingdom*, xiv–xviii; Bliss, *Encyclopedia of Social Reform*, 251–260. For more on Christian socialism in the United States, see Dombrowski, *Early Days of Christian Socialism*; Phillips, *Kingdom on Earth*; G. Smith, *Search for Social Salvation*; Behrends, *Christianity and Socialism*; Ely, *Social Aspects of Christianity*. It is beyond the scope of this book to address the complicated question of how the American social Christian movement and the American Social Gospel movement relate and intersect. For an excellent brief discussion see Phillips, *Kingdom on Earth*, xviii–xx, xxiii–xxiv, 12n31, 34, 74–76. For a different view, see Dorrien, *Making of American Liberal Theology*; White and Hopkins, *Social Gospel*. Addams is often described as a Social Gospeler.

44 Westcott, *Social Aspects of Christianity*, 90–91. Re Westcott, see Phillips, *Kingdom on Earth*, 16–17, 176–77; Himmelfarb, *Poverty*, 341. Westcott was also present at the launching of the settlement movement. H. Barnett, *Canon Barnett*, 2:34.

45 Marx and Engels, *Communist Manifesto*, 108.

46 Re the motto, see S. Barnett, "Town Councils and Social Reform," 181. Re the various cooperative Toynbee Hall projects, see H. Barnett, *Canon Barnett*, 1:139–40, 221, 256, 287–88, 335, 2:73. Re "Grand," see 1:315, 2: 37, 38, 41. See also Pimlott, *Toynbee Hall*, 47–48, 49. The references in *Canon Barnett* to the clubs' decision-making powers are vague. It is possible that Hull House's clubs were more formally self-governing (see below) than were those of Toynbee Hall.

47 Among the social Christians Jane Addams read were John Ruskin, Charles Kingsley, Francis Peabody, Frederick Jackson, Frederick Denison Maurice, Mary Ward, and Edward Caird. See JA, "Outgrowths," 11. She owned a copy of Charles Nordhoff, *The Communistic Societies of the United States* (New York: Harper and Bros., 1875). Rockford Acquisition List. Among those who became personal friends were Richard T. Ely, F. D. Huntington, Henry Demarest Lloyd, George Herron, and W. T. Stead. See Bliss, *Encyclopedia*, 252, 862.

48 JA to George Haldeman, November 24, 1889; JA, "Subjective Necessity," 20. See also JA, "Social Settlements: A Three Years' Test." Addams had at least a loose tie to the American Society of Christian Socialists. *Twenty*, 190. Re its founding principles, see Bliss, *Encyclopedia*, 258.

49 For details see Knight, "Jane Addams and Hull House," 125–41.

50 JA to AAH, June 27, 1888. JA to Laura Shoemaker Addams, July 4, 1888.

51 JA to AAH, July 3, 1888; JA to AAH, June 27, 1888; JA to AAH, July 5, 1888; JA to Laura Shoemaker Addams, July 4, 1888; EGS to Sarah Anderson [Ainsworth], July 15, 1888.

52 *Freeport Weekly Democrat*, July 2, 1888, 2, col. 6.

53 Hacking, "Autonmatisme Ambulatoire," 31–43. His book on the subject is *Mad Travelers*.

54 *Selected Papers*, 503–7; AHA to Henry Haldeman, December 24, 1895, file 5, HJP; MHJ to Weber Linn, July 25, 1935.

55 JA to AAH, November 23, 1889. Marcet Haldeman-Julius agreed with the wisdom of Jane Addams's decision. See *Jane Addams as I Knew*, 5.

56 JA, *Twenty*, 64. She first used the phrase "a really living world" in her 1892 essay "Subjective Necessity," 18. In *Twenty Years*, she also writes that in starting the settlement house she wished to "learn about life from life itself" (85). In the second observation, she is expressing her belief that experience is the best teacher of truth. For reasons conveyed in this book, I believe she was still an idealist, not a pragmatist, in 1888.

CHAPTER EIGHT: CHICAGO

1 JA, "Subjective Necessity," 1–2; "Tribute to Allen B. Pond," in "Memorial Service for Allen B. Pond, City Club, Chicago, Illinois, April 21, 1929," TS, 24, *JAPM*, 48:1156.

2 JA, "Outgrowths," 13; Briggs and Macartney, *Toynbee Hall*, 17; U.S. Bureau of the Census, *Report on Population of the United States at the Eleventh Census: 1890*,

table 23, 527. Adding the numbers in the "Foreign born" column for Chicago to the "Native[-born], white foreign parents" column produces 862,830. This is 78 percent of the total population of Chicago of 1,099,850; Department of Development and Planning, City of Chicago, *People of Chicago*, 21; Higham, *Strangers in the Land*, 87–88. Re their interest in certain nationalities, see JA to MAL, March 13, 1889; JA, *Twenty*, 446; JA, "Objective Value," 32. See also JA, "Commencement Address [Western Reserve College for Women]," 131.

3 JA, "Outgrowths," 2.

4 JA, *Twenty*, 38.

5 JA to MAL, February 26, 1889; EGS to Mary Starr Blaisdell, February 23, 1889.

6 EGS wrote, "I shall ask you to send this letter directly to Mrs. H [Alice Addams Haldeman], then Mrs. L [Mary Addams Linn] + Mr. A [John Weber Addams]." EGS to Mary Starr Blaisdell, February 23, 1889, EGSP.

7 EGS to Mary Starr Blaisdell, February 23, 1889; JA to AAH, August 31, 1889. Re EGS's income in the future, see Pond, "Personal Philanthropy," *Plymouth [Church] Review*, November 1890, Scrapbook 1.

8 EGS to Mary Starr Blaisdell, February 23, 1889. Recalling this theory in 1910, Addams writes, "We fatuously hoped that we might pluck from the human tragedy itself a consciousness of a common destiny which should bring its own healing." *Twenty*, 133. Her sentence structure neatly obscures the identity of those who would be healed. As a statement of what Addams hoped to gain personally from living at the settlement, it is particularly powerful. Re adversity, see *Twenty*, 159; EGS to Caleb and Susan Gates Starr, November 15, 1889, JAC.

9 EGS to Mary Starr Blaisdell, February 23, 1889; JA to MAL, February 19 and 26, April 1, 1889.The ministers were Frank Gunsaulus of Plymouth Congregational Church, M. Wolsey Striker of the Fourth Presbyterian Church, and David Swing of Central Church. See letters from Ellen Gates Starr and Jane Addams between January and April 1889.

10 EGS to Mary Starr Blaisdell, February 23, 1889; JA, "Alumnae Essay," 74. Re the desire to do good, see JA, "Outgrowths," 1, 5.

11 EGS to Mary Starr Blaisdell, February 23, 1889.

12 Ibid.; Mary Porter, *Advance*, July 11, 1889, Scrapbook 1, 2. In 1931 Addams credited Tolstoy, not Toynbee Hall, as their inspiration. See also JA, "Tolstoy and Gandhi," 1485.

13 JA, *Twenty*, 71. Her mother's mother, Sarah Weber, died in 1846. Her father's mother, Catharine Huy Addams, died in 1866 in Pennsylvania. *JAPCG*, 53, 45. It is likely, however, that JA heard about them both during her visits to Pennsylvania relatives in 1885–87, and this may explain her sudden interest in grandmothers.

14 JA, "Subjective Necessity," 20, 23; the second quotation is from JA, "Settlement as a Factor," 187. In 1910 she put the idea even more elegantly, saying that in the early years they had hoped to use the "power of cooperation" to nurture in neighbors a healing "consciousness of a common destiny." *Twenty*, 133.

15 JA, "Outgrowths," 2; Arnold, "Democracy," 68–69.

16 EGS to Mary Starr Blaisdell, February 23, 1889. See also JA to MAL, February 26, 1889 and EGS's letters to JA throughout the 1880s.

17 EGS to Mary Starr Blaisdell, February 23, 1889. In their correspondence for February and March, Addams and Starr refer to the neighborhoods that various churches wished them to serve and to possible church financing.

18 JA to EGS, June 7, 1889; for "while an enlivener," see Josephine Starr, "Josephine's Notes," 3, EGSP. Re EGS as co-founder, see JA, "Art-Work Done by Hull-House," 614; Linn, *Addams*, 132. Starr continued to speak of JA as "the founder of Hull House." EGS to T. C. Horsfall, April 25, 1895.

19 Gilbert, *Perfect Cities*, 16; U. S. Bureau of the Census, *Compendium of the Eleventh Census: 1890, Part II*, 604.

20 C. Warner, "Chicago," 208–9, 197, 200; R. Schneirov, *Labor and Urban Politics*, 299.

21 Paderewski, *Paderewski Memoirs*, 264. Arnold is quoted in J. Strong, *Our Country*, 163; Kipling is quoted in Evans and Boyte, *Free Spaces*, xviii; Wells is quoted in Miller, *City of the Century*, 195.

22 Re unskilled workers, see Mayer, "Private Charities in Chicago," 125; E. Hirsch, *Urban Revolt*, 9. Re skilled workers, see Wyckoff, "Workers," 99–105.

23 Keyssar, *Right to Vote*, 119; Sumner, *What the Social Classes Owe Each Other*, 106.

24 The only "votes" northern women had as of 1889 were in educational elections and for all municipal candidates in a few states. See Keyssar, *Right to Vote*, chap. 6. Re voting by immigrants, see ibid., Table A.12, 359; over a period of years after 1877, African Americans in the southern states lost the vote. See Hahn, *Nation under Our Feet*. Re resistance to immigrant voters, see C. Warner, "Chicago," 212–13; M. Schneirov, *Dream*, 28; Mink, *Old Labor and New Immigrants*, 125–26; J. Strong, *Our Country*, 215.

25 Lincoln is quoted in *Democratic Imagination*, 216. Dewey, "Ethics of Democracy," 246. Although the term "liberal democracy" is often used to discuss democracy in the nineteenth century, I avoid it because of the complexities it introduces regarding the meaning of "liberal." It had various meanings in the nineteenth century and has had additional ones in the twentieth and the twenty-first.

26 Re idea of social democracy, see Tocqueville, *Democracy in America*, vol. 2, pt. 3; Arnold, "Democracy," 9–10; Arnold, *Culture and Anarchy*, 52; Urbinati, *Mill on Democracy*, 190, 60; Kloppenberg, *Uncertain Victory*, chap. 6. This can be confusing because the phrase "social democracy" was also used as a synonym for political democracy, i.e., "universal" suffrage. See Sumner, "Socialism," 889; Adams, "Democracy," 771; Dewey, "Ethics of Democracy," 240. White is quoted in Kasson, *Rudeness and Civility*, 60.

27 JA, *Twenty*, 150–51. Addams starts to call this theory her "theory of nonresistance," but corrects herself: "or rather." She was right to retract the first term

because the two theories were not quite the same. In 1889 they may have been blurred together in her mind. See also McCree, "First Year of Hull House," 101–14.

28 Abell, *Urban Impact*, 88–117; Boyer, *Urban Masses*, 135, 139; Mapes, "Visions," 61–62; JA to MAL, February 12, 1889. Ralph E. Luker calls urban missions of the 1880s "proto-settlement houses" and the prototypes for institutional churches. See "Missions, Institutional Churches, and Settlement Houses," 103. See also his *Social Gospel in Black and White*. A closely related type of institution was the local branch of the Woman's Christian Temperance Union, which Addams visited. JA to MAL, April 1, 1889. Because Addams and Starr were Protestants, I focus on the Protestant movement. For more on Catholic efforts, see Oates, *Catholic Philanthropic Tradition* and Moloney, *American Catholic Lay Groups*. Re Chicago, see Skok, "Catholic Ladies Bountiful."

29 Mapes, "Visions," 71–78.

30 Re the absence of Christian education or conversion at Hull House, see JA, *Twenty*, 83–84; JA to Katharine Coman, December 7, 1891; Kirkland, "Among the Poor of Chicago," 17. Re not offending Catholics and Jews, see David Swing, "A New Social Movement," *Advance*, April 11, 1889, in Scrapbook 1, 1; JA. *Twenty*, 83. There has been some confusion among historians about the place of religion at Hull House because of a failure to distinguish between worship and instruction. (Mapes, to her credit, is clear about this distinction; see "Visions," 76–77, 77n19.) Although Hull House did not offer religious instruction, there are two known instances in the 1890s when religious worship was organized under its roof. One was for some members of the Working People's Social Science Club who were dissatisfied with church worship and wanted something different. *Twenty*, 190. The other was for interested settlement residents at their request. *Twenty*, 448–49; November 23, 1893, Hull House Minutes; JA, "College Woman and Christianity," 1853. Resident Edward Burchard, who lived at Hull House in 1891–92 and was the son of a minister, recalled this worship service forty-five years later: "Miss Addams led in evening Bible and prayers with everyone on their knees." Burchard to EGS, January 16, 1938, EGSP. This gives the impression that the service was devout and that Addams always led it. In fact, various residents led it and various forms of worship were used, some not involving kneeling, according to each leader's preference. Addams canceled this weekly gathering when attendance dropped off and was criticized for doing so. *Twenty*, 448–49; HII Minutes, November 23, 1893; JA, "College Woman and Christianity," 1853. Re Burchard, see N. Kelley, "Early Days at Hull House," 426. Scholars have also thought that Addams lost her enthusiasm for religion or for Christ as a teacher. The evidence rebuts this assertion. See, e.g., her remarks in "Whoso Liveth to Himself" (1923), 373. In 1926 her close friend Louise deKoven Bowen described her as a "deeply religious woman" who expressed her faith by "following in the footsteps of" Christ. Bowen, *Growing up with a City*, 92. In 1927

she asked her publisher, Macmillan, whether it would be interested in publishing a work on religion that she might write. W. H. Murray to JA, February 21, 1927.

31 Re the conservative evangelical community and JA, see Mapes, "Visions," 78; JA, *Twenty*, 84. A news clipping praised Addams for withstanding fierce "opposition" when Hull House opened. *Chicago Inter-Ocean*, November 16, 1894, Scrapbook, Graham Taylor Papers, Newberry Library, Chicago. See also *Advance*, September 6, 1895, n.p. JA is quoted in [Tribute to Graham Taylor on the 40th anniversary of Chicago Commons], May 3, 1934, TS, Graham Taylor Papers, Newberry Library; the evangelical paper is quoted in Mapes, "Visions," 78.

32 JA to MAL, February 12, 1889; EGS to Mary Starr Blaisdell, February 23, 1889.

33 Quoted in *Annals*, 69.

34 Re the CWC, see Ruegamer, " 'Paradise of Exceptional Women' "; Powers, "Chicago Woman's Club"; Flanagan, *Seeing with Their Hearts*, 31–33. The club used "Women's" in its title until 1895, but I use its post-1894 name throughout the book for simplicity's sake. *Annals*, 168; re Jewish members, see Ruegamer, "Paradise of Exceptional Women," 152. Re doctors, see Ralph, "Chicago's Gentle Side," 294. The number of working women who belonged to the club has never been carefully analyzed. Some former schoolteachers of working-class background such as Ella Flagg Young belonged to the club. *Annals*, 74.

35 Re presentations to club members, see JA to MAL, February 19, 1889. This letter describes the event in charming detail. See also JA to MAL, February 26, 1889; Chicago Woman's Club board minutes, April 10, 1889, CHS; JA to AHA, May 9, 1889. Re her recruitment speech, see JA, *Excellent*, 13. She would later retitle it "Outgrowths of Toynbee Hall." The earliest surviving version of this speech is from December 1890, *JAPM*, 46:0480; it hardly mentions Christianity. I suspect there were two versions of the speech, one distinctly Christian and one more secular. The former would have been given to the [Chicago] Young People's Missionary Club of New England, to whom JA also spoke. JA to MAL, March 13, 1889. These two speeches may have been combined in "The Subjective Necessity of Social Settlements" (1892), which treats Christianity at much greater length than "Outgrowths" does.

36 JA to MAL, April 1, 1889; JA, *Excellent*, 13, 114.

37 *Chicago Tribune*, March 8, 1889, 8.

38 The extensive publicity the new settlement received before it opened its doors was clearly orchestrated by Addams, using her new ties with the Chicago social Christian, missionary, and women's club communities. See Swing, "New Social Movement," *Advance*, April 11, 1889, Scrapbook 1, 1; Mary H. Porter, "A Home on Halsted Street," *Advance*, July 11, 1889, Scrapbook 1, 2; Leila G. Bedell. "A Chicago Toynbee Hall," Letter to the editor dated May 5, 1889, in *Woman's Journal* 20 (May 25, 1889): 162 (also in Scrapbook 1, 1). Bedell was a recent president of the Chicago Woman's Club. Re JA's strategies for press coverage

and Mary Porter's interest, see JA to EGS, June 4, 1889. For a discussion of the early press coverage of Hull House, see Scherman, "Jane Addams," 83–84. Re Chicago journalism in the 1890s, see McGrath, *Rose Man of Sing Sing.*

39 EGS to Mary Starr Blaisdell, February 23, 1889. The College Settlement Association was organized either in the fall of 1887 (Scudder, *On Journey,* 109) or January 1890. *First Annual Report of the College Settlement Association for the Year 1890* (New York: privately printed, 1891), 12. A history of the CSA has yet to be written.

40 JA to MAL, March 13, April 1, 1889. Despite many claims to the contrary, the historic record establishes that the College Settlement opened October 1, 1889, almost two weeks after Hull House. College Settlement Association, *Fourth Annual Report, 1894,* cited in Woods and Kennedy, *Handbook of Settlements,* x, 2; Susan Walker, secretary of the CSA, in Gavit, *Bibliography of College, Social, and University Settlements* [1897], 4; Woods and Kennedy, *Settlement Horizon,* 45. Although the two essentially opened at the same time, Hull House was technically the first American settlement house. The evidence that the College Settlement opened in September is based on much older memories. See Robbins, "First Year at the College Settlement," 1801; Scudder, *On Journey,* 135. Davis cites Bedell, "Chicago Toynbee Hall," for his claim that the College Settlement opened a week before Hull House, but the source does not mention the New York settlement. Davis, *Heroine,* 51. Nor was Neighborhood Guild the first. Stanton Coit held that his Neighborhood Guild, which opened in New York City in 1886, was in certain respects quite different from a settlement, and he was correct. Coit, *Neighbourhood Guilds,* 85–88; see also 7–16, 46–51. Knight, "Jane Addams and the Settlement Movement," 4. Re Fine's visit to Hull House, see JA to Jenkin Lloyd Jones, October 27, 1890.

41 Re the New York settlement "intended to be an organization," see EGS to Mary Starr Blaisdell, February 23, 1889. Scholars sometimes claim that residence at Hull House was open only to college graduates, but this was never the case. Mary McDowell, one of the earliest residents, did not attend college, and there were many others. See Appendix, 229. Re the benefits of informality, see "Subjective Necessity," 24. For "rigidity of method," see Lathrop, "Hull House as a Sociological Laboratory," 319. Perkins, a short-term resident at Hull House and the first woman cabinet member and first woman secretary of labor, serving under FDR, is quoted in Remarks, *Memorial Services for Jane Addams,* National Conference of Social Workers, June 1935, 18. Re endowments, see JA, "Subjective Necessity," 24; "Objective Value," 45–46. The Hull House Association did not gain an endowment until the early twentieth century.

42 JA to MAL, March 13, 1889; C. Brown, "Illinois Woman's Alliance," 110–11; Livermore, "Cooperative Womanhood in the State," 290; Flanagan, *Seeing,* 37, 39. For more about the IWA, see also Tax, *Rising of the Women;* R. Schneirov, *Labor and Urban Politics,* 272–74.

43 JA to MAL, March 13, 1889; JA, *Twenty,* 91–92; EGS to Mary Starr Blaisdell,

February 23, 1889. Her interest in the anarchists may have been sparked by her interest in Tolstoy. See E. Hirsch, *Urban Revolt*, 45, 83; Lerner, *Why History Matters*, 67–69. By 1886 an estimated twenty-eight hundred anarchists were in Chicago, organized into twenty-six different groups, with seven daily newspapers. R. Schneirov, *Labor and Politics*, 173.

44 JA to MAL, February 12, 1889; JA to AAH, February 19, 1889; JA to MAL, March 13, 1889.

45 JA to MAL, March 13, 1889. "Slum" was a British slang word widely in use by the 1880s in England and the United States. Mayne, *Imagined Slum*, 127–28. The definition I use comes from a Department of Labor Study of the period quoted in Ward, *Poverty, Ethnicity, and the American City*, 83.

46 EGS to Mary Starr Blaisdell, February 23, 1889.

47 Re their neighborhood explorations, see EGS to Mary Starr Blaisdell, February 23, 1889, EGSP; JA to MAL, February 26, 1889. Re ethnicities see *Maps*, 17. The *Maps* data, based on a DOL study, are not about the Nineteenth Ward as a whole but only about half of the Nineteenth Ward, that half east of Halsted Street, north of Twelfth Street and south of Polk and west of the Chicago River. The DOL data also include information for a small neighborhood east of the river, outside the Nineteenth Ward. For the acreage and the number of people in the ward, see "Chicago's Wards—What They Need," *Chicago Times-Herald*, March 8, 1898, 10. This has historical data going back to 1890. Re statistics for "colored," see *Maps*, 17, Nationalities Map #1 (folded inside book cover); U.S. Bureau of the Census, *Report on Population of the United States at the Eleventh Census: 1890*, pt. 1, table 23, 528. Nationalities Map #1 includes a neighborhood east of the Chicago River that is outside the boundaries of the Nineteenth Ward. Quite a number of African Americans lived there. For a map of the Nineteenth Ward's boundaries in 1890, see U.S. Bureau of the Census, *Report on Vital and Social Statistics in United States*, *11th Census*, pt. 2, *Vital Statistics*, map opposite page 180.

48 Re African Americans, see Spear, *Black Chicago*, 12. JA, "Objective Value," 28. By 1900, African Americans would still make up less than .5 percent of the *ward's* population. See Spear, *Black Chicago*, Map 1, following page 14.

49 C. Warner, "Chicago," 218; the information is drawn from the Nineteenth Ward businesses listed in Donnelley, *Lakeside Directory*.

50 JA, "Tribute to Allen B. Pond," 24–25; JA, *Twenty*, 92–94. Subsequent photographs show the piazza with plain Tuscan columns. Apparently the original columns were removed because the piazza was rotting. JA to Helen Culver, March 7, 1890. When the building was restored in the 1960s, the Corinthian columns of the piazza were not restored. Because Halsted Street was later widened, Hull House no longer stands well back from the street.

51 Hull obituary, February 14, 1889, Scrapbook 1, 1; Price, *Helen Culver*, 6–24; Goodspeed, "Helen Culver," in his *University of Chicago Biographical Sketches*,

92; JA to AHA, May 9, 1889. Charles Jerold Hull, orphaned and illiterate as a child, earned an M.D. and a law degree from Harvard University and became a successful real estate developer and entrepreneurial philanthropist, offering affordable housing on the installment plan to working-class people, including African Americans in the south. Helen Culver's mother was the sister of Charles Hull's father. Goodspeed, "Helen Culver," 80. Re the estate's value, see Schultz and Hast, *Women Building Chicago*, s.v. "Helen Culver."

52 JA, *Twenty*, 93; JA to Helen Culver, March 7, 1890.

53 JA to Helen Culver, March 7, 1890; Davis, *Heroine*, 106.

54 JA to Helen Culver, March 7, 1890; JA to AAH, August 6, 1889; Scrapbook 1, 3. The furnace was installed by early November. EGS to Susan Gates and Caleb Starr, November 3, 1889, EGSP.

55 Re visiting family, see JA to EGS, June 14, 1889; re Alice's visit to Genesco, see "Personal," Girard Press, June 6, 1889, 3, 5. JA came to Chicago briefly in August to inspect the kitchen renovations. JA to AAH, August 6, 1889. Re her sisters' support, see JA to EGS, January 24, 1889; *JA as I Knew*, 6. Re the Haldeman brothers' views, see ibid., 5; Harry Haldeman to George Haldeman, February 2, 1890. Re Anna's blaming JA, see *JA as I Knew*, 5.

56 Re Genesco, see "Personal," *Girard Press*, January 3, 1889, 3, col. 6. Re JA trying to stay in touch with Anna, see JA to AHA, November 23, 1889; JA to AHA, June 3, 1890; *JA as I Knew*, 5, 9; JA to AHA, July 4, 1890, November 9, 1891. MHJ writes that the estrangement ended after her father's death in 1905. Alice, who herself had been alienated from her mother-in-law, began to manage Anna's investments, as her husband once had, and was determined to accomplish a reconciliation, which she did. Jane joined in the reconciliation. *JA as I Knew*, 10–11. See also JA to AAH, May 19, 1899.

57 Minutes of the Board of Trustees, Rockford Female Seminary, June 21, 1889, 2:69, RCA. Re the date of Sill's retirement, see ibid., 2:13. Re the memorial service, see Minutes of the Rockford Seminary Alumnae Association, June 19, 1889, 1:149, RCA.

58 JA, "Alumnae Essay," 72.

59 JA to AAH, September 13, 1889. See also MAL to JA, February 6, 1888. Mary Keyser's brother Frank joined Hull House as a resident and, beginning in 1900, was superintendent of buildings and grounds. See clipping, [January 1940], *Genesco Republic*, Jane Addams Clippings file, FLHR. Florence Kelley incorrectly writes that Mary Keyser came from Cedarville. Kelley, "I Go to Work," *Survey Graphic* 58 (June 1, 1897): 271. For Addams's remarks at Mary Keyser's memorial service, January 10, 1897, see *JAPM*, 38:727. See also Stebner, *Women of Hull House*, 95–100.

60 JA, *Twenty*, 94.

61 JA to EGS, August 6, 1889; JA to AAH, September 13, 1889; "Work of Two Women," *Chicago Times*, July 8, 1890, Scrapbook 1, 3.

62 JA, *Twenty*, 108. Re the art, see John Dewey to Alice Chipman Dewey, October 7, 1894, JDC; Henry B. Learned, "Hull-House," *Lend a Hand* [Boston], May 1893, 328. Dewey does not give the Millet painting he saw at Hull House a title but describes it as depicting children at the door. I believe it was *Woman Feeding Her Children.*

63 JA, "Hull House as a Type of College Settlement." 97, *JAPM*, 46:0578.

64 Ibid.

CHAPTER NINE: HALSTED STREET

1 JA, "Objective Value," 27, 28, 31; Mayer and Wade, *Chicago*, 116–17, 137; Duis, *Challenging Chicago*, 274–86.

2 JA, *Twenty*, 286; JA, "Objective Value," 29–31; *Chicago Times-Herald*, July 5, 1895 (Scrapbook 3, 16); *Chicago Journal*, July 29, 1895 (Scrapbook 3, 17). Regarding rats, see Robins, *Tomorrow Is Beautiful*, 20–21; Loth, *Swope of General Electric*, 32. See also Holbrook, "Map Notes and Comments," in *Maps*, 3–6.

3 C. Warner, "Chicago," 201.

4 JA, "Objective Value," 30–31; *Maps*, 4–6, 10; Nelli, *Italians in Chicago*, 13–14. Re diseases, see ibid., 13–14; *Maps*, 6.

5 JA to George Haldeman, November 24, 1889.

6 JA to George Haldeman, December 21, 1890; re her disapproval of materialism, see JA, "How Would You Uplift the Masses?" 12; JA, "Social Settlements: A Three Years' Test," n.p. EGS shared this view. See Carrell, "Reflections in a Mirror," 113–14. Addams's attitude toward the material reform agenda had changed a great deal by 1910, when she wrote *Twenty Years*. Her memoir does not narrate that shift but incorporates her wider agenda into all her observations.

7 JA, "Washington's Birthday," 17; JA, "Recent Immigration: A Field Neglected by the Scholar," *University Record* 9, no. 9 (January 1905): 281. See also JA, *Newer Ideals*, 127, 141.

8 Re vermin, see Carrell, "Reflections in a Mirror," 206; EGS to [?], October 10, [n.y.], EGSP (the letter begins, "My dear I am tired"); Nelli, *Italians in Chicago*, 13–14; A. Hamilton, *Exploring the Dangerous Trades*, 251; Wolf, "Dr. A. Louise Klehn," 16. Re EGS's finances, see V. Brown, *Education*, 376n12. During the first three years Addams subsidized Starr's and the other residents' living costs by keeping the fee low and covering the resulting debt; JA's economic situation in the 1890s is discussed in subsequent chapters. Re her income in her final years, see Linn, *Addams*, 352, 393; Weber Linn to Esther Linn, May 27, 1935, "Letters to Esther," box 1, series 18, JAC. According to an obituary, at her death her personal property was worth $10,000 and her only real estate was the farm near Cedarville. *New York Times*, May 22, 1935, EGSP.

9 JA told a reporter in 1893, "We do not go to their houses uninvited." "In the White City," [November 1893], *Chicago Inter-Ocean*, Scrapbook 1; JA to Katharine Coman, December 7, 1891. For "first settlers," see JA, "Neighborhood Improve-

ment," 457; for "when you go," see JA, "English and American Social Settlements," 7.

10 JA, *Twenty*, 109. For " 'got a dodge,' " see JA, "English and American Social Settlements," 7. Re stones being thrown, see EGS to Susan and Caleb Starr, November 3, 1889, JAC; John Dewey to Alice Chipman Dewey, October 10, 1894, JDC. For "proselyte them," see JA to Katharine Coman, December 7, 1891.

11 JA, "Outgrowths," 16; JA to George Haldeman, December 21, 1890.

12 For "We have two boys clubs," see JA to AAH, October 8, 1889. Re clubs, see also JA, "Objective," 38; for additional clubs, see Scrapbook 3, 80; Linn, *Addams*, 113, 115; JA to AAH, November 23, 1889. Re kindergarten, see JA to AAH, October 8, 1889; EGS to Mary Blaisdell, December 17 and 21 [1890], EGSP; Linn, *Addams*, 147. Re Dow, see JA, "Jenny Dow Harvey," in *Excellent*. Hull House did not have the first free kindergarten; the Chicago Woman's Club began one in 1886. *Annals*, 80–81.

13 Re the receptions, see JA to AAH, November 23, 1889; JA to George Haldeman, November 24, 1889. Re ethnic and religious organizations in the neighborhood, see Lissak, *Pluralism and Progressives*, chap. 6; Polacheck, *I Came a Stranger*, 181; Skerrett, "Irish of Chicago's Hull-House Neighborhood," 21–63.

14 JA, *Twenty*, 183.

15 H. Barnett, *Canon Barnett*, 1:368–71. Chicago Commons, founded a few years later, kept the all-male Toynbee Hall model. Phelps, *Changing Faces*, 28. Re the Social Science Club, see JA to AAH, October 8, 1889; JA, *Twenty*, 178–79; McDowell, "Social Service in Chicago," 298. See also JA, "Chicago Settlements," 166. Re JA's service on the Executive Committee of the Working People's Social Science Club, see "Weekly Program of Classes, Clubs, Lectures, etc. January, 1891," Scrapbook 2, 5; Hull-House Program, March 1, 1892, RCA. See also Jackson, *Lines of Activity*, 73–79.

16 For lecture topics, see JA, *Twenty*, 179; *Chicago Times*, July 8, 1890, in Scrapbook 1, 3; "Hull House College Extension Classes, October, 1890," Scrapbook 2, 1; "Weekly Programme of Classes, Clubs, Lectures, etc. January 1891," Scrapbook 2, 5. Despite the 1891 date, this program includes the Working People's Social Science Club lecturers for December 1890.

17 JA, *Twenty*, 179–80; Blanc, *Condition of Women*, 77–81. (The lectures were not on Wednesday nights originally but were soon switched to that night.)

18 JA, *Twenty*, 179–80; Blanc, *Condition of Women*, 77–81; "Notes by a Woman" (interview with Jane Addams), June 28, 1894, *Chicago Herald*, Clippings, *JAPM*, 55:0025.

19 JA, *Twenty*, 196.

20 JA, "How Would You Uplift the Masses?" 12; JA, "Objective Value," 89–41. Re Starr's teaching responsibilities, see JA, *Twenty*, 101; JA, "Art Work," 615. Re the Mazzini class, see JA, *Second Twenty*, 409. Re adding classes, see JA, *Twenty*, 41; JA to AAH, June 3, 1890; Scrapbook 1, 17; JA to Loredo Taft, February 3, 1891.

Re the first college extension courses, see Appendix. The University of Chicago did not begin its extension program until it opened its doors in 1892.

21 JA, *Twenty*, 166–67.

22 Ibid., 110, 158.

23 JA, *My Friend*, 52–53.

24 JA, *Democracy*, 20–21. See also JA, "Ethical Survivals," 277.

25 JA, *Twenty*, 110.

26 Ibid., 168–69. In February 1890, JA wrote AAH, "[This week we] have started a little crèche." JA to AAH, n.d. Later, the settlement refused to take babies younger than two months. Scrapbook 3, 12. JA later erroneously gave the founding date of the crèche as the spring of 1891. *Twenty*, 169.

27 JA, "Ethical Survivals," 282; JA, "Social Settlements," 339–40.

28 JA, "Ethical Survivals," 282–83.

29 JA, "Settlement as a Factor," 184. She wrote the essay in 1894 and published it in 1895.

30 Re strikes in 1890 in Chicago, see Nutter, *Necessity of Organization*, 7–9; see also R. Schneirov, *Urban*, 306; Toynbee, *Lectures on the Industrial Revolution*. An 1887 edition of the book was in JA's library. Hull House Library List. Addams's first documented reference to the book appears in "Outgrowths," 3.

31 For "I am touched every night," see JA, "Sunday Rest," 1.

32 Re the garment industry in the Nineteenth Ward, see JA, "Julia Lathrop at Hull-House," 377; JA, "Social Settlements in Illinois," 164. Re sweatshop practices, see Sheppard, *London*, 293; Burrows and Wallace, *Gotham*, 1116. For statistics about Chicago, see Kirkland, "Among the Poor," 23. Re wives and children, see JA, *Twenty*, 220.

33 Re full-time work, see R. Schneirov, *Labor*, 188. Re the 1892 figure, see Kenney, "Address," 872. Re struggling to survive, see Commons, *Trade Unionism*, 293; Kirkland, "Among the Poor," 23.

34 JA, *Twenty*, 198, 148.

35 JA, *Newer Ideals*, 119–20; JA, *Excellent*, 73–75; R. Schneirov, *Labor*, 284. Re Tuley's first arbitration see ibid., 250. Re JA's early interest in girls who worked in factories and sweatshops, see JA to George Haldeman, November 24, 1889.

36 Bliss, *Encyclopedia*, s.v. "Arbitration and Conciliation, United States"; R. Schneirov, "Labor and the New Liberalism," 210–11; Ely, *Labor Movement*, 146–49; Beckner, *History of Labor Legislation*, 72–73; Westhoff, " 'A fatal drifting,' " 186.

37 Toynbee, *Lectures*, 74–75, 173–74, 84, 201, 19, 17.

38 I date the meeting of JA and Mary Kenney as the spring of 1890 on the basis of the following evidence. Kenney was in the midst of organizing the Bindery Girls' Protective Union, Local 1, when she met JA (see below), and the union held its first annual reception on April 30, 1891, which means that the union was formally organized in April 1890. *Gerritsen Collection*, text-fiche A258(1). Also, once Kenney had organized the bindery girls, she went on in 1891 to organize the women shirtmakers. JA, "Settlement as a Factor," 188. See also Nutter,

Necessity of Organization, 7–8; it seems likely that Addams met Lloyd in 1889 through Lydia Avery Coonley (later Coonley-Ward), who was a friend of EGS and an early supporter of the idea of a settlement house. JA to MAL, February 19, 1889; JA, *Excellent*, 114. Lloyd was friends with Coonley. Destler, *Henry Demarest Lloyd*, 221 (re Lloyd's friendship with Thomas Morgan, see 199). In any case, JA was certainly supporting Kenney's union organizing work by November 18, 1891, more than a month before FK arrived at Hull House. See JA to H. D. Lloyd, November 18, 1891

39 Nutter, *Necessity of Organization*, 2. The Mary Kenney O'Sullivan Papers, Schlesinger Library, Radcliffe Institute for Advanced Study, contain a photograph of Kenney as a child with her parents. All three are dressed quite fashionably.

40 Re the LFLU, see P. Foner, *Women and the American Labor Movement*, 227, 100; Kessler-Harris, *Out of Work*, 155; Buhle, *Women and American Socialism*, 71–72. Re Elizabeth Morgan, see Ritter, "Elizabeth Morgan," 241–51; Schultz and Hast, *Women Building Chicago*, s.v. "Elizabeth Morgan." Re CTLA, see Tax, *Rising*, 36; R. Schneirov, *Labor*, 71. Re Kenney, see Tax, *Rising*, chap. 3; and Nutter, *Necessity of Organization*, 7–8. There were 1,115 trade unions in the CTLA by 1893. *Chicago Tribune*, November 13, 1893, 2.

41 Mary Kenney O'Sullivan, "Autobiography," excerpt printed in Bryan and Davis, *One Hundred Years*, 21–22; Murolo, *Common Ground*, 1.

42 Re JA and Kenney meeting, see JA, *Twenty*, 212; Kenney O'Sullivan tells this story in her autobiography, an excerpt of which is reprinted in Bryan and Davis, *One Hundred Years*, 21–23. See also Graham Taylor's remarks, included in JA, "Settlement as a Way of Life," 156–57; Graham Taylor to JA, February 15, 1913. For "when I saw there," see Bryan and Davis, *One Hundred Years*, 23; re Kenney a resident, see *Twenty*, 212.

43 Stanton Coit, review of *Philanthropy and Social Progress*, ed. H. C. Adams, *International Journal of Ethics* (January 1894): 245. For "we find ourselves," see JA to Katharine Coman, December 7, 1891.

44 JA to Henry Demarest Lloyd, November 18, 1891, December 2, 1891. By February 1892, with Kenney's help, the IFLU had organized 24 women's unions in Chicago. P. Foner, *Women and the American Labor Movement*, 101.

45 JA to AAH, November 23, 1889, March 6, 1890; JA to Eleanor Smith, August 6, 1901. Re impressions of JA, see *JA as I Knew*, 19, 3; William Kent, "Jane Addams," 10, TS, file 2, box 55, William Kent Family Papers, Archives, Sterling Library, Yale University; JA, *Twenty*, 147–48.

46 JA, "Commencement Address," 130.

47 JA, *Twenty*, 147–48; see also JA, Address, Peace Congress Banquet, 261. She loved physical risk, too; she had what a friend called "sporting blood." Hull, "Jane Addams," 14.

48 EGS to Mary Allen, December 30, 1891, EGSP; JA, *Twenty*, 147. For "overwhelmed," see JA, "Tribute to Allen B. Pond," 30; for "moments of depression," see JA, "John Dewey and Social Welfare," 143.

49 JA to EGS, January 24, 1889.

50 EGS to Mary Allen, September 1, 15, 1889, EGSP. Starr is quoting a version of Hebrews 12:12.

51 JA to MAL, February 26, 1889; JA to AAH, [September 1890?]. *JAPM* dates this undated letter February 1890. Supporting a September date are references in the letter to a photograph that JA arranged for AAH to receive in August (JA to AAH, June 6, 1890) and to a photograph of Marcet that AAH had sent JA for her birthday on September 6.

52 JA to EGS, June 4, 1889.

53 EGS to Mary Allen, September 1, 15, 1889, EGSP; JA to EGS, January 24, 1889.

54 Faderman, "Nineteenth-Century Boston Marriage," 29–33. According to Faderman, the term "lesbian" did not become popularly known or reflect a widespread negative attitude until the second decade of the twentieth century (33–36). See also Jeffreys, *Spinster and Her Enemies*, chap. 6; L. Rupp, *Desired Past;* L. Rupp, "Imagine My Surprise," 61–70; D'Emilio and Freedman, *Intimate Matters;* Vicinus, *Intimate Friends.* On the question of whether "lesbian" applies only to relationships that are fully sexual, see Faderman, *To Believe,* 1–3; FK, 1:373n48; Cook, "Female Support Networks," 20.

55 Seidman, *Romantic Longings,* 7, 59–60. See also Davis, *Heroine,* 90; FK, 1:373 n48. Margaret Fuller emphasizes this kind of idealized romantic love. Fuller, *Woman in the Nineteenth Century,* 342. Exactly what proportion of American marriages aspired to such spirituality, let alone achieved it, is impossible to say. It is no doubt true that the ideal was more discussed, admired, and read about than consistently practiced. See Lystra, *Searching the Heart.* Re Boston marriages, see Faderman, *Surpassing the Love of Men,* chap. 4.

56 EGS to Mary Allen, September 15, 1889, EGSP. EGS mentions that they are sharing a bed. See EGS to Mary Allen, December 7, [1890], dated "Xmas Eve" [December 24, 1890]. Also, see below.

57 JA, *Spirit,* 16, 27–30. See also 16–17. She refers to Diotima and these ideas again in *Long Road,* 82. Emerson's most powerful statement on this subject appears in his essay "Love." Addams did not equate physicality with sensuality. She often hugged and kissed friends and family, held people's hands, enjoyed massages, and shared a bed with various people. *JA as I Knew,* 25, 30; Polacheck, *I Came a Stranger,* 86–87, 122, 149; EGS to JA, March 14, 1888; JA to EGS, [July or June? 1892, *JAPM,* 2:1317]; JA to AAH, October 28, 1894; Bowen, *Open Windows,* 226; Davis, *Heroine,* 256. In the 1880s passionate hugs and kisses between men were not taken to signify sexual feelings. N. Katz, *Love Stories,* 319, 33. Modern Americans tend to equate the act of two adults preferring to sleep together with a desire for sexual relations, but women of JA's day shared beds readily and casually. Close friendship, let alone a sexual relationship, was not implied. Re bed-sharing at Hull House, see EGS to Mary Allen, dated "Xmas Eve" [December 24, 1890], EGSP. See also V. Brown, *Education,* 376n5.

58 JA, *Spirit,* 30.

59 On the basis of discussions with Alice Hamilton, Allen Davis wrote in 1963 that there was "no open lesbian activity" involving Hull House residents although "unconscious sexuality" was involved in some close relationships. Davis, *Heroine*, 306n45. For other discussions of whether JA was a "lesbian"—the word is variously defined—see Cook, "Female Support Networks," 412–44; Faderman, *To Believe*, 1–3, 115–35; Smith-Rosenberg, "Female World of Love and Ritual," 53–76; Jackson, *Lines*, 164–44; V. Brown, *Education*, 194, 361n60. Re applying "lesbian" retrospectively, see Taylor and Rupp, "Lesbian Existence," 143–59.

60 Re MRS's large collection of JA's letters, see *JAPCG*, 69. There are 371 of JA's letters to MRS on the *JAPM*; 102 are from the period 1889 through 1898. About 114 letters from MRS to JA are on the *JAPM*; only seven are from the period 1889 through 1898. In 1935 JA destroyed "a good many" of her letters to MRS, particularly those about MRS's family or her own. But there were also a lot she did not destroy. JA to Weber Linn, March 5, 1935. Re other letters she destroyed, see JA to Weber Linn, March 8, 1935.

61 Elisabeth Young-Bruehl has written, "The partner is her mirror while she is . . . hers; their relationship may or may not be sexual in the narrow sense, but it will be full of erotic charge. . . . Such a mirroring relationship [is] nurturing to her creativity." *Creative Characters*, 238.

62 JA to Helen Culver, March 7, 1890; JA to AAH, March 23, 1890; JA, *Twenty*, 150; JA to AAH, January 5, 1890.

63 Re donors, see JA to AAH, November 23, 1889; re the Ten Account, see Henry B. Learned, "Hull-House," *Lend a Hand*, May 1893, 330. The Ten Account appears in the Hull House account books for the 1890s. Edward Hale, the idea's advocate, launched Ten Clubs all over the country to support charitable activities. See his novel, *Ten Times One Is Ten*. See also Huggins, *Protestants against Poverty*, 39, 41. Re JA's use of this method see Wise, *Addams*, 139; Scrapbook 1, 10; [M. Katharine Jones, comp.], *Bibliography on Settlements* (Philadelphia, 1891), s.v. "Hull House." Re in-kind donation, see EGS to Mary Blaisdell, May 18, 1890, EGSP; JA, *Twenty*, 149; Helen Culver to JA, March 3, 1890. By the fall of 1890 the free lease was for five years. *Twenty*, 149. Re naming Hull House, see EGS to Mary Starr Blaisdell, May 18, 1890. They used the spelling Hull-House. For earliest use of the name, see "College Extension Classes at The Hull-House, June [1890]," Clippings, *JAPM*, 50:0847. The word "The" had been dropped by October 1890. Scrapbook 2, n.p.

64 JA to AAH, August 12, 1890; JA to AAH, [September 1890; *JAPM* dates it to February 1890].

65 In June 1889, at least three women were considering residence but there is no evidence that any moved in. JA to EGS, June 4, 1889; Anna Farnsworth is mentioned in articles about Hull House in Scrapbook 1, 5½, 17. Re her father's disapproval, see EGS to Mary Allen, December 7, [1890], EGSP. See also F. Kelley, "I Go to Work," 271. Re Mary Keysar, see EGS to Mary Allen, December 7 [1890], EGSP. I date Starr's letter 1890 because Starr refers to Addams as having

just given a paper about Hull House to the Woman's Club and to the pending construction of the new "Art building." Also, EGS mentions Farnsworth as the new resident.

66 The editor of the *JAPM* dates "Outgrowths" to December 1891. The following sources document that the date was 1890: the manuscript itself (see *JAPM*), which is dated 1890 on its last page; Chicago Woman's Club Minutes, November 19, 1890, December 3, 1890, CHS; EGS to Mary Allen, December 7, [1890], EGSP; JA to AHA, December 9, 1890. A week later, on December 10, 1890, Addams gave a speech with the same title to the Working People's Social Science Club. "Weekly Programme of Lectures, Clubs, Classes, etc., January 1891," Scrapbook 2, 5 (events taking place in December 1890 were included in the program). Also, Addams refers in the speech to the Butler Art Gallery as currently under construction. "Outgrowths," 15. The gallery was built in the winter of 1890–91 and opened in the spring of 1891. Excerpts from the speech are reprinted in *Twenty Years*, 368–70. No description of JA delivering this speech exists. This description of her typical speaking style is drawn from Polacheck, *I Came a Stranger*, 102; Linn, *Addams*, 116–17; "Two Mothers," 7. For reporters' impressions, see clipping, Cincinnati, Ohio, 1894, Clippings, *JAPM*, 55:0022; *Cleveland Leader*, June 20, 1893, Clippings, *JAPM*, 55:0023.

67 JA, "Outgrowths," 2. The obvious sources for her thinking about democracy are Mazzini, Toynbee, and Arnold's essay "Democracy." But she had also recently been reading Carl Schurz's book-length review of the new biography *Abraham Lincoln: A History,* by John G. Nicolay and John Hay. Schurz's piece, first published in segments in the *Atlantic Monthly* between 1886 and 1890, was published in book form in 1891. Addams gave away copies at Christmas in 1891 (not 1889, as she states). *Twenty*, 35–36, 42. She may have also read John Dewey's 1888 essay "Ethics and Democracy," in which he asserts the need for a democratic theory of society to reflect historical trends (227), the point she is making in "Outgrowths." It is not a point that Mazzini, Toynbee, or Schurz makes. She had not met Dewey at this time, and his paper was published obscurely, but Henry Demarest Lloyd, a friend of Dewey's close colleague at the University of Michigan, Henry C. Adams, may have shared a copy with her. Re Lloyd and Adams's friendship, see Destler, *Lloyd*, 149, 155–56.

68 Re "good citizenship," see JA, "Outgrowths," 16. Although Addams focused on women, she was otherwise echoing T. H. Green. See Meacham, *Toynbee Hall*, 14. JA does not refer to Green in "Outgrowths" but she does in "Uplifting" (11). For "social matters," see "Outgrowths," 2–3. Also, she discusses the mutual benefit motive at Toynbee Hall (7).

69 Re club activities, see JA, "Outgrowths," 15.

70 Re "faculties," see ibid., 9. Addams's language is mild in this case. At times she and others used more apparently insulting phrases, such as "dwarfed and crippled," to describe the deficiencies of people lacking formal education. JA,

"Standards of Education for Industrial Life," 164. The language was typical for her day. JA quotes Samuel Barnett as writing of the "dwarfed and mutilated life in the East End of London." "Pioneer Philanthropist," 869. John Stuart Mill writes of how circumstances are "stunting and dwarfing human nature." *Autobiography*, 163. Plato was probably the original source of these vivid metaphorical adjectives. In his "Theatetus," he writes of a lawyer whose "slavish condition has deprived him of growth, uprightness and independence. . . . [H]e has become stunted and warped." Jowett, *Plato*, 333. See also Carlyle's views above, on p. 172.

71 JA, "Outgrowths," 9, 4–6; Mill, *Subjection of Women*, 98.

72 JA, "Outgrowths," 12–13. For a thoughtful analysis of the implications of JA's rural background to her work and thought in Chicago, see Spears, *Chicago Dreaming*, chap. 6.

73 JA, "Outgrowths," 13.

74 Ibid., 2, 1. Scholars disagree about whether JA was racially or ethnically prejudiced while at Hull House. The issue is complicated by the way that class, race, and ethnic prejudices camouflaged each other and by usage patterns in nineteenth-century vocabulary, a sometimes neglected subject. My assessment is that for the period through 1898, her prejudices were mainly class-based.

75 The classic text on social Darwinism is still Hofstadter, *Social Darwinism*. The second chapter, "The Vogue of Spencer," shows the fundamental contribution of Spencer's thought to American social Darwinism. JA appears to have read Spencer's *Principles of Sociology* by 1889. JA to MAL, February 12, 1889. There are many areas of agreement and disagreement between Spencer and JA; the topic is too complex to address here. See JA, *Twenty*, 347.

76 JA to George Haldeman, December 21, 1890. Re the Ewing Street Church, see Stebner, *Women of Hull House*, 77–78; Linn, *Addams*, 81. Farrell states that Addams attended the Fourth Presbyterian Church (a socially prominent church on Michigan Avenue) regularly and taught in its Sunday school. *Beloved*, 53. The letter he cites, JA to MAL, February 26, 1889, does not document these statements. JA writes that they met with Reverend Stryker, its minister, but she says nothing about membership or Sunday school.

77 JA to George Haldeman, December 21, 1890.

78 Re classes and clubs, see "Weekly Programme of Lectures, Clubs, Classes, etc., January 1891," Scrapbook 2, 5; re the number of visitors the previous spring, see the undated, unidentified newspaper article [September 1891], Scrapbook 1, 10. See also V. Brown, *Education*, 368n3. Farrell appears to be the source of the incorrect claim, which he does not document, that two thousand people per week came to Hull House in its second year. *Beloved*, 63n29. Re the number of volunteers, see JA, "Outgrowths," 15–16.

79 Re the Butler Art Gallery, see JA, *Twenty*, 149. Butler's gift is mentioned in JA to AAH [September 1890; *JAPM* dates it to February 1890]. Re Edward Butler, see *Book of Chicagoans*, s.v. "Edward Butler"; Waage, "Social Background of Set-

tlement Trustees," 27–29. Re Barnett's visit, see EGS to Caleb and Susan Gates Starr, June 14, 1891, EGSP; Scrapbook 1, 18. For publicity about the event, see V. Brown, *Education*, 379n34. Re gallery visitors, see JA to Katharine Coman, December 7, 1891; EGS to Caleb and Susan Gates Starr, June 14, 1891, EGSP. Re gallery hours, see Scrapbook 1, 53, 56.

80 "Weekly Programme of Lectures, Clubs, Classes, etc., January 1891," Scrapbook 2, 5; "Hull-House Program, October 1891," RCA; EGS to Mary Allen, December 7, [1890], EGSP.

81 Re the alcove, see EGS to Caleb and Susan Gates Starr, June 14, 1891, EGSP. Re the first gym, see JA, "Objective Values," 38. Re the gymnasium, see JA to AAH, ca. September 6, 1891. The diet kitchen opened October 8, 1891, at 221 Ewing Street. Scrapbook 2, 9. For details, see *Churchman*, July 20, 1892, and Scrapbook 1, 25. Various city missions, as well as the YMCA and the WCTU, already had diet kitchens.

82 See the 1890–1891 account, Account Book #1, "JA's Ledger," *JAPM*, Addendum 3 (reel 74). That year the fiscal year ran from October 1, 1890, to September 30, 1891. Calculations are the author's. See Helen Culver to Culver's cousin Nelly, January 19, 1891, Hull-Culver Papers, Special Collections, The University Library, University of Illinois at Chicago; Linn, *Addams*, 84.

83 Katharine Jones, news clipping, n.d., n.p. [September 1891], Scrapbook 1, 10; JA to Sarah Anderson, August 4, 1891; JA to Katharine Coman, December 7, 1891. See also *Commons*, June 1896, 9; unidentified news clipping from the Rockford newspaper in 1894, "They Study Poverty," *JAPM*, 55:0017. Re the working girls' education movement of the 1880s, see Murolo, *Common Ground*, 17–19, 56, 60.

84 Re the period of ten years, see JA, *My Friend*, 30. Re McDowell, see Wilson, *Mary McDowell*, 18. For more on McDowell, see Wade, "Heritage from Chicago's Early Settlement Houses," 411–41; James, James, and Boyer, *Notable American Women*, s.v. "Mary McDowell"; Schultz and Hast, *Women Building Chicago*, s.v. "Mary McDowell." Re Burchard, see Kelley, "Early Days at Hull House," 426. Burchard is listed as teaching Latin in the Hull House Extension Program in the fall of 1891. Hull House Program, October 1891, RCA. Burchard is not listed as one of the residents as of March 1, 1892, possibly because he was still in his six-month probationary period. *Hull House Programs, Lectures and Classes*, March 1, 1892, 12, RCA. Hence Addams's recollection in 1895 that "all the residents of Hull-House for the first three years were women." *Maps*, 229. For more on the male residents, see Scrapbook 1, 49; JA, *Twenty*, 448.

85 Re Hull House being the first coeducational settlement, see G. Taylor, *Pioneering on Social Frontiers*, 277–78; Linn, *Addams*, 191. The ratio of female to male residents fluctuated. For 1895, when the ratio was 7.5:1, see *Maps*, 206; for 1897, when the ratio was 5:1, see *Hull-House Bulletin* 1, 4 (April 1897), 4; for 1905–6, when the ratio was 1:1, see *Hull-House Year Book 1905–6*, 8; for 1910, when the ratio was 3:2, see *Hull-House Year Book, 1910*, 5–6; for 1921, when the ratio was

2:1, see *Hull-House Year Book, 1921,* 3–4; all are in JAMC. Some historians have stressed that Hull House was intentionally a predominantly women's community or a "separate female institution," e.g., Muncy, *Creating a Female Dominion,* 10; Sklar, "Hull House in the 1890's," 659; Smith-Rosenberg, "Female World of Love and Ritual," 254; Horowitz, "Hull-House as Women's Space," 4. It was certainly predominantly female in spirit and provided all the opportunities and benefits to women that have been noted. It was also an intentionally coeducational institution. Hull House was a "breakthrough" mixed-sex organization in a highly sex-segregated society. JA believed that the ideal arrangement was for men and women to work together. See Jane Addams [interview], "As I See Women," *Ladies Home Journal,* August 1915, 11, 54. Scholars have yet to examine closely the place of men at Hull House in the 1890s.

86 Linn, *Addams,* 139. Lathrop was a boarder during the first years of Hull House. JA, Remarks, Memorial Service for Julia Lathrop, *JAPM,* 38:0680. See also *Hull House Programs, Lectures, and Classes,* March 1, 1892, 15, RCA. Lathrop was first appointed a county visitor for Cook County in the winter of 1890–1, when she was a short-term resident. JA, *Twenty,* 311; JA to AAH, December 28, 1891. She began to live there year-round in the fall of 1892. JA to Jenkin Lloyd Jones, January 8, 1893. Linn (*Addams,* 139) believes that Lathrop was admitted to the bar. Addams fails to mention it in *My Friend.* See Anne Firor Scott's introduction to the 2004 edition of this book. Very few of Lathrop's letters to JA and JA's to her from the 1890s survive.

87 The COS was founded in London in 1869; by 1893, there were fifty-five COS groups in the United States. Cumbler, "Politics of Charity," 99. Re Hull House and the COS, see *Hull House Programs, Lectures, and Classes,* March 1, 1892, 15, RCA; Lathrop, "Hull House as a Sociological Laboratory," 318–19. For the complicated early history of the CRAS and the COS movement in Chicago see Mayer, "Private Charities," 58–109; JA, *Twenty,* 158, 306; Chicago Woman's Club Minutes, November 4, 1891, CHS. For JA's views in 1902, see JA, *Democracy,* chap. 2.

88 JA, *My Friend,* v–vi; Linn, *Addams,* 134; JA, *My Friend,* 61, 170.

89 JA, *Excellent,* 32; JA to MRS, April 26, 1890, June 14, 1890; JA to AAH, [June 1891].

90 JA to MRS, February 3, 1891. Re Addams and Starr's relationship and Addams and Smith's relationship, see also Jackson, *Lines of Activity,* 168–71. On MRS, see Schultz and Hast, *Women Building Chicago,* s.v. "Mary Rozet Smith."

91 There is confusion about the year of Smith's birth. Most evidence suggests that it was 1869. The 1880 census lists Mary Rozet Smith as ten years old. Since the census was taken in the spring and her birthday was in December, this would make her birth date December 1869. U.S. Bureau of the Census, *1880 Census,* Chicago data, S530, reel 199, vol. 15, ed. 185, sheet 54, line 12. Linn says that Smith was twenty years old in early 1890, which would also date her birth to

1869. *Addams*, 147. See also Linn, "Miss Mary," *Chicago Daily Times*, February 28, 1934, 25. However, the 1900 census lists Smith as being born in 1870. U.S. Bureau of the Census, *1900 Census*, S530, Reel 411, vol. 51, ed. 716, sheet 19, line 1. Was the thirty-one-year-old Smith beginning to hide her age? Kenney eventually moved to Boston and married. In the fall of 1893, however, she was a temporary resident at Hull House and attended a residents' meeting. HH Minutes, September 24, 1893.

92 JA, "Outgrowths," 9; JA to AAH, [June 1891].

CHAPTER TEN: FELLOWSHIP

1 Kelley, *Autobiography*, 77; *FK*, 1:168, 96, 122, 136, 171, 178, 223; FK to Henry Demarest Lloyd, January 4, 1892, Nicholas Kelley Papers, New York Public Library; *FK*, 1:156. Kelley knew Caro Lloyd, the sister of Henry Demarest Lloyd, from the Rivington Street Settlement. Blumberg, *Florence Kelley*, 125–26. Did Caro arrange for her brother to hide Kelley's children before Kelley had left New York? The note Kelley sent him on January 4 requesting a meeting is remarkably terse; she writes that she is a friend of Caro's and gives no other reason for the meeting. Perhaps it was the prearranged signal that Kelley had arrived and was ready to deliver the children in secret to the Lloyd home. Secrecy before the divorce was final was necessary because of her husband's legal right to take the children away. Sklar refers to Rivington Street (or College) Settlement as University Settlement, which is the name of a different settlement. Given that FK wrote Lloyd on January 4, her recollection of arriving at Hull House before New Year's and of going to meet Lloyd the following day is probably incorrect. *Autobiography*, 77, 82. FK to Henry Demarest Lloyd, January 4, 1892, Nicholas Kelley Papers.

2 Goldmark, *Impatient Crusader*, 22–23; *FK*, 1:176–78, 370n13; Destler, *Henry Demarest Lloyd*, 159, 199; Account Book #1, "JA's Ledger," *JAPM*, Addendum 3 (reel 74); "Hull House Program, March 1, 1892," 15, RCA; F. Kelley, *Autobiography*, 80, 82.

3 Sklar provides a complete list of Kelley's published writings from 1882 to 1899. *FK*, 1:409–10. Linn, *Addams*, 137. For "galvanized us all," see JA, *My Friend*, 116.

4 *FK*, passim; F. Kelley, *Autobiography*, 54; Linn, *Addams*, 136.

5 *FK*, passim. For "years of effort," see F. Kelley, *Autobiography*, 63. Re her thesis, see also Goldmark, *Impatient Crusader*, 5.

6 *FK*, passim; F. Kelley, *Autobiography*, 61 (for the quotation), 86.

7 *FK*, 1:136, 95, 123; for the quotation, see 132–33.

8 *FK*, 1:140–42, 156, 142. Tax, *Rising*, 81; P. Foner, *History of the Labor Movement*, 2:145; F. Kelley, *Autobiography*, 10–11. Re Campbell's influence, see *FK*, 1:122, 144–45.

9 For "I am . . . learning," see Blumberg, *Kelley*, 127; *FK*, 1:225. Although it is generally assumed that Kelley was a resident from the beginning, the evidence sug-

gests that she did not become one until the fall of 1893. She is first mentioned as attending a residents' meeting in January 1894. HH Minutes, January 14, 1894. Kelley had previous ties to labor reformers in Chicago. She read the newsletter of the Illinois Woman's Alliance (she wrote a letter to its editor in 1888), and the Woman's Christian Temperance Union published one of her child labor pamphlets. *FK*, 1:211, 380n12; Ann D. Gordon, "A Push from the Left: Hull House and Chicago Socialists, 1889–1899," TS, 7, 10 (1978), Special Collections, The University Library, University of Illinois at Chicago.

10 EGS to Mary Starr Blaisdell, July 26, 1892, EGSP, quoted in *FK*, 1:163.

11 JA, *My Friend*, 58; JA, *Twenty*, 186; Bisno, *Abraham Bisno*, 119, 118. Re Kelley's continuing Marxism, see FK to Henry Demarest Lloyd, June 18, 1896, Nicholas Kelley Papers.

12 Alice Hamilton, quoted in *FK*, 1:290. See also Linn, *Addams*, 134; Goldmark, *Impatient Crusader*, 210. Goldmark was a later colleague.

13 E. Abbott, "Notes and Comment," 306; Linn, *Addams*, 139, 138; Bisno, *Abraham Bisno*, 117; FK is quoted in *FK*, 1:167.

14 Linn, *Addams*, 133; JA, *My Friend*, 119.

15 Linn, *Addams*, 139–40.

16 Andrew Alexander Bruce, "Memorial Services for Julia Lathrop," 1927, 17, *JAPM*, 38:0673; re Bruce, see JA, *My Friend*, 58–59.

17 JA quotes this statement in *My Friend*, 119; EGS to Mary Allen, October 14 [1892], EGSP.

18 E. Abbott, "Grace Abbott," 377; JA, "Social Settlements," 341; JA, "Settlement as a Way of Life," 141.

19 Bisno, *Abraham Bisno*, 172–73.

20 *JA as I Knew*, 19. She told Marcet once that "constant contact with active minds" was necessary for her (27). For "quickness," see S. O. Levinson, *Unity* [Memorial issue on Jane Addams] 115, 10 (July 15, 1935): 196. For "completely suspended," see Caroline F. Urie to EGS, June 13, 1935, EGSP. Linn, *Addams*, 135. See also the statement of Charlotte Perkins Gilman, quoted in Hill, *Charlotte Perkins Gilman*, 275. For "One cannot talk," see Hackett, "Hull House—A Souvenir," 279. Re "gentle Jane," Alexander Bruce believed that Julia Lathrop gave Addams that title. Bruce, "Memorial Services for Julia Lathrop, 1927," 22, *JAPM*, 38:0673.

21 JA, *My Friend*, 117; "everyone was brave" is quoted in Goldmark, *Impatient Crusader*, viii.

22 *FK*, 1:183; N. Kelley, "Early Days at HH," 426.

23 JA, "Objective Value," 47–48; Visher, *Handbook*, 82; "Hull House College Extension Classes, Plans for Twelve Weeks, Beginning on Monday, January 11, 1892," Scrapbook 2, 13. Dewey's talk was titled "Psychology and History." Re attendance numbers, see JA, "Objective Value," 55.

24 Re the Social Science Club, see *FK*, 1:198; "Hull House Program, Lectures, Clubs, Classes, etc., March 1st, 1892," 4, RCA. Re the clubs, see "Hull House

College Extension Classes, Plans for Twelve Weeks, Beginning on Monday, January 11, 1892," Scrapbook 2, 12; Scrapbook 3, 66; JA, *My Friend*, 50. EGS to JA, May 17, 1892.

25 These numbers are calculated from Account Book #1, "JA's Ledger," *JAPM*, Addendum 3 (reel 74).

26 JA probably learned of Dewey from Henry Demarest Lloyd, who knew Henry C. Adams, Dewey's colleague at the University of Michigan. Destler, *Henry Demarest Lloyd*, 149, 155–56; Dewey, "Ethics of Democracy"; Westbrook, *John Dewey*, 43. For more about Dewey's early career, see Westbrook, *John Dewey*, 21, 33.

27 Re Dewey as a Christian in these years, see Dewey, "Christianity and Democracy," 3–10; Kloppenberg, *Uncertain Victory*, 43–44; Livingston, *Pragmatism*, 188. James T. Kloppenberg and Cornel West note the influence of T. H. Green, the British social Christian, on Dewey in these years. Kloppenberg, *Uncertain Victory*, 43; West, *American Evasion*, 78, 80. John Dewey to JA, January 27, 1892, JDC.

28 The quotation from *Outlines* is in Livingston, *Pragmatism*, 189. Kloppenberg notes the influence of William James's *Principles of Psychology* (1890) on Dewey. Kloppenberg, *Uncertain Victory*, 44. See also Feffer, *Chicago Pragmatists*.

29 John Dewey to JA, January 27, 1892.

30 Dewey joined the Hull House Association board of trustees in 1897. HHA Minutes, April 13, 1897. He served until April 1903, when he resigned to move to New York City. HHA Minutes, April 14, 1903. See Westbrook, *John Dewey*, for biographical details on Dewey. Many have noted in passing Addams's influence on Dewey and vice versa. Two detailed efforts are Leffers, "Pragmatists"; Seigfried, "Socializing Democracy." Both discussions focus on the twentieth-century writings of the two thinkers. Other thoughtful discussions include Whipps, "Philosophy and Social Activism"; Seigfried, *Pragmatism and Feminism*, especially pages 73–78; Ross, "Gendered Social Knowledge," 244–245; M. Fischer, "Jane Addams's Critique," 279–84; Randall, "John Dewey and Jane Addams," iii.

31 Re the Sunset Club, see R. Schneirov, *Labor*, 270; *Chicago Times*, February 5, 1892, Clippings, *JAPM*, 55:0010. Re Schilling, see R. Schneirov, *Labor*, 71, 77, 173. The CWC started the cross-gender hospitality by hosting Men's Night with the Sunset Club in April 1891. *Annals*, 96–97.

32 Schultz and Hast, *Women Building Chicago*, s.v. "Frances Willard"; R. Schneirov, *Labor*, 266–67; *Chicago Times*, February 5, 1892, Clippings, *JAPM*, 55:0010.

33 Schultz and Hast, *Women Building Chicago*, s.v. "Lucy Louisa Flower." For Flower's activities with the Chicago Woman's Club in 1887–1892 period, see *Annals*, 5, 70, 82, 88, 92–97, 102; Ruegamer, "Paradise," 155–58; *Chicago Inter-Ocean*, February 5, 1892, Clippings, *JAPM*, 55:0011. See also *Chicago Tribune*, February 5, 1892, 8, Clippings, *JAPM*, 55:0012.

34 Re Hirsch see Cutler, *Jews of Chicago*. For the Schilling quotation, see *Chicago Inter-Ocean*, February 5, 1892, Clippings, *JAPM*, 55:0011–12.

35 JA, "How Would You Uplift the Masses?" 11–12.

36 "Invaded the Sunset Club," *Chicago Times*, February [5, 1892], Clippings, *JAPM*, 55:0010; JA, "Outgrowths," 8; "How Would You Uplift the Masses?" 11.

37 Re the Nineteenth Ward, see JA, "Objective Value," 49. See also FK to Friedrich Engels, May 27, 1892, Nicholas Kelley Papers; *FK*, 1:218. Re Illinois law, see R. Schneirov, *Labor*, 272–73. See also *Annals*, 68–71, 96; Tax, *Rising*, 71, 76; Flanagan, *Seeing*, 44–46; *Woman's Journal* 22, no. 4 (January 24, 1891): 25.

38 Re the Chicago Board of Education, see JA, "Objective Value," 49; Scrapbook 3, 75b. The IWA often used petitions. JA, "Women's Work in Chicago," 506. Re the City Council, see *FK*, 1:221; Wade, "Heritage," 435; Davis, *Spearheads*, 152–53; Baker, "Hull-House and the Ward Boss," 770; Lissak, *Pluralism*, 51; *FK*, 1:225. Re the new school, see F. Kelley, "Hull House," 560–61; Lathrop, "Hull-House," 317. This was the Andrew Jackson School.

39 Re Sweet and the Municipal Order League, see *Chicago Tribune*, March 19, 1892, 9; *Annals*, 103, 124; Ralph, "Chicago's Gentle Side," 296. The Municipal Order League became the Municipal Reform League, the name that Ralph uses. See also JA, "Women's Work in Chicago," 506–7. For more about Ada Sweet, see Schultz and Hast, *Women Building Chicago*, s.v. "Ada Sweet." Re boodling, see Roberts, "Municipal Voters' League," 117–48. Re poor garbage collection services, see *Chicago Tribune*, June 1, 1894, 5.

40 Sweet is quoted in *Chicago Tribune*, March 19, 1892, 9. For more on the garbage campaign, see *FK*, 1:382n38; Ralph, "Chicago's Gentle Side," 296; Livermore, "Cooperative Womanhood," 290. Nongovernmental groups in Chicago had been organizing by ward as early as 1866. E. Hirsch, *Urban Revolt*, 113; re Kelley's efforts, see EGS to Mary Starr Blaisdell, July 25, 1892, EGSP; F. Kelley, "Hull House," 556–57; F. Kelley, *Autobiography*, 50; JA, "Objective Value," 50.

41 Flanagan, *Seeing*, 44, 234n73.

42 *FK*, 1:231–32.

43 The National Labor Union called for legislation to limit the hours of women and children and provide equal pay for women and men in 1869 and 1870 (Barrows, *Trade Union Organization*, 41). For the Massachusetts law, see Brown and Tager, *Massachusetts*, 239. Re state laws, see Trattner, *Crusade for the Children*, 33. For a summary of child labor legislation before 1890 see Foner and Chamberlin, *Friedrich A. Sorge's Labor Movement*, 196.

44 L. Gordon, "Women and the Anti–Child Labor Movement," 313. Illinois had adopted a law requiring an eight-hour day in 1867, but it had never been enforced. E. Hirsch, *Urban Revolt*, 113.

45 Re the 1884 proposal and the 1888 articles, see E. Hirsch, *Urban Revolt*, 56, 47; Tax, *Rising*, 66. Re Sweet, see *Chicago Tribune*, March 19, 1892, 9. Re the IWA, see Ritter, "Elizabeth Morgan," 250; R. Schneirov, *Labor*, 272–73; Flanagan, *Seeing*, 37–39.

46 Richard Schneirov claims that the IWA's efforts "created a far stronger impetus for state-building . . . than the [male] local labor movement [had]." *Labor*,

274. Re city ordinances, see *FK*, 1:212–14, 380n16, 382n29; Tax, *Rising*, 77–78; JA, "Women's Work in Chicago," 506. The alderman is quoted in the *Woman's Journal* 20, no. 31 (August 3, 1889): 244.

47 These events are covered in P. Foner, *Women*, 227–30; Tax, *Rising*, 78–80; Scherman, "Addams," 183–84; Ritter, "Morgan," 244–45, 251 (for details from the report see 247–50); P. Foner, *Women*, 116–17; *FK*, 1:209. Foner calls "The New Slavery" one of "the most important and influential reports in American labor history." *Women*, 115.

48 These events are covered in *FK*, 1:381n25, 217; Tax, *Rising*, 82; Destler, *Lloyd*, 254–55; Blumberg, *Kelley*, 127; Bisno, *Abraham Bisno*, 122–23.

49 Re Kelley's 1892 investigations, see Ritter, "Morgan," 246; Blumberg, *Kelley*, 128; *FK*, 1:206, 229–33, 410; EGS to Mary Starr Blaisdell, July 25, 1892, EGSP. Kelley's model for these reports was probably Carroll D. Wright, *The Working Girls of Boston* (1884; reprint, New York: Arno and the New York Times, 1969). He also published a report titled "Working Women in Large Cities" in 1888. See Scrapbook 1, 10. Re the *Seventh Biennial Report*, see *FK*, 1:410; EGS to Mary Starr Blaisdell, July 25, 1892, EGSP.

50 JA, *Twenty*, 136; Meyerowitz, *Women Adrift*, 96–97. Kenney is quoted in Bryan and Davis, *One Hundred Years*, 35; Scrapbook 1, 26. In *Twenty Years*, Addams misremembers the year the cooperative club opened as 1891 (136). Re launching the club, see ibid.; Bryan and Davis, *One Hundred Years*, 35; Scrapbook 1, 18, 24, 26, 43; *Hull-House Bulletin*, 1896, Scrapbook 3, 90; Meyerowitz, *Women*, 97. A copy of the constitution of the Jane Club for 1894 is in Scrapbook 2, 39. Re other so-called self-governing (nonresidential) working girls' clubs, see Murulo, *Common Ground*, 29–30. Re charitable boarding houses for working girls, see Meyerowitz, *Women*, 46.

51 JA to Katharine Coman, December 7, 1891; Abell, *Urban*, 102–3; *Old Colony Memorial*, July 9, 1892, 4.

52 Mary Heaton, "A Woman's Toynbee Hall," *Review of Reviews* [New York], July 1890; Eva H. Brodlique, "A Toynbee Hall Experiment in Chicago," *Chautauquan*, September 1890; "Hull-House," *Altruistic Review*, October 1890; Emily Kellogg, "Hull-House," *Union Signal*, January 22, 1891; Katharine Jones, "The Working Girls of Chicago," *Review of Reviews* [New York], September 1891; "Household Labor," *Union Signal*, February 4, 1892; Alice Miller, "Hull House," *Charities Review*, February 1892; Joseph Kirkland, "Among the Poor of Chicago," *Scribner's Magazine*, July 1892. Most of these are in Scrapbook 1, as are many of the newspaper articles.

53 The best single source for information about the nonreligious settlement houses founded in the United States in the 1890s is Gavit, *Bibliography*. For a list of settlements in existence in 1899, by year of founding, see *Chicago Tribune*, May 14, 1899, n.p. For "It is good," see *Springfield Republican* article, n.d., Scrapbook 1, 21.

54 Residents who wrote articles in the 1890s include Florence Kelley, Isabel Eaton, Dorothea Moore, Alzina Stevens, and Henry Learned. Alice Miller was a settlement volunteer. Joseph Kirkland and Caroline Kirkland were the children of EGS's former employer, Elizabeth Stansbury Kirkland, the founder of the Kirkland School. Elia Peattie and Leila Bedell were CWC members. As of the summer of 1892, Addams had published no articles herself, unless one counts a reprint of her Sunset Club speech in the *Advance* (March 1892); to compare Hull House's publicity to that of others, see the College Settlement Association bibliographies for the 1890s.

55 EGS to Mary Allen, August 13, 1892, EGSP. See also Carrell, "Reflections," 205; EGS to Mary Blaisdell, [Fall 1892], containing "Dear Mary, I don't suppose," EGSP. The letter can be dated from the reference it contains to the possibility that EGS might be appointed to the Chicago school board. Re EGS's trip to Europe, see JA to AAH, March 15, 1892 and JA to AAH, [March], 1892; Carrell, "Reflections," 205; Bosch, *Life of Ellen Gates Starr*, 59–61.

56 For "crisis," see EGS to Mary Allen, [July 1892]; EGS to Mary Blaisdell [Fall 1892]. See also EGS to Mary Allen, October 14 [1892], "Thanksgiving Day" [November 1892], December 3 [1892]. All are in EGSP.

57 EGS to Mary Allen, August 13, [1892?], EGSP. Earlier that summer, when EGS was in Europe, she had written to JA in the old affectionate way. EGS to JA, May 17, [1892]. JA replied with similar tender affection. JA to EGS, [July 1892], *JAPM*, 2:1317. See also V. Brown, *Education*, 254–55.

58 EGS to Mary Allen, October 14, [1892], EGSP. For "if the devil," see Wise, *Addams*, 171. For more on Starr's intense friendships, see Muncy, *Creating*, 7.

59 Carrell, "Reflections," 205–6. See EGS to Mary Allen, "Dearly Beloved," [September? 1891]; see also letters of October 14 [1892] and "Thanksgiving Day" [1892], EGSP.

60 EGS to Mary Allen, September 1891, September 5 [1895], EGSP.

61 EGS to JA, April 12, 1935; JA to MRS, July 21, 1892.

62 Weber Linn, "Miss Mary," *Chicago Daily Times*, February 28, 1934, 25. See also Linn, *Addams*, 147–48; Alice Hamilton to Agnes Hamilton, December 1, 1900, file 637, box 25, Hamilton Family Papers; Eleanor Smith, "Memoir," 7, *JAPM*, 52:0158; Sicherman, *Alice Hamilton*, 188.

63 *JA as I Knew*, 10; Linn, "Miss Mary," 25. Many of JA's letters to MRS include sentences along the lines of "I have so much to tell you" or "I have a new plan I want to tell you about." See JA to MRS, March 3, May 4, and October 1, 1894. See also V. Brown, *Education*, 258–59. For more on Smith's role as a partner in the Hull House enterprise, see Sklar, "Who Funded Hull-House?" 101–4.

64 JA to [AAH], [July 1892]; JA to AAH, July 8, 1892.

65 See Mill, *Auguste Comte*, 184–85; Bain, *English Composition*, 124–25. The titles given in the text were her original titles (*Boston Evening Transcript*, July 29, 1892, 3). The original manuscripts for the two lectures have not survived; the versions

published in the *Forum* constitute the most accurate record we have of what she said at Plymouth. About 40 percent of "Subjective Necessity" was drawn from "Outgrowths." Only a few sentences were drawn from "How Would You Uplift the Masses?" "Objective Value" appears to be an entirely original effort.

66 See Bonsanquet, "Principles and Chief Dangers," 249; Giddings, "Ethics of Social Progress," 231, 233; Carrell, "Reflections," 174–75; Huntington, "Philanthropy—Its Success and Failure"; Huntington, "Philanthropy and Morality." Re Huntington's career, see Carrell, "Reflections," 170–75, 215–16; Woods, "University Settlement Idea."

67 Those present included Vida Scudder, a founder of the College Settlement on Rivington Street in New York City, Robert Woods, founder of Andover House (later South End Settlement) in Boston, whose doors would open that fall, and Katharine Coman, Helena Dudley, and Emily Balch, who would found Denison House in Boston in early 1893. Randall, *Improper Bostonian*, 82, 67; JA, *Twenty*, 114, Scudder, *On Journey*, 141.

68 Addams attracted "the largest audience of the session" for her first lecture, and the one for her second lecture was "still larger"; a reporter said that 150 people were in attendance ("The Cool Reasoning at Plymouth," *Springfield Republican*, July 30, 1892, Scrapbook 1, 21); see also *Boston Evening Transcript*, July 29, July 30, 1892, Scrapbook 1, 21; "The Plymouth School," *Boston Evening Transcript*, August 5, 1892, Scrapbook 1, 23.

69 JA, "Subjective" 2. The speech is often quoted because JA reprinted excerpts from it as chap. 6 of *Twenty Years*. She did not reprint the entire speech, as some have assumed. See also V. Brown, *Education*, 263–68.

70 JA, "Subjective," 18–20. Re her speeches to Christian audiences, see, e.g., her "Social Settlements," March 28, 1895, Clippings, *JAPM*, 55:0039; "Claim on the College Woman," 59; "Objective of Social Settlements," 149; *Democracy*, 69–70; "Whoso Liveth," 373. In Addams's day, college audiences were considered self-evidently Christian (daily attendance at chapel was required).

71 JA, "Subjective," 18; Mazzini, "Thoughts on Democracy," 109–11; Lowell, "Democracy," 13, 21; Adams, "Democracy," 753.

72 Dewey, "Christianity and Democracy," 9; Coughlan, *Young John Dewey*, 89. Coughlan does not identify the borrowed phrases, but my analysis reveals them to be the following: "[Jesus] had no set of truths labeled 'Religious' "; "no dogma to mark it off from truth and action in general"; "a revelation"; "action is the only medium [Addams edited Dewey here; he had used the word "organ"] man has for receiving and appropriating truth"; and "man's action is found in his social relationships in the way in which he connects with his fellows." JA, "Subjective," 17–18. For a discussion of Dewey's paper, see Westbrook, *Dewey*, 78–79; Rockefeller, *Dewey*, 190–96.

73 JA, "Subjective," 7; JA, "Objective Value," 33, 50, 33, 49.

74 JA, "Subjective," 14. See also Scherman, "Jane Addams," 33.

75 If Addams borrowed the paired terms "family" and "social claims" from someone else, I have been unable to discover her source. One possible inspiration
is Greek classical democratic theory, which makes the same basic distinction.
Catherine Peaden was the first to propose this idea. See "Jane Addams," 188.
Addams was particularly knowledgeable about Cicero, a Greek-educated Roman
who argued that the only ethical life was the active public life. Of course, "social"
was also a major concept in social Christianity. Regarding Addams's theory of
the family and social claims, see also Elshtain, *Addams*, 293nn35, 36.

76 JA uses the word "duty" in the context of the patriarchal, benevolent ethic. See
"Modern Lear," 114, 115, 118, 119. Re JA's other writings on the family and so-
cial claims, see Knight, "Biography's Window," 126, 137n76. For her most ex-
plicit and fully developed discussion of the family and the social claims, see
JA, "Growth of Corporate Consciousness." Re her theory and its meaning, see
also Scherman, "Jane Addams," 102–11; Silver, "Jane Addams," 33–34; Elshtain,
Jane Addams, 97; Elshtain, "Jane Addams as a Civic Theorist," 504–20; Rudnick,
"Feminist American Success Myth," 155.

77 *FK*, 1:109–13. For "revolt of the daughters," see MacDonald, "American Social
Settlements," 4. MacDonald identifies the speaker he quotes only as "a sprightly
American." Given the boldness of the statement and its content, his source was
most likely Kelley, the daughter who rebelled against her father.

78 JA, "How Would You Uplift the Masses?" 11; JA, "Subjective," 22–23; JA, "Objective Value," 45–46; JA, "Subjective," 22, 24.

79 In his talk, Dewey stresses that God is the source of truth; action is the means
by which man grasps God's truth. Thus truth remains absolute. In 1892
Dewey's pragmatism was as nascent as Addams's. In his "Christianity and
Democracy" he endorsed "life" as a source of continuous knowledge about
truth, but he was thinking of Christian revelation, not experience. Rockefeller,
Dewey, 190–94. On Dewey's development as a pragmatist, see Kloppenberg,
Uncertain Victory, 44; Rockefeller, *Dewey*, 204, 215–17; Feffer, "Between Head
and Hand," 11.

80 JA, *My Friend*, 56–57.

81 The two speeches were published the following year in the collection Henry C.
Adams edited with the original titles and the word "settlement" made plural in
both. Adams, *Philanthropy and Social Progress*. Jane Addams updated a few facts
in both texts. The 1893 versions of both lectures have been reprinted in Elshtain,
Jane Addams Reader.

CHAPTER ELEVEN: BAPTISM

1 JA, *Twenty*, viii; JA, "Settlement as a Way of Life," 143.

2 Re Altgeld, see Howard, *Mostly Good*, 187–97; Altgeld, *Mind and Spirit*, editor's
preface. Re Altgeld's positions, see Gordon, "Women and the Anti-Child Labor
Movement," 314; Altgeld, *Live Questions*, passim. Re his campaign, see Howard,

Mostly Good, 182, 187; Altgeld, *Mind and Spirit*, 8; Pegram, *Partisans and Progressives*, 68. See also Wish, "Altgeld and the Progressive Tradition," 813–31.

3 Altgeld, "Inaugural Address," in *Mind and Spirit*, 59. Re Kelley's reports, see Dunne, *Illinois*, 140; Harmon, "Florence Kelley," 166; *Chicago Inter-Ocean*, January 13, 1893, 2.

4 Document 10, "Florence Kelley's Testimony on the Sweating System," *Report and Findings of the Joint Committee to Investigate the "Sweat Shop" System* (Springfield, IL: H. W. Rokker, 1893), 135–39, at http://www.binghamton.edu/womhist /factory/doc10.htm. Bisno presented a proposed bill to the joint committee that had been prepared by Kelley, Elizabeth Morgan, and members of the CTLA and other labor organizations. News clipping, Scrapbook 1, 29. Re the tour, see *Chicago Tribune*, February 11, 1893, 8, col. 1; February 12, 1893, 6, col. 2; February 13, 1893, 7, col. 1; and other clippings, Scrapbook 1, 29–39; *Woman's Journal* 24 (March 4, 1893): 69.

5 JA, *Twenty*, 201.

6 JA to Henry Demarest Lloyd, January 2, 1893; *Chicago Tribune*, February 20, 1893, 1–2; *Chicago Times*, February 20, 1893; *Chicago Inter-Ocean*, February 20, 1893, all in Scrapbook 1, 32–34; *Chicago Inter-Ocean*, April 4, 1893, Scrapbook 1, 39. For additional news coverage, see Scrapbook 1, 29–39. Regarding Toomey, see Scrapbook 1, 43. Lucy Flower was on the stage. Mary Wilmarth's membership in the Anti-Sweatshop League in 1893 suggests that she was involved labor reform earlier than has been previously noted. See also Schultz and Hast, *Women Building Chicago*, s.v. "Mary Wilmarth."

7 JA left Chicago February 13, 1893. See JA to AAH, February 10, 1893.

8 JA, *Twenty*, 202. Five years later, she was still a reluctant lobbyist. See JA to Madeleine Sikes, March 6, 1897.

9 Re Angelina Grimké's historic speech, see Perry, *Lift up Thy Voice*, 163–65. Clara Barton was the first woman to speak to a body of the U.S. Congress, in 1866. Pryor, *Clara Barton*, 147. Women began petitioning Congress, which was the earliest form of lobbying they undertook, in 1828. Zaeske, *Signatures of Citizenship*, 149.

10 For the Harbert quotation, see Buechler, *Transformation*, 124. Re suffrage efforts in Illinois, see *Woman's Journal* 22 (February 21, 1891): 5; Buechler, *Transformation*, 149.

11 See Bisno, "Economic and Industrial Condition: Chicago," 141; Tax, *Rising of the Women*, 83; JA, *Twenty*, 202. By 1893 the IWA had six hundred members, including about one hundred men, millionaires and workingmen among them. Ralph, "Chicago's Gentle Side," 296.

12 JA, *Twenty*, 33–34. Addams does not identify in *Twenty Years* the "good friend" who invited her to the lunch, but this story is told in William Colvin's obituary, "In Memoriam," *Hull-House Bulletin* (October 1896). The cost of the Gymnasium Building appears in Scrapbook 1, 43; Colvin is identified as a donor.

13 JA, *Twenty*, 33. She tells about her father's reputation as unbribable just before she tells her own bribe story.

14 *Annals*, 130, 126. Re club member Bertha Honoré Palmer's public criticisms of the sweatshops, see an 1893 speech in *Woman's Journal*, May 13, 1893, 150.

15 JA, *Twenty*, 202.

16 Ibid., 201–2. In 1898, JA praised the IWA as "the pioneer in various undertakings which more conservative bodies have since carried." JA, "Women's Work in Chicago," 506. For details of the trade union campaign, see Scherman, "Jane Addams," 193–94.

17 JA, "Objective Value," 30; JA, *Twenty*, 199.

18 JA, *Twenty*, 205.

19 Harmon, "Florence Kelley," 166. See also Zuck, "Florence Kelley." Historians have referred to the law by various titles. I use the one Addams and her colleagues used in *Maps*, 51.

20 Tax, *Rising*, 83; Harmon, "Florence Kelley," 166; *FK*, 1:233–36.

21 Kessler-Harris, *Out to Work*, 186; Brown and Tager, *Massachusetts*, 239. The 1893 law was the first state law in the United States to limit women industrial workers to eight-hour days. For earlier, less wide-reaching precedents, see Kessler-Harris, *Out to Work*, 182–83. Twenty-six years earlier, in 1867, Illinois had been the first state to pass an eight-hour law of any kind when it adopted legislation restricting the hours of work for state employees. Beckner, *History of Illinois Labor Legislation*, 179–80.

22 Dietz, *Turning Operations*, 35. I draw on Tilly and Gurin's definition of politics as efforts to "affect the distribution of power and/or resources in a state or community" in "Women, Politics, and Change," 4.

23 *Annals*, 114. For a history of the idea of the congresses, see Badger, *Great American Fair*, 77–78. Re the Art Palace, see Sewall, *World's Congress of Representative Women*, 1:67; *Annals*, 113, 108; *Chicago Times*, May 16, 1893, 5. Other congresses were held on the fairgrounds.

24 Re JA's proposal see Charles C. Bonney to JA, January 14, 1893. Re visits in the east, see Woods, *Robert A. Woods*, 72; College Settlement Association, *Fourth Annual Report* (Boston: privately printed, 1894), 92–93.

25 See the map in Badger, *Great American Fair*, after page 81; Miller, *City of the Century*, 383, 488.

26 See JA to AAH, April 10, 1893; AHA to Harry Haldeman, September 24, 1893, Lilly Library; Florence Kelley to Caroline Kelley, May 27, 1893, box 66, Nicholas Kelley Papers; Fry, *Generous Spirit*, 41. Re the cool relations between JA and Anna, see *JA as I Knew*, 5–9. Marcet dates the reconciliation between them to 1905 or 1906, soon after Marcet's father died.

27 Re the playground and public baths, see FK to Caroline Kelley, May 27, 1893; re the consumers' league, see *Annals*, 128; re the advisory committee for the social settlement congress, see JA's correspondence for May 1893. JA spoke to

the Women's Congress on May 19, 1893. Sewall, *World's Congress*, 1:83. The Anti-Sweatshop League was the first group to propose a consumer's league in Chicago; it did so to put pressure on Chicago's sweatshop and factory employers. See *Chicago Tribune*, February 20, 1893, 1–2. Re chairing the local peace committee, see the Women's International League for Peace and Freedom, United States Section Papers, JA's résumé, reel 19, frame 0738–9, SCPC.

28 *Annals*, 113. Re Henrotin, see Schultz and Hast, *Women Building Chicago*, s.v. "Ellen Henrotin." A number of congresses on subjects of interest to women were held at the Woman's Building on the fairgrounds. Excerpts from speeches were reprinted in Eagle, *Congress of Women*. The congresses discussed in Eagle's collection are not to be confused with the World's Congress of Representative Women. Badger, *Great American Fair*, 101–2; Williams, "Intellectual Progress of the Colored Women," 2:696–711; Kenney, "Organization of Working Women," 2:871–74.

29 Murolo, *Common Ground*, 15. The reform of domestic service was a much discussed topic in the early 1890s. See Wilkinson, "Household Economics," 234–36.

30 There are passing references in JA's college letters to Anna's difficulties with servants, who were regularly fired or who regularly quit. See also V. Brown, *Education*, 24, 46, 150, 311n21; Stebner, *Women of Hull House*, 95–98. The number of three servants at Hull House comes from Poole, *Giants Gone*, 221. Poole's interviewee, a Hull House servant, gives no dates; her reference to ten residents living in the house, including two men, suggests that she was speaking of 1892 or early 1893. See JA, "Domestic Service and the Family Claim," 2:626–31. "Domestic Service" is her first surviving speech on labor. The version in Sewall appears to be a lengthy excerpt from the complete speech. Many in the Sewall collection are excerpts. No complete text of Addams's speech survives.

31 JA, "Domestic Service," 628.

32 Ibid., 629. Addams's invocation of a "patriarchal altar" was likely inspired by her knowledge of ancient Roman religion, in which the altar was the family hearth and the religion was typically described as patriarchal.

33 She specifically elaborated on that role as being an important one for a social settlement in her 1899 essay "A Function of the Social Settlement."

34 JA, "Domestic Service," 626. For "primitive," see "Subjective Necessity," 8. For "less intellectual," see "Objective Value," 31. For "less intelligent," see JA, *Democracy*, 229. For an example of contemporary usage, see Bain, *English Composition* (which had been her textbook), 175.

35 Learned, "Social Settlements in the United States," 108–14. The proceedings of the congress were not published; a list of the papers is provided by Learned and Johnson, *History of the World's Columbian Exposition*, vol. 4, *Congresses*: 219–20. See also "The World's Fair Congress of Social Settlements," *Unity* 31 (July 27, 1893): 22:251–52. Re British settlements, see M. Katherine Jones, "Bibliography

of College, University and Social Settlements" [College Settlement Association 1894], CSA Papers, Wellesley Archives, Wellesley College, Wellesley, MA. Re the numbers of settlements, see *Chicago Sun Tribune,* May 14, 1899. The four Chicago settlements were Hull House, Northwestern University Settlement, Clybourne Avenue Settlement, and Maxwell Street Settlement. Although some religious settlements are included in these counts, they are probably significantly undercounted, particularly the Catholic ones.

36 R. Johnson, *History,* 4:219–20. Re FK, see *FK,* 1:237. Kelley was appointed on July 12, 1893. Kelley, "I Go to Work," 274. Re Lathrop's work with the state board of charities, see JA, *My Friend,* chap. 6. Re EGS, see *Annals,* 131; Stebner, *Women of Hull House,* 87. EGS chaired the planning committee for the Manual and Art Education Congress. *Annals,* 114.

37 The number of residents is drawn from HH Minutes. It does not include Florence Kelley, who became a resident in 1893–94. In 1894, Rivington Street Settlement in New York City had ten residents and the newer Andover House had five. For this and other statistics, see Ely, "Social Settlements in the United States," pts. 1–3. As of November 1896, Denison House in Boston had six residents. H. J. Gow Diaries, November 7, 1896, Rare Book, Manuscript, and Special Collections Library, Duke University. Re Hull House being the first coed settlement, see Linn, *Addams,* 191; G. Taylor, *Pioneering on Social Frontiers,* 277–78; Knight, "Jane Addams and the Settlement House Movement," 89. Re the seven men, see Scrapbook 1, 42. There were six men as of May 1893. See FK to Caroline Kelley, May 27, 1893, Nicholas Kelley Papers. Re John Linn, presumably the seventh male resident, see HH Minutes, November 12, 1893.

38 See Stead, *If Christ Came to Chicago,* 418; various articles in Scrapbook 1, 40½, 42, 43, 44; *Hull-House Brochure,* January 1, 1894, *JAPM,* 46:0612; FK, "Hull House," 554. Scholars have sometimes confused the diet kitchen with the Coffee House. The two were distinct in form and purpose. In the new building, the diet kitchen was located behind the Coffee House, on the lower level. Regarding the neighbors' dislike for the New England diet, see JA, *Twenty,* 129–31. Re JA's early, naïve enthusiasm for the concept, see *Chicago Inter Ocean,* August 24, 1893, 8, col. 3. For "education" and "the first buildings," see JA, *Twenty,* 150.

39 Learned, "Hull-House," 329.

40 Re the DOL study, see *FK,* 1:228–29; *Maps,* 7–8. The Chicago study was conducted in the city blocks east of Halsted Street to State Street and south of Polk to Twelfth Street. This was the eastern half of the Nineteenth Ward plus a small portion of an adjacent ward. *Maps,* 3; HH Minutes, August 27, 1893. According to the minutes of the Residents' Meeting for July and August, they had hoped to have some other maps as well, for example, an ownership map and a sanitary map.

41 The earliest minutes book that survives has a date of January 1, 1893, on its cover. Because this book starts at the beginning of a calendar year, it seems possible

that there was an earlier minutes book that was lost or destroyed. Many Hull House records were lost when the buildings were torn down in the 1960s to make way for the University of Illinois's new Chicago campus. Bryan, "Provenance," in *JAPCG*, 72. This earliest surviving minutes book is missing its first twenty pages; the first minutes that survive are dated July 16, 1893. Minutes survive through October 5, 1896. However, the meetings continued to take place after that date. See JA's calendar diary entry, "Residents Meeting," for April 25, 1898, *JAPM*, 29:0419. For more about the meetings, see Knight, "Jane Addams and Hull House," 131–32. No document exists that gives the formal name of the residents' governing body. In the earlier article, "Jane Addams and Hull House," I called it the Residents Committee. Subsequently, I noted that the cover page of the first surviving minutes book was labeled "Residents Meetings," so I have adopted the name Residents' Meeting. Furthermore, the meeting eventually acquired committees that reported to it.

42 Re other settlement houses and the governing role of residents, or lack of one, see Knight, "Jane Addams and Hull House," 131–33. Re the broader question of the influence of JA and Hull House on the American settlement movement, see Knight, "Jane Addams and the Settlement House Movement," 1–14.

43 HH Minutes, October 8, 1893. See also other minutes for 1893 and 1894. The first documented instance of the Residents' Meeting making decisions about admitting residents occurs in the minutes for August 13, 1893. For the residents' admission process, see the appendix to *Maps*, 229. By the fall of 1893, the meeting was also setting the fee that residents paid for room and board. See below. Toynbee Hall's probationary period was three months. Picht, *Toynbee Hall*, 30–31. Re JA and playground duty, see HH Minutes, July 23, 1893, August 6, 1893; re standing committees, see HH Minutes, September 10, 1893.

44 For examples of the various procedures, see HH Minutes, September 10, 1893, October 8, 1893, November 12, 1893, December 10, 1893. In one case, Addams supported having a former resident return but others defeated the motion. HH Minutes, May 25, 1896.

45 Knight, "Jane Addams and Hull House," 128–35.

46 Ibid., 128–31; Eliza Sunderland, "Hull-House Chicago: Its Work and Workers," *Unitarian*, September 1893, Scrapbook 1, 42–44.

47 "Constitution of the Hull House Men's Club," Scrapbook 2, 47. The club was separately incorporated. Re children's clubs being self-governing, see Stevens, "Life in a Settlement," 49; news clippings, Scrapbook 3, 3; JA, "Description of Hull House, January, 1, 1894"; JA, "Discussion of Social Settlements," 474; Hecht, "Hull-House Theatre," 24.

48 For "the dream," see JA, *Twenty*, 142. Re the fundraising, see JA to Henry Demarest Lloyd, [December 26, 1892], January 2 1892 [1893]. Re Coit's views, see Coit, *Neighbourhood Guilds*, 30. Re the Labor Congress, see "Women Dominate Morning Sessions," *Chicago Daily Tribune*, August 30, 1893, 3, col. 3. I am in-

debted to Julia W. Kramer and Ann Feldman for alerting me to this news item. See also *The Programme of the Labor Congress, World's Congress Auxiliary of the World's Columbian Exposition, 1893*, Miscellaneous Pamphlets Collection, Chicago Historical Society. Re the Cooperative Congress, see JA, *Twenty*, 142. See also Knight, "Jane Addams's Early Theory and Practice of Cooperation."

49 JA to AAH, March 15, 1892.

50 Account Book #1, "JA's Ledger," *JAPM*, Addendum 3 (reel 73).

51 The minutes do not say what she told them, but on October 8, 1893, the minutes observe that the house has a surplus, which meant that the residents knew about the deficit. HH Minutes, August 27, 1893, October 8, 1893, August 13, 1893.

52 Robert Woods to JA, June 20, 1893. Re "Saint Jane," see Ralph, "Chicago's Gentle Side," 295; Blanc, *Condition of Woman*, 70; "The Only Saint America Has Produced," *Current Literature* 40 (April 1906): 377–79. Weber Linn observed that JA was referred to as "Saint Jane" by the neighbors, which, he claims, prompted her close friends, in teasing fashion, to call her that, too. Linn, *Jane Addams*, 433; Adams, introduction to *Philanthropy and Social Progress*, ix; "The World's Fair Congress of Social Settlements," *Unity* 31, 22 (July 27, 1893): 251

53 "World's Fair Congress of Social Settlements," 252.

54 JA, "Subjective Necessity," 22. Balch is quoted in Foster, *Women for All Seasons*, 19.

CHAPTER TWELVE: COOPERATION

1 Steeples and Whitten, *Democracy*, 22–23, 1, 29–30, 32–34.

2 See Kindleberger, *Manias, Panics, and Crashes*, 43, 5, 113; Rezneck, "Unemployment, Unrest, and Relief," 324; Bliss, *Encyclopedia of Social Reform*, s.v. "Business Failures"; Rezneck, "Unemployment, Unrest, and Relief," 327; P. Foner, *History*, 2:234; Hoffman, *Depression of the Nineties*, 102–3; Feder, "Unemployment," 83.

3 Scrapbook 1, 58, unidentified news clipping, September 1894. Re Pullman employment, see C. Smith, *Urban Disorder*, 234; Hogan, *Class and Reform*, 20.

4 Adams is quoted in Steeples and Whitten, *Democracy*, 1.

5 For the quotations, see Burrows and Wallace, *Gotham*, 1190, 1184. Re churches, see Marks, "Polishing the Gem of the Prairie," 126. The group of economists was the American Economics Association, which was pro-labor in 1886, when the statement was made.

6 FK to Henry Demarest Lloyd, June 18, 1896, Henry Demarest Lloyd Papers, Wisconsin State Historical Society, Madison. She wrote, "I hold to the whole platform of . . . the International Socialist Party."

7 Nutter, *Necessity of Organization*, 27; Mayer, "Private Charities," 408. Re the figure of one-tenth, see Mapes, "Visions," 114.

8 See Scherman, "Jane Addams," 127; Marks, "Polishing the Gem," 114; Mayer, "Private Charities," 410, 435, 142.

9 See Rezneck, "Unemployment, Unrest, and Relief," 328. JA, "What Shall We Do for Our Unemployed?" 82; Lathrop, "Cook County Charities," in *Maps*, 145, 147. Lathrop subsumes the infirmary and the asylum under the title "poor house."

10 *Chicago Tribune*, September 2, 1893, 2. For "city officials" see Flanagan, *Seeing*, 38.

11 *Chicago Tribune*, August 27, 1893. See also P. Foner, *History*, 2:236–38.

12 *Chicago Tribune*, September 2, 1893, 2.

13 E. Woods, *Robert A. Woods*, 82. The author of the letter is not identified, but Starr was a friend and correspondent of Robert Woods and the letter's dramatic and playful tone is consistent with Starr's personality and letter-writing style. Account Book #1, "JA's Ledger," 40–57, *JAPM*, Addendum 3 (reel 74); JA to MRS, August 26, 1893.

14 JA, *My Friend*, 67. For "We all worked," see JA, *Twenty*, 259–60.

15 JA, "What Shall We Do for Our Unemployed?" 82.

16 Ibid.; box 94, Stephenson County Courthouse Records, Stephenson County Courthouse, Freeport, IL; Duis, *Challenging Chicago*, 327–29.

17 JA, *Twenty*, 259–60.

18 JA, "What Shall We Do for Our Unemployed?" 82.

19 HH Minutes, December 10, 1893. Addams told the residents that Powers had come to her to propose the collaboration.

20 HH Minutes, July 23, 1893. Re coal co-ops, see Coit, *Neighbourhood Guilds*, 30; HH Minutes, October 15, 1893; Scrapbook 1, 32; Scrapbook 2, 32; HH Minutes, September 14, October 14, November 12, 1893, December 2, 1893; JA, *Twenty*, 134. For more on the coal cooperative, see Jackson, *Lines of Activity*, 79–80; Scrapbooks 1 and 2; "Plans for the Poor," Scrapbook 1, 58; JA, "Hull-House Description, January 1, 1894," Scrapbook 2, 32.

21 Account Book #1, "JA's Ledger," 57–59, *JAPM*, Addendum 3 (reel 74). In 1935 Addams credited Lathrop with proposing cooperative systemized charity work. *My Friend*, 75. Lathrop, knowing that there would be resistance among the residents, probably thought it best for Swing to make the request to Hull House. HH Minutes, September 24, 1893, November 25, 1893; JA, *Twenty*, 161. Eventually Lathrop organized the bureau separately, with its own board of directors, which she chaired. JA, *My Friend*, 76, 79; JA, *Twenty*, 161; JA to MRS, August 26, 1893.

22 HH Minutes, August 13, 27, 1893; Visher, *Handbook*, 65; JA, "Hull-House Description, January 1, 1894." The neighborhood physician was Josephine Milligan. Scrapbook 1, 49. Re the nurse from the VNA and the Hull House physician, see Stead, *If Christ*, 418; Schultz and Hast, *Women Building Chicago*, s.v. "Harriet Alleyne Rice." Her status as a resident was unorthodox. She is listed as an "independent resident" as of November 4, 1894, in HH Minutes. She rarely attended Residents' Meetings (she did in the summer of 1896).

23 Lathrop, "The Cook County Charities," in *Maps*, 158.

24 Re canal jobs, see *Chicago Tribune*, May 8, 1895, 8; *First Annual Report, Civic Federation*, 34, CFMCR. Re the CRAS woodyard, see National Conference of Charities and Correction, *Proceedings of the National Conference of Charities and Correction, 1893* (Boston: Ellis, 1893), 103. Re men sleeping in police stations, see Duis, *Challenging Chicago*, 332. Re JA's proposal, see HH Minutes, December 10, 1893. Re lodging houses, see A. Warner, *American Charities*, 254.

25 JA, "Hull House Description, January 1, 1894." Re the December 13 meeting, see *Annals*, 117, 122–23. Re the workshop and lodging house, see HH Minutes, January 14, 1894. Re the work of forty clubs, see [Rochester] *Union Advertiser*, April 25, 1895, Scrapbook 3, 4. For more about the project see *Annals*, 169, 173; Kelley, "Hull-House," 559; "Women Are the Lodgers," *Chicago Tribune*, April 4, 1896, 16; JA, "Hull-House as a Type of College Settlement," 109. The lodging house was later named after Sarah Hackett Stevenson, who endowed it. Possibly the city's first private, nonreligious homeless shelter for women, it was still in operation in 1939. Powers, "Chicago Woman's Club," 122, 71; *Annals*, 169.

26 Board Minutes, CFMCR, box 3, December 9, 1893; Re the Relief Bureau, see JA, *Twenty*, 160. Re COS procedures, see Watson, *Charity Organization Movement*, 255. Re moving the main office, see JA, *My Friend*, 74–76. The Committee of 50 was appointed by the organizing committee of what would become the Civic Federation. The CRA became the first project of the federation, whose founding is described below. Re the number of CRA cases, see Mayer, "Private Charities," 144–45, 147, 154.

27 Re the COS system, see M. Katz, *In the Shadow of the Poorhouse*, 71; R. Brown, *Strength of the People*, 122–23; Bliss, *Encyclopedia*, 220. The settlement house philosophy led, for example, to Hull House volunteers' moving a family that was badly in debt to a new house or set of rooms with a month's rent paid. H. J. Gow Diaries, April 26, 1897, Rare Book, Manuscript, and Special Collections Library, Duke University. The quotation is from JA, *Twenty*, 162.

28 *Twenty*, 162; JA, *My Friend*, 75. When Addams writes in 1910 that there was no Charity Organization Society in Chicago twenty years earlier, she is referring to the state of things in 1889. *Twenty Years*, 158. The movement had died in the city. For more on COS and its operations in Chicago, see Mayer, "Private Charities," 74–79, 86, 89, 226–28, 232–38.

29 Re the Relief Bureau, which became the branch COS office, see HH Minutes, September 24, 1893, November 25, 1893; JA, *Twenty*, 161.

30 JA, *Twenty*, 162. See also JA, "Subtle Problems of Charity," 163. She writes in *Twenty Years* that the experience taught her that "life cannot be administered by definite rules and regulations," implying that she ceased from that time to approve of COS methods (162). I do not quote this statement in the text because I think she did not realize this at the time.

31 JA, *Democracy*, 15; JA's views of COS methods were complex and changed over time. She continued to try to improve organized charity throughout the 1890s

but also was very aware of the problems with its methods. See "For Systematic Charity," *New York Times*, December 10, 1897, 5; JA, *Democracy*, 13–70.

32 Re the subcommittee, see JA, *My Friend*, 74–76; JA, *Twenty*, 161. If a man worked full-time for $1.50 per day on a regular basis, he could earn just enough to support a family of four. Mayer, "Private Charities," 135, 448.

33 JA, *Twenty*, 161, 187.

34 Re Henderson, see Diner, *City*, 32–33. Re the title of his speech, see *Maps*, 217. For the quotations, see Blanc, *Condition of Woman*, 77–81, 83. For more on the event, see Blanc, "A Hull-House Scene," *Boston Transcript*, August 30, 1894; JA, *Twenty*, 182; Scrapbook 1, 44.

35 A. Warner, *American Charities*. JA to MRS, January 15, 1895. See also JA, "Child Labor and Pauperism," 116.

36 Toynbee, "Wages and Natural Law," in *Lectures*, 155–77.

37 Re Ely and his views, see Kloppenberg, *Uncertain Victory*, 265–66; Ely, *Labor Movement*, vii; *FK*, 1:108–9, 156, 162.

38 Re JA reading Lloyd's book, see JA to Henry Demarest Lloyd, December 1, 1894. Re his views, see Lloyd, *Wealth against Commonwealth*, 518, 521. For the quotation, see *Chicago Tribune*, September 4, 1893, 1. She also read the works of Werner Sombart, author of *Modern Capitalism*, and Achille Loria. JA, *Twenty*, 58.

39 JA, *Twenty*, 57, 187; Stead, *If Christ*, 401.

40 JA, *Twenty*, 186–87. In this discussion, JA deals with her thinking about Marxism as of 1893. For a discussion that ranges over a broader time period, see Deegan, *Jane Addams and the Men of the Chicago School*, 256–57.

41 JA, *Twenty*, 187. See also *JA as I Knew*, 28–29. Addams writes in *Twenty Years* (1910) that she could accept the theory that capitalists pursued overproduction. My assessment, based on the shift in consciousness she underwent in the year and a half after the strike, is that she did not accept it in the fall of 1893. She probably did by 1896. Marx, *Contribution*, preface.

42 JA, *Twenty*, 185. When some Chicago anarchists could not find a hall to rent for an Emma Goldman speech, JA agreed to let them use Hull House although she did not agree with anarchism. Polacheck, *I Came a Stranger*, 103.

43 JA, *Twenty*, 185.

44 Stewart, *Half-Century*, 2; White is quoted at 7–8. For more on the national history of municipal reform, see Schiesl, *Politics of Efficiency*; Stewart, *Half-Century*. For a view as of 1895, see Tolman, *Municipal Reform Movements*. On Chicago, see Komons, "Chicago, 1893–1907." Re corrupt alliances, see E. Hirsch, *Urban Revolt*, 49.

45 By 1873 almost half of the city's aldermen were Irish Americans. R. Schneirov, *Labor*, 52. Re the tendency of boodlers to be Democrats, see Wendt and Kogan, *Lords of the Levee*, 125; R. Schneirov, *Labor*, 58–63; E. Hirsch, *Urban Revolt*, 170.

46 Re MacVeagh and Gage, see Stewart, *Half-Century*, 11; R. Schneirov, *Labor*, 269–

70. Re JA attending the conferences and for more about them, see JA, "Chicago Settlements and Social Unrest," 166; Destler, *Henry Demarest Lloyd*, 199.

47 Re Gage's and MacVeagh's views, see R. Schneirov, *Labor*, 269–70; Westhoff, " 'A fatal drifting,' " 102–3, 106. Re labor's willingness to work with reformers see R. Schneirov, *Labor*, 282. For "with their hands," see MacVeagh in "Program of Municipal Reform," 562.

48 Re the first coalition, see R. Schneirov, *Labor*, 283; Gilbert and Bryson, *Chicago*, 227. Re the second coalition, see Miller, *City of the Century*, 483–87. See also Small, "Civic Federation of Chicago," 88.

49 Re Stead, see Phillips, *Kingdom on Earth*, 139–40; Miller *City of Century*, 535; Marks, "Polishing the Gem," 116; JA, "Julia Lathrop at Hull-House," 377; Baylen, "Victorious 'Crusade,' " 419–21; Stead, *Chicago Today*, xiii. See also C. Smith, *Urban Disorder*, 248–49.

50 Re Stead's talk at Hull House, see *Maps*, 217. Re JA's recollection, see JA, *Twenty*, 160. Re Stead's recollection, see Stead, *If Christ*, 419. For more on Stead's visit to Chicago, see JA, "Julia Lathrop at Hull-House," 377.

51 *Chicago Tribune*, November 13, 1893, 1. For JA's quotation, see JA, *Twenty*, 160. According to the *Tribune* coverage, Addams did not give a speech at either session, notwithstanding the claim made in Downey, "William Stead and Chicago," 160. Indeed, she is not mentioned in the *Tribune* story at all. Graham Taylor in *Pioneering on Social Frontiers* (28–33) lists categories of people on the stage but does not mention Addams.

52 *Chicago Tribune*, November 13, 1893, 1.

53 Ibid., 2; *Chicago Record*, November 13, 1893, 1–2.

54 *Chicago Tribune*, November 13, 1893, 2.

55 Ibid.; Board Minutes, CFMCR, box 3, November 23, 1893. Re O'Brien, see R. Schneirov, *Labor*, 318; see also Stead, *If Christ*, 465.

56 Stead, *If Christ*, 465 (Stead dates this information to February 1894, but some is from later that year); JA, *Twenty*, 160; Sutherland, *Fifty Years*, 1, 5, 7. Scholars have generally accepted this version. The Civic Federation's remarkable early history deserves more scholarly attention.

57 Baylen, "Victorian's 'Crusade,' " 425. For Gage's statement, see Civic Federation of Chicago, *First Annual Report* 25.

58 Civic Federation of Chicago, *First Annual Report* 8, 25. See also Marks, "Polishing the Gem," 121. Stead would be back in Chicago in December 1893 to organize a federation of ministers to "influence the affairs of the city through cooperative action." Stead, *If Christ*, 461–63.

59 Board Minutes, CFMCR, box 3, November 23, 1893. For the second quotation see the form letter, signed by Addams, from her ward's membership committee to invite individuals to join the ward council. Scrapbook 2, 41.

60 Sutherland, *Fifty Years*, 8. For the list of board members, see Stead, *If Christ*, 467. I am assuming that E. S. Dryer is a businessman, having no information

otherwise; E. B. Butler was a merchant (and a major donor to Hull House); L. C. Collins was a judge. George A. Adams was a missionary whom Addams first met soon after moving to Chicago. See her 1889 correspondence.

61 Re women in leadership, see Sutherland, *Fifty Years*, 8. See also 1894 letterhead stationery for the Civic Federation, Scrapbook 1, 41; Minutes for 1893–84, CFMCR. For its first members list, see Stead, *If Christ*, 468–69. Re visitors' comments, see Blanc, *Condition of Women*, 90; Ralph, "Chicago's Gentle Side," 297–98; John Dewey to Alice Chipman Dewey, October 7, 1894, JDC.

62 Re the membership of the organizing committee and the board, see Board Minutes, CFMCR, box 3, November 23, 1893; Stead, *If Christ*, 466–67. Re McGrath, see R. Schneirov, *Labor*, 351. Re the president of the State Federation of Labor, M. H. Madden, see Westhoff, "'A fatal drifting.'" Re the president of the Retail Clerks Association, L. T. O'Brien, see Stead, *If Christ*, 463. Re the president of the Building Trades Council, J. J. Ryan, see P. Foner, *Women and the Labor Movement*, 116. Re the initial membership list of the federation, see Stead, *If Christ*, 468–69. Some have characterized the federation as middle class, unaware of its labor membership and of the support among some working people for its reform agenda. As Gage and MacVeagh learned, Germans and other non-Irish trade union members, having been disenfranchised by the Irish-controlled political machine, shared it. Mayer, "Private Charities," 141. Westhoff, like Schneirov, stresses the Civic Federation's class diversity. "'A fatal drifting,'" 64.

63 Re Linehan and Carroll, see Sutherland, *Fifty Years*, 8. Re one-sixth membership, see R. Schneirov, *Labor*, 334. Re the Presbyterian group, see Marks, "Polishing the Gem," 133. Re the labor aristocracy, see Hirsch, *Urban Revolt*, 54, 114.

64 Re Kenney and Elizabeth Morgan, see Nutter, *Necessity of Organization*, 11, 27. Re Thomas Morgan's loss of power, see Tax, *Rising*, 36; R. Schneirov, *Labor*, 320; Westhoff, "'A fatal drifting,'" 70. Re the percentage of women, see Barrows, *Trade Union*, 32.

65 Committee of Five Minutes [Civic Federation], November 23, 1893; Executive Committee Minutes, CFMCR, box 3, December 9, 1893; Sutherland, *Fifty Years*, 15. Re Hirsch, see Gilbert and Bryson, *Chicago*, 819. Re Onahan, see Mayer, "Private Charities," 109. U.S. Bureau of the Census, *Report on Population of the United States at the Eleventh Census: 1890*.

66 The federation's precinct-and-ward structure had been used by the Citizens Association, as well as the IWA and the Municipal Order League. Re the CA's structure, see R. Schneirov, *Labor*, 58. Re ward councils, see form letter [1894], *JAPM*, 52:0525; Civic Federation of Chicago, *First Annual Report*, 8–9. For the by-laws, see Board Minutes, CFMCR, box 3, February 15, 1894. See also undated Civic Federation letter addressed "Sir," Scrapbook 2, 41. For the constitution, see Board Minutes, CFMCR, box 3, January 20, 1894. According to Frank Mann Stewart, as of 1895, nine of the fifty-two urban reform organizations had ward-and-precinct organizational structures. Stewart, *Half-Century*, 12.

67 See the constitution (January 20, 1894) and the by-laws (February 15, 1894), both in Board Minutes, CFMCR, box 3. The departmental structure imitated that of the CWC.

68 Stewart, *Half-Century*, 12.

69 Schiesl, *Politics of Efficiency*, 42; Stewart, *Half-Century*, 15–19; Board Minutes, CFMCR, box 3, November 22, 1894; McCormick, "Public Life in Industrial America," 104; Scherman, "Jane Addams," 124.

70 Stead, *If Christ*, 467. Because Addams was a member of the Board of Directors, she was also a member of the Central Council. Board Minutes, CFMCR, box 3, February 5, 1894. By 1895 she would be chair of the Industrial Committee. Industrial Committee Minutes, box 1, CFMCR, March 20, 1895.

71 Board Minutes, CFMCR, box 3, April 19, 1894.

CHAPTER THIRTEEN: CLAIMS

1 Re JA's paleness, see Blanc, *Condition of Woman*, 70; Stead, *If Christ*, 419. Re JA's Green Bay trip, see JA to MRS, December 27, 1893. Re her California trip, see JA, *Twenty*, 165.

2 JA, *Twenty*, 165; JA to MRS, January 27, 1894; EGS to [?], November 21, 1893, EGSP (this letter is misfiled under "Letters to Jane Addams"); JA schedule, February 1894–March 1895, series 6, box 1, JAC, *JAPM*, 55:0009.

3 JA to Sarah Anderson, February 17–20, 1894.

4 HH Minutes, February 11, February 18, 1894.

5 HH Minutes, March 5, 1894.

6 Re MAL's illness, see JA to MRS, December 27, 1893. Re John Manning Linn's struggles to support the family in 1893, see *Selected Papers*, 534. Paying Mary's debts subsequently occupied JA for more than a year. See her correspondence for 1895. See also Solon D. Wilson to JA, October 2, 1897; JA to AAH, April 27, 1894; JA to AAH, March 17, 1894.

7 Re her finances, see JA to MRS, September 4, 1895. She mentions receiving the farmer's rent; the farm was among her assets when she died in 1935. JA, obituary, *New York Times*, May 29, 1935; JA to Sarah Anderson, June 23, 1894. JA's speaking schedule shows that she was speaking at least twice a week during this period to clubs, societies, churches, and universities. JA, engagement diary, February 1894–March 1895, series 6, box 1, JAC, *JAPM*, 29:0201–1227. Re JA supporting the Linn children, see *JAPCG*, 98. Between 1894 and 1899, JA's correspondence with MRS includes frequent references to Mary's desire to support her and Jane's unwillingness to let her do so unless she became really desperate. For example, see JA to MRS, March 1, 1897. Weber Linn says that she had given "most of her money" away by 1900, but the evidence suggests that that happened several years earlier. *Addams*, 193.

8 JA to Sarah Anderson, June 23, 1894.

9 JA to MRS, March 3, May 1, May 4, 1894.

10 JA to MRS, May 4, 1894; Woods and Kennedy, *Handbook of Settlements*, 69.
There was another competitor on the horizon. Graham Taylor would launch
Chicago Commons, a new settlement on the Northwest Side, in October 1894.

11 For JA's letter to Alice, see JA to AAH, May 11, 1894. Re her schedule for May 9,
see JA engagement diary, May 9, 1894, *JAPM*, 29:0209. Re events leading up
to the strike, see Watts, *Order against Chaos*, 55. Lindsey, *Pullman Strike*, 92–95,
98–100. Rents in Pullman were roughly 33 percent higher than those in surrounding neighborhoods. Lindsey, *Pullman*, 92. Re workers living in Pullman,
see *Strike Commission Report*, 598. Re the foremen's threats, see Lindsey, *Pullman Strike*, 93; *Strike Commission Report*, 598. For the Wickes quotation and
dividends, see Papke, *Pullman Case*, 22–23. Re dividends, see also Wickes testimony, *Strike Commission Report*, 605.

12 Re the grievance committee, see *Chicago Daily Tribune*, May 6, 8, 10, 1894;
Watts, *Order against Chaos*, 55; *Strike Commission Report*, 598. Re layoffs, see
Strike Commission Report, xxxviii. For "We struck at Pullman," see Freeman, *Who
Built America?* 140.

13 Re Pullman's theory, see George Pullman, testimony, *Strike Commission Report*,
529–30; C. Smith, *Urban Disorder*, 180–203. The JA quotation is from "Modern Lear," 110. Re workers' dissatisfaction, see Lindsey, *Pullman*, 61–63, 66,
90, 84; C. Smith, *Urban Disorder*, 192, 199, 206, 234; Reiff, "Modern Lear and
His Daughters," 66. Re house ownership, see Lindsey, *Pullman*, 65–66, 91. Re
workers organizing and earlier strikes, see S. Hirsch, "Search for Unity," 46–48,
89; Leyendecker, *Palace Car Prince*, 216–17, 180–81.

14 Re Howard, see Bliss, *Encyclopedia*, 1150; Chapin, "Infamous Pullman Strike,"
181; *Chicago Tribune*, May 6, 8, 10, 1894. Howard attended the May 7 and May
9 meetings. Lindsey, *Pullman*, 104. For the ARU's stated purpose, see *The Constitution of the American Railway Union* [adopted June 5, 1893; revised June 24,
1894] (Terre Haute, IN: Moore and Langen, 1896). Re the Great Northern Railroad, see Filippelli, *Labor Conflict in the US*, s.v. "Pullman Strike and Boycott";
Chicago Tribune, May 5, 1894, 12, col. 4. Re the percentage of workers joining
the ARU, see Chapin, "Infamous Pullman Strike," 181; Brecher, *Strike*, 97.

15 For Debs's remarks, see Papke, *Pullman Case*, 22; In "Modern Lear" JA applied
the metaphors of the father and the feudal king to George Pullman. To charge
Pullman with feudalism was a more biting criticism than to charge him with
paternalism. See also C. Smith, *Urban Disorder*, 368n37.

16 Re the Conciliation Board, see *Strike Commission Report*, 645–47; Industrial
Committee of the Civic Federation of Chicago, *Congress on Industrial Concili-
ation and Arbitration* (hereafter cited as *Congress on Industrial Conciliation*), 94;
Westhoff, " 'A fatal drifting,' " 186; *Chicago Tribune*, May 8, 1894, 8, col. 5. The
members were Lyman J. Gage of First National Bank, J. J. P. Odell of the Union
National Bank, A. C. Bartlett, vice president of a wholesale druggist firm, E. B.
Butler, president of a wholesale notions company, the stockbroker Charles Hen-

rotin, the attorney Arthur Ryerson, an unidentified person from the building trades council, and an unidentified newspaper editor; M. H. Madden, William Pomeroy, and M. J. Carroll were all labor union activists or labor editors. The two professors were Charles Henderson and W. W. Bemis of the University of Chicago. The number of members fluctuated. I list its core membership, which I established by comparing different lists. See *Chicago Mail*, June 1, 1894, 1, col. 1; undated *Chicago Daily Inter-Ocean*, Scrapbook 1, 52. Carroll, Addams, and Palmer were members of the Industrial Committee of the Civic Federation. Re Gage's previous interest in arbitration, see R. Schneirov, *Labor*, 285. "Conciliation Board" is the name used in the Civic Federation's annual report, the *Strike Commission Report*, and newspaper accounts of the time. At one point Addams refers to the board as "a so-called 'Citizens' Arbitration Committee.'" *Twenty Years*, 215. Historians have sometimes claimed that the board intended to conduct the arbitration. According to Addams, the board desired to arrange for another board to do the arbitration. JA, testimony, *Strike Commission Report*, 645. Re boards of conciliation in England, see A. Toynbee, *Lectures*, 198.

17 [Jane Addams], introduction to *Congress on Industrial Conciliation*, 94. I ascribe the introduction to JA on the basis of the fact that she was the secretary of the Industrial Committee; also, those familiar with her style will see similarities in this document. JA was neither entirely in favor of strikes or entirely opposed to them. See also Scherman, "Jane Addams," 208; V. Brown, "Advocate for Democracy," 146–49.

18 JA, testimony, *Strike Commission Report*, 645–46; *Chicago Mail*, June 1, 1894, 1, col. 1; *Chicago Herald*, June 2, 1894, 4, col. 7. See also V. Brown, *Education*, 283; V. Brown, "Advocate for Democracy," 135, 151n15.

19 JA, testimony, *Strike Commission Report*, 646; *Chicago Mail*, June 1, 1894, 1, col. 1; *Chicago Times*, June 2, 1894, 5, cols. 4 and 5. In her testimony Addams made it clear that Bartlett missed the meeting, although the *Times* reported that he was there. Addams also stated that by the time she and Easley met with company representatives the "railroad convention had assembled in Chicago," but this does not jibe with the documented meeting date of June 1. She appears to have been speaking loosely. *Strike Commission Report*, 646. The convention opened on June 12, 1894. Salvatore, *Debs*, 128. Adding to the confusion, Addams's and Easley's first attempt to meet with Wickes on June 1 failed because he was out of the office. The *Chicago Mail*, an evening paper whose copy deadline was in the early afternoon, therefore reported as if no meeting took place with Wickes that day. *Chicago Mail*, June 1, 1894, 1, col. 1. The *Times* story, published the next day, refers to two attempts. For Bartlett's antipathy for those on both sides of the dispute, see John Dewey to Alice Chipman Dewey, July 14, 1894, JDC.

20 JA, testimony, *Strike Commission Report*, 646; *Chicago Mail*, June 1, 1894, 1, col. 1. JA told the Strike commission that her meeting with Debs took place "before the Pullman matter had been formally considered by the [ARU] convention,

although [it had by then been] much discussed." *Strike Commission Report*, 646. While this suggests that it may have been after the convention began, it seems more likely that she approached Debs with her request quite soon after he arrived back in town.

21 *Chicago Herald*, June 28, 1894, *JAPM*, 55:0025.

22 JA testimony, *Strike Commission Report*, 646.

23 Re Debs's announcement, see *Chicago Herald*, June 2, 1894, 4, col. 7. Stead, *Chicago Today*, 21. Stead does not name Addams but describes the speaker as "one of the shrewdest, brightest, and most sympathetic observers . . . [in] Chicago." Given the content of the quoted statement, his well-documented respect for JA, his ties to Hull House, and Addams's subsequent essay about the strike as a tragedy, I believe that he was quoting her.

24 Re the June 15 meeting, see Lindsey, *Pullman*, 129. Re Pullman's return, see Chapin, "Infamous Pullman Strike," 189–90. JA testimony, *Strike Commission*, 646–47. She lists the men who met with Pullman as Bartlett, Butler, Henderson, Carroll, and Ryerson.

25 Lindsey, *Pullman*, 130–31, 115 (for the quotation); Chapin, "Infamous Pullman Strike," 190. Re the announcement, see Salvatore, *Debs*, 130.

26 The quotation is from Eugene V. Debs Papers, Cunningham Library, Indiana State University, Terre Haute, IN (hereafter cited as Debs Papers), *The Papers of Eugene V. Debs*, 6:092. For statistics, see Papke, *Pullman*, 26.

27 JA, "Address at the Commencement Exercises," [1894], 129–31. The date of the speech appears in her travel schedule for February 1894–March 1895, box 1, series 6, JAC.

28 JA, *Twenty*, 216, 214.

29 For statistics, see Brecher, *Strike!* 101. Re moving mail cars, see Filippelli, *Labor Conflict*, 444, 221. Re men in railyards, see Laurie, "Anti-labor," 11; Lindsey, *Pullman*, 155.

30 Lindsey, *Pullman*, 153–54.

31 JA to MRS, June 29, 1894; re the GMA's actions, see Salvatore, *Debs*, 121, 132; R. Schneirov, *Labor*, 338.

32 Re the Linn family's travels, and the quotation, see Hulbert, "Autobiography," 11. Re the Linn family, see also JA, *Twenty*, 216–17. Addams fails to say in *Twenty Years* that Mary's family arrived before Mary died, leaving the erroneous impression that it did not. Mary died of a cerebral hemorrhage, according to her death certificate. Mary Lynn McCree Bryan, pers. comm., August 23, 2004.

33 Re federal troops, see Chapin, "Infamous Pullman Strike," 191; JA, *Twenty*, 217. Re violence in the railyards, see Lindsey, *Pullman*, 206–8, 144, 199, 211.

34 JA, *Twenty*, 217. See JA to MRS, July 10, 1894; Lindsey, *Pullman*, 313, 310, 312, 319–20.

35 JA, *Twenty*, 137, 214. When she spoke of maintaining avenues, JA was referring to Hull House, not herself, but the description certainly applied to her. Re Kelley, see *FK*, 1:273.

36 John Dewey to Alice Chipman Dewey, October 10, 1894, JDC. According to Dewey, JA said that this was "the first personal flagellation she had ever rec'd." I suspect, however, that she had been "flagellated" earlier by the Christian missionaries who disapproved of her secular settlement. Perhaps she felt that this attack was the most personalized. Re Edward Everett Ayer, see Finding Aid, Ayer Papers, Minnesota Historical Society; Bowen, *Growing Up*, 87; JA, *Twenty*, 228.

37 Hamilton, "Janc Addams: Gentle Rebel," 34; Debs is quoted in Salvatore, *Debs*, 137.

38 Alice Hamilton, "Jane Addams of Hull-House," 15. Hamilton joined Hull House as a resident in 1897, three years after the strike, and became a close friend of Addams. Either Hamilton talked with JA about it or Hamilton heard this from others.

39 JA, *Twenty*, 32. She is referring to the St. Gaudens statue at the south end of Lincoln Park, the "standing Lincoln." On its base are carved quotations from Lincoln's two inaugural addresses merged into one long sentence.

40 Salvatore, *Debs*, 137–38. He was later temporarily released but returned to jail in June to complete his sentence (138).

41 Lindsey, *Pullman*, 234, 270. Re the fate of the ARU, see Quint, *Forging of American Socialism*.

42 See *Strike Commission Report*.

43 JA, *Twenty*, 213; Board Minutes, CFMCR, box 3, July 19, 1894; Civic Federation of Chicago, *First Annual Report*, 75. See also JA, appendix to *Congress on Industrial Conciliation*, 94.

44 Program, Hull-House College Extension Summer School, July 10–August 10, 1894, Scrapbook 2, n.p.; JA to AAH, August 8, 1894, writing from Rockford, IL; Board Minutes, CFMCR, box 3, September 27, October 18, 1894; *First Annual Report, Civic Federation*, 17; *Congress on Industrial Conciliation*, 94, 29, 93, 2. Most of the members of the planning committee were also members of the Conciliation Board. Two people not on the board who served on the committee were Ada Sweet and Graham Taylor, the head of the new settlement, Chicago Commons.

45 John M. Linn to JA, July 20, 1894. Linn had resigned his job at Buena Vista College. *Selected Papers*, 534. Re the plans for the children, see JA to AAH, September 25, 1894; JA to MRS, July 10, 1894. Re John Linn as a resident, see HH Minutes, November 4, 1894; *Maps*, 206.

46 Esther Hulbert, "Autobiography," 6, SCPC. For the rest of their lives, the Linn children's ties to JA would remain close. Esther's son Eri Hulbert would become a valued resident at Hull House. Davis and McCree, *Eighty Years*, 215. Stanley, who married and moved to California, would name one of his daughters after Jane. Weber saw the most of his aunt because he stayed in Chicago and became a professor at the University of Chicago. John Linn died working as an ambulance driver during World War I. *JA as I Knew*, 7.

47 Re dinners at MRS's house, see Weber Linn, "Miss Mary," obituary of MRS, *Chi-*

cago Daily Times, February 28, 1934, 25. Re Stanley Linn relying on JA's advice, see Jane Linn Morse to Mary Lynn McCree Bryan and the author, November 1, 1988, in possession of the author. Re JA's knitting for her niece and nephews and their children, see Hart, *Pleasure Was Mine*, 84.

48 Scrapbook 2, 49½. That fall Dewey taught a course on social psychology in the Hull House College Extension Program.

49 John Dewey to Alice Chipman Dewey, October 10, 1894, JDC. Dewey reported that JA mentioned her father's "teaching" and the fact that he was a Quaker. In this context, this seems to imply that JHA advocated the avoidance of antagonism and that she (and he) associated it with his Quaker upbringing and inclinations. It is interesting that JA does not discuss this aspect of her father in *Twenty Years*. Given what we know about JHA—that as an older man, he generally did not lose his temper—her claim seems entirely plausible.

50 Ibid. Addams thought it possible that the story about the violent actions of Jesus in the temple was not true, but if it was true, she thought it had significant implications. Christ's loss of faith would explain, she told Dewey, the "apparent difference between the later years of Christ's ministry and his earlier years and also much of the falsity of Christianity since." Ibid. This is a stunningly radical view.

51 Ibid.

52 John Dewey to JA, October 12, 1894, JDC. See also Louis Menand's interpretation of this conversation in *Metaphysical Club*, 313–14, 330.

53 Robert B. Westbrook believes that in his psychological writings of the mid-1890s Dewey "hinted at the replacement of the Absolute with a naturalistic conception of 'life activity' as the basis of his philosophy." *John Dewey*, 71. Dewey did not publish anything on the subject, Westbrook notes, until 1903, when his *Studies in Logical Theory* appeared (71). Andrew Feffer explores the way Dewey's idealism mingled with his developing experimentalism during the 1890s. "Head and Hand," 176–214.

54 JA to MRS, [early November 1894], *JAPM*, 2:1482.

55 Ibid. A series of clues help date this crucial letter. JA mentions expenses related to the bakery; she had been fundraising for a new oven for the bakery since the previous March. JA to Mrs. Medill, March 20, 1894. She refers to Maggie Toomey, a young woman who lived at the Jane Club who, although unmarried, had become pregnant. Toomey would be mentioned in subsequent letters between JA and MRS as they became involved with the question of the baby's fate. See their correspondence for January and February 1895, *JAPM*, 2:1624; 2:1647; 2:1656. JA writes that she expected the house to be out of debt within a week. At the November 12, 1894, meeting of the residents, it was announced that the house was out of debt. HH Minutes. JA notes that she has been surprised by the debt. The previous spring, she had turned over the task of keeping the account books to someone else. The minutes of the first Residents' Meeting of the fall,

dated November 5, 1894, contain detailed committee reports about finances for the month of October, a new practice and an indication of JA's determination to turn over a new leaf.

56 Re AAH's unwillingness to help with the Linn children's expenses, see Gertrude Barnum to MRS, August 19, 1899, *JAPM*, 3:1410. Re JA's October schedule, see JA to AAH, October 28, 1894; for November, see JA, engagement calendar, 1894–95, *JAPM*, 29:0203; JA to Richard Ely, November 27, 1894.

57 The total includes those who would become residents as soon as they had been there six months and were voted in. There were also "independent residents" for a time. HH Minutes, November 4, 1894; Appendix, 206. Addams was inclined to be relaxed about whether certain people living at Hull House fulfilled residential responsibilities, and most of the time the residents allowed it. Re the composition of the residents' group in 1894–95, see Appendix, 229; JA to Enos M. Barton, November 6, 1896. John Dewey quotes JA's observation to Alice Chipman Dewey, October 9, 1894, JDC.

58 JA to Richard T. Ely, October 31, 1894; see the table of contents in *Maps*. The complete book is found at *JAPM*, 54:0019.

59 JA to Richard T. Ely, October 31, 1894; Linn, *Addams*, 376; JA to Henry Demarest Lloyd, December 1, 1894; JA to Graham Taylor, March 22, 1895.

60 JA, "Settlement as a Factor," 199–201, 194, 202.

61 Ibid, 195, 204.

62 Ibid, 200, 203.

63 Ibid., 193.

64 Ibid., 204, 201.

65 Ibid., 203.

66 Ibid., 199.

67 Hegner, "Scientific Value of the Social Settlements," 176. Hegner was a resident at Chicago Commons, which opened in October 1894.

68 JA is quoted in John Dewey to Alice Chipman Dewey, October 9, 1894, JDC.

69 JA, "Claim on the College Woman," 62.

70 JA, *Twenty*, 217.

71 For the quotation, see JA, "College Woman and Christianity," 1853. Re Huntington, see JA, *Twenty*, 181. JA reports that Huntington's 1893 speech was titled "Can a Free Thinker Believe in Christ?" Reporting on the speech, EGS quotes him as saying, "the essence of immorality is to make an exception of yourself." EGS to Mary Allen, December 13, 1893, EGSP. JA also refers to the speech in "Hull House as a Type of College Settlement," 104–5. She had heard him speak many times. In 1889 and 1890 she heard him speak twice, once at Hull House and once in the city. JA to AAH, December 22, 1889; EGS to Mary Allen, December 30, n.d., file 79, EGSP; JA to AAH, January 5, 1890. In the last year of her life Addams thought she had first heard him speak of "the essence of immorality" at Plymouth. JA, *My Friend*, 55. He did not offer this striking formulation in

either of his Plymouth speeches, however, although he did make more or less the same point. Those speeches were published in Henry Adams, *Philanthropy and Social Progress*.

72 JA, "Settlement as a Factor," 198.

73 JA, "Modern Tragedy," 1894, TS, *JAPM*, 46:0589.

74 The claim is often made that Addams delivered "A Modern Lear" to the CWC in the fall of 1894. In fact (see below) she did not finish the final version of the speech until at least 1895 and did not deliver a version of it to the CWC until 1896. The source of the 1894 date is a headnote supplied by the editor of the magazine that first published the essay in 1912. JA, "Modern Lear," 131. The editor was Graham Romeyn Taylor, son of Graham Taylor, JA's friend and colleague in the Chicago settlement movement. The former apparently assumed that she wrote it during the year of the strike, which was reasonable, if wrong (or perhaps JA misremembered). Relying on Taylor's headnote, Linn vaguely confirms the 1894 date for writing the essay. *Addams*, 167. Lasch used the 1894 date for the writing of the speech and mentions that she gave it to the CWC. Lasch, *Social Thought*, 105–6. Farrell dates the speech to the CWC as late 1894. *Beloved Lady*, 73.

75 The proceedings of the conference were subsequently published in *Congress on Industrial Conciliation and Arbitration* and reprinted in Civic Federation of Chicago, *First Annual Report*. Re the conference's planning, see ibid, 75. For a summary of some of the views presented, see Westhoff, " 'A fatal drifting,' " 187–204.

76 JA, "Address," *Congress on Industrial Conciliation*," 48. Several identical passages appear in the essay and the remarks she made at the arbitration conference.

77 Re the bill's drafting, see R. Schneirov, "Labor and the New Liberalism," 211. Re lobbying, see JA, *Twenty*, 214. Re the national commission, see *Congress on Industrial Conciliation*, 93; Civic Federation of Chicago, *First Annual Report*, 78. Westhoff describes some of the problems with the law in " 'A fatal drifting,' " 204–6. In the law's first year, eight unions and only one employer sought the arbitration board's assistance (206).

78 *Congress on Industrial Conciliation*, 93.

79 Menand, *Metaphysical Club*, 371.

80 JA to AAH, November 24, December 4, December 23, 1894.

CHAPTER FOURTEEN: JUSTICE

1 JA to MRS, December 23, 1894; JA to AAH, December 28, 1894.

2 Scrapbook 3, 94. A new lease between Hull House Association and Culver covered the period from May 1, 1895, to April 30, 1920. HHA Minutes, May 20, 1895. Re JA's election, see HHA Minutes, January 28, 1895. The petition for incorporation, copied into the April 6, 1895, entry in the Minutes book of Hull House Association, is dated March 28, 1895. For a list of members of the first

board and for the bylaws, see the petition and HHA Minutes, April 25, 1895. For a history of the HHA board during JA's lifetime, see a memo from Charles Hull Ewing to the trustees, November 23, 1935, folder 1, box 55, Edith and Grace Abbott Papers.

3 Re the trustees' gifts, see HHA Minutes; *JAPCG*, Correspondence Index, s.v. "H.H. Assn., financial contributions"; Sklar, "Who Funded Hull House?"; the Hull House Account Books, *JAPM*. The other rent-free leases are at *JAPM*, 49:1334 (for 1892–1900), 1340 (for 1895–1920), and 1360 (for 1900–1950). Re fundraising, see Linn, *Addams*, 192; Bowen, *Speeches*, 2:821; JA, *Twenty*, 138.

4 Bowen, *Speeches*, 2:821. Bowen joined the board in April 1903 to complete the term of John Dewey. HHA Minutes, April 14, 1903. Re Wilmarth, see JA, *Excellent*, 101, 104, 105; JA, dedication, *Peace and Bread;* JA, "Tribute to Allen B. Pond," 29–30. Re William Colvin, see *Chicago Commons* (August 1896): 4; *Chicago Times-Herald*, July 8, 1896, *JAPM*, 55:0190; "In Memoriam," *JAPM*, 55:0197.

5 The mission language comes from the petition for incorporation. HHA Minutes, March 28, 1895. These words are often quoted as summing up the settlement's mission in 1889. JA herself caused this confusion. See *Twenty*, 112.

6 JA, "Social Settlements: A Three Years' Test," n.p. For people's impressions of JA's face, see Polacheck, *I Came a Stranger*, 97; Hackett, "Souvenir," 58; Mary Simkovitch, commentary, *Pax International* 10, nos. 3–4 (May–June 1935): n.p.; Linn, "Interpretation of Life," 221.

7 Board Minutes, CFMCR, box 3, June 21, 1894. The committee is first referred to by name in the minutes of August 16, 1894. For a history of women's efforts to improve refuse services in Chicago through 1917, see McGurty, "Trashy Women," 27–43. See also Hoy, " 'Municipal Housekeeping.' "

8 JA, *Twenty*, 282. JA's letters confirm that Stanley was not living all the time at Hull House in 1894 and 1895. See, e.g., JA to MRS, February 3, 1895. Many have assumed that Addams was a leader of the early phases of the garbage campaign because she writes in *Twenty Years* about the efforts "we" made. See *Twenty*, 282–84.

9 Re JA and the Sanitation Committee, see Civic Federation of Chicago, *First Annual Report*, 46–47; *Chicago Inter-Ocean*, April 25, 1895, 7, col. 4. The article reports that the previous year Addams served the federation as garbage inspector in the Nineteenth Ward. Re federation pamphlets, see Civic Federation of Chicago, *First Annual Report*, 14. Re complaint statistics for the summer of 1894, see editorial, "The 'New Woman' Scavenger," *Chicago Tribune*, March 21, 1895, 6; *Twenty*, 284–85. The quotation is from *Chicago Herald*, interview with JA, June 28, 1894, Scrapbook 1, 18, 55:0025–26.

10 HHA Minutes, March 8, 1895.

11 Re JA's research into collection methods, see *Chicago Tribune*, March 21, 1895, 6, col. 3; JA to MRS, February 24, 1895. Re JA's bid, see *Chicago Tribune*, March

23, 1895, 7. The contract was for nine months. JA proposed to charge $1,472 per month.

12 Editorial, "The 'New Woman' Scavenger," *Chicago Tribune*, March 21, 1895, 6, col. 3. Re services in the summer of 1894, see *Chicago Tribune*, June 1, 1894, 5.

13 *Chicago Tribune*, March 21, 1895, 6, col. 3.

14 "Miss Addams Loses," *Chicago Tribune*, March 23, 1895, 7, 5. Re the affidavit, see JA, *Twenty*, 285. Re Powers blocking her bid, see Wade, "Heritage," 435.

15 Re members of the Executive Committee who also were members of the Central Council, see letterhead of stationery used for a form letter by R. M. Easley addressed "Dear Sir" [1894], regarding service as a member of the Nineteenth Ward Council, *JAPM*, 52:0525.

16 Re methods of increasing votes, see Roberts, "Municipal Voters League," 118; E. Hirsch, *Urban Revolt*, 200; Wendt and Kogan, *Lords*, 19. The city government licensed saloons, gaining 12 percent of its revenues in the 1880s from that source. Mapes, "Visions," 52–53. The Civic Federation took ward politicians to court for election fraud, and fifty were eventually convicted. Mayer, "Private Charities," 140l. Re ward statistics, see Mapes, "Visions," 52–53; E. Hirsch, *Urban Revolt*, 90–93, 168; Nelli, *Italians in Chicago*, 90; Nelli, "John Powers and the Italians," 72–73.

17 *Chicago Tribune*, March 4, 1895, 1; March 5, 1895; March 8, 1895, 2. See also Board Minutes, CFMCR, box 3, October 18, 1894. Re citywide meetings, see Wendt and Kogan, *Lords*, 125. Re corruption in the Democratic Party, see R. Schneirov, *Labor*, 140–41. The idea of forming ward improvement clubs may have originated with Kelley. See Lathrop, "Hull House as a Laboratory," 318.

18 Re anti-Irish prejudice, see Jacobson, *Barbarian Virtues*, 187; White is quoted in Beinart, "Pride of the Cities," 17.

19 E. Hirsch, *Urban Revolt*, 143; McCarthy, "Businessmen and Professionals."

20 Marks "Polishing the Gem," 165–169; *Advance*, March 28, 1895, 14; Addams, *My Friend*, 96–97.

21 Re Kelley as president, see Board Minutes, CFMCR, box 3, October 18, 1894. Re Lawler's candidacy, see Davis, *Spearhead*, 154; Davis, *Heroine*, 121. The number of 150 members comes from Lathrop, "Hull House as a Sociological Laboratory," 318. Re Lawler's political career, see R. Schneirov, *Labor*, 28, 53, 73–74, 91, 105, 169, 281; *Chicago Tribune*, March 11, 1895, 2.

22 Wendt and Kogan, *Lords*, 108, 125; *Chicago Tribune*, April 3, 1895, 1. Re the results for the Nineteenth Ward, see *Chicago Tribune*, March 17, 1895, 2; April 3, 1895, 1. Lawler died on January 17, 1896. *Biographical Directory of the United States Congress, 1874–Present*, s.v. "Lawler, Frank." See http:bioguide.congress.gov.

23 *Chicago Tribune*, April 25, 1895, 2; see also *Chicago Daily News*, April 24, 1895, 1; JA, *Twenty*, 285.

24 *Chicago Tribune*, April 25, 1895, 2. Johnson had a background in settlement work and in sanitation reform. See *Chicago Herald-Times*, July 5, 1895, Scrapbook 3, 14; JA, *Twenty*, 287.

25 JA, *Twenty*, 286; *Chicago Herald-Times* of July 5, 1895; *Chicago Evening Journal*, July 29, 1895, 2. For other coverage, see *Chicago Tribune*, March 21, 1895; *Chicago Times-Herald*, April 30, 1895, 12.

26 JA, *Twenty*, 285. See also *Chicago Times-Herald*, April 30, 1895, 12.

27 JA, *Twenty*, 286; *Chicago Tribune*, May 8, 1895, 9.

28 JA, *Twenty*, 286–87; *Chicago Times-Herald*, July 5, 1895, Scrapbook 3, 14; *Chicago Journal*, July 29, 1895, Scrapbook 3, 17; JA to MRS, August 8, 1895; JA to Henry C. Adams, June 28, 1895.

29 Re Chicago publicity, see *Chicago Daily News*, May 1, 1895; *Chicago Journal*, July 29, 1895, Scrapbook 3, 17; *Chicago Evening Post*, July 23, 1895, quoted in Davis, *Heroine*, 121; *Chicago Times-Herald*, July 4, 1895, Scrapbook 3, 14; *Chicago Evening Journal*, July 29, 1895, 2. Re non-Chicago publicity, see *Topeka* (Kansas) *Journal*, May 28, 1895, Scrapbook 3, 7.

30 JA, *Twenty*, 287.

31 Ibid., 288. The earliest documentation we have for Addams taking this perspective is a speech she gave in 1897 (published in 1898). See JA, "Social Settlements," 340.

32 "Progress and Poverty," *Omaha Bee*, June 2, 1895, Scrapbook 3, 8, *JAPM*, Addendum 10:0008. Starr taught three college extension courses that spring. Hull House Brochure, January 1895, RCA.

33 Polacheck, *I Came a Stranger*, 56–57, 67, 97. For "was the first," see JA, *Twenty*, 346.

34 Hard, "Chicago's Five Maiden Aunts," 489; JA, *Twenty*, 49; William Kent, "Jane Addams," 30, TS, Kent Papers, Yale University. See also Alden, "Social and College Settlements," 1090.

35 Re Holden, see Agnes Hamilton to "dearest mother," February 1, 1898, Folder 337, Hamilton Family Papers, Schlesinger Library on the History of Women in America, Radcliffe Institute for Advanced Study, Harvard University, Cambridge, MA. John Dewey to Alice Chipman Dewey, October 7, 1894, JDC; Stevens, "Life in a Settlement," 50; Kelley, "I Go to Work," 271.

36 "Progress and Poverty," *Omaha Bee*, June 2, 1895, Scrapbook 3, 8; Webb, *Beatrice Webb's American Diary*, 108; June Rader, "Jane Addams—A Fortnightly Treasure," Paper given to the Fortnightly Club of Chicago, September 28, 1989, 5. TS. Copy in possession of the author. She is quoting a "columnist for a Greek newspaper" who grew up in the Hull House neighborhood and was writing at the time of JA's death.

37 JA, "Settlement," 57.

38 Alice Hamilton to Agnes Hamilton, June 18, 1899, file 636, box 25, Hamilton Family Papers, M-24, Schlesinger Library, Radcliffe Institute for Advanced Study; FK to Caroline Kelley, May 27, 1893, Nicholas Kelley Papers, New York Public Library. Sicherman, *Alice Hamilton*, 143.

39 Schultz and Hast, *Women Building Chicago*, s.v. "Harriet Alleyne Rice." Re JA's efforts to fundraise for fellowships see JA to Henry C. Adams, June 28, 1895; JA

to Anita Blaine, December 11, 1895. See also Alice Hamilton to Agnes Hamilton, June 2, 1898, file 635, box 25, Hamilton Family Papers, Schlesinger Library, Radcliffe Institute for Advanced Study; *Maps*, 229; Muncy, *Creating a Female Dominion*, 17–18. For a list of those receiving fellowships see "enclosure," JA to Edward P. Barton, November 6, 1896, *JAPM*, 49:1467; Holbrook, "Hull-House," 172.

40 Robert Woods to JA, September 4, 1895.

41 Madeleine Sikes to [Dear Mother], November 5, 1896, folder "1895–96," box 1, Madeleine Wallin Sikes Papers, CHS; JA, *Twenty*, 160; JA, *My Friend*, 37.

42 Hulbert, "Autobiography," 5.

43 "Hull House . . . A Social Settlement," Program, January 15, 1895, *JAPM*, 50:0304. Appendix, 229. The best source of information about the clubs before 1910 is "The Value of Social Clubs," in JA, *Twenty*. See also W. Johnston, "New Social Movement," 56; Jackson, *Lines of Activity*, 70; Stevens, "Life," 49; Scrapbook 3, 3; JA, "Description of Hull House, January 1, 1894"; Hecht, "Hull-House Theatre," 24; Polacheck, *I Came a Stranger*, 94. In 1895 Hull House organized a congress of thirty Hull House clubs that met quarterly to address common concerns. *Hull-House Bulletin* 1 (April 1896): 4; Scrapbook 3, n.p.

44 JA, "Discussion on Social Settlements," 474–75; *Hull-House Program*, January 15, 1895, *JAPM*, 50:0304. Re a mixed-ethnicity neighborhood party held at Hull House, see *Chicago Record*, March 3, 1896, *JAPM*, 55:0144. See also Lissak, *Pluralism*, 42–43, 45, note to table 2, 43; JA, *Twenty*, 342.

45 JA, *Twenty*, 342. Addams does not name the club in *Twenty Years* but she names it in her letters to MRS. See below. In June 1894 the Lincoln Club performed a play as part of a social that it organized in cooperation with Hull House Men's Club. Scrapbook 2, 41; Scrapbook 1, 47.

46 Re its focus on debate, see JA, "Hull-House as a Type of College Settlement," 109; *Hull-House Program*, January 15, 1895, *JAPM*, 50:0304; JA, *Twenty*, 343; JA to MRS, August 8, 1895.

47 JA to MRS, August 8, 1895; JA *Twenty*, 343.

48 JA, *Twenty*, 344. She describes herself as vainly attempting to persuade them of her viewpoint. By 1910 she concluded that the club's "wholesome bourgeois position . . . was most reasonable" (345). Murolo describes the same issue arising in working girls' clubs. *Common Ground*, 21.

49 JA to MRS, August 8, August 17, 1895. Addams writes that the discussion she had with the Men's Club that evening "has always remained with me as one of the moments of illumination which life in a Settlement so often affords." *Twenty Years*, 344. Judging from her letters to MRS, the conversation's larger meaning only became clear to her in retrospect.

50 JA, "Claim on the College Woman," 62.

51 Ibid.

52 The full speech, which is primarily about settlements, does not survive in her papers. The two newspaper clippings, titled "Pullman Follows Lear" and "Miss

Addams' Striking Characterization of Pullman; Likens Him to Lear," are loose items, see *JAPM*, 55:0047. Re the conference, see *Outlook*, May 11, 1895, 767, Scrapbook 2, 60.

53 JA to MRS, September 4–6, 1895. JA started her letter to MRS on September 4, delivered the speech on September 5, then finished the letter September 6. Re her speech, see *The Kingdom* (the national paper of the Congregational Church), September 6, 1895; *Advance*, September 6, 1895.

54 EGS to AHA, September 10, 1895, *JAPM*, 2:1764; EGS to John Weber Addams [September 11, 1895], quoted in AHA to Henry Haldeman, September 13, 1895, *JAPM*, 2:1769.

55 AAH to Sarah Anderson, September 16, 1895, Sarah Anderson Papers, Rockford College, *JAPM*, 2:1771; EGS to John Weber Addams [September 11, 1895], *JAPM*, 2:1769. After her surgery, the *Chicago Tribune* ran a long near-obituary on Addams headlined, "Jane Addams Is Ill." *Chicago Tribune*, September 12, 1895, 16; JA, *Twenty*, 261.

56 Mary Keyser to AAH, October 6, 1895; Mary Keyser to AHA, October 16, 1895, *JAPM*, 2:1787; JA to AAH, October 31, 1896.

57 EGS to JA, April 12, 1935; EGS to Mary Allen, September 5, [1895].

58 JA to EGS, September 14, 1907; JA to EGS, November 2, 1931.

59 Starr traces her religious history in her essay "Bypath," 3–44. JA to Sarah Anderson, June 23, 1894. Beginning in 1896, Starr would become active in various strikes, using more radical methods than JA did. See Carrell, "Reflections," 232–35. Starr would also become a Catholic and a radical socialist.

60 JA, *Excellent*, 33; JA, *Twenty Years*, 262. Four versions of her Pullman strike talk survive. Three are in her papers in manuscript form, all with the title "A Modern Tragedy." The first, dated 1894, is one page in length. It is clearly the first page of a longer paper. *JAPM*, 46:0589. The second (*JAPM*, 46:0648) and the third (*JAPM*, 46:0723) are complete, typed, and dated 1895. The third has footnotes and refers to "the writer," which makes it clear this version was intended for publication. The fourth version survives only in its published form and is titled "A Modern Lear." Practically all of her revisions to version 3 to create version 4 are in the first three pages. They include fresh material for the first five paragraphs. "A Modern Lear" has been subject to various interpretations. These include that JA was favoring Pullman's position rather than that of the workers (Abbott, *States of Freedom*, 180), that she was offering a critique of unions and strikes, that she was dodging the economic issues (Conway, "First Generation," 140), that she was championing unions (D. Levine, *Jane Addams*, 165; Scherman, "Jane Addams," 226; Elshtain, *Jane Addams*, 102), and that both sides were equally to blame (Reiff, "Modern Lear and His Daughters"). Victoria Brown believes that JA's sympathy for George Pullman grew out of her sympathy and affection for her own father and that JA's criticisms of Pullman stemmed from her frustrations with her stepmother. *Education*, 288–92. Michael McGerr shares the view that "Lear" was influenced by JA's feelings about her father. *Fierce Discon-*

tent, 58. Bob Pepperman Taylor offers an interpretation that astutely grasps the complexity of JA's democratic vision. *Citizenship and Democratic Power*, 64–69. For rhetorical analysis, see Leff, "Lincoln among the Nineteenth-Century Orators"; Sargent, "Jane Addams's Rhetorical Ethic," 191–234. See also Knight, "Biography's Window."

61 William Shakespeare, *King Lear*, act I, scene 1, lines 1–120, 213–17.

62 JA, "Modern Lear," 107. All citations to this speech are from Lasch, *Social Thought of Jane Addams*.

63 See A. Toynbee, *Lectures*, 148. H. D. Lloyd's *Wealth against Commonwealth* was published in 1894. JA, "Modern Lear," 120–21. References to justice in "Lear" attach the ethic to the workers' or Cordelia's cause (113, 114).

64 To trace JA's earlier narrower or not-always-approving references to justice or injustice, see "Outgrowths" (9), "Subjective Necessity" (5–6, 8), and "Settlement as a Factor" (184). In "Modern Lear" for the first time since college she embraces justice as a positive, guiding moral principle to be applied to more than education.

65 JA, " Modern Lear," 121.

66 Ibid., 109, 120, 117 (her exact words were "self-righteousness" and "egoism"), 122, 116.

67 Ibid., 122, 113.

68 Ibid., 116. JA's critique of individualism in "Modern Lear" is foreshadowed in her 1894 commencement speech, in which she criticizes the workers' narrow individuality. JA, "Address at the Commencement Exercises at Western Reserve College for Women," 130. Also, Fremantle's ideas about selfishness and justice, stated in *The World as the Subject of Redemption*, are strongly echoed in "Modern Lear." See Fremantle, *World as Subject*, 29–30, 32, 35, 37, 97.

69 JA, "Modern Lear," 118, 122, 118. See also Leff, "Lincoln," 149.

70 JA, "Modern Lear," 117, 113, 120, 116, 118, 122–23, 107.

71 JA, "Claim on the College Woman," 60. This is JA's first published reference to Lincoln. For subsequent ones, see *Democracy*, 151–52; chap. 2 in *Twenty Years;* "If Men Were Seeking the Franchise," in E. Johnson, *Centennial Reader*, 110; *Spirit*, 11; "Modern Lear," 118, 122; *Opening Address* [1924], 3; "Book That Changed My Life," 1196.

72 JA, *Twenty*, 36, 40. For possible sources of JA's "idea of greatness," see Schurz, *Abraham Lincoln*, 20–21, 31, 36, 64, 90–91. Edward Caird's lecture on Lincoln has been lost to history. Re his lecture at Toynbee Hall, see Jones and Muirhead, *Life and Philosophy of Edward Caird*, 180, 211. JA quotes the phrase by Caird that begins "content merely" in *Twenty Years* when she writes about meeting him (40). He likely read Schurz's work on Lincoln, since these ideas closely match Schurz's and are the same ones that Addams expresses in the Rockford Commencement speech and in "Modern Lear."

73 JA, *Twenty*, 39; Caird, *Evolution of Religion*, 1:ix, x. Famous as a leading British idealist, Caird nonetheless had nascent pragmatist leanings. One philosopher

solves the problem by calling him, at this stage of his career, a "developmental absolutist." See Mander, "Caird's Developmental Absolutism," 51–63. JA had first encountered what might be called "moral developmentalism" much earlier. Cicero, for example, also argued that historical change led to ethical change. In Josiah Royce's *The Spirit of Modern Philosophy* (Boston: Houghton Mifflin, 1892), the author argues in a chapter titled "The Rise of the Doctrine of Evolution" that the doctrine is "about experience, a theory founded on observation," and thus it "subordinates its original idealism." Royce, *Spirit*, 288. She read the book sometime in the 1890s and quite possibly in 1895. *Twenty*, 347 (she gives a slightly wrong title). In 1904, Addams quotes a passage from it without attribution. "Recent Immigration," 279. Re Caird's ties to Toynbee Hall, see Meacham, *Toynbee Hall*, 19–20; Jones and Muirhead, *Life and Philosophy of Edward Caird*, 180, 211.

74 In earlier speeches, Addams makes direct links between kings and daughters and Rockford Seminary's motto. See Knight, "Biography's Window," 126–27.

75 JA, "Modern Lear," 113, 121, 111. I have borrowed two phrases from a later revision of the "filial" part of the speech. See JA, *Democracy*, 100.

76 JA, "Modern Lear," 119. This interpretation of Lear as selfish was standard, of course. See Bate, *Romantics on Shakespeare*, 384.

77 JA, "Modern Lear," 108, 107. Re "king gentleman," see Linn, *Addams*, 21. In "Settlement as a Factor," when she describes the "individualist," she adds, "there is much in our inheritance that responds to this" (191). See also Knight, "Biography's Window."

78 JA, "Modern Lear," 109.

79 JA, *Twenty*, 261. For the poem, see *JAPM*, 45:1599. Linn reprints part of the poem. *Addams*, 289. In the poem Addams sees her intense, motherly love of Hull House (which she characterizes as her child) as too obsessive and pitiful in its dependency. It seems a commentary, perhaps, on Anna's approach to mothering.

80 Horace Elisha Scudder to Mary Wilmarth, April 18, 1896, *JAPM*, 3:0104. JA had her friend Mary Wilmarth submit her piece, because Wilmarth knew Scudder. Other rejection letters were Albert Shaw to JA, January 18, 1896; A. E. Keet to JA, February 1, 1896, Lloyd Bryce to JA, February 6, 1896.

81 Watts, *Order against Chaos*, 69, 73.

82 John Dewey to JA, January 19, 1896, JDC. Re her speech to the CWC, see *Chicago Record*, March 5, 1896, *Chicago Tribune*, March 5, 1896, 12, *Chicago Chronicle*, March 5, 1896, *JAPM*, 55:0145; Chicago Woman's Club Minutes, March 4, 1896. Chicago Woman's Club Papers, CHS. As noted above, erroneous secondary sources have misled scholars to believe that she gave this speech to the club in 1894.

83 Linn, *Addams*, 167; JA, *Twenty*, 218; Henry Demarest Lloyd to JA, February 23, 1896.

84 Linn, *Addams*, 167, 173; William Kent, "Notes: Miss Addams, June 8, 1904,"

William Kent Family Papers, Yale University Library; Smith, *Urban Unrest*, 277; JA, "A Modern Lear," *Survey* 29, no. 5 (November 2, 1916): 131–37; Linn, *Addams*, 167.

CHAPTER FIFTEEN: DEMOCRACY

1 JA, "Modern Lear," 122, 120. She elaborates on this point in *Democracy*, 139, 144. See also JA, "Settlement as a Factor," 196–98.

2 Scholars often assume that she was leading the aldermanic campaigns from the beginning, apparently either because she was the head resident or because of her subsequent involvement in later campaigns. But without documentary evidence, I am not persuaded. Kelley's early leadership role, on the other hand, is documented.

3 Re labor, see Mink, *Old Labor and New Immigrants*. See also Boyer, *Urban Masses*, pt. 4. Re the AFL, see P. Foner, *History of the Labor Movement*, 2:287–88, 300–344. Re African Americans, see Hahn, *Nation under Our Feet*. Re women, see Keyssar, *Right to Vote*, table A.20. "National-American" is hyphenated in the stationery of the NAWSA of the period.

4 Re the nine franchises and the mayoral veto, see Roberts, "Municipal Voters' League," 122, 127. Re the formation of the MVL, see R. Schneirov, *Labor and Urban Politics*, 349–51; Roberts, "Municipal Voters' League," 129–37; JA, *Twenty*, 322; *Hull-House Bulletin*, March, 1896, 4, Scrapbook 3, 89–91. Re endorsing candidates of both parties, see *Chicago Tribune*, April 15, 1898, 5, cols. 2, 3. For the best history of the first several years of the MVL's work, see E. Smith, *Municipal Outlook*.

5 Allen F. Davis has written and published extensively on Hull House's anti-Powers campaigns. See especially "Jane Addams versus the Ward Boss." See also Scott, "Saint Jane and the Ward Boss," 12–17, 94–99; F. Kelley, "Hull House," 565; Addams and Kelley began to plan the campaign long before the league was organized. See JA to Henry Demarest Lloyd, December 22, 1895. Re the MVL, see *Hull-House Bulletin* (March 1896): 4; *Hull-House Bulletin* (April 1896): 4.

6 Re JA's desire for Sikes to run, see George Sikes to Madeleine Wallin [Sikes], February 29, 1896, box 6, Madeleine Sikes Papers, CHS. Re Kelley's views, see F. Kelley, "Hull House," 565. Re Gleeson, see Davis, *Spearheads*, 155; *Chicago Tribune*, April 4, 1896, 9. According to the *Tribune*, Gleeson was the former president of the Chicago Bricklayers' Union. The union's leadership helped found the MVL. Re that union and the Civic Federation, see R. Schneirov, *Labor*, 351. Many have assumed, on the basis of her letter to Lloyd, that Addams led the fight, but it seems more likely that the campaign was a cooperative effort in which Kelley played the key role. For JA on the 1896 campaign, see JA, "Settlement," 55.

7 JA is quoted in *Chicago Evening Post*, February 19, 1896, 4, col. 1. Lissak argues that Addams was opposed to Powers because he was a lower-class immigrant

with influence and he sought to perpetuate ethnicity. *Pluralism and Progressives,* 63, 66. Re the number of jobs, see JA, "Ethical Survivals," 279. Re Power's largesse, see JA, *Twenty Years,* 316; JA, "Ethical Survivals," 279–81. For the quotation, see George Sikes to Madeleine Wallin [Sikes], February 29, 1896, box 6, Madeleine Wallin Sikes Papers, CHS. Re Hull House's intent to educate, see *Hull-House Bulletin* (March, 1896): 4; JA, "Tribute to Allen B. Pond," 30–31.

8 Re trade union support for Gleeson, see R. Schneirov, *Labor,* 352; JA to Henry Demarest Lloyd, December 22, 1895 *Hull House Bulletin* 1, no. 1 (January 1896), Scrapbook 3, 82. For other campaign efforts, see *Hull-House Bulletin* (March 1896): 4; JA, *Twenty,* 322. Most of the *Bulletin*'s short notices were unsigned, but judging from the ideas expressed and the prose style, it appears that Addams authored many.

9 Re Powers on Gleeson's candidacy, see F. Kelley, "Hull House," 565; JA, *Twenty,* 316. Re the congress and the newspapers, see R. Schneirov, *Labor,* 352; JA, *Twenty,* 317–18; Linn, *Addams,* 215. Re Yerkes, see "Lively Chicago Politics," *New York Times,* February 13, 1898, 13.

10 Nelli, "John Powers and the Italians," 72; F. Kelley, "Hull House," 565; *Chicago Tribune,* April 7, 1896.

11 Roberts, "Municipal Voters' League," 138; R. Schneirov, *Labor,* 350; "Jane Addams in London," *Chicago Post,* June 17, 1896, n.p., a reprint of an interview conducted in London by a staff reporter for the *London Daily News, JAPM,* 55:0184.

12 F. Kelley, "Hull House," 565; JA, *Democracy,* 257; Davis, *Spearheads,* 156. Re Power's personal wealth, see "Chicago Wards—What They Need," *Chicago Times-Herald* (March 8, 1898), 10.

13 JA, *Democracy,* 222. She writes in *Twenty Years* that the discussion with the Lincoln Club "has always remained with me as [providing] one of the moments of illumination which life in a Settlement so often affords" (344).

14 JA, *Twenty,* 290; JA, "Ethical Survivals," 190.

15 Caird, *Evolution of Revolution,* 2:155, 1–2; JA, *Twenty,* 39.

16 JA, "Social Settlements," 343.

17 Peattie, "Women of the Hour," 1004; Kent, "Jane Addams," 10; Mary Simkovitch, Remarks, Jane Addams Memorial Service, *Proceedings, National Council of Social Workers,* June 1935, 6, Social Welfare History Archive, University of Minnesota; Madeleine Wallin Sikes to her father, October 27, 1896, box 6, Madeleine Wallin Sikes Papers, CHS; Linn, *Addams,* 34.

18 MRS to JA, [March] 1896, March 5, 1896.

19 JA, *Twenty,* 261–62, 39. Re JA's plans for learning about European social reforms, see JA to Henry Demarest Lloyd, March 11, 1895; JA to EGS, May 29, 1896; JA to Weber Addams, June 1, 1896. Re Johnson, see Scrapbook 3, 77; Superintendent of the Bureau of Street Alley Cleaning to JA, May 26, 1896; John C. Rhode to JA, May 26, 1896; JA to Gertrude Barnum, July 25, 1896. For Barnum's arrival at Hull House, see HH Minutes for 1893.

20 Re JA's travel plans, see *Hull-House Bulletin* (May 1896): 5, Scrapbook 3, 91.

21 Linn, *Addams*, 290; Carrell, "Reflections in a Mirror," 236; tickets, *JAPM*, 28:0829; JA to Weber Addams, June 1, 1896.

22 Henrietta Barnett to JA, June 14, 1896; JA, "Social Settlements," 341.

23 JA, *Twenty*, 40. My interpretation of this obscure passage has been influenced by the fact that the discussion preceding it is about her sense of competition and superiority when her country's settlements are compared with the British settlements (38–39). In regard to her conversation with Caird, Addams writes that "vision and wisdom as well as high motives must lie behind every effective stroke in the continuous labor for human equality" (41). I believe she had not quite reached this conclusion as of 1896.

24 Maude, "Talk with Jane Addams," 205; JA, *Twenty*, 276; JA, "Tolstoi and Gandhi," 1485 (see also *Twenty*, 409); JA, "Object of Social Settlements," 149. She is quoting an essay by William Dean Howells on Tolstoy, as she acknowledges.

25 JA to MRS, September 4, 1895; JA, *Twenty*, 262.

26 JA to Gertrude Barnum, July 17, 1896; Maude, "Talk with Jane Addams," 203–5; Maude refers to MRS as Addams's niece, a misunderstanding that highlights the difference in their age and, possibly, the nature of the relationship as he discerned it.

27 Maude, *Tolstoy*, 2:328, 333, 362.

28 JA, *Twenty*, 267–68. Tolstoy's underlying Puritanism was probably the real source of his disapproval. He believed that stylish women's dresses were meant to excite sexual desire, which he considered a "base act." *What I Believe*, 402, 404.

29 "Reception to Miss Addams," *Woman's Journal*, February 1897, 60.

30 JA, *Twenty*, 268.

31 Ibid.

32 JA, *Twenty*, 274; Maude, "Talk with Jane Addams," 212.

33 JA, *Twenty*, 274–75.

34 JA's letter quoted in Maude, "Talk with Jane Addams," 216. Maude eventually agreed with Addams's assessment of Tolstoy's theory. See Maude, *Tolstoy*, 2:370.

35 Maude, "Talk with Jane Addams," 216–17. See also JA to Aylmer Maude, [July 30, 1896], reprinted in *Humane Review*, June 1902, 216–17.

36 JA, *Twenty*, 273; JA, "Miss Addams [on the family and the state]," 112.

37 Maude, "Talk with Jane Addams," 215; JA, *Twenty*, 268, 276–77 (see also 274).

38 JA, "Social Settlements," 342. She gave the first of the Tolstoy speeches to the Hull House residents on October 8, 1896. Madeleine Wallin [Sikes] to George Sikes, October 9, 1896, Madeleine Wallin Sikes Papers, CHS. Re other speeches, see *Commons*, February 1897, 7, 10; *Annals*, 173–74. JA spoke about Tolstoy at least three times at Chautauqua, in 1898 and 1902. See *Chautauqua Assembly Herald* for those years. See also *JAPCG*, 132–75 for other writings about Tolstoy. For "blundering," see JA, "Tolstoi," 7; JA, *Twenty*, 262.

39 H. J. Gow Diaries, May 3, 1897, Rare Book, Manuscript, and Special Collections Library, Duke University. Gow kept a three-volume diary of her visit to the United States and Canada. Two of the three volumes are at Duke University. Gow writes about visiting a number of settlement houses in the United States. Re Gow's ties to WUS, see the entry for April 28, 1897.

40 See H. J. Gow Diaries for April 26 (for lunch with JA), April 30 (for writing JA), May 14 (for JA offering Gow a job), May 27 (for the first quotation), and June 2 (for the second quotation and for Gow's views on her "nearest" duty), 1897, Rare Book, Manuscript, and Special Collections Library, Duke University. Addams sometimes sounds as if she thinks that the family and social claims are morally equal, but she clearly states that the social claim is the higher claim in "Belated Industry," 540; my sense is that she thought both had a "real moral basis" (JA, *Democracy*, 76) and were part of life but that, as she told Gow, the social claim asked a higher morality of a person.

41 MRS to JA, December 1, 1896. In January 1897 letters between Jane and Mary begin to contain puzzling references to "Toomey" and "little Jane." Mary Toomey was a bookbinder, labor activist, and a member of the Jane Club. When Toomey discovered she was pregnant, MRS paid for her to travel to Boston to stay with O'Sullivan and have the baby. In January 1897, Toomey, back in Chicago, fell ill and decided to give the baby up for adoption. JA and MRS worked together to find a home for it, but MRS seriously considered adopting the baby herself. JA appears to have talked her out of it.

42 Bowen, *Speeches*, 2:833.

43 *JA as I Knew*, 10. For JA's views of Mary's willingness to criticize her closest friends, see "Dedication of the Mary Rozet Smith Cottage." This speech is Addams's only known description of MRS. JA to AAH, December 4, 1896. For two particularly tender letters that Addams sent to Smith, see January 18, 1896 and May 31, 1899. For "You can never," see MRS to JA, Dec. 1, 1896. Evidently, JA was willing to consider that MRS might marry and even to encourage her, but she also understood that MRS's love for her might present an obstacle in MRS's mind. See JA to MRS, August 24, 1899.

44 Susan B. Anthony to JA, December 19, 1895.

45 JA spoke at the Twentieth Century Club in Boston on February 10, 1897. JA to AAH, February 11, 1897. For the Livermore quotation, see "Reception to Miss Addams," *Woman's Journal*, February 20, 1897, 60.

46 Susan B. Anthony to JA, December 19, 1895.

47 "Reception to Miss Addams," 60. She may have drawn this idea from her reading of John Stuart Mill. Urbinati, *Mill*, 167.

48 The *Boston Globe* article is quoted in "Reception to Miss Addams," 60; JA to AAH, February 28 and March 1, 1897.

49 Keyssar, *Right to Vote*, 198–99. Re JA's views, see Scherman, "Jane Addams," 292–94; JA, "As I See Women" [interview], *Ladies' Home Journal*, August, 1915,

11. Re Addams's motives in favoring votes for all women, see V. Brown, "An Introduction to 'Why Women Should Vote,'" 192. The quotation is from JA, "Neighborhood Improvement," 457.

50 Buechler, *Transformation*, 152–53, 178, 176. JA became first vice president of the Illinois Equal Suffrage Association in 1912. Trout, "Sidelights on Illinois Suffrage History," 93–116; *JAPCG*, 14.

51 For "public agitation," see JA, *Democracy*, 170.

52 JA, "Subjective Necessity," 20.

CHAPTER SIXTEEN: ETHICS

1 For a fine discussion of issues surrounding the historiography of the progressive movement, see Robert Johnston, "Re-Democratizing the Progressive Era."

2 Re Armstrong, see Davis, *Spearheads*, 161. Re Powers's action against Johnson, see Baker, "Hull-House and the Ward Boss," 770; Powers is quoted at 769.

3 Baker, "Hull-House and the Ward Boss," 770–71; Davis, *Spearhead*, 159. JA appears to have given the same speech in December 1897 to the Social Reform Club. *American Fabian* (November–December 1897), box 3, series 4, JAC. The published version, "Ethical Survivals in Municipal Corruption," appeared in the *International Journal of Ethics* in April. It was excerpted in the same month in *Outlook*, whose editor gave the speech its best title: "Why the Ward Boss Rules." Elshtain reprints this excerpt (not the complete speech) in *Jane Addams Reader*. Re the Ethical Culture Society and its journal, see Abell, *Urban Impact*, 102–3.

4 Addams gave a speech in Minneapolis in January 1898 in which she made this point even more explicitly. *Minneapolis Journal*, January 12, 1898; JA, "Ethical Survivals," 276, 282, 286.

5 JA, "Ethical Survivals," 288; JA, *Twenty*, 204.

6 JA, "Ethical Survivals," 290, 273; JA, *Democracy*, 270; JA, "Pragmatism in Politics," 268.

7 JA, *Twenty*, 317–18.

8 Alice Hamilton to Agnes Hamilton, March 30, 1898, file 635, box 25, Hamilton Family Papers, M-24, Schlesinger Library, Radcliffe Institute for Advanced Study. Cambridge, MA.

9 *Chicago Tribune*, April 6, 1898, 6, col. 2. Davis gives a slightly different number for Armstrong. *Spearhead*, 161. Alice Hamilton to Agnes Hamilton, April 5, 1898, file 635, box 25, Hamilton Family Papers, M-24, Schlesinger Library, Radcliffe Institute for Advanced Study. Re Addams's continuing tight income situation in the twentieth century, see Linn, *Addams*, 393, 352.

10 Re Rice staffing the dispensary, see *Hull-House Bulletin*, January 1896, n.p., *JAPM*, 81:0008; JA to MRS, February 3, 1895; Schultz and Hast, *Women Building Chicago*, s.v. "Harriet Alleyne Rice."

11 JA, "Anti-Lynching Address," December 12, 1899, TS, JAC. For another speech about lynching, see *Chicago Inter-Ocean*, November 18, 1900; JA, "Respect for

the Law," 18–20. Re black middle-class people assuming that the rape charge was true, see I. Wells, "Southern Horrors," 389–419; for the rebuttal, see ibid., 403. See also Wells-Barnett, "Lynching and the Excuse for It," 1133–36. Re Wells's friendship with JA, see Wells, *Crusade for Justice,* 259.

12 JA, "Subjective Necessity," 3. See also Deegan, *Race, Hull House and the University of Chicago,* 53–58. Fanny Barrier Williams was admitted in September 1895, after the CWC had adopted a nondiscrimination policy. *Annals,* 145; *Chicago Tribune,* September 12, 1895. Re the luncheon at Hull House, see Wells, *Crusade for Justice,* 259. Re the National Convention of Women's Clubs, see Davis, *Heroine,* 129.

13 Photographs of Hull House activities from 1906 and from the 1920s and 1930s show African American children and women participating. Bryan and Davis, *One Hundred Years,* 81–82, 230; M. Johnson, *Many Faces of Hull House,* 24, 52, 53. Scholars who claim that Hull House did not welcome African Americans usually cite as their evidence the statement that blacks "were not always welcomed warmly." This observation is commonly attributed to a credible source— JA's good friend Louise deKoven Bowen, a Hull House trustee. See, e.g., Lasch-Quinn, *Black Neighbors,* 15; McGerr, *Fierce Discontent,* 196. These words, however, were written not by Bowen but by Allen F. Davis and Mary Lynn McCree (later Bryan), editors of *Eighty Years,* in a headnote introducing an excerpt from an essay by Bowen. Davis and McCree write, "Those few blacks who did appear at a Hull-House club or class were not always welcomed warmly" (121–22; the same statement is repeated in Bryan and Davis, *One Hundred Years,* at 133). Bowen's essay itself does not address the subject of African Americans at the settlement. See *Eighty Years,* 121–22; Bowen, "Colored People of Chicago," 117–20. Davis and McCree may be referring to the house's failure in the 1930s to actively overcome African Americans' doubts that they would be welcome at a white institution. See Dewey Jones's comments to the Welfare Council of Metropolitan Chicago, excerpted in *One Hundred Years,* 230–32. Re the KKK, see Spear, *Black Chicago,* 85–86. Re the NAACP and the Chicago Urban League, see Davis, *Heroine,* 129. Re the Progressive Party, see Scott, *Natural Allies,* 169. Re Haiti, see JA, *Second Twenty Years,* 195. For other views of JA and racism, see Philpott, *Slum and the Ghetto,* 293–95, 297–300; Lasch-Quinn, *Black Neighbors,* 13–15, 20. For the views Addams held in 1930 about racism in the United States, see *Second Twenty Years,* 396–404. In 1913 she published "Has the Emancipation Proclamation Been Nullified by National Indifference?"

14 Re the federal commission's creation and FK's being named to it, see Lyman Gage to JA, July 11, 1898; JA to MRS, July 18, 1898. Re the commission's charge, see *Report of the Industrial Commission on the Relations and Conditions of Capital and Labor, Report of the Secretary, 1900* (Washington, D.C.: GPO, 1901), 1. Re FK's work with the National Consumers' League, see James, James, and Boyer, *Notable American Women,* s.v. "Florence Kelley."

15 Re Addams's work to improve the Illinois child labor law, see Board Minutes, CFMCR, box 3, March 20, 1895; JA to Henry Demarest Lloyd, March 16, March 21, 1897. Re the new Illinois law, see "Child Labor Act of 1903," in *Laws of Illinois*, 187–93; *Twenty Years*, 210; G. Abbott, *Child and the State*, 1:265; Farrell, *Beloved Lady*, 126; JA, *Twenty*, 357. For more on Addams's efforts at the state and federal levels see *Columbus Dispatch*, March 9, 1895, *JAPM*, 55:0148; *Annals*, 162; JA, *Twenty*, 209; JA, "Ten Years' Experience in Illinois," 144. Re federal actions, see JA, "Woman's Conscience and Social Amelioration," 46; Farrell, *Beloved*, 97; G. Abbott, *Child and the State*, 1:463–68.

16 The speech is mentioned in the *Woman's Tribune* 15, no. 14 (July 9, 1898), 1. It was published in the *Machinist's Monthly Journal*, September 1898, 551–52. See also JA, "Trade Unions and Public Duty," 448–62; JA, *Twenty*, 229.

17 Re the founding of the WTUL, see Kessler-Harris, *Out of Work*, 165–66; Boone, *Women's Trade Union Leagues*, 63; P. Foner, *Women and the American Labor Movement*, 290. Re WTUL activists in Illinois, see Kessler-Harris, *Out of Work*, 165–66; re WTUL activities in Illinois, see Buechler, *Transformation*, 159–60.

18 JA, *Twenty*, 139.

19 JA, "Modern Lear," 122–23; JA, "College Woman and Christianity," 1855. See also JA, *Democracy*, 153, 275. Regarding Addams's refusal to seek credit for her accomplishments see Dunn, "Jane Addams as a Political Leader," 151–52.

20 Matthew 10:38–39; the saying is repeated in Luke 9:23–25. Emerson, "The Over-Soul," in *Emerson*, 387. Marcus Aurelius, *Meditations*, chap. 5, passage no. 3. See also JA, *Twenty Years*, 308–9, and JA, "Growth of the Corporate Consciousness."

21 Robert Woods to JA, April 28, 1898.

22 JA to MRS, October 6, 1898.

23 Re her settlement speech, see Davis, *Heroine*, 139–40. JA, "What Peace Means," 11–14.

24 Re JA's participation and for the resolution, see "Protest against Imperialism," *Springfield Republican*, May 1, 1899, 3, col. 1. Re JA's participation, see also "Loyalists Are Aroused," *Chicago Tribune*, May 1, 1899, 2, col. 3. Re the October conference, see Harrington, "Anti-Imperialist Movement," 223; *Chicago Tribune*, October 18, 1899, 7, col. 1, and October 19, 9, 14. Re Addams's peace speeches, see *JAPCG*, 135–75. Her writings on peace (including her books) have been published in four volumes. See Fischer and Whipps, *Jane Addams's Writings on Peace*. Re the New York City march, see Davis, *Heroine*, 212.

25 Davis, *Heroine*, 216–17, 258, 285–86.

26 Quint, *Forging of American Socialism*, 289, 320.

27 Tolman, "League for Social Service," 473–74.

28 Bliss, "Union Reform League Activities," 111–12; Bliss, "Unite or Perish," *Arena* 22, no. 1 (July 1899): 83–85. The league was initially a California organization, but by early 1899 it had added "of America" to its name.

29 Pomeroy, "How the Conference Was Started," 33–34 (for "what to do next," see 34). For use of the term "radical," see Buchanan, "Referendum for Reform," 455. Re JA and others serving on the general committee, see Members List, *Direct Legislative Record* 6, no. 3 (Special Number) (July 1899): 49–56.

30 Re JA's signing of the call, see *Springfield Republican*, June 9, 1899. Re her hope to attend, see her calendar entry for June 28, 1899 ("Buffalo conference, may attend"), *JAPM*, 29:0509. Re the National Social and Political Conference's statement of principles, see "Militarism and Plutocracy," *Springfield Republican*, July 10, 1899. For a restatement of the principles, see *Statement of Objects, Results and Actions of the National Social and Political Conference Held at Buffalo, New York, June 28–July 23, 1899* (pamphlet), Richard Ely Papers, Wisconsin State Historical Society, Madison. The National Civic Federation, a direct outgrowth of Chicago progressivism and the organization that would have the staying power to shape progressivism in the twentieth century, was founded in 1900. Cyphers, *National Civic Federation*, 19.

31 For "free, just and progressive society," see "Militarism and Plutocracy," *Springfield Republican*, July 10, 1899, 8. For the five planks and names of the leaders, see Bliss, "Social Reform Union," *Arena* 22, no. 2 (August 1899): 272–74.

32 JA to Henry Demarest Lloyd, December 1, 1894. [Iowa College] *Scarlet and Black*, n.s., 4, no. 2 (February 5, 1898): 4; *Scarlet and Black*, n.s. 4, no. 9 (March 2, 1898): 1.

33 The five evenings of lectures were briefly summarized in the Iowa College campus newspaper. "The Social Philosophy of Count Tolstoï" and "Ethical Survivals in the Efforts of Charitable Organizations," *Scarlet and Black*, 4, no. 9 (March 2, 1898): 1; "Ethical Survivals in Municipal Corruption," "Ethical Survivals of Pullman Strike," and "Ethical Survivals in the Labor Movement," *Scarlet and Black*, 4, no. 10 (March 5, 1898): 1, 4. She may have had a book in mind even earlier. In 1894 and 1895 she gave a series of six lectures titled "Hull-House and Its Civic Influences" at Knox College; *JAPM*, 42:0013.

34 Re Chautauqua, see *JAPM*, 38:0643. In 1898 she also gave a six-lecture version of the series, its theme unknown, at the All Souls Church in Chicago, box 3, series 4, JAC. The syllabus for the University of Chicago course is found in the Edith and Grace Abbott Papers, Archives, Regenstein Library, University of Chicago, and the Anita McCormick Blaine Papers, Wisconsin State Historical Society, Madison. Re teaching the course, see also JA to MRS, June 22, 1899; J. J. Gurney to JA, August 8, 1899. Re her schedule, see JA's calendar, *JAPM*, 29:0509; see also *Twenty*, 140. Re the Davenport series, see JA to Richard Ely, November 8, 1899. In this letter she first proposes turning the lectures into a book. *Democracy* is quite similar in structure to the University of Chicago lecture series.

35 JA, *Democracy*, 13

36 The textual history of the chapters of the book is as follows. Chapter 1, "Introduction," is based on her introductory lecture for the University of Chicago course.
Chapter 2, "Charitable Effort," is based on remarks she made for a panel discussion titled "Why Is Systematic Charity Disliked?" presented at the Nineteenth
Century Club in New York City on December 9, 1898 and on the next version of
that speech, "Subtler Problems of Charity." An excerpt was published as "The
Charity Visitor's Perplexities," *Outlook*, March 11, 1899. Chapter 3, "Filial Relations," is based on her various speeches concerning the claim on the college
woman, combined with the father-daughter material from "Modern Lear." The
core of the chapter (with new opening and closing) comes from "The College
Woman and the Family Claim." See also "College Women and Christianity."
Chapter 4, "Household Adjustment," is a revision with additions of "Belated
Industry," which is itself a revision with additions of "Domestic Service and
the Family Claim." Chapter 5, "Industrial Amelioration," draws its ideas mainly
from "Trade Unions and Public Duty" and from "Lear" but is for the most part
newly written. Chapter 6, "Educational Methods," draws on "Foreign-Born Children in the Primary Grades." (See also her "Social Education of the Industrial
Democracy.") Chapter 7, "Political Reform," is a revision with additions of "Ethical Survivals." Addams wrote a short essay, "Democracy and Social Ethics," in
McLaughlin and Hart, *Cyclopedia of American Government*, that casts interesting
light on her intentions in the book by that name. Addams was quite nervous
about whether the book was good. When she received the first copy, she had to
go off by herself to look at it, fearing she would be greatly disappointed. *JA as I
Knew*, 12. A few of the scholars who have explored Addams's *Democracy* in more
detail than I can do here include Seigfried, introduction to *Democracy*, ix–xxxviii;
B. P. Taylor, *Citizenship and Democratic Doubt*, 70–85; Fischer, "Jane Addams's
Critique of Capitalism"; Nackenoff, "Gendered Citizenship"; Schwartz, *Fighting
Poverty with Virtue*, chap. 4; Scott, introduction to *Democracy*.

37 JA, *Democracy*, 6.

38 JA, *Democracy*, 10. Elsewhere in the book she would develop Huntington's point
in more detail, even invoking the phrase that had made such an impression on
her, "an exception of himself" (177). JA, "Respect for the Law," 18.

39 JA, *Democracy*, 10.

40 Ibid., 5, 6, 9. Joseph Conrad used the same road metaphor in *An Outcast of the
Islands* to make a similar point: that people traveling a narrow road are "fenced
in by their . . . prejudices" and "full of contempt" for others (152). Addams, a
great admirer of Conrad's work, may have borrowed from him.

41 JA, *Democracy*, 153, 93, 9–10. See also 177.

42 Ibid., 214, 219, 12, 102; the 1902 quotation is from JA, "Newer Ideals of Peace,"
22.

43 JA, "Social Obligations of Citizenship," 2. This Chautauqua speech, which appears to have been delivered extemporaneously because its language is more di-

rect and less obscurely poetic than the language of *Democracy and Social Ethics*, makes fascinating background reading for the book. For the quotation from the Denver speech, see JA, "Significance of Organized Labor," 551. For "What is the human?" see JA, "Recent Immigration," 279. This is a direct quote, unacknowledged, from Royce, *Spirit of Modern Philosophy*, 280. See also JA, "College Woman and Christianity," 1853; JA, *Twenty*, 359. Lois Rudnick discusses this point in her essay "Feminist American Success Myth," 151. See also "Address of Miss Addams," 55.

44 JA, "Function of the Social Settlement," 32; Coughlin is quoted in Wendt and Kogan, *Lord of the Levees*, 18.

45 JA, Remarks, "Proceedings of the Twenty-Fifth Anniversary of the University Settlement Society," 23–24.

46 Linn, "Interpretation of Life," 221. See also his comment in *Addams*, 193.

47 JA, *Democracy*, 13; JA, *Newer Ideals*, 186–87; JA, *Long Road*, 101; JA, "Function of the Social Settlement," 48.

AFTERWORD: SCHOLARSHIP AND JANE ADDAMS

1 Linn's *Jane Addams* was recently reissued by the University of Illinois Press, with a new introduction by Anne Firor Scott. Remarkably, this was the only adult popular biography of Addams ever written until 1999. In that year Gioia Diliberto published *A Useful Woman*, a short, readable half-life treatment, and Barbara Garland Polikoff published the equally readable part-family-history *With One Bold Act*. For John C. Farrell's, Daniel Levine's, Allen F. Davis's, and Jean Bethke Elshtain's books on Addams, see the discussion below.

2 Commager, "Jane Addams: 1860–1960," reprinted as the foreword to *Twenty Years at Hull-House*, xvi.

3 Also, Staughton Lynd cites a centennial selection of Addams's writings published that year (Johnson, *Jane Addams: A Centennial Reader*) as a source in his 1961 essay "Jane Addams and the Radical Impulse" (56). Also published in 1960 was Tims, *Jane Addams of Hull House*. It is a study of JA's peace philosophy with some biographical introductory chapters. Historians had been making passing references to Jane Addams for decades, of course. See C. Beard and M. Beard, *American Spirit*, 478; Hofstadter, *Age of Reform*, 209, 274; Schlesinger, *History of American Life*, 10:351–52.

4 Commager, foreword to *Twenty Years*; Curti, "Jane Addams on Human Nature," 240–53; Scott, "Saint Jane and the Ward Boss," 12–17, 94–99; Davis, "Jane Addams versus the Ward Boss," 247–65. Scott published another essay about Addams in the 1960s in *American Heritage*. Davis also published "The Social Workers and the Progressive Party, 1912–1916" prior to his book on the same subject, discussed below.

5 Unger, "The 'New Left' and American History," 1237–63; Wiener, "Radical Historians," 399–434.

6 S. Lynd, "Jane Addams and the Radical Impulse," 54–59; D. Levine, "Jane Addams." Levine wrote a revised version of this essay that was included as a chapter in his book *Varieties of Reform Thought*.

7 D. Levine, "Jane Addams," 210, 200. Although historians have long used the terms "middle class" and "working class," they are just beginning to develop a sophistication regarding class comparable to that which they have developed regarding gender, race, ethnicity, and sexuality. Important contributions outside of labor history (for which see below) include Blumin, *Emergence of the Middle-Class*; Zunz, *Making America Corporate;* Vinovskis, "Stalking the Elusive Middle Class," 582–87; Burke, *Conundrum of Class*; R. Johnston, *Radical Middle Class*. Like Johnston and some others, I understand class as a "process" embedded in and shaped by history and centered on issues of power.

8 Conway, "Jane Addams," 248–50; see also Conway, "Women Reformers and American Culture," 166. She also wrote a dissertation about seven educated women, including Addams. Conway, "First Generation of American Women Reformers."

9 Lasch, *New Radicalism*, 30, xiv–v, 31. He cites as his source for this idea a passage in Richard Hofstadter's *Age of Reform* (151–52) in which Hofstadter raises such a question regarding the clergy's new interest in reform after the Civil War.

10 Lasch, *New Radicalism*, 27, 62, 65.

11 D. Levine, *Jane Addams*, xiv–xv.

12 Davis, *Heroine*, 74, 110. In addition to his article about Addams and the ward boss, John Powers, Davis published *Spearheads for Reform*.

13 I call *American Heroine* the first scholarly biography because it has been perceived that way. In fact, the claim that it is a biography is arguable. Despite the subtitle, Davis is careful to point out in the preface that his book "is in no sense a definitive account of her life or times" or even "an intellectual biography" (xi). He describes it as being primarily focused on "motivation," on the "development of Jane Addams' personality, and . . . her relationship with other people" (xi). Davis's assessment that he had not written a full biography of Addams seems a fair one. As he notes in his preface, while the first four chapters are biographical, the remaining chapters are concerned "with her reputation and her public image" (xiii). They appear, however, to continue the chronological story, which may explain why his book is usually seen as a biography despite his disclaimer. Interestingly enough, Davis began work on this biography as early as 1960, making him another scholar whose interest was apparently sparked by the centennial (See editor's note to Davis, "Jane Addams versus the Ward Boss," 247).

14 Scott, "Heroines and Heroine Worship" 142–43, 146.

15 Rosemarie Scherman, review of *American Heroine* by Allen F. Davis, *New York Times Book Review*, October 28, 1973. See Scherman, "Jane Addams and the Chicago Social Justice Movement." Regarding Jean Bethke Elshtain's book about Addams, see the discussion below.

16 It is impossible to cite here all the important work on Addams that has been done in these fields. Among the more substantial are Elshtain, "Self/Other, Citizen/State"; Elshtain, "Return to Hull House"; Cavallo, "Sexual Politics and Social Reform"; Carson, *Settlement Folk*; Crunden, *Ministers of Reform*; Jackson, *Lines of Activity*; Stebner, *Women of Hull House*; Sklar, "Hull-House in the 1890's"; Sklar, "Hull-House Maps and Papers"; Sklar, "Who Funded Hull House?"; V. Brown, "Advocate for Democracy"; Knight, "Authoritative Voice"; Knight, "Biography's Window"; Knight, "Jane Addams and the Settlement House Movement"; Knight, "Jane Addams' Views"; Knight, "Jane Addams and Hull House." Other works are cited below. For reasons of space, I leave aside all the excellent work that has been done regarding Addams's memoir, *Twenty Years at Hull House*, as a piece of literature and regarding her speeches as rhetoric.

17 Spear, *Black Chicago*; Philpott, *Slum and the Ghetto*; Lasch-Quinn, *Black Neighbors*; Lissak, *Pluralism and Progressives*; Cook, "Female Support Networks"; Smith-Rosenberg, "Female World of Love and Ritual"; Faderman, *To Believe in Women*.

18 Deegan, *Jane Addams and the Men of the Chicago School*; Lageman, *Jane Addams on Education*; Davis, *Jane Addams on Peace*; Seigfried, *Pragmatism and Feminism*; M. Fischer, "Jane Addams's Feminist Ethics"; M. Fischer, *On Addams*. Addams's ideas about ethnicity remain to be carefully studied. She wrote a good deal about the subject after 1898 but not much about the subject before that.

19 Elshtain, *Jane Addams Reader*; Elshtain, *Jane Addams and the Dream of American Democracy*. The first collection of Jane Addams's writings, now out of print, was edited by Christopher Lasch. *Social Thought of Jane Addams*. Fischer and Whipps, *Jane Addams on Peace*.

20 Bryan, *Jane Addams Papers*, microfilm edition; Bryan, Bair, and de Angury, *Selected Papers of Jane Addams*, vol. 1, *Preparing to Lead*.

21 These are *Twenty Years at Hull-House*, *Spirit of Youth and City Streets*, *Peace and Bread*, *A New Conscience and an Ancient Evil*, *The Long Road of Woman's Memory*, and *Democracy and Social Ethics*.

22 V. Brown, *Education*, 105. As *Citizen* was going to press, a "literary biography" of Addams was published that deals mainly with her life as a writer after 1900 and the books she wrote after that date. It traces the development of Addams's style as a writer as manifested in her books and in essays that were published in books. It also considers her in relation to other Chicago writers of the period. See Joslin, *Jane Addams*.

23 Horowitz, *Power and Passion*; Horowitz, *Culture and the City*; Sicherman, "Sense and Sensibility"; Winterer, *Culture of Classicism*.

24 Ethington, *Public City*; Lebsock, "Women and American Politics"; Keyssar, *Right to Vote*; Skocpol and Fiorina, *Civic Engagement*; Schudson, *Good Citizen*; Cott, *Bonds of Womanhood*; Kerber, *Women of the Republic*; Baker, "Domestication of American Politics"; Hewitt, *Women's Activism and Social Change*; Ginzberg,

Women and the Work of Benevolence; M. Ryan, "Gender and Public Access"; M. Ryan, *Women in Public;* Isenberg, *Sex and Citizenship;* Monoson, "Lady and the Tiger"; Muncy, *Creating a Female Dominion;* Gullett, *Becoming Citizens;* Weld, *Concept of Political Culture;* Sklar, *Florence Kelley;* Deutsch, *Women and the City;* Flanagan, *Seeing with Their Hearts;* Tax, *Rising of the Women;* Spain, *How Women Saved the City;* Nackenoff, "Gendered Citizenship"; Zaeske, *Signatures of Citizenship.*

25 Montgomery, "To Study the People." See also Moody and Kessler-Harris, *Perspectives on American Labor History;* Fink, *In Search of the Working Class;* Dubofsky, *Industrialism and the American Worker;* D. Montgomery, *Fall of the House of Labor;* Licht, *Industrializing America.*

26 Works particularly relevant to any studies of Addams in the 1890s are R. Schneirov, *Labor;* Schneirov et al., *Pullman Strike;* Tax, *Rising of the Women;* Scherman, "Jane Addams and the Chicago Social Justice Movement"; Kessler-Harris, *Out of Work.* On the subject of women, class, and labor, see Kessler-Harris's "New Agenda for American Labor History."

27 Scholars have been contesting for some time when the Progressive Era began and how to define "progressivism." See Rodgers, "In Search of Progressivism"; Kloppenberg, *Uncertain Victory;* Mattson, *Creating a Democratic Public;* Rodgers, *Atlantic Crossings.* Re the early history of progressivism in Wisconsin, see Thelen, *New Citizenship.* A number of other books cited in this essay address this important question.

BIBLIOGRAPHY

This bibliography is divided into three sections. First, writings by Jane Addams that are cited in this book are listed in alphabetical order (for a complete bibliography of Jane Addams, see *JAPCG*); next is a list of the manuscript collections whose holdings are cited. The final section provides information about the cited books, articles, and microfilms.

Selected Writings of Jane Addams

BOOKS

Democracy and Social Ethics. New York: Macmillan, 1902.
The Excellent Becomes the Permanent. New York: Macmillan, 1932.
The Long Road of Woman's Memory. New York: Macmillan, 1916.
My Friend, Julia Lathrop. New York: Macmillan, 1935.
A New Conscience and an Ancient Evil. New York: Macmillan, 1912.
Newer Ideals of Peace. New York: Macmillan, 1907.
Peace and Bread in Time of War. New York: Macmillan, 1922.
The Second Twenty Years at Hull-House: September 1909 to September 1929, with a Record of a Growing World Consciousness. New York: Macmillan, 1930.
The Spirit of Youth and City Streets. New York: Macmillan, 1909.
Twenty Years at Hull-House with Autobiographical Notes. New York: Macmillan, 1910.

OTHER WRITINGS

"Address." In *Congress on Industrial Conciliation and Arbitration, November 13, 14, 1894*, by the Industrial Committee of the Civic Federation of Chicago. Chicago: Hollister, 1894. Reprinted in Civic Federation of Chicago. *First Annual Report of the Central Council*, 48–49. Chicago: privately printed, 1895.
"Address of Miss Addams." In *University Settlement Society Annual Report, 1903*. New York: privately printed, 1903.
"Address on Illinois Geography." May 26, [1878]. *JAPM*, 45:1779.
Address, Peace Congress Banquet, University Peace Congress, Boston, October 7, 1904. *Official Report* (1904): 161–62.
"Alumnae Essay." In [Rockford Seminary Endowment speeches], *Memorials to Anna P. Sill* [June 1889], *First Principal of Rockford Female Seminary, 1849–1889*, 70–75.
"Anti-Lynching Address." December 12, 1899. TS, JAC.
"Appendix: Outline Sketch Descriptive of Hull-House." In *Hull-House Maps and Papers*, by Residents of Hull-House. New York: Crowell, 1895.

"The Art-Work Done by Hull-House, Chicago." *Forum* 19 (July 1895): 614–17.

"A Belated Industry." *American Journal of Sociology* 1 (March 1896): 536–50.

"Bellerophon." [Spring 1880.] *JAPM*, 46:0090.

"A Book That Changed My Life." *Christian Century* 44 (October 13, 1927): 1196–98.

"Breadgivers" [Opening Address]. *Rockford Seminary Magazine* 8 (April 1880): 110–11; *JAPM*, 46:0195.

"Cassandra." *Essays of Class of '81, Rockford Seminary*, June 22, 1881. *JAPM*, 27:0458.

"The Chicago Settlements and Social Unrest." *Charities and the Commons* 20 (May 2, 1908): 155–66.

"Child Labor and Pauperism." In *National Conference of Charities and Corrections Proceedings, 30th Annual Conference, Atlanta, Georgia, May, 1903*, 114–21. N.p.: Privately printed, 1903.

"Claim on the College Woman." *Rockford Collegian* 23 (June 1895): 59–63.

"The College Woman and Christianity." *Independent* 53 (August 8, 1901): 1852–55.

"The College Woman and the Family Claim." *Commons* 3 (September 1898): 3–7.

"Commencement Address [Western Reserve College for Women]." *College Folio* 2 (June 1894): 129–31.

"Comments to Open Discussion, at Seventh Session, July 12, 1897." In *Proceedings of the National Conference of Charities and Corrections, Twenty-Fourth Conference, July 7–14, 1897*, 464–66. Boston: n.p., 1898.

Commonplace book [1877–83?] Series 6, JAC; SCPC; *JAPM*, 27:0143.

"Darkness versus Nebulae." June 14, 1880. *JAPM*, 46:0207.

"Dedication of the Mary Rozet Smith Cottage, Bowen Country Club [Waukegan, IL]." [1935.] TS. JAC, SCPC; *JAPM*, 49:0516.

"Democracy and Social Ethics." In *Cyclopedia of American Government*, edited by Andrew C. McLaughlin and Albert Bushnell Hart, 1:563–64. New York: n.p., 1914.

"Description of Hull House, January 1, 1894" [pamphlet]. *JAPM*, 46:0608.

Diary of Jane Addams (1875). SCPC; *JAPM*, 28:1483.

"Discussion of Social Settlements." *Proceedings of the National Conference of Charities and Corrections, Twenty-Fourth Conference, July 7–14, 1897*, 472–76. Boston: n.p., 1898.

"Domestic Service and the Family Claim" [excerpt]. In *World's Congress of Representative Women*, edited by Mary Wright Sewall, 2:626–31. Chicago: Rand McNally, 1894.

"English and American Social Settlements," *Chautauqua Assembly Herald* 23, no. 24 (August 12, 1898): 3, 6–7.

"Ethical Survivals in Municipal Corruption." *International Journal of Ethics* 8 (April 1898): 273–91.

"Follow Thou Thy Star." *Rockford Seminary Magazine* (July 1879): 183–85 (written

February 1879); *JAPM*, 45:1831 (MS); 46:0030 (published version); *Selected Papers*, 284–85.

"Foreign-Born Children in the Primary Grades." *Journal of Proceedings and Addresses, National Educational Association* 36 (1897): 104–12.

"A Function of the Social Settlement." *Annals of the American Academy of Political and Social Science* 13 (May 1899): 33–55 (second numbering system: 323–45).

"Growth of Corporate Consciousness." In *Illinois State Conference of Charities and Corrections Proceedings, 1897,* 2:40–42. Springfield, IL: n.p., 1897.

"The Gypsies of Romance—Meg Merrilies Their Queen." October 15, 1879. *JAPM*, 46:0049.

"Has Nationalism Become a Dogma?" TS, January 14, 1927, *JAPM*, 48:0212.

"Has the Emancipation Proclamation Been Nullified by National Indifference?" *Survey* 29 (February 1, 1913): 565–66.

"How Would You Uplift the Masses?" [Speech to the Sunset Club, February 4, 1892.] Reprinted as "With the Masses." *Advance* (February 18, 1892): 10–13; *JAPM*, 46:0498.

"Hull House as a Type of College Settlement" [assigned topic]. In *Wisconsin State Conference of Charities and Corrections, Proceedings, 1894,* 98–115. N.p.: privately printed, 1894; *JAPM*, 46:0578. Delivered December 1894.

"If Men Were Seeking the Franchise." *See* "Miss Addams [on the family and the state]."

[Introduction] to *Congress on Industrial Conciliation and Arbitration, November 13, 14, 1894,* by the Industrial Committee of the Civic Federation of Chicago. Chicago: Hollister, 1894. Reprinted in Civic Federation of Chicago, *First Annual Report of the Central Council,* 94. Chicago: privately printed, 1895.

Introduction to *Religion in Social Action,* by Graham Taylor, xi–xxxv. New York: Dodd, Mead, 1913.

Introduction to *What Then Must We Do?* by Leo Tolstoy. Translated by Alymer Maude, vii–xiii. Oxford: Oxford University Press, 1934 .

"John Dewey and Social Welfare." In *John Dewey: The Man and His Philosophy,* edited by [Graduate School of Education, Harvard University], 140–50. Cambridge: Harvard University Press, 1930. Delivered October 1929.

"Julia Lathrop at Hull-House." *Survey Graphic* 24 (August 1935): 373–77, 410–11.

"The Magnificence of Character." October 5, 1880. *JAPM*, 46:0219.

"Miss Addams [on the family and the state]," *Ladies' Home Journal,* June 1913. Reprinted as "If Men Were Seeking the Franchise" in *Jane Addams: A Centennial Reader,* edited by Emily Cooper Johnson, 107–13. New York: Macmillan, 1960.

"A Modern Lear." [1895.] *Survey* 29 (November 2, 1912): 131–37. Reprinted in *The Social Thought of Jane Addams,* edited by Christopher Lasch, 105–23. New York: Bobbs-Merrill, 1965, and in *The Jane Addams Reader,* ed. Jean Bethke Elshtain, 163–76. New York: Basic, 2002.

"A Modern Tragedy." 1894. TS, *JAPM*, 46:0589.

"Neighborhood Improvement." *Proceedings of the National Conference of Charities and Correction, 31st Annual Conference, Portland, Maine, June 15–22, 1904,* edited by Isabel C. Barrows, 456–58. N.p.: privately printed, [1904].

"The Newer Ideals of Peace." *Chautauqua Assembly Herald* 27 (July 8, 1902). Reprinted in *Jane Addams on Peace, War, and International Understanding, 1891–1932,* edited by Allen F. Davis, 19–25. New York: Garland, 1976.

"The Objective of Social Settlements." *Union Signal* 22, no. 16 (March 5, 1896): 148–49.

"The Objective Value of a Social Settlement." In *Philanthropy and Social Progress,* edited by Henry C. Adams, 27–56. New York: Crowell, 1893.

Opening Address as President of the Women's International League of Peace and Freedom at the Fourth Biennial Congress, Washington, May 1–8, 1924. Geneva: privately printed, 1924.

"Our Debts and How We Shall Repay Them." October 1887. *JAPM*, 46:0104.

"Outgrowths of Toynbee Hall." TS, December 1890, 6. *JAPM*, 46:0480.

"A Pioneer Philanthropist." [Review of H. Barnett's *Canon Barnett.*] *Yale Review* 9 (July 1920): 869; *JAPM*, 48: 0310.

"Plated Ware." *Rockford Seminary Magazine* 6 (April 1878): 60–62; *JAPM*, 45:1756.

"Pragmatism in Politics." *Survey* 29, no. 1 (October 5, 1912): 267–68.

"The Present Policy in Congress." December 1877. *JAPM*, 45:1684–90; *Selected Papers,* 200–201.

"Presidential Address." [WILPF Congress, Zurich, 1919.] TS, SCPC; *JAPM*, 48:0022.

"The Progressive Party and the Negro." *Crisis* 5 (November 1912): 30–31.

"Recent Immigration: A Field Neglected by the Scholar." *University Record* 9, no. 9 (January 1905): 274–94.

Remarks in "Proceedings of the Twenty-Fifth Anniversary of the University Settlement Society, December 7, 1911." *Annual Report for the University Settlement Society, 1912,* 21–24. N.p.: privately printed, 1912.

"Resolved: That the Invention and Use of Machinery." [November 1877]. *JAPM*, 45:1644–52; *Selected Papers,* 255–57.

"Resolved: The Civilization of the Nineteenth Century Tends." February 18, 1880; *JAPM*, 48:0181.

"Respect for the Law." *Independent* 53 (January 3, 1901): 18–20.

"The Settlement." *Illinois State Conference of Charities and Correction Proceedings, 1896,* 54–58. Springfield, IL: privately printed, 1896.

"The Settlement as a Factor in the Labor Movement." In *Hull-House Maps and Papers,* by Residents of Hull-House, 183–204. New York: Crowell, 1895.

"The Settlement as a Way of Life." *Neighborhood* 2 (July 1929): 139–46.

"Significance of Organized Labor." *Machinists' Monthly,* September 1898, 551–52.

"Social Education of the Industrial Democracy." *Commons* 5 (June 30, 1900): 17–20.

"The Social Obligations of Citizenship." *Chautauqua Assembly Herald* 23, no. 22 (August 10, 1898): 2–3.

"Social Settlements." In *Proceedings of the National Conference of Charities and Corrections, Twenty-Fourth Conference, July 7–14, 1897*, 338–46. Boston: n.p., 1898.

"Social Settlements: A Three Years' Test." *Union Gospel News*, March 28, April 11, 1895; *JAPM*, 55:0039, 0043.

"Social Settlements in Illinois." *Transactions of the Illinois State Historical Society*, pub. no. 11 (1906): 162–71.

"Standards of Education for Industrial Life." *Proceedings of the National Conference of Charities and Corrections, June 7–14, 1911, Boston, Mass.* Fort Wayne, IN: n.p., 1911.

"The Subjective Necessity of a Social Settlement." In *Philanthropy and Social Progress*, edited by Henry C. Adams, 1–26. New York: Crowell, 1893.

"The Subtle Problems of Charity." *Atlantic Monthly*, February 1899, 163–78.

"Sunday Rest and the Character of Working People." In *The Sunday Problem: Papers Presented at the International Congress on Sunday Rest, Chicago, September 28–30, 1893*, 156–58. New York: Baker and Taylor, 1894.

"Ten Years' Experience in Illinois." In *Uniform Child Labor Laws: Proceeding of the Seventh Annual Conference, March, 1911*, by the National Child Labor Committee, 144–48. New York: National Child Labor Committee, 1911. Reprinted as a supplement to *Annals of the American Academy of Political and Social Science*, no. 32. Philadelphia: American Academy of Political and Social Science, 1911.

"Tolstoi." *Chautauqua Assembly Herald* 23, no. 21 (August 9, 1898): 3, 6–7.

"Tolstoy and Gandhi." *Christian Century* 48 (November 25, 1931): 1485–88.

["Tonight Is Walpurgis Night." 1880]. *JAPM*, 45:1615; *Selected Papers*, 354–56.

"Trade Unions and Public Duty." *American Journal of Sociology* 4 (January 1899): 448–62.

"Tramps." April 4, 1878. *JAPM*, 45:1757.

"Tribute to Allen B. Pond." In "Memorial Service for Allen B. Pond, City Club, Chicago, Illinois, April 21, 1929," TS, 24–32. Michigan Historical Collections, Bentley Historical Library, University of Michigan; *JAPM*, 48:1155.

"The Uncomfortableness of Transition." *Rockford Seminary Magazine* 11 (July 1883): 215.

"Unexpected Reactions of a Traveler in Egypt." *Atlantic Monthly*, February 1914, 178–86.

"Washington's Birthday." February 23, 1903. In *Modern Eloquence: A Library of the World's Best Spoken Thought*, edited by Ashley H. Thorndike, 16–19. New York: Lincoln Scholarship Fund, 1929.

"What Peace Means." [1899.] In *Jane Addams on Peace, War, and International*

Understanding, 1889–1932, edited by Allen F. Davis, 11–14. New York: Garland, 1976.

"What Shall We Do for Our Unemployed?" [assigned topic.] *Sunset Club Yearbook, 1893–94,* 81–82. Chicago: privately printed, 1894. Delivered December 21, 1893.

"Whoso Liveth to Himself." *Survey* 51 (January 1924): 373.

"Woman's Conscience and Social Amelioration." In *The Social Application of Religion,* by Jane Addams, Charles Patrick Neill, Graham Taylor, and P. O. Eckman. Cincinnati: Jennings and Graham, 1908, 41–60. [The Merrick Lectures, 1907–8, Ohio Wesleyan University, April 5–9, 1908.]

"Women's Work in Chicago." *Municipal Affairs* 2, no. 3 (September 1898): 502–8.

LOCAL HISTORY RESOURCES IN STEPHENSON COUNTY
Freeport Local History Room, Freeport Public Library, Freeport, IL.
Cedarville Historical Society, Cedarville, IL
Stephenson County Historical Society, Freeport, IL
Stephenson County Courthouse, Freeport, IL

Manuscript Collections

Chicago Historical Society
Chicago Bureau of Charities Papers
Chicago Relief and Aid Society Papers
Chicago Woman's Club Papers
Civic Federation of Metropolitan Chicago Records
Lucy Flower Papers
Madeleine Wallin Sikes Papers
Rare Book, Manuscript, and Special Collections Library, Duke University
H. J. Gow Diaries
Cunningham Library, Indiana State University
Eugene V. Debs Papers
Lilly Library, Indiana University
Sarah Alice Addams Haldeman Mss
Manuscripts and Archives Division, Astor, Lenox, and Tilden Foundations, New York Public Library
Nicholas Kelley Papers
Special Collections and University Archives, Leonard Axe Library, Pittsburgh State University, Pittsburgh, KS
Emanuel Haldeman-Julius Collection
Haldeman-Addams Collection
Rockford College Library, College Archives
Anna Sill Scrapbook
Julia Lathrop Papers
Sarah Anderson Papers

Schlesinger Library, Radcliffe Institute for Advanced Study
    Alice Hamilton Papers
    Hamilton Family Papers
Sophia Smith Collection, Smith College
    Ellen Gates Starr Papers
Stevenson County Historical Society, Freeport, IL
    Jane Addams Papers
Swarthmore College Peace Collection, Swarthmore College
    Jane Addams Collection
Special Collections, Regenstein Library, University of Chicago
    Edith and Grace Abbott Papers
The University Library, Special Collections, University of Illinois at Chicago
    Jane Addams Memorial Collection
Center for Dewey Studies, University of Southern Illinois at Carbondale
    John Dewey Correspondence
Wisconsin State Historical Society, Madison
    Henry Demarest Lloyd Papers
    Richard Ely Papers
Yale University Library
    William Kent Family Papers

Books and Articles

Abell, Aaron Ignatius. *The Urban Impact on American Protestantism, 1865–1900.*
    Cambridge: Harvard University Press, 1943.

Abbott, Edith. "Grace Abbott: A Sister's Memories." *Social Service Review* 13, no. 3
    (September 1939): 351–407.

———. "The Hull House of Jane Addams," *Social Service Review* 26 (September
    1952): 334–37.

———. "Notes and Comment: Julia Lathrop and the Public Social Services."
    Social Service Review 6 (June 2, 1932): 301–9.

Abbott, Grace. *The Child and the State.* Vol. 1, *Legal Status in the Family*
    Apprenticeship and Child Labor. Chicago: University of Chicago Press,
    1938.

Abbott, Philip. "Reforming: Charlotte Perkins Gilman and Jane Addams." In
    States of Perfect Freedom: Autobiography and Political Thought, 159–81. Amherst:
    University of Massachusetts Press, 1987.

Adams, Henry Carter. "Democracy." *New Englander* 40, no. 163 (November 1881):
    752–72.

———, ed. *Philanthropy and Social Progress.* 1893. Reprint, Freeport, NY: Books
    for Libraries Press, 1969.

Alden, Percy. "The Social and College Settlements of America." *Outlook* 51 (June
    22, 1895): 1090–91.

Allen, Howard W., and Vincent A. Lacey. *Illinois Elections, 1818–1990: Candidates*

and County Returns for President, Governor, Senate and House of Representatives.
Carbondale: Southern Illinois University Press, 1992.

Altgeld, John Peter. *Live Questions.* Chicago: Donohue and Henneberry, 1890.

———. *The Mind and Spirit of John Peter Altgeld.* Edited by Henry M. Christman.
Urbana: University of Illinois Press, 1965.

Andreas, A. T. *History of Chicago.* 1884. Reprint, New York: Arno, 1975.

Arnold, Matthew. *Culture and Anarchy: An Essay in Political and Social Criticism.*
Edited by Ian Gregor. 1869. Reprint, Indianapolis: Bobbs-Merrill, 1971.

———. "Democracy." In *Mixed Essays, Irish Essays and Others.* 1879. Reprint,
New York: Macmillan, 1924.

———. *Literature and Dogma.* 4th ed. London: Smith, Elder, 1874.

Badger, R. Reid. *The Great American Fair: The World's Columbian Exposition and
American Culture.* Chicago: Nelson Hall, 1979.

Bae, Youngsoo. *Labor in Retreat: Class and Community among Men's Clothing
Workers of Chicago, 1871–1929.* Albany: SUNY Press, 2001.

Bailey, Richard W. *Nineteenth-Century English.* Ann Arbor: University of Michigan
Press, 1996.

Bain, Alexander. *English Composition and Rhetoric: A Manual.* 4th ed. London:
Longmans, Green, 1877.

Baker, Paula M. "Domestication of American Politics: Women and American
Political Society, 1780–1920." *American Historical Review* 89 (June 1984):
620–47.

Baker, Ray Stannard. "Hull-House and the Ward Boss." *Outlook* 58 (March 28,
1898): 769–71.

Barbour, Hugh, and J. William Frost. *The Quakers.* Westport, CT: Greenwood,
1988.

Barker-Benfield, G. J. " 'Mother Emancipator': The Meaning of Jane Addams's
Sickness and Cure." *Journal of Family History* 4, no. 4 (Winter 1979): 395–420.

Barnett, Henrietta. "The Beginnings of Toynbee Hall." In *Practicable Socialism:
New Series,* by Samuel Barnett and Henrietta Barnett, 107–20. London:
Longmans, Green, 1915.

———. *Canon Barnett: His Life, Work and Friends.* 2 vols. Boston: Houghton
Mifflin, 1919.

———. "Charitable Efforts." [1884.] In *Practicable Socialism: Essays on Social
Reform,* by Samuel Barnett and Henrietta Barnett, 157–72. London: Longmans,
Green, 1888.

Barnett, Samuel. "Education by Permeation." *Charities and Commons* 16 (May 5,
1906): 186–88.

———. "Settlements of University Men in Great Towns." [1883.] In *Practicable
Socialism: New Series,* by Samuel Barnett and Henrietta Barnett, 96–106.
London: Longmans, Green, 1915.

———. "Town Councils and Social Reform." [1883.] In *Practicable Socialism:*

Essays on Social Reform, by Samuel Barnett and Henrietta Barnett, 62–75. London: Longmans, Green, 1888

————. "University Settlements." [1884.] In *Practicable Socialism: Essays on Social Reform*, by Samuel Barnett and Henrietta Barnett, 96–108. London: Longmans, Green, 1888.

Barnett, [Samuel], and [Henrietta] Barnett. *Practicable Socialism: Essays on Social Reform*. London: Longmans, Green, 1888.

Barr, Eleanor M., ed. *The Women's International League for Peace and Freedom, United States Section, 1919–1959*. Microfilm. Wilmington, DE: Scholarly Resources, 1988.

Barrett, Mrs. John W., and Philip L. Keister, eds. *History of Stephenson County, 1970*. Freeport, IL: County of Stephenson, 1972.

Barrows, Emily. *Trade Union Organization among Women in Chicago*. Chicago: University of Chicago Press, 1927.

Basler, Roy, ed. *The Complete Works of Abraham Lincoln*. 2 vols. New Brunswick, NJ: Rutgers University Press, 1953.

Bate, Jonathan, ed. *The Romantics on Shakespeare*. London: Penguin, 1992.

Baylen, Joseph O. "A Victorious 'Crusade,' 1893–94." *Journal of American History* 50, no. 3 (December 1964): 418–34.

Beam, Ronald H. *Cedarville's Jane Addams . . . Her Early Influences*. Freeport, IL: Wagner Print Company, 1966.

Beard, Charles, and Mary Beard. *The American Spirit: A Study of the Idea of Civilization in the United States*. New York: Macmillan, 1942.

Beard, George M. *A Practical Treatise on Nervous Exhaustion (Neurasthenia)*, 5th ed. New York: E. B. Treat, 1905. Reprint, New York: Kraus Reprint Co., 1971. First published 1880. Page references are to the 1971 edition.

Beaver, I. M. *History and Genealogy of the Bieber, Beaver, Biever, Beeber Family*. Philadelphia: privately published, 1939.

Beckner, Earl R. *A History of Labor Legislation in Illinois*. Chicago: University of Chicago Press, 1929.

Bedell, Leila G. "A Chicago Toynbee Hall" (letter), *Woman's Journal* 20 (May 25, 1889): 162–63.

Behrends, A. J. *Christianity and Socialism*. New York: Baker & Taylor, 1886.

Beinart, Peter. "The Pride of Cities." *New Republic*, June 30, 1997, 16–24.

Berlin, James. *Writing Instruction in Nineteenth Century American Colleges*. Carbondale: Southern Illinois University Press, 1884.

Berry, Christopher J. *The Social Theory of the Scottish Enlightenment*. Edinburgh: University of Edinburgh Press, 1997.

Biographical Dictionary of the American Congress, 1774–1971. Washington, D.C.: Government Printing Office, 1971.

Bisno, Abraham. *Abraham Bisno, Union Pioneer*. Madison: University of Wisconsin Press, 1967.

———. "Economic and Industrial Condition: Chicago." In *The Russian Jew in the United States,* edited by Charles Bernheimer, 135–46. Philadelphia: John C. Winston, 1905.

Blair, Karen J. *The Clubwoman as Feminist: True Womanhood Redefined, 1868–1914.* New York: Holmes & Meier, 1980.

Blanc, Marie Therese de Solms. [Bentzon, Theresa]. *The Condition of Women in the United States.* Translated by Abby Langdon Alger. Boston: Roberts Bros., 1895.

Bliss, W. D. *The Encyclopedia of Social Reform.* New York: Funk & Wagnalls, 1897.

———. "The Social Reform Union." *Arena* 22, no. 2 (August 1899): 272–75.

———. "Union Reform League Activities." *Arena* 21, no. 4 (April 1899): 111–14.

———. "Unite or Perish." *Arena* 22, no. 1 (July 1899): 78–89.

Block, James E. *A Nation of Agents: The American Path to a Modern Self and Society.* Cambridge: Harvard University Press, 2002.

Blumberg, Dorothy Rose. *Florence Kelley: The Making of a Social Pioneer.* New York: August M. Kelley, 1966.

Blumin, Stuart. *The Emergence of the Middle-Class: Social Experience in the American City, 1760–1900.* New York: Cambridge University Press, 1989.

Boas, Louise Schutz. *Woman's Education Begins: The Rise of the Woman's Colleges.* 1935. Reprint, New York: Arno, 1971.

Bonsanquet, Bernard. "The Principles and Chief Dangers of the Administration of Charity." In *Philanthropy and Social Progress,* edited by Henry C. Adams, 249–68. New York: Crowell, 1893.

The Book of Chicagoans. Chicago: Marquis, 1905.

Boone, Gladys. *The Women's Trade Union Leagues in Great Britain and the United States of America.* New York: Columbia University Press, 1942.

Bordin, Ruth. *Woman and Temperance: The Quest for Power and Liberty, 1873–1900.* Philadelphia: Temple University Press, 1981.

Boris, Eileen. *Home to Work: Motherhood and the Politics of Industrial Homework in the United States.* New York: Cambridge University Press, 1994.

Bosch, Jennifer Lynne. "The Life of Ellen Gates Starr, 1859–1940." Ph.D. diss., Miami University, 1990.

Bowen, Louise deKoven. "The Colored People of Chicago." *Survey* 31 (November 1, 1913): 117–20.

———. *Growing up with a City.* New York: Macmillan, 1926.

———. *Speeches, Addresses and Letters.* Ann Arbor: Edwards Bros., 1937. Vol. 2.

Bowker, R. R. "Toynbee Hall, London." *Century* 24 (May 1887): 158–59.

Bowles, Samuel, and Herbert Gintis. *Democracy and Capitalism: Property, Community, and the Contradictions of Modern Social Thought.* New York: Basic Books, 1987.

Boyer, Paul. *Urban Masses and Moral Order in America, 1820–1920.* Cambridge: Harvard University Press, 1978.

Brackett, Anna C. "Liberal Education for Women." *Harper's Monthly* 54, no. 323 (April 1877): 695–96.

Brands H. W. *The Reckless Decade: America in the 1890s*. Chicago: University of Chicago Press, 1995.

Brandt, Thompson A., ed. *The Jane Addams Papers in the Collection of the Stephenson County Historical Society*. Freeport, IL: privately printed, 2001.

Brecher, Jeremy. *Strike!* Rev. ed. Boston: South End, 1977.

Briggs, Asa, and Anne Macartney. *Toynbee Hall: The First Hundred Years*. Boston: Routledge, 1984.

Brown, Corrine S. "The Illinois Woman's Alliance." *American Magazine* 3, no. 2 (March–April 1891): 110–11.

Brown, Mary Jane. *Eradicating This Evil: Women in the American Anti-Lynching Movement, 1892–1940*. New York: Garland, 2000.

Brown, Richard D. *The Strength of the People*. Chapel Hill: University of North Carolina Press, 1996.

Brown, Richard D., and Jack Tager. *Massachusetts: A Concise History*. Amherst: University of Massachusetts Press, 2000.

Brown, Victoria Bissell. "Advocate for Democracy: Jane Addams and the Pullman Strike." In *The Pullman Strike and the Crisis of the 1890s: Essays on Labor and Politics*, edited by Richard Schneirov, Shelton Stromquist, and Nick Salvatore, 130–58. Urbana: University of Illinois Press, 1999.

———. *The Education of Jane Addams*. Philadelphia: University of Pennsylvania Press, 2004.

———, ed. Introduction to *Twenty Years at Hull House*, by Jane Addams. Abridged. Boston: Bedford/St. Martin's, 1999.

———. "An Introduction to 'Why Women Should Vote.'" In *One Woman, One Vote: Rediscovering the Woman Suffrage Movement*, edited by Marjorie Spruill Wheeler, 182–95. Troutdale, OR: New Sage, 1995.

Bryan, Mary Lynn McCree, ed. *Jane Addams Papers*. Microfilm. Ann Arbor, MI: University Microfilms International, 1985–86.

Bryan, Mary Lynn McCree, Barbara Bair, and Maree de Angury, eds. *The Selected Papers of Jane Addams*. Vol. 1, *Preparing to Lead, 1860–1881*. Urbana: University of Illinois Press, 2003.

———. *The Selected Papers of Jane Addams*. Vol. 2, *1881–1888*. Urbana: University of Illinois Press, forthcoming,

Bryan, Mary Lynn McCree, and Allen F. Davis, eds. *One Hundred Years at Hull-House*. Bloomington: Indiana University Press, 1990.

Bryan, Mary Lynn McCree, Nancy Slote, and Maree de Angury, eds. *The Jane Addams Papers: A Comprehensive Guide*. Bloomington: Indiana University Press, 1996.

Bryan, William Jennings, and Mary Baird Bryan. *The Memoirs of William Jennings Bryan*. Chicago: Winston, 1925.

Buchanan, Joseph. "A Referendum for Reform." *Arena* 22, no. 4 (October 1899): 454–62.

Buckley, Jerome Hamilton. *The Victorian Temper*. New York: Vintage, 1951.

Buechler, Steven M. *The Transformation of the Woman Suffrage Movement: The Case of Illinois, 1850–1920*. New Brunswick: Rutgers University Press, 1986.

Buenker, John. *Urban Liberalism and Progressive Reform*. New York: Scribner's, 1973.

Buhle, Mari Jo. *Women and American Socialism, 1870–1920* . Urbana: University of Illinois Press, 1981.

Bulwer-Lytton, Edward. *Last Days of Pompeii*. New York: G. Routledge & Sons, 1876.

Burke, Martin J. *The Conundrum of Class: Public Discourse on the Social Order in America*. Chicago: University of Chicago Press, 1995.

Burrows, Edwin G., and Mike Wallace. *Gotham: A History of New York City to 1898*. New York: Oxford University Press, 1999.

Caird, Edward. *The Evolution of Religion*. Vol. 1. New York: Macmillan, 1893.

Carrell, Elizabeth H. "Reflections in a Mirror: The Progressive Women and the Settlement Experience." Ph.D. diss., University of Texas at Austin, 1981.

Carson, Mina. *Settlement Folk: Social Thought and the American Settlement Movement, 1885–1930*. Chicago: University of Chicago Press, 1990.

Carwardine, Richard. *Evangelicals and Politics in Antebellum America*. New Haven: Yale University Press, 1993.

Cavallo, Domenic. "Sexual Politics and Social Reform: Jane Addams from Childhood to Hull House." In *New Directions in Psychohistory,* edited by Mel Albin. Lexington, MA: Lexington Books, 1980.

Cedarborg, Hazel. "Early History of Rockford College," M.A. thesis, Wellesley College, 1926.

Chapin, John R. "The Infamous Pullman Strike as Revealed by the Robert Todd Lincoln Collection." *Journal of Illinois State Historical Society* 74 (Autumn 1981): 179–98.

Chernow, Ron. *Titan: The Life of John D. Rockefeller, Sr.* New York: Random House, 1998.

City of Chicago. Department of Development and Planning. *The People of Chicago: Who We Are and Who We Have Been; Census Data on Foreign Born, Foreign Stock and Race, 1837–1970*. Chicago: City of Chicago, 1976.

Civic Federation of Chicago. *First Annual Report of the Central Council*. Chicago: privately printed, 1895.

Clark, Eleanor Grace. "Ellen Gates Starr, O.S.B." *Commonweal*, March 15, 1940, 444–47.

Cohen, Nancy. *The Reconstruction of American Liberalism, 1865–1914*. Chapel Hill: University of North Carolina Press, 2002.

Coit, Stanton. *Neighbourhood Guilds*. 2d ed. London: Swan Sonnenschein, 1892. First published 1891.

Cole, Charles C., Jr. *The Social Ideas of the Northern Evangelists, 1826–1860*. New York: Columbia University Press, 1954.

Combination Atlas Map of Stephenson County, Illinois. Geneva, IL: Thompson and
Everts, 1871.

Commager, Henry Steele. "Jane Addams: 1860–1960." *Saturday Review*,
December 24, 1960. Reprinted as the foreword to *Twenty Years at Hull-House*.
New York: New American Library Signet Classic, 1961.

Commons, John. *Trade Unionism and Labor Problems*. Boston: Ginn, 1905.

Conrad, Joseph. *Almayer's Folly: A Story of an Eastern River*. Introduction by
Nadine Gordimer. 1895. Reprint: New York: Modern Library, 2002.

———— *An Outcast of the Islands*. Edited with an introduction by J. H. Stape.
First American edition, 1896. Reprint: New York: Oxford University Press,
1992.

Conway, Jill [Ker]. "The First Generation of American Women Graduates." Ph.D.
diss., Harvard University, 1968. Reprinted as *The First Generation of American
Women Graduates*. New York: Garland, 1987.

Conway, Jill Ker. "Jane Addams: An American Heroine," *Daedalus* 93 (Spring
1964): 761–80. Reprinted in Robert J. Lifton, ed. *The Woman in America*.
Boston: Houghton Mifflin, 1965.

————. "Women Reformers and American Culture: 1870–1930." *Journal of
Social History* 5 (Winter 1971–72): 164–77.

Cook, Blanche Wiesen. "Female Support Networks and Political Activism: Lillian
Wald, Crystal Eastman, Emma Goldman, Jane Addams." In *A Heritage of Her
Own: Toward a New Social History of American Women*, edited by Nancy F. Cott
and Elizabeth H. Pleck, 412–44. New York: Simon & Schuster, 1979.

Cotkin, George. *William James: Public Philosopher*. Baltimore: Johns Hopkins
University Press, 1989.

Cott, Nancy. *Bonds of Womanhood: "Woman's Sphere" in New England, 1780–1835*.
New Haven: Yale University Press, 1977.

Coughlan, Neil. *Young John Dewey: An Essay in American Intellectual History*.
Chicago: University of Chicago Press, 1973.

Cronon, William. *Nature's Metropolis: Chicago and the Great West*. New York:
Norton, 1991.

Crunden, Robert M. *Ministers of Reform: The Progressives' Achievement in American
Civilization, 1889–1920*. New York: Basic Books, 1982.

Cumbler, John T. "The Politics of Charity: Gender and Class in Late 19th Century
Charity Policy." *Journal of Social History* 14 (1980): 99–112.

Curti, Merle. "Jane Addams on Human Nature." *Journal of the History of Ideas* 22,
no. 2 (April–June 1961): 240–53.

Cutler, Irving. *The Jews of Chicago*. Urbana: University of Illinois Press, 1995.

Cyphers, Christopher J. *The National Civic Federation and the Making of a New
Liberalism, 1900–1915*. Westport, CT: Praeger, 2002.

Davis, Allen F. *American Heroine: The Life and Legend of Jane Addams*. New York:
Oxford University Press, 1973.

———. Introduction to *Spirit of Youth and City Streets*, by Jane Addams. Urbana: University of Illinois Press, 1972.

———, ed. *Jane Addams on Peace, War and International Understanding, 1899–1932*. New York: Garland, 1976.

———. "Jane Addams versus the Ward Boss." *Journal of the Illinois State Historical Society* 53, no. 3 (Autumn 1960): 247–65.

———. "The Social Workers and the Progressive Party, 1912–1916." *American Historical Review* 69 (April 1964): 671–88.

———.

Spearheads for Reform: The Social Settlements and the Progressive Movement, 1890–1914. New Brunswick, NJ: Rutgers University Press, 1984.

———. "The Women's Trade Union League Origins and Organization." *Labor History* 5 (Winter 1964): 3–17.

Davis, Allen F., and Mary Lynn McCree. *Eighty Years at Hull-House*. Chicago: Quadrangle, 1969.

Debs, Eugene V. *The Papers of Eugene V. Debs, 1834–1945*. Microfilm. Glen Rock, NJ: Microfilming Corporation of America, 1982.

Deegan, Mary Jo. *Jane Addams and the Men of the Chicago School, 1892–1918*. New Brunswick, NJ: Transaction, 1988.

———. *Race, Hull House and the University of Chicago: A New Conscience against Ancient Evils*. Westport: Praeger, 2003.

———. "W. E. B. DuBois and the Women of Hull-House, 1895–1899." *American Sociologist* 19, no. 4 (Winter 1988): 301–11.

D'Emilio, John, and Estelle Freedman. *Intimate Matters: History of Sexuality in America*. New York: Harper & Row, 1988.

Dennehy, C. "Childhood Bereavement and Psychiatric Illness." *British Journal of Psychiatry* 112 (1966): 1049–69.

De Quincey, Thomas. "The English Mail Coach." In *Collected Writings, New and Enlarged Edition in Fourteen Vols.* Vol. 8, *Tales and Prose Phantasies*. Edinburgh: Adam and Charles Black, 1890.

Destler, Chester McArthur. *Henry Demarest Lloyd and the Empire of Reform*. Philadelphia: University of Pennsylvania Press, 1963.

Deutsch, Sarah. *Women and the City: Gender, Space and Power in Boston, 1870–1940*. New York: Oxford University Press, 2000.

Dewey, John. "Christianity and Democracy." In *John Dewey: The Early Works, 1882–1898*. Edited by Jo Ann Boydston. Vol. 4, *1893–1894*, 3–10. Carbondale: Southern Illinois University Press, 1969.

———. *The Correspondence of John Dewey* [electronic resource]. General editor: Larry A. Hackman. Editors: Barbara Levine, Anne Sharpe, and Harriet Furst Simon. Charlottesville, VA: Windows version, InteLex Corp, [2000] Past Masters Series.

———. "The Ethics of Democracy." University of Michigan Philosophical Papers, 2d ser., no. 1. Ann Arbor: Andrews, 1888. Reprinted in *John Dewey: The*

Early Works, 1882–1898. Edited by Jo Ann Boydston. Vol. 1, *1882–1888*, 227–49. Carbondale: Southern Illinois University Press, 1969.

———. *John Dewey: The Early Works, 1882–1898*. Edited by Jo Ann Boydston. Carbondale: Southern Illinois University Press, 1969.

———. *Outlines of a Critical Theory of Ethics* (1891). In *John Dewey: The Early Works, 1882–1898*. Edited by Jo Ann Boydston. Vol. 3, *1891–1892*, 237–357. Carbondale: Southern Illinois University Press, 1969.

Dietz, Mary G. *Turning Operations: Feminisim, Arendt, and Politics*. New York: Routledge, 2002.

Diggins, John Patrick. *The Lost Soul of American Politics: Virtue, Self-Interest, and the Foundations of Liberalism*. New York: Basic Books, 1984.

Diliberto, Gioia. *A Useful Woman: The Early Life of Jane Addams*. New York: Scribner's, 1999.

Dombrowski, James. *The Early Days of Christian Socialism in America*. New York: Columbia University Press, 1936.

Donald, David Herbert. *Lincoln*. New York: Simon & Shuster, 1995.

Donnelley, Reuben, comp. *Lakeside Directory of the City of Chicago*. Chicago: Chicago Directory Company, 1889.

Dorfman, Joseph. *The Economic Mind in American Civilization*. Vol. 3, *1865–1918*. New York: Viking, 1959.

Dorrien, Gary. *The Making of American Liberal Theology: Imagining Progressive Religion, 1805–1900*. Louisville: Westminster John Knox Press, 2001.

Downey, Dennis B. "William Stead and Chicago: A Victorian Jeremiah in the Windy City." *Mid-America* 68, no. 3 (October 1986): 153–66.

Dubofsky, Melvin. *Industrialism and the American Worker, 1865–1920*. Arlington Heights, IL: Davidson, 1985.

Duis, Perry R. *Challenging Chicago: Coping with Everyday Life, 1837–1920*. Urbana: University of Illinois Press, 1998.

Dunn, Margaret Carol. "Jane Addams as a Political Leader." M.A. thesis, University of Chicago, 1926.

Dunne, Edward Fitzsimmons. *Illinois: The Heart of the Nation*. Vol. 2. Chicago: Lewis Company, 1933.

Eagle, Mary Kavanaugh Oldham. *The Congress of Women*. 1893. Reprint, New York: Arno, 1974.

Edward, Norman R. *The Victorian Christian Socialists*. New York: Cambridge University Press, 1987.

Edwards, Lee R. *Psyche as Hero: Female Heroism and Fictional Form*. Middletown, CT: Wesleyan University Press, 1984.

Edwards, Rebecca. *Angels in the Machinery: Gender in American Party Politics from the Civil War to the Progressive Era*. New York: Oxford University Press, 1997.

Eliot, George. *Daniel Deronda*. 1876. Reprint, New York: Signet, 1979.

———. *The Mill on the Floss*. 1860. Reprint, New York: New American Library, 1965.

————. *Romola.* 1863. Reprint, New York: Penguin, 1980.

Elshtain, Jean Bethke. "Jane Addams: A Pilgrim's Progress." *Journal of Religion* 78, no. 3 (July 1998): 339–60.

————. *Jane Addams and the Dream of American Democracy.* New York: Basic Books, 2002.

————. "Jane Addams as a Civic Theorist: Struggling to Reconcile Competing Claims." In *History of American Political Thought,* edited by Bryan-Paul Frost and Jeffrey Sikkenga, 504–20. New York: Lexington, 2003.

————, ed. *The Jane Addams Reader.* New York: Perseus, 2002.

————. "A Return to Hull House: Reflections on Jane Addams." In *Power Trips and Other Journeys: Essays in Feminism as Civic Discourse,* 3–12. Madison: University of Wisconsin Press, 1990.

————. "Self/Other, Citizen/State: G.W.F. Hegel and Jane Addams." In *Meditations on Modern Political Thought: Masculine/Feminine Themes from Luther to Arendt.* New York: Praeger, 1986.

Ely, Richard T. *The Labor Movement in America.* New York: Crowell, 1886.

————. *Social Aspects of Christianity and Other Essays.* New ed. New York: Crowell, 1889.

Emerson, Ralph Waldo. *Ralph Waldo Emerson: Essays and Lectures.* New York: Library of America, 1983.

Erwin, Edward, ed. *The Freud Encyclopedia: Theory, Therapy, and Culture.* New York: Routledge, 2000.

Eschbach, Elizabeth Seymour. *The Higher Education of Women in England and America, 1865–1920.* New York: Garland, 1993.

Ethington, Philip J. *The Public City: The Political Construction of Urban Life in San Francisco, 1850–1900.* New York: Cambridge University Press, 1994.

Evans, Sarah. *Born for Liberty: A History of Women in America.* New York: 1989.

Evans, Sarah, and Harry C. Boyte. *Free Spaces: The Sources of Democratic Change in America.* New York: Harper & Row, 1986.

Faderman, Lillian. *To Believe in Women: What Lesbians Have Done for America; A History.* Boston: Houghton Mifflin, 1999.

————. "Nineteenth-Century Boston Marriage as a Possible Lesson for Today." In *Boston Marriages: Romantic but Asexual Relationships among Contemporary Lesbians,* edited by Esther D. Rothblum and Kathleen A. Brehony, 29–42. Amherst: University of Massachusetts Press, 1993.

Fanning, Charles, Ellen Skerrett, and John Corrigan. *Nineteenth-Century Chicago Irish: A Social and Political Portrait.* Chicago: Center for Urban Policy, Loyola University, 1980.

Faragher, John Mack. *Sugar Creek: Life on the Illinois Prairie.* New Haven: Yale University Press, 1986.

Farrell, John C. *Beloved Lady: A History of Jane Addams's Ideas on Reform and Peace.* Baltimore: Johns Hopkins University Press, 1967.

Farwell, Harriet S. *Lucy Louise Flower, 1837–1920: Her Contributions to Education and Child Welfare in Chicago.* Chicago: privately printed, 1924.

Feder, Leah. *Unemployment Relief in Periods of Depression.* New York: Russell Sage, 1936.

Feffer, Andrew. "Between Head and Hand: Chicago Pragmatism and Social Reform, 1886–1919." Ph.D. diss., University of Pennsylvania, 1987.

———. *The Chicago Pragmatists and American Progressivism.* Ithaca: Cornell University Press, 1993.

Ferris, James H. "The Buffalo Conference, I. Plan and Scope." *Arena* 22, no. 1 (July 1899): 71–73.

Filippelli, Ronald L., ed. *Labor Conflict in the US: An Encyclopedia.* New York: Garland, 1990.

Fink, Leon. *In Search of the Working Class: Essays in American Labor History and Political Culture.* Urbana: University of Illinois Press, 1994.

———. *Progressive Intellectuals and the Dilemmas of Democratic Commitment.* Cambridge: Harvard University Press, 1997.

Fischer, David Hackett. *Historians' Fallacies.* New York: Harper & Row, 1970.

Fischer, Marilyn. "Jane Addams's Critique of Capitalism as Patriarchal." In *Feminist Interpretations of John Dewey,* edited by Charlene Haddock Seigfried, 279–84. University Park: Pennsylvania State University Press, 2002.

———. "Jane Addams's Feminist Ethics." In *Presenting Women Philosophers,* edited by Cecile T. Tougas and Sara Ebenreck, 51–57. Philadelphia: Temple University Press, 2000.

———. *On Addams.* Belmont, CA: Wadsworth, 2004.

Fischer, Marilyn, and Judy Whipps. *Jane Addams on Peace.* Bristol, UK: Thoemmes, 2003.

Fishman, W. J. *East End 1888: Life in a London Borough among the Labouring Poor.* Philadelphia: Temple University Press, 1988.

Flanagan, Maureen. *Seeing with Their Hearts: Chicago Women and the Good City, 1871–1933.* Princeton: Princeton University Press, 2002.

Foner, Eric. *Free Soil, Free Labor, Free Men: The Ideology of the Republican Party before the Civil War.* New York: Oxford University Press, 1970.

Foner, Philip S. *History of the Labor Movement.* Vol. 2, *From the Founding of the A.F. of L. to the Emergence of American Imperialism.* 2nd ed. New York: International, 1975.

———. *Women and the American Labor Movement: From the First Trade Unions to the Present.* New York: Free Press, 1979.

Foner, Philip S., and Brewster Chamberlin. *Friedrich A. Sorge's Labor Movement in the United States: A History of the American Working Class from Colonial Times to 1890.* Westport, CT: Greenwood, 1977.

Forbush, Bliss. *Elias Hicks: Quaker Liberal.* New York: Columbia University Press, 1956.

Foster, Catherine. *Women for All Seasons: The Story of WILPF*. Athens: University of Georgia Press, 1989.

Frank, Henriette Greenebaum, and Amalie Hofer Jerome, comps. *Annals of the Chicago Woman's Club for the First Forty Years of Its Organization, 1876–1916*. Chicago: Chicago Woman's Club, 1916.

Fraser, Nancy. "Rethinking the Public Sphere: A Contribution to the Critique of Actual, Existing Democracy." In *Habermas and the Public Sphere*, edited by Craig Calhoun, 109–42. Cambridge: MIT Press, 1992.

Freedman, Estelle. "Separation as Strategy: Female Institution Building and American Feminism, 1870–1930." *Feminist Studies* 5 (Fall 1979): 512–29.

Freeman, Alan. *Who Built America?* New York: Oxford University Press, 1967.

Fry, Paul E. *Generous Spirit: The Life of Mary Fry*. Rev. ed. Freeport: Stephenson County Historical Society, 2003.

Fuller, Margaret. *Woman in the Nineteenth Century*. 1845. Reprint, New York: Norton, 1971.

Fulwider, Addison L. *History of Stephenson County, Illinois*. Chicago: Clarke, 1910.

Furbank, P. N. *Unholy Pleasure: The Idea of Social Class*. New York: Oxford University Press, 1998.

Gamwell, Lynn, and Nancy Tomes. *Madness in America: Cultural and Medical Perceptions of Mental Illness before 1914*. Ithaca: Cornell University Press, 1995.

Gavit, John Palmer. *Bibliography of College, Social and University Settlements*. 3rd ed. Cambridge, MA: Co-operative Press, 1897.

The Gerritsen Collection: Women's History Online. Ann Arbor: Bell & Howell, 2000.

Giddings, Franklin H. "The Ethics of Social Progress." In *Philanthropy and Social Progress*, edited by Henry C. Adams, 205–48. New York: Crowell, 1893.

Gienapp, William E. *The Origins of the Republican Party, 1852–1856*. New York: Oxford University Press, 1987.

Gilbert, James. *Perfect Cities: Chicago's Utopias of 1893*. Chicago: University of Chicago Press, 1991.

Gilbert, Paul, and Charles Lee Bryson. *Chicago and Its Makers*. Chicago: Felix Mendelsohn, 1929.

Ginzberg, Lori D. " 'Moral Suasion Is Moral Balderdash': Women, Politics and Social Activism in the 1850s." *Journal of American History* 73 (December 1986): 601–22.

————. *Women and the Work of Benevolence: Morality, Politics, and Class in the Nineteenth-Century United States*. New Haven: Yale University Press, 1990.

Golden, Stephanie. *Slaying the Mermaid: Women and the Culture of Self-Sacrifice*. New York: Harmony Books, 1998.

Goldmark, Josephine. *Impatient Crusader: Florence Kelley's Life Story*. Urbana: University of Illinois Press, 1953.

Goodspeed, Thomas Wakefield. *The University of Chicago Biographical Sketches*. Chicago: University of Chicago Press, 1922.

Goodwin, Henry D. *Memorials, 1849–1889.* Rockford, IL: Daily Electric Register Print, 1889.

Goodwin, Jean. "Forms of Authority and the Real *Ad Verecundiam.*" *Argumentation* 12 (1998): 267–80.

Goodwyn, Lawrence. *Democratic Promise: The Populist Movement in America.* New York: Oxford University Press, 1976.

———. *Populist Moment: A Short History of the Agrarian Revolt in America.* New York: Oxford University Press, 1978.

Gordon, Ann D. "A Push from the Left: Hull House and Chicago Socialists, 1889–1899." TS (1978).

Gordon, Lynn. "Women and the Anti–Child Labor Movement in Illinois, 1890–1920." *Social Services Review* 51 (June 1977): 228–48.

Gorn, Elliott. *Mother Jones: The Most Dangerous Woman in America.* New York: Hill & Wang, 2001.

Gosling, F. G. *Before Freud: Neurasthenia and the American Medical Community, 1870–1910.* Urbana: University of Illinois Press, 1987.

Graham, Sara Hunter. *Woman Suffrage and the New Democracy.* New Haven: Yale University Press, 1996.

Greenstone, David. "Dorothea Dix and Jane Addams: From Transcendentalism to Pragmatism in American Social Reform." *Social Service Review* 53, no. 4 (December 1979): 527–59.

Grob, Gerald. *The Mad among Us: A History of the Care of America's Mentally Ill.* New York: Free Press, 1994.

———. *Mental Illness and American Society, 1875–1940.* Princeton: Princeton University Press, 1983.

Gullett, Gayle. *Becoming Citizens: The Emergence and Development of the California Women's Movement, 1880–1911.* Urbana: University of Illinois Press, 2000.

Hackett, Francis. *American Rainbow: Early Reminiscences.* New York: Liveright, 1971.

———. "Hull-House—A Souvenir." *Survey* 54, no. 5 (June 1, 1925): 275–80.

Hacking, Ian. "Autonmatisme Ambulatoire: Fugue, Hysteria, and Gender at the Turn of the Century." *Modernism/Modernity* 3, no. 2 (1996): 31–43.

———. *Mad Travelers: Reflections on the Reality of Transient Mental Illnesses.* Charlottesville: University Press of Virginia, 1999.

Hahn, Steven. *A Nation under Our Feet: Black Political Struggle in the Rural South.* Cambridge: Harvard University Press, 2003.

Haldeman-Julius, Marcet. *Jane Addams as I Knew Her.* Reviewer Library no. 7. Girard, KS: Haldeman-Julius Publications, [1936].

Hamilton, Alice. *Exploring the Dangerous Trades.* Boston: Little, Brown, 1943.

———. "Jane Addams: Gentle Rebel." *Political Affairs,* March 1960, 33–35.

———. "Jane Addams of Hull-House." *Social Service* 27, no. 1 (June–August 1953): 12–15.

Hamilton, Edith. *The Echo of Greece.* New York: Norton, 1957.

Handy, Robert T. "The Influence of Mazzini on the American Social Gospel." *Journal of Religion* 29, no. 2 (April 1949): 114–23.

———, ed. *The Social Gospel in America, 1870–1920.* New York: Oxford University Press, 1966.

Hanson, Russell L. *The Democratic Imagination in America: Conversations with Our Past.* Princeton: Princeton University Press, 1985.

Hard, William. "Chicago's Five Maiden Aunts." *American Magazine* 62 (September 1906): 481–89.

Harmon, Sandra D. "Florence Kelley in Illinois." *Journal of the Illinois State Historical Society* 74 (Autumn 1981): 163–78.

Harrington, Fred H. "The Anti-Imperialist Movement in the United States, 1898–1900." *Mississippi Valley Historical Review* 22, no. 2 (September 1935): 211–30.

Harrington, Maurice. "Jane Addams and a Politics of Embodied Care." *Journal of Speculative Philosophy* 15, no. 2 (2001): 114–16.

Harris, Kenneth Marc. *Carlyle and Emerson: Their Long Debate.* Cambridge: Harvard University Press, 1978.

Harris, Maxine. *The Loss That Is Forever: The Lifelong Impact of the Early Death of a Mother or Father.* New York: Plume/Signet/Penguin, 1995.

Harris, William T. "Educational Conference Address." *Smith College: Quarter Centennial.* [Northampton, MA: privately printed, 1900].

Hart, Sara L. *The Pleasure Was Mine.* Chicago: Valentine-Newman, 1947.

Havlike, Robert J. "Abraham Lincoln and the Reverend Dr. James Smith: Lincoln's Presbyterian Experience in Springfield." *Journal of the Illinois State Historical Society* 92, no. 3 (Autumn 1999): 222–37.

Hawkins, Mike. *Social Darwinism in European and American Thought, 1860–1945: Nature as Model and Nature as Threat.* New York: Cambridge University Press, 1997.

Hayes H. G., and C. J Hayes. *A Complete History of the Trial of Guiteau, Assassin of President Garfield.* Philadelphia: Hubbard Bros., 1882.

Hecht, Stuart Joel. "Hull-House Theatre: An Analytical and Evaluative History." Ph.D. diss., Northwestern University, 1983.

Hegner, Herman. "Scientific Value of the Social Settlements." *American Journal of Sociology* 3, no. 2 (September 1897): 171–82.

Hewitt, Nancy A. *Women's Activism and Social Change: Rochester, NY, 1822–1872.* Ithaca: Cornell University Press, 1984.

Hicks, Elias. *Journal of the Life and Religious Labours of Elias Hicks.* 2nd ed. New York: Hopper, 1832.

Higham, John. *Strangers in the Land: Patterns of American Nativism, 1860–1925.* New Brunswick, NJ: Rutgers University Press, 1992.

Hill, Mary A. *Charlotte Perkins Gilman: The Making of a Radical Feminist.* Philadelphia: Temple University Press, 1980.

Himmelfarb, Gertrude. *Poverty and Compassion: The Moral Imagination of the Late Victorians*. New York: Knopf, 1991.

Hindman, Hugh D. *Child Labor: An American History*. Armonk, NY: Sharpe, 2002.

Hirsch, Eric L. *Urban Revolt: Ethnic Politics in the Nineteenth-Century Chicago Labor Movement*. Berkeley: University of California Press, 1990.

Hirsch, Susan E. *After the Strike: A Century of Labor Struggle at Pullman*. Urbana: University of Illinois Press, 2003.

―――. "The Search for Unity among Railroad Workers." In *The Pullman Strike and the Crisis of the 1890s: Essays on Labor and Politics*, edited by Richard Schneirov, Shelton Stromquist, and Nick Salvatore, 43–64. Urbana: University of Illinois Press, 1999.

Hoffman, Charles. *The Depression of the Nineties: An Economic History*. Westport, CT: Greenwood, 1970.

Hofstadter, Richard. *Social Darwinism in American Thought*. Rev. ed. Boston: Beacon, 1955.

Hogan, David. *Class and Reform: School and Society in Chicago, 1880–1930*. Philadelphia: University of Pennsylvania Press, 1985.

Holmes, Richard. *Coleridge: Darker Reflections, 1804–1834*. New York: Pantheon, 1998.

Holt, Michael. *The Rise and Fall of the American Whig Party*. New York: Oxford University Press, 1999.

Horowitz, Helen Lefkowitz. *Alma Mater*. Boston: Beacon, 1984.

―――. *Culture and the City: Cultural Philanthropy in Chicago from the 1880s to 1917*. Chicago: University of Chicago Press, 1976.

―――. "Hull-House as Women's Space." *Chicago History* 12 (Winter 1983–84): 40–55.

―――. *The Power and Passion of M. Carey Thomas*. New York: Knopf, 1984.

Howard, Robert P. *Mostly Good and Competent Men: Illinois Governors, 1818–1988*. Springfield: Sangamon State University and Illinois State Historical Society, 1988.

Howe, Daniel Walker. *Making the American Self: Jonathan Edwards to Abraham Lincoln*. Cambridge: Harvard University Press, 1997.

Hoy, Suellen M. *Chasing Dirt: The American Pursuit of Cleanliness*. New York: Oxford University Press, 1995.

―――. " 'Municipal Housekeeping': The Role of Women in Improving Urban Sanitation Practices." In *Pollution and Reform in American Cities, 1870–1930*, edited by Martin V. Melosi, 173–98. Austin: University of Texas Press, 1980.

Huggins, Nathan. *Protestants against Poverty: Boston's Charities, 1870–1900*. Westport, CT: Greenwood, 1971.

Hull, Hannah Clothier. "Jane Addams." *Pax International* 10, nos. 3–4 (May–June 1935): 14.

Hunt, James B. "Jane Addams: The Presbyterian Connection." *American Presbyterians* 68 (Winter 1990): 231–44.

Huntington, James O. S. "Philanthropy—Its Success and Failure." In *Philanthropy and Social Progress,* edited by Henry C. Adams, 98–204. New York: Crowell, 1893.

———. "Philanthropy and Morality." In *Philanthropy and Social Progress,* edited by Henry C. Adams, 98–204. New York: Crowell, 1893.

Industrial Committee of the Civic Federation of Chicago. *Congress on Industrial Conciliation and Arbitration, Held at Chicago Tuesday and Wednesday, November 13 and 14, 1894.* Chicago: Hollister, 1894. Reprinted in Civic Federation of Chicago. *First Annual Report of the Central Council.* Chicago: privately printed, 1895.

Ingle, H. Larry. *Quakers in Conflict: The Hicksite Reformation.* Knoxville: University of Tennessee Press, 1986.

Ingram, J. S. *The Centennial Exposition, Described and Illustrated.* Chicago: Hubbard Brothers, 1876.

Isenberg, Nancy. *Sex and Citizenship in Antebellum America.* Chapel Hill: University of North Carolina Press, 1998.

Jackson, Shannon. *Lines of Activity: Performance, Historiography, Hull-House Domesticity.* Ann Arbor: University of Michigan Press, 2000.

Jacobson, Mathew Frye. *Barbarian Virtues: The United States Encounters Foreign Peoples at Home and Abroad, 1876–1917.* New York: Hill and Wang, 2000.

———. *Whiteness of a Different Color: European Immigrants and the Alchemy of Race.* Cambridge: Harvard University Press, 1998.

Jaher, Frederic Cople. *The Urban Establishment: Upper Strata in Boston, New York, Charleston, Chicago and Los Angeles.* Urbana: University of Illinois Press, 1982.

James, Edward T., Janet Wilson James, and Paul S. Boyer, eds. *Notable American Woman, 1607–1950: A Biographical Dictionary.* Cambridge: Harvard University Press, 1971.

Jeffreys, Sheila. *The Spinster and Her Enemies: Feminism and Sexuality, 1880–1930.* Boston: Routledge/Pandora, 1986.

Jensen, Richard J. *Illinois: A History.* 1978. Reprint, Urbana: University of Illinois Press, 2001.

Johnson, Emily Cooper, ed. *Jane Addams: A Centennial Reader.* New York: Macmillan, 1960.

Johnson, Mary Ann, ed. *The Many Faces of Hull House: The Photographs of Wallace Kirkland.* Urbana: University of Illinois Press, 1989.

Johnson, Nan. *Gender and Rhetorical Space in American Life, 1866–1910.* Carbondale: Southern Illinois University Press, 2002.

Johnson, Rossiter, ed. *History of the World's Columbian Exposition.* Vol. 4, *Congresses.* New York: Appleton, 1898.

Johnston, Robert. *The Radical Middle Class: Populist Democracy and the Question of Capitalism in Progressive Era Portland, Oregon*. Princeton: Princeton University Press, 2003.

———. "Re-Democratizing the Progressive Era: The Politics of Progressive Era Political Historiography." *Journal of the Gilded Age and Progressive Era* 1, no. 1 (January 2002): 68–92.

Johnston, W. D. "The New Social Movement." *Brown Magazine*, November 1894, 54–60.

Jones, Henry, and John Muirhead. *The Life and Philosophy of Edward Caird*. Glasgow: Maclehose, Jackson, 1921.

Jones, Peter d'A. *The Christian Socialist Revival, 1877–1914: Religion, Class and Social Conscience in Late-Victorian England*. Princeton: Princeton University Press, 1968.

Joslin, Katherine. *Jane Addams: A Writer's Life*. Urbana: University of Illinois Press, 2004.

———. "Literary Cross-Dressing: Jane Addams Finds Her Voice in *Democracy and Social Ethics*." In *Nouvelle Femmes de Conscience: Aspects du Feminisme Americain (1848–1975)*, 217–37. Paris: Presses de la Sorbonne, 1994.

Kadish, Alan. *Apostle Arnold: The Life and Death of Arnold Toynbee, 1852–1883*. Durham: Duke University Press, 1986.

Kagan, Jerome. *Unstable Ideas: Temperament, Cognition, and Self*. Cambridge: Harvard University Press, 1989.

Kasson, John F. *Rudeness and Civility*. New York: Hill & Wang, 1990.

Katz, Jonathan Ned. *Love Stories: Sex between Men before Homosexuality*. Chicago: University of Chicago Press, 2001.

Katz, Michael B. *In the Shadow of the Poorhouse: A Social History of Welfare in America*. New York: Basic Books, 1986.

Keillor, Steven J. *Cooperative Commonwealth: Co-ops in Rural Minnesota, 1859–1939*. St. Paul: Minnesota Historical Society Press, 2000.

Keister, Philip L., ed. *History of Stephenson County, 1970*. Freeport, IL: County of Stephenson, 1972.

Kelley, Florence. *The Autobiography of Florence Kelley: Notes on Sixty Years*. Edited by Kathryn Kish Sklar. Chicago: Kerr, 1986.

———. "Hull House." *New England Magazine* 18, no. 5 (July 1898): 550–66.

———. "I Go to Work." *Survey Graphic* 58 (June 1, 1897): 271–74, 301.

Kelley, Nicholas. "Early Days at Hull House." *Social Service Review* 28, no. 4 (December 1954): 424–29.

Kenney, Mary. "Organization of Working Women." In *The Women's Congress of Representative Women*, edited by May Wright Sewall, 871–74. Chicago: Rand McNally, 1894.

Kerber, Linda. "Separate Spheres, Female Worlds, Woman's Place: The Rhetoric of Women's History." *Journal of American History* 75 (June 1988): 9–39.

————. *Women of the Republic: Intellect and Ideology in Revolutionary America.* Chapel Hill: University of North Carolina Press, 1980.

Kessler-Harris, Alice. "A New Agenda for American Labor History: A Gendered Analysis and the Question of Class." In *Perspectives on American Labor History: The Problems of Synthesis,* edited by J. Carroll Moody and Alice Kessler-Harris, 217–34. DeKalb: Northern Illinois University Press, 1989.

————. *Out of Work: A History of Wage-Earning Women in the United States.* New York: Oxford University Press, 1982.

Keyssar, Alexander. *The Right to Vote: The Contested History of Democracy in the United States.* New York: Basic Books, 2000.

Kindleberger, Charles P. *Manias, Panics and Crashes: A History of Financial Crises.* New York: Basic Books, 1989.

King, John Owen. *The Iron of Melancholy: Structures of Spiritual Conversion in America from the Puritan Conscience to Victorian Neurosis.* Middletown, CT: Wesleyan University Press, 1983.

Kirkland, Joseph. "Among the Poor of Chicago." *Scribner's Magazine* 12, no. 2 (July 1892): 1–27.

Kloppenberg, James. "Pragmatism: An Old Name for Some New Ways of Thinking?" *Journal of American History* 83, no. 1 (June 1996): 100–138.

————. *Uncertain Victory: Social Democracy and Progressivism in European and American Thought, 1870–1920.* New York: Oxford University Press, 1986.

Knight, Louise W. "An Authoritative Voice: Jane Addams and the Oratorical Tradition." *Gender and History* 10, no. 2 (August 1998): 217–51.

————. "Biography's Window on Social Change: Benevolence and Justice in Jane Addams's 'A Modern Lear.'" *Journal of Women's History* 9, no. 1 (Spring 1997): 111–38.

————. "Jane Addams." *Encyclopedia of Women's Autobiography.* Westport, CT: Greenwood, 2005.

————. "Jane Addams and Hull House: Historical Lessons in Nonprofit Leadership." *Nonprofit Management and Leadership* 2 (Winter 1992): 125–41.

————. "Jane Addams and the Settlement House Movement." In *American Reform and Reformers: A Biographical Dictionary,* edited by Randall M. Miller and Paul A. Cimbala, 1–14. Westport, CT: Greenwood, 1996.

————. "Jane Addams's Early Theory and Practice of Cooperation." In *Women's Experiences Shaping Theory,* edited by Wendy Chmielewski, Carol Nackenoff, and Marilyn Fischer. Urbana: University of Illinois Press, forthcoming.

Komons, Nick A. "Chicago, 1893–1907: The Politics of Reform." Ph.D. diss., George Washington University, 1961.

Koven, Seth. "Henrietta Barnett, 1851–1936: The (Auto)biography of a Late Victorian Marriage." In *After the Victorians: Private Conscience and Public Duty in Modern Britain,* edited by Susan Pedersen and Peter Mandler, 31–53. New York: Routledge, 1994.

Koven, Seth, and Sonya Michel. "Women's Duties: Maternalistic Politics and the Origins of the Welfare State in France, Germany, Great Britain, and the United States, 1880–1920." *American History Review* 95 (October 1990): 1085–1112.

Kraditor, Aileen S. *The Ideas of the Woman Suffrage Movement, 1890–1920.* Garden City, NY: Anchor Books, 1971.

Kraus, Harry P. *The Settlement House Movement in New York City, 1886–1914.* New York: Arno, 1980.

Ladd-Taylor, Molly. *Mother-Work: Women, Child Welfare, and the State, 1890–1930.* Urbana: University of Illinois Press, 1994.

Lagemann, Ellen Condliffe, ed. Introduction to *Jane Addams on Education.* New York: Teachers College Press, 1985.

Landes, Joan B., ed. *Feminism, the Public and the Private.* Oxford: Oxford University Press, 1998.

Lasch, Christopher. *The New Radicalism in America, 1889–1963: The Intellectual as a Social Type.* New York: Vintage, 1965.

———. *The Social Thought of Jane Addams.* Indianapolis: Bobbs-Merrill, 1965.

Lasch-Quinn, Elisabeth. *Black Neighbors: Race and the Limits of Reform in the American Settlement House Movement, 1890–1945.* Chapel Hill: University of North Carolina Press, 1993.

Lathrop, Julia. "The Cook County Charities." In *Hull-House Maps and Papers by the Residents of Hull House, A Social Settlement,* 143–61. New York: Crowell, 1895.

———. "Hull House as a Sociological Laboratory." [assigned topic] *Proceedings of the National Conference of Charities and Correction, May 23–29, 1894, Nashville, Tennessee,* edited by Isabel C. Barrows, 313–18. Boston: Ellis, 1894.

Laurie, Clayton D. "Anti-labor Mercenaries or Defenders of Public Order?" *Chicago History* 20, nos. 3 and 4 (Fall and Winter 1991–92): 4–31.

Laws of Illinois, 1903. Springfield: State of Illinois, 1903.

Learned, Henry B. "Hull-House." *Lend a Hand* [Boston], May 1893, 318–31.

———. "Social Settlements in the United States: The Settlement Congress of 1893." *University Extension World* 3, no. 4 (April 1894): 108–14.

Lebsock, Suzanne. "Women and American Politics, 1880–1920." In *Women, Politics, and Change,* edited by Louise A. Tilly and Patricia Gurin, 35–62. New York: Russell Sage, 1990.

Leff, Michael C. "Lincoln among the Nineteenth-Century Orators." In *Rhetoric and Political Culture in Nineteenth-Century America,* edited by Thomas W. Benson, 131–55. East Lansing: Michigan State University Press, 1997.

Leffers, M. Regina. "Pragmatists Jane Addams and John Dewey Inform the Ethic of Care." *Hypatia* 8, no. 2 (Spring 1993): 64–77.

Leibowitz, Herbert. "The Sheltering Self: Jane Addams's Twenty Years at Hull House." In *Fabricating Lives: Explorations in American Autobiography,* 115–55. New York: Knopf, 1989.

Levine, Daniel. "The City Federation of Chicago." In *Varieties of Reform Thought*. Madison: State Historical Society of Wisconsin, 1964.

———. *Jane Addams and the Liberal Tradition*. Madison: State Historical Society of Wisconsin, 1971.

———. "Jane Addams: Romantic Radical, 1889–1912," *Mid-America* 44, no. 4 (October 1962): 195–210.

Levine, Lawrence. *The Opening of the American Mind*. Boston: Beacon, 1996.

Leyendecker, Liston Edington. *Palace Car Prince: A Biography of George Mortimer Pullman*. Niwot: University Press of Colorado, 1992.

Licht, Walter. *Industrializing America: The Nineteenth Century*. Baltimore: Johns Hopkins University Press, 1995.

Lindsey, Almont. *The Pullman Strike: The Story of a Unique Experiment and of a Great Labor Upheaval*. Chicago: University of Chicago Press, 1964.

Linn, James Weber. *Jane Addams: A Biography*. New York: Appleton-Century, 1935.

———. "Interpretation of Life." *Religious Education* 32 (July 1937): 217–21.

Lissak, Rivka Shpak. *Pluralism and Progressives: Hull House and the New Immigrants, 1890–1919*. Chicago: University of Chicago Press, 1989.

Livermore, Mary. "Cooperative Womanhood in the State." *North American Review* 153, no. 418 (September 1891): 283–95.

———. *The Story of My Life*. Hartford, CT: Worthington, 1898.

Livingston, James. *Pragmatism and the Political Economy of Cultural Revolution, 1850–1940*. Chapel Hill: University of North Carolina Press, 1994.

Lloyd, Henry Demarest. "The New Conscience. [1888.] In *Henry Demarest Lloyd's Critiques of American Capitalism, 1881–1903*. Edited by Alan Munslow and Owen R. Ashton, 45–64. London: Edwin Mellon, 1995.

———. *Wealth against Commonwealth*. New York: Harper & Brothers, 1894.

Loth, David. *Swope of General Electric: The Story of Gerard Swope and General Electric in American Business*. New York: Simon & Schuster, 1958.

Lowell, James Russell. "Democracy." In *The Works of James Russell Lowell*. Vol. 6, *Literary and Political Addresses*, 7–37. Boston: Houghton Mifflin, 1886.

Lovett, Robert Morss. *All Our Years*. New York: Viking, 1948.

Luker, Ralph E. "Missions, Institutional Churches, and Settlement Houses: The Black Experience, 1885–1910." *Journal of Negro History*, 69, nos. 3–4 (Summer–Fall, 1984): 101–13.

———. *The Social Gospel in Black and White: American Racial Reform, 1885–1912*. Chapel Hill: University of North Carolina Press, 1991.

Lusk, Bridget. "Monstrous Productions or the Best of Womanhood? Progressive-Era Women in Medicine." *Chicago History* 28, no. 2 (Winter 2000): 4–21.

Lyman, Darryl. *Civil War Wordbook, Including Sayings, Phrases, and Expletives*. Conshocken, PA: Combined Books, 1994.

Lynd, Helen Merrell. *England in the Eighteen-Eighties: Toward a Social Basis for Freedom*. London: Frank Cass, 1945.

Lynd, Staughton. "Jane Addams and the Radical Impulse." *Commentary* 32, no. 1 (July 1961): 54–59.

Lystra, Karen. *Searching the Heart: Women, Men, and Romantic Love in Nineteenth-Century America.* New York: Oxford University Press, 1989.

Maas, John. *The Glorious Enterprise: The Centennial Exhibition of 1876 and H. J. Schwarzmann, Architect-in-Chief.* Glen, NY: American Life Foundation, 1973.

MacDonald, Ramsey. "American Social Settlements." *Commons* 2 (February 1898): 4–6.

MacVeagh, Franklin. "A Program of Municipal Reform." *American Journal of Sociology* (March 1896): 561–63.

Mander, W. J. "Caird's Developmental Absolutism." In *Anglo-American Idealism, 1865–1927.* Westport, CT: Greenwood, 2000: 51–63.

Mapes, Mary Lynne. "Visions of a Christian City: The Politics of Religion and Gender in Chicago's City Missions and Protestant Settlement Houses, 1886–1929." Ph.D. diss., Michigan State University, 1998.

Marks, Donald. "Polishing the Gem of the Prairie: The Evolution of Civic Reform Consciousness in Chicago, 1874–1900." Ph.D. diss., University of Wisconsin, 1974.

Marsden, George. *The Evangelical Mind and the New School Presbyterian Experience: A Case Study of Thought and Theology in Nineteenth-Century America.* New Haven: Yale University Press, 1970.

Marshall, T. H. *Class, Citizenship, and Social Development: Essays by T. H. Marshall.* Chicago: University of Chicago Press, 1977.

Marty, Martin. *Protestantism in the United States: Righteous Empire.* 2nd ed. New York: Charles Scribner's Sons, 1986.

Marx, Karl. Preface to *A Contribution to the Critique of Political Economy.* In *Selected Works by Karl Marx and Friedrich Engels,* 1:304–22. Moscow: Foreign Languages Publishing, 1951.

Mattson, Kevin. *Creating a Democratic Public: The Struggle for Urban Participatory Democracy during the Progressive Era.* Philadelphia: University of Pennsylvania Press, 1998.

Maude, Aylmer. *The Life of Tolstoy.* Vol. 2, *The Later Years.* 1930. Reprint: New York, Oxford University Press, 1987.

———. "A Talk with Jane Addams." *Humane Review* [London], (October 1902): 203–18.

Mayer, Harold M., and Richard C. Wade, *Chicago: Growth of A Metropolis.* Chicago: University of Chicago Press, 1969.

Mayer, John Albert. "Private Charities in Chicago from 1871–1915." Ph.D. diss, University of Minnesota, 1978.

Mayne, A. J. C. *Imagined Slum: Newspaper Representation in Three Cities, 1870–1914.* New York: St. Martin's, 1993.

Mazzini, Joseph. *The Duties of Man and Other Essays.* Introduction by Thomas Jones. First published in Italian in 1860. New York: Dutton, 1907.

————. "Thoughts upon Democracy in Europe." In *Life and Writings of Mazzini*, 6:98–149. London: Smith, Elder, 1847.

McCabe, David. "Knowing about the Good: A Problem with Antiperfectionism." *Ethics* 110, no. 2 (January 2000): 311–38.

McCabe, James D. *Illustrated History of the Centennial Exposition.* Philadelphia: n.p., 1876.

McCarthy, Michael Patrick. "Businessmen and Professionals in Municipal Reform: The Chicago Experience: 1887–1920." Ph.D. diss., Northwestern University, 1970.

McCloughlin, William G. *Revivals, Awakenings, and Reform: An Essay on Religion and Social Change in America, 1607–1977.* Chicago: University of Chicago Press, 1978.

McCormick, Richard L. "Public Life in Industrial America, 1877–1917." In *The New American History*, edited by Eric Foner, 93–117. Philadelphia: Temple University Press, 1990.

McCree, Mary Lynn. "The First Year of Hull House, 1889–1890, in Letters by Jane Addams and Ellen Gates Starr." *Chicago History*, n.s., 1, no. 2 (Fall 1970): 101–14.

McCusker, John J. *How Much Is That in Real Money?* Charlottesville: University Press of Virginia, 1992.

McGerr, Michael. *A Fierce Discontent: The Rise and Fall of the Progressive Movement in America, 1870–1920.* New York: Free Press, 2003.

McGrath, James Morris. *The Rose Man of Sing Sing: A True Tale of Life, Murder, and Redemption in the Age of Yellow Journalism.* New York: Fordham University Press, 2003.

McGurty, Eileen. "Trashy Women: Gender and the Politics of Garbage in Chicago, 1890–1917." *Historical Geography* 26 (1998): 27–43.

McIlhaney, Asa K. "Historical Notes from the Writings of Asa K. McIlhaney." 2 vols. Easton, PA: Easton Public Library, 1956.

McMurry, Linda O. *To Keep the Waters Troubled: The Life of Ida B. Wells.* New York: Oxford University Press, 1998.

McPherson, James M. *Battle Cry of Freedom: The Civil War Era.* New York: Oxford University Press, 1988.

Meacham, Standish. *Toynbee Hall and Social Reform, 1880–1914: The Search for Community.* New Haven: Yale University Press, 1987.

[Mearns, Andrew.] *The Bitter Cry of Outcast London: An Inquiry into the Condition of the Abject Poor.* Edited with introduction by Anthony S. Wohl. 1883. Reprint, New York: Humanities, 1970.

Mearns, David C. *The Lincoln Papers.* Vol. 1. Garden City, NY: Doubleday, 1948.

Melosi, Martin V. *Garbage in the Cities: Refuse, Reform, and the Environment, 1880–1980.* Chicago: Dorsey, 1981.

Meyerowitz, Joanne J. *Women Adrift: Independent Wage Earners in Chicago, 1880–1930.* Chicago: University of Chicago Press, 1988.

Mill, John Stuart. *Auguste Comte and Positivism*. 1865. Reprint, Ann Arbor: University of Michigan Press, 1973.

———. *On Liberty*. 1859. Reprint, Indianapolis: Hackett, 1978.

———. *The Subjection of Women*. 1869. Reprint, Cambridge: MIT Press, 1970.

———. The Subjection of Women *and* On Liberty. New York: Henry Holt and Sons, 1885.

Miller, Donald. *City of the Century: The Epic of Chicago and the Making of the Nation*. New York: Simon & Schuster, 1996.

Miller, Paul, and Kathleen Miller. *Borough of Sinking Spring, 1913–1988*. [Sinking Spring, PA: Sinking Spring Historical Society, 1989.]

Million, Joelle. *Woman's Voice, Woman's Place: Lucy Stone and the Birth of the Woman's Rights Movement*. Westport, CT: Praeger, 2003.

Mink, Gwendolyn. *Old Labor and New Immigrants in American Political Development: Union, Party and State, 1875–1920*. Ithaca: Cornell University Press, 1986.

Mintz, Steven. *A Prison of Expectations: The Family in Victorian Culture*. New York: New York University Press, 1983.

Mitchell, B. R., ed. *International Historical Statistics: Europe, 1750–2000*. 5th ed. New York: Palgrave Macmillan, 2003.

———. *International Historical Statistics: The Americas, 1750–2000*. 5th ed. New York: Palgrave Macmillan, 2003.

Mitchell, S. Weir. *Lectures on Diseases of the Nervous System*. Philadelphia: Henry Clea's Son, 1881.

Moloney, Deirdre M. *American Catholic Lay Groups and Transatlantic Social Reform in the Progressive Era*. Chapel Hill: University of North Carolina Press, 2002.

Monoson, S. Sara. "The Lady and the Tiger: Women's Electoral Activism in New York City before Suffrage." *Journal of Women's History* 2 (Fall 1990): 100–135.

Montgomery, Caroline, comp. *Bibliography of College, University and Social Settlements*, 5th ed. Philadelphia: College Settlements Association, 1905.

Montgomery, David. *Citizen Worker: The Experience of Workers in the United States with Democracy and the Free Market during the Nineteenth Century*. New York: Cambridge University Press, 1994.

———. *The Fall of the House of Labor: The Workplace, the State and American Labor Activism, 1865–1925*. New York: Cambridge University Press, 1987.

———. "To Study the People." *Labor History* 21 (Fall 1980): 341–67.

Montgomery, Morton L., comp. *Historical and Biographical Annals of Berkshire County, Pa*. 2 vols. Chicago: Beers, 1909.

Moody, J. Carroll, and Alice Kessler-Harris, eds. *Perspectives on American Labor History: The Problems of Synthesis*. DeKalb: Northern Illinois University Press, 1989.

More, Hannah. *The Works of Hannah More: A New Edition*. Vol. 1, *Sacred Dramas and Poems*. London: n.p., 1830.

Morris, Richard B., ed. *Encyclopedia of American History*. New York: Harper & Brothers, 1961.

Mosier, Richard D. *Making the American Mind: Social and Moral Ideas in the McGuffey Readers*. 1947. Reprint, New York: King's Crown Press, Columbia University Press, 1965.

Mott, Frank Luther. *A History of American Magazines, 1865–1885*. Vol. 3. Cambridge: Harvard University Press, 1938.

Muncy, Robyn. *Creating a Female Dominion in American Reform*. New York: Oxford University Press, 1990.

Munro, Petra. " 'Widening the Circle': Jane Addams, Gender, and the Re/definition of Democracy." In *"Bending the Future to Their Will,"* edited by Margaret Smith Crocco and O. L. Davis Jr., 74–91. Lanham, MD: Rowman & Littlefield, 1999.

Murolo, Priscilla. *The Common Ground of Womanhood: Class, Gender, and Working Girls' Clubs, 1884–1928*. Urbana: University of Illinois Press, 1997.

Nackenoff, Carol. "Gendered Citizenship: Alternative Narratives of Political Incorporation in the United States, 1875–1925." In *The Liberal Tradition in America*, edited by David F. Ericson and Louisa Bertch Green, 137–69. New York: Routledge, 1999,

Nein, Jacqueline B. "An Alphabetized Compilation of Records, First United Church of Christ, Reading, Pennsylvania." N.p.: privately printed, 1986.

Nelli, Humbert S. *The Italians in Chicago, 1880–1930: A Study in Ethnic Mobility*. New York: Oxford University Press, 1970.

———. "John Powers and the Italians: Politics in a Chicago Ward, 1896–1921." *Journal of American History* 57, no. 1 (June 1970): 67–84.

Nelson, Hal. *Rockford College: A Retrospective Look*. Rockford: Rockford College, 1980.

Noll, Mark A. "Revolution and the Rise of Evangelical Social Influence in North American Societies." In *Evangelicalism: Comparative Studies of Popular Protestantism in North America, the British Isles, and Beyond, 1700–1900*, edited by Mark A. Noll, David W. Bebbington, and George A Rawlyk, 113–36. New York: Oxford University Press, 1994.

Nordhoff, Charles. *The Communistic Societies of the United States*. New York: Harper and Bros., 1875.

Northcote, J. Spencer, and W. R. Brownlow. *Roma Sotteranea; or, Some Account of the Roman Catacombs, compiled from the works of de Rossi*. London: Longmans, 1869.

Nutter, Kathleen Banks. *The Necessity of Organization: Mary Kenney O'Sullivan and Trade Unionism for Women, 1892–1912*. New York: Garland, 1999.

Oates, Mary J. *The Catholic Philanthropic Tradition in America*. Bloomington: Indiana University Press, 1996.

Oppenheim, Janet. *"Shattered Nerves": Doctors, Patients, and Depression in Victorian England*. New York: Oxford University Press, 1991.

Pagels, Elaine. *The Gnostic Gospels*. New York: Vintage, 1979.

Paine, Judith. "The Women's Pavilion of 1876." *Feminist Art Journal* 4, no. 4 (Winter 1975–76): 5–12.

Palmer, Alan. *The East End: Four Centuries of London Life*. London: John Murray, 1989.

Palmieri, Patricia Ann. *In Adamless Eden: The Community of Women Faculty at Wellesley*. New Haven: Yale University Press, 1995.

Papke, David Ray. *The Pullman Case*. Lawrence. University Press of Kansas, 1999.

Peaden, Catherine. "Jane Addams and the Social Rhetoric of Democracy." In *Oratorical Culture in Nineteenth-Century America*, edited by Gregory Clark and S. Michael Halloran, 184–207. Carbondale: Southern Illinois University Press, 1983.

Peattie, Elia M. "Women of the Hour: Miss Jane Addams." *Harper's Bazaar* 38, no. 10 (October 1904): 1003–8.

Pegram, Thomas R. *Partisans and Progressives: Private Interests and Public Policy in Illinois, 1870–1922*. Urbana: University of Illinois Press, 1992.

Phelps, Sarah O'Connell. *The Changing Faces of the Chicago Commons*. Chicago: privately printed, 1974.

Phillips, Paul T. *A Kingdom on Earth: Anglo-American Social Christianity, 1880–1940*. University Park: Pennsylvania State University Press, 1996.

Philpott, Thomas. *The Slum and the Ghetto: Neighborhood Deterioration and Middle-Class Reform, Chicago 1880–1930*. New York: Oxford University Press, 1978.

Picht, Werner. *Toynbee Hall and the Settlement Movement*. London: n.p., 1914.

Pierce, Bessie Louise. *A History of Chicago*. Vol. 3, *The Rise of a Modern City, 1871–1893*. New York: Knopf, 1957.

Pierson, George Wilson. *Tocqueville in America*. 1938. Reprint, Baltimore: Johns Hopkins University Press, 1996. (Originally titled *Tocqueville and Beaumont in America*.)

Pimlott, J. A. R. *Toynbee Hall: Fifty Years of Social Progress, 1884–1934*. London: Dent and Sons, 1935.

Platt, Anthony M. *The Child Savers: The Invention of Delinquency*. 2nd ed. Chicago: University of Chicago Press, 1977.

Plutarch. *Selected Essays and Dialogues*. Translated by Donald Russell. Oxford: Oxford University Press, 1993.

Poirier, Suzanne. "The Weir Mitchell Rest Cure: Doctor and Patients." *Women's Studies* 10, no. 1 (1983): 15–40.

Polacheck, Hilda Satt. *I Came a Stranger: The Story of a Hull-House Girl*. Edited by Dena J. Polacheck Epstein. Urbana: University of Illinois Press, 1989.

Polikoff, Barbara Garland. *With One Bold Act: The Story of Jane Addams*. Chicago: Boswell, 1999.

Pomeroy, Eltweed. "How the Conference Was Started." Special number, *Direct Legislation Record* 6, no. 3 (July 1899): 33–35.

Poole, Ernest. *Giants Gone: Men of Chicago*. New York: Whittlesey House, 1943.

Portrait and Biographical Album of Stephenson County, Illinois. Chicago: privately printed, 1888.

Potter, Beatrice. *The Cooperative Movement in Great Britain*. 1891. Reprint, London: George Allen & Unwin, 1930.

Potter, Caroline. "Dear Friend." *Rockford Seminary Magazine* 12, no. 2 (February 1884): 53–55.

———. "Intercollegiate Literary Contests." *Rockford Seminary Magazine* 3, no. 1 (January 1875): 37–40.

———. "The Madonna of the Future." Reprinted in "The Alumnae Meeting." *Rockford Seminary Magazine* 11, no. 7 (July 1883): 218–19.

Powers, Dorothy E. "The Chicago Woman's Club." M.A. thesis, University of Chicago, 1939.

"Presbyterianism, Reformed." *Encyclopedia of Religion*. New York: Macmillan, 1987.

Price, Tricia. "Helen Culver: A Biography of a Chicago Philanthropist." M.A. thesis, University of Chicago, 1974.

Ralph, Julian. "Chicago's Gentle Side." *Harper's Magazine* 87 (June 1893): 286–98.

Randall, Mercedes M. *Improper Bostonian: Emily Greene Balch*. New York: Twayne, 1964.

———. "John Dewey and Jane Addams" [Introduction]. In *"Pan the Logos and John Dewey: A Legend of the Green Mountains by Herbert W. Schneider and "The Realism of Jane Addams," by John Dewey*. Philadelphia: Jane Addams House, Women's International League for Peace and Freedom, 1959.

Reed, Thomas B. Introduction to *Modern Eloquence: Library of After-Dinner Speeches, Lectures, Occasional Addresses*, edited by Thomas B. Reed, 1:v–xiv. Philadelphia: Morris, 1901–3.

Reid, Daniel G., Robert D. Linder, Bruce L. Shelley, Harry S. Stout, and Craig A. Noll, eds. *Concise Dictionary of Christianity in America*. Downers Grove, IL: InterVarsity, 1995.

Reiff, Janice. "A Modern Lear and His Daughters: Gender in the Model Town of Pullman." In *The Pullman Strike and the Crisis of the 1890s: Essays on Labor and Politics*, edited by Richard Schneirov, Shelton Stromquist, and Nick Salvatore, 65–86. Urbana: University of Illinois Press, 1999.

Report of the Industrial Commission on the Relations and Conditions of Capital and Labor, Report of the Secretary, 1900. Washington, D.C.: Government Printing Office, 1901.

Residents of Hull-House. *Hull-House Maps and Papers*. New York: Crowell, 1895.

Rezneck, Samuel. "Unemployment, Unrest and Relief in the United States during the Depression of 1893–1897." *Journal of Political Economy* 61, no. 4 (August 1953): 324–45.

Richter, Melvin. *The Politics of Conscience: T. H. Green and His Age.* Cambridge: Harvard University Press, 1964.

Ritter, Ellen M. "Elizabeth Morgan: Pioneer Female Labor Agitator." *Central States Speech Journal* 22, no. 4 (Winter 1971): 241–51.

Robbins, Jane Fine. "The First Year at the College Settlement." *Survey* 27 (February 24, 1912): 1800–1802.

Robbins, Sarah. "Rereading the History of Nineteenth-Century Women's Higher Education; A Re-examination of Jane Addams's Rockford College Learning." *Journal of the Midwest History of Education Society* 21 (1994): 27–43.

Roberts, Sidney I. "The Municipal Voters' League and Chicago's Boodlers." *Journal of the Illinois State Historical Society* 53 (Summer 1960): 117–48.

Robins, Lucy Lang. *Tomorrow Is Beautiful.* New York: Macmillan, 1948.

Rockefeller, Steven C. *John Dewey: Religious Faith and Democratic Humanism.* New York: Columbia University Press, 1991.

Rodgers, Daniel T. *Atlantic Crossings: Social Politics in a Progressive Age.* Cambridge: Harvard University Press, 1998.

———. "In Search of Progressivism." *Reviews in American History* 10 (1982): 113–32.

Rosenberg, Charles E. *The Trial of the Assassin Guiteau: Psychiatry and the Law in the Gilded Age.* Chicago: University of Chicago Press, 1995.

Ross, Dorothy. *Gender and American Social Science: The Formative Years.* Princeton: Princeton University Press, 1998.

———. "Gendered Social Knowledge: Domestic Discourse, Jane Addams and the Possibilities of Social Science." In *Gender and American Social Science: The Formative Years,* edited by Helen Silverberg, 235–64. Princeton: Princeton University Press, 1998.

———. "Socialism and American Liberalism: Academic Social Thought in the 1880s." *Perspectives in American History* 11 (1977): 5–79.

Rothman, Sheila M. *Woman's Proper Place: A History of Changing Ideals and Practices, 1870 to the Present.* New York: Basic Books, 1978.

Royce, Josiah. *The Spirit of Modern Philosophy.* Boston: Houghton Mifflin, 1892.

Rudnick, Lois. "A Feminist American Success Myth: Jane Addams's *Twenty Years at Hull-House.*" In *Tradition and the Talents of Women,* edited by Florence Howe, 145–67. Urbana: University of Illinois Press, 1990.

Rudolph, Frederick. *Curriculum: A History of the American Undergraduate Course of Study Since 1636.* San Francisco: Jossey-Bass, 1977.

Ruegamer, Lana. " 'The Paradise of Exceptional Women': Chicago Women Reformers, 1863–1893." Ph.D. diss., Indiana University, 1982.

Rupp, I. Daniel. *History of Lancaster County.* Lancaster, PA: Gilbert Hills, 1844.

Rupp, Leila J. *A Desired Past: A Short History of Same-Sex Love in America.* Chicago: University of Chicago Press, 1999.

————. "Imagine My Surprise: Women's Relationships in Historical Perspective." *Frontiers* 5 (1980): 61–70.

Ruskin, John. "Of Queen's Gardens." In Sesame and Lillies, Unto This Last, *and* The Political Economy of Art. London: Cassell, 1907.

Ryan, Alan. *John Dewey and the High Tide of American Liberalism.* New York: Norton, 1995.

Ryan, Mary P. "Gender and Public Access: Women's Politics in Nineteenth-Century America." In *Habermas and the Public Sphere,* edited by Craig Calhoun, 259–88. Cambridge: MIT Press, 1992.

————. *Women in Public: Between Banners and Ballots, 1825–1880.* Baltimore: Johns Hopkins University Press, 1990.

Sandel, Michael J. *Democracy's Discontent: America in Search of a Public Philosophy.* Cambridge: Harvard University Press, 1996.

Sargent, Kevin. "Jane Addams's Rhetorical Ethic." Ph.D. diss., Northwestern University, 1996.

Schacter, Daniel. *Searching for Memory: The Brain, the Mind and the Past.* New York: Basic Books, 1996.

Scherman, Rosemarie Redlich. "Jane Addams and the Chicago Social Justice Movement, 1889–1912," Ph.D. diss., City University of New York, 1999.

Schiesl, Martin J. *The Politics of Efficiency: Municipal Administration and Reform in America, 1800–1920.* Berkeley: University of California Press, 1977.

Schiller, Francis. "Spinal Irritation and Osteopathy." *Bulletin of the History of Medicine* 45, no. 3 (May–June 1971): 250–66.

Schirmer, Daniel B. *Republic or Empire: American Resistance to the Philippine War.* Cambridge, MA: Schenkman, 1972.

Schlesinger, Arthur M. *A History of American Life.* Vol. 10, *The Rise of the City, 1878–1898.* New York: Macmillan, 1933.

Schmider, Ellen Heian. "Jane Addams's Aesthetic of Social Reform." Ph.D. diss., University of Minnesota, 1983.

Schneirov, Michael. *The Dream of a New Social Order: Popular Magazines in America, 1893–1914.* New York: Columbia University Press, 1994.

Schneirov, Richard. "Labor and the New Liberalism in the Wake of the Pullman Strike." In *The Pullman Strike and the Crisis of the 1890s: Essays on Labor and Politics,* edited by Richard Schneirov, Shelton Stromquist, and Nick Salvatore, 204–31. Urbana: University of Illinois Press, 1999.

————. *Labor and Urban Politics: Class Conflict and the Origins of Modern Liberalism in Chicago, 1864–97.* Urbana: University of Illinois Press, 1998.

Schneirov, Richard, Shelton Stromquist, and Nick Salvatore, eds. *The Pullman Strike and the Crisis of the 1890s: Essays on Labor and Politics.* Urbana: University of Illinois Press, 1999.

Schudson, Michael. *The Good Citizen: A History of American Civic Life.* New York: Free Press, 1998.

Schultz, Rima Lumin, and Adele Hast. *Women Building Chicago, 1790–1990.* Bloomington: Indiana University Press, 2001.

Schurz, Carl. *Abraham Lincoln: An Essay.* Boston: Houghton Mifflin, 1891.

Schwartz, Joel. *Fighting Poverty with Virtue: Moral Reform and America's Urban Poor, 1825–2000.* Bloomington: Indiana University Press, 2000.

Scott, Anne Firor. "Heroines and Heroine Worship. " In *Making the Invisible Woman Visible,* 142–58. Urbana: University of Illinois Press, 1984.

———, ed. Introduction to *Democracy and Social Ethics,* by Jane Addams, vii–lxxiv. Cambridge: Harvard University Press, 1964.

———. *Natural Allies: Women's Associations in American History.* Urbana: University of Illinois Press, 1991.

Scudder, Vida. *On Journey.* New York: Dutton, 1937.

Seidman, Steven. *Romantic Longings: Love in America, 1830–1980.* New York: Routledge, 1991.

Seigfried, Charlene Haddock, ed. *Feminist Interpretations of John Dewey.* University Park: Pennsylvania State University Press, 2002.

———. Introduction to *Democracy and Social Ethics,* ix–xxxviii. Urbana: University of Illinois Press, 2002.

———. *Pragmatism and Feminism: Reweaving the Social Fabric.* Chicago: University of Chicago Press, 1996.

———. "Socializing Democracy: Jane Addams and John Dewey." *Philosophy of the Social Sciences* 29, no. 2 (June 1999): 207–30.

Sewall, May Wright, ed. *World's Congress of Representative Women.* Vol. 1. Chicago: Rand McNally, 1894.

Sherrick, Rebecca. "Their Fathers' Daughters: The Autobiographies of Jane Addams and Florence Kelley." *American Studies International* 27 (Spring 1986): 39–53.

Shook, John R. *Dewey's Empirical Theory of Knowledge and Reality.* Nashville: Vanderbilt University Press, 2000.

Sicherman, Barbara. *Alice Hamilton: A Life in Letters.* Cambridge: Harvard University Press, 1984.

———. "Reading and Ambition: M. Carey Thomas and Female Heroism." *American Quarterly* 45 (March 1993): 73–103.

———. "Sense and Sensibility: A Case Study of Women's Reading in Late Victorian America." In *Gendered Domains: Rethinking Public and Private in Women's History,* edited by Dorothy O. Helly and Susan M. Reverby, 71–89. Ithaca: Cornell University Press, 1992.

———. "The Uses of Diagnosis: Doctors, Patients, and Neurasthenia." *Journal of the History of Medicine and Allied Science* 32 (January 1977): 33–54.

[Sidwell, Annie.] "Sage and Sibyl." *Rockford Seminary Magazine* 9 (July 1881): 193–94.

Silver, Regene Henriette. "Jane Addams, Peace, Justice, Gender, 1860–1918." Ph.D. diss., University of Pennsylvania, 1990.

Skerrett, Ellen. "The Irish of Chicago's Hull-House Neighborhood." *Chicago History* 30, no. 1 (Summer 2001): 21–63.

Sklar, Kathryn Kish. *Florence Kelley and the Nation's Work: The Rise of Women's Political Culture.* Vol. 1. New Haven: Yale University Press, 1995.

———. "Hull House in the 1890's: A Community of Women Reformers." *Signs* 10, no. 4 (Summer 1985): 658–77.

———. "Hull House Maps and Papers: Social Science as Women's Work in the 1890's." In *The Social Survey in Historical Perspective, 1880–1940,* edited by Martin Bulmer, Kevin Bales, and Kathryn Kish Sklar, 111–47. New York: Cambridge University Press, 1991.

———. "Who Funded Hull-House?" In *Lady Bountiful Revisited: Women, Philanthropy, and Power,* edited by Kathleen D. McCarthy, 94–115. New Brunswick: Rutgers University Press, 1990.

Skok, Deborah Ann. "Catholic Ladies Bountiful: Chicago Settlement Houses and Day Nurseries, 1892–1930." Ph.D. diss., University of Chicago, 2001.

Skocpol, Theda, and Morris P. Fiorina, eds. *Civic Engagement in American Democracy.* Washington, D.C.: Brookings Institution Press, 1999.

Small, Albion W. "The Civic Federation of Chicago: A Study in Social Dynamics." *American Journal of Sociology* 1, no. 1 (July 1895): 79–103.

Smith, Adam. *A Theory of Moral Sentiments.* 1759. Reprint, Washington, D.C: Regnery, 1997.

Smith, Carl. *Chicago and American Literary Imagination.* Chicago: University of Chicago Press, 1984.

———. *Urban Disorder and the Shape of Belief: The Great Chicago Fire, the Haymarket Bomb, and the Model Town of Pullman.* Chicago: University of Chicago Press, 1995.

"Smith College," *Scribner's Monthly* 14, no. 1 (May 1877): 9–17.

Smith, Edwin Burritt. *The Municipal Outlook: An Address.* Chicago: Municipal Voters' League, 1896.

Smith, Gary Scott. *The Search for Social Salvation: Social Christianity and America, 1880–1925.* New York: Lexington Books, 2001.

Smith, Timothy L. *Revivalism and Social Reform: American Protestantism on the Eve of the Civil War.* New York: Abingdon, 1957.

Smith-Rosenberg, Carroll. "Female World of Love and Ritual: Relations between Women in Nineteenth-Century America." In *Disorderly Conduct: Visions of Gender in Victorian America,* 53–76. New York: Oxford University Press, 1985.

Spear, Allan H. *Black Chicago: The Making of a Negro Ghetto, 1890–1920.* Chicago: University of Chicago Press, 1967.

Starr, Ellen Gates. "A Bypath into the Great Roadway." *Catholic World* (May–June 1924): 177–90.

Stead, William T. *Chicago Today.* London: Clowes, 1894.

———. *If Christ Came to Chicago.* Chicago: Laird & Lee, 1894.

Stebner, Eleanor J. *The Women of Hull House: A Study in Spirituality, Vocation and Friendship*. Albany: SUNY Press, 1997.

Steeples, Douglas, and David O. Whitten. *Democracy in Desperation: The Depression of 1893*. Westport, CT: Greenwood, 1998.

Stein, Leon, ed. *The Pullman Strike and American Labor: From Conspiracy to Collective Bargaining*. New York: Arno, 1969.

Stennett, W. H. *Yesterday and Today: A History of the Chicago and North Western Railway System*. 3rd ed. Chicago: Winship, 1910.

Stevens, Alzina P. "Life in a Settlement—Hull-House Chicago," *Self-Culture* 9 (March 1899): 42–51.

Stevenson, Louise L. *The Victorian Homefront: American Thought and Culture, 1860–1880*. New York: Twayne, 1991.

Stewart, Frank Mann. *A Half-Century of Municipal Reform: The History of the National Municipal League*. Berkeley: University of California Press, 1950.

Stimson, F. J. *Handbook to the Labor Law of the United States*. New York: Scribner's, 1896.

Storr, Anthony. *Solitude: The Return to the Self*. New York: Free Press, 1988.

Strong, Douglas M. *Perfectionist Politics: Abolitionism and the Religious Tensions of American Democracy*. Syracuse: Syracuse University Press, 1999.

Strong, Josiah. *Our Country: Its Possible Future and Its Present Crisis*. Rev. ed. New York: Baker & Taylor, 1891. Facsimile edition edited by Jürgen Herbst. Cambridge: Belknap Press of Harvard University Press, 1963. First published 1885. Page references are to the 1963 edition.

Sumner, William Graham. "Socialism." *Scribner's Monthly* 16, no. 6 (October 1878): 887–93.

———. *What Do the Social Classes Owe Each Other?* New York: Harper & Brothers, 1883.

Sunderland, Eliza. "Hull-House Chicago: Its Work and Workers." *Unitarian* (September 1893): 400–402.

Sutherland, Douglas. *Fifty Years on the Civic Front*. Chicago: Civic Federation, 1943.

Swart, Koenraad W. " 'Individualism' in the Mid-Nineteenth Century (1826–1860)." *Journal of the History of Ideas* 23, no. 1 (January–March, 1962): 77–90.

Tax, Meredith. *The Rising of the Women: Feminist Solidarity and Class Conflict, 1880–1917*. New York: Monthly Review Press, 1980.

Taylor, Bob Pepperman. *Citizenship and Democratic Doubt: The Legacy of Progressive Thought*. Lawrence: University Press of Kansas, 2004.

Taylor, Graham. "Jane Addams: The Great Neighbor." *Survey Graphic* 24, no. 7 (July 1935): 338–41, 368.

———. *Pioneering on Social Frontiers*. Chicago: University of Chicago Press, 1930.

Taylor, Verta, and Leila J. Rupp. "Lesbian Existence and the Women's Movement: Researching the 'Lavender Herring.'" In *Feminism and Social Change: Bridging Theory and Practice*, edited by Heidi Gottfried, 143–59. Urbana: University of Illinois Press, 1996.

Teaford, Jon C. *The Unheralded Triumph: City Government in America, 1870–1900*. Baltimore: Johns Hopkins University Press, 1971.

Terr, Leonore. *Too Scared to Cry: Psychic Trauma in Childhood*. New York: Harper & Row, 1990.

Thayer, H. S. *Meaning and Action: A Critical History of Pragmatism*. 2nd ed. Indianapolis: Hackett, 1981.

Thelen, David. *The New Citizenship: Origins of Progressivism in Wisconsin, 1885–1900*. Columbia: University of Missouri Press, 1972.

Theriot, Nancy. *Mothers and Daughters in Nineteenth-Century America: The Biosocial Construction of Femininity*. Lexington: University Press of Kentucky, 1996.

Thiem, E. George. *Carroll County, "A Goodly Heritage."* Mt. Morris, IL: Kable, 1968.

Tilden, M. H., comp. *The History of Stephenson County, Illinois*. Chicago: n.p., 1880.

Tilly, Louise A., and Patricia Gurin. "Women, Politics, and Change." In *Women, Politics, and Change*, edited by Louise A. Tilly and Patricia Gurin, 3–32. New York: Russell Sage, 1990.

Tims, Margaret. *Jane Addams of Hull House, 1860–1935: A Centenary Study*. London: George Allen & Unwin, 1960.

Tocqueville, Alexis de. *Democracy in America*. Translated by George Lawrence. Edited by J. P. Mayer. 2 vols. New York: Anchor, 1969.

Tolman, William H. "The League for Social Service." *Arena* 21, no. 4 (April 1899): 473–74.

——. *Municipal Reform Movements in the United States*. New York: Revell, 1895.

Tolstoi, Lyof N. *My Religion*. In *The Works of Lyof N. Tolstoi*. Vol. 17, *My Confession, My Religion, and The Gospel in Brief*. New York: Charles Scribner's Sons, 1899.

——. *What to Do?* Translated by Isabel F. Hapgood. New York: Crowell, 1887.

Townsend, Lucy. *The Best Helpers of One Another: Anna Peck Sill and the Struggle for Women's Education*. Chicago: Educational Studies Press, 1988.

——. "The Education of Jane Addams: Myth and Reality." *Vita Scholasticae* 5, nos. 1–2 (1986): 225–46.

——. "The Gender Effect: The Early Curricula of Beloit College and Rockford Female Seminary." *History of Higher Education Annual* 10 (1990): 69–90.

——. "Jane Addams Abroad: Travel as Educational 'Finish.'" *Vitae Scholasticae* 6 (Spring 1987): 185–206.

Townsend, Lucy, and Linda O'Neil. "Things Beyond Us: A Freirean Analysis of Jane Addams's Seminary Education." *Midwest History of Education Society* 21 (1994): 13–26.

Toynbee, Arnold. "Industry and Democracy." [1881.] In *Lectures on the Industrial Revolution of the 18th Century in England*, 178–202. New York: Longmans, Green, 1890.

————. *Lectures on the Industrial Revolution of the 18th Century in England*. New York: Longmans, Green, 1890.

————. "Wages and Natural Law." In *Lectures on the Industrial Revolution of the 18th Century in England*, 155–77. New York: Longmans, Green, 1890.

Toynbee, C. M. Prefatory note to *Lectures on the Industrial Revolution of the 18th Century in England*, by Arnold Toynbee, xxx–xxxi. 3rd ed. London: Longmans, Green, 1890.

Trachtenberg, Alan. *The Incorporation of America: Culture and Society in the Gilded Age*. New York: Hill & Wang, 1982.

Trattner, Walter I. *Crusade for the Children: A History of the Child Labor Committee and Child Labor Reform in America*. Chicago: Quadrangle, 1970.

Trout, Grace Wilbur. "Sidelights on Illinois Suffrage History." *Transactions of the Illinois State Historical Society for the Year 1920* (1920): 93–116.

Tucker, Beverly. *S. Weir Mitchell*. Boston: Badger, 1914.

Turner, Frank. *The Greek Heritage in Victorian Britain*. New Haven: Yale University Press, 1981.

Turner, Glennette. *Underground Railroad in Illinois*. Glen Ellyn, IL: Newman Educational Publication Company, 1998.

Unger, Irwin. "The 'New Left' and American History: Some Recent Trends in United States Historiography." *American Historical Review* 72, no. 4 (July 1967): 1237–63.

U.S. Bureau of the Census. *1850 Census*. Microfilm.

————. *1870 Census*. Microfilm.

————. *1880 Census*. Microfilm.

————. *1900 Census*. Microfilm.

————. *Compendium of the Eleventh Census: 1890, Part II*. Washington, D.C.: Government Printing Office, 1894.

————. *Report on Population of the United States at the Eleventh Census: 1890*. Washington, D.C: Government Printing Office, 1895.

————. *Report on Vital and Social Statistics in United States, 11th Census, Part II, Vital Statistics*. Washington: Government Printing Office, 1896.

U.S. Congress. House. *Report of the Industrial Commission on the Relations and Conditions of Capital and Labor, Report of the Secretary, 1900*. 56th Cong., 2nd sess. H. Doc. 495. Washington, D.C.: Government Printing Office, 1901.

U.S. Strike Commission. *Report of the Chicago Strike, June–July, 1894*. 53rd Cong., 3rd sess. S. Exec. Doc. 7. Washington, D.C.: Government Printing Office, 1895.

Urbinati, Nadia. *Mill on Democracy*. Chicago: University of Chicago Press, 2002.

Venturi, Emilie Ashurst. *Joseph Mazzini: A Memoir by Emilie Ashurst Venturi with Two Essays by Mazzini*, Thoughts on Democracy *and* The Duties of Man. 2nd ed. London: King, 1875.

Vicinus, Martha. *Intimate Friends: Women Who Loved Women, 1778–1928*. Chicago: University of Chicago Press, 2004.

Vinovskis, Maris A. "Stalking the Elusive Middle Class in Nineteenth-Century America: A Review Article." *Comparative Studies in Society and History* 33 (July 1991): 582–87.

Visher, John. *Handbook of Chicago's Charities*. Chicago: Illinois Conference of Charities and Corrections, 1892.

Vogeler, Martha S. *Frederick Harrison: The Vocations of a Positivist*. Oxford: Clarendon, 1984.

Waage, Marilyn Jean. "Social Background of Settlement Trustees, 1890–1914." M.A. thesis, University of Chicago, 1965.

Wade, Louise C. "The Heritage from Chicago's Early Settlement Houses." *Journal of the Illinois State Historical Society* 60 (1967): 411–41.

Waggenspack, Beth Marie. *The Search for Self-Sovereignty: The Oratory of Elizabeth Cady Stanton*. New York: Greenwood, 1989.

Walker, Margaret Urban. "Seeing Power in Morality: A Proposal for Feminist Naturalism in Ethics." In *Feminists Doing Ethics*, edited by Peggy DesAutels and Joanne Waugh, 3–14. New York: Rowman & Littlefield, 2001.

Ward, David. *Poverty, Ethnicity, and the American City, 1840–1925: Changing Conceptions of the Slum and the Ghetto*. New York: Cambridge University Press, 1989.

Warne, Colston Estey. *The Consumer's Co-operative Movement in Illinois*. Chicago: University of Chicago Press, 1926.

Warner, Amos G. *American Charities: A Study in Philanthropy and Economics*. 1894. Reprint: New Brunswick: Transaction, 1989.

Warner, Charles Dudley. "Chicago." In *The Complete Writings of Charles Dudley Warner*. Vol. 8, *Studies in the South and West*. Hartford: American Publishing, 1904.

Watt, N. F., and A. Nicholi. "Early Death of a Parent as an Etiological Factor in Schizophrenia." *American Journal of Orthopsychiatry* 49 (July 1979): 465–73.

Watts, Sarah L. *Order against Chaos: Business Culture and Labor Ideology in America, 1880–1915*. New York: Greenwood, 1991.

Webb, Beatrice. *Beatrice Webb's American Diary, 1898*. Edited by David A. Shannon. Madison: University of Wisconsin Press, 1963.

Webb, Catherine. *Industrial Cooperation: The Story of a Peaceful Revolution*. 4th ed. Manchester, UK: Co-operative Union, 1910.

Webber, F. R. *Church Symbolism*. Cleveland: Jansen, 1938.

Weld, Stephen. *The Concept of Political Culture*. New York: St. Martin's, 1993.

Wells, Anna Mary. *Miss Marks and Miss Woolley*. Boston: Houghton Mifflin, 1978.

Wells, Ida B. *Crusade for Justice: The Autobiography of Ida B. Wells*. Chicago: University of Chicago Press, 1970.

———. "Southern Horrors: Lynch Law." 1892. Reprinted in Kathryn Kohrs Campbell, *Man Cannot Speak for Her*. Vol. 2, *Key Texts of the Early Feminists*, 389–419. Westport, CT: Praeger, 1989.

Wells-Barnett, Ida B. "Lynching and the Excuse for It." *Independent* 53 (May 16, 1901): 1133–36.

Wendt, Lloyd, and Herman Kogan. *Lords of the Levee*. New York: Bobbs-Merrill, 1943.

Wernick, Andrew. *Auguste Comte and the Religion of Humanity*. New York: Cambridge University Press, 2001.

West, Cornel. *The American Evasion of Philosophy: Genealogy of Pragmatism*. Madison: University of Wisconsin Press, 1989.

Westbrook, Robert B. *John Dewey and American Democracy*. Ithaca: Cornell University Press, 1991.

Westhoff, Laura Mane. " 'A fatal drifting apart': Social Knowledge and Civic Identity in Chicago Social Reform, 1890–1907." Ph.D. diss., Washington University, 1999.

Whipps, Judy Dee. "Philosophy and Social Activism: An Exploration of the Pragmatism and Activism of Jane Addams, John Dewey and Engaged Buddhism." Ph.D. diss., Union Institute, 1998.

White, Arthur M., and Jerome A. Schofferman. *Spine Care*. Vol. 2, *Operative Treatment*. St. Louis: Mosby Year Book, 1995.

White, Horace. *The Life of Lyman Trumbull*. Boston: Houghton Mifflin, 1913.

Wiebe, Robert H. *The Search for Order, 1877–1920*. New York: Hill & Wang, 1967.

Wiener, Jonathan. M. "Radical Historians and the Crisis in American History, 1959–1980." *Journal of American History* 76, no. 2 (September 1989): 399–434.

Wilkinson, Laura S. "Household Economics." In *The Congress of Women*, edited by Mary Kavanaugh Oldham Eagle, 234–46. 1893. Reprint: New York: Arno, 1974.

Williams, Fanny Barrier. "The Intellectual Progress of the Colored Women of the United States Since the Emancipation Proclamation." In *World's Congress of Representative Women*, edited by May Wright Sewall, 2:696–711. Chicago: Rand McNally, 1894.

Wilson, Howard E. *Mary McDowell, Neighbor*. Chicago: University of Chicago Press, 1928.

Winterer, Caroline. *The Culture of Classicism*. Baltimore: Johns Hopkins University Press, 2002.

Wintle, Justin, ed. *Makers of Nineteenth-Century Culture, 1800–1914*. Boston: Routledge, 1982.

Wise, Winifred E. *Jane Addams of Hull-House*. New York: Harcourt, Brace, 1935.

Wish, Harvey. "Altgeld and the Progressive Tradition." *American Historical Review* 46 (July 1941): 813–31.

Withrow, W. H. *The Catacombs of Rome and Their Testimony Relative to Primitive Christianity*. New York: Nelson & Phillips, 1877.

Wohl, Anthony S. Introduction to *The Bitter Cry of Outcast London*, by Andrew

Mearns, edited by Anthony S. Wohl. 1883. Reprint, New York: Humanities Press, 1970.

Wolf, Gillian. "Dr. A. Louise Klehn: Skokie's First Lady of Family Practice." *Illinois Heritage* 4, no. 1 (Fall 2001): 13–16.

Woods, Eleanor Howard. *Robert Woods: A Champion of Democracy.* 1929. Reprint, Freeport, NY: Books for Libraries, 1971.

Woods, Robert A., and Albert J. Kennedy, eds. *The Handbook of Settlements.* New York: Charities Publications, 1911.

———. *The Settlement Horizon: A National Estimate.* New York: Russell Sage, 1922.

———. "The University Settlement Idea." In *Philanthropy and Social Progress,* edited by Henry C. Adams, 57–97. New York: Crowell, 1893.

Woody, Thomas. *A History of Women's Education in the United States.* 2 vols. New York: Science, 1929.

Wrobel, Arthur. *Pseudoscience and Society in Nineteenth-Century America.* Lexington: University Press of Kentucky, 1987.

Wyckoff, Walter. "The Workers—The West: Among the Revolutionaries." *Scribner's* 24 (July 1898): 99–105.

Yeich, Edwin B. "Jane Addams." *Historical Review of Berks County* 17 (October–December 1951): 10–13.

Young-Bruehl, Elisabeth. *Creative Characters.* New York: Routledge, 1991.

Zaeske, Susan. *Signatures of Citizenship: Petitioning, Antislavery and Women's Political Identity.* Chapel Hill: University of North Carolina Press, 2002.

Zuck, Janet. "Florence Kelley and the Crusade for Child Labor Legislation in the United States, 1892–1932." Ph.D. diss., University of Chicago, 1946.

Zunz, Olivier. *Making America Corporate, 1870–1920.* Chicago: University of Chicago Press, 1995.

INDEX